CONTENDING
WITH
DESTINY

The Caribbean in the 21st Century

CONTENDING WITH DESTINY

The Caribbean in the 21st Century

Edited by

KENNETH HALL | DENIS BENN

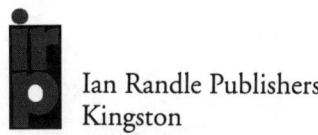

Ian Randle Publishers
Kingston

First published in Jamaica 2000 by
Ian Randle Publishers
11 Cunningham Avenue
Box 686, Kingston 6

© The Office of the Principal, UWI, Mona campus

While copyright in the selection and editorial material is vested in the Office of the Principal, UWI, Mona campus, copyright in individual chapters belongs to their respective authors and no chapters may be reproduced wholly or in part without the express permission in writing of both author and publisher.

ISBN 976-637-009-5 paper
     976-637-010-9 cased

A catalogue record for this book is available from the National Library of Jamaica

Set in Adobe Garamond 11/15 x 27
Book and cover design by Robert Harris (Jamaica)
Printed and bound in the United States of America

Contents

Preface / ix
Acronyms and Abbreviations / x
Introduction / xiii

Part 1: Strategic Perspectives for the Future

1   Reconfiguring the Matrix of Caribbean Development / 1
    Basdeo Panday, Prime Minister of Trinidad and Tobago

2   Mobilising Human Resources in Support of
    Caribbean Development / 7
    P J Patterson, Prime Minister of Jamaica

3   Economic Policy Options in the Twenty-first Century / 12
    Owen Arthur, Prime Minister of Barbados

4   The Challenge of Change / 26
    Edwin Carrington, Secretary General, CARICOM

Part 2: The Caribbean – Geography, Culture, History and Identity

5   Creating and Recreating the Caribbean / 31
    Norman Girvan

6   Identity, Space and The West Indian Union / 37
    Havelock RH Ross-Brewster

7   The Caribbean – Geography, Culture, History
    and Identity: Assets for Economic Integration / 45
    and Development
    Byron Blake

8   Image, Representation and the Project of Emancipation:
    History and Identity in the Commonwealth Caribbean / 53
    Verene A Shepherd

9 Migration, National Identity and Regionalism in the Caribbean: A Leeward Islands Case Study / 80
Jessica Byron

Part 3: Economic Policy Options in the 21st Century

10 Economic Policy Options for the 21st Century / 93
Omar Davies

11 The Global Economy, Market Confidence and Development Goals: The Dilemmas of Macroeconomic Policy in the Caribbean / 96
Clive Thomas

12 Economic Policy Options for the Caribbean in the 21st Century: Priority Challenges / 114
Felipe Noguera

Part 4: Science, Technology and Sustainable Development

13 Information Technology and Sustainable Development in the Caribbean / 125
Han Reichgelt

14 Current Trends in Higher Education and the Implications for UWI / 137
Anthony Clayton

15 Growth and Sustainable Development Through University and Industry Collaboration in Biotechnology / 147
Mohammad Ahmad

16 Science, Technology and Sustainable Development: Will We Get It Right This Time? / 154
Anthony Johnson

Part 5: Social Integration/ Disintegration: The Caribbean Experience

17 Diversity and Liberation in the Caribbean: The Decentralist Policy Challenge in the New Millennium / 161
Ralph Premdas

18 Those Two Jamaicas: The Problem of Social Integration / 179
Barrington Chevannes

| 19 | Social Disintegration in the Context of Adjustment and Globalisation: The Caribbean Experience / 185
Tyrone Ferguson |
| 20 | City Limits: Urbanisation and Gender Roles in the Caribbean into the 21st Century / 196
Patricia Mohammed |
| 21 | Social Integration and Disintegration: The Caribbean Experience: Jamaica / 204
Carol Narcisse |

Part 6: Caribbean Thought and the Political Process

| 22 | Caribbean Thought and the Political Process / 237
Trevor Munroe |
| 23 | Caribbean Political Thought, from Westminster to Philadelphia / 248
Selwyn Ryan |
| 24 | Independent Thought, Policy Process / 274
Lloyd Best |
| 25 | The Politics of Principled Proactive Pragmatism / 286
David Panton |

Part 7: The Caribbean in the International System

| 26 | The Caribbean in the International System: Outlook for the first 20 years of the 21st Century / 295
Richard Bernal |
| 27 | Looking from the Inside Outwards: The Caribbean in the International System After 2000 / 326
Vaughan Lewis |
| 28 | Caribbean International Relations: A Retrospect and Outlook for a New Millennium / 347
Anthony Bryan |
| 29 | Global Neoliberalism, The Third Technological Revolution and Global 2000: A Perspective on Issues Affecting the Caribbean on the Eve of the 21st Century / 382
Hilbourne Watson |

30 An Experiment in Supra-National Governance:
The Caribbean Regional Negotiating Machinery / 447
Cedric Grant

31 Reflections on the Caribbean Diaspora and
Its Policy Implications / 500
Orlando Patterson

Part 8: The Caribbean and the Creative Imagination

32 The Lost Literature of the West Indies / 513
Kenneth Ramchand

33 Caribbean Creative Achievement: Preserving the
Record/Extending the Influence / 530
Ian McDonald

34 Fostering the Creative Imagination / 534
Jean Small

35 Change and Prophecy in the Trinidad and
Tobago Calypso Towards the 21st Century / 542
Gordon Rohlehr

36 Art, Comrade, Makes Nothing Happen Here / 575
Bernadette Persaud

Conclusion / 587

Afterword: *"The Way Ahead"* / 590
  Rex Nettleford

List of Contributors / 596

Index / 601

Preface

The Caribbean faces a number of fundamental challenges as it enters the twenty-first century against the backdrop of the profound changes taking place in the international system. There is an urgent need, therefore, to initiate an exchange of views on the nature of these challenges and also to identify suitable strategic responses by the region in dealing with these challenges.

It was against this background that the University of the West Indies, in cooperation with the CARICOM Secretariat and the Caribbean Development Bank, decided to organise a conference on the Caribbean in the Twenty-first Century which was held on the Mona Campus of the University from September 3–5, 1999. The conference brought together scholars from the region, policy makers in government, the private sector and the NGO community as well as representatives of regional institutions in the Caribbean, in order to reflect upon the challenges facing the region and to identify strategic responses which could inform policy. I would like to take this opportunity to express the appreciation of the organisers of the conference for the generous financial assistance provided by the UNDP in support of the conference.

This volume, which is based on the presentations made at the conference contains a number of practical proposals for responding to the challenges facing the region. As such, it will serve as a ready reference on a number of important issues relevant to contemporary realities as well as future possibilities for the Caribbean.

I take great pleasure in introducing the volume and commend it to policy makers in the region, the serious student of Caribbean politics, economics and society as well as to members of the public.

Professor Kenneth O Hall
Pro Vice Chancellor and Principal,
University of the West Indies, Mona campus
January 31, 2000

Acronyms and Abbreviations

ACCP	Association of Caribbean Community Parliamentarians
ACP	Africa Caribbean and Pacific
ACS	Association of Caribbean States
BIT	Bilateral Investment Treaty
CAIC	Caribbean Association of Industry and Commerce
CAPE	Certificate of Advanced Proficiency in Education
CARDI	Caribbean Agricultural Research and Development Institute
CARIBCAN	Caribbean/Canada Trade Agreement
CARICOM	Caribbean Community
CARIFORUM	Caribbean Forum
CARIFTA	Caribbean Free Trade Area
CAST	College of Arts, Science and Technology
CATA	Central American Trade Agreement
CBI	Caribbean Basin Initiative
CBO	Community Based Organisation
CCE	Caribbean Council for Europe
CCP	Caribbean Community Parliamentarians
CCS	CARICOM Secretariat
CCST	Caribbean Council for Science and Technology
CDB	Caribbean Development Bank
CDCC	Caribbean Development and Cooperation Committee
CD&W	Colonial Development and Welfare
CEDAW	Convention on the Elimination of all forms of Discrimination Against Women
CERN	Conseil Européen pour la Recherche Nucléaire (European Organisation for Nuclear Research)
CET	Common External Tariff
CFCR	Council for Foreign and Community Relations
CHSD	Council for Human and Social Development
CIT	Caribbean Institute of Technology
CMO	Caribbean Meteorological Organisation
CN	Chief Negotiator
COMECON	Council of Mutual Economic Assistance
COTED	Council for Trade and Economic Cooperation
CRDC	Construction Resource and Development Centre
CRIDNET	Caribbean Rice Industry Development Network
CRT	CARICOM Review Team

CSEC	Caribbean Secondary Education Certificate
CSME	Caribbean Single Market and Economy
CTP	Caricom Trade Project
CUSFTA	Canada-United States Free Trade Agreement
CXC	Caribbean Examinations Council
DR	Dominican Republic
DRFTA	Dominican Republic Free Trade Area (with CARICOM)
ECLAC	Economic Commission for Latin America and the Caribbean
EDI	Electronic Data Interchange
EFT	Electronic Fund Transfer
EMU	European Monetary Union
EPZ	Export Processing Zone
ESSJ	Economic and Social Survey of Jamaica
EU	The European Union
FDI	Foreign Direct Investment
FHH	Female-Headed Household
FTAA	Free Trade Area of the Americas
GATT	General Agreement on Tariffs and Trade
GCC	Georgetown Cricket Club
GDP	Gross Domestic Product
G7	Group of Seven
G20	Group of Twenty
GATS	General Agreement on Trade-in-Services
GDP	Gross Domestic Product
GNP	Gross National Product
HDI	Human Development Index
HEART	Human Employment and Resource Training Trust
HLAG	High Level Advisory Group
IAST	Institute of Applied Science and Technology
IADB	Inter-American Development Bank
IDS	Institute for Development Studies
IFI	International Financial Institutions
ILO	International Labour Organisation
IMF	International Monetary Fund
IT	Information Technology
JLP	Jamaica Labour Party
KRC	Kingston Restoration Company
LAC	Latin America and Caribbean
MAI	Multilateral Agreement on Investment
MERCOSUR	Mercado Común del Sur (Southern Cone Market)
MIDA	The Micro Investment Development Agency Ltd
MNC	Multinational Corporation
NAFTA	North American Free Trade Agreement
NAR	National Alliance for Reconstruction
NCTVET	National Council on Technical and Vocational Education and Training

NDM	National Democratic Movement
NGO	Non-Governmental Organisation
NIP	National Industrial Policy
NTA	National Training Agency
NVQ-J	National Vocational Qualification of Jamaica
NWG	Negotiating Working Group
OAS	Organisation of American States
OAU	Organisation of African Unity
OECS	Organisation of Eastern Caribbean States
OECD	Organisation for Economic Cooperation and Development
ONR	Organisation for National Reconstruction
P-IC	Prison-Industrial Complex
PMSC	Prime Ministerial Standing Committee
PNC	People's National Congress
PNM	People's National Movement
PPP	People's Political Party
PSIP	Public Sector Investment Programme
PSOJ	Private Sector Organisation of Jamaica
PTA	Parent Teachers Association
R&D	Research and Development
REPA	Regional Economic Partnership Agreement
RNM	Regional Negotiating Mechanism/Machinery
ROSE	The Reform of Secondary Education
SAP	Structural Adjustment Policy
SGR	Strategic Global Repositioning
STEP	Special Training and Employment Programme
TNC	Transnational Corporations
TRIPS	Trade Related Intellectual Property
TRIMS	Trade Related Investment Measures
TTR	Third Technological Revolution
UF	United Front
ULF	United Labour Front
UNCED	United Nations Conference on the Environment and Development
UNCTAD	United Nations Conference on Trade and Development
UNDP	United Nations Development Programme
UNUDHR	United Nations Universal Declaration of Human Rights
UWI	University of the West Indies
VAT	Value Added Tax
WGE	Working Group of Experts
WHFTA	Western Hemisphere Free Trade Area
WIC	West Indian Commission
WICR	West Indian Commission Report
WTO	World Trade Organisation

Introduction

At the beginning of the twenty-first century, the Caribbean stands literally at the crossroads of history, reflecting upon its past while contemplating its future and seeking in the process to fashion its destiny. In fact, the region faces the dual challenge of formulating suitable national and regional policies and strategies designed to accelerate the pace of development, to strengthen governance structures, to promote social stability and to nurture its cultural creativity while at the same time, seeking to respond effectively to the challenges presented by the phenomena of globalisation and economic liberalisation which have exercised a dominant influence on the structure of contemporary international relations.

In terms of domestic economic policy, beginning in the 1980s most of the countries of the region embarked at one stage or another, on IMF/World Bank sponsored economic stabilisation and structural adjustment programmes. The programmes emphasised increased private sector involvement in the economy and a corresponding reduction in the role of government, together with increased reliance on market forces in the regulation of the economy. The adoption of a viable exchange rate regime and an appropriate interest rate policy geared to controlling inflation constituted essential elements of the overall adjustment framework. The results of the various adjustment programmes were, however, mixed. While some governments have succeeded in controlling inflation and reducing public sector deficits, the achievement of a sustained level of growth has proved elusive and the social impact of adjustment has borne heavily on the population in these societies.

Against this background, there is an urgent need to revisit conventional economic policies and to adopt creative strategies capable of generating higher levels of growth with equity. This will require not only the formulation of a more expansionary macroeconomic policy framework but also the adoption of specific strategies geared to increased economic diversification based on the identification of new patterns of production of goods and services, including the promotion of niche manufacturing and other knowledge-based industries. Such a strategy would also require the development of adequate human resources and the incorporation of new and innovative forms of technology and also the application of techniques for the organisation of production, such as flexible specialisation and cross functional management principles, in order to increase productivity and the overall competitiveness of the economies.

At the political level, there is a growing debate on the need to re-orient existing governance structures by promoting effective constitutional change and suitable public sector reforms designed to modify some elements of the Westminster Model which has served as the dominant constitutional form in the region since political independence. Indeed, the establishment of an effective system of governance, based on people empowerment and increased decentralisation of decision making is seen as a critical element in promoting an optimal level of human development.

Similarly, the demand for increased social equity as a basis for social stability will require that greater attention be paid to the equitable distribution of the benefits of development and the adoption of specific measures to ensure the increased allocation of resources to the poor and vulnerable in the society.

In the area of culture, the region has developed vibrant and dynamic expressions of art and music which have achieved international recognition and acclaim. This cultural vitality must therefore be sustained and enriched through the adoption of suitable policies designed to promote art and culture as an integral aspect of the overall development of the region.

The challenges facing the Caribbean have been further complicated by the fundamental changes that have occurred in the traditional structure of international relations during the past decade. The end of the Cold War, in the wake of the collapse of the Soviet Union and the emergence of a hegemonic order in which the USA as the sole remaining superpower exercises virtually unchallenged power and influence, has fundamentally altered the overall power equation in the international system. This development has, in turn, diminished the geo-political and geo-strategic significance of the Caribbean region and has therefore reduced its bargaining position in both the hemispheric and the wider global system. As a result, the Caribbean is faced with increased competition for scarce resources and already there is evidence of a significant decline in external resources made available to the region.

The implication of this development is that in the future, the bulk of the resources for development would need to be generated from domestic sources, hence the need not only to optimise the use of such resources but also to adopt suitable investment strategies that will generate increased returns to the region.

At the same time, the process of globalisation which has exercised a profound influence on international economic relations also has major implications for the Caribbean. A number of the philosophical elements of the newly emerging global order are in fact embodied in the series of far reaching agreements concluded during the Uruguay Round of Multilateral Trade Negotiations on issues such as investment, services, intellectual property rights and agriculture which, if the developed countries have their way, are likely to be supplemented by additional agreements on new issues such as competition policy, environment, labour standards and procurement. At the institutional level, the World Trade Organisation (WTO), has been established as a forum to facilitate negotiations on trade related issues and as an instrument for the promotion of a liberalised global trading regime. The process of globalisation and liberalisation, which together define the content and orientation of the emerging global economic order, is therefore likely to result over time in the creation of a predominantly reciprocity based international trading system and thus progressively erode the preferential trading arrangements previously accorded to the Caribbean and other developing countries in recognition of their special needs and circumstances.

These developments have important consequences for the Caribbean which has benefited from a wide range of preferences under the ACP/EU Lomé Convention, the Caribbean Basin Initiative (CBI) and the Caribbean/Canada preferential accord (CARIBCAN). Indeed, the strictures contained in the WTO ruling against the preferential arrangements for Caribbean banana exports to the European Union are likely to have an adverse impact on banana exports which play such a central role in the economies of the Eastern Caribbean.

However, as recent events in East Asia have shown, globalisation is not an unmixed blessing and in fact has major implications for the Caribbean and other developing countries, particularly in terms of the liberalisation of financial markets. In light of the East Asian experience, which sent ripples throughout the international financial system, serious concerns have been raised regarding the efficacy of the neo-classical economic assumptions which inform the process of globalisation. In view of the importance of these issues and their implications for the region, the Caribbean cannot afford to stand aside from the debate but must instead become intellectually engaged in the process in an effort to influence the content of international development policy.

Given the realities described above, the Caribbean is forced to deal not only with the broad issue of globalisation in the context of the WTO but would also need to address, simultaneously, its specific relations with the European Union in the context of the ACP/EU Lomé Convention and also its participation in the negotiations on the proposed Free Trade Area of the Americas (FTAA). In so doing, the region would need to reconcile its commitment to the integration process within CARICOM with the obligations to be incurred in the context of the various arrangements mentioned above. In this regard, it should be pointed out that CARICOM remains an important instrument for optimising the development potential of its member states. However, there is an urgent need to make the transition from trade integration to production integration in order to rationalise the use of resources within an integrated development framework and thus strengthen the capacity of the region to deal with the external economic environment.

Indeed, faced with these challenges, the Caribbean would need to pursue a policy of *concentric diplomacy* systematically aimed at reinforcing its relations with economic and trading groups as well as functional co-operation arrangements involving the countries of the wider Caribbean, the Association of Caribbean States (ACS), Latin America as a whole, the hemispheric system as well as extra-regional groupings and ultimately, the global system. At the political level, the countries of the region would also need to participate actively in the work of the Group of 77 which exercises important diplomatic influence in the international system. The forging of such alliances with other groupings will not only enable the region to secure economic benefits from such arrangements but would also enable it to pursue joint diplomatic initiatives with such groups aimed at influencing the shape and content of the emerging global order in a manner consistent with its interests. Finally, the region would need to strengthen its negotiating capacity both at the national and regional level based on arrangements such as those embodied in the Regional Negotiating Machinery (RNM) or an appropriate variation of it.

The Caribbean therefore faces a number of major challenges in the twenty-first-century in seeking to ensure that it not only survive economically but that it lays the foundation to participate as a viable actor in the international system.

Apart from adopting appropriate macroeconomic policies geared to the promotion of an accelerated pace of development, it will also need to address on an urgent basis, specific issues such as production and employment, education, health, human resources development, environmental protection and poverty eradication as well as social stability and cultural cohesion, particularly in societies such as Guyana and to some extent, Trinidad and Tobago, which are characterised by ethnic polarisation, and the strengthening of governance structures designed to improve efficiency in decision making and promote increased popular participation, all of which are critically important in the promotion of the well being of the people of the region, who are the ultimate beneficiaries of development. In addition, the region would need to fashion increasingly sophisticated strategies for dealing with the external environment which exercises an important influence on its economic viability and political survival.

All of these issues are addressed in one way or another in the various papers which make up this publication. Indeed, the papers cover a wide spectrum of issues ranging from broad philosophical concerns relating to the conception and definition of the Caribbean, the validity of conventional assumptions and categories of analysis, to more specific questions such as economic policy options, governance structures, science and technology, including information technology, education, social integration, political theory, international relations, gender, art, literature and the creative imagination.

Part I which is entitled *Strategic Perspectives for the Future* sets out the ideas expressed by Prime Minister Basdeo Panday of Trinidad and Tobago, Prime Minister Percival J. Patterson of Jamaica, Prime Minister Owen Arthur of Barbados and Edwin Carrington, Secretary General of CARICOM on strategies that should be adopted by the Caribbean in the future. In this regard, Prime Minister Panday sees the creative imagination of the Caribbean people as is reflected in the contributions of Sir Arthur Lewis, CLR James, Vidia

Naipaul, Derek Walcott, Bob Marley, The Mighty Sparrow and others, as the region's greatest asset. For this reason, he laments the fact that despite its tremendous creative talents, the region is dominated by the hegemony of the American media. He therefore poses the question whether the region should not contemplate the establishment of a major film and video production industry, with the University of the West Indies providing appropriate training in this area. Prime Minister Panday also emphasises the importance of the development of human capital in order to enable the people of the region to contribute to the development of twenty-first century technologies. He therefore calls upon the University of the West Indies to lead the way in effecting this vital transformation of Caribbean societies.

Prime Minister Patterson underlines the fact that in the face of increased competition at the global level, the Caribbean would need to improve economic efficiency and also develop new lines of production designed to capitalise on niche market opportunities. He also identifies technological change as a critical element of the overall development process and therefore calls for increased attention to be paid to the training of science and technology personnel by the University of the West Indies and other tertiary institutions in the region. Prime Minister Patterson calls upon the region to harness the creative energies of its people in order to lay the foundations for increased economic prosperity in the twenty-first century.

Prime Minister Arthur believes that the Caribbean faces unprecedented challenges as it enters the twenty-first century which would require a number of strategic responses. In seeking to formulate such responses, he rejects many of the assumptions of the Washington Consensus with its uncritical reliance on market forces and the imposition of a number of limitations on the role of the state in the economic sphere. On the contrary, Prime Minister Arthur feels that the role of the state is critical in putting in place the necessary infrastructural and institutional arrangements to ensure the development of a competitive capacity in the economies of the region. Similarly, he argues that current approaches to globalisation also threaten a number of Caribbean economies with marginalisation. He therefore advocates a more strategic approach by countries of the region towards integration in the global economy. In the face of these challenges, Prime Minister Arthur identifies a number of elements that could form the basis of a comprehensive strategy, namely, the adoption of long term strategic planning instead of crisis intervention, the abandonment of the primacy accorded to the traditional North Atlantic economic relationship, based on preferential arrangements, in favour of a new global focus, the adoption of a 'managed market' approach in the formulation of economic policy, the pursuit of new forms of governance based on consensus building and increased popular participation as key elements of the overall political culture.

Edwin Carrington, Secretary General of CARICOM highlights the profound nature of the changes that have occurred in recent years at both the regional and international level. He feels therefore that the Caribbean will need to master the art of managing change which will involve major adjustments in the polity, economy and culture of the region. He believes that a successful response to the challenge of change will also depend on the mobilisation of the human resources of the region which will in turn require the removal of the obstacles that have traditionally stood in the way of the more effective participation of women in all aspects of the society. Carrington also emphasises the need for the Caribbean to establish creative relationships at the regional, hemispheric and international level in order to deal effectively with the challenges that it will face in the twenty-first century.

It should be pointed out that all four of the papers call upon the University of the West Indies to play a leading role in assisting the region to articulate a vision and strategy for coping with the challenges of the twenty-first century.

In Part II dealing with *The Caribbean – Geography, Culture, History and Identity*, Norman Girvan raises a number of questions regarding the traditional conception of the Caribbean as a geographical entity. He argues that in the future, it may be more appropriate to conceive of the Caribbean as an 'ethno-cultural zone' encompassing not only the countries within the purely geographical limits of the region but also the Caribbean diaspora located in various metropolitan centres. Havelock Ross-Brewster advocates the creation of a Union of West Indian States based on the 'cultural capital' existing in the region. He nevertheless sounds a pessimistic and cautionary note since he questions the efficacy of the single market and economy on which CARICOM governments have embarked. For Ross-Brewster, the region would need to fashion a common vision and philosophy to give direction to the various negotiations being conducted in the context of the ACP/EU Lomé Convention, the FTAA and the WTO. Byron Blake, on the other hand, feels that the Caribbean governments should give priority to the management of the Caribbean Sea and that they should also seek to widen the current integration process in CARICOM. Moreover, he feels that the University of the West Indies should spearhead the development of a programme of educational exchange between universities in the anglophone Caribbean and those in the Spanish and French Caribbean as well as in Central America. Verene Shepherd, focusing on a somewhat narrower aspect of the Caribbean reality, deals with the 'identity crisis' within the Afro-Caribbean segment of the population, which she feels will need to be resolved urgently if the region is to enter the twenty-first century with a truly liberated psyche. She feels that this could be achieved by ensuring that history education is not based solely on Eurocentric texts of the imperial historians but is instead grounded in the alternative perspectives of the new generation of historians who bring a more indigenous appreciation to bear on the interpretation of the Caribbean historical experience. For her part, Jessica Byron identifies migration as an integrative force in the region. She feels that the focus on intergovernmental structures as a means of promoting regional integration has distracted attention from the possibilities of migration as instrument for the promotion of Caribbean integration. Byron also believes that the integration effort has focused too narrowly on the English-speaking Caribbean and has therefore tended to perpetuate the divisions of the colonial past.

In respect of **Part III**, *Economic Policy Options in the Twenty-first Century*, Omar Davies sees the challenge of economic policy in terms of the establishment of a balanced relationship between the government and the private sector in support of development objectives. In fact, he believes that economic progress will depend critically on the forging of a creative partnership between government and the private sector. Davies also argues that the increased emphasis on individualism has detracted from the commitment to a national and Caribbean regional identity which he feels is an important issue to be resolved during the twenty-first century. Clive Thomas, on the other hand, advances the proposition that in response to the changes in the global economy, Caribbean governments have adopted a model of macroeconomic management which impacts adversely on the trajectory of growth and threatens the reversal of development priorities with negative consequences for mass based democratic politics. He feels therefore that urgent steps will need to be taken to correct this policy stance if the Caribbean is to realise its full potential in the twenty-first century. Reflecting a private sector perspective, Felipe

Noguera argues that the profound scientific and technological revolution that has occurred in recent years has spawned a new social formation in the form of the Info-Media Society grounded in the concept of a borderless world in terms of communication and commerce and has also created new modes of production. He feels that in order to respond to these challenges, the public and private sectors as well as civil society in the region must forge a 'smart partnership' and that a transformed education system, under the leadership of the University of the West Indies, should serve as the engine for innovation and the transformation of the economies in the region into high quality, competitive exporters of refined products.

Part IV, which deals with *Science, Technology and Sustainable Development* highlights the importance of human capital formation and technology in the development process. Han Reichgelt points to the fact that the 'open nature' of the internet and the comparatively low cost involved in setting up e-business operations, offer new possibilities for the region. However, in order to exploit these possibilities, it will be necessary for the region to make a concerted effort to put in place arrangements for the training of programmers and software engineers who are currently not available in sufficient numbers. Anthony Clayton examines the impact of technological change on higher education, with special reference to the development of the multi-media mega-university along the lines of the model of the Open University in Britain which was designed specifically to deliver mass distance education. He advances the provocative thesis that these developments could lead to the demise of the traditional teaching university with lectures and students in a fixed location, which are likely to lose market share to powerful consortia of research universities and communications corporations which increasingly see themselves as having a role in knowledge distribution. Clearly, the region would need to monitor closely, developments in these areas which are likely to have a profound impact on the model of knowledge creation and distribution in the twenty-first century. Similarly, Mohammed Ahmad emphasises the importance of biotechnology and predicts that the twenty-first century will witness a struggle between information technology and biotechnology in terms of their relative importance and their overall impact on development. Based on the experience of the experiments in biotechnology carried out by the University of the West Indies, Ahmad argues, that in order for the region to capitalise on this technology, it will need to focus attention on the rapid commercialisation of successful research in an effort to achieve what Ahmad has termed the 'bio-industrialisation' of small economies. Anthony Johnson advances the thesis that the main challenge facing the region in the twenty-first century is to apply scientific methods to improve the standard of living of the people of the region on the basis of long term sustainability.

Part V, *Social Integration and Disintegration*, focuses upon the important issue of social cohesion and stability which have come under increased pressure in a number of societies in the region as a result of increasing levels of economic and social deprivation and also, in some cases such as Guyana, as a result of ethnic rivalry. Ralph Premdas starts from the proposition that 'Caribbean people are new arrivals who have had to reconstruct their identities, having lost most of what they had in the transmigration from the Old World'. Like Girvan, he sees the Caribbean as extending beyond the confines of the Caribbean Sea and also embracing Caribbean communities located in various metropolitan centres, mainly the USA, Canada and the UK. He feels therefore that the region will need to make a special effort to overcome the imperially constructed barriers and differences that have been consolidated into ethno-linguistic compartments in order to achieve a viable social integration. Taking a cue from Philip Curtain, Barry Chevannes analyses the problem of social integration in the context of his conception of 'two Jamaicas' separated by wealth, class and culture. In so doing, he rejects the validity of MG Smith's concept of 'cultural pluralism' as well as the Marxist praxis as satisfactory explanations of this complex reality. Instead, he advances the concept of 'code-switching' to explain how the two Jamaicas 'have not only coexisted but have together formed an apparent status quo which gives the appearance of social integration through a common value system' although, in his view, the reality is quite different. In his paper, Tyrone Ferguson focuses on the issue of social integration in the context of adjustment and globalisation. He argues that the implementation of structural adjustment programmes in Caribbean societies has proved to be socially disruptive, particularly in multi-ethnic societies such as Guyana in which it 'introduces serious tensions in inter-ethnic relations'. He therefore asserts that, in the context of the negative impact of a reliance on market forces implicit in adjustment programmes, the government should play a critical role in promoting social integration and cohesion in order to avoid the dangers of social disintegration. What is required in his view, therefore, is a 'new functional synthesis of state, market and civil society'. In examining gender roles in the Caribbean, in the context of a process of increasing urbanisation, Patricia Mohammed asserts that the quality of human life is the fundamental question that should preoccupy the region in the twenty-first century. She feels that urbanisation and technological innovation have blurred the traditional sex-based division of labour and therefore new approaches will need to be adopted in order to further clarify gender roles in Caribbean society as a basis for promoting social integration. Carol Narcisse, in reflecting upon contemporary social realities in the region, identifies a number of factors such as race and ethnicity, political tribalism and patronage, economic crisis and widening income gaps, which have contributed to social disintegration. Given this reality, she documents a number of survival strategies that have been adopted by various segments of the society, most notably the poor and vulnerable, to cope with economic and social deprivation.

In **Part VI** dealing with *Caribbean Thought and the Political Process*, Trevor Munroe affirms the virtues of transparency, accountability, participation and consensualism as the foundation of effective governance. He also confidently asserts that in the same way that the Caribbean contributed to the transition from political dependence to political independence during the course of the twentieth century, so too will the region succeed in the twenty-first century in transforming globalisation from a system delivering benefits to a privileged minority to a more regulated and managed process with the potential to benefit the majority of mankind. In his review of the history of Caribbean political thought, Selwyn Ryan boldly asserts that 'with the possible exception of Rastafarianism, Caribbean political thought has not distinguished itself by its originality'. Instead he points to the proliferation of various 'isms' which have been indiscriminately transferred from other contexts and applied as an explanation of the social experiences of the region. Ryan poses a fundamental question as to whether in the twenty-first century, Caribbean societies should continue to structure their political systems along Westminster lines or along consociational lines. Ryan argues persuasively that, based on the experience with the 'winner takes all' politics in Guyana and Trinidad and Tobago, that these societies should probably re-examine the merits of the Westminster model and opt for the consociational formulas proposed by writers such as Arend Lijphart, W. Arthur Lewis and others. Ryan's eloquent exposition of the merits of the consociational model as opposed to the majoritarian ethic of the Westminster model is certainly instructive and will doubtless inform further debates on the nature of the constitutional architecture to be constructed in the Caribbean in the twenty-first century, particularly in ethnically plural societies such as Guyana and Trinidad and Tobago where, in the words of Clive Thomas, electoral politics in effect, reflect 'ethnic censuses', given the demographic realities of the societies in question. Ryan also concedes the need to ensure the involvement of civil society in restructured governance arrangements but, unlike some who see their role as central to the democratic equation, Ryan believes that their role should be complementary to that of government. Based on his overall analysis of the political challenges facing the region, Ryan systematically documents a number of recommendations for constitutional change which are quite pertinent to the Caribbean reality. In his usually provocative style, Lloyd Best posits that the 'fractal societies' in the Caribbean face the double problem of 'chronic unviability' and 'endemic illegitimacy' of the political regime, regardless of their ideology or method of installation. Best is also disdainful of the 'new imperialism of the self-avowed neo-liberals who preach the merits of globalisation with its soaring inequities'. Like Wilson Harris, who advocates a new philosophy of history, Best asserts the need for 'independent, innovating thought to meet the reality' in which the region finds itself. David Panton argues that the profound changes that have taken place in the international economic system under the broad rubric of 'global liberalisation' have important implications for the Caribbean in that they have limited the scope of national policies. He feels therefore, that while seeking to strengthen the integration arrangements within CARICOM, the region should also seek to establish wider alliances with other groupings in an effort to improve their development prospects. Moreover, he feels that in responding to the challenges facing the region in the new century, Caribbean leaders should adopt what he terms the 'politics of principled proactive pragmatism' (PPP) which is based on the notion that political decisions should be guided not by prior ideological assumptions but whether the decisions make sense in terms of promoting the national interest.

In **Part VII** which deals with *The Caribbean in the International System*, Richard Bernal advances a number of innovative but controversial propositions regarding the strategies to be pursued by the countries in the region in response to changes in the international economic system. Bernal argues that the end of the Cold War produced a period of 'ideological entropy' but rejects

Fukuyama's 'end of history thesis' as an accurate characterisation of the new global reality. He states that the revolution in the global economy during the past two decades or more has resulted in increasing disparities, as evidenced by a widening development gap, economic concentration and increasing heterogeneity of national economies. Moreover, he notes that the decline in the strategic importance of the Caribbean has led to an increased attack on the preferential arrangements traditionally accorded to the region. Bernal therefore advocates a strategic global repositioning based on the increased diversification of exports and the pursuit of new patterns of international economic and political relations. In this context, he advances a new paradigm of small states in international relations which is premised on the assumption that the increasing differentiation among the developing countries has rendered less effective traditional developing country groupings such as the Group of 77. He therefore urges the formation of a coalition among small states and also a 'new transnational strategic alliance' between small states and small firms in the developed countries which he sees as going beyond the limits of the 'old North-South and South-South axes'. Bernal also advocates significant changes in the approach to regionalism. His ideal is the creation of 'a seamless regional economic space conducive to globally competitive economic activities' and based on 'market – driven corporate integration' which should take precedence over 'government – induced market integration'. In this context, he proposes a 'flexible integration' which would allow governments to integrate beyond the core agreement. He also argues that small states should pursue a policy of 'niche diplomacy' based on the concentration on a select number of priority issues. In order to pursue such a strategy, Bernal proposes a radical transformation of the existing orientation of the Foreign Service of the region, geared towards its greater involvement in commercial and financial negotiations and also based on the increased professionalisation of staff.

Although innovative and well argued, the strategy advanced by Bernal is quite problematical and will certainly provoke debate and controversy. For one thing, the alliance of small states which he has proposed is likely to be diplomatically insignificant without the support of the larger developing countries. Secondly, the assumption of an inherent commonality of interests between small economies in the developing world and small firms in the developed countries is debatable. Finally, while there are stresses within the Group of 77 based, for example, on the existence on differing views on current approaches to globalisation, which are not unrelated to differences in economic structure and overall levels of development, many would argue that the Group of 77 is still a viable entity, as is evidenced by the fact that the first Summit of all the developing countries will be held in Havana in April 2000.

In his paper, Vaughan Lewis raises the question of the nature of the evolution of the traditional relationships between the Caribbean and Europe and whether the region will continue to benefit from this relationship in the future. He feels that in light of its declining strategic significance and potential loss of markets for its traditional exports, the region could lapse into a period of benign neglect. Moreover, the Caribbean is also likely to face increasing pressures 'to dissolve the traditional and defining regional boundaries that they have partly inherited and partly constructed for themselves'. Faced with these challenges, Lewis believes that the small states of the Caribbean will need to reassess the effectiveness of the strategies they have pursued in respect of regional integration in order to determine whether changes in the international system have rendered them irrelevant. By way of a solution, Lewis proposes, on pragmatic grounds, a 'cession of elements of state sovereignty in favour of a new regime (or new regimes) of regional governance' and the reinvigoration of the Association of Caribbean Community Parliamentarians (CCP).

In reviewing the political economy and the security dimensions of contemporary international relations of the Caribbean, Anthony Bryan notes that the economies of the region have been historically integrated in the international economic system based on product specialisation, but that what is different in the present era is the increasing vulnerability of the economies of the region under the impact of globalisation. Moreover, given the fact that traditional preferential arrangements are likely to disappear, he points to the possibility of pursuing 'niche market' opportunities as part of a strategic response to globalisation. Bryan also advocates the adoption of a new integrationist culture based on corporate integration which he states involves a fundamental 'paradigm shift' in traditional integration theory from a virtual preoccupation with North America and Europe towards the establishment of horizontal links between the wider Caribbean and Latin America. He also feels that the region faces increased vulnerability deriving from drug trafficking and threats to the environment, which also pose major security problems. For this reason, the region will need to embark on a new diplomacy based on recognition of the relative decline of national governments.

Hilbourne Watson's exposition on global neo-liberalism in the context of technological change is premised on the notion that the Caribbean has been forced to function in 'an international environment shaped largely by the decisions of the World Bank and key agencies of the US government which in fact serve as surrogates of a global state and ruling class'. He feels therefore, that it will be important to counter the central assumptions of the neo-liberal ideology as a pre-condition for articulating a strategy geared to promoting the interests of the region in the international economy.

Cedric Grant's paper focuses on the Regional Negotiating Machinery (RNM) as an experiment in supra-national governance. Grant examines the factors which led to the establishment and elaboration of the functions of the RNM and its relationship with the CARICOM secretariat structure and other key sectors including individual member states in the negotiating process. Against this background, he also presents a critical assessment of the functioning of the RNM acting as an interpositioning authority. Grant's analysis contains a number of controversial propositions and is therefore likely to generate debate on the subject.

In reflecting upon the Caribbean diaspora, Orlando Patterson sees the existence of large West Indian communities in North America and, to some extent, in the UK as offering important political and economic opportunities on which the region can capitalise. He feels that at the political level, these communities can be mobilised to lobby Congress in the case of the US, to support Caribbean positions. Moreover, he feels that the existence of what he terms the West Atlantic diaspora can also make an important contribution to the economies of the region through remittances. Patterson believes that the proximity of the region to the USA provides an opportunity to establish in the region, nursing home facilities to cater for clients from the USA, given the latter's inability to provide an adequate quota of nursing personnel in the context of the development of an increasingly aging population. In fact, Patterson emphasises that Caribbean countries should seek to train an increasing number of nurses to cater for domestic needs as well as those of the external market, bearing in mind that nurses working in metropolitan countries will be in a position to send back remittances to the region. In Patterson's view, the opportunity exists to establish a large number of private educational institutions to cater for the education of children in the West Atlantic diaspora, given the unsatisfactory nature of education in some of the public schools in the USA which the children of migrants are often forced to attend. In elaborating his argument, Patterson suggests that such opportunities will allow the Caribbean to leap-frog the industrialisation process and to specialise in high technology and other service areas. He points out, of course, that these proposals assume an increased level of investment in education. In passing, Patterson also advances the notion that the traditional model of the nation state is no longer relevant and therefore the Caribbean must think increasingly in transnational terms. Clearly, this is a controversial proposition which is unlikely to find universal acceptance in the region.

In **Part VIII** Kenneth Ramchand examines the role of the creative imagination, defined in terms of literature, music, dance, song, story, painting, carving, sculpture and many other forms, in engendering 'self-knowledge, cultural confidence and regional self-affirmation'. He therefore advances specific suggestions designed to retrieve the literature of the region currently located in a number of different places and to minimise the loss and non-recognition of current literary output. He also sees the need for a complete revamping of the region's education system with a view to ensuring that every person is tri-lingual in order to widen communication and create the possibility of accessing the rich literature of the region. A major recommendation advanced by Ramchand is the need to establish departments of Philosophy and Intellectual History on all the campuses of the University of the West Indies in order to stimulate a culture of thought and to consolidate a philosophical tradition in the region. Ian McDonald, for his part, makes a powerful plea for the systematic preservation of Caribbean literature and artistic output which he feels face the danger of being lost to the region. He argues that this effort is critical to ensuring the expression of an integrated vision of the Caribbean through the arts. Similarly, Jean Small laments the disadvantage faced by the region in terms of the lack of access to the resources necessary for the full expression of the creative imagination. In his paper on 'Change and Prophecy in Trinidad and Tobago Calypso Towards the Twenty-first Century', Rohlehr analyses the role of calypsonians in dealing with societal change. He sees calypsonians as prophets in a universe where social class relations are characterised by inequality. He reviews the work of calypsonians such as the Mighty Spoiler, Stalin, Chalkdust, David Rudder and the Mighty Sparrow to support his thesis. Rohlehr, in effect, sees calypsoes as 'texts of survivalism' and argues that millennium economists, sociologists and political scientists might learn much from a study of the attitudes that are engrained in the calypso. Finally, Bernadette Persaud presents a critical appraisal of the evolution of art in the region. She expresses a clear preference for the postmodernist tradition based on its eclectic character, its democratic definition of art as well as its accommodation of the figurative and the use of a wide range of innovative techniques. In her view, its importance is further accentuated by its appropriateness for articulating the peculiar existential conditions of Caribbean man – 'isolated, restless, marginalised, with his multiple perspectives of reality, more varied than Picasso's'. She also feels the avant-garde school of art, which has emerged in Jamaica and also Barbados and Trinidad and Tobago, fits neatly into the postmodernist theoretical framework and can in fact become a major area of focus for Caribbean art in the new century. Despite Veerle Poupeye's famous work on Caribbean art which provides a comprehensive review of major trends in the development of art in the region, Persaud argues that the region itself must seek to provide an 'insider's mapping of the inner landscape of its own territory'. In other words, she sees the post modernist task in terms of an effort to construct an indigenous interpretation of the region's artistic heritage.

The various papers contained in this volume present a rich array of ideas and practical suggestions covering a wide range of topics. It is clear, however, that the papers reflect differing perspectives and interpretations of the Caribbean reality. Be that as it may, taken together, the papers constitute a solid basis for formulating strategies for advancing the interests of the region in the twenty-first century.

Kenneth O Hall
Denis M Benn
Janaury 31, 2000

Part 1
Strategic Perspectives for the Future

1 | BASDEO PANDAY
Prime Minister of the Republic of Trinidad and Tobago

Reconfiguring the Matrix of Caribbean Development

As I understand it, the mission of this conference is to produce a roadmap that will chart the direction of the Caribbean in the new century. This must surely be the most challenging assignment ever to have been undertaken by any group of scholars and policy makers in this, or in any other region; in this, or in any other century. I make this judgement in the knowledge that perhaps the most predictable dimension to the character of the people of this region is that they are utterly unpredictable.

Should there be any challenge to this assertion, we need only to look at the recent history of the West Indies cricket team. We may also look at the cheekiness of that young lad from a tiny Caribbean island, who has proceeded to make himself the top soccer striker in the European Union – Trinidad and Tobago's Dwight Yorke. Now, the ultimate in the unpredictable, the people responsible for such things have bestowed the accolade 'Best Dressed Man in Britain' on this Caribbean son. Who could have predicted that Dwight Yorke would be scoring such conquests, both on and off the field?

You have been set a difficult task, and I am about to make it even tougher for you. My responsibility is to present for the consideration of the conference, and particularly for the consideration of the plenary session, some of the critical perspectives of CARICOM. In my Trinidad and Tobago Independence Day Message on August 31, I made reference to this conference and to the significance that I expect it will have in shaping the fortunes of the Caribbean in the next century. Now, in my capacity as Chairman of CARICOM, I again underline my expectation that from this conference will come the new Caribbean paradigm.

At the Twentieth Meeting of the Conference of Heads of the Caribbean Community in Port of Spain in July 1999, I submitted that in examining the perspectives for the new century, CARICOM should set itself the obligation of bringing the business of the twentieth century to effective closure, as an essential prelude to the twenty-first century.

Of major and immediate concern is CARICOM's low score in the implementation of programmes which are fundamental to the integration movement in the region. We are behind in the preparations that are necessary for the establishment of the Caribbean Single Market and Economy, and not all member countries are ready for its implementation in 2000. It is now clear that some must move at a pace different from others. We must find the mechanism to facilitate this.

CARICOM's undertaking for the development of computer skills, nationwide in member states, is far from being realised. Within the forum of the Free Trade Area of the Americas, a number of CARICOM states are the only countries of the Americas that are yet to convert to the amended 1996 Harmonised Commodity Description and Coding System. The introduction of Spanish at the primary level in the region's education system is still in the 'mañana' mode.

Among the regional groupings of the world, Central America, Mexico, South America and the Caribbean make up Latin America, with an aggregate population close to 500 million, which is predominantly Spanish-speaking. The importance of Spanish as a second language in the region should thus be obvious, and should be urgently implemented. In this framework, the benefits of bilingualism in the Free Trade Area of the Americas will be significant.

Another area of overdue implementation is the national arrangement for the free movement of UWI graduates and the graduates of other designated institutions, as well the arrangements for the free movement of skilled workers. We also have to accelerate the process for the establishment of the Caribbean Court of Justice. These are key concerns which will be in critical focus during the Special Meeting of the Conference of Heads of Government in Port of Spain in October, 1999 when we will discuss the closing of the twentieth century as the platform for the commencement of the twenty-first.

It would be most propitious if this conference were to commit to participation in a series of task forces to tackle the most critical undertakings on CARICOM's twentieth century agenda. The Secretary General will be in an excellent position to network with volunteers in laying the groundwork for the establishment of those task forces. Though I am confident that there will be no shortage of volunteers, I shall, nonetheless, seek the agreement of my colleague prime ministers for the vesting of the Secretary General, Dr Carrington, with the power to conscript volunteers, should it be necessary to do so. It is my strong conviction that the requisite task forces are precisely what is needed to facilitate the processes necessary to ensure that CARICOM will enter the new century with increased momentum. CARICOM needs your assistance to bring this century to its close, as much as we need your counsels to navigate the next.

While my concerns are geared to the anglophone Caribbean, we must begin to gear up for the transition to the full Caribbean Basin community. This thrust flowed from the 1992 Special Heads of Government Conference, which was called to consider the West Indian Commission report, 'Time For Action'. From that initiative has come the establishment of the Association of Caribbean States, which is headquartered in Port of Spain.

In the broader regional context, CARICOM has established a network of new Caribbean relationships, with negotiations for a Free Trade Agreement with the Dominican Republic; a Trade and Investment Agreement with Venezuela; a Trade and Economic Co-operation Agreement with Colombia; and a Joint Commission with Mexico. We are also committed to the negotiation of a CARICOM/Central American Trade Agreement. Within this framework of new relationships, the time has come for a Caribbean 2000 Conference that will involve the major policy makers from the public and the private sectors, and visionaries from the wider Caribbean.

The Caribbean Basin grouping places the region in a stronger position in inter-American relations. The Caribbean, Latin America and the United States have found common ground in the battle against drugs, the defence of democracy and the promotion of freer trade. At the same time, the Caribbean must negotiate new relationships with Europe and with the World Trade Organisation. While we seek continued access to support from the European Union, we have to be prepared for the total dismantling of preferential relationships. I trust that from this conference will come an agenda for the mobilisation of the region's thinkers in ongoing strategic planning to enable the Caribbean to arrive at a secure destination in the new century. Future symposia such as this will be valuable, and would be greatly enhanced by strong participation of the private sector, the labour movement and the NGOs.

There is, as well, urgent need for a review of the relationship between the University of the West Indies and an important stakeholder group, the governments, which some of us believe to be entitled to greater consideration from the governors of UWI than we currently receive. There are recurring questions as to the cost-benefit relationship between the university and the government, and some of us in government are concerned about getting better value for money. These are concerns which should be speedily addressed. In any event, there seems to be a need for the university and the governments to come to the table to work out the bases for a new relationship in the new century.

To configure the matrix for the first century of the new millennium, it is necessary to examine a central question: In what way did the Caribbean most greatly affect the twentieth century? What was our forte? My thesis is that the Caribbean's greatest impact on the twentieth century was, essentially, the creative imagination of our people: Bob Marley; CLR James; Gary Sobers; Sir Arthur Lewis; Vidia Naipaul; Peter Minshall; Viv Richards; Marcus Garvey; Frank Worrell; Derek Walcott; Dwight Yorke; Brian Lara. Whatever the mode of expression, can there be any question that the creative imagination of the Caribbean people has most powerfully impacted this century? Reggae and Rastafari . . . songs of freedom . . . dreadlocks . . . culture colours . . . 'ice, green, and gold' . . . calypso and carnival – major musical forms invented in the twentieth century . . . The steelband and The Mighty Sparrow, whose celebrated creative imagination the University of the West Indies has recognised with an honorary PhD.

All of this brings to mind an observation which Professor Rex Nettleford made ten years ago, and which, without Professor Nettleford's permission, I now quote: 'The region has more artists per square inch than is probably good for it.' But Professor Nettleford was not dismissing the artist in Caribbean society. He had more to say on the subject, and I again quote him as he continued on the region's artists:

. . . this merely speaks of that need to survive with dignity where the creative imagination offers a particular kind of freedom of expression and self-fulfilment on a personal as well as on a collective level.

With the greatest respect, Rex, what we create for ourselves and for the world is something indeed as grand as you suggest, but I do believe it to be grander yet. Much, much grander.

From this abundance of creative imagination issues forth not only intrinsic cultural richness, but virtually unlimited commercial wealth. I am told that Eddie Grant dropped out of the bidding for Bob Marley's musical works when the figure reached US$50 million. That is a measure of the great potential of our creative imagination. The millennium question for the Caribbean might therefore be, 'How do we mine all of this wealth?'

Let us look to the extraordinary paradox in which a region endowed with such immeasurable creative intelligence, such genius, is regarded as the region of the world most dominated by imported cultural product. Television programming consumed in the Caribbean region is said to have a higher imported content than all other countries, somewhere around 95 per cent. In essence, the Caribbean has been recolonised by the hegemony of American media, much of it delivering a surfeit of gratuitous violence. Much of that programming also contributes to the identity crises afflicting many of our young people. With the abundant talent in this region, we should be global leaders in the export of cultural product, not the captive consumers of imported lifestyles and attitudes that we largely are. Is there the opportunity for a top level degree in film and video production at UWI? Is there the potential for a major film and video production industry in the Caribbean?

We need new industries for a new Caribbean. We must look to the university to provide our people with the grounding that will give them a kick-start in electronic commerce and in international financial services. We leave a century in which Dolly, the first mammal cloned from an adult cell, has given birth to a healthy female lamb named Bonnie. We are hurtling to a century in which a warp-speed IBM computer, capable of carrying out ten trillion operations per second, will be installed and running at the United States Department of Energy's Lawrence Livermore National Library. If any one of us now were to take a handheld calculator and attempt to do the same number of calculations that this computer will carry out in one second, it would take ten million years. Another computer, ten times as fast, will shortly follow.

One of the challenges which this conference on the Caribbean in the twenty-first century must address is the obligation to so rapidly develop the region's human capital that the people of the Caribbean, will be masters and producers of twenty-first century technologies, not just consumers. The mission of this conference, I propose, is that none of us, and none of the people whose futures and fortunes will, we hope, be shaped here, should even have to contemplate the first decade of the first century of the next millennium, with a handheld calculator. I challenge our collective creative imagination to save the peoples of the Caribbean from such a future.

Of all the institutions and estates of our region – the Church, the media, the governments, and CARICOM – it is to the University of the West Indies we must look for divination and direction such as this conference sets out to provide. At the turn of the century, and the millennium, the University of the West Indies is, and will continue to be, the essential fount and fulcrum for West Indian leadership in virtually every area of Caribbean society.

If we, the people of the Caribbean, are ever to be all that we can be, we must now call upon the University of the West Indies to lead the vital transformation that must take place in the West Indian psyche.

If the people of the Caribbean are to take the position in the new millennium to which our intrinsic worth entitles us, we must enter the twenty-first century a confident people. To this end, we must free ourselves from the psychology of colonialism, slavery and indentureship which shackles us to the past. Only in this way will we have the confidence to seize the twenty-first century as the Caribbean century, and to make it a century enriched by the singular creative imagination, the immense energy and the great humanity of the peoples of the Caribbean.

2 | PJ PATTERSON
Prime Minister of Jamaica

Mobilising Human Resources in Support of Caribbean Development

I regard your invitation to address the launch of this symposium as a special privilege. It is most fitting that we should gather on the Mona campus, the foundation site of a university that was cradled to illuminate the path of Caribbean development and which must serve throughout the next millennium as a beacon in the process of regional integration.

I wish to congratulate the University of the West Indies, the CARICOM Secretariat and the Caribbean Development Bank for their foresight in organising this conference. I commend their success in marshalling such a formidable array of political and institutional leaders, academicians, captains of the private sector and distinguished representatives of civil society. Your objective is to critically examine the challenges which face the Caribbean on the threshold of a new century; to consider what policy options are available and suggest what programmes we can implement to ensure our survival and our progress.

We can hardly claim that the new millennium is catching us by surprise. For the past decade, we have been talking about little else. As is the case of political independence, the change from one century to another is not so much a magic incident of time, but a defining moment in a process of total transformation. However we view it, let us recognise that we are entering an entirely different 'ballpark'. It will be technologically driven and interest alliance ridden.

International Prospects

We in the Caribbean are painfully aware that the conditions for international trade will substantially alter our prospects in the years ahead. For all practical purposes we have to envisage a future when, quite early in the next century, trade preferences may altogether disappear. Development aid, on any meaningful scale, is rapidly disappearing everywhere. Several of our number have been deprived of access to concessional lending and one international agency, the World Bank, is attempting to redefine small island states that would remove Jamaica from this category.

In the light of all this, we have to confront the global forces of competition and strive more than ever before to increase efficiency throughout the economy and look for new lines of production and trade which are profitable. We are working assiduously to negotiate new arrangements for engaging in international trade, both in goods and services. Over the coming months we hope to make major progress in negotiations of a successor to the Lomé IV Convention, the Free Trade Area of the Americas and the New Millennium Round under the WTO.

These are tough negotiations. We are applying all of our political and diplomatic skills to get the situation of small, vulnerable economies recognised and appropriate provisions established for them.

A Knowledge-based Economy

It has also become patently clear that the challenge of the next century will not be confined to worldwide trade liberalisation. The technological revolution and the emergence of economic activities which rest primarily on the pillars of knowledge, rather than the spread of natural resources, pose formidable demands for all of us. The Caribbean economy has never been blessed with an abundance of natural resources, but we have survived on such as we have. We are now adrift in an unfamiliar world, dominated by knowledge created through scientific and technological effort. We cannot reverse history, but the contemporary situation obliges us to undertake urgent collaborative action simply in order to cope. Our situation is destined to worsen sharply unless we take corrective measures immediately. This is best done on a collective basis, so as to share costs, attain critical masses and afford worthwhile coverage.

The old hierarchial ways of management, organisation, education, training and internalisation, must give way to more wide-based, flexible and knowledge-oriented interrelationships, where all concerned are part of an information-led learning environment. Except in very few instances, low skills and low technologies with low expectations, have restricted economic possibilities. Many of our industries still follow a traditional production line; trading in low value, mass produced commodities which are incapable of commanding competitive positions in world markets. The result in the new globalised and liberalised environment, has been declining fortunes, loss of jobs and generally pessimistic prognostications. Few Caribbean businesses, as well as supportive public institutions, have grasped the overwhelming importance of scientific approaches and technological advancements, in gaining and maintaining competitive positions. A culture of innovation has yet to take hold in our societies. Rigid old fashioned thinking will never solve complex rapidly moving problems.

Technological Changes

Remaining abreast of technological changes and determining their consequences on local effort and traditions must be major goals of all societies. This will not happen by chance, or by the flows of the market. Instead this will require purposefully trained and nationally sensitive science and technology workers, and in turn this depends on active research and development efforts, in key areas of domestic importance. I would suggest that many more of our teaching institutions take a systematic approach to this question and prepare specialists in order to address the unique problems of the Caribbean. The 'scatter shot' approach to education and training will simply not suffice.

Not only must scientists be wisely groomed, our political, social and economic systems will have to undertake and undergo the necessary adjustments. Managers and other leaders must also be properly alerted to appreciating the value of technological innovations and scientific inventiveness. The technological challenges will, among others, involve new computer applications, advances in telecommunications, bio-technological breakthroughs and new forms of doing business. Quite early in the twenty-first century one can expect electronic commerce to become established as the predominant form of doing business, particularly in the wholesale and retail fields. The Caribbean has to be ready to utilise the new technologies so that we can join the ranks of state-of-the-art exporters.

We have to see how far we can take advantage of niche opportunities in fields such as professional services (architecture, consulting engineering, legal research, market research); back-office operations with higher value added than basic data entry, e.g. software programming, data capture and repair, adjudication of claims, management of electronic medical records; and services that leverage cultural or linguistic strengths (e.g. provision of multi-lingual, off-shore call centre services).

Niche opportunities, however, change rapidly, driven largely by rapid technological changes. This requires a capacity for prompt and rapid adaptation to new market circumstances. Once we have succeeded in marking out the playing field, the private sector must move into the game. Among other things, this requires higher standards of human capability and risk taking.

A New Orientation

Speaking as I am at UWI, I cannot stress too strongly the need for the graduates of today to have the skill requirements of the new era in fields such as science, technology, international business and languages. It is important that our students are taught to think. But it is also imperative that they develop simultaneously an orientation for problem solving, for teamwork and a deep commitment to their country and region.

A large part of the economic success of the future resides in the hands of the UWI and our other universities and tertiary institutions. These institutions are required to deliver both in the range and quality of their teaching and research programmes, so that we make the first step towards sustained success. A critical factor to our success has to depend on the growing involvement of youth in entrepreneurship and business development. We have already a number of elements that provide support to youth entrepreneurs. Graduates of today should not only be asking about the jobs available, but also about what business opportunities they can themselves create.

Our Resolve

No matter what position each of us may occupy, or the role in which we participate here, it is incumbent upon us, as Caribbean people, to accept that we are all facing severe difficulties which require major and overdue adjustments. Unless we make them, we will never achieve the substantial levels of self-sustaining growth which are necessary to reduce unemployment and remove the endemic poverty that has been for so long entrenched. These impediments threaten social stability – they pose a real danger to democracy itself.

As a regional society, we have to build and harness the creative energies of all our people, embracing the masses and our youth in particular, to foster hope rather than despair. Since whatever systems we create – political, economic, social or cultural – must exist to serve people, and not the other way round, the emphasis and absolute priority must always be placed on the primacy of our human resource.

As we stand on the threshold of a new century, this must be a moment of resolve, of new decision-making, of new visions, of new confidence. I call upon this conference to begin a new wave of ideas generation, of optimism, and of collective endeavour. I assure you that my government, both nationally and at the CARICOM level, will leave no stone unturned in giving leadership and in contributing decisively to unearthing those factors that can make Jamaica and the region as a whole, a new land of opportunity, boundless with the confidence and capability which are needed to turn the tide, and to achieve the highest levels of performance in economic, social and human terms.

We dare not enter the twenty-first century, overcome by defeatism and a sense of hopelessness. However intractable the problems, it is for us to find the requisite solutions. I know this is not beyond our collective capacity and I am confident that flowing from these deliberations will be reflected our resolve and ability to build a brighter future for us all.

3 | OWEN ARTHUR
Prime Minister of Barbados

Economic Policy Options in the Twenty-first Century

Many years ago, I had the very good fortune to be schooled on these premises as a graduate student in economics. I was expected then to be rigorous. I return today in an entirely different capacity; a position which has afforded me certain academic liberties in preparing myself to treat with an issue which has been the focus of the most rigorous analysis and the most overwhelming outpouring of policy advice ever imposed on any single issue pertaining to the Caribbean society – the future of the Caribbean economy in the twenty-first century.

I found everything that I perhaps need to say today summed up in VS Naipaul's graphic introduction to his novel, *A Bend in the River*: 'The world is what it is, men who are nothing, who allow themselves to become nothing, have no place in it.'

The twentieth century has, in economic terms, not been the Caribbean's century. We stand now on the threshold of a new century which, in every respect, will usher in a new era in the conduct of man's affairs.

It will expose us to challenges of unprecedented dimensions and opportunities of vast and exciting proportions.

The essential issue is whether we will choose to remain mired in the volatility and inertia that, on balance, exemplify so much of the Caribbean economic experience at the end of this century, or whether we will grasp the initiative and become robust and successful economies in the decades ahead.

It is to this essential issue that I seek to treat in the discursive manner of the politician, orienting my exposition to deal with the following issues:

1. What is the economic situation in which the Caribbean finds itself at the end of the twentieth century, and what does that forebode regarding our capacity to face the economic realities with which we will have to grapple in the decades ahead?
2. And what are the essential changes in our strategic perspectives, our mix of policies, and our way of conducting our affairs that must be embarked upon immediately and sustained over the long haul to maximise our chances of economic success in the new dispensation that lies ahead?

The Caribbean's Economic Conditions and Challenges

As mentioned earlier, the twentieth century has not been the Caribbean's century. While some other small societies which occupied the same rung on the development ladder as the leading Caribbean economies at mid century have gone on to acquire the attributes of fully developed and successful economies, the Caribbean will end the twentieth century essentially occupying the status that it held at the beginning – the world's most volatile and vulnerable economic region. To be sure, it has not all been unrelieved economic and social gloom.

Some Caribbean societies have come to enjoy very high rankings in the global human development index. The region also shows up favourably in the global index of poverty. Some countries have also successfully initiated processes of economic diversification, and have come to occupy niches, especially as export service economies, which have redounded to their favour in the form of sustained internal and external stability, rising incomes and improved standards of living. Trinidad shows real signs of emerging as a highly competitive and successful example of the export manufacturing and mineral economy at the turn of the century.

In the corporate economy there have also been a few cases, though far too few, of cross-regional synergies being harnessed to create companies with the diversity, the critical mass and the financial conditions to prosper regionally, and to successfully operate on a hemispheric and a global plateau.

On balance, however, the performance of the Caribbean economy in general has been anaemic and spasmodic, reflecting both market and policy failures, a slowness and failure to adjust in line with changing circumstances, and an inability to attain a path of sustained and sustainable growth and development.

Our business cycles are not things to be commended to the fainthearted, reflecting random bouts of economic growth followed by declines sufficiently large to cancel the earlier economic gains. Typically, when the international economy has been growing, the Caribbean has generally recorded slower growth than almost every region, and when the world has experienced recession, our decline has been sharper than the average. The Caribbean has also been fond of playing an indigenous stroke, going into depression in circumstances where robust growth is being realised in most of the other countries of the world.

This record of macro instability has generated the typical Caribbean economic syndrome – mass unemployment, fiscal difficulties, recurring external imbalances, and major distortions in resource allocation in favour of highly subsidised state enterprises or highly protected private firms, all leading to a tendency for the economies to lurch from crisis to crisis; pepetuating mass poverty and raising of the spectre of societal disintegration. Elsewhere, I have called attention to the fact that economic decay in some Caribbean economies has been so severe and corrosive as to set in train social and political disorder which, unchecked, will create a new Caribbean species of 'failed society' among the family of nations.

A debt crisis of overwhelming proportions in the larger economies has, at the turn of this century, contributed massively to this, draining those economies not only of the foreign exchange needed to support sustained development but also causing them to replace strategic planning and sound macroeconomic management with policy expedients which can only be charitably described as crisis intervention. By contrast, the economic circumstances of the OECS countries have reflected an element of sustained stability, however camouflaging two potentially unsettling aspects to their structure which might have dire implications for the years immediately ahead.

The first is that these economies have higher ratios of trade preference induced activity to GDP of all Caribbean economies, and probably of all global economies, raising the spectre of a traumatic period of adjustment if trade preferences are abruptly terminated. The second is that these economies have evolved with very narrow fiscal bases, reflecting an overwhelming dependence on custom revenues. Again, the vulnerability of these economies is likely to be exposed in a new economic dispensation that has at its core the international dismantling of tariff barriers.

Added to these, there are general aspects of the structure and functioning of the Caribbean economy at the end of the century which would immediately be recognised by anyone who was with us at the beginning of the century – a heavy concentration in the agricultural sector on primary production for exports, a distributive sector dominated by import-intensive oligopolies, the prevalence of state and private monopolies in critical service sectors, narrow specialisation in the production of a few goods and services and the like. In such a context, the need for structural and functional adjustment in the Caribbean has been recognised and acted upon, particularly in the last two decades.

Generally, however, this adjustment has been prompted by the severity of the external strains experienced by some leading Caribbean economies and carried out in accordance with the Washington Consensus, featuring trade and financial liberalisation, privatisation, flexible exchange rates, the setting of user fees, the market determination of prices for inputs and outputs, and a recourse to market-driven, private sector led, export-oriented activities. There is, however, no discernible evidence that the policy mix associated with the Washington Consensus has been successful or recommends itself as the policy menu to embrace for a new century.

It can therefore be fairly said that the end of the century finds us with a gap between the current conditions of the region and what is required to support sustained and sustainable development. The need to address this longstanding deficiency in the structure and functioning of the region's economy would have meant that this period would have to be one in which far reaching adjustments had to be carried out in the Caribbean.

A special urgency has been added to the need for reform because of the emergence of another gap which is looming larger and larger. It is the gap between the current conditions of the region and what is required for it to function successfully in the emerging global economic order. It is now commonplace to observe that those aspects of the international economic environment which bear most directly on the functioning of the Caribbean economy have changed in ways which do not appear to be to our advantage. The region therefore finds itself on the threshold of a new century relatively unprepared for the new dispensation and caught up in a desperate rear guard action to either secure the status quo, or to arrange new transition mechanisms to reposition itself in the evolving new order. These matters have enjoyed the favour of such a rich literature that I will avoid the technicalities and focus merely on the strategic dimensions of what is portended.

The first is that in the course of our economic evolution, we have given a largely North Atlantic focus to our international economic relationships. The result has been the development of special relationships with Europe and the Americas, having at their core our preferential access to their markets and access to aid and other concessional financial resources whose flow these societies have effectively influenced. These 'development props' are incrementally being dismantled and it is envisioned that in the decades after 2005, under the auspices of a new Lomé Convention and the proposed FTAA, a new model of cooperation will be phased in that replaces preferences with reciprocal relationships, and access to aid with new forms of decentralised cooperation.

The essential issue must now be the extent to which, and the means by which, our region – which has embedded the main aspects of its former special relationships deeply into its economic structure – should make the transition to a new dispensation, especially given the short period over which the transition has to be made. But there is evidence of a determined resolve simply to maintain the status quo. It is of course always a very dangerous thing to look a gift horse in the mouth. It has to be recognised properly however that trade preferences, even before the turn of the century, have become massively depreciated assets. The margin of protection offered to the Caribbean by Europe through the Lomé Conventions has been eroded by the extension of equivalent preferences to other countries. In addition, the liberalisation of trade under multilateral trade arrangements has, and will further strip such preferences of their residual worth, if there is any. The same applies to the preferences traditionally extended by our North America partners under the CBI and CARIBCAN.

In a broader sense, the Lomé Convention is but one of several frameworks for development cooperation that Europe has put in place with other developing and emerging economies. In many respects, it is probably not the most favourable; Europe's new framework relationship with its Mediterranean neighbours is more advantageous. In a similar vein, it would be uniquely difficult to demonstrate that our relationship with the USA, as expressed through the CBI, is more advantageous than that extended to Mexico under NAFTA.

The point is that the conventions which have bound us to the North Atlantic economy, like the preferences which have been at their core, have also been made depreciated development assets. It would therefore be a matter of the greatest hazard for a future relationship between the Caribbean and its North Atlantic partners to be forged without taking into account the need for new modalities of cooperation that can be more beneficial to Caribbean development. To rest a relationship with the North Atlantic economy on preferences would be to hope their incantations can create what reality denies. Perhaps the lesson in all of this, waiting to be acted upon, is that the Caribbean can no longer, in this age of globalisation, see the world as a strip of North Atlantic economies.

We need a new global focus. This is made all the more compelling by our need to accommodate the new forces of globalisation as a factor in shaping the Caribbean's economic destiny in the twenty-first century.

Again, I will spare the technical details on this matter and speak to the strategic dimensions as they concern the Caribbean economy. The first is that globalisation has at its core certain new geopolitical dimensions which have devalued the Caribbean from a security and strategic point of view in the eyes of the dominant coalition of nations. This is except in so far as our security interests coincide with theirs in our mutual battle against illegal drugs and associated forms of international criminal activity.

The geopolitics of globalisation, however, on balance predispose the Caribbean towards economic marginalisation. It is a matter which can only successfully be addressed in the resilience we exercise to ensure that our cooperation in the international fight against illegal drugs has as its focus the meshing of that cooperation in an interrelated network of relationships which are conducive to the general development of the Caribbean society.

The second strategic dimension is the dominant and legitimising ideology of globalisation – unbridled liberalisation – particularly as espoused by the principles intended to inform the workings of the WTO.

The Caribbean cannot stand splendidly in isolation from the new forces of liberalisation. It is my judgement, however, that the unbridled application of the forces of liberalisation has to be guarded against for reasons which will be outlined when we consider the mix of policies appropriate to our present and evolving circumstances.

The strategic dimension of the new forces of globalisation that must most concern us is the technological one. Contemporary globalisation has been underpinned by technological revolutions in information, communications and transport. It has caused a transition in the global society from the Industrial to the Information Age. Indeed, one of the key features of the emerging global economy is that information has replaced energy, commodities and natural resources as the basic raw material in the production process. In its wake, it has thrown up a whole welter of new knowledge-based, skill intensive, service-oriented production possibilities which can readily be exploited by all societies that spare the effort to develop the human capital and the institutional capacity required to master the use of information.

Globalisation in this context has virtually therefore reconfigured the bases of the comparative and competitive advantage of nations. It has neutralised the supposed disabilities arising from small size, the lack of a wide array of natural resources and the absence of scale economies which have hitherto been regarded as effective constraints to the transformation of the Caribbean economy, individually and collectively. Hence, while other aspects of globalisation will confront the Caribbean economies with severe competitive challenges (especially those arising out of the obligation to the WTO, which will alter the market context within which our development will take place), there can be no doubt that the technological underpinning of globalisation will facilitate the viability of thousands of new producers in the Caribbean, provided we are prepared to respond positively and proactively.

I am led therefore to the judgement that the Caribbean need not perpetuate the development stalemate that has characterised so much of its twentieth century experience, and that we can and should face the future with the confidence of being able to attain sustained and sustainable growth and development.

New Strategic Perspectives, Policies and Arrangements

It is against such a background that I now turn succinctly to the new strategic perspectives, the mix of policies and changes in our institutional and other arrangements affecting the conduct of business which will make that possible. First, the character of the management of our economic affairs, especially in those national economies which are under the greatest stress, must move away from crisis intervention to strategic planning. Too much of our economic energy and far too much of our scarce financial resources have been deployed in support of stop-gap, short term expedients in a self defeating way and in a manner that is pre-emptive of the accomplishment of long term strategic goals.

The fear of reporting failure in small societies, or the fear of antagonising entrenched interest groups, has caused many Caribbean governments to intervene, at points of perceived crisis, to prop up failed systems long after any justification for their continued support could be advanced. In the interim, the few key strategic things that must be done to underwrite sustained development get starved of the required resources and attention. I believe that a classic case in point has been Jamaica's crisis intervention to stave off the difficulties in its financial sector. The evidence suggests that the conditions for sustainable macro economic stability had been established in Jamaica immediately prior to the financial crisis. The resulting deployment of billions of dollars, largely to protect depositors and directors of institutions against losses, have compromised Jamaica's capacity to underwrite the restructuring of its economy that coincides more with its long term strategic interest.

Voltaire expressed it well in *Candide*: 'it is often necessary to shoot a general in order to encourage the others'. By way of comparison, Barbados has made a strategic choice that it should reform what might still be the best education system in the Caribbean to make it more appropriate to the requirements ushered in by globalisation. We have determined that the programme 'Edutech 2000' should have first claim on our domestic resources, and should be the principal purpose for which we borrow internationally. I believe that the exercise of strategic choices such as these by countries which in fact have only a few strategic options, will make all of the difference.

The second and third aspects of our policy requirements are interrelated. We must go beyond the Washington Consensus for the substance and direction of our macroeconomic management and development strategies and we must adopt a carefully balanced and properly sequenced approach to the implementation of schemes for liberalisation. The policy mix arising out of the Washington Consensus proposed that in economies where part of the problem was located in state domination and the inward orientation of the economic system, a menu of measures intended to induce a market-driven, private sector-led outward orientation should be instituted.

The market forces of this agenda required that appropriate prices should be set – for capital and for inputs to foreign exchange – reflecting conditions of scarcity or international conditions. It also required the reduction in the role of the state, the dismantling of barriers to trade, privatisation, de-regulation and the like. Some of these measures have proven disfunctional in their own right. For example, it is very difficult to induce sustainable development in the face of very high, real interest rates, and there can be no doubt that flexible exchange rates, by increasing the degree of risk and uncertainty, can retard investments in Caribbean economies. The more compelling criticism is that while these measures may create the parameters of a market, they do not deal with fundamentals such as the development of human resources, institutional capacities, the creation of technological assets and the like which are really the building blocks upon which our development efforts must rest.

It is also a very serious error to presume that the role of the state in the Caribbean should be so marginalised. Such would prevent it from playing a creative role in the redesign of the Caribbean infrastructure that will enable it to move from the Industrial to the Information Age; from attending to longstanding deficiencies in the development of our human institutional and technological capabilities, from creating a framework within which non-traditional enterprise can emerge, and from carrying out those vital programmes to enhance and protect our environment in support of our sustainable development.

After 30 years of independence, the state cannot retreat as a force for good in Caribbean development. It must reform its way of doing business. It must reinvent itself to be relevant to today's purposes and tomorrow's needs. It must build new strategic alliances with the private sector, the non-governmental institutions, and all the institutions of our civil society to create a new Caribbean, ordered in accordance with the precepts of a just and equitable and good society, which can take its place among the family of nations in today's challenging age as a competitive, productive and prosperous region. But it cannot retreat.

In a similar vein, it would be tragic if we were to be beguiled by the magic of the supposed workings of free markets. A market is not an institution unto itself governed by invisible forces of demand and supply. At its best, it is a social institution governed in accordance with clearly defined rules and regulations. Indeed, the experience in the financial markets of East Asia and Russia clearly indicates that wherever liberalisation precedes the clear definition of regulatory and supervisory systems, the rest is economic and financial chaos.

Our task now is to build market structures and to sensitively apply a 'managed market' approach to our economic affairs. In all of this, the Caribbean must be very careful in relating to the existing economic orthodoxies regarding free international trade. In many respects it is a con game. If I may illustrate, the right of capital to be mobile globally and to seek its highest reward is not extended to labour. There are also many important examples where powerful developed societies provide substantial protection to their sensitive agricultural sectors, provide domestic subsidies to their food producers in the name of food security, place restraints on the importation of industrial goods such as textiles, create barriers to the movement of labour, and use non-tariff barriers such as environmental, social and human rights conditionalities to prevent the flood of imports to their markets. The Caribbean would be unwise to participate in a new global society with its eyes shut to these practices.

Our general response to this is that we should devise and implement our own phased and appropriately structured programmes for trade, financial liberalisation and privatisation, and support these with institutional and productive capacity building initiatives, and human resource and technological developments, as the core of programmes on which to base our quest for international competitiveness.

The fourth crucial aspect in our new way forward will be to successfully carry out the measures to create a Single Caribbean Market and Economy both as a response to regional economic inertia and as one of the means of better preparing the Caribbean economies to compete in the global arena. The 1973 concept of a limited common market, with no provision for capital and labour movement, nor rights of establishment, embedded itself in the structure of Caribbean economy since then, and has been a major factor in explaining some of the realised deficiencies in its functioning.

It was based on the premise that the mere freeing of the movement of goods could in itself be a positive, major force, independent of other adjustments necessary to make trade liberalisation work. We have come to understand otherwise. Hence the decision at Grand Anse in 1989 to move from a limited version of a common market to a fully-fledged Single Market and Economy was a crucial initiative in Caribbean development.

The effort to create the legal framework within which the Caribbean Single Market and Economy (CSME) will function is now virtually completed, and should be in place by the Year 2000. Protocol 2, which has already been signed, provides for the removal of restrictions on capital and skills within the region, the provision of services and the rights of establishment. These are especially important in creating the transition from a limited common market to a single economy.

It is also vital that the work to amend the Treaty of Chaguaramas to create a legal framework for the CSME be complemented by measures, already underway, to harmonise the development of our capital markets, to put in place a system for the avoidance of double taxation, to harmonise our fiscal systems and our incentives, to put in place arrangements for the portability and harmonisation of our social security arrangements, the convertibility of our currencies and the convergence of our economic policies with the intention of creating conditions of regional internal and external stability capable of supporting a common currency. It will take some doing, but it must be done. In all of this, we must remain sensitive to the limitations in the mechanisms of the CSME as conceived, and be flexible enough to improve upon them.

In particular, it is to be recognised that the formal instruments of regional integration such as the CET and trade liberalisation will be of less value in promoting Caribbean development than concerted efforts to promote region-wide, human resource development capabilities, and technological, infrastructural and institutional capabilities that are attractive to both domestic, regional and international enterprise. In addition, the long term relevance of the CET as an instrument of regional policy may also reside more in its capacity as a negotiating chip than as an instrument of effective protection, and will be reduced as we enter hemispheric and extra regional trade arrangements.

Furthermore, many of the matters to be addressed by Caribbean societies in their international negotiations, especially intellectual property rights, government procurement, environmental and labour standards, have not been provided for under the CSME, although it is not beyond our intellectual capacity to do so. Unless these are treated in the development of the CSME, it will be less useful as an instrument for making a more successful integration of the Caribbean economy in the global economy.

Above all, in our efforts to create a CSME, we would do well to remember that enterprises compete internationally, not countries.

Economic integration for us in the twenty-first century will be less important for the regional trade it will promote than for the creation of an environment that can conduce the development of globally competitive enterprises. Such synergies across the Caribbean are slowly being created. But it must increasingly become the principal focus of the efforts to carry a CSME into the twenty-first century as an instrument of Caribbean progress.

The fifth aspect of our new economic dispensation must be the proactive measures we employ to integrate the Caribbean into the new global society. Our focus must become global and must not be constrained as exclusively as it has been to maintaining the status quo or improving our relationship with our North Atlantic traditional partners. There are exciting strategic alliances that we must forge and develop with Latin and Central America, Asia and Africa.

We must look to express our relationship with our global partners more in terms of modalities of cooperation that can improve our own efforts to build our human resources, our institutional and technological capabilities, promote services, permit decentralised forms of cooperation that facilitate private sector to private sector strategic alliances and encourage the development as an investment beach-head for enterprises looking to expand into emerging markets, than clinging to the depreciated asset of trade preferences. I qualify this only by the recognition that the recourse to preferences over the medium term for the OECS economies particularly may be a transitional measure that they cannot entirely do without.

The sixth is that in the new global arena, the Caribbean's best option, having regard to the changing configuration of international demand and the direction of technological change, is to set in train the measures that will ensure that we become high quality producers of the range of services which meet our resource capabilities. The Caribbean's relative political stability, its long standing investment in its human resources, its strategic location, all make a strategy in support of the development of 'intelligent exports' both feasible and highly desirable. The informatics industry is now a $3 trillion industry into which we must tap.

Not enough has been made of our tourism potential, both as a generator of income employment and foreign exchange in its own right, and as a catalyst for the transformation of other sectors. I am immediately struck by the enormous potential that Jamaica possesses, were it to be structured and unrelenting in realising its capacity to be one of the leading tourism destinations of the world. The development of our traditional and non-traditional services as our most feasible option will require that we put a premium on those elements of Caribbean development that have hovered on the fringe – human resource development, a new business-friendly environment intended to reduce the transaction costs and encumbrances to doing business, the commercialisation of our intangible assets, and the acquisition of capabilities to develop, apply and absorb new technologies.

It will especially require that we also place a premium on the development and enhancement of the Caribbean's social capital. There is now a growing literature that has documented that the stock of a society's social capital, the norms, interpersonal trust, social networks and organisation, which is created when institutions, groups and organisations develop the ability to work together for mutually productive gain, makes a decisive difference as to whether a society transforms positively or not. To face the challenge posed by globalisation we must systematically enhance such social capital in the Caribbean.

However, Francis Fukuyama's most recent work, *The Great Disruption*, warns us that such enhancement will not necessarily be easy.

With globalisation, freedom of choice has exploded. Hierarchies of all sorts, political and corporate, will come under pressure, and large rigid bureaucracies will be undermined. There will be a disruption of the old social order as the practice of excessive individualism and the notion of 'no limits' are introduced increasingly. This culture of intense individualism, bereft of a sense of community, that will feature increasingly as a facet of our new information age has carefully to be managed if we are not to incur social disintegration as a by-product of our integration into the new global order.

Finally, to realise its full potential, the Caribbean needs to move to a new form of governance.

No Caribbean society can succeed unless all of its resources are mobilised in support of national development. However, the unfortunate aspect of the Westminster model of governance we have inherited is that it has encouraged a 'to the victors, the spoils' mentality that has ensured that at any time almost half of the population of any given Caribbean society is marginalised and alienated from participation in the development of their society.

It has also reasonably been argued that, in our region, there has been too destructive a competition for political office; too heavy a concentration of power in the hands of the ruling elites, an unhealthy preservation of anti-developmental party and tribal divisions, a focus on short term partisan, political concerns rather than long term strategic objectives, and a patronage and spoils systems which work against sound and progressive government. Alienation, cynicism and marginalisation have been the results, all leading to a perpetuation of underdevelopment. We have to change that.

It surely must be part of our mission to make consensus building the foundation of a new form of governance; to make popular and effective participation and inclusion the key facets of our political culture, and to fashion a society in which the people's business and the government's business are one and the same thing. It is what the social contract in Barbados is intended to be about. It is the factor, perhaps more than any other, which has enabled Barbados to rebound from economic adversity and to be able to explore new paths of social and economic progress. I commend it to all.

I conclude on this note. The twenty-first century is not a chronological milestone. It is a set of social and economic relations that have a dynamic that is already with us, and is irreversible. It represents a new way of doing old things, and new ways of doing new things. As I said earlier, in preparation for this address, I delved into disciplines other than those in which I was schooled in these premises twenty-five years ago.

I took stock of Naipaul's view that the future of the Caribbean is Haiti. I took note of Walcott's words, on receiving a Nobel Prize, 'That a day may come when people may ask not only what became of our shores and our bays, but of a whole people.'

As a product of this institution, I do not share this pessimism. I also have the honour to lead a nation which essentially has entered the social relations of the twenty-first century before it has chronologically departed the twentieth. So can all of the Caribbean. I have a responsibility to close by urging you, in the words of Arthur Clough, 'But westward look; the land is bright.'

4 — EDWIN CARRINGTON
Secretary General of CARICOM

The Challenge of Change

I have been paid the signal honour of being invited to chair the opening session of this important conference and I do so with unmitigated joy. Let me begin by welcoming this initiative and the initiators of this exercise, the University of the West Indies, spearheading a venture supported by the Caribbean Secretariat and the Caribbean Development Bank.

As I understand it, the objective of the conference is to bring together regional leaders in various fields of Caribbean life, to help chart the course of regional development in the early twenty first century. It is my hope that it will help to generate even greater commitment to the cause of regional development than exists at present. I am hoping it that will generate some militancy for Caribbean development. I also hope that there will be a wide-ranging multiplier effect to ensure that what happens here this weekend impacts upon the wider Caribbean society. Indeed, I am hoping that there will be many more initiatives of this kind. If I have any regrets, it is that we have not done this earlier or that we have not taken more initiatives of this nature.

Since I will not be presenting a paper at the conference as originally planned, I hope you will permit me to say a few words about the role and contribution of this conference. First of all, in an audience like this, one hardly needs to draw attention to the rapid pace of change in today's world at virtually every level. Indeed even the proverbial ostrich with its head in the sand can hardly avoid taking note of the changes around us as the very sand itself is shifting, and not only by weather patterns. It is now impossible for us, for example, to avoid the computer, dare I say 'dead or alive' and to be without an e-mail address today is to run the risk of being classified as a vagrant. So let us face it, change is coming fast and furious and we have to face up to it. To do so effectively however, one has to master the art of managing change. This capacity has to be one of the cultural attributes of our lifestyle in the early twenty-first century. That process will certainly involve a number of adjustments to our current *modus vivendi*; for one, it will require us to recognise within our selves the need to make changes in our way of relating and reacting to the changing environment around us. Most importantly, it will require us to be able to determine what changes we must make to our way of life and our various relationships. This process would relate in fact, to all processes of our lives the – polity, the economy, the culture and all else. Most importantly, it is not simply a matter of requiring government action, but a general societal action.

How are we to achieve these changes and which of them should be achieved in what time frame? These are questions which we are going to have to grapple with as a society. In the world in which we live and in which, in the context of our history, many forces impact our societies continually and continuously, it is a factor which points most dramatically, to the necessity for the entire society to be awake to these developments and, if we are to empower our societies to respond effectively to this situation, certain approaches are clearly inevitable. One such, approach which is urgent is to remove the legal and, even more so, the social constraints to the full contribution and participation of that half of our society which is still impeded in this contribution by sexually based limitations. I refer to our women. Of no less importance is the requirement to organise our societies in such a way that the fullest possible involvement and contribution of our people are assured.

To enter the twenty-first century, culturally constraining our female population and delaying the full involvement of the young people in the development of our society is an underutilisation of our most precious resource – our human resource, which we cannot afford. It is as economically unaffordable as it is culturally unacceptable.

These concerns also highlight the fact that the development of our societies, is not merely a matter of economics and, even where the economics is concerned, it is vulnerability that is vital. The quality of life to which our societies aspire in the early twenty-first century requires much more.

A no less critical dimension of our region's development in the twenty-first century is certainly the nature of the regional, hemispheric and wider international relations to be established by the countries of the Caribbean. This consideration brings squarely to the fore the question of what Caribbean we have in view. We certainly cannot afford to think of a Caribbean without Cuba or Haiti or the Dominican Republic or Suriname for that matter. Whatever the Caribbean that we speak of, it is certain that the international environment, and in that context, Inter-American relationships are certain to assume increased importance on the region's agenda. The most critical and, in a sense, the most sensitive and decisive consideration is the nature of the regional relationships which we will design, construct and sustain. Speaking lucidly and authoritatively on this matter in parliament last month, during his budget presentation, the Honourable Prime Minister of Barbados had this to say among much else. "The real constitution of the Caribbean economy as a single market and a single economy will therefore be the first great challenge that we will face in the new century and the creation of such a single market economy is not a pipe dream. We have a revised timetable set to have the main elements in place by 1999, we are scheduled to meet that objective".

The achievement of such a goal and indeed of many others, marked by critical analysis, widespread public discussion, insightful policy formulation, wise decision taking and effective and thorough implementation, for example in regard to the establishment of the Caribbean Court of Justice, are steps which commend themselves to us in respect of social, economic, political and cultural development in the twenty-first century. Are we up to it?

We have here in the gathering today, many of the key actors, political leaders, university professors, national and regional administrators, bankers, creative thinkers and cultural and human development specialists on whom the answers to these problems will depend. It is for that reason that I attach great importance to this conference and the opportunity for it to provide for an in-depth consideration of many of the issues relevant to the transition from the closing of the twentieth century to the commencement of the twenty-first, a subject which itself will engage the full attention of the Heads of Governments of the Caribbean Community. It is against this background that I extend a warm welcome to all participants. I extend a particularly warm welcome to the three distinguished prime ministers of Jamaica, Trinidad and Tobago and Barbados for taking time out from their busy work schedules to attend this conference. It is most fortunate that they have done so, for much rests on their shoulders if the region is to find and secure a place of honour in the international environment of the twenty-first century, worthy of the aspirations of the peoples of the Caribbean. I therefore wish this conference the greatest possible success, not just with regard to its deliberations over the next few days, but with regard to its impact on the broader Caribbean region and the wider civil society.

Part 2

The Caribbean: Geography, Culture, History and Identity

5 | NORMAN GIRVAN

Creating and Recreating the Caribbean[1]

As we begin our deliberations on the Caribbean in the twenty-first century, it is worth noting that the term 'Caribbean' itself is used in many ways with many meanings. Anglophones like ourselves are in the habit of talking as if we *are* the Caribbean. We go about the place calling our regional organisation the 'Caribbean Community' and christening a host of other primarily anglophone organisations with the name 'Caribbean', displaying a degree of cultural arrogance that is exceeded only by our geographic ignorance and strategic myopia. Many, if not most of us, seem to be blissfully unaware of the fact that we are less than one-fifth of the population, land area and GDP of the island Caribbean. While I am aware that this is not the case with the organisers of this conference, I hope that they will forgive the comment that its scope and content tends to reflect the traditional anglo-centric view of the region – this is a *West Indian* rather than a *Caribbean* gathering. In this presentation I will attempt to loosen our thinking and widen the discourse somewhat by making some observations on alternative conceptions and definitions of the Caribbean, on the question of identity, and socioeconomic characteristics.

We can identify at least four broad notions of what constitutes the 'Caribbean'. First is the Caribbean as the *island chain* lying in the Caribbean Sea. Second is the Caribbean as *basin*, comprising the countries lying in and around the Caribbean Sea. Third is the Caribbean as an *ethno-historic zone*, comprising the islands and the adjacent coastal communities in South and Central America sharing a similar history, culture and ethnicity. The fourth, and most recent, is the idea of the Caribbean as a *transnational community* that embraces the Caribbean diaspora overseas.

These conceptions correspond roughly to stages in historical development and geopolitical perspective. The island Caribbean is *las Antillas, les Antilles,* the *Antilles,* the *West Indies* (though this included the mainland Guianas) – the strategically located islands encircling the shipping lanes that became the locus of intense European rivalry and subsequently the heartland of the sugar plantation system. The Caribbean defined as basin was the product of US expansionism – the area at the turn of the nineteenth century, as argued persuasively by the Puerto Rican historian Antonio Gaztambide-Geigel. It was around this time that the word 'Caribbean' came into general use to refer to the region. If this name was taken from one of the indigenous people of the region – unfairly demonised by the Spanish as cannibals – Gaztambide-Geigel argues that its superimposition on a zone that was in reality extremely diverse and heterogeneous reflected an imperial conception and design.

It was not at first accepted by the actual inhabitants of the region – who in the main continued to speak of 'Central America', the 'Isthmus', the 'Antilles' and the West Indies. The process by which this definition became internalised within the region may have started with the formation of the Anglo-American Caribbean Commission based in Puerto Rico in the early 1940s, continued with US President Reagan's Caribbean Basin Initiative in the 1980s and culminated with the establishment of the Association of Caribbean States in the 1990s.

For us anglophones, the transition is expressed by the replacement of the colonial term 'West Indies' – as in West Indies Federation – by the postcolonial term 'Caribbean' – as in *Caribbean* Community and *Caribbean* Development Bank. Yet we remain uncomfortable with the perceived threat of loss of cultural identity from the more numerous Hispanics which might be connoted by an unambiguous acceptance of the term 'Caribbean' to describe ourselves. Notably, we have retained the colonial appellations of the West Indies cricket team and of course the University of the West Indies. Perhaps more significantly, when the leaders of the Caribbean Community set up a commission on the future of the Community in 1992, they took care to name it the Independent West Indian Commission. In doing so they seemed to signal a conscious or subconscious wish to retain the primarily anglophone character of CARICOM while at the same time opening the way to the formation of the looser Association of West Indian States.

I have suggested elsewhere that analogous ambiguities are detectable among Hispanic, Francophone and Dutch-speaking Caribbeans associated with self-perceptions of their own ethnicity and linguistic cultural heritage. Hence while we anglophones see ourselves as being at one and the same time Caribbean and *West Indian,* Hispanics might to see themselves as Caribbean and *Latin American.* Moreover, for anglophones 'West Indian' might also incorporate elements of pan-Africanism or even pan-Hinduism that are either muted or non-existent in the Hispanic societies. The term 'West Indian' is itself problematic to many anglophones of East Indian descent, insofar as it is connotes an African-centred cosmology and is implicitly opposed to the identity of 'East Indian'. In summary, the formation of a common Caribbean psycho-cultural identity that transcends barriers of language and ethnicity is a slow and uneven process that has yet to realise its potential.

Hence the significance of conceptions of the Caribbean that are not rooted in the geopolitical perspectives of external powers but are rather based on assertions of shared historical experience. Prominent among these is the Caribbean as a zone of Plantation America or as 'African Central America'. This Caribbean comprises the islands and the adjacent mainland coastal areas of South and Central America with a history characterised by extermination of the majority of the pre-Colombian population, sugar and the plantation system, and slavery and indenture; and which have ethnically diverse populations with a strong or predominantly African base. The initial characterisation of this zone as a 'culture sphere' is widely attributed to the American anthropologist, Charles Wagley. However in the anglophone Caribbean this conception has a strong nationalist and regionalist flavour and is associated with the work of people like CLR James, Eric Williams, Lloyd Best, George Beckford, George Lamming and the New World Group. Similar perspectives are evident in the work of the Haitian scholar Jean Casimir and the Puerto Rican Gaztambide-Geigel. It constitutes a powerful source of psycho-cultural identity revealing commonalities of experience that transcend divisions of language, political status and to some extent ethnicity. Its main drawback is its lack of close correspondence with a defined state system, as it includes some portions of the mainland states and excludes others – Cartagena but not Bogota or Puerto Limon but not San Jose.

In recent years we have seen the emergence of a broader socioeconomic conception of the Caribbean as embracing the Caribbean diaspora abroad. For example in a short paper I did on Rethinking Development some ten years ago, I suggested that being a Jamaican is more a state of mind than a legal status, and that 'Jamaica' is more a transnational community than a nation state. The same holds for the Caribbean. With continued migration and the growing economic, and to some extent political, role of overseas Caribbeans, the diaspora Caribbean must be considered to be a real phenomenon.

For instance, Haiti, Cuba, Jamaica and Puerto Rico each had close to one million of their native-born population living abroad at the close of the 1980s. In relation to the resident population, the overseas population at the end of the 1980s stood at 40 per cent for both Jamaica and Guyana, 36 per cent for Suriname, 23 per cent for Puerto Rico, 21 per cent for Trinidad and Tobago, 15 per cent for Haiti, and 10 per cent for Cuba. By the early 1990s the overseas population was sending home in remittances an amount equal to 71 per cent of the value of exports in the case of the Dominican Republic, 32 per cent in the case of Haiti, 29 per cent in Jamaica and 17 per cent for Barbados. In Jamaica, remittances have been the fastest growing source of foreign exchange inflows in the 1990s.

So from the conceptual point of view we have at least four Caribbeans – the islands, the basin, the ethno-historical Caribbean and the Caribbean as diaspora. This is mirrored in the scope and membership of the prominent 'Caribbean' institutions. As mentioned before, CARICOM is a minority fraction even of the islands only and will remain so even after the full admission of Haiti at the beginning of 2000 doubles its population. Then you have CARIFORUM, which includes both Haiti and the Dominican Republic for the purposes of Lome; the CDCC of ECLAC, which includes most of the non-independent countries; and finally the Association of Caribbean States, whose membership embraces the entire basin although some of the non-independent countries have yet to join.

In summary, the very notion of Caribbean was not only invented but has been continuously reinterpreted in response both to external influences and to internal currents. We can draw several lessons from this. One is the extreme difficulty of imagining what the Caribbean might be in 100, or 50 or even 20 years. It is a sobering thought that a conference like this one held 100 years ago could almost certainly not have anticipated the events of the first half of the twentieth century: two world wars, the rise of labour and nationalist movements, black nationalism and decolonisation, let alone the break up of the empires of Central Europe and the Russian Revolution. At most, we can talk about certain trends and suggest strategies for the next ten to twenty years.

That said, two trends appear to be irreversible, at least into the foreseeable future. One is the erosion of traditional language and other barriers in the region, based on colonial legacies under the impact of hemispheric and global trade liberalisation. The other is the growing importance of the diaspora as the transnationalisation of the labour force continues apace, in spite of officially erected barriers to migration. If I were to respond to the requests of the organisers to make practical recommendations, I would say two things. To students I would say, 'Learn Spanish, and visit our Spanish-speaking neighbours at every opportunity.' To policy-makers I would say, 'Besides paying more attention to our Spanish-speaking neighbours, which many are already doing, turn your departments of foreign investment into departments of diaspora relations to tap into the skills, capital and expertise of overseas citizens.'

More generally, let us consider that in the same way that much of the ideological and institutional legacy of the nineteenth century was blown away within the first few decades of the twentieth, the same could happen as we make the transition from the twentieth to the twenty-first. For instance, today capitalist globalisation and the ideology of progress are being questioned, as was imperialism 100 years ago. But so are the ideas and institutions associated with national sovereignty and the nation state, national development, and regional (inter-state) co-operation. Increasingly, the notions of 'sovereignty' and 'identity' are being detached from a defined physical space. Culture and common interest are emerging as important frames of reference. May I suggest that *to be 'sovereign' in the age of global community will be less a matter of formal state authority and more a matter of developing the capacity for autonomous and proactive strategies at all levels, from the community upwards*. To be regional will imply discovering shared identity and interests and acting in their function.

If the 'Caribbean' was an invention of the twentieth century, it seems certain to be reinterpreted and perhaps transcended in the twenty-first. I believe that the Caribbean of tomorrow will not be an exclusively anglophone or Hispanic conception, and it will not be tied exclusively to geographic space or definition. If it survives at all, it will be a *community* of shared economic, social and political interests and strategies that encompasses different languages and cultures and the Caribbean diaspora. Interstate co-operation will be only one of a number of spheres of interaction.

Note

1. These remarks are based on a paper titled 'Reinterpreting the Caribbean', in *New Caribbean Thought*, Folke Lindhal and Brian Meeks, eds, (forthcoming, UWI Press).

6 | HAVELOCK R H ROSS-BREWSTER

Identity, Space and the West Indian Union

'If you don't know where you are going, look back at where you are coming from.'[1]

Scale, Sovereignty and Functionalism

Geographic and economic space has been the dominant, indeed virtually the only, rationale offered for Caribbean integration. This may be because the subject has been treated mainly by economists and political scientists. For example, William Demas gives as the 'basic rationale of integration' the creation of greater economic space so as to create a critical mass. Traditionally integration has thus been viewed as making possible the pooling of markets and resources, greater efficiency of production and trade, and enhanced cost-effectiveness in the provision of common services. In an earlier period, federation was considered equally beneficial for a similar reason – it would improve the viability of small colonies by securing economies of scale in government and administration.

True, cultural affinity often has been the inspiration of regional cultural events, but it has never been viewed as providing an essential raison d'être for integration. But scale has not delivered the expected benefits. Its failure seems to derive from the fact that it is a second-best rationale for integration, predicated, on the economic side, on willingness to accept the cost of protection, and on the political side, some loss of sovereignty. Common services too, or functional cooperation, as it has been called, seem to have lost their way. For the most part, they have consisted of limited, discrete acts of cooperation in selected areas, mostly exchanges, reviews and the organisation of training. Functionalism, as practised up to now, has lacked a premeditated design. The low-level forms of functional cooperation practised seem to be merely surrogates for integrated common services. There has not been the expected spillover into higher levels of collective organisation.

In all these respects suboptimal solutions rarely prove to be successful. Individual states are always ready, in deed if not in words, to defect whenever better opportunities are available. And so it has been in the Caribbean Community. Defections *de facto* have taken place whenever cost/benefit assessments did not seem favourable to the individual state, whether it be in respect of trade flows, joint foreign policy stances, tertiary education, shipping, joint food production, or agricultural research. Further, commitments on paper to advance the process of integration, in ways that in reality do not conform to member-states' perception of the first-best, are not being put in place. For example, most of the foundations of a single economy, such as the coordination of fiscal policy, harmonisation of tax regimes and production incentives, coordination of exchange rate and interest rate policy, and the free movement of persons.

Cultural Identity, Kinship and Unity

The West Indian Commission's attempt to chart a new course in the run-up to the new millennium, though diverse in scope and rich in proposals, did not offer novel ideas for Caribbean integration. Instead, it sought ways to perfect the existing economic integration instruments of CARICOM. Confining its sights to conventional notions of political integration (parliamentary union) and economic integration (single market), it preserved a false dichotomy between them, and failed to address the essential issue that states are unlikely to implement and, when they can, will defect from, suboptimal solutions.

Yet a way forward might be found through a rather different route. This would be by capitalising on those unifying features already present in West Indian life, and focusing on those forms of regional integration for which there are no superior alternatives – in other words on first-best solutions. The premises here are that if better cannot be done, the 'compulsions to regional engagement', to use Shridath Ramphal's words, should be positively enhanced, and the temptation to defect should be minimised.

Cultural identity and a sense of history and kinship are already to a good extent part of West Indian reality and are thus the core of any institutional expression of political unity. Indeed, these essential ingredients are far more developed in West Indian society than are reflected in its political institutions. Political expression needs to catch up with social reality. For example, in Gordon Rohlehr's discussion of the compositions of calypsonians on regional unity,[2] impressive material is presented on the history and extent of their involvement in this matter. It is remarkable that while these authentic voices of the masses have expressed a variety of views – disappointment, anger, disillusion, hope, pride – in not a single instance is the dream of a unified West Indies ridiculed, or considered unwelcome, nonsensical, unfeasible or unworthy. For example, an interesting composition by Ashanti in 'Carifesta Regional Unity' (1992) begins by dismissing CARIFTA and CARICOM and then relates the hope of unity uniquely to our 'cultural foundation'.

> *We celebrating in song and dance*
> *The family reunion*
> *The exponents of the Arts*
> *Will highlight this grand occasion*
> *Displaying their talents in a way to bring Unity*
> *Where some of the people tried and failed very miserably*
> *So we have to bridge the gap on a cultural foundation*
> *If we really want to unite the Caribbean*

A more formal expression of West Indian cultural identity, history and kinship, representative, as they are, of a 'distinctive society', would not only correspond better to reality but would have positive psychological benefits in enhancing our people's pride, self-esteem, and confidence. There are also practical benefits, such as those associated with the development of civil society and social capital, enhanced negotiating status, more prominent international diplomatic, intellectual, cultural and sporting profiles, and more effective self-protection.

Such a political expression, in this era of globalisation and liberalisation, may have become a more real and urgent necessity, at least for those who value our distinctive heritage. Indeed, even much larger societies like France, and Canada, are struggling to ward off absorption into homogeneity. CARICOM states have become, in economic and political terms, peripheral to and estranged from the outside world. Even the links to our own external communities are becoming tenuous. The migrant ties to Europe and North America that were established over the last half-century are fast loosening. The diaspora is becoming more remote, culturally less recognisable with succeeding generations, and even less accessible as racial fortresses are erected around Europe and North America.

We have thus enormous cultural capital. The creation of a union of West Indian states – 'The West Indian Union' – might be a good investment of that capital. Such a union would not be a unitary or federal state, in the traditional sense, with a unified parliament, defence force, administration and so on. It would have the meaningful attributes that we agree among ourselves to give it. For example, it might include West Indian citizenship, carrying with it generally agreed rights and duties, coexisting with citizenship of the individual member states – in much the same way as the European Union (Maastricht Treaty) and European Citizenship were selectively defined to suit the peculiar needs and limits of the European states concerned.

For example, the European Union coexists with statehood and sovereignty of the individual states; states continue to maintain individual defence forces and diplomatic representation, have individual representation in international organisations, including the United Nations, participate as individual states in international sporting events like the Olympics. Monetary union permits individual member states to opt out. It coexists with individual membership in the IMF. European citizenship has even been proclaimed before complete freedom of movement of people and employment has been achieved. And while selected functions of governance have been assigned to the European parliament, it does not have legislative powers.

Evidently, the European Union is different in significant ways from the United States of America, or the United Kingdom for that matter. But it confers on the membership the benefits of a unity that is being shaped over time to meet its needs while respecting its limits. Thus the West Indian Union could be an indigenous, dynamic and meaningful concept. Statehood and sovereignty need not be fixed, indivisible and determined wholly by external norms, as has been the traditionally accepted view.

Space and Economic Integration

Geography has been kind to the West Indies in many respects, but it has also imposed severe constraints to economic development. Recognising the limits of small scale territory and population, and the protectionism then existing in world markets, our approach has been to create larger geographic and economic space by removing internal barriers to trade, harmonising economic systems, and erecting common protection against the outside world. The centrepiece of this integration strategy is the 'single market and economy'.

However, if we apply the first-best test, serious doubts would arise, in a contemporary setting, about its incremental benefits to the Caribbean. In an age of progressive liberalisation, world markets offer far greater opportunities. By that measure, access to the CARICOM market makes little difference to the viability of production. Moreover, the common external tariff (CET) is certainly not common in terms of the protection it affords to CARICOM industries, nor is it effective as a tool of industrial development. Under external pressure, it is in any case declining. Further, when account is taken of differences in tax regimes, industrial incentives, interest rates, transport cost, and uncoordinated movements in exchange rates, it becomes difficult to make a really compelling case that the creation of a single market, even if were to be perfected, would bring significant benefits to the region and thus should be a high priority for Caribbean integration and development.

If trade policy were to be viewed in first-best terms the focus would have to be on the most efficacious and development-compatible means of eventually integrating into the world trading system, a concept that has been endorsed by all CARICOM member states. Our future international trading relationships are now being designed – with the hemisphere (the Free Trade Area of the Americas or FTAA), the European Union (renegotiation of the Lome Convention), Latin America (Mercosur and the Andean Group), and the World Trade Organisation (Millennium Round). These relationships will determine the strength and quality of our integration into the world economy and how harmonious they are going to be with our development aspirations.

However, at the present time, coherent policies and strategies towards this end do not exist. The CARICOM Single Market is more like a fifth wheel to a coach. It is not much of a hindrance to development, nor is it much of an aid. It is being fashioned, in any case, more by external forces than by

CARICOM itself. We are pursuing simultaneously negotiations with the European Union, in the wider African-Caribbean-Pacific (ACP) Group context, and hemispheric arrangements for an FTAA, but in ways that do not seem to be interrelated. Even less understood is how an approach to the Latin American blocs would fit into the overall pattern. Three states (Guyana, Suriname and Trinidad & Tobago) have announced first-steps towards Mercosur. The Association of Caribbean States (ACS) also has trade policy intentions but their details are yet to be revealed. There are as well sundry bilateral treaties with States of the Caribbean Basin. And now, we are about to enter the new WTO round of multilateral trade negotiations, without clear objectives, and without analysis of the options for an efficient, development-compatible CARICOM international trade policy and strategy. An important task therefore should be to bring greater coherence to this mosaic of trade initiatives, in a way that would help pave the way for our eventual integration into the world economic system, on terms that satisfy, to the extent negotiable, our development capacities and needs.

Regional Commons and Public Goods

Geography has also imposed severe disadvantages in organising some of the most essential services and the use of some of our resources. In almost every field – education, health, culture, gender issues, sports, youth, drugs, legal affairs – much regional activity is found. While this activity is mostly helpful to national administrations, in very few cases has it actually resulted in functional regional integration. The most notable exception is the University of the West Indies. But even in this respect there has been defection, with several member states – Barbados, Guyana, Jamaica, Trinidad & Tobago – organising and financing selected faculties on national campuses. A good illustration, indeed, of individual states defecting from integration arrangements where they are not judged to be in their first-best interest.

The activities that are inherently first-best are those that from each state's viewpoint are better pursued regionally, rather than nationally or internationally. They will be activities that are unique or least-cost or for which there are no alternative options. They necessarily require regional solutions. Analytically they may be categorised as regional commons, regional public goods and regional resource complementarity. Regional commons are commonly shared resources, benevolent or malevolent, such as the sea, airspace, weather, disease, pest infestation, and narcotics. Regional public goods are goods and services which, if not provided regionally, would not be provided at all such as regional security, regional social infrastructure (such as high technology and advanced scientific research and training), specialised medical services, meteorological services, and regional physical infrastructure (such as sea and air transportation and telecommunications). Regional resource complementarity is the combining of resources that are unlikely to be exploited other than through regional arrangements, such as mineral smelting/hydroelectricity or diversified financial services.

The task of identifying these activities more precisely, promoting their development as truly first-best activities and, where appropriate, energising the participation of the private sector in them, should now assume far greater importance in the integration process. On the whole, too much time, effort and resources, not only of the community secretariat but of the national administrations, seem to be consumed in the routine management of the various instruments that constitute and support the Common Market, and in the proliferation of low-level functional activities. Rationalisation and outsourcing, including to non-governmental organisations, should be beneficial. The test of functional integration will be whether or not member states, or groups of them, are ready to allocate national resources to regional commons and regionally organised public goods, replacing national with collective decision-making and management.

Policy Agenda

This is a convenient time for CARICOM to:-

– Consider advancing toward some form of union that would give expression to the West Indian people's distinctive cultural and historical identity. Innovative approaches to Union, for example those that break out of the straitjacket of static and indivisible concepts of statehood and sovereignty, could facilitate its attainment.
– Develop coherent policy and strategic options for development-compatible integration into the world economy, given overlapping and conflictive bilateral, regional, hemispheric, bi-regional and world trade initiatives.

– Give greater emphasis to functional integration, designed to meet the test of the first-best, and exploit the potential inherent in regional commons, regional public goods and regional resource complementarity.

The author is Ambassador of Guyana to the European Union. The views expressed in this paper are those of the author and should not be attributed to the government of Guyana. Some of the ideas presented here are drawn from recent papers by the author.

Notes

1. Paraphrase of an African proverb.
2. William Demas, *West Indian Development and the Deepening and Widening of the Caribbean Community* (IRP/ISER, Kingston, 1997)
3. The Report of the West Indian Commission – *Time for Action* (Black Rock, Barbados, 1992)
4. For example, Gordon Rohlehr, *These Islands Now* (CARICOM Perspective, Georgetown, 1998, No. 68)

7 | BYRON BLAKE

The Caribbean – Geography, Culture, History and Identity:
Assets for Economic Integration and Development

The Caribbean is one of the most Balkanised regions in the world. The machinations of imperial powers from the sixteenth to eighteenth, and even the nineteenth centuries superimposed hegemonic partitions on a geography of islands. In the words of Elsa Goveia, 'The history of the area is one of fragmentation and separation and throughout that history the division within each territory has been compounded by the division across territories.'

One result of this history in service of imperialist objectives has been geographically neighbouring countries, with different cultures and identities, facing different metropoles across the Atlantic. These have parallel but similar historical experiences characterised by:

- a high degree of integration into particular metropolitan economies
- plantation socioeconomic systems based on stratification, exploitation and deprivation
- pluralistic cultures and linguistic divisions – a patchwork quilt of societies wherein each individual society is a separate patchwork
- limited or no official economic or social interaction

The challenge for the Caribbean in the twenty-first century, the first part of which will be dominated by the economic ideology of globalisation, is to convert these factors of division – identity, geography, culture and history – into assets for economic integration and development.

In this brief paper we seek to:
- define the Caribbean

- identify the challenges to integration in a 'wider' Caribbean framework
- analyse some opportunities for integration and co-operation
- make some recommendations

What is the Caribbean?

The theme of the session – 'The Caribbean: Geography, Culture, History and Identity' – poses the issues as if the Caribbean is a uniquely defined concept. Upon reflection, there has been confusion even with a geographic definition ever since the mistaken identity attributed to the area by the lost European mariner, Christopher Columbus, as the West Indies or lands on a western route to the Indian subcontinent.

A search for a definition might be pursued through the geography, the culture or political association.

A Geographic Definition

Central to any physical or geographic definition of the Caribbean is the sea. The Caribbean Sea has been defined by some cartographers as an area of about 1.02 million square miles (2.64 million square kilometres) between 9 and 22 degrees north and 60 to 89 degrees west. With those coordinates the Caribbean would be bounded to the south by the coasts of Venezuela, Columbia and Panama; to the west by Costa Rica, Nicaragua, Honduras, Guatemala, Belize and Mexico; to the north by the Greater Antilles chain of Cuba, Jamaica, Hispaniola and Puerto Rico; and to the east by the Lesser Antilles chain of islands. This, however, raises two questions: first, what is the position of countries and territories such as The Bahamas, Barbados and Guyana, which are included in so many organisations and arrangements described as Caribbean, for example the Caribbean Community? Second, can large countries such as Colombia, Mexico and Venezuela, with a relatively small part of their perimeters washed by the Caribbean Sea, be considered geographically Caribbean? Here the word 'relatively' is important, since Venezuela's Caribbean coastline of over 1,000 miles is greater than that of Cuba, and Columbia's 600 miles is much greater than that of Jamaica.

A Cultural Definition

A definition of the Caribbean through cultural identity is no less challenging. Pre-European 'Caribbean' boasted indigenous but diverse cultures deriving from, among others, the Carib, Arawak, Ciboney, Maya and Aztec peoples. Superimposed on these indigenous cultures have been the Christian religious-based cultures of the European colonisers – Spain, England, France, Holland and Denmark – and more recently of the United States of America. The European colonisers created a complex socioeconomic system in their quest to cultivate or capture a range of tropical produce such as tobacco, cotton, and sugar for an expanding temperate market. In that quest they decimated the indigenous population and imported, among others, large numbers of African, East Indian and Chinese people. Coming from large continents, each of these groups brought a multiplicity of cultural practices – including religion and languages – many of which have survived to add to the cultural diversity of the Caribbean. The Caribbean now has, in addition to indigenous 'Amerindian' cultural roots, strong cultural ties with Europe, Africa and Asia. The boundaries of this cultural Caribbean are not easily demarcated.

A Political Definition

There have been several concepts of the Caribbean for 'political' purposes. The framers of the Caribbean Community Treaty employed a concept which focused on the insular Caribbean. The Treaty of Chaguaramas establishing the Caribbean Community lists, in Article 2 on Membership, eleven island states and territories and two mainland states and then adds, 'any other state of the Caribbean Region that is in the opinion of the Conference able and willing to exercise the rights and assume the obligations of membership . . .'[1] Dr Eric Williams, historian and political practitioner and one of the original signatories to the Treaty of Chaguaramas, used a similar concept in 1974 when he encouraged the formation of the Caribbean Development and Co-operation Committee (CDCC) within the United Nations Economic Commission for Latin America and the Caribbean (UNECLAC).

A more recent articulation of a political concept of the Caribbean is in the construct of the Association of Caribbean States (ACS). This definition incorporates all the countries in Central America plus Mexico and Panama; all the countries on the northern coast of South America – Colombia, Venezuela, Guyana, Suriname and Cayenne; and all the island countries and territories in and around the Caribbean Sea, including the Bahamas and Barbados. This definition has much in common with that used by the Caribbean Hotel Association (CHA) and the Caribbean Tourism Organisation (CTO) as the basis of qualification for membership. There is however an often asked question with this concept of the Caribbean, namely the basis of the inclusion of El Salvador.

Definitions of the Caribbean have thus depended on the user and purpose, although there is a universally accepted concept which lends identity. For example, there is a 'Caribbean Rum' and a 'Caribbean Tourism', which are accepted without question in the market place. For the purposes of this conference, a wider and more inclusive definition might be more useful. In spite of the significant challenges there will be an effort in the next twenty-five years to give substance to a grouping based more on the definition in the Association of Caribbean States.

Challenges to Integration in a Wider Caribbean Framework

The wider political definition of the Caribbean creates a significant space for economic integration. As stated earlier this will involve many challenges deriving from the history of division and the cultural cleavages. We focus on three of these:

1. Territorial disputes, claims to the Caribbean Sea and the continued metropolitan presence are deep in the political and cultural psyche and can emerge at anytime to stymie co-operation. The Venezuelan claim to significant areas of the Caribbean Sea based on Spain's renunciation of its rights to Venezuela in 1845, and to areas of Guyana and Colombia based on decisions of 1777, are well documented in Dr Eric William's famous speech to the 1975 Special Convention of The People's National Movement (PNM) in Chaguaramas on 'The Threat to the Caribbean Community'. The history led Dr Williams to conclude that the efforts of President Carlos Andres Perez of Venezuela to integrate with the Caribbean, including Central America, had sinister or hegemonic undercurrents. Dr Williams was concerned about the implications of the various proposed integrated projects. In the event neither the integrated aluminium smelter project in

Trinidad and Tobago nor the integrated aluminium smelter and other projects between Venezuela and other Caribbean and Central American countries came to fruition. Yet integrated projects based on the use of complementary resources are among the most practical ways of building cooperation between countries. President Perez was to restate this at an informal meeting with the Caribbean tourism ministers in New York in 1989, shortly after regaining the presidency of Venezuela.

France, Holland, the United Kingdom and the United States are still active metropolitan powers in the Caribbean. In fact France, Holland and the United Kingdom are participants within the Association of Caribbean States while the refusal of the United States to participate in that body – because of Cuba's membership – has kept Puerto Rico and the United States Virgin Islands out of the Association. This metropolitan presence can adversely affect the effectiveness of the body. Official invitations to the physically-based Caribbean entities often must be directed through the metropolitan capital or representative. This is not always appropriate. For example, in the Caribbean developing its technical position for the 1994 United Nations Conference on the Sustainable Development of Small Island Developing States, the French ambassador in Trinidad and Tobago took exception to participating as an observer, while the representatives from Cayenne, Guadeloupe and Martinique participated as full members. The tension can also be seen in the effort to protect the Caribbean Sea. While the physically-located Caribbean states are anxious, the Association's ability to strongly urge the international community to recognise and treat the Caribbean Sea as a special area in the context of sustainable development has been constrained by the attitude of outside states such as France.

2. The historical cleavages have created a situation in which there are three formal economic groupings and three independent countries – Cuba, the Dominican Republic and Panama – which do not belong to any grouping. Colombia and Venezuela belong to the Andean Community, which also includes other Spanish-speaking countries of South America; the Caribbean Community – which includes the autonomous grouping of the Organisation of Eastern Caribbean States (OECS) – is the grouping of English-speaking Caribbean countries (which has only recently admitted Dutch-speaking Suriname and French-speaking Haiti); and the Central American Common Market, which groups the Spanish-speaking Central American countries.

There is also a less formal grouping – the Group of Three – the larger Spanish speaking economies of Colombia, Mexico and Venezuela. One challenge will be to get these established groupings to permit and facilitate effective co-operation across the wider ACS region.

3. The decision of 34 of the 35 independent countries in the hemisphere in December 1994 to move to the creation of a hemisphere-wide Free Trade Area of the Americas (FTAA) beginning in 2005 and to promote economic cooperation in other areas, such as energy and transportation, created an immediate challenge for the ACS launched in August of that year. Some members have privately, if not publicly, questioned the economic rationale for an ACS or even the established subregional grouping in the face of an FTAA. The strength of the argument for an ACS as a strong negotiating sub-group in the FTAA is weakened by the presence of Mexico, which is simultaneously a full and active participant of the three member North American Free Trade Area (NAFTA).

The question as to whether the ACS can be configured and structured to be an effective sub-group in the FTAA might be resolved as the incongruity of Mexico's full participation in the NAFTA and the ACS becomes clearer.

Opportunities for Integration and Cooperation Created by the Diversity

The rich diversity of the wider Caribbean, physical and cultural, can provide a significant basis for integrated development. We discuss three broad areas:

1. The history of the Caribbean has created strong cultural, and in some cases economic, links into the vast North American, European, Asian and African continents. There are Caribbean countries which are members of the 54-independent member English-speaking Commonwealth,[2] the 21-member Spanish-speaking IBERIO-American Conference and the 52-member French-speaking La Francophonie Group.[3] These cultural and linguistic links when added to the indigenous cultures, provide a strong basis for investment in the integrated development of services such as tourism. The cultural diversity can be packaged not only to exploit the natural linkages but also to provide additional experiences. For example, a Spanish-based experience could be packaged to include Cuba – with its Spanish – and

Jamaica – with its predominantly English, but early Spanish connection. As a group, the countries of the wider Caribbean provide a natural basis for multilingual training and for services such as interpreting. These services will be increasingly important in a global economy.

2. While the resource base of individual Caribbean countries might be limited, that of the region as a whole is extensive. This is the case with biodiversity resources for example, when the resources of Central American countries such as Costa Rica, the Caribbean islands and South American countries such as Guyana and Suriname are considered. It is also the case with mineral resources including hydrocarbons and natural gas. The Caribbean Sea, including the seabed, is a major shared resource. These are resources, which can be transformed into assets for integrated development.

3. Globalisation and even the creation of mega-trading blocs are forcing countries to seek increased space for their enterprises to create competitive bases. The globalisation and FTAA pressures could encourage Caribbean countries to submerge their other concerns and work together to create an effective wider Caribbean space. The network of subregional and bilateral treaties and agreements already in place could provide an important initial base.

Recommendations

The development of a viable movement in the wider Caribbean to meet the challenges of the twenty-first century will depend on action by all the countries and subregional groupings. It is a medium to long term project which will only be successfully achieved through a web of actions. We will make three recommendations:

1. Caribbean governments should give priority to the management of the Caribbean Sea. The sea links all the countries and any threat to its integrity in one area will quickly impact on other areas. The current effort initiated by CARICOM and now adopted by the ACS, to have the Caribbean Sea recognised as a special area in the context of sustainable development, is an important entry point. This should be complemented by internal initiatives to jointly manage the sea, delineate or settle boundaries and, in time, develop the resources. We would recommend the establishment of a technical commission on the management of the Caribbean Sea.

2. We recommend a systematic effort to widen the current processes of economic integration in CARICOM and Central America. CARICOM as well as Central America are currently finalising the negotiation of free trade agreements with the Dominican Republic. Cuba should be the next target even as CARICOM and Central America seek to negotiate a free trade agreement between the two economic groupings. The free trade thrust should be complemented by other initiatives building, for example, on the arrangements for cooperation in tourism. The Caribbean Hotel Association and the Caribbean Tourism Organisation have the institutional capacity and should be encouraged to take the lead to this area.

3. We recommend that the University of the West Indies spearhead the development of a programme of educational and cultural exchanges for implementation between different universities in the anglophone Caribbean and universities in the Spanish and French Caribbean including Central America.

Conclusion

The twenty-first century will pose a major challenge for the Caribbean as the region seeks to maintain its identity in a globalised and more homogenised world. The prospects of success will be increased to the extent that the region can overcome its history of fragmentation and use its varied experience as assets for economic integration and development.

Notes

1. The states named in Article 2 are Antigua and Barbuda, Bahamas, Barbados, Belize, Dominica, Grenada, Guyana, Jamaica, Montserrat, St Kitts – Nevis – Anguilla, St Lucia, St Vincent and the Grenadines, Trinidad and Tobago.
2. There are also 14 non-independent members of this group.
3. These create links to the other two continents, Australia and South America.

8 | VERENE A SHEPHERD

Image, Representation and the Project of Emancipation:
History and Identity in the Commonwealth Caribbean

". . . why should only one man have a mirror image of you that you do not want to have of yourself?" (Errol Barrow, 1986)[1]

The Commonwealth Caribbean continues to battle with several problems and challenges as it approaches the twenty-first century. Some, like volcanic activity, the state of the banana industry, and extremely high murder rates, are confined to specific territories although they have wider regional repercussions. Others assume more pan-Caribbean dimensions, such as the pros and cons of a Caribbean Court of Appeal; drug trafficking; debt; the macroeconomic environment; the future of the regional integration movement; the issue of economic citizenship; the future of the nation state in an age of globalisation (especially in small states lacking a powerful white or coloured elite with which 'First World' countries can form alliances); the increasing pressure to adapt to a global system characterised by competitive and efficient economic integration;[2] poverty; gender relations; the vicissitudes imposed by ethnic, cultural, linguistic and religious diversity; and the state of the West Indies cricket team. There also seems to be a view among some elements in the contemporary Commonwealth Caribbean, particularly in societies which are categorised as multi-ethnic, that 161 years after the coming of 'full free', there is an identity crisis among the African-Caribbean segment of the regional population, and a disrespect for black-skinned peoples which, if not addressed with the same vigour applied to solving problems related to tourism and the gross economic output, will drag us, still enchained, into the twenty-first century.[3]

Those who argue that there is a crisis in black identity cite numerous examples as proof. Two of the most recent examples, based on the public debates in the local, regional and international media (including the internet) are skin bleaching and beauty contests, both of which send out signals, it is argued, that black is not seen as beautiful and that black people have internalised the myth of black inferiority and white superiority. The phenomenon of skin bleaching, in which countless, mostly young black men and women engage supposedly to lighten their complexion to achieve a whiter shade of black, make themselves more appealing to those who uphold caucasian standards of beauty, and gain the 'rewards' which seem to fall to 'brownings', has outraged many (as did Buju Banton's 1992 song, 'Browning')[4], and has been the focus of much debate, particularly in the Jamaican media. Most have condemned the practice, despite the 'advantages which those who practise it claim to achieve. For example, Serge F Kovaleski's investigation revealed that, 'despite youthful good looks, . . . (name withheld) was bothered by her dark skin. The 17-year-old felt it was a hindrance to attracting boyfriends and finding opportunities for a better life . . . ; so (she) set her mind on becoming a "browning".' Her reason? "'It looks pretty . . . when you are lighter, people pay more attention to you. It makes you more important.'" Another young woman added, "'I want people to think I am more than a ghetto girl . . . I want to walk into dance halls and feel like a movie star, a white one.' (name withheld)."[5]

FIG. 1

Similarly, in some Caribbean territories, despite the strides made by beautiful black women like Lois Samuels, Wendy Fitzwilliam, the Botswanian Mpule Kwelagobe, the Dinka beauty Alek Wek and others, there is still a tendency to select only women who conform to caucasian standards of beauty to compete in the annual Miss World beauty pageant. In condemning this tendency, Barbara Ellington noted that 'the brainwashing that short hair, dark skin, thick lips and flat noses are ugly, has taken root and many people do not like what they see in the mirror'.[6]

Afua Hirsch, an 18-year-old British girl confirmed the persistence of this trend, saying ". . . it is still the case that the more European you look, the more beautiful you're considered to be." Most black women in the public eye – in music videos, say – are light-skinned with weaves or straight hair.[7]

Certainly, British Tory peer and novelist Jeffrey Archer's recent 'racist claptrap' about black women has been regarded in some quarters as giving credence to such a view. Archer is reported to have said, in an interview with Spectrum radio, that 30 years ago, 'Your head did not turn in the road if a black woman passed because they were badly dressed, probably overweight and probably had a lousy job.'[8]

Barbara MacLeod and Ngozi Omambala, two women asked to respond to Archer's comments, indicated the longstanding nature of the negative stereotyping of black people, especially black women, over a century after the abolition of slavery.[9] MacLeod recounted her days living in Cambridge when: The white men in Cambridge didn't want us as girlfriends, they just wanted to sleep with us. Some white men would say, "I'm sure you're good in bed", because there was this false assumption that black women were sexually voracious. Ngozi Omambala recalled more recent experiences:

as a black woman I am aware that even today white men think my looks are exotic. I was queuing outside a club recently and this white guy stood in my way, said I had beautiful hair and tugged it. I slapped his hand off; it (his action) was rude and I felt like an object.

The majority of those who have entered the debate over bleaching, beauty contests and the persistence of racial stereotypes about black people, in particular black women, have blamed these practices on the legacies of slavery, maintaining that we have not fully emancipated ourselves from that 'mental slavery' to which Marcus Garvey referred in 1937[10] and Bob Marley later popularised in song. For example, while medical doctors warn of the harmful physical side effects of the creams taken to lighten skin and the 'fowl pill', containing arsenic, taken to correct other perceived 'deficiencies';[11] Morris Cargill 'soothes' that bleaching is a fashion fad that will go away as did women's fad of 'pygidial protuberance', 'bustles' and 'corsets';[12] counsellors blame the disintegration of the family; others link the practice to the legacies of slavery and the persistence of 'mental slavery'.[13] In Jamaica, the most recent version of the bleaching debate probably started off with Dawn Ritch's June 1999 article in the Jamaican *Gleaner*,[14] but widened thereafter. Attorney-at-Law

Audley Foster, in his insightful ontribution to the debate, attributes the practice to the fact that Jamaicans 'have internalized the lie that being black is to be ugly', and lamented Jamaican's seeming inability to 'correct 300 years of mental servitude'.[15] Avia Ustanny, while suggesting several possible reasons for the phenomenon, nevertheless also concludes that,

> Black Caribbean women continue to seek all that they think is desirable in the eyes of males and a society in love with the Caucasian look . . . the black-skinned majority continue to betray a self-contempt and a lack of self-confidence . . .[16]

The selection of girls with long hair, light skin and straight noses (if not blue eyes and thin lips) to be entrants in beauty pageants like Miss World and Miss Universe, is regarded as a present day manifestation of centuries of racial conditioning in which beauty was colour coded and race was a marker of social status. Kamau Brathwaite confirms the tyranny of a sort of 'pigmentocracy' among the people of colour during the period when black Africans were enslaved, shades (and contingent status) ranging from octoroon (child of quintroon and white) through mustee (child of quadroon/native Caribbean and white) to sambo (child of mulatto and black) and black.[17]

There are numerous other phenomena/themes which invoke the 'legacy of slavery' model to explain their persistence: male marginalisation, African-Caribbean family structure, the preference for imported goods and things 'foreign', hatred of service (equated with servitude), the commodification of the bodies of black men and women, negative aspects of the tourist culture, the tendency towards monopoly, the expropriation of Caribbean resources (including underground/undersea resources), poor social infrastructure and inequitable/differential access to social services, male/female relations, the system of education, domestic violence perpetrated by the supposed male ex-slaves, police violence, the treatment of street people and the poor and marginalised, the mentality of some current rulers/administrators, elite alienation, the treatment of domestic helpers, praedial larceny, the selection of heroes and the location of statues, employer/employee relations, black-white relations in the work place, access to land, the relationship between Caribbean states and the former imperial power, crime and (in)justice . . . And the list goes on.

For novelist Jamaica Kincaid, it is the Hotel Training School in Antigua that 'teaches Antiguans how to be good servants, how to be a good nobody', which is reminiscent of the mentality of slavery; for in Antigua, 'people cannot

FIG. 2 ©The Jamaica Observer Ltd.

FIG. 3 ©The Jamaica Observer Ltd.

see a relationship between their obsession with slavery and emancipation and their celebration of the Hotel Training School.[18]

But perhaps it was the capture and forced transportation to St Elizabeth on July 15 1999 of 35 of Montego Bay's street people by 'phantom people in the dead of night' which has brought this 'legacy of slavery' debate most sharply into focus in the Caribbean. People used various terms to describe the unforgivable action, but all made comparisons with one aspect of enslavement or the other. It was characterised as 'Operation Get Tough' by one cartoonist in the *Daily Observer*'s official emancipation day edition who, like the Prime Minister PJ Patterson, pointed to the irony of this happening so close to the celebration of emancipation day.[19] (See fig. 2)

Jamaica Labour Party leader Edward Seaga went even further, invoking the image of the 'Middle Passage', saying that the act was 'reminiscent of the way men and women were captured in Africa, bound in chains and transported 3,000 miles away to lands unknown'.[20] This comparison with the Middle Passage also appeared in cartoons, as fig. 3 illustrates. Thus, despite the abolition of the system of African enslavement in 1834 and Britain's premature ending of that system of neo-slavery euphemistically called 'Apprenticeship' in 1838, references to slavery and the ideologies/legacies of slavery are constantly used to frame and contextualise public debates and discussions among the people of the region, as, indeed, they are within the wider Atlantic World. And though the descendants of the formerly enslaved now occupy the highest political offices in societies radically transformed by the slavery and post-slavery struggles for freedom and justice, the 'up from slavery' concept in public life is strong and indicates that there is a strong opinion that the process of emancipation is not complete; that, in Swithin Wilmot's terms, emancipation is somehow, still 'in action'.[21] Indeed, although emancipation day is celebrated in most parts of the Commonwealth Caribbean as an official public holiday, with Trinidad and Tobago now embarking, albeit not unproblematically, on plans to build an appropriate memorial in the year 2000 to mark the end of African enslavement,[22] the annual rhetoric which accompanies emancipation day commemorations is very often located within the discourse of slavery rather than within the discourse of anti-slavery and freedom. It would therefore almost seem as if the attempts in the period of modernity to bring about a level of wellbeing within social formations and to create human rights communities in former slave colonies have failed.

Of course, the fact that slavery survives in the collective consciousness of people in the Caribbean should be no surprise, given the long history of this brutal system of human exploitation in the region, dating back to the Columbus dispensation and the period of conquest and colonisation. The emergence of western Europe as the political centre of an Atlantic economy signalled the importance of imperial exploitation to its development. Indeed, development discourse, centering around the discipline of political economy, privileged colonialism as the transformative engine of capitalist growth. It is within this context that six European powers – Spain, England, France, Sweden, the Netherlands, and Denmark – targeted the Caribbean segment of the Atlantic world for their imperial designs and colonisation enterprises. Having conquered the land resources of the indigenous Caribbeans, European colonisers turned to coerced labour to extract returns from this captured land. Indeed, European colonial capitalism could see no way to ensure profitable economic activity other than with the mass deployment of servile labour. As the intensity of economic accumulation gripped colonial élites, and the pressures of profits, power and glory fuelled the colonising enterprise, chattel slavery became the preferred form of servile labour. Other labour institutions like indigenous and white servitude (mainly of the Irish) and white slavery were tried for varying periods in most places, but with the development of the productive activities in all colonies, the incompatibility between continued white (Irish) labour exploitation and the colonial ideological project, the enslavement of Africans was centred as critical to economic accumulation and the cultural imperatives of white supremacy. In doing so, Europeans, ignored the multi-ethnic model of slavery in the Caribbean as well as in the ancient world and in western Europe, and opted to reinvent chattel slavery exclusively for black Africans. By the mid-eighteenth century, the enslavement of Africans had become an integral part of North Atlantic capitalist accumulation and defined the economy and society of all Caribbean societies regardless of the ethnicity or religious affiliation of the imperial power. Over the entire period of the transatlantic trade in African captives (fifteenth to nineteenth centuries), about 15.4 million Africans were exported to the Americas with perhaps another 15 million dying from the trauma of capture and shipment and the inhumane actions of enslavers.[23] The English-colonised Caribbean imported about two million Africans, the majority going to Barbados and Jamaica.

Of particular relevance to this discussion is that those who use the 'legacy of slavery' explanation for racial stereotyping and the perpetuation of myths about black people have some historical basis for their view. For conquest and colonization were not only accompanied by the decimation of the indigenous population, the introduction of a brutal system of exploitation, denigration and 'othering' of 'natives' and enslaved blacks comparable within the region only to apprenticeship and post-slavery indentureship, but also by the textual invention of the Caribbean. During the colonial era large parts of the non-European world were *produced* for Europe through the accounts of those who either visited, lived in, heard about, or targeted the Americas for their writings. Indeed, each new arrival went through what Peter Hulme refers to as a 'gesture of discovery'. This 'gesture of discovery' was repeated over a period of three centuries and gave rise to a series of narratives and histories, the first being the encounter between European and 'native'.[24]

The articulating principles of the Columbian discourse are those of conflict and accommodation with the indigenous people as well as of mild censure for the simplicity/primitiveness of their lives. The impression of innocent transgressors of the rules of civilisation is also evident. Indigenous women were characterised as open to sex, a stigma that continued in the period of African enslavement and in the post-slavery period with the historical literature, particularly of the former period, presenting black women as ugly, lacking in intelligence and promiscuous.[25] Such negative representation of indigenous and black people served the purpose of justifying the conquest and colonisation of so-called 'inferior, uncivilised' people by a so-called 'superior, civilised' race.[26]

Since the Columbus dispensation, others have continued the project of representation and textual invention of black people. The early narratives and histories reveal a certain racism and ethnocentrism towards people regarded as 'other'; and those of male writers reflected prevailing ideas of patriarchy and male dominance. Many of these narratives were written without reference to the historical Caribbean and its inhabitants, and fall into the realm of historical (even fictional) literature, a sure indication, according to Veronica Gregg, that the invention of the Caribbean as a European enterprise required little knowledge of the region and in fact depended upon 'a willed ignorance'.[27] Most of the writers of the eighteenth and nineteenth centuries, as well as demonising black people, supported a social hierarchy that venerated whiteness and, ignoring the reality of the existence of working class, poverty-stricken white women in the Caribbean, particularly in Barbados, dichotomised the black and white woman in terms of perceived 'moral attributes'. Charles Leslie's *A New and Exact Account of Jamaica*, published in 1739 and reissued in two expanded editions in 1740,[28] painted a picture of shameless black women who had no qualms about exposing their bodies, offending the sensibilities of Europeans:

The negro women go many of them quite naked; they do not know what shame is and are surprised at an European's bashfulness who perhaps turns his head aside at the sight. Their masters give them a kind of Petticoat but they do not care to wear it. In the towns they are obliged to do it; but these are the favourites of young squires who keep them for a certain use.[29]

The main contribution to the ideology of racism and sexism is essentially that of Edward Long who wrote when the pro-slavery ideology had reached its zenith. Obsessed with racial purity, he inveighed against white male miscegenative habits and decried the black woman in the most negative and racist of terms. He constructed a hierarchy among women in Jamaica based on his racist and classist notions. Predictably, he placed white women at the top of this social ladder and black women at the base; and the faults he found with white women were almost always attributable to a) lack of education, b) lack of sufficient association with Europeans and c) their too close association with black women. Among other things, he accused slave domestics of having a bad influence on the language of the white children, and generally blamed black women for certain social ills in the society such as immorality and creolisation of the white population.

Cynric Williams similarly showed his preference for coloured women and the superiority of European features.[30] He waxed almost lyrical over the 16-year-old quadroon girl, Diana, daughter of a wealthy white planter and an enslaved woman, whose complexion he described as 'very little darker than the European'. He studiously avoided too much reference to her African origin, extolling those aspects of her physique which reminded him of European, classical Greek and Roman women. In fact, though he regarded Diana as a beautiful coloured woman, her features were only 'near' perfect; for 'the features (of the quadroon) retain too often the inclination to the African lips, or cast of countenance that reminds one of their origin'. In his view, as in the view of many other visitors, 'the European cast of countenance is vastly superior to the African'.[31]

Maria Nugent, despite her typically elite benevolence to the 'underclass' manifested during slavery in her habit of forever 'teaching the blackies their catechism', shared the white stereotype of the African, on two occasions describing them as savages and cannibal-like, yet somehow contented with their enslavement. Of the new African recruits in the West India Regiment, she wrote, 'They made a most savage appearance, having just arrived from Africa'. And on another occasion:

In returning home from our drive this morning, we met a gang of Eboe negroes, just landed and marching up the country. I ordered the postilion to stop, that I might observe their countenances . . . and see if they looked unhappy; but they appeared perfectly the reverse . . . The women in particular seemed pleased . . . One man attempted to shew more pleasure than the rest by opening his mouth as wide as possible to laugh, which was a rather horrible grin. He showed such truly cannibal teeth, all filed as they had them, that I could not help shuddering.[32]

In similar vein, according to Bridget Brereton, Elizabeth Fenwick described blacks in Barbados as 'a sluggish, inert, self-willed race of people, apparently inaccessible to gentle and kindly impulses'.[33]

Legislative emancipation did not signal the end of this negative stereotyping, judging by the writings of such nineteenth century figures as Thomas Carlyle, Stephen Harmer, Lafcadio Hearn, James Anthony Froude, William Sewell, Charles Augustus Stoddard and Anthony Trollope, and early twentieth century figures like William Burn.[34] The nineteenth century was a period in which freedpeople in the Caribbean sought to actualise their hard-won freedom through refusal to continue in a capital-labour relationship with former enslavers; when work was equated with plantation labour; when 'idle' and 'lazy' were terms applied to those who tried to carve out a life which did not involve full-time estate labour. It was also a period when whites, influenced by developments in Haiti where blacks were in power by 1804, feared what they termed the threat of the 'Haitianisation of the region' (a sentiment resurrected in some parts of the region in the 1980s). The so-called 'negatives' of the peasant mode of production and the 'civilising' possibilities of the plantation system were influential ideologies. The demonisation of black people was thus crucial to the maintenance of white power in the region. Proprietors actively sought to import additional white immigrants and north Asians who were themselves socialised into a caste/colour hierarchy to 're/place' black labourers and bolster white ideologies in the Caribbean. Their project was helped by the Euro-Christian missionaries and elites in charge of education (mis-education); so that even where descendants of the enslaved eventually took power, 'slavery mentalities' continued. This context is crucial for understanding the continued textual invention and imaging of the black Caribbean in the post-slavery period.

Carlyle, Trollope, Froude and Harmer all supported a delayed freedom and the paying of compensation to the former enslavers for the loss of their property. They were united on the reasons freedpeople abandoned the plantations, the site of their former enslavement, to seek alternative occupations. Almost without exception, they attributed the new mobility of the freedpeople to 'the laziness and idle disposition' of black people, ignoring their tremendous industry during the period of slavery when black women formed the bulk of the field labour force and contributed to the industrialisation of the core and the personal enrichment of many English people.[35] The overall picture painted by nineteenth and early twentieth century historians was that of blacks observing planters' impending economic ruin 'with an ironic grin of malicious pleasure'.[36] William Sewell, while giving a fairly accurate survey of labour conditions across the English-colonised Caribbean, showing some understanding of the actions of the newly freed, demonstrated his biases in his discussion of black's culture and gender relations, supporting stereotypes about family and sexual habits. According to Sewell, 'the inhabitants (of Jamaica) taken en masse, are steeped to the eyelids in immorality; promiscuous intercourse of the sexes is the rule...'[37] Hearn, who visited several territories in the French and English Caribbean in the late nineteenth century, remarked of the black Barbadian population, 'the darkest in the West Indies', that 'It is by no means an attractive population, physically – rather the reverse, and frankly brutal as well...'[38] Hearn also lamented the fast decline in the white population of the Caribbean, particularly in Guyana where 'the future tendency must be to universal blackness, if existing conditions continue – perhaps to universal savagery.'[39] Stoddard, finally, resurrected the stereotypical images of black women so reminiscent of the period of African enslavement, describing black women in St Thomas in the Virgin Islands as 'Black, rough, coarse in face and feature beyond description, they seemed like huge human beasts of burden'.[40]

There were only a few nineteenth century writers who opposed the dominant representation of the newly freed pushed by Carlyle, Trollope and those of their ilk, an outstanding example of the beginning of Caribbean counter-discourse being JJ Thomas' *Froudacity*.[41] The twentieth century has also seen the emergence of texts that continue to reflect the influence of Eurocentric and planter-centric views grounded in the 'official' voice of the colonisers. An example is William Green's pro-planter text which is quite popular among sixth form history students across the Caribbean, some of them styling it the 'A' Level Bible.[42] A more recent book, Sherlock and Bennett's, *The Story of the Jamaican People*, while to be lauded for the bold, African-centric objectives, has not managed to rid itself totally of remnants of the colonialist ideology, presenting in many aspects only the 'official' view of Caribbean history.[43]

Interestingly, as various other non-European groups entered post-slavery Caribbean society to further the capitalistic enterprises of the British, racialised representations were broadened to include the Asian population, Indians for example, variously being described as people who were 'docile', 'weak/fragile', 'penurious', 'liars', 'clannish', 'heathenish', 'promiscuous' (the women), and so on.[44] More recently, many people in Britain and the Asian diaspora were shocked by the Duke of Edinburgh's racist remark that messy electrical wiring in parts of the UK looked 'as though it was put in by an Indian'.[45]

There is a widespread view that it is these images and representations which still circulate in the educational material available in the schools, which are transmitted via the various media and which, locally and globally, still inform the attitude to, and treatment of black people as 'other', which are largely responsible for the present feeling among some elements that there is a 'crisis in black identity'. The question, then, of how to construct a Caribbean identity that would negate the images and representations of the colonial and present eras and challenge the epistemic violence of the imperial project thus remains an important and pressing one. Debates over solutions ebb and flow particularly during the annual observance of emancipation day and independence day, as well as during the very quick dash to the shrine of blackness when Black History Month and Marcus Garvey's birthday come around; but judging from the on-going preoccupation with the issue of black identity, despite the obvious achievements of black people in the region, there has been no satisfactory resolution to the matter.

While I agree that after more than 400 years of the slavery experience the 'legacy of slavery' model must be still applicable to Caribbean society, I wish for us to be very clear about why it persists. There seem to be four reasons:

1. The mentalities and ideologies of past enslavers and past managers of enslaved people have been perpetuated by those, some the descendants of enslaved ancestors, who have voice and authority and who inherited and exercised (and still exercise power) in the immediate post-slavery and in the post-colonial periods. Their lingering slavery ideologies are often reflected in their failure to educate the population away from a colonial education which emphasised social control, to respect the human rights claims of the masses and their failure to improve the social infrastructure and address the increasing economic gap between rich and poor.
2. We have failed to make a part of more sustained public debate, the positive images, achievements, representations and lessons from the slavery and post-slavery eras left by our ancestors; so that what is being projected about the 'legacy of slavery' is really only part of the total legacy, the ways in which our ancestors survived centuries of exploitation, marginalisation and 'othering' and sought to live decent and dignified lives being submerged, if not muted.
3. We have failed to make history education more widespread inside and outside of formal educational institutions.
4. The images passed on through film and television are not empowering enough for black-skinned people.

Up from slavery: The Project of Emancipation

I wish to suggest that we need not enter the twenty-first century chained to the neo-slavery of the negative images and representations of the slavery, post-slavery and post-colonial periods that seeks to keep us in mental slavery, but should align ourselves to, and promote, a project of true emancipation –

emancipation as process rather than as event, momentous as that was. For the Caribbean cannot afford to leave the scene of action at the moment of redemption. There are several possible solutions but, owing to space limitations, I shall elaborate only on two strategies: recovering and publicising that lost legacy of slavery which is not often taught and transmitted and reimaging Caribbean people through public education, using the media (especially television) as fundamental tools.

I shall begin with what I consider to be a crucial and non-negotiable strategy of using the media to project more positive images of black people. Media representations are powerful cultural forces through which audiences receive cues about themselves. As several cultural historians like Stuart Hall have noted, the media produce and transmit ideologies because the rituals and myths they produce for public consumption justify practices and institutions. They can thus be transformative or they can serve to oppress. In the Caribbean as elsewhere in the black diaspora affected by colonialism, media messages do not do enough to challenge dominant ideologies about racial hierarchies, black inferiority and white superiority. A cable-crazy population tune in to white images from North America and 'even local TV offers mostly regurgitated imports from that Continent'.[46] There are insufficient television programmes that contest and oppose, by their visual imagery, the stereotypical representations of black characters. Instead they often lend support to them. These tendencies no doubt led Wycliffe Bennett, after working for over 50 years in cultural fields to conclude that 'television is helping to de-Jamaicanise the country',[47] and Amina Blackwood-Meeks to argue that,

> The television stations still cannot find it possible to produce or facilitate programmes celebrating our glorious past, pre-Columbus or our many achievements in spite of him. Instead they topple over one another to bring us soap operas featuring beautiful, rich white people steeped in their dirty lifestyles. And they attract top advertising dollars in prime time so to do. Issues relating to Independence, Heroes Week and Emancipation (and she could add Black history) get the now-you-see-it-now-you-don't treatment on the day of the event.[48]

It is hypocritical to tell young black men and women that skin-bleaching is self-denigrating; that black is beautiful, yet fail to provide the cultural environment in which 'blackness' is truly seen as beautiful. Equally, self-confidence and self-esteem cannot be expected to develop and thrive if the images presented through films, documentaries and advertisements are about rich, successful white people, presentations of blacks being confined to sports, comedy, crime, the police force and music. Some of these areas are important of course, but they reflect only a part of the reality. Despite the present ill-health of the macroeconomic environment and the competition for advertising dollars, the various media houses, in collaboration with each territory's Ministry of Education and Culture must endeavour to promote programmes which seek to enlighten (other than through bleaching) and educate African-Caribbean people about the black diaspora. Greater care must also be taken to prevent the elite association of black working class people with certain products like white rum, guinness and 'big bamboo' Irish Moss, while light-skinned models push wine, champagne, vodka and certain supposedly 'finer products'.

I should also like to suggest that the project of emancipation of the mind requires a greater knowledge of, and engagement with, history and modern historiography and that history education must be expanded at all levels of our society. I would go as far as to suggest that African and Caribbean history should be made compulsory in our secondary schools as well as at the tertiary level so that all future leaders, journalists and public policy-makers/shakers will have a greater understanding of our historical legacy. It is not quite clear to me that all of those who write in the newspapers and who make public speeches on emancipation and independence days have a full grounding in the history of the region from pre-Columbian times to the more modern period even though the information is available, though admittedly not always in easily accessible form; for no-one familiar with Caribbean history would continue to perpetuate the myth of black inferiority. I should also like to see public/adult education taken more seriously in the region, more money not only being made available for the eradication of illiteracy in countries with unacceptable levels of illiteracy, but to fund public history lectures. And these public lectures, following the excellent example being set by some of my colleagues, should be held outside of the walls of academia to encourage wider public participation. Experience has shown that it is not enough for us to announce that the various lectures on the campuses are 'open to the public'. We only end up talking among ourselves or to the converted.

Before going into more detail on the various strategies of history education, I should like to explain why I have singled out history as a tool for helping to solve what has been described as an 'identity crisis' among African-descended people in the region. One overarching reason is that history and historical evidence are crucial to a people's sense of identity. Second, only the project of history has the ability to elucidate the future through an understanding of the past. Indeed, as some scholars point out, 'what historians do best is to make connections with the past in order to illuminate the problems of the present and the potential of the future.'[49] Third, history is increasingly being used as a form of cultural enquiry in many societies. The view is that history and historical consciousness belong to culture, and no questions can meaningfully be asked about the usefulness of culture. Culture, of which historiography is a part, is the background against which we can form opinion about the usefulness of, say, certain scientific research or political objectives.[50] As Kevin Yelvington, Neill Goslin and Wendy Arriaga observed in a recent paper:

... the wider world, currently overrun with the passions of regionalism, ethnicism and nationalism, and in the throes of both modernization and development, has made history the privileged ground of individual and collective identity.[51]

History education should not be based solely on the Eurocentric texts of the imperial historians (which unfortunately seem better known by students and many engaged in public debates), but should be grounded in the alternative discourse of the new generation of historians which at present seem familiar only to academics. There is a view, particularly in post-colonial societies that are multi-ethnic and which are emerging from modernism into postmodernism, that there are contested versions of history. The twentieth century represented the era of burgeoning nationalism when nationalist histories written in what William Green refers to (and opposes) as the 'Creole genre' were being written[52] and perhaps were needed, as Patrick Bryan observes, 'to plant the first seeds of a collective consciousness'.[53] The end of World War Two, the escalation of decolonisation, the globalisation of western culture and the re-empowerment of non-western states, all signalled a new age. Not surprisingly, much of the scholarship of twentieth century, professional (and cultural/nationalist) historians, some influenced by Marxist ideology, continued to intervene in the hegemonic and authoritative discourse which ascribes 'rationality' and 'legitimacy' to its own discursive practice. They questioned the essentialism of traditional historiography and replaced the eurocentric history which had as part of its mandate the imposition of a kind of 'master narrative' on formerly colonised people, with writings that oppose the epistemic violence of the imperial project; for, in the postmodernist era, they support the realisation that Europe is no longer the unquestioned and dominant centre of the world. Additionally, influenced by the democratising appeal of social history, many sought, in Spivak's terms, to develop a strategy of reading that spoke to the historically muted subject;[54] to present 'the vision of the vanquished' rather than the 'vision of the victors'.[55]

Not everyone is happy with the post-colonial writings of cultural nationalist professional historians, of course, and many find the fact that the empire is writing back extremely destabilising and unsettling, as is evidenced by Green's caution about history written in the 'Creole genre'. Similarly, Canadian historian Donald Akenson, while observing that 'how Montserratians of the twenty-first century should invent their own history is no business of professional historians such as myself,' nevertheless could not resist the swipe at nationalist perspectives, saying that 'the Montserratians have the right to create whatever fiction makes it easier for them to get through the day'.[56] Nevertheless, the reality is that in the post 1970s period, the old intellectual absolutisms have been dethroned and the post-independence generation in the Caribbean has constructed what Appleby *et al*, describe as 'sociologies of knowledge, records of diverse peoples, and histories based upon groups and gender identities'. The question 'Whose history and for what purpose?' is now heard frequently by students and that generation of scholars who became historians after the 1970s and who have now 'made skepticism and relativism common currency in intellectual life'.[57] Our own UWI history departments have not been immune from these developments and faculty now have to answer tough questions from our students who are becoming militant about the need for a greater attention to the history of traditionally marginalised groups and the former 'objects' of our discourse.[58]

Despite Akenson, Green and those who support their perspective, 'the present', as Glenn Sankatsing has observed, 'should never be opposed to history, because the contemporary is a special case of history'.[59] Whether we like it or not, as many societies, influenced by the post-colonial discourse, become increasingly historicised, struggles over history and its representation are implicated. A few years ago when white English people contemplated honouring John Hawkins, the slave trader, there was an angry outcry from the black population at the insensitivity of some whites to the slavery experience that affected African people. As Yelvington *et al* reveal, when, as part of a strategy of urban redevelopment, white elites in Tampa, Florida, in the 1990s attempted to attract a museum with a piracy theme based on artifacts recovered from *The Whydah Galley,* an eighteenth century pirate ship (which, as it turned out, was originally used in the slave trade) there was an outcry from local African-Americans. The protesters used a counter-discourse that challenged interpretations of 'history' by addressing issues of identity, partially through references to slavery.

Both at the secondary and tertiary levels and at the level of the wider public, means must be found to re-educate Caribbean people about the contested versions of Caribbean history.[60] The secondary schools, however, will be the crucial place to begin. Caribbean history as presented through the CXC history syllabi (CSEC and CAPE) is not a 'baby-mild form of West Indian history', as Michael Burke has charged. He is also wrong that '(But) the present way in which (so-called) West Indian history is taught, one would be led to believe that the black man's history began with slavery'.[61] Admittedly, the present syllabi are far from perfect; but they are recognised, even by their competitors, as superior to the alternatives, covering the history of the region from pre-Columbian times to the present. If necessary, as has been done in the United States where recent controversy over history has centred on school textbooks,[62] new teams of reviewers must be established by the Ministry of Education in each territory to scrutinise existing history texts to see the extent to which they reinforce the worst racial and sexual stereotypes in our children, and where deemed crucial, produce alternative texts.[63]

A textbook-writing project may, in any case, be vital, for much of the work which will assist Caribbean people to have a more inclusive version of Caribbean history resides in the so-called 'academic' books unintelligible to secondary school students and the masses. As Appleby and others found in their own case in the United States, professional historians have been so successfully socialised by demands to publish that most of us have little time or inclination to participate in general debates about the meaning of our work; and writing textbooks and seeking to answer questions about the role of history in shaping national identity are often dismissed as irrelevant to our work which we mostly define as researching in archives and writing scholarly books and articles.[64] The solution might be for the universities and regional presses to stop hierarchising publications and encourage more faculty (junior or senior) to engage in writing for the schools and a more popular audience. It is disrespectful and a reflection of elitist snobbery and our monopolistic tendencies to continue to attach more importance to academic works than to textbooks and popular writing. Our people who toil, and through their taxes, help to facilitate the careers of academics, are deserving of exposure to cutting-edge historical information which can only come from the scholars. In this regard, I applaud those on the three campuses who defy the academic culture (which has been slow to change) and not only write for the schools, but also engage in public lectures, schools' outreach programmes, syllabus construction and examination duties for the CXC, and in teacher training workshops. Such involvement in educational ventures outside of the walls of the university will only contribute to the liberating project of emancipation as process instead of as event.

Exposure to the newer historical works will facilitate a more inclusive view of Caribbean history and, above all, will recuperate that part of the historical legacy which hardly features in public debates but which is vital if Caribbean people are to be anchored firmly to a more positive beginning. The newer works show that Caribbean history neither began with slavery nor with Columbus. Indigenous Caribbean society had its own internal logic, dynamism and culture. The early Caribbeans had an economic system, a developed cosmology, a political system, their own family structure, gender system, ways of settling disputes and communication system. The presence of descendants of the indigenous Caribbeans should remind us that despite the effort to exterminate them, they never collaborated with colonialism, fighting wars of resistance and engaging in maroon activities as survival strategies. Kalinago women fought rape and the attempts by Europeans to treat them as loose and promiscuous. Instead of writing about the indigenous peoples as 'problems' and 'disasters' for European colonisation,[65] historians should laud them for preventing Europeans from completely establishing their monopolistic economic system in the region when they introduced structural discontinuity, reinvented the Caribbean as a colonised space and attempted to abolish indigenous people's internal social dynamism and their command over the engine of development and creation and embarked on a project of 'othering' which was to affect the region for centuries.[66] Regional governments are urged to ensure that the present day communities of indigenous peoples are not subject to neo-colonialist attitudes; that their environments are not sacrificed at the altar of eco-tourism.

Those who engage in the debates over slavery and its legacies and make official speeches every emancipation day should also familiarise themselves with the revisionist works on slavery so that they do not rely only on the traditional texts but engage with comparative material. The revisionist works are more focused on people's agency, while not, of course, negating the brutality of the slavery experience. They reveal the danger of invoking the 'legacy of slavery' model too narrowly through focusing solely on the perpetuation of colonialist mentalities, and urge that the actions of the enslaved be revisited. They project the African's struggles against capture in Africa, shipment across the Middle Passage and enslavement in the Caribbean – topics which hardly form a part of public discussions on slavery. They negate the view that was pushed by black Jamaican sociologist Orlando Patterson that 'slaves in the West Indies mated promiscuously and sometimes in outright prostitution'; that 'the family was unthinkable to the vast majority of the population' and that 'the nuclear family could hardly exist within the context of slavery'.[67] Instead they stress the enslaveds' search to reconstitute family and African culture; to negotiate terms and conditions of work, even wages; engage in collective bargaining despite the system of slavery; their search for personal and group economic autonomy through provision grounds and marketing; their personal efforts to defeat the monopolistic tendencies of slave society and promote economic and socio-cultural diversification; women's resistance to sexual exploitation; enslaved men's resistance to plantation owners' efforts to negate their masculinity and the anti-slavery actions which brought down slavery within an economic environment of declining importance of the Caribbean to Britain.

In aligning ourselves with the project of true emancipation, we must also negate the association of Africa with slavery, savagery and barbarism. The view that Africa was more than a land from which slaves were captured and that blacks did not begin their lives in the Caribbean as slaves must be more widely circulated. Ivan van Sertima's controversial book, *They Came Before Columbus*, may suffer from many deficiencies; but we should not find it so offensive to contemplate that Africans were in the Americas before Columbus as he argues.[68]

During the early period of colonisation, many blacks were classified as 'indentured labourers' rather than slaves; and they were not all engaged as agricultural labourers. Equally, the historical dichotomisation of blacks as powerless and whites as powerful must be corrected. Many whites started their lives in the Caribbean as enslaved people or indentured labourers. And even after the end of white indentured servitude, many remained poor and powerless, sometimes, particularly in urban centres, relying on enslaved people for economic assistance.

It is also vital that black women realise that their role in the Caribbean was first and foremost that of producers – not reproducers; outnumbering enslaved men in the crucial field gangs, as works by Mathurin-Mair, Higman, Beckles and others have shown.[69] It is also false to project an image of the loose and promiscuous black woman and the pure and moral white woman. White women cannot be homogenised into one class and social status. The reality of Caribbean slave society was that there were unmarried white European women, some of whom cohabited with black men and had children for them. European racism dictated that the progeny of these women could not be enslaved because while white women could reproduce the slavery ideology in order to protect the myth of white supremacy, their bodies were not allowed to reproduce slaves, an act reserved for black women. Great efforts were made in places like Barbados, for example through poor relief efforts, to prevent these women from relying on black men.

It should also be exposed that slaveholding was not an exclusive white, male project, though it was overwhelmingly so. Women - freed black, free coloured, whites – were slave holders and managers; and they were not all kind and gentle unlike the so-called 'savage blacks' mentioned by Lady Nugent and others. Free coloured women were described as harsh slave owners and they were among the first to be 'dissed' by ex-slaves in 1838. The narrative of Mary Prince demonstrates unambiguously the cruelty of white European women who were slave holders or managers. Prince said that her mistress,

... caused me to know the exact difference between the smart of the rope, the cartwhip, and the cowskin, when applied to my naked body by her own cruel hand. And there was scarcely any punishment more dreadful than the blows I received on my face and head from her hard, heavy fist. She was a fearful woman, and a savage mistress to her slaves.[70]

Indeed, if those who are really keen to invoke the 'legacy of slavery' model should embark on a serious research project to reclaim marginalised people's voices which would provide them with much to counter the hegemonic discourse and master narrative; for it was not only through violent rebellions and day-to-day acts of non-cooperation that blacks demonstrated their opposition to slavery and racism. In other words, blacks did not only fight back;

despite the endemic anti-intellectual culture bred by slavery, they wrote and spoke back as part of an ontological positioning with colonialism that brought slavery under their literary gaze. The literary output, written or narrated, of people like Olaudah Equiano, Mary Prince, Juan Francisco Manzano and Esteban Montejo, serves to situate anti-slavery ideology at the core of enlightenment modernity.[71]

Statements like: 'I am a Prince. I was much greater in Guinea.' 'I am a prince. For the time being, I am in your power, but nothing will ever persuade me to serve you; I would rather end my life by voluntary death.' 'I was much greater in Guinea than you are here. Now you expect me to be your slave?' are powerful reflections of positive self-identification by Africans captured for enslavement in the Caribbean.[72]

Part of the work coming out also reveals the pitfalls of the wholesale application of the plantation economy model to the Caribbean. Much of this negates the fact that diversification is the real Caribbean experience. During slavery, those without the capital to invest in sugar, turned to other ways of making a living. Despite the desire of colonisers to plant sugar all over the region, the physical environment did not always cooperate. Thus crops like coffee and cotton thrived, as did livestock farming. The pre-conquest economic model which Europeans tried to exterminate and reconfigure upon conquest, therefore continued in many places like Jamaica and the Windward Islands. The implications were internal capital generation, internal trade and a low rate of absenteeism among non-sugar producers not engaged in the export trade. Some inputs were obtained locally and outputs sold locally or intra-regionally.[73] Thus the role of indigenous people and 'new Creoles' in challenging the ideologies and institutional arrangements/economic imperatives of the mercantilist system must form a part of public discussion. This might make us more conscious of our multi-cultural heritage and encourage us to stop playing monopoly in the Caribbean. Monopoly is evident in ethnicised politics, inter-ethnic relations, ethnic stereotyping, the elitist attitude to Caribbean nation languages and so-called 'lower class culture'; the attempt to homogenise a diverse population along the lines of a hegemonic culture and in the disregard of the needs of the Caribbean masses. The dangers of the continuation of monopolistic tendencies should be equally obvious to Caribbean policy-makers; for every form of bondage generates an opposing struggle for liberation. History teaches this, and as we know, those who do not learn from history are destined to repeat it.

Black African and Indian men and women's resistance to apprenticeship, indentureship and the inequities of the free order so that they could actualise freedom and pursue 'perfect personal freedom',[74] are also not in the forefront of public debates and discussions – except, perhaps, at emancipation and Indian arrival day lectures by academics when the commitment of the descendants of slaves and indentured workers to freedom and justice manifested in the anti-colonial struggles of the nineteenth are stressed.

Works which must be more widely disseminated are Swithin Wilmot on counter-discourse in which he opposes the mythical representations of the views about the newly freed people and the black working class; Woodville Marshall and Douglas Hall's revisionist work on what was popularly termed the 'labour problem' in the post-slavery period; and works by Satchell, Marshall and others on the search for land and the political implications of its acquisition and non-acquisition.[75] These works on the post-slavery Caribbean reveal what freedom meant for the newly freed as opposed to what it meant for the former enslavers. Certainly, for the newly freed, as Wilmot pointed out in a recent lecture, emancipation meant more than the absence of slavery.[76] It meant freedom to bargain for fair and equitable wages, freedom to buy land, to take part in the political process, to live where they wished and work for whom they wished. Women wanted the right to choose flexible estate labouring hours so that they could juggle family responsibilities with other productive activities. Freedpeople thus ultimately recognised that emancipation legislation did transform the nature of their lives in such drastic ways that it constituted a revolutionary experience. On the other hand, former enslavers and their imperial allies sought ways to diminish the potential for radical transformation and curb the freedom of blacks by retaining control of government. Thus the role of labour as a factor of production within the economics of emancipation and the rights and expectations of labourers as 'citizens' within the politics of freedom proved contradictory and pitched freedpeople and ex-slaveholders in a battle for terrain that exists to modern times. In this regard, the legacies of planter mentalities proved the obstacle to Caribbean freedom and continue to do so.

The suggestions that I have made in this paper concerning possible ways to educate Caribbean people about their rich and diverse historical legacy with a view to broadening and contextualising the 'legacy of slavery' debate and anchor us to a more positive past, may not solve the so-called 'crisis of black identity' which many feel exists among African-descended people. Considerations about this issue may even be dismissed as 'dated' and not the 'real problem' by those to whom self-confidence is a birthright; to those who are preoccupied with the macroeconomic environment, regional integration, expanding CARICOM, tourism, regional airlines, WTO and the banana industry, the huge external debt, crime and violence, the social infrastructure, and the increasing racial tensions in some of our societies (in themselves part of the legacy of slavery). Indeed, attention to ethnic-specific issues may seem unwise to those who regard the forging of unity and the subordination of cultural diversity to economic imperatives like economies of scale, critical mass and so on in the context of globalisation as being more vital. But this 'old' debate will not go away; and in any case, no discourse is ever closed; so to submerge this much talked-about issue of 'black identity' beneath the concern with so-called 'larger macroeconomic issues' would be myopic. To do so would be to indeed condemn Caribbean societies to continue to suffer the consequences of that part of the legacy of slavery which results in 'othering' and 'desmadification'.

I would like to thank Hilary Beckles, Patrick Bellegarde-Smith, John Campbell, Juan González-Mendoza, Richard Goodridge, Veronica Gregg, Janice Mayers, Keith Nurse, Rita Pemberton, Glen Richards, Bramwell Shepherd, and Pedro Welch for finding the time to exchange views with me about several of the issues raised in this paper.

Notes

1. Quoted in Alissandra Cummins *et al*, *Art in Barbados: What Kind of Mirror Image?* (Kingston, 1999)
2. Andrés Serbin, *Sunset Over the Islands: The Caribbean in an Age of Global and Regional Challenges* (Warwick, 1998), p. 1
3. Black-skinned Indians in the region are also said to be affected by the colour/caste hierarchy, the legacy of the Indian caste system and the north/south divide on the subcontinent.
4. Part of the lyrics of Buju Banton's song, 'Browning', read: 'Me love mi car, me love mi bike/Me love mi money and t'ing/But most of all me love mi Browning'. But it

seems that Buju's intention has been much misunderstood as he penned these lyrics for one 'browning' only!
5. 'Shades of an Indentity Crisis', *Washington Post*, August 5, 1999, p. A15
6. *Flair Magazine*, May 31, 1999, p. 4. This debate of course does not engage with the tanning craze of whites and the increasing tendency among some white women of thickening their lips by plastic surgery.
7. *The Guardian*, August 12, 1999, p. 9
8. Michael White, 'Archer accused of racist claptrap', *The Guardian*, August 10, 1999, p. 2
9. *The Guardian*, August 12, 1999, p. 8. MacLeod is a 54-year-old retired nurse who went to the UK at age 17.
10. See, for example, Michael Burke's piece in the *Daily Observer*, August 2, 1999, p. 17
11. 'Taking the Fowl Pill is suicidal', Dr Neil Persadsingh, *Daily Observer*, August 2, 1999, p. 17
12. Morris Cargill, 'Bleaching, etc', *The Gleaner*, July 29, 1999, p. A4
13. See, for example, the report on Carolyn Cooper's address at the St Mary Emancipation function, August 9, 1999.
14. *Sunday Gleaner*, June 27, 1999
15. 'The bleaching craze', Weekend Observer, July 23, 1999, p. 7. Interestingly enough, the wish to be white/lighter is confined, by most of those who enter the debate, to 'ghetto people'. As Juan González-Mendoza pointed out in a recent conversation, the issue of 'biological bleaching' and 'social engineering' through deliberate selection of marriage partners who are whiter/lighter does not enter the public debates. Additionally, as Patrick Bellegarde-Smith wrote to me in an e-mail, we seem to forget that other ethnic groups apart from black Africans engage in the practice of bleaching. The sun-tan craze of whites and light-skinned people should also form part of the debate, says Jennifer Keane-Dawes. See Fig. 1.
16. 'The best for the browning', *Outlook Sunday Magazine*, August 29, 1999, p. 11
17. Kamau Braithwaite, *The Development of Creole Society in Jamaica, 1770–1820* (Oxford, 1971), p. 167
18. Jamaica Kincaid, *A Small Place* (New York, 1988), p. 55
19. *Daily Observer*, August 2, 1999, p. 6
20. *Sunday Gleaner*, August 1, 1999, p. 2A
21. Swithin Wilmot, 'Emancipation in Action: Workers and Wage Conflict in Jamaica, 1838-1848', *Jamaica Journal*, Vol. 19, No. 3 (1986), pp.55–61
22. Ricky Singh, *The Gleaner*, August 3, 1999, p. A8
23. This figure by the Nigerian scholar Joseph Inikori, overturns Philip Curtin's long-accepted figure of 9.6 million. See Philip Curtin, *The Atlantic Slave Trade: A Census (Madison, 1969)*, and Joseph Inikori, 'Africa in World History: The Export Slave Trade From Africa and the Emergence of the Atlantic Economic Order', in BA Ogot, ed., *General History of Africa*, Vol. 5 (UNESCO, Paris, 1992).

24. Peter Hulme, *Colonial Encounters: Europe and the Native Caribbean, 1492–1797* (London and New York, 1986), p. 1
25. DJR Walker, *Columbus and the Golden World of the Arawaks* (Kingston, 1992), p. 270. As Veronica Gregg observed in her 1993 gender symposium paper on Edward Long, the view of the sensual, promiscuous, 'easy going' and 'exotic' black woman still persists and is manifested in overseas popular culture, particularly in posters and brochures which push tourist destinations in the Caribbean.
26. Jurgen Osterhammel, *Colonialism: A Theoretical Overview*, transl. Shelley L Frisch (Princeton and Kingston, 1997), pp. 107–112
27. Veronica Gregg, *Jean Rhys's Historical Imagination: Reading and Writing the Creole* (North Carolina, 1995), p. 11
28. Charles Leslie, *A New and Exact History* (London, 1739, 1740), Letter XI, pp. 305–306. See a more detailed discussion in Elsa Goveia, *A Study of the Historiography of the British West to the end of the Nineteenth Century* (Washington DC, 1980), p. 53
29. Leslie, Letter XI
30. Cynric Williams, *A Tour Through the Island of Jamaica* (London, 1824), p. 53
31. Ibid., p. 255
32. Philip Wright, ed., *Lady Nugent's Journal of her Residence in Jamaica, 1801–1805* (Kingston, 1966), February 22, 1805, p. 220
33. Bridget Brereton, 'Text, Testimony and Gender', in Verene Shepherd, Bridget Brereton and Barbara Bailey, eds., *Engendering History: Caribbean Women in Historical Perspective* (Kingston, 1995), p. 68
34. See Thomas Carlyle, *The Occasional Discourse on the Nigger Question, Fraser's Magazine*, 1849; James A Froude, *The English in the West Indies: The Bow of Ulysses* (London, 1888); William Sewell, *The Ordeal of Free Labour* (New York, 1861); Anthony Trollope, *The West Indies and the Spanish Main* (New York, 1860); L Hearn, *Two Years in the French West Indies* (New York, 1890); Charles Stoddard, *Cruising Among the Caribbees: Summer Days in Winter Months* (New York, 1895); and William Burn, *Emancipation and Apprenticeship in the BWI* (London, 1937). For Harmer's comments see MS 65, National Library of Jamaica.
35. See Eric Williams, *Capitalism and Slavery* (North Carolina, 1944)
36. Karl Marx, *Grundrisse: Foundations of the Critique of Political Economy* (New York. 1973), pp. 325–326, in Gregg, *Jean Rhys's Historical Imagination*, p. 13
37. Sewell, *The Ordeal of Free Labour*, p. 175
38. Hearn, 'A Midsummer Trip to the Tropics', in *Two Years in the French West Indies*, p. 69
39. Ibid, p. 98
40. Stoddard, Cruising Among the Caribbees, p. 30
41. JJ Thomas, *Froudacity: West Indian Fables by James Anthony Froude, explained by JJ Thomas* (London, 1889)
42. William Green, *British Slave Emancipation: The Great Experiment* (Oxford, 1976)

43. Philip Sherlock and Hazel Bennett, *The Story of the Jamaican People* (Kingston, 1997). This book has the potential to be a good history of Jamaica, but needs to be consistent with its 'Afri-centric perspective'. It also needs a good historiographical overhaul in order to include more recent works on Caribbean/Jamaica history.
44. See, for example Rhoda Reddock, 'Indian Women and Indentureship in Trinidad and Tobago, 1845–1917: Freedom Denied', in Hilary Beckles and Verene Shepherd, eds., *Caribbean Freedom: Society and Economy from Emancipation to the Present* (Kingston, 1993), pp. 225–244 and Verene Shepherd, 'Emancipation Through Servitude?', in Beckles and Shepherd, eds., pp. 245–249.
45. Mark Lawson, 'Not Bigoted, Just Barking', The Guardian, August 14, 1999, p. 18
46. Ustanny, 'The Best for the Browning', p. 11. Interestingly enough, African-Americans, upset by the paucity of black actors and actresses on TV shows, have recently called for a boycott by black people of prominent US TV stations like NBC and CBS.
47. Interview with Howard Campbell in *The Sunday Observer*, August 29, 1999, p. 6
48. 'Emancipation without Apology', *The Gleaner*, July 30, 1999, p. A8
49. Joyce, Appleby, Lynn Hunt & Margaret Jacob, 'Telling the Truth About History', in Jenkins, ed., *The Postmodern History Reader*, p. 216
50. FR Ankersmit, 'Historiography and Postmodernism', in *The Postmodern History Reader*, Keith Jenkins, ed., (London, 1997), pp. 277–297
51. Kevin Yelvington *et al*, eds., 'Whose History? Museum-making and Struggles Over Ethnicity and Representation in the Sunbelt' (August 1999, draft)
52. William Green, 'The Creolisation of Caribbean History: The Emancipation Era and a Critique of Dialectical Analysis', in Hilary Beckles and Verene Shepherd, eds., *Caribbean Freedom: Economy and Society and Emancipation to the Present* (Kingston, 1993), pp. 28–40
53. Patrick Bryan, 'History in the Tropics', Inaugural Professorial Lecture, 1999, p.11
54. Gayatri Chakravorty Spivak, 'Can the Subaltern Speak?', in P Williams and L Chrisman, eds., *Colonial Discourse and Post-Colonial Theory: A Reader* (London, 1993), pp. 66–111
55. Stephen Greenblatt, ed., *New World Encounters* (Berkeley, 1993), pp. vii–viii
56. Donald Akenson, *If the Irish Ran the World: Montserrat, 1630–1730* (Montreal and Kingston), p. 186
57. Appleby, *et al*, 'Telling the Truth About History', p. 217
58. This is also the generation which will refuse to sing 'Amazing Grace', no matter how 'sweet the sound' as long as that sound came from a slave trader, albeit a converted one.
59. Glenn Sankatsing, 'The Caribbean: Archipelago of Trailer Societies', Seed Paper of the inaugural Allan Harris Conference, ISER, UWI, St Augustine, November 1998, p. 6
60. Despite the need to listen to a 'chorus of voices' in this age of postmodernism, I am still not convinced that Caribbean historians can avoid a more activist approach to the teaching of Caribbean history. History needs to be more than an 'academic exercise'

in postcolonial societies. In this regard, I am not sure that I can support totally the view of my white, English colleague who told me recently that Afro-centric history should not be pushed down the throats of our students; that students should be allowed to believe in UFOs or planter-centric versions of histories if they wish. I am sorry if my response to this view upset him; but perhaps I have been too influenced by that great teacher of Caribbean history, Kamau Brathwaite.

61. *The Daily Observer*, August 119, 1999, p. 6
62. Appleby, *et al*, 'Telling the Truth About History', p. 212
63. The Bureau of Women's Affairs in Jamaica has already started on such a project with respect to the gender biases in school textbooks.
64. Appleby, *et al*, 'Telling the Truth about History', p. 215
65. Akenson's *If the Irish Ran the World* smacks of this kind of representation in sections
66. Sankatsing, 'The Caribbean: Archipelago of Trailer Societies'
67. Orlando Patterson, *The Sociology of Slavery* (London, 1967), pp. 9, 167
68. Ivan va Sertima, *They Came Before Columbus* (New York, 1976)
69. See for example, Lucille Mair, *Women Field Workers in Jamaica* (UWI, Mona, 1989); Mair, *Rebel Woman* (Kingston, 1975); Barry Higman, *Slave Populations of the British Caribbean, 1807–1834* (Baltimore, 1984); Hilary Beckles, *Natural Rebels* (New Jersey, 1989) and *Centering Woman: Gender Discourses in Caribbean Slave Society* (Kingston, 1999), Verene Shepherd, *et al*, eds., *Engendering History: Caribbean Women in Historical Perspective*, and Verene Shepherd, compl/ed., *Women in Caribbean History* (Kingston, 1999).
70. Moira Ferguson, ed., *The History of Mary Prince, A West Indian Slave, Related by Herself* (London, 1987), p. 56
71. See Hilary Beckles and Verene Shepherd, eds., *Slave Voices: The Sounds of Freedom* (UNESCO, Paris, 1999)
72. CGA Oldendorp, *History of the Mission of the Evangelical Brethren on the Caribbean Islands of St Thomas, St Croix and St John* (Michigan, 1987), p. 220
73. See Barry Higman, *Slave Population and Economy in Jamaica, 1807–1834* (Cambridge, 1976) and Higman, *Slave Populations of the British Caribbean*. See also Verene Shepherd, 'Pens and Penkeepers in a Plantation Society', Ph. D. dissertation, Cambridge 1988 and Shepherd, guest editor, *Slavery Without Sugar*, special issue of Plantation Society in the Americas, Vol. V, Nos, 2 and 3 (Fall, 1998).
74. Quoted in Glen Richards, 'The Pursuit of "Higher Wages" and "Perfect Personal Freedom": St Kitts-Nevis, 1836-1956', Mary Turner, ed., *From Chattel Slaves to Wage Slaves: The Dynamics of Labour Bargaining in the Americas* (Kingston; Bloomington; London, 1995), pp. 275–301
75. The relevant articles can be read in *Caribbean Freedom: Economy and Society from Emancipation to the Present* (Kingston, 1993), sections 1–3.
76. Lecture delivered to the Jamaican Historical Society, July 1999

9 | JESSICA BYRON

Migration, National Identity and Regionalism in the Caribbean:
A Leeward Islands Case Study

A number of recent publications have highlighted the relationship between migration, the state and international relations in a globalised world and have drawn attention to the role of migration in shaping the peculiar nature of state, citizenship and identity in the Caribbean. I begin with a quotation from Mary Chamberlain's 1998 edited collection, *Caribbean Migration: Globalised Identities*, which speaks volumes on the subject:

International migration strikes at the heart of nationhood and the nation-state, questioning the civic virtue of loyalty, the political certainty of citizenship, the patriotic basis of identity and the geographical security of the border. International migrants are, by definition, global people whose horizons and allegiances, education and enterprise, family and friendship are both portable and elastic. What, finally, unsettles about international migration is that it internationalises the nation-state and globalises identity. Fluidity, not fixity, characterises the migrant . . . few if any people are more global and more migratory than those from the Caribbean. For them, the nation is 'unbound'.

In our attempts to construct a Caribbean region, we have never acknowledged the extent and the power of migration among Caribbean societies as an integrative force. Many factors have contributed to shaping the fragmentation, multiplicity and complexity of Caribbean identities, including ethnicity, colonial history, geography and so on. We know them only too well. I wish to focus on migration, a factor which has tremendous implications for the nature of Caribbean societies in the twenty-first century and the types of connections we will have with the international system through our many diasporas. Let me make it clear that I am not a student of demography or geography, but rather of international relations. My interest in this subject derives primarily from having observed during the past decade the tremendous consequences of migration for the Caribbean state and society in a globalised world.

The role of migration was traditionally understated in Caribbean policy-making circles. However, as ECLAC points out in a 1998 study, in the closing years of the twentieth century, officialdom's view of migration has changed and there have been attempts to formulate new policies, mainly to address return migration issues. The attention of our academics and policy-makers has been focused primarily on extra- Caribbean migration to Europe and to North America. They recognise its economic significance for remittance flows, in-flows of investment and new skills, the growing importance of these diasporas as political lobbies overseas and the need to maintain good relations with such segments of Caribbean societies. Undoubtedly, our metropolitan diasporas will be a vital part of our insertion into the global community in the twenty-first century and they deserve major attention from the policy-makers. However, our approaches to Caribbean migration have been at best partial and have not embraced all aspects of the movement. Intra-Caribbean migration has received far less public attention although its impact is equally significant for Caribbean societies. Such migration, both historically and in the contemporary period, transcends the linguistic, cultural and political boundaries in the region and weaves a complex network of human linkages across Caribbean societies that is largely ignored at the official level.

My current research looks only at a small dimension of this phenomenon, namely the movement between the Dominican Republic (DR) and the Leeward Islands in the twentieth century. However, some of the issues raised may well be applicable to a number of other cases, including Haiti and its neighbours, and in the longer term, possibly Cuba and its neighbours. Also, when I was gathering data on the presence of the Dominicano population in Antigua in particular, I was struck by the magnitude of the foreign-born population there overall. Migrant labour accounts for 23 per cent of the Antiguan workforce. Most migrants come from Dominica, Montserrat, Guyana, Jamaica, and the Dominican Republic. The DR citizens, who number approximately 7,000, are a small part of this overall movement. In neighbouring St Kitts and Nevis, there are 1, 500 to 2, 000. They, as well as their fellow migrants, are gradually bringing about significant change in the island's society.

Aaron Segal (1998) projects that a number of factors in the global political economy will cause the overall rate of Caribbean migration to continue to increase. I argue here that intra- and extra-Caribbean migratory patterns are linked in several ways, and that migration is likely to be a major element shaping the composition of Caribbean societies in the early twenty-first century. It will influence changes in gender and ethnic relations, give us multiple national identities and force an expansion of our concepts of regionalism. There has been relatively little public discussion of migration issues in recent years, much of that occurring in the context of the signing of Protocol 2 of the Treaty of Chaguaramas and the CARICOM commitment to allow UWI graduates and certain categories of skilled CARICOM nationals to work in member territories. Despite this gap in the debate, intra-Caribbean migration poses several burning policy issues, including the social service provisions for migrant workers, land ownership rights on small islands, labour force needs and policies of various countries, citizenship issues, law and order issues in the regional context, and other regional integration issues.

Objective Conditions Propelling Migration

Much of the present intra-Caribbean migration flows from the larger, more heavily populated Caribbean territories which have been trapped in economic decline for several years (Guyana, Jamaica, Haiti and to some extent the Dominican Republic), into some of the smallest territories. Although explicit government policies have been aimed mostly at the migration of professional workers, much of the migration that is occurring consists of manual and technical workers. Demographers have noted this phenomenon in the European and US dependent territories and have pointed out the demographic policy implications posed by the very small indigenous populations and large influxes of migrant workers.

There are similar implications for independent states like Antigua and St Kitts and Nevis. The migrants travel to economies dominated by service industries (tourism and entertainment, offshore finance), where the indigenous workforce is smaller than a high economic growth rate dictates, and where nationals are no longer attracted to low-paid jobs. In host territories, such as

Antigua, for example, the rate of migration by nationals to North America or to Europe is also high. There is therefore a dearth of certain categories of labour which creates an additional opening for migrant workers.

Migration is also encouraged in some cases by the geographical proximity of sending and receiving territories, and by historical links. The latter is certainly true of the movement between the DR and the Leeward Islands, which is the return cycle of a much earlier pattern of seasonal migration from the Leeward Islands to work on the sugar estates of the DR in the first three decades of this century. That created kinship networks which have been reactivated since independence offered citizenship possibilities for DR descendants of those earlier migrant workers, in the 1980s. They came to Antigua and St Kitts and Nevis in search of work, in search of better economic opportunities and possibly in search of new opportunities to emigrate to North America with new national identities. Many have remained, appreciating not only the economic opportunities but the comparatively peaceful, stable environment.

Societal Changes Generated – Positive and Negative

Language and communication

Spanish is increasingly becoming a second language in the Leeward Islands, as it is the mother tongue of approximately ten per cent of the Antiguan population and three per cent of the population of St Kitts and Nevis. This is reflected in changes in both print and radio media: three radio programmes in Spanish broadcast on Antiguan radio stations, one Spanish newspaper (*Hoy*) in Antigua and two weekly newspapers in St Kitts and Nevis which publish a Spanish summary of their news in the centre pages. Likewise, there is an increasing shift in Antigua towards disseminating public information in both Spanish and English, for example disaster preparedness information, immigration and citizenship procedures, public health and education information.

Sports and culture

We witness the emergence of baseball leagues in the Commonwealth Caribbean. There are three in Antigua, one in Nevis, one in St Kitts and a number of inter-island tournaments. The Dominicanos also participate in carnival and other cultural festivals. In some instances, their presentations have generated much debate and some conflict over what is local culture.

The Dominicano presence has added to the number and range of religious communities in the Leeward Islands. There are now eight Spanish-speaking churches in Antigua. Additionally, the populations of the Catholic Church and some other churches have swelled tremendously in all three islands. Even in those churches which have not explicitly started Spanish branches (sometimes a controversial move with the traditional membership bodies), there have been attempts to offer some services to the Spanish congregation, such as free English classes and special services and meetings in Spanish at designated times.

Entertainment

One of my interviewees, in response to a question about the establishment of Dominicano-owned businesses, described his community as being best at selling happiness ('*vendedores de alegria*'). There is evidence of a number of bars opened by members of the Dominicano community, a couple of merengue bands which perform among the Leeward Islands, including in St Martin and Anguilla. There are instances of some major hotels contracting entertainment groups from DR for specific periods. This trend has certainly added to the range and quality of entertainment available in these islands.

Agriculture and food

In this area, it is not only the Dominicanos, but other migrants, including the Guyanese, who feature. As the service industries attract more and more young people, one notes that many gardeners and landscapers in the Leeward Islands are either Guyanese or Dominicano, and that some are now trying their hands at market gardening. I was struck in the market in Nevis at the sight of vegetables which were not traditionally a part of the Nevisian diet, such as bodi. They are now being grown, marketed and bought by the Guyanese community. For the past few years, the St Kitts Sugar Manufacturing Company has recruited seasonal labour from both Guyana and the Dominican Republic during the sugar cane harvesting period each year.

Intermarriage and gender relations

There are mixed signals here, as gender relations seem to have generated as many flash points of conflict as integration in the short run. The longer term effects should be integrative. There is evidence in all the islands of intermarriage taking place, primarily between local men and women from the immigrant community.

Influx of new technical/service skills

The migrants tend to be employed mainly in domestic service, sanitation services, construction and maintenance, agriculture, hairdressing, and hotel work. In case of the Dominicanos, their employment prospects seem to be limited both by recent migrant status and by language barriers. Several had many years' experience in export processing zones in the DR but have not been able or have not wanted to exploit this work experience in the new environment. They have definitely made a positive impact on technical and service skills available in St Kitts and Nevis and in Antigua. With farsighted labour policies, the impact could be even greater.

Criminality

There has been recent evidence of a rising violent crime rate in Antigua, associated especially with some Jamaican migrants, and there has also been some evidence of passport and visa fraud by some migrants in all the Leewards. There is the ever-present possibility of people with criminal records in their own countries seeking to enter these islands through this route. Increased regional mobility and more flexible immigration policies pose the need (as they did in the European Union, for example) for much closer collaboration among the region's police forces to prevent circulation of criminal elements across the Caribbean.

Nascent new political constituencies emerging?

Throughout the Leeward Islands, the issue of migrant workers and minority communities has become a focus for public discussion during the last three to five years. A priority for the migrant communities is to regularise their status and gain recognition and goodwill from the local community. DR nationals appear to be the best organised of the immigrant communities in terms of having national associations and strengthening their lobbying capacity. Also, many among them have a firm claim to citizenship by descent that the CARICOM nationals do not have. In general, the presence of the migrant communities has attracted additional attention from political parties around election times. Migrant communities are aware that they have increased bargaining power at those times when political parties are anxious to win over new constituencies. So, in the longer term, their presence has introduced new issues and new actors into the local political spectrum of the Leeward Islands.

Policy Responses

The clearest policy responses are evidenced in Antigua where there is an explicit policy of encouraging the influx of migrant workers: 'The national policy on citizenship and extended residency for migrant workers has turned a transient emigration process into a progressively more permanent one, including the movement of migrant families.' (Departments of Labour and Immigration Alliance statement, March 1999.) The economic argument is that Antigua's service-oriented economy and small population of 65,000 need an additional workforce for sustainability. Some political controversy has been generated by this as evidenced in claims after the last elections that the ruling party's advantage may have come from winning the votes of Dominicanos and Commonwealth Caribbean citizens. The spate of violent crime in March and April 1999 led to a tightening up of Antigua's immigration regulations and much closer collaboration between the labour department and the immigration authorities. Despite this move to increased regulation, the end result is still a more liberal policy than in many other Caribbean countries. Health policies are mostly evident in the dissemination of information on HIV and other sexually transmitted diseases in Spanish and the organisation of classes three times each year for DR sex workers in Antigua.

As far as education policies are concerned, there have been efforts, spearheaded by the labour authorities in Antigua, to ensure that places in public schools are available for children of migrant workers. However, there is little evidence yet, in either Antigua or St Kitts and Nevis, to focus on special pedagogical problems that may be experienced by Dominicano children who come in from a different educational system, taught in a different language. Interviewees in Nevis and Antigua agree that there are problems for some secondary school-age children and that the education system is not fully meeting their needs. There have been few attempts up to now by local authorities to take remedial action, or to seek to employ people from the Spanish-speaking community as teachers. It appears that there are not yet arrangements in place for the recognition of equivalent diplomas and certification across the Caribbean.

Another example of an active policy response comes from the Ministry of Home Affairs in Antigua, which has employed since April 1998 liaison officers drawn from the Dominicano community for the following purposes:

- to assist the Spanish-speaking community with processing residence, citizenship and work permit documents
- to ensure that the children go to school
- to translate and disseminate public information to the Spanish-speaking community and to relay their concerns back to the government
- to promote the organization of welfare-related activities among the DR community and especially to organise the youth

Antigua also has an honorary consul in the DR and there may soon be a Dominicano counterpart in Antigua.

Few such clear-cut policies exist in St Kitts and Nevis, where there has a been a much slower and less open policy towards DR nationals despite a recognition of the legitimate claims of many to citizenship and the economic value of their labour. Successive governments appear to have been ambivalent on citizenship, residence and work permit policies. At times the processing of citizenship applications has slowed markedly and there have been instances of expulsions. There was a period of amnesty granted for illegal aliens to regularise their status in Nevis in April 1998. However, there is no evidence of specifically targeted education policies or government attempts to disseminate official information in Spanish. Both in Antigua and in St Kitts and Nevis, work permit and residence fees are quite high and DR nationals are obliged to pay them for an extended period of time while their citizenship applications are undergoing processing.

Dominicano residents point to areas where they would like to see policy shifts. These include the need for a greater focus on education policies, and for the pace of processing citizenship applications to be speeded up. In some communities there is a great desire for more classes in English and for more public information to be made available in Spanish. In both countries, there is still a lack of consular services available to the DR communities from their own government. Representation has been made by the communities to the DR authorities. In the perception of many migrants, they continue to rely primarily on their own close-knit communities and their own organising capacity to ensure their welfare in the host societies.

Implications for National Identity and Regionalism in the Caribbean

National identity

It seems obvious to me that such migratory movements will significantly change the composition of the host societies during the first decade of the twenty-first century. These societies will be, at the very least, much more heterogeneous, and many of their residents may feel allegiance to at least two countries. Ironically, my interviews with Dominicanos of St Kitts or Antiguan descent suggested that their sense of identity as Dominicanos has been intensified by their sojourn in the English-speaking islands, although they may have originated from a part of the DR characterised by its Commonwealth Caribbean heritage. Settlement in the Eastern Caribbean is a pragmatic individual or household response to the political and economic pressures of life, but they retain active links with the DR and they travel there frequently. Responses of locals varied between Antigua and St Kitts and Nevis. The former accepted the presence of foreign minorities more and there appeared to have been more social integration. In St Kitts and Nevis, although there has been some flexibility and integration is gradually taking place, people appeared more ambivalent and more inclined to feel threatened by the influx. Much of the resentment was expressed by people who might be competing for similar categories of jobs to the migrants.

Moreover, the foreign presence seems to have induced people to examine more seriously their own sense of identity and appreciation of their local culture. In neither country was there much evidence of more locals speaking Spanish fluently or having a better understanding of the culture of the DR. Although all the Leeward Islands are now aware in a more tangible way of the Spanish-speaking Caribbean, many locals still express ignorance and lack of interest about the DR, such as its size, economy, politics. They merely think that it must be a small, backward and impoverished place for all these people to have come to their country! The DR national associations work to dispel such impressions with their cultural activities in the host societies.

Regionalism

During the past 40 years Caribbean regional integration has often faltered or stagnated because there was too great an emphasis on building intergovernmental structures and insufficient involvement of people. Likewise, we focused on too small an area of the region, and perpetuated the divisions of the colonial period. We are now required to rapidly integrate with the rest of the western hemisphere, and interact intensively with Latin America. This process is portrayed as being externally imposed and a product of the push of globalisation. Little or no attention has been paid to the real people networks that exist between the English- and Spanish-speaking Caribbean as a result of historical and contemporary migration. Few attempts have been made to use them as the base for building more meaningful and productive interaction between the societies concerned. During the 1998 negotiations on a CARICOM/DR FTA, no reference was made to the Dominicano communities in the Eastern Caribbean. There are few examples of diplomatic or consular representation between the DR and the receiving societies and few initiatives to use these people's presence as the basis for constructing commercial and cultural exchanges or to establish new transport and communication routes.

Conclusion

My conclusions are that migration is an untapped resource for promoting Caribbean integration. Moreover, there is a regional labour market which informally incorporates the entire insular CARIFORUM area and Cuba. However, up to now, policy-makers and researchers do not officially acknowledge its existence, do not gather data or make projections about labour needs on that basis and do not formulate regional policies for human resource development and deployment.

Policy Recommendations based on the foregoing

i. Use migration to promote the use of the Spanish language, to promote cultural exchanges between English and Spanish-speaking Caribbean.

ii. Rework school curricula (such as social studies or history) to incorporate more teaching about migratory patterns and our links with Hispanic and French-speaking Caribbean.

iii. Develop programmes of public education to address some of the issues and minimise the tensions caused by migration; and develop appropriate institutions to facilitate the integration of the migrant communities.

iv. The UWI, as a leading institution of regional integration, should continue and indeed rapidly increase its collaboration with sister institutions in the Spanish- and French-speaking Caribbean, should seek to attract each year a quota of students from the Dominican Republic, Haiti, Cuba, and maybe Central America, and should develop new research programmes designed to support the integration of the wider Caribbean.

v. The lack of diplomatic and consular representation that is designed to serve the needs of the populations should be speedily addressed.

vi. CARICOM societies should explore the extent to which the existence of the migrant communities can serve as a base for acquiring an understanding of their societies and for constructing trade and investment links with the Hispanic Caribbean.

vii. Caribbean governments and populations should openly acknowledge that regional integration involves the movement of labour and seek to develop appropriate regional labour market policies for the twenty-first century.

References

Basch L, Glick Schiller N, Szanton Blanc C, *Nations Unbound: Transnational Projects, Post-Colonial Predicaments and Deterritorialised Nation-States* (Gordon and Breach Publishers, Amsterdam, 1994)

Chamberlain M, ed., *Caribbean Migration: Globalised Identities* (Routledge, London, 1998)

Segal A., 'The Political Economy of Contemporary Migration' in Klak T, ed., *Globalisation and Neoliberalism : the Caribbean Context* (Rowman and Littlefield Publishers, Maryland, 1998)

United Nations Economic Commission for Latin America and the Caribbean, *A Study of Return Migration to the OECS Territories and the British Virgin Islands in the Closing Years of the Twentieth Century: Implications for Social Policy* (General LC/CAR/G.550, December 1,1998)

Part 3

*Economic Policy Options
in the Twenty-first Century*

10 | OMAR DAVIES

Economic Policy Options for the Twenty-first century

In regard to the policy options for the twenty-first century for the Caribbean countries, certain economic and financial imperatives continue to be relevant; these include low inflation, the need for a fiscal surplus, increased competitiveness and the fact that there will be diminished external support, either in terms of concessionary loans or grants. I place special emphasis on the need for a fiscal surplus because in the Caribbean, particularly in Jamaica and Guyana, the problem of the debt burden has not been adequately linked to loose fiscal policy. We have had a tendency to see the phenomenon of external debt as being separate and apart from the need for a conservative fiscal policy. A friend of mine argues that, whether at the individual, household or national level, having a fiscal surplus gives you that most important bargaining tool – options. Operating with a fiscal deficit limits one's ability, not only in terms of allocating additional resources to those areas which are clearly in need of support, but it also forces a country into crisis decision making – to which Prime Minister Arthur made reference. So the objectives of low inflation and the tight fiscal policy leading to a fiscal surplus and increased competitiveness, remain relevant. I assert that these are non-negotiable imperatives for the future.

I now address a question which should be of interest and importance to this gathering, particularly given where we are located – that of human resource development. Whilst all of us accept this as a necessity, sometimes even at the heart of the institutions which should be at the forefront of human resource development, there is a lack of focus. There has to be a greater awareness that investment in human resource development, is not only aimed at fostering social mobility, but also geared to the training of persons suitable for gainful and productive employment.

I recall recently when I raised the issue of greater accountability in the education sector, a spokesperson for the Jamaica Teachers' Association ridiculed my position by suggesting that I was arguing as if education were a 'cash crop' in that I expected a given output from a given level of investment. My response is simple; 'yes, we do!' If I may be bold enough to say so, this institution represents one where we could start with that realisation that there needs to be accountability for the output, given the cost of the input. So the issue of human resource development, to which Prime Minister Arthur made reference, is one which I would emphasize, in terms of its importance for the twenty-first century.

I turn next to the issue of the form of organisation of the economy, in particular the relationship between the state and the private sector. For a very long time, the 'Washington Consensus' originating in the period of the Reagan/Thatcher axis, held the view, and many of us bought into this idea, that we should simply privatise the main areas of the economy, with the government concentrating on support services: the prisons, and perhaps the education system, and all would be well. This led many countries, including Jamaica, to embark on a privatisation timetable without any careful analysis as to whether those to whom we were selling assets were capable of running these institutions, or indeed running them any better than the state had. Jamaica has several unfortunate examples of failed privatisation schemes. One, I will mention, is the sugar industry. What the twenty-first century will demand, is a recognition, within our countries, of the need for collaboration between the state and the private sector in certain strategic enterprises. That observation leads me to the matter of an approach to mature industries. There is often a tendency to think that once problems arise in a mature industry, the only solution is to abandon it and move one. I do not wish to take issue with Prime Minister Arthur, because I do not think that he meant this in an extreme sense. There is a thin line between recognizing when a country has exploited a mature industry to the maximum extent possible, as opposed to recognizing that whilst there are indeed significant problems, if one were to focus one's energies on reducing unit costs, it would be possible to return it to viability. I have, in the last year, attempted to learn more about the sugar industry. I am not one who subscribes to its abandonment because I think there are several basic steps, which can be taken in terms of reducing unit costs as well as increasing the range of products from this industry.

I wish to make a final point, and in so doing, raise a fundamental but perhaps disturbing question, which is: 'what is the future of small nation states such as those of the Caribbean'? In speaking to the issue of the future of the Caribbean, we assume away a fundamental problem, which is one which I consider the most important economic and social question for the future. What is a Caribbean state? What will be the nature of the Jamaican or Barbadian state for the future? What will make us identifiable entities? What will be the result of our proximity to North America or our use of English? These two factors combine to pose a major problem to us, even as they present us with opportunities. Prime Minister Arthur made reference to the increasing development of an 'intense individualism' in our countries. If there is a difference between twenty-five or thirty years ago and now, it is the decrease in a commitment to our nation states by our young population. Economic policies are not designed in the abstract. They must relate to a people. Therefore, I am convinced that the identification of the factors needed to give us all a sense of a common identity will be the critical underlying factor in determining our economic policies and options for the twenty-first century.

11 | CLIVE THOMAS

The Global Economy, Market Confidence, and Development Goals:

The Dilemmas of Macroeconomic Policy in the Caribbean

Approaching the new millennium, a list of economic development priorities in the Caribbean would include: the alleviation of poverty; the reduction of unemployment; sustained improvements in the health, education, skills, and standard of living of the broad mass of the population; economic diversification and the attenuation of economic fluctuations, vulnerability and insecurity; and a more equitable distribution of incomes, wealth, productive assets, and access to economic opportunities, along with the removal of gender and other forms of discrimination. These items appear in many official pronouncements in the region. They also would find wide acceptance as global priorities.

However, in the face of unprecedented changes in the global economy, CARICOM authorities have been adopting, either deliberately or by default, independently or in 'consultation' with the IFIs and major bilateral donors, a model of macroeconomic management which impacts adversely on the trajectory of its growth. This threatens the reversal of these developmental priorities leading to far-reaching negative consequences for mass-based democratic politics. I shall now seek to argue the bare bones of this thesis.

The Policy Trilemma

In market-based open economies, it is not possible to sustain both *internal balance* (defined as potential full employment non-inflationary growth with the smallest possible deviations in the long run in the size and duration of economic fluctuations as a result of shocks, taking into account society's trade-off between price and output stability), and *external balance* (defined as a zero balance on the current account of the balance of payments), as independent targets, unless the authorities pursue some combination, or all of the policies below:

i. An independent monetary/fiscal policy (as distinct from automatic monetary and fiscal adjustment to shocks) and/or direct controls
ii. Some degree of flexibility in the exchange rate (at the minimum a 'dirty float')
iii. Some regulation of international transactions (in particular private short term flows such as bank debt, bonds, and portfolio equity)

An independent monetary/fiscal policy is essential for pursuing internal balance as an independent target. This is therefore, a *necessary* inclusion for all workable combinations of these policy instruments. Thus we have at all times two policy instruments directed at the two independent targets. These instruments are capable of influencing *both* the magnitude and composition of aggregate expenditure and output flows.

This policy condition is established in the literature as the only way of resolving the contradictions of the so-called 'impossible trinity', or the 'policy trilemma', which faces all open economies pursuing macroeconomic stability. It recognises that, while the authorities may have a monopoly in the supply of base money (currency and bank deposits with the central bank), in the absence of administrative controls they cannot control both the supply and price of money. Further, because the price of money has two aspects to it – the interest rate and the exchange rate – the authorities can set only one of the following: the interest rate, the exchange rate, or the supply of base money. In effect therefore, monetary policy and exchange rate management are integrated.

If the open economy is small, and its financial/capital markets are effectively integrated into world markets, as in the Caribbean, the condition described here applies *a fortiori*. Furthermore, if we took into account certain special characteristics of Caribbean economies, the condition becomes literally, a policy straightjacket. These characteristics include a rapid process of trade liberalisation; high export concentration in markets and products combined with a relatively dispersed sourcing of imports; high cost and uncompetitive exports, so that quite apart from the economic rents obtained from their preferential marketing, they depend on these preferences for their very survival (sugar and bananas); high frequency of external 'exogenous' shocks; a significant debt overhang (particularly acute in Guyana, which qualifies for special IFI concessions – HIPC Initiatives, Lyons terms, and the Cologne Initiative; a high dependence on concessional capital flows for infrastructural projects; high opportunity costs attached to holding international reserves; a restricted scope for administrative (direct) intervention and/or moral suasion in domestic markets, as the role of state operated enterprises in the economy has shrunk; and a large diaspora with continuing significant levels of outward migration.

Past experiences with the strict gold standard/currency board mechanism of fixed exchange rates and free capital flows show that an independent fiscal policy is ruled out *a priori*. In this situation, the money supply is fully backed by foreign reserves and is regulated to adjust completely to changes in the balance of payments (foreign exchange availability). Balance of payments surpluses therefore automatically induce monetary expansion, and deficits the reverse. Here the money supply is endogenous, as the authorities are required to provide either foreign or domestic currency, as demanded, at the fixed exchange rate and they are precluded from exercising any sterilisation functions. The government cannot then monetise public debt. There is, in effect, no lender-of-last-resort. Indeed one can say that there is really no point in such circumstances in having one's own currency, which is the basis of the present day appeal of dollarisation and a return to the currency board mechanism.

In this setting, any external balance is achieved at the expense of internal balance. This is without regard to either the size or duration of the deviations of domestic output and prices from their long-run trend, or to society's preferred trade-off between employment and inflation. In regard to the former, it is worth noting that the adjustment is easier the more flexible the wage rate and other prices upwards and downwards. Such flexibility requires weak unionism and the absence of wage indexation. In regard to the latter trade-off, the pursuit of strict output stability will involve a large amount of inflation loss. Similarly, the pursuit of strict price stability will involve a large amount of output/employment loss. An uncompromising either/or approach is therefore clearly unsuitable, as this does not take into account the big reductions in opportunity costs which accompany any movement away from either extreme position on the trade-off curve.

In CARICOM, there is a revealed preference for *fixed exchange rates* as the centrepiece of macroeconomic management. Ten countries formally practise fixed exchange rates, and five others formally proclaim some form of floating. In reality, however, the latter five aspire to fixed rates, and envy their counterparts who have been able to maintain such a system. With varying degrees of emphasis, their desire is to make the exchange rate as fixed as possible. A similar revealed preference has been identified in Latin America, where even in the period of large real shocks last year, stable exchange rate policies were pursued (see Hausmann, 1999). This practice, in effect, converts the exchange rate from a policy instrument into a target (parameter).

Alongside this tendency to fixed exchange rates, there has also emerged in recent times a preference for an *open capital account* or the progressive removal of all forms of controls on inward and outward capital flows, long term and short term. Concurrent with these two policy stances, CARICOM countries have already acceded to the WTO liberalisation process for trade in goods and services.

The combined effect of these three linked policy stances is to revert the region towards the gold standard/currency board-type adjustment mechanism, whose economic and political consequences we need to explore in the contemporary world. Before doing so, let me comment on some of the matters raised so far.

Fixed Exchange Rates

First, why is there a revealed preference for fixed exchange rates? In theory, with a rigidly fixed exchange rate the authorities have no freedom to control their foreign exchange reserves, as they stand ready to provide or accept foreign currency on demand, against domestic funds. In effect, therefore, the authorities take on the responsibility to finance the balance of payments in contrast to the other extreme of a freely floating exchange rate. Here, there will be no flows into or out of reserves held by the authorities; private agents finance the balance of payments. In practice, regional authorities have fixed their exchange rates in relation to the US dollar, so that although the rate is fixed some variation does occur. That variation, however, is dependent on the variation of the US exchange rate with regard to other countries. As a practical matter also, the authorities have declared their intention to use their foreign exchange reserves to guard against currency speculation and to intervene, if required, in order to 'sterilise' undesired effects on the domestic economy arising from outflows and inflows of foreign funds. This, however, is usually a costly exercise as the authorities have to carry fiscal losses arising from the difference between interest earned on foreign exchange reserves and debt denominated in domestic currency. More importantly, however, although international reserves are growing in absolute terms, they are becoming smaller relative to the size of foreign funds with a potential for rapid movement into and out of the country, as domestic capital markets become integrated into world markets. The practical scope for effective 'sterilisation' is at present very limited.

A survey of official statements and analyses indicates that among the reasons advanced in support of a fixed exchange rate is that the fixed rate is like an autopilot for guiding the macroeconomy. Once established, it requires monetary and fiscal discipline to safeguard it, which would not be otherwise forthcoming. A fixed rate therefore, generates 'market confidence' and provides 'credibility' for the authorities' policy positions, thereby stabilising private markets. Moreover, since the rate is fixed to the US dollar, and the US is committed to a low domestic inflation policy, this reinforces the deflationary bias of fixed exchange rates in the local economy. In this way it helps to contain wage-price inflation. This is of particular importance, since the export sector is largely uncompetitive, the wage rate is de facto indexed, and there is already a large value of dollar denominated liabilities in the domestic market.

By removing exchange rate volatility, a fixed rate is also expected to reduce the disruption to trade and production, which occurs when exchange rates change frequently. Also, because of the growing tendency for local financial intermediaries and other savers and investors to denominate their assets and liabilities in foreign currency, exchange rate stability helps to reduce risk in the financial system, lengthen the investment horizon, reduce transactions costs, and minimise the risk of divorce between market expectations about the exchange rate and 'economic fundamentals'. The combined effect of all these considerations is that the domestic economy would be secured against destabilising speculation and contagion from financial and currency crises emanating elsewhere.

As seen from the perspective of these advantages, the fixed rate constitutes a desired automatic adjustment transmission mechanism – one in which changes in foreign currency lead to changes in the domestic money supply, which in turn affect real money balances, the interest rate, domestic spending, output, wages and prices, and the competitiveness of traded goods. Monetary policy and its outcomes are therefore determined above all, by this commitment to a fixed exchange.

Open Capital Account

The second matter concerns the regional movement towards an open capital account. Controls on capital movement represent the most common form of insulation of the domestic economy from the operations of the world financial and monetary system and its forms of governance. They have been used by authorities as the most common way of permitting the domestic interest rate, adjusted for risk and expected exchange rate movements, to vary from the world rate – an insulation is considered to be a necessary condition for the independent regulation of the domestic economy. Controls have been placed on all types of capital flows: foreign direct investment (FDI); real estate; domestic bank borrowing in foreign exchange; corporate and individual holdings of foreign exchange assets and liabilities positions; forward market transactions; and derivatives. These flows can either be short term or long term, although in recent times this distinction is becoming blurred. Capital controls are permitted under current IMF Articles, and indeed the Fund itself can recommend their implementation.

Over the past decade or so, CARICOM countries have taken considerable steps to dismantle their capital controls, complementing this with WTO-type liberalisation of trade in goods and services. Thus quotas and import licencing have been removed. Free currency convertibility has been promoted. Residents are now permitted to purchase financial instruments or raise funds by selling financial instruments in overseas markets. Foreigners can buy/sell/borrow/lend in the local financial market. Such developments, together with local stock market initiatives, the development of foreign currency accounts in local banks, and regular public offerings of local financial dealers, provide evidence of this freedom of inward and outward capital flows. If we also take into account the growing use of the US dollar in domestic transactions (such as US dollar loans to firms) and credit card purchases of tourist services, then we have to admit that dollarisation and currency substitution are already fairly well advanced.

Separate research by Bennett (1995) and Doyle (1997) confirms the high level of capital mobility in the four larger regional economies. For example, in Barbados, where some express the belief that capital controls are most highly developed, Doyle concludes, 'capital is still relatively mobile across the Barbadian economy and arbitrage operations are operative.' The tests used to measure this derive from the theoretical conclusion that with high capital mobility, interest rate equalisation will occur at the world rate or that of the USA, adjusted for expected exchange rate changes, whereas in Barbados there is no expected exchange rate change and high capital mobility changes in domestic interest rates should pattern those in the US.

Among the arguments advanced for an open capital account is that capital controls lead to a suboptimal global allocation of capital. This is an extension of the arguments in favour of free trade. In any event it is pointed out that, with new technologies, cross-border flows are virtually unstoppable. As a related benefit the open capital account avoids the administrative/political arbitrariness of capital controls. This is also in keeping with the global process towards increasing financial liberalisation and the more or less complete integration of world capital markets. In this process, free capital mobility offers portfolio diversification and risk spreading, for both domestic and foreign investors. It therefore yields higher risk-adjusted rates of return. It is also trade promoting, as trade and capital flows go together. Capital mobility is also expected to smooth out fluctuations in the level of national consumption expenditures and domestic business cycles, through permitting borrowing when there is a need to do so and repayment when the economy is able to do so. It is usually conceded that portfolio flows are more volatile than FDI flows, but it is argued that these may nevertheless encourage the less volatile FDI flows. As for FDI flows, these are seen as capacity-expanding, including capacity in the trade sector, thereby making them sustainable. Finally, it is advanced that an open capital account is accommodating to the IMF's recent change in direction, as now expressed in its support for full capital account liberalisation.

Monetary/Fiscal Policy

Why monetary/fiscal policy and not monetary and fiscal policy as separate policy instruments? The answer is simple. Practice in the region has shown that fiscal policy, even when including an incomes and price policy component, is administratively and legislatively inflexible as a macroeconomic stabilisation instrument. The lag in effecting fiscal policy changes are considerable and this makes them impractical. Moreover, concern has been expressed in the region about other related matters, such as sending the 'wrong signals' to domestic and foreign economic agents; the danger of compensating private behaviour as the private sector responds to anticipated fiscal changes; fears of crowding-out the private sector; and the politics of frequent government spending and tax changes. Because of these concerns, most of the burden for short term stabilisation of the economy falls on monetary policy, which has tended to become somewhat overloaded.

This observation, however, does not rule out the expectation that, from time to time, fiscal policy will be used as an effective response to certain shocks. In countries that have undergone stabilisation programmes, fiscal adjustments have played a leading role. And, in terms of long term structural adjustment, fiscal policy also has a major role to play.

The Global Economy

How do tendencies in the global economy impact on these policy stances in favour of a fixed exchange rate and an open capital account? Over the past three decades, fragmented national economic and financial systems have given way to an integrated global one. This has been partly as a result of developments in technology, and partly due to policy changes led by the major industrial countries. The present management of the global economy through the IFIs and the WTO is premised on the view that national systems are now more or less subordinate to it. These are translated into certain rules of the game. In trade, this is seen in the presumption of reciprocity and national treatment. And in finance, it is premised on the expectation that with uncovered interest parity, domestic interest rates will more or less follow world rates or that of the country in which the local currency is anchored, and tend towards global interest rate equalisation. The expectation is that optimal global allocation of savings and a tendency towards convergence of all economies will result. The belief is that only market imperfections can prevent this outcome. If such imperfections persist, then at least in theory, global cooperation can devise a global facility to act as lender-of-last resort and to provide liquidity to oil the wheels of this system and maintain the rules of the game. Since for all practical purposes this is unlikely, the result has been that efforts are focused on removing market imperfections. In the region the movement towards a fixed exchange policy, open capital account, and trade liberalisation is driven in large measure by this global perspective. But before turning to examine the consequences of this, we must first identify the chief elements of the present global configuration.

To begin with there are elements that centre on global trade, which strongly impact on the region. These include the transition to a post-preferences WTO-type world trading system, based on reciprocity and equal national treatment. The expectation is that these principles will be embodied in future trade arrangements, particularly the renegotiated Lomé Convention and the FTAA. Indeed, in anticipation of joining NAFTA some CARICOM countries were led to adopt a hasty, ill-considered, and un-programmed process of liberalisation, which the others subsequently followed. Today, we are still living with some of the adverse consequences of this in some of our fledgling domestic sectors. Other global trade elements to bear in mind include the impact of exogenous technological change on the region's export performance; the drastic decline in the prices of primary commodities vital to the region; the growing linkage of global trade to transnationalised production and the consequent rise of intra-TNC trade relative to traditional arms-length trade.

There are also elements that centre on the behaviour of financial agents at the global level. These include the much talked about surge in hot-money flows and the threat this brings of financial and currency crises. Experience has shown that these flows are volatile, producing sharp swings and reverse flows, and strong evidence of herding behaviour. During the 1990s, at approximately two-yearly intervals, there have been major episodes of financial and currency crises with their attendant contagion effects. This result contrasts sharply with the stabilising speculative behaviour in response to 'economic fundamentals' anticipated from policies of financial liberalisation and the adoption of floating exchange rates in the major industrial countries. Some analysts trace this unanticipated outcome to the nature of financial markets. In these markets information is intrinsically asymmetric – borrowers will always generally know more about a financial transaction than lenders do. This asymmetry gives rise to certain forms of market behaviour recognised in the literature as moral hazard, adverse selection, herding behaviour, and gambling for redemption through taking risky loans to bail out enterprises in distress. There is an old adage about stock market activity: what goes up must come down. Similarly, one might say that capital flows are never intended to be permanent one-way flows – what goes out must return.

Financial agents also behave in a manner which suggest that FDI flows to developing countries are a 'reward' for pro-market liberalisation policies. 'Market confidence' as defined by financial agents has become the operative factor in capital flows. In this relation, macroeconomic stability no longer guarantees market confidence. In fact it may be the other way around - market confidence is required as a condition for macroeconomic stability. This market confidence may be affected by actual, perceived or expected changes in interest rates, exchange rates, or inflation rates; or by declines in export earnings, whether or not these are related to the country's economic fundamentals. It has also displayed a marked preference for certain situations: small government, low taxes, low social insurance expenditures, flexible labour markets, and credible authorities. The decline in official concessional flows, and the rise in profit-motivated private capital flows to the region, have given an added edge to this outlook of financial agents. (At present private global financial flows are more than 60 times greater than global trade, and nine times greater than global GDP.)

There are also elements which centre on the global governance of the international financial system. These include recurring situations where the burden of adjustment to global financial and currency crises is carried principally by borrowers and not lenders. This has invariably occurred when the IFIs and governments of the major industrial countries are required to intervene in a crisis. This has raised complaints about the moral hazard of providing bail-outs to international creditors, which is seen as encouraging their revealed lack of prudence in lending.

In the governance of the international financial system there has been a noticeable shift in favour of the influence of financial capital over other forms of capital and labour. Also, to all intents and purposes small developing countries are marginalised in the decision-making process over global financial events. Indeed, with the increased risk of financial crisis among these countries, this has added further leverage which the IFIs can exercise over the direction and management of their economic policy. It is for this reason that the IMF's recent reversal of position on capital flows is so important. The Declaration of the Interim Committee at the 1997 IMF/World Bank Annual Meeting states that liberalisation of the capital accounts in the balance of payments is desireable overall, but that risks need to be carefully managed.

In sum, the overall determination of the international events is such that the present global financial system and the process of trade liberalisation emerge as the pivotal factors in the nexus between CARICOM and the wider world. These define the rules of the game internationally and determine, therefore, what scope there is for national efforts directed at fostering economic and social development. The conduit for the influence of the new liberal trade order on the region is the WTO obligations entered into by CARICOM countries. The conduit for the enhanced power and influence of finance capital at the global level on the national economy is the extent of integration of local financial markets into the world markets. The scope for national/regional manoeuvre in relation to the former conduit I have addressed in a recent paper (see Thomas, 1999). The latter conduit explains why the model of macroeconomic management that the authorities pursue emerges as so important to the trajectory of regional growth. As we have seen, that model is premised on the view that interest rate parity anchors the exchange rate in the balance of payments and domestic price levels. With free capital mobility, the economy is expected to converge towards the world interest rate and inflation rate, or that of the lead currency to which it is fixed. From one perspective, this epitomises the optimal global allocation of savings and welfare. But for this to be even theoretically plausible, certain very restrictive conditions approximating to perfect competition and perfect information flows, will have to apply. But, as we have pointed out, systemic risks and their associated asymmetric information flows are intrinsic to financial markets. Indeed, contemporary global financial markets no longer focus primarily on the traditional intermediation between savers and investors and the provision of stabilising speculation aimed at managing future risks. Many new instruments, like derivatives and highly leveraged hedge funds, create the opportunity for short term profits based solely on taking gambles on minute-to-minute, day-to-day changes in security prices.

Consequences

What are the consequences of the region's macroeconomic policy stance in the context of the global economy? The major proposition I wish to advance from this is that these consequences are in the first instance economic, having to do principally with the likely success or not of macroeconomic management and the trajectory of economic growth in the region. In the final instance, however, because of the relationship between these two considerations to economic development in the broadest sense, they take on a fundamentally disturbing political character.

The economic consequences can be summarised as follows. In light of the potential for increased volatility of both inward and outward capital flows under conditions of an open capital account and experience of large fluctuations in export earnings, macroeconomic stability takes precedence over all other economic concerns. With repeated shocks occurring, the pressure to preserve this focus on macroeconomic stability is strengthened. However, because the exchange rate is managed as the centrepiece for maintaining stability and the open capital account for securing market confidence, a self-fulfilling cycle of expectations and actions is set in train, disregarding its growth consequences. The view that there is no alternative to this neo-classical monetarism then becomes deeply entrenched – which is true if the parameters of the model are taken as given. The result is that what are essentially short-run considerations take precedence over medium- and long term growth issues unless, by coincidence, these happen to converge.

The effect is that economic growth and diversification, productivity enhancement, innovation, and resource mobilisation become de facto second-order priorities – even if the authorities present it as otherwise. The inner dynamics of this process is revealed in the way political power accretes to the ministry of finance as the front-line, fire-fighting ministry facing continuing economic emergencies, of macroeconomic instability, and scarce resources. Frequently, this ministry also controls the PSIP, thereby enabling it to impose its primary concerns on the government's long term capital programme. I must point out that the situation I describe is systemic. It is not being suggested that ministers of finance set about to accumulate political power in this way, or for that matter that, the authorities are uncaring about medium and long term development of the economy.

The next question we have to consider is how economic growth/development is articulated. By default, if not design, medium and long term growth and development are left to the private sector – local and foreign. It is in this sense that the claim governments now routinely make is true – that the private sector is the engine of growth. The need to ensure market confidence among private investors, which this almost exclusive reliance on them entails, reinforces the macroeconomic policy stance described earlier. In the meantime, the situation has emerged where even those private sector firms that are engaged in long term productive enterprises have a significant short term capacity to move capital into and out of the country, as can readily be measured in the growth of their dollar denominated debt and holdings of domestic financial assets that are readily convertible.

We need also to bear in mind that the dynamic element in regional private sector activity is foreign. The trajectory of the region's growth is therefore really dependent on how foreign investors see opportunities in the local economy. This is an exogenous factor, which despite expectations to the contrary is not under the control of the local authorities. There is therefore an element of the lottery syndrome in all this. Each country hopes that it will be picked as a winner by foreign investors. In this lottery the tickets are purchased through offering competitive encouragements to foreign capital. But it is useful to note the results of a recent IDB study (Hausmann, 1999), which shows that volatility in the magnitude and cost of capital flows to Latin America has been highly correlated across disparate countries, suggesting that global factors were of greater significance than domestic policies in each economy.

In sum, the model of macroeconomic management pursued gives rise to increasing constraints on the exercise of economic options. Policies that promote integration into the global economy narrow the scope for national control and, simultaneously widen the scope for global events to determine domestic economic outcomes. The higher the degree of permitted capital mobility, the smaller the window of opportunity for flexibility in the pursuit of a domestic agenda and, simultaneously, the greater the fixity of the exchange rate regime. In order to keep this system going, the national economy must earn market confidence at the global level. It is therefore constrained to anticipate and meet the wishes of the market. We have already identified some of the fiscal and financial elements on which this market confidence seems to hinge: small government, privatisation, low taxes, competitive tax concessions, and financial openness. These policies, however, are being extended to other politically sensitive areas including flexible labour markets and constrained trade unionism; mild and non-confrontational environmentalism; non-punitive regulatory and incentive frameworks for enterprise operation; low social insurance; and easy work permit policies.

If the present scenario continues, only reforms at the global level directed at the regulation of hot-money flows and the provision of lender-of-last-resort balance of payments support on a principled and ordered basis, will be in a position to provide a resolution of these contradictions. The prospect for this, however, is dim at best. In this situation of apparent hopelessness and helplessness, political debate and choices are progressively reduced to one between the choice of which political party can best provide the needed accommodation since, as the saying goes, there is no alternative. The result is, as Friedman (1999) notes:

Once your country puts on the Golden Straightjacket, its political choices get reduced to Pepsi or Coke – to slight nuances of taste, slight nuances of policy, slight alterations in design to account for local traditions, some loosening here or there, but never any major deviation from the core golden rules. (ibid. p. 87)

This political situation contrasts sharply with the strong alternative – mass-based politics – Caribbean electorates have known for most of the twentieth century, until the 1980s. Some portray this outcome as a mark of the growing sophistication of politics. To my mind it is the opposite. Politics without mass involvement, and in which there are neither clear alternative options nor a strong national consensus in favour of one, represents a weakening of the democratic political culture. This the region can ill afford, in light of the massive problems that it presently faces. If this persists politics will become shallow, symbolic, ritualised and routinised. Formal democracy may widen to cover excluded minorities. It will not, however, deepen to embrace mobilisation for development and economic and social equality.

The Way Forward

Do we end on a depressing note? Is there a way forward? The formulation of the impossible trinity/policy trilemma suggests the need to rethink either the policy of fixed exchange rates, or that of promoting an open capital account, or both, in order to give some ease to the macroeconomic constraints. I do not propose, however, to make the case for freely floating/flexible exchange rates, as I think that this would be impractical. What I do believe is feasible, is sustaining what has been termed a 'dirty float' or some approximation to it. A dirty float, as the description implies, is a combination of intervention by the authorities and reliance on private markets. What is sought is a rate flexible enough to respond to underlying economic conditions and so give some measure of autonomy for domestic monetary policy, but not so stable as to constitute a permanent deflationary bias. This places a high premium on skill and judgement. The risk with such an endeavour is the danger of falling between two stools, and therefore ending up with the worst, and not the best of both worlds.

As recommended here also, a flexible rate policy requires that exchange rate issues figure prominently in framing domestic policies. There is a trade-off in the role of the exchange rate as an instrument of macroeconomic adjustment and international competitiveness, as well as a trade-off between monetary contraction/expansion and nominal exchange rate depreciation/appreciation in response to changes in capital flows. Most of the macroeconomic shocks in the region have been external or can be sourced to real changes in the domestic economy. In such circumstances, some flexibility in exchange rates is preferred because it permits relative price changes to reallocate resources in response. Also, a flexible rate more readily than a fixed rate reveals the costs of unsustainable domestic policies through changes in the exchange rate and price movements. It therefore expands not only the scope for autonomous monetary policy, but gives the authorities more control over the real exchange rate than its fixed rate counterpart, thereby allowing for better cyclical management. While it is true that several exported items from the region are price-takers and their prices will remain fixed in foreign currencies, variations in the domestic currency equivalent will occur, boosting domestic income. These may eventually evaporate because of domestic price level changes, but there are techniques that the authorities can use to slow this process.

It may be useful on this point to ponder the following quotation from none other than the first deputy managing director of the IMF made on August 7, 1999:

The crises in Thailand, Indonesia, Korea, Russia and Brazil were all associated with exchange rates that had become more or less fixed. Other hard-hit countries, among them South Africa, Mexico, and Turkey, used their exchange rates to absorb part of the adjustment burden, and suffered less. (Fischer, 1999, p. 2).

An open capital account combined with financial liberalisation tends to propel investments into riskier assets, because barriers to the entry of new firms are reduced and the increased competition lowers operating margins. In Jamaica this helped produce a severe banking crisis, weakened the entire financial infrastructure, hampered financial deepening, and has created much uncertainty. In Jamaica also, the policy of fixed exchange rates has been tied to high interest rates for sometime now. This presents speculators with a one-way option for any serious rate change. This is a destabilising situation. It is worsened because of the already large sustained losses of growth and investment from the high interest rate policy.

Capital controls designed to restrain short term inflows to the carrying-capacity of the financial infrastructure and to prevent their use as fuel for a consumption boom are therefore essential. Again I do not now seek to present a call to revert to the capital control regimes of the 1970s. These have proven to be administratively and politically unworkable. I am also not appealing for sands in the wheel of capital flows, as advocated by Tobin and others. The call here is for the authorities to be selective and market-friendly in their choice of controls.

Market-friendly capital controls seek to alter price incentives which include many elements. One set is based on prudential and protective regulations for investors, such as the provision of adequate insurance and lender-of-last-resort facilities. Another set is based on regulations governing open positions in foreign exchange-based transactions between residents and non-residents; the holding of external bond and equity issues; the liabilities of commercial banks in foreign currency and their short term obligations to non-residents; and the status of non-performing loans in the banking system. A third set refers to regulations governing transparency, corporate governance, and the provision of adequate information for private markets to function efficiently, and for the government to be kept informed so that preventative action can be taken as necessary. These regulations also facilitate IMF surveillance, which is an obligation of international governments.

Experience elsewhere suggests that it would be unwise to take a single menu approach towards the specific forms of the capital controls. That experience also suggests that the best sequencing of these controls is to begin with the strengthening of the domestic financial system, through implementation of the necessary prudential/regulatory/accounting/data-dissemination/accounting standards. The next vital step would then be establishing good macroeconomic fundamentals. The third step would be broad liberalisation of FDI flows. It is only then that a policy of retention of capital controls on the short term flows can best be adumbrated. It is also better if this sequencing is pursued in periods of boom rather than recession and crisis.

By way of conclusion, there are two other additional areas of policy reform to which I wish to draw attention. One of these relates to the influence of country size. Many of the difficulties identified in this paper stem from small country size. Because of this, regionalisation within the CARICOM framework emerges as more than just another preferred option. In the age of globalisation, Caribbean regionalisation is an indispensable necessity. Without this, the trajectory of regional economies, no matter how well managed nationally, will be the by-product of initiatives taken elsewhere without regard to our strategic national interests.

Finally, it is worth emphasising that the potential benefits of globalisation are awesome. What we have had so far, however, is increasing internationalised production, accompanied by an explosion of finance capital (and the short term profits that go with it). This has occurred with increasing joblessness, a dramatic skewing in the distribution of global income, and an increasing concentration of wealth among a few countries, firms, and people, while billions remain in poverty. Globalisation and its negative features are, however, not immutable results. They are ultimately subject to human regulation, once the political will to do so can be found. Regrettably, however, at this point in time the prospects for an equitable and harmonious management of the forces of globalisation are extremely dim. In the face of this reality, I believe that as we enter the new millennium, efforts to reinvent the United Nations, and in particular its economic and social charter mandates, remain the best available option open to remedy these deformations. Just, therefore, as regionalisation is presented here as necessary for regional survival, so too is a reformed United Nations. The implication of this is that activity within and through the United Nations should be the principal platform for the region's international diplomacy. Unfortunately, maintaining a good client status with the USA – whose strategic interest in general, and in particular within the UN system, is not the same as ours – remains the main plank of Caribbean diplomacy as we enter the new millennium.

References

Bennett, K, 'International Capital Mobility and the CARICOM Economies', XXVII Annual Conference of Monetary Studies, 1995

Doyle, M, 'Capital Mobility: Estimate and Implications (The Case of Barbados)', paper presented to the XXIX Annual Conference of Monetary Studies, Barbados, 1997

Fisher, S, Remarks at the Inauguration of the Governor of the Reserve Bank of South Africa, Mr Tito Mboweni, South Africa, August 7, 1999

Friedman, TL, *The Lexus and the Olive Tree: Understanding Globalisation* (New York, 1999)

Harris, L, 'International Financial Markets and National Transmission Mechanisms' in J Michie and J Smith, eds., *Managing the Global Economy* (Oxford University Press, 1995)

Hausmann, R, 'The Exchange Rate Debate', Latin American Economic Policies, Vol 7, Second Quarter, 1999

Michie, J and Smith, J, eds., *Managing the Global Economy* (Oxford University Press, 1995)

Schor, J, Introduction to T Banuri and J Schor, *Financial Openness and National Autonomy: Opportunities and Constraints* (Clarendon Press, Oxford, 1995)

Swinburne, M, 'Capital Controls, Exchange Rates and Monetary Policy – Towards an Integrated Framework', paper presented to the XXIX Annual Conference of Monetary Studies, Barbados, 1997

Thomas, CY, 'CARICOM and the New Liberal Trade Order', paper presented to the 17th Annual Conference of the Institute of Chartered Accountants of the Caribbean, Barbados, 1999

12 | FELIPE NOGUERA

Economic Policy Options for the Caribbean in the Twenty-first Century:
Priority Challenges

If civilisation and development are the goals of the next generation of Caribbean people, then both fostering and balancing scientific and technological progress on the one hand, and indigenous cultural preservation and promotion on the other, must be the focus of our attention.

At first glance, in much of western civilisation, science has seemed in conflict with peaceful relations in the human community. While scientific advances and technological change are leading the transition towards a knowledge-based economy, successful Caribbean adaptation and integration into this global process requires cultural grounding. For example, the present, available resources of the Caribbean public and private sector and the rest of civil society, singularly are insufficient to foster the necessary investments in research and development (R&D) to provide competitive advantages. Working together however, the possibilities become real. Moreover, emphasis on the 'knowledge factor' in our educational system from primary to tertiary levels will nurture an awareness of the role and importance of applications-oriented science and technology in every aspect of the lives of people in Caribbean society. This cultural change is conducive to the formation of human capital.

Thus, we can continue to teach and study classic neo-classical market economics and dialectical materialist political economy for an historic perspective, and review development theory and neo-liberal economic policies to appreciate the rationale for contemporary market globalisation trends. We cannot ignore the fact that more than a 'paradigm shift' is taking place in the world economy. The information revolution has spawned a new social formation – 'The Info-Media Society' – grounded in a 'borderless world' concept for communications and commerce. This revolution is producing in turn new modes of production that are neither capitalist nor socialist, and which beg for definition in praxis.

New social and economic relationships to the means of production and communications or information infrastructures are being formed; as are new socioeconomic classes. Alvin Toffler, in his work *Power Shift* described the new knowledge worker as the 'cognitariat'. We must devise our own lexicon, reflecting our interpretation of the new reality.

Methodology

In prioritising challenges and opportunities which should inform the economic policies of the Caribbean in the next century, a practical methodology seems relevant at this time – one which confronts key economic issues on the horizon from a perspective of collective, Caribbean community self-reliance regionally and recognises global interdependence.

Not long ago, here in Jamaica, UNCTAD and the UWI co-hosted an expert seminar on Bilateral Investment Treaties (BITs). The US government has been campaigning in the Caribbean to promote the signing of BITs on intellectual property. Interestingly, these proposed BITs on intellectual property with the US go well beyond the terms that have been negotiated for Trade Related Intellectual Property Rights (TRIPs) at Marrakesh which are in compliance with WTO requirements.

This means, therefore, that as former president of the CAIC, Ken Gordon, advised CARICOM heads of government in Barbados three years ago, the Caribbean community might still have negotiating leverage which we must exercise on the question of intellectual property. In fact, as Gordon stated, that leverage could be exerted in other areas of economic trade in terms of market access. US market access to Caribbean goods and services, indeed Caribbean intellectual property, should be the quid pro quo for the signing of BITs on intellectual property with the US. Furthermore, this should be a consultative CARICOM strategy, negotiated in the context of the CARICOM regional negotiating machinery.

As knowledge becomes a critical factor of production and the main source of competitive advantage, wealth creation, and improved standards of living, Caribbean public and private sectors and the rest of civil society must forge 'smart partnerships'. We can ill afford to foster the class antagonisms which characterised previous epochs and continue to plague and impair social cohesion in the metropolis.

Linked to economic production of competitive quality goods and services, a transformed Caribbean educational system, with UWI at the helm, can carve a share of the international market as the 'engine of innovation'. Since science is the key driver of innovation and local culture is a primary element for long term social development, a 'smart partnership' must also exist and be fostered between technology and culture in the Caribbean.

Where technology transfer from the north to the south has been traditionally viewed as a source for development, onerous licensing arrangements and commercial strategies linked to trade policies which foster dependence have rendered this an ineffective developmental tool. Rather than continuing to view and act as if technology transfer is a panacea to cure the ills of underdevelopment, it must be viewed as a series of negotiating tactics in the campaign to foster appropriate indigenous technology development strategy and policies.

One way to facilitate this is through the involvement of youth in scientific research. Institutions such as the UWI's Faculty of Agriculture, CAST in Jamaica, the John Donaldson Technical Institute in Trinidad, and the Arthur Lewis College in St Lucia are working in tandem with CARICOM governments, labour and the private sector. They should serve as the knowledge engines of innovation for the transformation of our plantation economies into high quality, competitively priced suppliers of refined products, organic foods, and drinks from our own agricultural produce, to feed ourselves and export to international markets.

Whether in pure or applied research, hardware engineering or software design, artificial intelligence or super conductivity, the flower of the region – our youth – must be motivated and inspired. They must be provided with the opportunities to pursue scientific studies with the confidence that their knowledge can be relevant to the world of work.

Globalisation and interdependence pose many threats to the traditional ways of conducting business in the region. Yet they also present intriguing opportunities as the removal of barriers to cooperation and innovation lead to the enhancement and diffusion of knowledge, technology, and people across the region. In particular, the CARICOM single market and economy must be not only a priority in policy. There must also be a commitment to action by the leaders of CARICOM, supported by our citizens, if necessary through popular education campaigns, to remove all impediments that limit the mobility of Caribbean personnel across the region. This is a critical factor to enhancing regional competitiveness. Strategically, because so many future developments will be knowledge-dependent, intellectual property represents the most important economic policy option to develop as patents and royalties provide untapped wealth for Caribbean industry and services.

Regional Integration

In late 1998, the Asian financial crisis illustrated how precarious small economies can be and how vulnerable they are to the effects of economic dislocation elsewhere in the world. However, globalisation seems to have shortened the recovery period from cyclical crises, at least for some.

A key priority, from an economic policy as well as a foreign trade policy point of view, must be the strengthening of relationships between CARICOM and Central America. First CARICOM must formally expand, fully embracing CARIFORUM members, as well as Cuba, and then speak with one voice, albeit in different languages. While CARICOM moves to approve the remaining protocols that would establish a single market and economy, Central America's economy grew by 10 per cent from 1997–1998, in spite of a reduction of foreign direct investment and exports. Exports grew intra-regionally, being responsible for the regional aggregate growth.

The WTO ruling on the EU/US banana trade dispute is indicative of the magnitude of the task which lies before the Caribbean in working with its developing country allies to transform the metropolitan orientation of the WTO, which has thus far been biased in favour of the developed countries. To quote the Secretary General of UNCTAD, Rubens Ricupero,

. . . a balance needs to be struck between the desirability of a common and uniform set of rules, privileges and obligations applicable in the same way to all members of WTO, and the inescapable fact that WTO members are at very different stages of development.

In the WTO's ministerial round of negotiations in Seattle in December 1999, explicit adaptation of obligations and the timing of the implementation to the needs and capacities of the poorest, smallest, and most vulnerable members of the WTO must be addressed. A notion of special and differential treatment for small economies like the Caribbean is an indispensable tool of regional trade policy to address the real needs of the Caribbean.

Although neither Central America nor the Caribbean are direct parties to the WTO banana panel dispute, both are adversely affected by the outcome, which weakens the potential trading block solidarity of the Association of Caribbean States. A glimpse of the declining value of Windward Island banana exports is sufficient to persuade us that economic diversification and agro-industrial development must be economic policy priorities in the coming century.

Change in the Value of OECS Banana Exports, 1993–1997

St Lucia US$51m – US$28m
Grenada US$2m – US$0M
St Vincent US$23m – US$14m
Dominica US$24m – US$15m

By way of illustration, projections for economic diversification in the Caribbean subregion must factor in the pivotal role of tourism in the economy. According to the ACS, in 1996 tourism represented 63 per cent of all imports to the OECS and was 35 per cent of GDP. It represented 43 per cent of all imports in the wider CARICOM and 20 per cent of GDP. These figures were very much lower for Central America, where tourism represented 10 per cent of all imports and only 3 per cent of GDP.

Using what we can refer to as the 'openness indicators' (the degree to which countries are exposed to export and import trade), the OECS is double (97 per cent versus 50 per cent) Central America. The implication here is that liberalisation will significantly impact upon the domestic economy of the OECS because CARIFORUM and CARICOM are 8 per cent more open than Central America (but with tourism increases to 20 per cent). There are crucial opportunities to link agribusiness services to the hotel and tourism sector.

The foregoing analysis should provide a compelling rationale for regional integration – from the OECS to CARICOM to CARIFORUM to ACS –

taking advantage of the economies of scale, increasing functional cooperation, preserving the environment and conserving natural resources. In a recent statement the UNCTAD Secretary General tacitly reinforced the need for developing countries to collaborate in order to achieve equal opportunities to benefit from the global trading system:

Equality of opportunity requires that systems be adapted so as to ensure that benefits theoretically available to all are in fact within the grasp of all, i.e. an 'equitable playing field'. This will require some flexibility in rules and procedures. Equality of opportunity also requires that systems have built into them educational, training, and other activities designed to help developing countries to secure the knowledge and skills required to obtain maximum benefits from the system.

Beyond the ACS region, the developing countries of Africa and Asia have proven to be effective trading allies in the ACP group of states in negotiating preferential market access into Europe under the Lome Convention. As Lome IV ends in 2000, we must seek ways to expand and deepen our trading alliance into a partnership with ACP by seeking to foster south to south trade links and market access.

Some of the constraints to achieving regional integration from the private sector standpoint relate to:

- the slow pace of including private sector and civil society in the former consultative process;
- the need for increased transparency and accountability of actors directly involved;
- the need to appreciate the spectrum of countries involved in the integration process which necessitates fair, flexible, responsive and – where possible – complimentary approaches to achieving the objectives of increasing the living standards of Caribbean people;
- the sequential and phased removal of preferences for the poorest and least developed members of the Caribbean community;
- a fast track reciprocity for those countries whose industries are already prepared for global competition
- targeted technical assistance and training to convert traditional sectors into centres for production of value added services
- the need for a bottom-up approach to increase dialogue with civil society in trade negotiations related to the WTO, FTAA, Lomé, and so on (for

example, the regional private sector, via the CAIC, relates to the WTO through the Coalition of Service Industries; relates to the FTAA through the Business Network for Hemispheric Integration; and the FTAA through the ACP Business Forum)
– the need to organise a Caribbean 'Reverse the Brain Drain' conference to capture the scattered human resources of the Caribbean diaspora.

Conclusion

Lacking a crystal ball, one dares to advance economic policy options and priority challenges by limiting them to the dawn of the twenty-first century. Using a 10-year trajectory, based on the current activities and preoccupations of the private sector, I would advance the following:

1. Economic diversification and agro-industrial development.
2. Consolidation of regional and international airlift infrastructure, by merging BWIA and Air Jamaica.
3. Activation of the newly-formed Caribbean Coalition of Service Industries, with special attention to the following sectors:
    i) tourism – currently the most significant sector of the regional economy, because of its linkages to other sectors, providing more jobs and linkages than any other (eco, cultural and intra-regional, expanded support from indigenous financial institutions)
    ii) financial services – offshore competitiveness is threatened by new eu policies which have declared their intention to terminate them
    iii) telecommunications services – liberalisation and regulation regionally. Cable and Wireless are now softening to competition; government, private, public (small) shareholders in national and international carriers to take advantage of low-cost, high revenue traffic refile activities now characterising the sector
    iv) professional/consultancy services – providing equal opportunities and even preferential treatment for qualified Caribbean contractors and consultants to bid on large development projects
    v) electronic commerce – challenging the non-tariff barriers of North America (US and Canada) in not allowing access to encryption technology to secure financial transactions, which gives them an unfair trade

advantage fostering Caribbean dependence in this sunrise sector, and stultifies the development of our capacity

vi) entertainment – perhaps the area with greatest comparative advantage of the Caribbean, due primarily to the prolific Caribbean creative imagination. But even with Bob Marley, Black Stalin, the steel band, salsa, merengue, zouk, and Island Records, no serious indigenous Caribbean entertainment booking agency or preparatory academy exists. We have to begin to factor in and marshal regional telecommunications infrastructures – the means of communication – and electronic commerce to support and bolster the viability of the Caribbean entertainment sector.

If CARICOM governments disagree with the conservative approach to local and regional programming of Caribbean private sector media houses, which argue (myopically) that it is cheaper to import foreign used violence in programming to foster and inspire West Indian 'gangstas', it should set the example. CARICOM governments can offer fiscal incentives, encourage regional script-writing competitions and use the media at their disposal to prove that our talented writers, producers and directors cannot only create material to satisfy Caribbean audiences (including the youth), but can, like Cuba, export them (in high definition formats) as well.

CARICOM governments have been reacting to the pressures of globalisation defensively. We must move to the counter offensive, designing policies which support and improve domestic and regional innovation capacity. We can use this occasion as the point of departure to reinforce the basic framework conditions for innovation, without adopting a xenophobic or isolationist posture, and concentrate on the promotion of a highly skilled labour force and dynamic research base. The UWI should play a leading role in collaborating with government and the private sector of the region in illustrating that planning and implementation of science and technology activities should be regional and transcend national considerations. Moreover, these activities, especially in R&D, should be applications-oriented and attuned to Caribbean culture and realities, embrace women's efforts to enter these exclusive fields and reach out to and involve our youth.

Perhaps this forum can be institutionalised to promote the conduct of detailed analyses of several high priority areas, resulting in the formulation of recommendations and policy options for consideration by government. By this means strategies can be devised, for example, to protect access by Caribbean astronomers to the electromagnetic spectrum, increasingly threatened by radio emissions from low earth orbiting communication satellites controlled by the North. We can develop a work plan for an ACS-regional, biodiversity data base that can improve connections between CARDI-related information facilities in the Caribbean, such as CRIDNET. This will be a powerful tool for scientific research to contribute to the development of agro-industrial public policy formulation and strengthen the preservation and utilisation of the region's biodiversity resources.

In this regard, the proposal of Trinidad and Tobago prime minister Panday for this conference to generate task forces related to CARICOM twenty-first century development is most welcome. We need Caribbean brain-storm centres, not talk shops. These task forces should operate as think/action tanks, linked through the UWI and CARICOM (two seminal regional institutions) to public policy apparatus.

This will enable the UWI to be both a purveyor of 'what is new in the world', linking its activities to the demands and requirements of Caribbean society in the new millennium. This will give greater real value and return for the investment, not of government money, but of tax payers' hard-earned resources and the efforts of students and teachers to help define the new economic paradigm in the interests of our people.

Part 4
Science, Technology and Sustainable Development

13 | HAN REICHGELT

Information Technology and Sustainable Development in the Caribbean

There are clearly problems facing the various societies in the Caribbean and other papers in this volume have identified many of them. However, many of the problems they pinpoint can be explained in terms of a single underlying cause – namely the relative poverty of the region. Two examples will suffice. First, without wishing to minimise the importance of history in these matters, it seems to me that a more likely explanation for the so-called bleaching phenomenon in Jamaica is economic. The most probable reason that some women from lower income groups in Jamaica wish to lighten their skin colour is their perception, rightly or wrongly, that women of a lighter hue are more likely to attract more affluent partners. Second, criminologists will attest that one of the factors most highly correlated to levels of crime and violence is the difference in levels of income. The Caribbean is unlikely to be an exception in this respect and the appalling levels of crime and violence in some Caribbean societies would seem to be a direct consequence of their extremely high differences in income levels.

If the above analysis is correct, then the main task facing the Caribbean in the immediate and medium future is to raise the income levels of its populations. While the Caribbean does not have the levels of abject poverty of other developing countries, primarily in sub-Saharan Africa, it is clear that such socially desirable goods as better health care and a better education system can only be achieved if the countries region increase their GDP. Moreover, in order to ensure any form of permanence in whatever increases can be achieved, it is clearly important that any economic improvements be sustainable.

Volumes have been written about sustainable development, and this is not the place to review the literature. However, it seems to me that for development to be called sustainable it has to meet at least two requirements. The first requirement is that it must be financially feasible for the foreseeable future. It would hardly make sense for a country or a region to make substantial investments to enable economic activities whose value is likely to disappear in the very near future. The second requirement that an economic development must meet to be called sustainable is that it does not consume vast amounts of non-renewable resources. In other words, it must be environmentally friendly.

As a brief digression, while continued economic feasibility and a limited consumption of non-renewable resources would seem to be necessary conditions for development to be called sustainable, they are not sufficient. One would probably wish to include some requirement that the activity also bring money into an economy, rather than merely redistributing it within the economy. In Jamaica, casino gambling should probably be regarded as an activity leading to sustainable development; the lotto probably should not.

Clearly, each country strives for sustainable development. After all, each country wants to increase its GDP without consuming vast amounts of non-renewable resources. Many countries, including, Barbados and Jamaica, have looked at the provision of information technology (IT) services for export as a possible sphere of economic activity. It is therefore important to have a closer look at IT and to examine the factors that have led governments in the Caribbean to identify it as one of the major elements in their development plans.

Information Technology and Sustainability

IT can be defined as the tools and techniques for gathering, manipulating, analysing and disseminating information. The IT services that a country can provide are wide ranging. They include hardware manufacture and data entry, an activity in which data initially collected on paper is recaptured electronically by re-entering it into the computer. They also include data conversion applications. For example Mona Informatix Ltd, a company on the Mona campus of the University of the West Indies, has created a very successful business converting data from one format to another. We need not be concerned with why this is such an important activity. The only thing that is important for the present discussion is that Mona Informatix is extremely profitable.

Another IT service is software engineering and programming, the specification and/or production of software for third parties. India is a well-known example of a poor country that makes a substantial amount of money out of software engineering and computer programming services for export. A final IT service worth mentioning is the provision of so-called content on the internet. The belief is that internet users are willing to pay for access to interesting material and that making such material available is therefore a lucrative activity. Indeed, some of the economically most successful internet sites do indeed do so, even if one may object to the material on moral grounds: many of the economically most successful internet sites get their income from selling pornographic material.

Clearly, the question arises as to why so many governments see providing IT services for export as such an attractive economic activity which to be involved in. If we go back to our two requirements for sustainable development, let us first observe that IT meets the second of our two requirements. Computers require few non-renewable resources. Indeed, IT can considerably lessen the strain on the environment. For example, IT makes it possible for people to telecommute, that is to work from home, thereby not requiring them to consume resources travelling to and from work. Moreover, the past year or so has seen the emergence of on-line auctions on the internet to sell perishable commodities, be they airline tickets, advertising space or cargo on trucks. The latter is of particular interest: it has been estimated that, at any one time, about half the trucks on American roads are empty.[1] The setting up of on-line services to sell such commodities has led to a more efficient use of resources, which is clearly attractive from an environmental point of view.

But most IT services also meet the first requirement, namely that their provision remain economically feasible. It has to be admitted that data entry, an activity that has provided significant economic benefits to many Caribbean countries, is unlikely to be sustainable in the economic sense as more and more data is already captured electronically at source. There is also some doubt about data conversion services, but it is certain that most other IT services, including hardware manufacture and software engineering and programming, will remain economically viable for the foreseeable future.

There are many reasons that can be advanced for this proposition, but I will restrict myself to two. First, as the world learns more about IT, it becomes more aware of the importance of information or rather a lack thereof, for many of its problems and the contribution that IT can provide make it their solution. The second reason is the emergence of the internet and in particular the emergence of e-business, the use of the internet for economic purposes. Let us examine both in some detail.

One simple example, drawn from the Jamaican context, will serve to illustrate the first point. Some years ago, I had occasion to speak to the managing director of one of the leading manufacturers of condiments and sauces on the island. During our conversations it emerged that there was a much greater international demand for its guava jelly than the company could meet. The company could not get its hands on sufficient numbers of guavas. At first sight, this might seem like a simple supply problem: there simply are not enough guavas to turn into jelly. However, when we discussed the matter further, we discovered that the problem was really an information problem. The company sourced its guavas by sending personnel to market towns all over the island to buy all available guavas. Clearly, this is not the optimum way to obtain raw materials. However, since the company did not have a better way of knowing where to find guavas, it was the only option open to it. So, the problem was not that there were not enough guavas around; the problem was that the company did not know where to find them. Such simple IT as telephones in the rural areas would obviously have been a great help.

The increasing realisation of the importance of information will clearly result in an increased demand for information systems to gather, analyse and disseminate information more efficiently. Hence, it seems clear that the production of information systems, such as software engineering and programming, will remain an important economic activity for the foreseeable future.

The second development that convinces me of the continued viability of IT services is the explosive growth of the internet, a development that is the culmination of the integration of computer and telecommunications technology, at least for the time being. We know that the numbers of internet users is growing at an enormous rate. Moreover, we are seeing a dramatic increase in commercial activity on the internet, also called e-business, and there is no doubt that commercial activity on the internet will continue to grow significantly. We have already seen the emergence of alternative ways of receiving already available services (for example, on-line banking or ticket reservation), as well as the creation of new services (such as the on-line auctions for all kinds of commodities alluded to above), and this trend will certainly continue. Accurate estimates are extremely hard to come by (most of the organisations that publish estimates on the size of e-business also provide e-business consultancy services). However, the OECD estimates the size of e-business in the year 2001 to be some US$300 billion and expects it to grow to US$1 trillion by 2005 (OECD, 1998).

While the use of networks to electronically interchange information between companies has been around a long time in the form of Electronic Data Interchange (EDI) and Electronic Fund Transfer (EFT), it is the open nature of the internet that has been responsible for the dramatic increase in e-business. EDI and EFT rely on the establishment of proprietary networks between collaborating organisations for the exchange of information. Such networks are expensive to set up and maintain. Because of the expense, the benefits tend to be limited to large organisations that can afford the investment. Moreover, again because of the expense of setting up such networks, organisations engaged in EDI or EFT are more or less locked together as the exit costs or indeed the cost of switching are very high.

The open nature of the internet has changed this. Establishing a presence on the internet is cheap and merely requires access to a computer, a telephone line and an internet Service Provider. Establishing an internet presence is therefore within the financial reach of virtually any business, no matter how small, and indeed most individuals. Moreover, the growth in the number of internet users means that using it for commercial activities will become financially more attractive. Producers will be able to find cheaper suppliers for their raw materials. On-line banking will enable banks to decrease staff numbers and possibly to close branches without decreasing the size of their business operations. Potential customers will come into shops, having researched the product that they are interested in on the internet and will therefore be better informed, hence increasing the productivity of sales staff. Airlines will be able to auction empty seats over the internet, increasing the average number of passengers on their flights and so increasing revenues with very limited increases in operating costs. In other words, electronic commercial activity that will drive down the cost of doing business significantly and hence it will grow as dramatically as the OECD estimates suggest.

The open nature of the internet and the resulting low cost of setting up e-business operations clearly allows possibilities for the region as well. Businesses that can provide compete with the best in the world in offering services and/or products and businesses that have hitherto had problems marketing themselves can clearly use the internet to improve their sales. Clearly, this applies to producers anywhere in the world, including the Caribbean. Moreover, earlier I mentioned the importance of providing content on the internet. Clearly, the region has a rich cultural heritage, much of which could be sold to the world over the internet. In other words, the internet may well provide the region with an opportunity to obtain greater economic benefits from one of its most important assets, namely its cultural diversity.

So, IT is clearly here to stay for the foreseeable future. As stated, many governments in the region have made the provision of IT services for export an important element in their development policies. They have rightly excluded hardware manufacture, as this requires enormous capital investments and it is unlikely that investments of this magnitude can be lured into the region. Most regional governments have also realised that data entry is probably an activity whose economic value will rapidly disappear. Instead, they have concentrated on computer programming. The argument seems to be almost purely market driven: there will be a continuing demand for programming services and entry into the market is very cheap. All you need is a group of well-trained programmers and a set of computers. Moreover, the salaries in the region are generally lower than in the developed world, and salaries are one of the major costs in the production of software. It might therefore seem reasonable to assume that the region could make an important contribution to meeting the continuing demand for information systems, and hence increase their GDPs. Most governments have also realised the potential of e-business and have encouraged their private sector to get involved in this type of activity. In the remainder of this paper, I will critically evaluate these policy positions.

Information Technology in the Caribbean

It is obvious that the region has no choice but to embrace the new technology for its existing economic activities to grow, indeed to survive. More and more commercial activity will take place over the internet and organisations that are not set up for e-business, whether they are in tourism, agriculture, light manufacturing or financial services, are unlikely to survive. Moreover, the increased integration of computing and telecommunications, of which the internet is but one example, and the resulting globalisation will force local organisations to compete with rivals from all over the world. They will therefore have to ensure that they are competitive with the best in the world. This, in turn, will force them to embrace more and more sophisticated information systems.

However, agreeing that the Caribbean has no choice but to make extensive use of IT in order to ensure its economic survival does not mean that the policies outlined at the end of the previous section can be adopted without any further thought. Both the position that the region can solve many of its economic woes through the adoption of electronic business and the belief that the region can make significant amounts of money out of the provision of software engineering and programming services for export are not without its problems. I shall turn to the issue of e-business first.

The enthusiastic embrace by some government ministers and other decision-makers of the opportunities provided by e-business is to a large extent based on the estimated size of e-business, and I argued above that the internet opens up important possibilities for local firms. However, there are a few caveats that one needs to keep in mind. As stated, the OECD reckons that the size of e-business in the year 2001 will be some US$300 billion. Clearly, this is not to be sneezed at, but it is important to put this figure in context. First, the estimated size of e-business worldwide in 2001 is merely twice the size of Wal-Mart sales in 1996. Second, while business-to-customer e-business, or e-retail, is probably the most visible aspect, some 80 per cent of e-business is in fact business-to-business. E-business makes it easier for companies to widen their range of business partners. However, as the OECD points out, an important, if usually hidden, cost of business is the cost of establishing business relationships. It is not clear to me to what extent local firms, which have not been able to establish business partnerships with other firms before, can use the internet to do so. Even when local organisations can compete with the best in the world, in terms of price and quality, the lack of established business relationships may mean that they may not be able to take advantage of the undoubted opportunities that e-business opens up for the creation of new business.

Turning to e-retail, one needs to be aware (and perhaps wary) of some complicating factors. First of all, it is important to keep the demography of the population of internet users in mind, at least as far as the largest market is concerned, the US. Most internet users are rich (an income of more than US$70,000). Moreover, there seem to be some racial biases. For some reason, African-Americans, even when they have similarly high incomes, seem far less likely to buy computers. Such considerations are clearly important in the formulation of marketing strategies. A marketing strategy that targets the African-American market, as has been done by the Jamaica Tourist Board, or indeed the West Indian community overseas, is clearly fraught with difficulties if it makes internet advertising an important element.

Another issue of relevance is the change in government tax revenue that e-retail is likely to bring. Governments all over the world have moved from indirect taxation, taxation on income, to direct taxation, taxation on sales. One reason has been that sales taxes are much easier to collect than taxation in income. However, e-retail is hard to tax. After all, the internet is truly a medium without borders. E-retail sites can be set up anywhere in the world and can be accessed from anywhere else. It is therefore hard to determine where goods or services sold over the internet come from and who has bought them, especially if the goods sold are content and can be delivered over the internet. The US Federal Government and many state governments in the United States have already committed themselves to not taxing e-retail. If one assumes that other governments will adopt similar policies, then a dramatic growth in e-retail will see a significant drop in government incomes. There is also the inequity that the beneficiaries of this change in tax basis are likely to be the richer in the population as it is that group which is more likely to have access to the internet and hence can reap the benefits of the tax-free nature of e-retail.

A final complicating issue also is a direct consequence of the global and cross-border nature of the internet. In most countries, governments regulate the behaviour of their citizens. For example, in most countries gambling is a highly regulated industry. Many governments have also banned certain forms of pornography. The global nature of the internet makes the enforcement of such regulations almost impossible. For example, the US government has banned internet gambling. This has not resulted in the end of internet gambling in the United States. Instead, providers of this service have simply moved their operations to countries that did not have such prohibitions in place. In other words, governments and societies in general seem to want to regulate their citizens, either by making certain behaviours illegal or by imposing restrictions on the type of material that their citizens have access to. However, the global and cross-border nature of the internet will make it extremely difficult for governments to enforce such regulations.

Clearly, the above arguments are merely meant to be words of caution to those who believe that e-business will solve all the economic problems of the region. It is not intended as a counter-argument to the position that organisations in the Caribbean have to incorporate e-business into their daily operations. The arguments against the position that the region can make substantial amounts of money out of software engineering and programming services for export are stronger. Without putting in place additional measures, the most important of which is already being piloted in Jamaica, it is more a matter of wishful thinking rather than realistic and rational analysis to believe that the region can become a major player in the international software engineering and programming market.

There are many factors that have to be in place for a region to be able to make money out of IT services of this type.[2] However, in most of the relevant literature, it is overlooked that programming is an extremely labour intensive activity, and one that requires highly trained professionals, typically university graduates. There is a myth of a programmer being a loner. However, nothing could be further from the truth. Almost all programmers work in relatively large groups;[3] in this sense, information technology is different from other scientific and technological endeavours. A group of 50 research chemists is, by international standards, a large group of research chemists; a software house of 50 programmers is, by international standards, a small software house.

Moreover, once a piece of software has been developed, it needs to be maintained in the sense that faults in it, or bugs, have to be fixed and additional functionality may have to be added. It is estimated that maintenance requires about one month of effort for every year that the system is being sold for every year of effort that went into its development. In other words, a piece of software that took 12 months to develop by a team of 25 software engineers requires two full time software engineers per annum for maintenance for each year that the product is being maintained.

Another dramatic illustration of the labour intensive nature of software engineering and programming is provided by the size of the two largest software companies in terms of revenues in the world. Microsoft, the largest, employs 20,000 technical personnel;[4] Oracle, the second largest, 25,000.[5]

It is the labour intensive nature of software engineering that throws doubt on the belief that the Caribbean can become a significant player in the international software engineering market, at least without putting in place some additional measures. First, the population is extremely small. The English-speaking Caribbean has a population of a mere six million. Moreover, the proportion of the population that receives post-secondary education (something that is essential if one is to become a programmer) is also extremely small. The percentage of the population that received post-secondary education differs between the countries in the region. However, in all, it is less than that of the developed countries. Moreover, the small size of the population means that, no matter what the percentage, absolute numbers remain small. Thus, the three campuses of the University of the West Indies each graduate about 50 majors in computer science each year. However, this means a new intake of computer science graduates of merely 150 per year. This is hardly sufficient to start a vibrant software engineering and programming industry. Moreover, this shortage of skilled human resources is made worse by continuing migration out of the region, especially of its skilled and well-trained people. In other words, a necessary condition for becoming a provider of programming and software engineering services for the international market is that there is a large pool of programmers and software engineers. Currently, the region is not producing them.

Clearly, if a region fails to produce the resources necessary for a particular economic activity itself, then an alternative strategy would be to import them. Thus, despite the shortage of indigenous human resources, the region can still establish itself as a provider of software engineering and programming services for the international market if it can import these resources from elsewhere. A variety of companies in the region have indeed followed this strategy by importing programmers primarily from India with varying degrees of success.

However, there is some doubt whether this strategy is likely to be successful in the long term. It is important to realise that there is a serious shortage of programmers internationally. For example, even by conservative estimates there are at least 200,000 IT related positions in the United States remaining vacant, and, like so many other countries, the United States is trying to solve its human resource problem in this area by importing software engineers and programmers from elsewhere. If the region is therefore to follow the strategy of attracting IT personnel from elsewhere, it has to compete with other, richer, countries. The problem is that one of the factors that would make the Caribbean attractive to set up software houses, namely its generally lower salaries, make it unattractive when it comes to competing for scarce human resources from elsewhere. It therefore seems unrealistic to believe that the problem of the shortage of skilled software engineers and programmers in the Caribbean can be solved by hiring such personnel from outside the region.

Should the region therefore give up on programming services as an important element in its development policy? Fortunately, the situation is not as desperate as it may appear. If the major hurdle to overcome is the lack of qualified staff, then clearly setting up more training opportunities might solve the problem. In general, entry level positions in software engineering firms have been filled by people with a university degree. Certain aspects of the construction of information systems (such as the identification of the problem the new information system is to solve and the initial specification of the system) almost certainly require people trained to this level, and probably beyond. However, it may well be the case that entry-level programming positions can be filled with people with a lower level of training. Indeed, this is the hypothesis underlying the recent establishment of the Caribbean Institute of Technology (CIT) in Jamaica. CIT is a joint venture between three universities, namely UWI, Furman University from the United States and the University of Hertfordshire from the UK, a software house based in Atlanta, HEART, the Jamaican national training agency and the Ministry of Commerce and Technology, Jamaica. CIT takes in young people with good 'O' Levels in English and Mathematics and provides an intensive nine month training programme to turn them into entry level programmers. CIT started operations in Montego Bay in Jamaica in February 1999 with a group of about 60 students and the first set of students is expected to graduate soon. If successful, then CIT will set up similar operations in other places in Jamaica as well, and may also establish a presence in other countries in the Caribbean. Encouragingly, the industrial partner involved in the enterprise had already committed to hiring most of the graduates from the programme and, equally important, has been able to attract offshore programming contracts from a variety of firms based in the United States. It is clearly too early to say whether CIT will be a success, but it seems to be one step in the right direction. If the lack of a sufficient number of programmers is the main obstacle to overcome for the region to establish itself as a major player in the international software engineering and programming market, then an organisation that can seriously address this problem is critically important.

Conclusion

It is clear that the Caribbean will have to embrace IT in its existing economic activities for its survival. The ever increasing globalisation of economies partly brought about by the emergence of the internet will force local firms to compete with firms from all over the world. Clearly, this entails that they must achieve the highest possible efficiency in their operations, which in turn, will require them to accept more and more sophisticated information systems.

The emergence of the internet also opens up new economic possibilities for the region. I have pointed to some complications that may arise from the wholesale adoption of e-business in the region, but, bearing these in mind, there is no reason to believe that the region cannot take advantage of the opportunities opened up by these technological innovations.

Moreover, providing IT services for export is an attractive option to pursue for a region interested in sustainable development. On the one hand, it is likely that it will remain a lucrative activity for a long period to come, while on the other, it uses very few non-renewable resources. I have however argued that blindly pursuing this policy is likely to run into difficulties, especially because of the lack of trained human resources. Fortunately, there are encouraging signs that this problem is being addressed. One can only hope that we are not greeting summer because we have seen a single swallow.

Notes

1. *The Economist,* June 26, 1999
2. *The Economic and Social Impacts of Electronic Commerce: Preliminary findings and Research Agenda* (OECD Press, 1989)
3. Schware, R, and Hume, S, *Prospects for Information Service Exports from the English-Speaking Caribbean* (The World Bank, 1996)
4. Summerville, I, *Software Engineering,* 3rd edn., (Wokingham, England: Addison Wesley, 1989)
5. Source: www.microsoft.com/jobs/guide/emstats.html
6. Source: www.oracle.com/corporate/annual_report/html/ao.htm

14 | ANTHONY CLAYTON

Current Trends in Higher Education and the Implications for the UWI

The world is currently undergoing a profound economic, social and political restructuring. The collapse of state socialism, the global ascendancy of democracy and liberal capitalism, the end of the cold war and its associated political realignments have reshaped the geopolitical landscape. The globalisation of international markets for goods, services and capital is starting to reshape every national economy in the world. Rapid technological innovation, in areas such as informatics, biotechnology, microfabrication techniques and nanotechnology is creating the basis for the next generation of globally dominant industries.

These developments are transforming our world, and have profound implications for this region. If we understand these changes, and the forces that drive them, we will be able to shape our future. If we fail to grasp the situation, our destiny will be largely determined by forces beyond our control. This paper will review one particular set of current technological developments to illustrate both how and why they will affect us, and how we might respond positively to turn them to our advantage – using the UWI as an example.

Many of the world's universities are facing a crisis, for three reasons:

1. Demand is rising. On the basis of the current growth in world population, it would be necessary to open about one new university per week from now until the mid-twenty-first century to maintain even the current level of provision of higher education.[1]
2. Expectations are rising. Universities are being asked to provide tertiary-level education to an increasing percentage of the population, as nations are faced

with the new demands of competing in a high skill, knowledge-based world economy.
3. Public funding for the majority of universities is being eroded, as many countries are faced with more urgent demands from other sectors.

This presents the universities of the world with a challenge. How is it going to be possible to increase the scale of provision of higher education, on the basis of reduced resources, without sacrificing quality? Some of the world's universities will probably not survive this crisis, at least in their current form. A 1996 World Bank report on Africa concluded that 'tertiary institutions in their present form – overwhelmed with problems related to access, finance, quality, internal and external efficiency – are not up to the challenge'.

Sir John Daniel, Vice Chancellor of the Open University in the UK, has argued that the answer must lie in the intelligent use of new technologies and the development of the multimedia mega-university.[2] The Open University was the first university in the world founded specifically to take advantage of new technology to deliver mass distance education, but, since it was established three decades ago, nearly 50 more universities have been created on this model. Eleven of these are now mega-universities, with enrolments of more than 100,000 students. One of the largest, the China Television University, now has well over half a million enrolled students. Collectively, the 11 mega-universities now have nearly three million enrolled students.

One obvious advantage of the mega-model is lower costs. On a country-by-country basis, the cost per student at a mega-university is about half that of the provision elsewhere. The potential aggregate savings are therefore substantial. The average cost today for the 14 million students at US colleges and universities is about US$12,500 per year, while the average cost for the 1.6 million students at UK higher education institutions is about US$10,000 per year. This suggests that a move to use mega-universities to deliver the bulk of higher education courses could, in principle, save the US nearly US$87.5 billion per year, while the potential saving to the UK could be some US$8 billion per year.

The Changing Technology

The 50 mass-distance education universities created to date still rely largely on television as their primary communication medium. All of this, however, is about to change, and the pace of events is about to accelerate sharply. We are still at a relatively early stage in a series of technology-driven changes that will fundamentally transform our understanding of the process of education and of the role of universities.

In the US, some 21 per cent of the population now have internet access. Percentages in Europe and Japan are about half the US total, but growth and sector by sector penetration rates are higher. About 45 per cent of Japanese companies now maintain web sites, for example, compared with 41 per cent in the US and 37 per cent in the UK.[3] One current projection suggests that by the end of 2000 there will be roughly 550 million internet users, nearly 10 per cent of the population of the planet.[4]

Business to business e-commerce is expanding particularly rapidly. In 1997–98 perhaps US$20 billion in trade was transacted over the internet.[5] By the end of 2000 the total is projected to be between US$100–200 billion. Another recent projection suggests that by 2020 more than half of all working, learning and commerce will take place over the internet, at least in the OECD nations, although the concurrent removal of the remaining legal and logistical barriers to international working, learning and commerce, as part of the wider process of economic globalisation, should in principle enable developing nations to participate fully.

This rapid extension of internet use is driven primarily by Moore's law, which states that the cost of a given unit of processing power roughly halves every eighteen months. The pace of events recently accelerated, however, as several internet service providers started offering free internet access last year. This was followed by the first mass offer of free computers, then by the first offer of free phone calls (including long distance), in both cases in return for accepting advertising. The companies involved now intend to make their profits on selling access to affluent consumers and on commissions on sales generated. As the CEO of Dixons, the first service provider to offer free access put it, 'We don't normally charge people to enter our shops'. Within the next decade, the cost of the hardware, software and network access is likely to become negligible (at least in OECD nations). The progressive erosion of the remaining costs is likely to increase the rate of new connections still further.

The Implications for Education

The process of education is already being transformed by these developments. The UK, Australia and the US are currently leading the process of change. In the UK today, some 20 per cent of the students at UK universities are overseas students. This brings in US$7 – 8 billion per annum in revenue for the UK, about half of the UK's total foreign exchange earnings from education.[6] The great majority of these students are resident in the UK. There is a very rapidly growing subset, however, now totalling nearly 150,000 students, who do their entire degree in their home country. The great majority of this last group are currently being taught in 'overseas validated courses', or franchised degrees. This group alone now generates nearly US$0.5 billion in foreign exchange for the UK.

So there are three distinct groups of students at UK universities: domestic students, foreign students in the UK, and foreign students based overseas. All three groups are expected to migrate onto the internet, but the group with the most obvious expansion potential is the third group – students who want to take a UK degree but who, for various reasons, do not find it convenient to leave their home countries.

This third group is already expanding rapidly, having grown from practically zero to nearly 150,000 in just ten years. The number of foreign students resident in the UK doubled over the same period, which suggests that the groups are not mutually exclusive. The number of resident foreign students in Australia also increased eight-fold over the same period (albeit from a much lower base), which suggests that the world market is nowhere near saturation.

Most studies suggest that the move to internet delivery will trigger a much faster rate of growth. Birkbeck College in London, for example, moved a complete degree course in the specialised subject of crystallography onto the internet, and immediately quadrupled the number of enrolled students.[7] The Open University, another market leader in this regard, had fourteen complete internet courses by July 1998, and intends to expand this further.

The total world market for higher education through distance learning is now worth some US$300 billion per annum,[8] most of which is currently domestic rather than international. This market is expected to grow rapidly as it becomes increasingly globalised. This is for a number of reasons, one of which is that the number and range of courses can be enormously extended.

Even highly specialised courses can become economically viable when a sufficient number of enrolled students can be attracted from around the world.

Several universities have therefore now started to ask whether they should move themselves, at least partially, into cyberspace. There is an obvious attraction in being able to dramatically expand the number of enrolled students while simultaneously realising capital by selling off redundant buildings. There are, however, even more profound implications for universities. A recent discussion document from the University of Technology in Sydney questioned, for example, whether universities would always need to retain permanent teaching staff. If the majority of students are taught by remote learning in future, the taught courses could also be bought in. This would allow universities to become global educational programme marketing organisations. They could buy in the best available courses, from researchers, lecturers and educators that could be based at other institutions, then market and administer them for a student body that could be dispersed over the world.

The University of Edinburgh has extended this discussion to the relationship between teaching and research. It has become clear that a small number of universities and advanced research institutions have effectively captured particular fields of research. The cost of equipment required to undertake advanced research in certain fields is now so high that it is almost impossible for other universities to gain entry to those fields. Even the United States, for example, balked at the cost of the proposed national particle accelerator, and decided not to try to duplicate the CERN facilities in Switzerland. Thus particular universities and advanced research institutions now dominate certain fields, with the most advanced programmes of research, and with relatively secure leads. Once dominance has been established, of course, leads tend to extend, as a leading position and high reputation help to attract the best possible staff and additional resources. Thus leads, once established, can become increasingly locked-in and stable.

This raises a question, of course, as to the role of those universities that cannot match these resources. The Vice Chancellor of the University of Edinburgh suggested recently that many university staff might hold dual appointments in future; undertaking their research at one university, but contracted to provide teaching material and course content for another. This suggests that universities would polarise further, dividing into a first group of elite research establishments, and a second group of educational programme managers. The process of restructuring is unlikely to stop there, however, as there is now a question as to whether the traditional teaching universities are necessarily the only organisations capable of packaging and delivering educational material.

Disney, Time Warner and Microsoft do not believe that they are. These three corporations are currently exploring links with major research universities (respectively; Berkeley, Michigan and Columbia). They have proposed that the universities would create the materials and validate the courses, and the communications corporations would package and deliver them. All three corporations have, of course, far greater capital, technological and media resources than any of the world's teaching universities, which suggests that they will present the universities with a new and completely unprecedented level of competition. This in turn suggests that a number of teaching universities, worldwide, might actually decrease, with the elite research universities becoming even more dominant than they are now.

It is important to note that the delivery of educational material over the internet offers positive returns. Given that the technology itself represents a sunk cost, most of the cost of each individual course is incurred in the development of the material. The cost (in terms of administration) of each new student added thereafter is negligible. Staff/student ratios change dramatically as there is little restriction on class sizes, and other fixed costs (such as building maintenance) can be slashed. This creates a powerful incentive to recruit more students, and to add to the portfolio of profitable courses.

This means that the new educational market has a very strong dynamic for further growth, which is what will drive the transformation of the structure and process of higher education over the next few years. One indicator of the current pace of change is that the UK's total foreign exchange earnings from education and training increased by nearly 30 per cent between 1997 and 1998 alone. Australia and the US are achieving similarly rapid growth, and others (such as Canada) are starting to catch up.

The Implications for the UWI

Bennell and Pearce of the Institute for Development Studies (IDS) at the University of Sussex produced a report in late 1998 which predicted that trade in knowledge and skill is set to grow exponentially. This is partly because the resolution of the remaining trade barriers under WTO rules will allow multinational corporations (MNCs) to further accelerate the rate at which they are expanding their share of world trade, and the extension of MNC trans-boundary production systems around the world will strongly favour those with internationally recognised qualifications. International companies need to recruit personnel with training and education they recognise and understand, especially when production systems are integrated across borders. This means that portable qualifications from prestigious institutions will become increasingly essential to those competing in the job market. People in developing and transitional countries, in particular, will need the competitive advantage of a recognised qualification from a prestigious institution. Similarly, governments in developing and transitional countries will be under increasing pressure to create high skill societies in order to attract inward investment, and many will have to rely increasingly on foreign provision of the necessary education and training.

The IDS report also predicts that the majority of the developed industrial economies will follow the lead of the UK, US and Australia over the next five to ten years, as there are already clear signs that universities in these other countries are becoming increasingly active in exploiting overseas education and training markets. This process will be dramatically accelerated by the further extension of internet access, as this will allows universities to offer their courses directly to a student body that can be scattered around the world.

The IDS report therefore predicts 'potentially dire' effects for institutions in developing countries, which are likely to lose out to universities based in the developed industrial economies. The universities based in the developed industrial economies will be far better able to offer the kind of prestigious and portable qualifications that will be increasingly required. More specifically, elite research universities and specialist research institutions will flourish as they will be able to use these technological and related changes to expand their role in the supply of course content and the validation of degrees. The traditional teaching universities, however, will come under increasing pressure, both from research universities and from communications corporations. It is likely that communications corporations will succeed in taking over an increasing share of the packaging and delivery of courses, in collaboration with the research universities.

The main losers in this process, therefore, are likely to be (a) traditional teaching universities, which are likely to lose market share to powerful consortia of research universities and communications corporations, and (b) universities in developing or transitional nations, few of which will be able to offer qualifications of the same perceived value as those from the elite research universities in the advanced industrial nations.

The UWI, as a predominantly teaching university in a developing/transitional nation, is therefore threatened on several fronts. However, it is important not to be trapped into a beleaguered frame of mind. The current process of technological and economic change will profoundly reshape the nature and process of higher education, but this will open up many new opportunities for UWI. Whether we succeed in turning this process of change to our advantage will depend on whether we have sufficient strategic vision and tactical agility. We will have to cede ground in areas where we have no comparative advantage, but we may be able to gain increasing market share in areas where we can develop a role at the cutting edge. Consider the following two scenarios:

1. UWI fails to adopt a strategy for managing the process of change. The extension of franchising and internet delivery is primarily seen as a threat, with staff reacting negatively to the incursion by other universities onto 'our' territory. Other universities and countries continue to set the pace of change and shape the outcomes.

   Result: The UWI of 2020 may suffer a massive erosion of its student intake. As other universities extend their franchise arrangements, and as the cost of internet access becomes negligible, most students are increasingly likely to opt for better, cheaper courses from more prestigious, research-oriented universities beyond the region, perhaps packaged and delivered by communications corporations with immense technological, capital and human resources. This would probably precipitate a funding crisis, as the governments of the region might be increasingly disinclined to support an institution that was perceived to be both failing and catering for a rapidly declining percentage of the domestic student base. The funding crisis would in turn make it increasingly difficult for the University to attract or retain the calibre of staff needed to turn the situation around, thus precipitating a further phase of decline.

2. UWI adopts a proactive strategy to stay fully abreast of the process of change. The University relinquishes the idea that universities are primarily defined by geographical locus, defines and focuses on its areas of excellence, establishes collaborative partnerships with other universities, and moves teaching and research collaboration onto internet delivery.

Result: The UWI of 2020 may well be smaller (in terms of staff numbers) than today, yet be dealing with a significantly larger student body, the majority of which could be based beyond the region. The University would probably be much more focused, on a few (perhaps half-dozen) core areas in which it had international recognition for cutting-edge research. Provision in other areas would be left to those institutions that had specialised accordingly. Franchised and inter-university joint degrees would therefore be the norm, as would the supply of specialist degree components to other universities, with franchising and related arrangements increasingly seen as a way of ensuring collaboration within strategic alliances of universities. The university would undertake routine benchmarking against other leading institutions in order to ensure that its courses retained the necessary quality and relevance.

Choosing Core Areas

This raises, of course, an important question as to what our areas of excellence might be – and it is important to think carefully about the University's wider strategic interests before making any irrevocable decisions. It seems likely, however, that the choice of core area would have to take into account the following factors:
- an assessment of the potential to establish an internationally recognised lead in the chosen areas, taking into account the extent to which particular strategic areas may already be dominated by other institutions
- the need to support a wider process of wealth creation and improved social welfare in the region, and an assessment of the potential contribution of the University through research, teaching or outreach programmes
- the existing skill base at UWI, an assessment of which of the existing centres, units, institutes and departments could be restructured as part of a refocusing exercise, and of which of the existing research, teaching or outreach programmes could be reoriented for delivery under the new structure

We should also note the recent comment from Sir John Daniel, the Vice Chancellor of the Open University, which currently has some 40,000 networked students. Sir John has argued that the universities that make a successful transition to the new information age will be those that have four fundamental qualities:
- excellent learning materials

- strong support for students
- efficient logistics
- the intellectual vitality that comes from a profound commitment to scholarship and research

Conclusion

It is important to recognise that the changes outlined in this paper will happen anyway, with us or without us. If we have sufficient resolution and agility, we can adapt successfully to the changing global environment. If we do so, UWI can look forward to an exciting era of intellectual expansion and wider engagement at global level. It is also clear, however, that if we ignore these changes, then we do so at our peril. The price of failure could be very high.

Notes

1. Halweil and Brown of the Worldwatch Institute have calculated that it will be necessary to create 30 million new jobs per year, on average, for the next 50 years in order to absorb the projected increase in the world population onto the labour markets. They also argue that many of the traditional outlets (such as agriculture) for surplus labour are no longer viable, as mechanisation and cheap imports have rendered these activities uneconomic. This suggests that relatively high-skilled service sector activity may be one of the few areas capable of generating the growth required, which has profound implications in terms of the commitment of resources required to raise the average skill level in the societies concerned.
2. Interview with the Vice Chancellor of the Open University, *Guardian Weekly*, August 7, 1999
3. 'Moving into the information age', UK Department of Trade and Industry report, April, 1998
4. C Anderson, 'In search of the perfect market', *The Economist*, September 14, 1997
5. Estimates as to the amount of e-commerce currently transacted vary widely, largely because the figures have to be partly imputed. The OECD estimate just US$3 billion per annum, but industry estimates range as high as US$50 billion per annum. US$20 billion is a recent, mid-range estimate. All sources agree, however, that the rate of growth is extraordinarily rapid.
6. UK Department of Trade and Industry statistics, reported in *Guardian Weekly*, November 17, 1998
7. Interview with the Master of Birkbeck College, *Guardian Weekly*, June 5, 1998
8. Interview with the Vice Chancellor of Southampton University, *Guardian Weekly*, May 2, 1999

15 | MOHAMMAD H AHMAD

Growth and Sustainable Development Through University and Industry Collaboration in Biotechnology

From the Lab into the Fields to the Market: Business & University Partnerships Promoting Biotechnology Commercialisation for Agro- and Environmentally related Industries

University-industry collaboration in biotechnology implies the transformation of the results obtained from the lab into a marketable product. Such collaboration is an important factor in the bio-industrialisation of small countries such as those of the Caribbean. The collaboration must be effective and positive because it acts as a catalyst in the process of the development of novel biotech-based industries that can contribute to sustainable economic growth and also improvement of the quality of life.

Some of the work that has come out of the Biotechnology Centre through university-industry collaboration will be presented. Also, some income generating ideas and strategic vision for future biotech-based industries will be discussed.

The world's population today is about 5.8 billion people. About 1.5 billion live in conditions of abject poverty. These people spend their time trying to find food in order to survive. As many as 800 million people are so severely malnourished that they can neither work nor participate in normal family life. It is expected that the world's population will double by the year 2030. The twenty-first century will, therefore, be a world of mass migration and environmental degradation on an unimaginable scale. The question is, can we enable the Caribbean to achieve prosperity in the twenty-first century? The answer is yes – by the introduction of science and emerging technologies at the grass roots level, where they are needed most.

In the twentieth century, we were able to feed people by bringing more acreage into production and by increasing agricultural productivity with the application of fertilisers, pesticides, and irrigation. However, we have lost 15 per cent of our top soil over 20 years. Irrigation is increasing the salinity of soil. Petrochemicals for fertiliser production are not renewable. Use of pesticides are becoming increasingly unacceptable, causing fear of pollution and deadly diseases such as cancer. Even if we are prepared to accept an unsustainable way, no technology today would let us double our productivity. With best practices applied to all the acreage in the world, we can only feed a third of the population of the world. So the only alternative is the use of new technology and one such technology is biotechnology.

Biotechnology is one example of several new industries that have recently been developed. Over a 12 year period from 1980 to 1992, worldwide sales of biotechnology-derived products grew to US$6 billion. By the end of the twentieth century, sales in the USA alone are estimated at US$50 billion. In the USA there are 300 biotechnology companies generating more than 100,000 high-skilled jobs. In addition, 400 companies in 16 European countries generate more than 40,000 high skilled jobs. When compared with data from the developing countries, hardly any biotechnology based companies or ventures are found with the exception of a few in the more advanced Asian and Latin American countries.

University-industry cooperation in biotechnology is considered to be a virtually indispensable mechanism for economic and social progress. Universities which have existed long before the advent of organised industry, will continue to be an important source of basic and applied knowledge which is vital for socio-economic progress. The striking advances made in molecular biology and biochemistry, various applications of DNA technology such as production of bio-pharmaceuticals, gene therapy, production of new vaccines, new hybrid plants and disease resistant transgenic plants have been driven by human curiosity to apply knowledge of biotechnology to ensure an optimal quality of life.

In University-industry collaboration, universities make an important contribution by generating new information. The contribution of universities to technology transfer through people transfer of top-level graduate and post-graduate students and competent staff into the industrial labour force is worth mentioning. Universities support research and new ideas with enthusiasm, stimulating imagination and creativity for the development of new products and services.

Attention was drawn to the various functions of a university education, research, training, and the provision of services in the development of human resources and technology transfer. Over a decade, collaboration between academia and industry was fundamental to the development of biotechnology and its related industries. CELLTECH, a biotechnology company in the UK established with private and public sector finance, is a good example of interaction and collaboration with a university.

Many such examples of biotechnology industries have been generated in the USA on the basis of university-industry collaboration. While this kind of collaboration is vital, there are some critical problems that have to be solved for its development, with special reference to the developing countries.

1. **Technical constraints:** The inability of many scientists to transform basic lab findings into pilot scale bio-industrial processes
2. **Economic loans:** The lack of economic loans, incentives and risk capital for the development of small scale biotechnological enterprises
3. **Professional experience and facilities:** The lack of experienced researchers, extension services, production facilities, marketing managers and a local market large enough for biotechnology-based business
4. **Public perception:** Insufficient public sector perception, and a low appreciation of the general public
5. **Strategic planning:** Long-term strategic planning by the university and industry executives of small nations for future development and growth.

In order to assist the Caribbean islands to participate effectively in the regional and international economy, the private sector with its financial muscle must fund competitive innovative research of biotechnology in the academic sectors.

Let us take some examples of research projects in biotechnology that we have been developing at the Biotechnology Centre. Our young scientists and lecturers are doing excellent work on various agro-biotechnology projects. To name a few: Dr Helen Asemota and Mrs Sylvia Mitchell on yam biotechnology; Dr Wayne McLaughlin and Dr Marcia Roye on the gemini virus affecting local vegetables; Dr Paula Tennant working on the papaya ring spot virus; and my own research group working on biodiversity and the development of natural products from plants to be used as pesticides, and as disinfectants.

Our research groups have several collaborative projects with the local industries. Some examples include:

1. Collaboration with the Best Dressed Chicken on the monitoring of microbial quality of locally processed chicken
2. Assessment of effectiveness of various disinfectants used in the food processing industry sponsored by the Jamaica Broilers Group
3. Studies on the bio-remediation of impurities in local bauxite – supported by Alcan Jamaica
4. Understanding the power of biorganics as an organic fertiliser – supported by Content Agriculture Ltd
5. Commercialisation of minisett yam production – supported by the Jamaica Poultry Breeders
6. Development of embryo transfer technologies for the improvement of dairy cattle – supported by ALCAN Jamaica Ltd
7. Use of natural products as disinfectants in a local patty producing factory – supported by Juicy Beef Patties
8. Technical assistance given to Polydiagnostics to set up a microbiological analytical laboratory in order to use DNA technology
9. For the first time in the Caribbean, the Biotechnology Centre is carrying out research on the production and field testing of transgenic papaya supported by the JADF and the UWI

University-industry collaboration is characterised by a decision-making process, and these decisions influence the transformation of basic knowledge into applications with commercial potential. Such processes demand rigorous monitoring of research projects for national economic development. We need to have a long term goal and well defined objectives. Realistic cost-benefit estimates and consumer demands are to be considered for prioritisation of the research agenda and final outputs of the biotechnological venture. The long term national biotechnology plans and performance involve the objective of socio-economic research which generates income and employment at the national level. The production, creation and dissemination of new information and new knowledge has always been the highest priority of any high quality university. However, in the developing countries linking fundamental and applied research to development is still considered a second class activity. The experimental work on plant biotechnology at the university laboratory (test tube grown plants) needs to be field tested. New products have to be registered and patented, the trade names need to be defined and projected and finally the products need to be marketed. In the final analysis, it should always be kept in mind that to launch new products in the market place is much more difficult than to develop a new product.

Let us speak of sustainable development – sustainability in terms of economic growth and environmental preservation. Global warming, acid rain, deforestation, urbanisation, unpredictable weather, intense droughts, and severe floods have drawn the attention of political leaders and international scientists to the need for a change in their planning and strategic thinking. The high incidence of disease including the increasing number of allergies is definitely symptomatic of environmental problems. Pollution and catastrophic environmental disasters will affect small islands more rapidly than large countries whose economies are not as fragile. For us, tourism is the key foreign exchange earner and any environmental disaster which has an adverse effect on the sector will immediately affect the economy.

Can we continue to enjoy clean air and water? Millions of people in the developing world expect the quality of their lives to improve. Is sustainability becoming an important component of strategic thinking? In some business, sustainability is not so critical as in agro-business. In agricultural production, information technology and biotechnology are the key technologies to be applied for sustainability. We can genetically code a plant to destroy or repel insects and pests. In future, we do not have to spray the crop with pesticides. Up to 90 per cent of what is sprayed on crops is wasted. Most of it ends up in the soil. We genetically alter the DNA encoded information on the plants so that plants do not need to be sprayed with deadly chemicals. In this regard, the scientists of the Biotechnology Centre have formulated and developed a natural product bio-pesticide from the neem (*Azactarichta indica*) plant. The oil is extracted from the neem seed and is used as an active ingredient in the formulation of bio-pesticides. Our field test results on various pests and diseases are quite encouraging, and soon we will be able to commercialise our bio-pesticide. Neem oils are not only useful as natural pesticides, but also as a natural disinfectant. Soap and shampoo can also be prepared from neem oil as an alternative to chemicals.

I think in the early twenty-first century we will see a struggle between information technology and biotechnology. While information technology will lead us to the super information highway to speed up our knowledge dissemination and market information, biotechnology will allow us to develop several new products for better health, better food, better feed, better water, air and, most importantly, will save us from environmental degradation.

Recommendation

Biotechnology will lead the way towards making that goal attainable. Genetically superior corn, wheat, tomatoes and soybean will create a revolution in modern agriculture and in new agro-industries. New knowledge of biotechnology and its application will benefit the Caribbean countries by boosting their economies due to enhanced agricultural production and new product development. However, the most limiting factors in the development of biotechnology-based industries in the Caribbean are the lack of skilled human resources to create, develop and market new biotechnology products. In order to produce the right managers and skilled workers, the university-industry cooperation in biotechnology is considered a most important mechanism for economic and social progress in the Caribbean. The various Caribbean islands need to embark on a number of biotech-intensive agro-based industries ranging from the commercial production of tissue-culture medicinal or herbal plants, to ornamental plants, transgenic crops, and various flavoured and fragranced plants for extraction of essential and natural oils. Some of the examples of herbal and medicinal plants are periwinkle (*Catharanthus rosens*), *Dioscorea deltoidea, Dioscorea floibunda, D composita, Plantago Ovata, Ricinus communis, Cassia angustifolia, Cephaelis ipecacuanha, Papaver somniferum, Mentha arvensis, Cymbopogan winterianus, Pelargonium graveolens* (geranium), *Eucalyptus citriodora, Cinnamom zeylanieum*, and many others.

Caribbean islands are known for the production of various spices. The commercial production of high quality spice can be produced economically by the use of biotechnology. The spice market is growing rapidly and demand is increasing for high quality and value added products. Can we produce the quantity with quality to meet the demand of the sophisticated spice export market? Similarly, volatile oils such as pimento oil, cardamom oil, lemon grass oil, ginger oil, lime oil, turpine oil, clove oil, and dill oil are needed for pharmaceutical and cosmetic industries. There are various phytochemicals, for example menthol and peppermint, that can be produced of the highest quality to fetch a premium price.

Conclusion

It is clear that biotechnology will play a central role in the development process in the twenty-first century. In fact, it has been argued that future developments in the realm of biotechnolgy will provide the next great frontier in the ongoing technological revolution. The Caribbean will therefore need to seek to develop its biotechnological potential as a critical element of its development strategy in the twenty-first century.

16 | ANTHONY S JOHNSON

Science, Technology and Sustainable Development
Will We Get It Right This Time?

Regarding the vexed question of science, technology and sustainable development in the Caribbean, the only thing we are guaranteed to agree upon is that we did not get it right in the twentieth century, and that we should get it right in the next one. I would argue that basic to the problem is what we mean by science and technology. That we should adopt the principles of sustainable development is not in doubt, since we are so small and vulnerable, we will not survive at a reasonable standard of living. Some see it as the expenditure on certain physical facilities, typically laboratories and computers. Others see it as a sort of talisman to be called upon whenever things do not go right. Yet others see it as pure research of whatever type or as the science of measurement, while I will claim that it is simply the application of scientific method for solving human problems.

I suspect that some may not be pleased with this definition, since it might not guarantee resources into pure science or laboratories. But since the region has a certain stock of resources, and these have to be allocated by the various institutional processes, it is not scientifically justified to simply declare on whatever grounds that we should spend a certain percentage of such resources on any specific area, be it research, information technology, agriculture, education, planning or heritage studies, to name just a few which are constantly proclaimed by various interests to be entitled to such treatment.

From my perspective, our main failing, and the main challenge before us, is to use scientific methods to provide what we need: an acceptable minimum standard of living for the vast majority of our people on bases that are sustainable in the long run. In the instances where this has been applied, we have succeeded. Where it has not, we have failed. I would therefore argue that the best approach for the twenty-first century would be to get back to basics: ordered collection of facts, keen recording and observation, analysis and observation, formation of preliminary ideas, a process of rigorous testing, drawing of conclusions, and repeating the process if the results are unacceptable.

If this seems too simple, I would suggest that it is the non-application which has led us into the path of inappropriate policies and foolish programmes which have sapped so much of our energies in the past century. Not all of us, since, generally, the region has been experiencing economic growth, and most CARICOM states are in the top third of the HDI scale, and four are in the upper-middle income band of economies listed according to gross domestic product.

Whatever the figures might show, the people of the region are not satisfied that our countries are offering a standard of living commensurate with their desires, and we have an inherent instability in several areas:

- persistently high levels of unemployment, even in the success stories of Barbados and Trinidad and Tobago
- migration, leading to the loss of our best trained and most highly skilled personnel
- dependence on high-cost exports; constantly threatened by closure of protected markets
- threat of victimisation by externalities from the new globalisation process
- the rape of our conch beds, marine pollution by cruise ships, contamination of our water supplies, atmospheric pollution from our industries, loss of endemic habitat, and much more
- the fall-out from global climatic change – rising sea levels, more powerful hurricanes, shifts in rainfall patterns, and so on.

These and other problems are repeated ad nauseum, and will continue to be repeated in the twenty-first century, and while I am not suggesting that we have made no progress, we ought to be doing much better. Certainly, our largest members – Haiti, Guyana and Jamaica – are prime examples of economic failure. Perhaps, therefore, we should have a look at some of the differing perspectives we might use in our search for solutions.

Instead of looking at our inputs from a traditional view-point, we might look from a perspective suggested by the paradigm of sustainable development. So that we would not see only agriculture, manufacturing, or tourism, but rather energy, natural resources, recoverable waste, labour resources, and heritage resources. The industries, institutions and capital resources could then be seen as adjuncts or sub-sets of these inputs, and assist us in plotting a development path with a far greater possibility of success.

In terms of the desired outputs, I suggest we look not merely at the components of the HDI – per capita income, life expectancy, access to water, health care and education – but look at wider constructs – productivity, national stability, social equity and environmental enhancement.

This would allow us to view our problems more rationally, less emotionally, and cut out the traditional rivalry between various sectors, such as manufacturing versus tourism, or agriculture versus education. It would also remove some major policy problems, such as determining optimal levels for research, whether research should be pure or applied, and the extent to which we should depend on imported or local resources of manpower, products, services, or culture. However, if we do not apply scientific methods to our decision-making processes, but continue to depend on hunches, general ideas, or what appears to be a consensus or popular view, we will not solve the major challenges which lie ahead.

My view of the twenty-first century is that:

1. The new opportunities being offered by globalisation will far outweigh the negatives.
2. Small countries will have a better chance of success than large ones (look at the performance of small states such as Luxembourg, Hong Kong, Bermuda, Holland and Singapore)
3. Countries with unique heritage profiles such as the Caribbean have tremendous potential in a world in which travel will continue to be the largest industry for some time to come.
4. In the past century the region has been the major producer of bananas (Jamaica), sugar (Cuba), bauxite (Jamaica), nutmeg (Grenada), ammonia and aromatic bitters (Trinidad and Tobago), and much more. The region has produced world class scientists – Frazer-Reid, TP Lecky, Cicely Williams, Trevor McMorris, our own Bunny Lalor, Lawson Douglas, and I could go on. What has been missing is a consistency of performance and a

linkage between our undoubted ability, and a focus on adapting the opportunities to solving our problems. I suggest that we have not been using a scientific approach, and this has caused us to waste resources of time, money and manpower. I also suggest that we have tended to use an institutional construct which, by focusing on existing institutions and industries, might have given us a bias, or led us into, unnecessary rivalries and antagonisms and also the adoption of false positions.

5. We can use the opportunity of a new century to reflect, assess and start perhaps not by setting new goals, but by setting up new systems for thinking, assessing and planning. For some countries this might seem optional. For us it is not. It is quite clear that we are totally dissatisfied with our overall performance as a region: poverty, illiteracy and general hopelessness should have been abolished, given our resources.

Let us unleash the power that comes from scientific thinking. Let us not forget about the past failures and frustrations, but greet the new century with a dedication to the sometimes lengthy, tedious and rigorous process set out in the fourteenth century by Roger Bacon, but clearly needed by us for the twenty-first.

Part 5
Social Integration/Disintegration: The Caribbean Experience

17 | RALPH R PREMDAS

Diversity and Liberation in the Caribbean:
The Decentralist Policy Challenge in the New Millennium

After nearly a half century of independence for most countries of the Commonwealth Caribbean (as well as almost two centuries of independence for Haiti and nearly a century for countries like Cuba), what have we achieved in terms of forging a unified region with a consciously shared Caribbean identity that defines us as a unique people living in a separate space with a distinctive culture? Colonised and consolidated into ethno-linguistic compartments, are the imperially constructed barriers and differences which trammel our potential for full cooperation being overcome so that we know each other better, sharing in our collective sufferings and joys? Or are we becoming more different and differentiated, less regionally integrated, not only along the linguistic-metropolitan divide, but in other political and economic ways in all parts of the Caribbean including the Commonwealth Caribbean? Are we now more intensely and intimately linked to our respective imperial cities of the west than before, becoming more like them and less alike among ourselves, even as we indulge heavily in the ritual rhetoric of sameness in identity and interests?

Is there a unified Caribbean? Has there ever been one? Is it all an imaginary construct serving as a functional fantasy for our divided and insular insecurities? What are the costs of preserving illusions of non-existent relationships and fictions? Since colonisation and the extermination of the Amerindians in the insular Caribbean, many fissures in race, ethnicity, religion, and language have configured in the construction of our internally differentiated identity. Indeed, differences and diversity have come to define our identity and uniqueness. While there is a geographical expression called 'the Caribbean', often associated with a site, a sea, and several islands, the truth is that the Caribbean even as a regional entity is a very imprecise place, difficult to define by consensus. Some analysts include Florida, the Yucatan, Nicaragua, Colombia, and Venezuela, while others exclude them altogether. In this region, however and wherever we choose to locate its boundaries, it is usually visualised as an area populated by a diverse polyglot of peoples. There are whites, blacks, browns, yellows, reds, and an assortment of shades in between. There are Europeans, Africans, Asian Indians, Chinese, Aboriginal Indians, and many mixes. There are Christians, Hindus, Muslims, Jews, Rastafarians, Santeria, Winti, and Vudun. They speak in a multitude of tongues – Spanish, English, Dutch, French, English, and a diverse number of Creoles such as Papiamentu, Sranan, Njuka, Kromanti, or Kreyol. In whatever combinations of race, religion, language, and culture they cohere and coexist, Caribbean people dwell on small islands and large, some poorly endowed with natural resources, others abundantly. To social and cultural diversity are compounded differences in physical and natural endowment. Perhaps no other region of the world is so richly differentiated and diverse with a proliferation of all manner of pluralisms.

To be sure, there have been unifying forces and experiences in our history in slavery, indentureship, and plantations of sugar, bananas, and coffee, in our economic dependence and external domination. But the interplay of centripetal and centrifugal forces, always present, seems permanently to place our survival and identity on shifting sands, up for grabs, exposed mercilessly to unpredictable external powers and pressures. It is clear, however, even as we chant the mantra of a community-shared Caribbean space, today it is our differences which stand out most starkly against the landscape of the new millenium. Some of these differences have assumed proportions which truly interrogate our collective sense of 'Caribbeanness'. Many of the main countries or clusters of countries spin in their own orbits and create their own trajectories. Cuba, the most populous of Caribbean states with over ten million of the Caribbean's estimated total of about 33 million souls, is Spanish-speaking and Marxist-Leninist with a one party system and a planned economy which still relies heavily on sugar. The Dominican Republic and Puerto Rico, both

Spanish-speaking, account for about a fourth of the Caribbean population, and are both liberal democratic, capitalist and tied closely to the US economy. Haiti, French patois-speaking, is almost anarchistic politically with an economy that has been reduced to shambles by civil strife. Taken together, these four large states in the Caribbean are deeply different from each other in their political and economic structures. They do indeed spin in their own orbits with few significant links among them. Then there are the Dutch and French territories which are economically and politically attached by a virtual umbilical cord to their respective metropoles. These are prosperous islands which relate most intimately to France and the Netherlands respectively for much of their literature and learning. Nearly half of their population lives in their 'metropolitan motherland'. Even in the Commonwealth Caribbean, sharp differences proliferate. Guyana probably fits more closely to countries outside the Caribbean such as Northern Ireland, Bosnia and Sri Lanka because of the politics of ethnic hate that have left the place pathetically prostrated and poor.

While Trinidad and Suriname may bear some socio-cultural similarities with Guyana, economically they could not be further apart. Suriname is practically run by the long shadow of the military *caudillo* strongman, Desi Bouterse, who has been placed by the Dutch on drug smuggling charges and is liable to be arrested outside Suriname. Trinidad's polity is an ethnically bifurcated democracy. Its economy is based on petroleum, methanol, and other minerals coupled with a vibrant industrial base which sets the island apart in significant ways from the rest of the Commonwealth Caribbean. Barbados has converted from a sugar-based economy to tourism and enjoys a high standard of living which separates it from impoverished Jamaica which, although also dependent on tourism, is culturally unique, drug ridden, and politically unstable.

Overall, these differences point to deep, persistent, numerous, and formidable cleavages. They portray a region that is more a geographical expression than a culturally, economically, or politically unified entity. Levels of inequality in poverty and prosperity are stark, from Haiti, Guyana and Suriname at one end of the continuum to the Bahamas, the French and Dutch Antilles and Puerto Rico on the other. Political systems vary widely, from parliamentary democracies to presidential dictatorships to virtual anarchism in Guyana and Haiti. Cultural differentiation is also marked not only along linguistic spheres but in relation to ethnically and racially plural societies in such countries as Guyana, Trinidad, and Suriname to more homogenous places like Nevis, St Kitts, and Grenada. In many ways, the separate orbits and trajectories suggest that for the most part the majority of the Caribbean states are of little relevance to each other in their quest for survival and prosperity.

If all of this is true, what does it amount to? Is this only a prism of pessimism? Are we truly flying apart? Should we be afraid? Should we scrap the myth of a Caribbean imaginary? Is it just a freight of frustrations? Is there nothing redeeming in all of our rich diversity? Are there assets in our diversity to be recognised, encouraged and celebrated? Isn't our diversity indeed our strength, and not our weakness and the source of our problems? Where do we go from here into the next millennium? What needs to be done? Before answering some of these questions and offering a new challenge for change in a possible solution, it will be useful to clear the ground in defining what we mean by 'Caribbean'. Since the paper is largely about identity, it is also necessary to shed some light into its definition and significance.

Identity and the Caribbean

Identity emerges from a collective group consciousness that imparts a sense of belonging derived from membership in a community bound putatively by common descent and culture. As a subjective phenomenon, it imparts to the individual a sense of belonging, and to the community a sense of solidarity, which is a vital need of human existence. Belonging plays a pivotal part in human life:

. . . just as people need to eat and drink, to have security and freedom of movement, so too they need to belong to a group. Deprived of this dimension in life, they feel cut off, lonely, diminished, unhappy. To be human means to be able to feel at home somewhere, with one's own kind.[1]

Identity as belonging can be acquired through membership in various communities bound by one or more social attributes such as race, language, religion, culture, or region. Often this identity is formed in contradistinction to the claims of other groups to a similar sense of uniqueness, so that in a real sense identity formation is a relational and comparative phenomenon locked into 'we-they' antipathies which may be mildly benign or overtly hostile. To belong is simultaneously to include and exclude, to establish a boundary, even though this line of demarcation may be, as Barth noted, composed of fluid and situational social constructs that are 'subjectively held categories of ascription and identity by actors themselves'.[2]

Caribbean identities are, like many other group constructs, aimed at meeting instrumental and expressive needs wherever Caribbean peoples find themselves. In this regard I have devised for conceptual analysis four levels into which Caribbean identity can be conceived:

1. The trans-Caribbean
2. The regional
3. The insular
4. The ethno-local universal

Most Caribbeans are carriers of multiple identities, which points to a differentiated citizenship and loyalty. We shall return to these categories of identity later in the paper. But before we proceed to describe them, some exploration into the Caribbean is necessary to point to tensions, contradictions, and overlaps in identity formation.

In all this diversity, the concept of a Caribbean people and the construction of a Caribbean identity is caught up in many contradictions. It is easy to assert a Caribbean identity if that person does not have to meet their compatriots and has no hope of this ever happening. It is because of this fact that we can maintain the fiction of a collection of people with an all-encompassing Caribbean identity, for in enlarging the ambit of one's interaction beyond the village or town, one is quite likely to encounter Caribbean 'brothers' and 'sisters' whom one will instantly disown. It is in part because of this reason that Benedict Anderson titled his renowned book on ethnicity *Imagined Communities*. Anderson argued:

It (ethnic or communal identity) is imagined because the members of even the smallest nation will never know most of their fellow-members, meet them, or even hear of them, yet in the minds of each lives the image of their communion.[3]

It is easy to understand that people from an imaginary region designated 'the Caribbean' may want an identity that is much bigger than a relatively small island. It imparts some sense of security in size and numbers. It bestows belonging, and the larger the tribe the greater the warmth imparted. However, some of these designations can be dangerous when ascribed collective identities assume the form of hegemonic cultural claims that omit or marginalise other communities. Identities are potentially dangerous constructs and can be manipulated for oppressive ends. I believe that the Caribbean is suffused with an assortment of conflicting claims and overlaps that demonstrate the difficulty of defining identity claims. The many sites of struggles are located in relationships of 'we-they' claims to power and privileges. Most of these are low key and institutionalised, but with a few periodically breaking the bounds of their normality and becoming quite controversial. The very fact of racial as well as linguistic, regional and religious diversity embedded in the pattern of settlement and in the social structure of the twenty-odd states populated by some 33 million people in the Caribbean predisposes them to the process of identity formation and consciousness. Beneath the veneer of Caribbean homogeneity lurk numerous identities around the axes of race, culture, language, religion, and region. Political mobilisation has played on these cleavages so that identity sensitivity and assertiveness pervade these states like blood the body.

What and where is the Caribbean? Where are its boundaries? Even though these are seemingly innocent questions, they have evoked diverse and sometimes controversial answers. In the contemporary period, the Caribbean states have been carved out of the functional plantation zone and has assumed its regional centre of gravity in the insular areas. A few continental coastal countries are usually appended to this Caribbean region, including Belize and the Guianas. The islands include two great chains: the Greater Antilles, which cover 90 per cent of the land and peoples of the region and includes Cuba, Hispaniola (Haiti and the Dominican Republic share this island), Puerto Rico, and Jamaica; and the Lesser Antilles, which incorporate the other smaller islands. The Caribbean region has been truncated into sub-linguistic subsets reflecting the early pattern of colonisation by an assortment of European powers. Hence, the Spanish area includes Cuba, the Dominican Republic, and Puerto Rico – which is part of American territory. Spanish is spoken by about 60 per cent of the 33 million people who inhabit the Caribbean. The French portion includes Martinique, Guadeloupe, and French Guiana, which are currently departments of France, and Haiti which has been independent since 1804. A French-based Creole is spoken in Dominica and St Lucia. The Dutch parts include Suriname, which has been independent since 1976, Curacao and The Netherlands Antilles – comprising the islands of Curacao, Aruba, Bonaire, Saba, St Maarten and St Eustatius, which are part of the Dutch state. The English-speaking areas include an assortment of independent and dependent islands linked to Britain, collectively called the Commonwealth Caribbean. The independent ones include Jamaica, Barbados, Guyana, Belize, the Bahamas, Antigua, St Kitts-Nevis, Grenada, Dominica, St Lucia, and St Vincent. The dependent ones include the British Virgin Islands, Montseratt, Anguilla, Barbuda, and the Cayman Islands, and the Turks and Caicos islands. Linked to the United States are the American Virgin islands, while one anomalous island, St Maarten, which is a condominium jointly run by The Netherlands and France.

In the late twentieth century, a substantial part of the Caribbean peoples resided in North America, Britain, the Netherlands, and France in what has been referred to as the 'Caribbean diaspora'. It has been argued that this phenomenon, which includes substantial retentions of Caribbean cultural forms in predominantly Caribbean residential areas in the metropolitan countries, has created a new meaning of the Caribbean region to include all areas of the world where Caribbean peoples have migrated and reconstituted themselves as discrete sub-communities. In this sense, the Caribbean is located wherever Caribbean peoples congregate in tropical and temperate parts of the world, in industrial and agrarian regions, among white and black communities anywhere and everywhere.

The contemporary Caribbean displays in its raw statistics some of the variations in the region. Cuba has about 10.3 million people, while the Caicos has only about 10,000. The per capita income in Haiti, the poorest country in the western hemisphere, is about $300 while it is $7,600 in the Bahamas and a high of about $13,421 in Bermuda. Franklin Knight sums up this array of differences well: 'The contemporary Caribbean, less a melting pot than a melange, remains a strangely fascinating fusion of race, ethnicity, class and cultures-and the inescapable legacies of slavery and the plantation system have enormously complicated the social stratification of the region.'[4]

Diversity and Liberation

'Diversity and difference' define the Caribbean as a unique region in the world. While at one level it seems that the internal differentiation threatens to rend the region asunder at its many cleavages, it is paradoxically true that this very factor constitutes its greatest potential strength in its future development. It should be the role of public policy to recognise the differences and diversities, tapping them to our greater advantage. Policy directs the future. It is human agency and a matter of will. Policy can harness the plentitude of differences to the end of turning them into the lode site to be mined for the greater good. How this can be done will be illustrated in one main example below. It is necessary however to underscore that not all cleavages and differences are of positive value to the challenge of development in the Caribbean. Several differences have turned pathological and clearly dysfunctional. Take for example, the differences in ethnicity in Guyana. Here, differences in the rival ethno-cultural communities have been organised and mobilised in a manner that has brought the country to the brink of sectional civil war. Instead of ethnic differences being converted into a resource for collective enrichment, it has instead been turned into a destructive monster of communal hate that has practically destroyed Guyana.

Another negative example relates to religious diversity. In a number of cases, Pentecostalism and main stream Christianity have drawn swords so that discord defines much of a public culture among citizenry. Religious differences in Trinidad and Guyana have also become a source of discord. In other places, indigenous religions such as voodun, rastafari, and wenti still fail to receive public recognition and are often stigmatised. These are only a few cases of differences turned into disadvantages. There are many others. What is needed is a public policy that recognises legitimate differences (as against pathological ones), and encourages their expression, molding them into instruments of public gain and enrichment. Liberation from poverty can come from capitalising on the differences that define us. No instance better illustrates the need for recognising and empowering diversity than in the sphere of local democracy and decentralisation. To this we turn.

Decentralisation and Local Autonomy: Against Dispowerment of Place

The Caribbean landscape is rich in local diversity. Even though it has been constructed on the crossroads of trade and migration and has been endowed with a bequest of small and open systems which were always easily pierced and penetrated by external forces, even on the shifting sands of constant change, the Caribbean people were able to construct a stable identity around local communities and townships. An 'ethno-local' identity pervades all parts of the

Caribbean, conferring not only uniqueness to the region but to separate clusters of settlement, all constructed on a familiar landscape and history in slavery, indenture, and plantations. In the contemporary world where new massive forces of globalisation strongly buffet the Caribbean, these ethno-local identities, which provide deep anchorage in survival and pride, are threatened in unprecedented ways. Centralised governments and their domineering administrative systems have compounded the difficulty in preserving local identities.

The first demand is for recognition of place-based communities so as to return power to the people, developing more effective decision-making based on local needs, broadening political responsibility, and simultaneously preserving Caribbean traditions at the grassroots, thereby accommodating local diversity and accelerating development as a broadly conceived multi-faceted project. The fact of prevailing Caribbean democracy is that in its practices it is a farce. It barely exists except as a pretence parading in the form of public obeisance to centralised political and administrative authorities which bear little accountability to the populace. Everywhere, the main motif of governance is a top-down format of government-citizen relations. Authoritarian practices inhere in the centralised structures of administration which daily touch the lives of citizens who for the most part have been reduced to supplicants. A culture of pleading and clientelism, not effective participation and control, defines citizen orientation to the public administration and the system of political decision-making throughout the region.

The need exists at policy level to decentralise power meaningfully to local communities. Decentralisation does not refer to administrative devolution of duties to smaller units, but to the transfer of meaningful power and decision-making as well as funds and taxing capabilities to local communities. Over the years of top-to-bottom directed dominance by both the colonial and nationalist governments, centralisation has proceeded apace, depriving local communities of their autonomy and pride. Statistics can easily be adduced to show that the pattern of central government growth as a percentage of GNP has continued unabated, even though recently stifled by the market theology of divestment and privatisation.

If local particularities are recognised and encouraged, grass roots diversity will no doubt thrive. Julius Nyerere used to say that development is not what is done for people but what people do for themselves by themselves. The opposite is to do development for them, administer it from above and let them take it or leave it. At present, the level of participation is mainly confined to the act of lining up and voting every four or five years. Centralisation in politics and economy has disempowered local communities, reducing most to backwater enclaves of underdevelopment. Decentralisation is about evolving a more participant system.

Participation is about inclusion in the process of decision-making of a society as a matter of right. It is a proven and effective strategy of development. Participation permits individuals and communities to articulate their interests by speaking, petitioning, organising, and mobilising support. Such participation tends to confer a sense of belonging and efficacy and often fosters an open order with an ethos of equality, opinion exchange and compromise. In a meaningful sense, a democratic order is a system which recognises equality and fairness in the representation of rival viewpoints conferring a tenor of participation in membership. The benefits of inclusionary membership in the practices of collective decision-making at all levels of government, especially at small scale face-to-face local levels, are incontestable. To begin with, it bestows a sense of belonging and loyalty to communities. It curtails anomie and structural dissatisfaction which have accompanied the centralisation of governments, providing open fora for the articulation and redress of interests and grievances. It releases civic energy to serve the collective good. It encourages sacrifice in service of a transcendental public interest for the sustenance of a social psychology of collective identification in membership. Each democracy designs its own institutions to embody the ideals of participation in full membership. In the context of our discussion, participation refers mainly to the sharing of power and responsibilities in a decentralised political order in the Caribbean. The denial of participation in access to decision-making tends to weaken the state and delegitimise a political order. Throughout the Caribbean, centralised state power has witnessed widespread citizen cynicism regarding their belonging in the state and efficacy in influencing public decisions. Centralisation has meant exclusion and exclusion is often expressed in distortions of social existence in marginalisation and disempowerment. Exclusion can extend to individuals as well as entire communities, degrading and diminishing their identity, their way of life, self images and economic well being.

When added together, the exclusionary features of membership in the polity through practices of centralisation of power demonstrate a mountain of potential discontent and alienation tending to human disaster of major proportions. Caribbean citizens have been literally disenfranchised from their own land by their own leaders. The practices of exclusion are often institutionalised as a routine part of a regime of knowledge that justifies the order and organisation of the state that is accepted unquestioningly as natural. Victims come to accept their condition and recite the ideology of justification of the hegemonic group that normalises their marginalisation. Centralisation assumes the form of a natural and inevitable order. It has become deeply entrenched and ideologised.

For those who truly know the Caribbean, it is indeed a place of a multiplicity of local cultures and communities every where different, with local accents, resources, games, natural sights, stories, meeting places, and cuisines. When a Caribbean person speaks of their identity, in a very meaningful sense, they are frequently referring to the small localities and communities where life was first nurtured. Homeland meant an area of common communication and interaction in familiarity.[5] But it is much more than that, for it suggests a shared consciousness, a spatial structure in temporal depth – historical memory, and the veritable mental and emotional environment of the individual.[6] It is a 'home' with biological connection inscribed in images of the motherland. The idea of homeland then, is pregnant with powerful symbolism of belonging. For most Caribbeans their images of a separate and unique identity is derived from their association with the shores and scenes, the special sights and sounds, of their particular Caribbean localities. It is these local communities and neighbourhoods in all their diversity which are the physical expression of home that has nurtured their identity. And wherever they are found away from home, the images of these localities in the Caribbean assume the shape of a metaphor for life itself. Many Caribbean peoples who have migrated for decades and not returned home live in a sort of nostalgic dreamland of their ancestral local environment that sustains their claim to a separate identity. Many make periodic treks back home as if enacting a life-reinvigorating ritual to an ancient mystic Mecca.

The Caribbean homeland localities are recent inventions born on the anvil of struggle which instills a special pride of place. Homeland had to be reinvented in the localities of the New World and transformed into a moral architecture of the mind and memory. Into these new insular spaces, narratives and myths would be infused with memories constructed out of the recent painful past and attached to the land rendering it sacred and historical. Thus would deep attachments be constructed in the many diverse communities throughout the Caribbean.

Caribbean peoples are new arrivals who have had to reconstruct their identities, having lost most of what they had in the transmigration from the Old World. St Lucian Nobel laureate, Derek Walcott, noted:

"That is the basis of the Antillean experience, this shipwreck of fragments, these echoes, these shards of a huge tribal vocabulary, these partially remembered customs. They survived the Middle Passage and the *Fatel Razack*, the ship that carried the first indentured Indians from the port of Madras to the cane fields, that carried the chained Cromwellian convict and the Sephardic Jew, the Chinese grocer and the Lebanese merchants selling clothes samples on his bicycle".[7]

This melody of memory applies to the polyglot descendants of the new Caribbean natives, separated from their Old World roots even though cultural residues persist in one form or the other.[8]

In the face of centralised administrations, local pride in the homeland communities and neighbourhoods has diminished and indigenous diversity slighted. Delocalisation and disempowerment of place-based communities stimulated migration to cities where all the fun and jobs exist. With the virtual collapse of local government throughout the Caribbean, a story of de-democratisation is implicated. Central rationality is the only legitimate mode of development that is recognised. Local knowledge and particularities are peripheralised and belittled. Local communities need to be offered political space to speak for themselves, to find their own voices, and present their own authentic local needs and interests.

The importance of resuscitating local pride and local government in part is accentuated by the diminishing salience of the state in the face of globalisation. Local spaces are now becoming the areas of true participant citizenship. These diverse communities must be encouraged to become the locus of a vibrant participant Caribbean life. Policy directs the future and this is clearly an area where policy can construct the conditions of recovering Caribbean pride and citizenship in all of its rich grassroots diversity. Place-based communities and local knowledge must be given incentives to voice their interests, to free themselves from central directives in all details of their lives, to recover their autonomy and to take control of their destiny. Local power is about liberation. The suffrage which was once fought for by our independence movements has been lost in the labyrinth of centralised political and administrative power placed in the hands of our own leaders. A second revolution is required in the decentralisation of power and administration in returning power to the people. How can this be done? It is essential that the politics of this sort of change be understood.

Decentralisation and devolution of power and responsibilities will not be easy. The process is deeply implicated in the struggle for power. The decentralisation of a system of government is not like the shuffling of a deck of cards, but in a more appropriate metaphor, can be likened to the dismantling of a pyramid of power. It entails the redistribution of power and privileges and the creation of new politically powerful and competitive actors at the periphery of the polity. It is like a zero-sum game in which the distribution of powers results in some actors losing at the same time that others gain power. The centre will lose to the local. For this reason the decentralisation exercise must be seen as a sort of radical and revolutionary rearrangement of the internal configuration of power arrangements in the state. Few states and their established leaders readily concede the decentralisation of powers so that those who wish to see the devolution of meaningful power transfers must be willing to struggle for it. Once decentralisation has been conceded, a new form of consultative politics marked by constant bargaining must take place for the system to be preserved. Decentralisation calls for a system of accommodation and a moderate leadership at all levels of the government.

Existing practices by central governments underscore and reflect the asymmetrical relations between the dominant centre and the weak local communities across the Caribbean. Current policies of the state entrench the distribution of power and resources in the relations between the state and place-based groups. Most local groups are prevented from gaining significant access to the state and are likely to see the state and its policies as the instrument of their oppression. Where these communities have organised their demands and agitated for change, they therefore seek a redefinition of their relationship to the state so as to control policies related to their own needs. In this regard, they frequently seek greater internal autonomy in an extensively decentralised political system. Failing this seek, many simply live in passive ineffective languor.

At one level, the issue broadly turns on the challenge of redefining the heterogenous state as the appropriate unit of citizenship and international organisation. At another level, the focus is on the problem of resource allocation, identity, and recognition within the distributive dimension of the polity. How are the claims of regions and place-based communities for representation and equity to be reconciled with the equally powerful imperative of the central government for efficiency and internal unity of the state? The arguments of both centre and periphery are powerful and often attached to strong emotions. In a few notable cases involving larger local communities such as Tobago, Barbuda, and Nevis, the conflict has assumed the form of a protracted struggle that can cripple the state. While these cases are dramatic examples of larger units seeking greater autonomy, they only attest to a less visible demand by numerous small scale communities for a more meaningful sharing of power between centre and periphery throughout the Caribbean. The problem raises fundamental theoretical questions on the nature of the state as a site of conferring community and belonging. There is one factor among the many forces which can address the problem of the neglect of local power and that is a variety of public policies and institutional practices which can encourage community formation for political purposes and claims for material shares and symbolic recognition. At a more general level, the problem of uneven development and the associated issues of relative deprivation, neglect, and exploitation and discrimination of local communities can be pointedly corrected by public policies aimed at decentralising the state.

Decentralisation, Social Movements and Civil Society

Connected to decentralisation of political power is the area of social movements. These are autonomous citizen bodies which are organised around gender, environmental, cultural and other interests. These voluntary associations are often referred to as 'civil society'. They constitute an intermediate tier of citizen life which occupies the zone between individual life and the state. They often strive to represent local interests in all of its diversity bringing vibrancy and accountability to public discourse and life. Public policy should aim at fostering the emergence of these bodies. They are likely to arise in the spaces which are created by an extensively decentralised political order.

Civil society needs to be revived in the Caribbean. Centralised governance has tended to become insensitive to citizens' interests. Community associations and local movements can best respond to the needs of their specific environments in diverse locations. Numerous small communities are threatened by large corporations which exploit local resources in logging, minerals, natural sights like beaches, reefs, and other items. Small scale social movements, such as environmental bodies, can best protect local interests by making corporations into sensitive citizens. These social movements often can tap into similar groups internationally for support. Indigenous, environmental, womens', and other groups have done this with great effect. Local civil movements offer the critical space where the local and global meet.

Social movements are best able to identify the particularities of our diversity for representation, protecting them as well as promoting them. They are best equipped to ensure that accountability in the performance of public duties are carried out. They can mobilise local citizens, educate them, and pressure governments and corporations to respond to public opinion. The interests which social movements can represent can cover a vast array of our diverse interests. These groups can identify and organise groups around cultural interests in music, dance, culinary expressions, historic sites, and language forms. Indigenous cultural forms are an endangered species in the Caribbean as cable TV grabs more and more of the recreation time of our citizens. The loss of local pride helps this process of self-destruction. Local movements are best equipped to point to and protect the cultural interests which are involved in the destruction of ancient sites, natural sanctuaries and sights, and historic locations used for traditional functions. Our diverse cultural heritage and practices linked to various sites and events are our finest forms of wealth. Indigenous social movements are best attuned to these interests and can act to protect them.

No government is large enough to cater to citizen demands in all the areas which require attention. This gap is best filled by voluntary associations in civil society. The governmental order needs to encourage and be sensitive to social movements. A decentralised order can provide the political space for citizen activity and government accountability at all levels of Caribbean society.

Conclusion: Diversity and a Multiple Caribbean Citizenship in a Globalised International Order

To understand how peoples in the Caribbean cohere into cultural communities, how they differ, how they act in solidarity and individually, one may look at the diverse bases on which they have tended to define themselves. These bases include such factors as homeland, language, religion, race, and customs, or what Clifford Geertz called the 'givens of social existence'.[9] These bases have a tendency to organise life into identity and solidarity formations which command the behavior of its members.[10] It is in the analysis of their identities especially at the level of locality and region constructed from real or imaginary claims that we shall also be able to evaluate how these identities can be mobilised for intra-regional and extra-regional effects with repercussions on international politics and society.

A multiple-headed Caribbean identity has now been forged by both residents in the Caribbean and those overseas attesting to the truism that to survive in the global present requires simultaneity in several spaces. While this schizophrenic split at one time described only a small Caribbean group overseas, today it applies with few exceptions to practically every home, village, and township throughout the Caribbean. The Caribbean is truly wherever Caribbean peoples reside in the insular areas of the Caribbean Sea as well as in metropolitan areas everywhere.

In effect, in the Caribbean as elsewhere, the contemporary state can now no longer lay on its citizens any sort of exclusive claim to cultural identity or attempts to impose one.[11] The massive movement of Caribbean peoples to metropolitan centres has created another sphere of contest in the construction of an identity. Caribbean peoples insist that they are 'Caribbean' regardless of where they live, holding on to all their partial alien identities as well. As elsewhere it all points to the restructuring of the state as an artifact of meaningful human association. The modern person in quest of personal identity finds that the old homeland increasingly assumes the form of a fragmented place of exile challenged as the very center of its gravity in a sea of new global contests. While from the inside the state is assaulted as a repository of personal meaning, from the outside it is buffeted by globalising transnational forces that ignore its sphere of governance. The secure self needs new boundaries of belonging. Caribbean peoples have now been forced to renegotiate their identities creating new mental mixes from their old insular spheres and new metropolitan residences.

Among the identities which the typical Caribbean person ascribes to self, is what can be called the ethno-local identity. It refers to consciousness of oneself as belonging to some community or neighbourhood. The decentralised self finds solace and meaningfulness in these communities. A policy of decentralisation, cutting across all services normally found in the central government such as health services, education, housing, community development, and agriculture, should be decentralised as is happening in the area of health services throughout the Caribbean. Such an event would more than likely add vibrancy to localities. This level of identity will coexist with a national, regional, and an overseas identity each offering a different level of loyalty to citizenship attachment to the state.[12]

Multiple identities are a reality of life and attests to the plural habitats of the Caribbean citizen. There are similarly other aspects of pluralism which needs to be accommodated in the identity structure of the Caribbean person apart from territorially-based communities. Decentralisation is about recognition of spatial and territorial expression of attachment at the grassroots. It is about participation, pluralism and development. In a similar vein, other forms of pluralism need to be accommodated in the diversity kaleidoscope of the Caribbean, among these gender, religious, language, and cultural differences. Structures of dominance and hierarchy which operate in these areas should be dismantled in general pattern of recognising and celebrating diversity in the Caribbean. It is the general strategy used to tap all of the varied resources for collective and individual development. Rather than seeing diversity and difference among the 33 million residents of the Caribbean as a threat to unity, it should be viewed as fundamental to our identity and the foundation for development and liberation of our physical and spiritual potential. This spirit should permeate all aspects of public policy.

Notes

1. N Gardels, 'Two Concepts of Nationalism: Interview with Isaiah Berlin', *New York Review of Books*, November 21, 1991, p. 19
2. F Barth, ed, 'Introduction', in *Ethnic Groups and Boundaries* (1969), p. 9
3. B Anderson, *Imagined Communities* (London: Verso Publications, 1991), revised edition, p. 6
4. FW Knight, 'Societies of the Caribbean Since Independence', in *Democracy n the Caribbean*, JI Dominguez et al, eds (Baltimore: Johns Hopkins Press, 1993), p. 38
5. See Steven Grosby, 'Territoriality: The Transcendental, Primordial Features of Modern Societies', *Nations and Nationalism*, July 1995, pp. 145-6
6. Ibid

7. Derek Walcott, *The Antilles: Fragments of an Epic Memory* (New York: Farrar, Strauss, Giroux, 1992), p. 9
8. Ibid
9. C Geertz, 'Primordial Sentiments and Civic Politics in the New States: The Integrative Revolution', in *Old Societies and New States*, C Geertz, ed (Free Press, 1963), p. 109. See also Ralph R Premdas, 'The Anatomy of Ethnic Conflict' in *The Enigma of Ethnicity: An Analysis of Race and Ethnicity in the Caribbean and the World*, R Premdas, ed. (Trinidad: University of the West Indies Press, St Augustine, 1993), p.2
10. Ibid
11. See Crawford Young, *The Rising Tide of Cultural Pluralism: Twilight of the Nation State?* (Madison: University of Wisconsin Press, 1994)
12. See Ralph Premdas, *Ethnic Identity in the Caribbean: Decentering a Myth* (Notre Dame: Kellogg Institute of International Studies, University of Notre Dame, 1996), monograph no 234

18 | BARRINGTON CHEVANNES

Those Two Jamaicas:
The Problem of Social Integration

Social integration has been central to the social sciences ever since MG Smith. To be more precise it concerns the place of the Africans/blacks in the post-emancipation societies of the anglophone Caribbean, and the place of Indians in Guyana and Trinidad and Tobago, where they once formed a significant, and now a majority, ethnic grouping.

Social and cultural pluralism was based on two premises. One was an institutionalised formulation of culture. Thus cultural differences are differences in institutional patterns - marriage, family, religion, education, sports and recreation, and so on. The other was that only state power held culturally diverse groups together.

Pluralism was vigorously attacked since its inception. At the beginning Lloyd Braithwaite, basing his attack on the premise that no society can exist without a shared value system, maintained that even in culturally diverse Trinidad, values such as education and colour preferences transcended class and ethnicity. Thirty years later Don Robotham carried on a bitter debate with Smith, exposing pluralism as a cover-up for the failure of the brown middle class to acculturate the black populace, and hence premised on a pessimistic post-independence future. In between, many had difficulty with the idea of race and colour as some sort of social glue, and not one serious Caribbean scholar was won over by pluralism, with the exception of a few who used the model to explain the bitter cleavages between Africans and Indians in Guyana. No school of cultural pluralism developed among Caribbean intellectuals.

Why not? Most scholars, I believe, sensed in pluralism an extremism which, except for Guyana and a very brief period around the time of emancipation, did not reflect the lived reality of the Caribbean. The withdrawal of colonial power did not result in the disintegration of the social order. And yet, most had to agree that there were indeed differences in the institutional life of the peoples. That these differences also paralleled class differentiation allowed some to offer a short-lived Marxist paradigm which, by reducing cultural differences to differences of class, explained social disintegration as an inherent feature of class-divided society, and social integration, wherever it existed, by hegemony. The failure of Marxist praxis to achieve working class hegemony, and therefore a new social integration, in the Caribbean was quickly followed by the demise of Marxism as an explanatory tool. It had been quite weak on the cultural question, and was never at home with the folk culture, African or Indian.

We are still faced with the task of explaining the basis of social integration among societies that are internally culturally differentiated, and of identifying the threats to it. Using the Jamaican experience, I propose an angle from which I believe light can be shed on the problem.

Code Switching

Our scholars in linguistics use the concept of code switching to identify a sort of bilingualism among Caribbean Creole speakers. The 'Creoles', or patois, are generally agreed to be languages with a largely anglophone, francophone or Hispanic lexicographical base, but with underlying structures that are closer to African than to European languages. That Creole speakers are also fluent in European languages make them bilingual. However, linguists speak not of bilingualism but of code switching. Creole and European languages are, among Creole speakers, not merely languages, but codes. They are not just media for the expression of thoughts, but their uses are codes for class positioning, orientation and meaning, or for personal advantage and power. Code switching is an expression of the inequality between languages. Speakers know the codes, and know when and when not to use them.

In Jamaica, it is this ability to switch from patois to English that misleads both those who are arguing for some sort of official recognition of patois, as well as those who believe that it is simply some form of perversity why people do not use English. The unfortunate result of the latter tendency is to assume that English need not be taught.

Code switching as a paradigm can explain why two Jamaicas have not just merely coexisted but have together formed an apparent status quo which gives the appearance of social integration through a common value system. Nothing could be further from the truth. Two Jamaicas do exist, but because the other Jamaica, the Jamaica of the Creole speakers, knows how to code switch, both Jamaicas appear to exist on the same plane. The people take advantage of both worlds, seeking to maximise opportunities.

I would argue that there are three prerequisites to code switching. First there must be inequality. If the languages are equal, then it matters little which is used, when. I know of no island of the region where the Creole has equal status, not even in Curacao where *papiamento* is used freely by political and religious leaders, or in St Lucia, where the same may be observed about *kweyol*. Second, there must be some value to the subordinate language, other than sheer ignorance, to explain its persistence. A sense of identity may provide ample reason for the persistence. But where, as in the Jamaican patois, new words are constantly being invented, it would appear that the language is also valued for its aptness. Third, an advantage must be discerned which would cause a speaker to switch codes. Let me now give three examples of cultural practices which I believe may be understood by using the device of code switching.

The first pertains to land tenure. An enterprising couple worked their way up and managed to buy an 11-acre property of coffee, cocoa and timber, which they put to commercial use. They bought a smaller property of four acres, on which they set up their home. After the death of her husband, the wife – now old and retired and the head of the family – subdivided the first property into equal plots for her children, with new titles, but the second she willed as family land.

Family land, which is found all over the Caribbean, is land bequeathed by an ancestor, male or female, to his or her descendants in perpetuity. It functions as a source of identity and security for members of the lineage group. All lineage members have usufruct and burial rights on family land. As Jean Besson argues, family land gives symbolic unity to the lineage; the living, their ancestors, and those yet to be born.

Here we have side by side, in one and the same family, two different uses of land and two different meanings of tenure. In one, land can be owned, like a horse or pig or house. In the other, land can only be used. The legal system recognises the former, but not the other. One can acquire a legal title over land, but there is no system that allows title to a lineage. From newspaper research of death announcements carried out a few years ago, in which nearly 30 per cent of interments took place in 'family plots', I am led to believe that a significantly large number of parcels of land are either family land or earmarked as such. The process begins when persons with legal tenure bequeath land as family land. The land probably reverts to legal tenure after a few generations. The point I am making is that quietly, without making any big fuss, the African-Jamaican peasants, living in a world structured by others, take advantage of it, while retaining an understanding and use of land all their own, with a different function. In the language of pluralism they practice the same institution in two different ways.

My second example is marriage and the family. It is astonishing that with all of the studies on the black family in the Caribbean, so little is understood of the value system underlying it. But it is not really astonishing, because it has largely been diagnosed as pathological. For a pathology it is extraordinarily persistent. Even in the most Roman Catholic of countries, where the majority of people are black, and where sex before marriage is a mortal sin, the overwhelming majority of births are to unwed mothers, many not yet separated from their families of orientation. Conjugal relations pass from the more unstable to greater and greater stability, from casual to visiting to common law unions, to legal marriage. It is not that people are not legally married, but they understand legal marriage, not as the legitimising of sexuality, but as the bestowing of social respectability. With marriage come things other than the mere joining of a couple as man and wife. Both increase their standing in the eyes of the community and are expected to behave in a manner befitting this status. Men, particularly, do not rush, but grow into marriage. When they do, they seldom divorce. Both Church and state, on the other hand, see marriage as the gateway to sexual cohabitation.

As for the concept of family itself, it is understood not as a nuclear unit but as an extended network connected by blood. Blood does not mean the same thing to the English as it does to the black Jamaicans. For one thing, there is no such thing as a 'half-sister' or a 'half-brother'. One is recognised as 'sister by mi father side', or 'brother by mi mother side'. This is why family land legacies include 'outside' children as well.

A third example is drawn from religious practice. Observers used to talk of 'dual membership' to describe the adherence by one and the same people to two different, almost opposing, religious orientations. People used to claim nominal membership in the establishment churches – Anglican, Baptist, Methodist, Moravian, and so on – but at the same time practice a spirituality that was unmistakably African – belief in the powers and possession by the powers. They attended church on Sunday morning and the Revival or balm yard on Sunday night. The church, with all its respectability, gave them access to social mobility, the Revival yard, for all its low social standing, gave them spiritual fulfillment. Culturally speaking, these are two different traditions, although Revival borrowed extensively from Christianity. Their belief systems are different, their rituals are different, and all their underlying worldviews are different.

Dual membership has disappeared now, because by making internal adjustments and by making external linkages with North American Pentecostalism, Revival has gained in respectability. Only now is it possible for the people Rex Nettleford likes to refer to as 'ladies of quality' to fall in the aisles, writhing in the spirit. Pentecostalism has grown by leaps and bounds since these developments. In 1960 it accounted for no more than 13 per cent of the nominal church membership, with the Anglican and Baptist denominations accounting for nearly 40 per cent between them. Forty years later, Pentecostalism accounts for nearly 30 per cent, while the Anglican and Baptist churches together barely account for 20. Now it enjoys equal status with the establishment churches.

As with these examples in the institutional life of the Jamaican people, so with other areas. They know how to operate in two worlds at the same time, switching from one to the other, as it suits. Fundamentally, I believe they retain a world outlook that has been derived from African world outlooks brought here and renewed over the centuries by incoming Africans, but reconfiguring and incorporating elements from the new social and physical environment.

What are the implications of all this? Where Jamaica appears to be a socially integrated society, it is because the people code switch. It is sad to think that law has attracted the brightest minds, judging by 'A' Level applicants to the University and by the number of Rhodes Scholars who turn to law. Yet in forty years of independence there has not developed a jurisprudence capable of reflecting our Caribbean realities. Law, unfortunately for us, means English Law. From a sociological point of view, law is the codification of social and culturally meaningful practice. Lawyers, politicians (most of whom are lawyers) and jurists who value the people as a resource cannot but be concerned at the deficiency of the legal system and become advocates for its reform in the direction of reflecting the culture of the people. It is remarkable that the things we highlight and value as markers of our national identity are things which for the most part derive from the people: music, the performing arts, cuisine, language, even the people we salute as heroes. Social integration is not possible without social recognition.

This also suggests that the social disintegration which some see taking place in Jamaica, to the extent that one can classify murders as such, is a function of our failure to recognise by legitimisation the *other* Jamaica. After 160 years, this country remains not one but *two* Jamaicas, divided not so much by social class as by thinking.

19 TYRONE FERGUSON

Social Disintegration in the Context of Adjustment and Globalisation:
The Caribbean Experience

This presentation has two focal points. It will first look at the issue of social disintegration in the Caribbean within the context of political economy adjustment and globalisation. Second, it will examine the international response, reflected in donor consensus, on the strategy and policy options to deal with this issue.

The interlinked processes of adjustment and globalisation are having devastating perverse outcomes in Caribbean countries, pushing many to the verge of societal breakdown. It should be noted that this condition is not unique to Caribbean countries, but is widespread within the developing world. The basic argument is that, in face of growing socioeconomic instabilities, after nearly two decades of adjustment experimentation in these countries, the donor community, as is its wont, is once again evolving a new consensus, revolving around issues of equity and social justice. In other words, we are on the verge of another redefinition of the development problematic, effectively captured in the concept of 'globalisation with a human face'.

It should come as no surprise to anyone familiar with the evolution of donor outlook on development that this is so. The history of post-World War II donor involvement in development, as gleaned from the ideological and operational aspects, is the fundamental change in perspectives on a decade-by-decade basis. Going back to the 1960s, each decade has been marked by new outlooks in this regard. For instance, in the 1970s, the prevailing wisdom was embodied in the strategy of poverty alleviation, but a decade on, there was more poverty and inequality. In the 1980s, it was structural adjustment, but by the end of that decade, there was still more poverty and inequality. Going back to the drawing-board, donors stressed that structural adjustment was absolutely necessary, but that they had missed a crucial insight – the imperative of good governance. So, the 1990s have been the era of structural adjustment and good governance. Now as the twenty-first century unfolds, notwithstanding the fact, in the words of World Bank president James Wolfensohn that 'we are putting a lot of money into developing countries', poverty and inequality are increasing (*Annual World Bank Conference on Economic Development, 1998*). The time is ripe, therefore, for a new outlook on development. In a sense, developing countries have served essentially as guinea pigs for constantly shifting donor-preferred strategies as the prevailing strategy fails miserably. The concern for us in the Caribbean, therefore, particularly in light of the extremely fragile social frameworks in so many of these countries is: how do we respond to this evolving consensus?

The presentation begins by a brief setting of the context generating social dislocation and disintegration in the Caribbean. It then briefly surveys the complex of interacting social disabilities with which these countries are beset. Next, it identifies the basic sources and orientation of the emerging consensus which I mentioned earlier and it concludes by essaying some thoughts with regard to potential lines of action and an approach for Caribbean countries facing this situation.

The Context of Social Dislocation and Disintegration

As our various Caribbean societies and peoples expectantly approach the historical milestone of a new millennium – the beginning of the twenty-first century – it is appropriate that we take stock of our existing condition and try to come to some conclusions about what is in store for us. Such a stock-taking necessarily has to take account of domestic factors, but also of international factors, for the obvious reason that the global transforming environment in which we are living is a decisive influence on both our existing condition and the prospects for our future. For our purposes, the stress is paid to global developments which have come to exert a decidedly determinative influence on the options we have, the shaping of our responses and the outlook in terms of how we will fare in the evolving circumstances.

The essential point of departure of this brief presentation is a hard-nosed awareness of certain fundamental realities in the overall operating environment of Caribbean countries. We live in a global transforming environment of unprecedented complexity and scope, dominated by certain transcending ideological trends. This is a world of the preeminence of the market, a world dominated by the forces of global integration, liberalisation, deregulation and privatisation. In contrast, it is a world of a retreating state, a devalued state. It is a world also of expanding democratisation within the Western democratic traditions. Today, we are all capitalists and we are all democrats.

We live in an exceedingly harsh world – a world without a soul, it would seem. We are required unavoidably to function in the hard fact of a globalised world. It is a world that is intolerant of and impatient with failure to adjust – whether within the framework of externally imposed and supervised structural adjustment or self-induced reform measures to equip countries to function, to survive and ideally to exploit the opportunities of globalisation. Adjustment and globalisation are the defining parameters of our operating contexts. It is a world, moreover, dominated by certain multilateral institutional forces that are exceptionally influential in policy-making in many of our countries. Some would say they have usurped it.

In a lecture delivered on the occasion of the UWI's 50th Anniversary in 1998, entitled 'West Indian Space in the Twenty-first Century', Sir Shridath Ramphal captured the fundamental dilemma that this global transforming context poses for us in the Caribbean: 'The world would certainly miss us were we gone, yet it would survive. But we could not survive without the world – not as we are or as we want to be . . .'

This historic point of departure for us, as he put it,

will involve challenges we have not faced before . . . They are not about staying as we are at home and enlarging our chances abroad. They are about enlarging those chances through adapting ourselves at home to new realities in the global economic scene – through influencing those realities as best we can, of course; but in the end through being a part of what is unquestionably a new global economic scene. (p.14)

The choice for us, therefore, is whether we are going to be helpless, resigned, conforming to externally imposed definitions of our political-economy condition and the resultant prescriptive remedies emanating from these sources – as has been the case for most of the 1980s and 1990s. Or, rather, on the basis of a concerted, but pragmatic assessment of that environment, are we going to assert a decisive role for ourselves in crafting the types of appropriate responses to deal with our condition? In short, are we going to insist on a voice in seeking sustainable and workable solutions for our conditions? I dare say that one of the evident social disruptions caused by adjustment and globalisation is a popular perception, particularly among the young, that we are not in control, that we have no role in defining our reality, that the immense sacrifices that are being borne by the vast majority of our peoples are at the behest of external forces and reward only a few, primarily foreign interests. The upshot is growing incidences of social alienation.

This ideological context of a pre-eminent market and a retreating state – the so-called minimalist state – represents a tremendous problematic for social integration, cohesion and stability, particularly in societies such as ours in the Caribbean. As the issue was posed by Dani Rodrik in his book,

the most serious challenge for the world economy in the years ahead lies in making globalisation compatible with domestic social and political stability – or to put it even more directly, in ensuring that international economic integration does not contribute to domestic social disintegration. (*Has Globalisation Gone Too Far?*, p.2)

The fact of the matter is that markets do not have a soul or a conscience. From a historical vantage-point, it has been recognised that unfettered or unconstrained markets are inimical to such basic human values as equality, equity and social justice, even as they are naturally oblivious to undesirable social outcomes. Markets do not have in-built mediating mechanisms to deal with such outcomes. In fact, markets are effectively reflective of a social Darwinism that can be cruelly destructive in the context of developing societies where compensatory institutions and mechanisms are generally minimal and inadequate.

It was in recognition of this crucial reality that in the past a consensus developed around the vital role to be played by the state in terms of strategic interventions to mitigate the pernicious social effects of market functioning. From this perspective, then, the primacy of markets in the framework of structural adjustment, on the one hand, and globalisation, on the other, has confronted Caribbean countries with the powerful dilemma of how to address the inevitable social dislocations that have come in their wake in the face of an increasingly disabled state.

If we agree with John Maynard Keynes that, 'The political problem of mankind is to combine these things: economic efficiency, social justice and individual liberty', then the globalisation process, as it is inexorably unfolding before our eyes in practical terms, embodies a glaring deficiency that is of acute relevance to the topic at hand – social integration and disintegration in the Caribbean. Its driving imperatives of economic efficiency and the triumph of individual liberty in a world of expanding democratisation and more extensive and profound webs of civil society were not, until relatively recently, matched by any articulated concern by the major governors of the global political economy for the third prong of this tripod – social justice.

A tremendous irony of the present conjuncture for us in the Caribbean is the fact that post-colonial Caribbean societies have generally had public policy frameworks that have been suffused by a worthy social ethos – an ethos at the core of which have been the fundamental values of equality, equity, social justice and the like. There have been societies, like Guyana, where they have been constitutionally underwritten, where social and economic rights were given pride of place in terms of constitutional aspirations.

Let us recall that structural adjustment, as implemented by several Caribbean countries, was particularly destructive in relation to the social foundations. It forced on them an inhumane abrupt retrenchment from their generally strong commitment to state provisioning in such key basic social sectors as education and health, as well as in general programmes of social security relief. It catapulted into societal marginalisation a whole new class of poor. In multi-ethnic contexts such as Guyana's, it introduced severe tensions into inter-ethnic relations on the basis of perceptions by discrete groups of being severely disadvantaged by adjustment programmes, while others were substantially privileged. It has had substantial fall-out in terms of gender relations, as already disadvantaged women have had to bear a disproportionate share of the adjustment burden.

Very late in the process, the external sponsors of structural adjustment, the bilateral and multilateral donors, conceded the negative social consequences of adjustment, but saw these undesirable outcomes as essentially short-run in duration. The experience of countries such as Guyana and Jamaica – the former enmeshed in adjustment programmes for more than a decade to date and the latter for more 15 years – have confounded that claim since the social dislocations have not merely persisted, but have intensified and worsened throughout the life of the implementation of adjustment.

Globalisation has contributed to the severe rending of the social fabric in Caribbean societies by way of various instruments. It is apposite at this point to pinpoint the extensive range of socially disintegrative forces that are being fed by some of the operational elements of globalisation. These forces include the rise of ethnic tensions in multi-ethnic societies such as Guyana, growing inequality and poverty, the tragic and destructive prevalence of drugs, crime and arms trafficking, such troubling health issues as the HIV/AIDS epidemic that is wreaking havoc on so many of our people, particularly the young, and the pernicious fact that women have been the biggest losers of the destabilising forces of adjustment and globalisation.

Globalisation significantly expands the threats to the social integrity, social cohesion and stability in Caribbean societies. It reinforces the inherent vulnerability associated with small size and openness. It seriously weakens public policy formulation in regard to social concerns and concomitantly it narrows the scope for effective social provisioning. As stated by the 1999 UNDP *Human Development Report*:

Uneven globalization is bringing not only integration but also fragmentation – dividing communities, nations and regions into those that are integrated and those that are excluded. It not only results in social fragmentation, but represents clear threats to human security.

Social Disintegration in the Caribbean

This leads us to capture the essential social condition that confronts our various Caribbean societies in the present conjuncture. How can we characterise the disintegrating social milieu in which we live today in the Caribbean? Widespread poverty, ethnic breakdown or rising ethnic tensions in certain countries, crime, violence, a culture of drugs, marginalisation, rampant HIV/AIDS, increasing alienation of youth. This is the harsh reality. In the southern extremities of the Caribbean, the three neighbouring countries – Suriname, Guyana and Venezuela – teeter on the edge of complete breakdown, attributable in a significant degree to a complex of social disfunctions. In the northern part of the Caribbean, Haiti is largely non-functioning, and Jamaica faces its own severe social dislocations. In between, who knows where Trinidad and

Tobago will go, even as the other countries of the region confront social disabilities of varying degrees of severity, linked to selected aspects of the above listing?

It is a social condition that, while not characterised by actual social collapse, is one of severe and growing social dislocation and disintegration. It is a social condition where the social deficit widens inexorably as we face the immensely destabilising forces of contemporary globalisation and adjustment. Caribbean countries face a combustible mix of social disabilities. Unacceptable levels of poverty coexist with growing unemployment in many societies and together they are the breeding ground for a host of potentially socially explosive problems. The poor and unemployed are exploited in terms of their involvement with the scourge of drug trafficking and drug abuse, drug-related crime of unprecedented proportions in some of these countries, the presence of increasingly sophisticated and illegal arms, the disturbing HIV/AIDS epidemic – in all of which so many of our young people are significantly implicated as purveyors or victims. The effects of structural adjustment and globalisation also rent the social fabric in another severe manner in multi-ethnic contexts, as exists in some Caribbean countries. Inter-ethnic relations are casualties as major tensions are introduced in the body politic in these societies.

It is true that the issue of ethnic relations is not widespread in the Caribbean – that in terms of the CARICOM countries, the main areas of concern are Guyana, Trinidad and Tobago, and Suriname, the former above all, as it is perched so precariously on the razor's edge of total ethnic breakdown. But ethnic explosions tend to have extensive cross-border consequences; they are not easily confined within national boundaries, and in a subregion of intensifying economic regionalism, this becomes an even more serious probability.

The collapse of the cold war, coupled with the functioning of a globalised political economy, has loosened the shackles of ethnic control. The ethnic genie that was so relatively controlled during the cold war, is out of the bottle in all its stark ugliness, brutality and inhumanity in so many places around the world. Markets can and do impact negatively on inter-ethnic relations and this is especially so in contexts and circumstances where discrete ethnic groups congregate around, and are identified with, discrete economic activities, as is the case in Guyana. The upshot is that the implementation of market processes in this situation has deleterious effects on one group, even as in the perception of that group, it privileges the competing other group. It is a clear recipe for a tension-filled political economy at best, ethnic breakdown and conflagration at worse, especially where passions are inflamed and perceptions reinforced by ethnically-directed political operatives.

Pranab Bardhan captures the issues involved thus:

. . . market expansion may accentuate ethnic problems by increasing inequality, polarisation, dislocation, social fragmentation and the attendant group anxieties. When a country moves to a market system from a system of controls and regulations or from a traditional patron-client system, the consequent resource reallocation rewards the more enterprising and more efficient (and often those who are already better endowed), leaving other individuals and groups behind. (*The Role of Governance in Economic Development*, p 74)

In contexts where the drug syndrome has emerged as a severe destabilising social force, there is the as yet unexplored nexus between the politics of inter-ethnic relations and drugs in several of its crucial manifestations – penetration of political parties via funding and illegal arms that are closely associated with the drug trade. Senior security officials in some Caribbean countries are concerned about this factor, whether in terms of 'tribal' politics in Jamaica or harsh ethnic competition in Guyana. In other words, the drug problem interacts with a range of social disintegrating forces in our societies to complicate the governance efforts in Caribbean societies. The lure of drugs, whether in terms of serving as purveyors or succumbing as victims, is understandably a great attraction for the poor and unemployed. Expanding levels of drug-related crime and violence have been the result. They are fertilised by another aspect of the transnationalised organised drug culture – the illegal trafficking in arms of an increasingly sophisticated type, often beyond the capacity of domestic security establishments to match. Along with poverty, lack of information and resources, this also explains to some extent the disturbingly high prevalence of HIV/AIDS in many Caribbean countries.

The Emerging New Consensus

The dominant donor community has played a pivotal part – and will continue to do in the foreseeable future – in meeting the challenge of development in the developing world. The current fad of adjustment within the framework of globalisation has clearly been a failure. The donor community is acutely seized of the potentially destabilising fall-out from globalisation since they have to deal with rising levels of legal and illegal immigration into their countries, increasing ethnic breakdown, and a burgeoning drug trade, all of which severely disrupt their own social contexts. From that perspective, globalisation's disintegrative effects in large parts of the developing world will increasingly contaminate these countries if left unmanaged.

As the new century approaches, a great sense of urgency is suddenly being shown in the authoritative sectors of the donor community with regard to the issue of social disintegration in the developing world. As the G8 countries noted in their summit communiqué in Cologne last June,

> ... rapid change and integration have left some individuals and groups feeling unable to keep up and have resulted in some dislocation, particularly in developing countries. We therefore need to take steps to strengthen the institutional and social infrastructure that can give globalization a 'human face' and ensure increasing, widely shared prosperity.

World Bank president James Wolfensohn (see *Annual World Bank Conference on Economic Development, 1998*) in noting that the Washington Consensus is dated, has remarked on the emergent general agreement for a new consensus which, while acknowledging that 'it is crucial to have economic growth and to adhere to tried and true monetary and fiscal policies', also conceded,

> ... as we go forward, the larger concerns are for equity and social justice. That is, how can we ensure that market-led economic growth benefits all members of society? And how can we deal with poverty in a framework that promotes environmental sustainability and popular participation and that generates significant results?

The most recent human development report of the UNDP (1999) graphically sums up the dilemma in the heading 'Globalization with a Human Face', in the process representing a not unintended reprise of an earlier UNICEF study of the devastating social consequences of structural adjustment, 'Adjustment with a Human Face'. As that report captures this dilemma,

> When the market goes too far in dominating social and political outcomes, the opportunities and rewards of globalization spread unequally and inequitably – concentrating power and wealth in a select group of people, nations and corporations, marginalizing the others.

It then argues for a globalisation that 'works for people – not just for profits'. This, to my mind, is going to be the fundamental challenge for us in the Caribbean in the years immediately ahead as we continue the necessary and unavoidable path of adjusting to the global transforming environment in which we live. The basic contention is that we are on the verge of a new formulation of the development problematic – as seen from the donor side – derived from insights into the perverse social impacts of globalisation. The argument here is not that there is any disavowal of the basic adjustment strategy that has been at centre-stage for two decades now. Rather, it is that there has been the recognition of the need for its appropriate revision to capture in a more centrally direct and substantive way a solution to social disintegration.

The emergent outlook within the donor community is encapsulated in the laudable goals of equity and social justice. From this perspective, it goes to the heart of the topic at issue today that I have to deal with. Let it be clear that this follows another pattern that has become the norm in the interaction between the donor community and developing countries. The former generally lags behind the latter in terms of some of the key insights into the development problematic. This emergent insight is really nothing new for us in the Caribbean and the wider developing world. Our countries, at both public policy and academic-intellectual levels, have argued incessantly that economic objectives of efficiency, competition and the like are not ends in themselves, but should serve a higher or larger social purpose – that of ensuring that the human element is neither bypassed nor subordinated to them. Issues of equity and social justice have been governing values, at least for us in the Caribbean, as reflected in the laudable efforts in the social areas on a comparative basis within the developing world context. From this perspective, then, we should welcome this emergent ideological change and insofar as we are in agreement with the overall ideological reformulation, we need to ensure that we are in the forefront of elaborating the operational bases for what I perceive to be a new emerging consensus.

Conclusion

In terms of the correlation between the market and the state, it is evident that the state has to play a critical role in assuring social integration and cohesion against the risks of social disintegration. An interventionist state is clearly absolutely necessary. The need, therefore, is for a new synthesis that creates a comfortable working relationship between state and market. And it is here that civil society can emerge to play a vital mediating role between state and market.

There must be a new functional synthesis of state, market and civil society, which collaborates with external donor sources to define and formulate an orientation to economic reform that places issues of equity, equality and justice as the pivotal core of a human value-laden approach to development without prejudice to the proper functioning of markets and efficiency considerations. This would be accompanied by the devising, on an indigenous basis, of an appropriate operational framework of action. The university community, with its comparative advantages in the intellectual realm, would be prevailed upon to contribute in terms of its teaching, research, and consultancy work to play an active part in this regard. A definitive engagement of the multilateral donor community under the framework of globalisation with a human face would fashion new lending arrangements to this end. Civil society would then play a critical role in terms of equity and social justice outcomes. This conference must be seen as the start of this new approach and as a reminder that specific action should be agreed upon to carry forward a defining programme of action regarding collaboration with various sectors.

References

Barhan, Pranab, The Role of Goverance in Economic Development: A Political Economy Approach, OECD, Paris, 1997.

Group of 8, Cologne Summit Communique, 1999.

Ramphal, Shridath, West Indian Space in the Twenty-first Century, Distinguished Lecture on occasion of the 50th Anniversary of the University of the West Indies, July 1998.

Rodrik, Dani, Has Globalisation Gone Too Far? Institute of International Economics, 1997.

UNDP, Human Development Report 1999, Oxford University Press

Wolfensotin, James, Address at Annual World Bank Conference on Development, 1998.

20 | PATRICIA MOHAMMED

City Limits:
Urbanisation and Gender Roles in the Caribbean into the Twenty-first Century

The last decade of the twentieth century marks a major watershed in the evolution of human settlement, for it encompasses the period during which the location of the world's people has become more urban than rural . . . No longer are towns and cities exceptional settlement forms in predominantly rural societies – the world has become an urban place. (David Clark, *Urban World/Global City*)

The Moral Geography of Time and Space

The quality of human life is the fundamental question which should preoccupy us into the twenty-first century. As we pondered on progress from the eighteenth to the twentieth century, the ideas of humanity informed by individual rights and freedoms, of material comfort and being, of well-fed stomachs and enlightened minds, and of technological and scientific revolutions, represented the apogee of progress. At the turn of a new century, there is so much, but owned and commandeered by too few. Rapid strides in technology in the latter half of the twentieth century have not solved many of the problems which beset world populations, even while technological progress itself cannot and should not be reversed. The distance between nations richer and poorer, and between people rich and poor, is not simply a question of the haves and have nots, nor the result of some 'inescapable whim', as observed by

Ernest Mandel (1962, p 441). It is, as Marx wrote in the nineteenth century, a 'history of expropriations'.

The expropriation of the agricultural producer, of the peasant, from the soil, is the basis of the whole process. The history of this expropriation assumes different aspects in the different countries, and runs through its various phases in different orders of succession. (Karl Marx, *Capital*, Vol 1, pp 875–876: 1976)

In the Caribbean, expropriation came in the form of colonial expansion, varying in time and by colonisers in the different territories, but nonetheless variations on a common theme. There is no simple economic, social or political explanation for the existing continuum of development which now places societies that have engineered colonial expansion at the more advantaged end, and those whose labour power and resources were extracted at the more deprived end. These discussions have preoccupied thinkers and scholars for generations, and will continue to do so. At the same time, even while complexity increases, we must find the ways through the labyrinth to understand and deal with them, or else be immobilised by confusion. I am not equating development with computers per capita, sky scrapers or pristine suburban housing. It seems to me that the essence of development is the capacity of a society to provide gainful employment for its population, and to satisfy basic needs such as food, housing, education and health care for all its population. Even while a greater satisfaction of such basic needs has, in the twentieth century, created new ones, the fundamental goals of development will remain fairly fixed as long as these have not yet been met. The question which must confront us as small states in the Caribbean is, how do we achieve the kind of progress, which keeps apace with technological and global advances so that we are not left behind, while ensuring that we do not reproduce the patterns of income distribution and privilege which characterised our earlier and formative years?

One of the more salutary aspects of progress in the twentieth century was that we at least appeared to have some control over our resources and decision-making. A major revolution which has crept up insidiously in the twentieth century, shuffling its feet at times, assuming more strident paces at others, has been the reordering of the social relations of gender. Gender scholarship and activism should not have to spend its time laboriously convincing the uninitiated that masculinity and femininity are two sides of the same coin, both having equal value in the market place. The idea that one sex contributes to the creation of surplus value, while the other has a secondary relationship to production, is primitive baggage to take into the twenty-first century. The majority of the migrant male and female populations introduced into this region were agricultural or industrial wage workers. The notion of a sexual division of labour which protected women and children from either the rigours of field labour as Lucille Mathurin Mair and others have proven, or from the harsh realities of sexual exploitation on the plantations, is a myth that has been sufficiently exploded. What is more accurate is that a blueprint generated by biology for sexually differentiated tasks and responsibilities was more firmly kept in place by ideology and the limits of technology. By the 1960s a profound upheaval occurred in gender relations themselves, in the private and public lives of individual men and women. The capacity for women to effectively control their child bearing, and to defer or space the birth of children, has generally been overlooked in the more populist debates around the question of 'women's liberation'. The metaphor of 'bra burning' which came to symbolise these heady days of women's liberation in the sixties is generally interpreted as a sexual liberation and the ushering in of an era of declining morals among women. It overlooked a more significant long term result. If childbearing and rearing confined women to the home and to jobs which were consistent with their nurturing roles, then a capacity to control 'nature' itself at one level allowed other possibilities to a femininity which had been restricted by the female body. This revolution was by no means geographically bound. Capitalism thrives on the dissemination of its product. One of the first testing grounds for contraception was in the Caribbean itself. In the 1950s the Lippy's loop and later the birth control pill, both devices in their early stages of development, were tested on a large scale on Puerto Rican women and other societies of the region.

The gradual impact of reproductive technology coupled with other harsh twentieth-century economic realities, with increasing female access to education and training and further challenges from marginalised groups, conspired to allow women the framework from which they could confront the question of gender inequality. During this time, masculinity has been largely unwilling or unable to shed its traditional boundaries, its privileges or authority. Understandably so. What the gender revolution offers men and masculinity is not transparent. It is in fact intimidating to many men. Two young female colleagues of mine described their experiences of dealing with their contemporary male peers. Young men are afraid to be chivalrous for fear that they will step on feminist corns. Others, while respecting, or even dependent on the earning power of women, also resent women's independence and new-found confidence. The world has moved on, particularly in the last three decades accelerating into a fast lane, leaving behind those who are either resistant or unwilling to accept change. At the same time, those who take the helm must also carry their passengers cautiously into a new era. In this brave new world of the twenty-first century, feminism and gender must also come of age, shedding victorian secrets and an early self-conscious clothing, to reveal a silken texture of concern about the lives of both sexes.

Recasting the Boundaries of Masculinity and Femininity in the Caribbean

The idea of an idyllic rural Caribbean past, a countryside replete with happy farming communities of extended family networks, where grandmothers and aunties are always willing to look after children, and childhood is passed in pastoral innocence, where men and women knew their place in the domestic life of the household and the social life of the village, is a dominant one in the popular imagination of the region. This narrative lent support to the existence of a naive gender order where work and life was deemed to be more compatible with childbearing and rearing. That this clear-cut, ideal typology never existed has been demonstrated again and again by the voluminous anthropology of the region. On the other hand, agricultural labour, as well as extended family networks, did accommodate the division of labour which entrusted childcare responsibility almost totally on women's shoulders. The Caribbean, like the rest of the world, is no longer entirely dependent on the rural economy, nor can these societies be neatly divided into rural and urban spaces. In some societies such as Trinidad and Barbados, there is little differentiation between town and country, in others there may still be apparent distinctions. But cable television, electricity and the ubiquitous Coca Cola have globalised the villages of Jamaica as much as they have the little townships of Namibia in Southern Africa. Production of goods and services has moved more into the urban setting, where remunerative work is sought daily by men and women migrating from the countryside.

To speak of urbanisation in the Caribbean is not to equate the relatively small cities in our territories with the large metropolitan cities found elsewhere. At the same time, the problems of urbanisation are much the same if scaled down. A large number of people are clustered in a small area, living in close proximity to each other. There are obvious benefits, such as access to services and opportunities for education and leisure, which outweigh the drawbacks of crowding, congestion, noise and pollution. Despite the infinite cultural variations found in each society, cities appear to have more in common than at first meets the eye. City dwellers face similar problems wherever they are – common concerns over scarce housing, limited playground facilities in high rise or overcrowded housing estates, problems with childcare, schooling and finding fit work. David Clark, in *Urban World/Global City*, reminds us that 'Although towns and cities have existed for over eight millenia, the wholesale transition to urban location and urban living is of very recent origin' (Clark, 1996, p 4). One of the major differences now is that cities are points of production and reproduction of a distinctively urban culture, offering freedom and opportunities for the young and the adventurous. What is distressing, however, is the increasing violence of this urban culture, as if the 'concrete jungle' has brought out the beast in man – the latter used generically, of course.

Cities have created their own forms of social culture. The idea of organised and informal female and male prostitution for example, or 'sex work' as it is has euphemistically been dubbed, is itself a product of an increasingly steady supply of, and demand for, this service in the city. Prostitution has always existed, but the manifest forms it takes, and the exploitation and danger inherent in the sex trade, has become one more concern in the urban planner's nightmare. In this sense the city now, as in the past, has represented freedom and a certain loosening of morals, providing opportunities for individual growth away from the confines of a provincial village life. Growth, however, comes with a price. The city also spews up its rejects without mercy – child beggars, drug addicts, vagrants, the unemployed, increasing street crime, territorial violence, and single young mothers who are incapable of looking after their children alone.

Most importantly for gender roles, urbanisation and technological innovation has blurred the lines of the traditional sexual division of labour. Demographers Jack Harewood and George Roberts, of Trinidad and Jamaica respectively, point to fluctuations in the female labour force participation in the first half of the twentieth century. This was due to increased access to education for boys and girls and, as in the case of Trinidad, the end of the Indian indentureship system, where many women were no longer counted as part of the active labour force. (A process Reddock refers to as the 'housewifisation' of women.) The second half of the century demonstrates fluctuations in the occupational categories and participation rates of women in the labour force in both societies, but despite occasional dips, there is a trend of ever-increasing education and formal and informal employment among women, alongside declining participation rates for men in the formal systems of education or employment. The colleges and universities are crowded with women seeking educational and professional advancement, a situation which has been treated with great alarm. Interestingly enough, there was no such similar outcry against the under-representation of females in relation to males in the education system in the past centuries. Society implicitly colluded with the Aristotlian view that females were, by and large, 'weak and morally unprincipled creatures who could not take education and should not be allowed to mix indiscriminately with the opposite sex'. To cut a long story short, these days are over. Education, work, and career opportunities are generally not a preference but a right, and often a necessity, for both sexes. At the same time other things have remained constant. Man, generically again, is still of woman born, and the reproduction of the new labour force still depends on the care and nurturing of the young and the challenge of changing family systems in a mode of production which requires both male and female labour outside of the home. The question which must be faced squarely in the new century is how are members of society, both men and women, prepared to reorganise the sexual division of labour and the tasks which must be carried out in the public and private sphere?

Women have conventionally been viewed as gatekeepers of the morality and culture of the family and its traditions, as if men were an invisible part of this culture. Traditional gender roles may have applied and worked in a situation of female dependency of one sort or another. Now a wide range of problems such as juvenile delinquency, particularly male delinquency, domestic violence and an increasing liberalisation of sexuality are attributed to women's negligence of their traditional roles. To many these shifts in gender relations appear to be temporary aberrations of some norms to which we should return in the future. This may very well be so, but it is myopic to suggest that family life now is a neatly structured package of male and female couples and children tied into nuclear parcels. There are single mothers and fathers, working couples with children, working grandmothers and grandfathers, and non-working couples, populating overcrowded cities. What resources will be allocated in future dispensations of state and private funds for childcare centres within institutions, playgrounds around housing estates, low cost and efficient transportation systems for school age children, adequate community health care, and an enlightened judiciary system which is discriminating towards the problems of gender relations in the private sphere? There are models to choose from in other societies, but it is vitally important that each society works with its own cultural norms and preferences, thus taking account of differences in class and ethnicity within the society.

The recognition of a tangled relationship between public and private spheres was one of the major struggles waged by feminism in the twentieth century. The fact that domestic violence Acts have been created in three countries in the region and that rape victims may now give their evidence in camera appear minor victories as we face the new millennium, but in fact they are not. Consider that in 1899, one hundred years ago, the idea that a black or Indian female judge would be privy to the courtrooms in which these matters are heard was unthinkable. The resolution and demarcation of gender relations, gender roles and responsibilities cannot be won primarily through legislation and through conscious women in the right places – the transactions of the market place and the polity are elementary compared to those which we make to each other in our homes and private lives. The fundamental challenge of gender is the extent to which we can metaphysically and physically shift our ideas and practices of femininity and masculinity to allow each sex a wholesome future, rather than to deny one to our children.

Bibliography

Anderson, Patricia, 'Conclusion WICP' in *Social and Economic Studies*, 35 no 2, 1986, pp. 291–324

Barrow, Christine, *Family in the Caribbean, Themes and Perspectives* (Jamaica: Ian Randle and London: James Currey, 1996)

Chevannes, Barry, *What We Sow and We Reap: Problems in the Cultivation of Male Identity in Jamaica*, The Grace Kennedy Foundation Lecture Series, 1999

Clark, David, *Urban World/Global City* (London: Routledge, 1996)

Galbraith, JK, 'For richer, for poorer', *Guardian Weekly*, July 8-14, 1999, p. 11

Hobsbawm, Eric, *Age of Extremes: The Short Twentieth Century 1914–1991* (London: Michael Joseph,1994)

Kazin, Michael, 'Birth of a Moral Age', review of *The Great Disruption* by Francis Fukuyama, in *Guardian Weekly*, June 1999

Leo Rhynie, Elsa, *The Jamaican Family: Continuity and Change*, The Grace Kennedy Foundation Lecture Series, 1993

Mandel, Ernest, *Marxist Economic Theory*, Vol. 11, Monthly Review Press, 1962

Mair, Lucille Mathurin, 'A Historical Study of Women in Jamaica from 1655 to 1844', PhD dissertation, University of the West Indies, Mona, 1974

Marx, Karl, *Capital*, Vol. I (Penguin, 1976)

Mohammed, Patricia and Perkins, Althea, *Caribbean Women at the Crossroads: The Paradox of Motherhood among Women of Barbados, St Lucia and Dominica* (Canoe Press, University of the West Indies, 1999)

Reddock, Rhoda, *Women Labour and Politics in Trinidad and Tobago: A History* (London: Zed Books, 1994)

21 | CAROL NARCISSE

Social Integration and Disintegration — The Caribbean Experience:
Jamaica

There is a growing consciousness in Jamaica, among all sectors of society, that the country is faced with an economic and social crisis of enormous proportions. There is a consciousness that the roots of the crisis are deep, systemic and that it is a crisis that could destroy us as a nation, as a people. It is a crisis that requires our undivided, diligent and collective attention. It can end. But only if and when we can be honest in our analysis of its genesis and so be able to devise appropriate solutions.

Building on a foundation of injustice

African-Jamaicans were granted 'full free' on August 1, 1838. This date marked the beginning of a journey to create a new society. Not an easy task, since the one which existed up to that time was created out of injustices – conquest and appropriation of resources, genocide of the first occupants of the country, the *tainos* – and reliance on enforced social and economic inequality, brutality and racism, to survive.

What were the newly freed slaves and the former enforcers of slavery to make of their new situation, a situation that demanded renegotiated terms of engagement and coexistence? What kind of society would be created from the existing structures? In these structures human worth or status, wealth, decision-making, access to opportunities for social advancement and access to the resources and benefits of society were closely tied to whiteness, to shades in between white and black and to gender. And, the relationship with the colonial empire was, by definition, unequal.

Within that context our ancestors set about the task of trying to create a new society. Their instinct to survive was strong. African humanism and traditions of cooperation and mutual aid had survived despite the dehumanising experience of slavery. With these traditions they set to work to build communities and secure a better future for their children. They received important help from different groups. In the Christian church, which had participated in slavery, there were some clergy who knew and acted on what was right. They created educational institutions that were one means to liberation and progress. And there were people from different social backgrounds who worked for an end to colonial rule. So despite the harshness and uncertainty of the time, our ancestors nonetheless set out on the journey to 'make a way'.

But, from the colonial era to the present, the story of Jamaica's development has been an illustration of the difficulty of achieving social integration, nationhood and human development within a national, regional and international context that is rife with inequalities, and where there is no sustained effort to redress and end these inequalities. For example, almost 100 years after 1838, in the 1930s, Jamaica existed in a context in which, Girvan writes,

world-wide economic depression had pushed export prices down . . . already low agricultural wages were cut even further . . . West Indian workers were sent home from countries where they had found employment. Three-quarters of the population lived in acute poverty in the rural areas where illiteracy, malnutrition, substandard housing and absence of the most basic health and educational facilities were widespread desperation and discontent stalked the land; protest demonstrations and rioting swept the region.[1]

Clearly, not a lot in life had changed for the majority of people in this society. Still, our people continued to hold on to a vision of, and work to create, a better society. From their efforts a strong labour movement was built, as was a dynamic and successful movement for political independence. Many worked hard to create a 'nation spirit' and to achieve community development. In this latter regard, the Jamaica Welfare Ltd founded in 1937 by Norman Manley, is a sterling example of the praiseworthy efforts of Jamaicans of different social backgrounds to work together to fashion a new society out of the creative intellect and energies of the people themselves.

We, today, would do well to revisit the strategies of Jamaica Welfare which, thanks to Norman Girvan, have been well documented. Such a revisit ought to give us pause the next time we reach for a packaged-in-North America kit on 'participatory methodologies' and 'community animation techniques'. And it should make us stop ourselves the next time we attempt to say that we do not know what the solution to our social and economic problems could be.

With the slogan 'We are out to build a new Jamaica', and with the involvement and leadership of people from different social backgrounds, Jamaica Welfare built upon and strengthened the survival strategies of the people who had created and sustained 'free villages' after emancipation. These strategies were based on self-help and the reciprocal human relations of family, friends and neighbours exchanging services, goods, labour, moral and emotional support as a basis for community building.

DTM Girvan, who spearheaded the community development programmes of Jamaica Welfare between 1939 and 1951, had a set of ideas and principles which guided his work and the approach to community development and nation building which was taken. These principles were to:

Listen to the people: find out their needs and aspirations. Stimulate group action and build community organisations. Motivate them to study, and provide training facilities. Develop local leadership and individual character. Coordinate external services to the community. Incorporate community development into national development.[2]

Except in the 1970s, when the People's National Party attempted to reconcile the processes of economic growth with social equity as a framework for national development, the exhortation to 'incorporate community development into national development' has hardly ever been followed. The long-standing disjoint between community and national development strategies and policies; insufficient attention to and support for policies and programmes to redress historical legacies of race, class and gender inequalities, and, a process of political tribalisation which has used any and all means for achieving and keeping state power, have been the main barriers to social integration and the main contributors to social disintegration in Jamaica.

Despite the interventions of Jamaica Welfare, in the 1930s through to the 1950s and 1960s, Thom Girvan, by 1961, was beginning to sound the warning. He said,

We have achieved so much in so short a time. We have built up so many democratic organisations which play a vital role in our economic and social life. We have political parties and labour unions. We have an expanded industrial programme. We know the problems of population growth, the migration trends, the economic limitations But what is a great shock to us is to realise that somewhere along the road we lost something of the vision we once shared. We need to ask ourselves: At what stage did we become less united, less tolerant, less confident in our friends, in ourselves and in our future? [3]

Girvan's words signalled that the process of social disintegration and alienation had already begun.

The Main Factors Contributing to Social Disintegration in Jamaica

Inequalities based on race and class

Race and ethnicity have, historically, been strong determinants of access to economic and political power in Jamaica. Racial and ethnic minority groups and a mulatto or 'brown' elite have had distinct social and economic advantages as part of an historical legacy of colonialism and slavery. With strong networks of mutual aid based on kinship bonds and connections, these groups have been able to consolidate their historical privilege into successful corporations which are supported by government incentives such as generous licenses and government contracts. They are a powerful interest group, many members of which influence national policies in ways that redound to their benefit.

In the post-emancipation period a 'middle class' of 'coloureds' and educated Jamaicans emerged. This class has dominated the civil service, political party leadership, managerial levels of the private sector, the professions, the hierarchy of traditional religious institutions, the legislature and the judiciary. This group, therefore, has considerable influence and control over a range of productive sectors and resources of the country.

The influence and control which these groups exert however have not been confined to capital and other material resources and to decision-making. For much of Jamaica's history, the upper and middle classes have exerted a cultural hegemony in the society – defining what is 'proper' in taste, morality, religious and political principles, language and other norms of social relations and defining the moral and intellectual connotations of these relationships.

In contrast, Austin (1984) refers to 'a history of divergent cultural forms among black working class Jamaicans . . .' which reflect 'a certain creative autonomy among the oppressed'. But this stubborn survival of the cultural mores of the majority of Jamaicans which retains many African features is subject to constant criticism and denigration by the minority classes who show preference for a culture which reflects a more distinctly European quality. Intelligence and worth are ascribed to people in the society on the basis of how they look (how dark/how light skinned), speak, dress, or worship, and on the basis of these factors people are exposed to privilege or disadvantage in the society.

Political tribalism and patronage

Growing out of differences of opinion about the development path which Jamaica was to take, from the 1940s onwards contests for political and trade union power and leadership became increasingly divisive, eroding the spirit of 'building a new Jamaica' and of putting national and community interest before party and individual interest. Jobs, money, infrastructural development and other scarce benefits became, by the 1950s and 1960s, the 'carrot and stick' of the political process promised and given in return for political support to enable state power and withheld as punishment for non-support of the winning party. This system thrived through the use of organised violence and the creation of politically homogenous enclaves where allegiance could be tightly controlled, nurtured and when necessary, enforced. Poverty and dependence became the prerequisites for that system's success.

An unsustainable economic framework

Anderson and Witter note that well into the first half of the twentieth century the Jamaican economy 'typified the colonial model of dependent underdevelopment an open, import-dependent, monocrop economy'.[4] Both the inherited and the subsequent national economic policies were disconnected from the cultural and social realities of Jamaica. From the 1930s to 1960s there were efforts to restructure and diversify the economic base of the country, so that by the 1960s, mining, tourism and manufacturing had emerged as leading sectors. But these sectors operated as import dependent enclaves with insufficient linkages to the rest of the economy.[5]

Therefore, note Anderson and Witter, while in that period there was economic growth there was not, for example, a commensurate impact on employment and the majority of the labour force continued to be engaged in low waged labour on plantations, in sugar factories and in small farming. Although economic opportunities opened up, particularly for those who had an advantage of education and capital, the majority of rural small and subsistence farmers, and the emerging urban working class faced increasing social and economic pressure. The distribution of the benefits of economic growth was highly skewed with the income of the minority growing while that of the majority declined (Freckleton and Anderson, 1999, p 16). The majority of the population who were black, poor and from the working class or peasantry remained on the fringe of the development process. Indeed, the social conditions and relations between the classes in the 1950s and 1960s were not much better than they had been in the previous century. In the late 1960s, 30 years after the riots and strikes of 1938, there were mass riots in Kingston.

In the 1970s, the government sought to achieve economic growth with social equity. When foreign and local business interests, owners of capital and the political opposition responded negatively to what, they purported, were signs of communism, one of the results was greatly increased external migration and capital flight. The government in turn relied on increased foreign borrowing and turned to the IMF in 1977 for balance of payments support.

Much has already been said about the structural adjustment policies of the IMF and other international lending agencies. What is important to note here is that these policies, as Anderson and Witter note, have been 'as much a social process as an economic one'.[6] So much so that by 1985, the then prime minister, Edward Seaga, speaking to the annual meeting of the World Bank and IMF at Seoul, South Korea, said:

... the prevailing wisdom of the international institutions, emphasises adjustment programmes through tight demand management. The result is severe austerity which, in the final analysis, cuts services and reduces growth ... this austere path carries social and political costs which are often counter-productive to the final objective of achieving adjustment without sacrificing stability, we do not (just) adjust economic systems, we adjust the lives of people who make these systems work . . . it is short-sighted in the least to ignore the human element . . .[7]

Despite this realisation, successive governments have remained on the path. The policies have exacerbated economic and social inequalities in the country.

Widening income inequality

A small number of people have benefited from the economic policies of the last two decades. Specifically, they have benefited from high interest rates and privatisation programmes. At the same time, a large number of people have suffered from redundancy, cuts in public expenditure on social services and infrastructure; the introduction of user fees for public services which has limited access for those who without financial means and, many have faced ruination from the high cost of capital to carry out businesses or own homes.

There has been, as a result of the macroeconomic restructuring of the period, an even greater level of income inequality. One manifestation of this is the wide disparities in levels of consumption expenditure evident in the country. Data from surveys of living conditions indicate that in 1995 the wealthiest 10 per cent of the population had a mean per capita annual consumption expenditure which was ten times greater than that of the poorest 10 per cent ($102,091 compared to $10,294). In 1995 the Gini Coefficient was 0.3624, in 1997 it reached 0.04164. The Gini Coefficient is a measure of the degree of equality in consumption/income. A Coefficient of 0 indicates perfect equality, a coefficient of 1 indicates total inequality.

A report on the preliminary findings of a recent study by Henry-Lee, Chevannes et al,[8] shows how a sampling of workers earning the minimum wage are coping with declining real incomes. The study's sample included security guards, domestic workers and garment factory workers. Of the total 2014 individuals surveyed, the study found that 56.3 per cent (1067 people) considered their income to be 'less than adequate'. Of that number the coping strategies employed were as follows:

Coping Strategies	%
Minimised spending in some areas	77.4
Borrowed money	18.1
Did nothing	15.7

Sold possessions	4.0
Other (not specified)	3.2

Spending is minimised on essential items as listed below:

Areas in which spending is minimised	%
Health	72.5
Clothing,	46.6
Food	31.1
Transport	30.8
Payment of bills	24.2
Loans	7.6

These coping strategies may be useful in the short term but may be bad for longer term development. The cuts in spending, on health for example, have significant implications for the long term capacity of the individuals or their family to escape vulnerability, and there are implications for the general health of the nation and consequently its productive capacity.

Increased vulnerability and social distance

All the factors discussed above have resulted in an increased vulnerability among the majority of the population and more so among specific groups. One consequence of being vulnerable for a prolonged period is a growing sense of abandonment by the 'powers that be' (employers, political leaders and so on) and an alienation from the formal processes within society, for example the electoral process and the formal labour market.

Robert Chambers (1989) defines vulnerability as 'defencelessness, insecurity and exposure to risks, shocks and stress; exposure to contingencies and difficulty in coping with them'.[9] Many individuals, households and communities in Jamaica have become physically, economically and psychologically at risk of harm or loss even when they are not necessarily faced with income poverty. A sense of security and well-being is fostered not only by adequate financial means, but also by the quality and extent of human relationships, the support systems and services which exist and their accessibility. The words of one rural Jamaican woman recalling life in past decades, illustrate the point.

If you have a dead . . . you didn't have undertakers and such, you only have the people in the house; people running around giving food, board for the coffin, money and rum. Women come and cook; people bring cocoa . . . everyone loving, not like these days – now if you don't have money, you die like a dog . . .[10]

Community spirit and social relations have been severely undermined in the last two decades. The economic policies of the last twenty-five years coupled with, among other things, extreme income inequality and limited social policies which promote equity, have exacerbated asymmetries of power and inequalities in access to resources and opportunities for different groups in society.

Gender-based inequalities differentials

In addition to race/ethnicity and class, gender is a significant factor in determining access to power and resources which influences social relations. Traditional definitions of women's and men's roles and responsibilities and different expectations for their position in society persist. Despite advances in education and relatively high workforce participation rates, women in Jamaica have fewer options for securing their well-being and have considerably less access to the resources and benefits of society and to the processes of decision-making than men. In this society women and men are expected to have different degrees of power and autonomy.

Men are expected to have higher levels of achievement than women, earn more and have more 'authority'. The dominant view in society (especially in powerful social institutions such as the church and religious institutions) is that men are the 'head' of the household (and by extension the rightful 'head' of the nation in business, politics, and leadership in general) and that men should have and are entitled to more power than women.

In this context:

1. Women's individual voice carries less weight with males of whatever age in the home and wider community than a man's, but some 44% of women are heads of households, and female-headed households have more children than male-headed, and two-parent households (SLC 1995). In this society a boy who 'listens to his mother' can very likely be ridiculed as being a 'sissy'.
2. Labour is still divided along very strict gender lines though some women and men have been able to break out of the mould. Women have less access to earned income than men (39% compared to men's 61% share; 1995

HDR), have a higher rate of unemployment and are predominantly low-waged. Children in female-headed households are therefore more likely to live in poverty, even where their mothers work. Generally women have less economic power than men – they access less credit, are under-represented at the highest levels of corporate society in terms of ownership and decision-making and are over-represented in small, own-account businesses.

3. Women dominate in caring roles – in their homes, in community groups, PTAs, voluntary organisations/civil society groups and so on, and in the economic realities of the times, they must also find employment. With still too few men taking on domestic and caring roles, many children are being left to their own devices. With no assistance, it is impossible for women to give adequate supervision to children.
4. Women are more vulnerable than men to a wider array of crimes against them, at home and in public. Domestic violence, which includes beatings, verbal and psychological abuse, is common in relationships between men and women. Men are socialised with a sense of right to discipline women and often resort to physical dominance when their sense of manhood is undermined by inability to provide, as much or more than women as society communicates they should. Rape and carnal abuse often have a higher incidence than murder and shootings but cases are less likely to be 'cleared up' than other crimes (ESSJ, 1996, p 23.1).
5. In no area of the society are women fairly represented at the pinnacles of power and decision-making. Not in NGOs, unions, the church and religious institutions, business and the corporate sector, judiciary, educational institutions, or local or national government. Women therefore have least access to and are least able to influence formal mechanisms for economic, social or political policies.

Gender socialisation has a negative and limiting impact on men in society to the extent that they believe that they are defined by what they are able to 'provide' rather than as a person working in partnership with another to carry out any and all functions needed to make a unit viable and strong. A society that defines masculinity by qualities of aggressiveness, power 'over' another, material provisions and sexual prowess and which disseminates this message must take responsibility for both its positive and negative manifestations.

Neglect of senior citizens, children and youth

Along with women, senior citizens, children and youth are among the most vulnerable in the society. According to the *Economic and Social Survey of Jamaica* (ESSJ) of 1998, based on a combined dependency ratio for children and seniors, in 1998 Jamaica had a societal dependency ratio of 636 per 1000 of workforce age. Meeting the needs of dependent children, youth and the elderly has become a major challenge for families, communities and the state.

Senior citizens now face a number of difficulties in the present economic and social context in Jamaica. These include health insecurity, loneliness and social isolation, inadequate finances/income poverty, and changing family dynamics as families become smaller and more dispersed. Older women are more poor, less healthy and less educated than older men, but they participate more in social activities and so have more social support and contact and are more easily reached for services. Older men have fewer social supports and are more isolated. Older women are more likely than men to be in multi-generational households caring for grandchildren, and are more often heads of households than older men. A society that neglects its elders neglects its memory and weakens an important link connecting the past to the present and the future.

Children aged 0-14 comprise 31.4 per cent of the Jamaican population and youth aged 15–24 comprise 27.5 per cent. Together they account for 58.9 per cent of the population (ESSJ 1998). Most live in rural areas where educational resources, jobs and social infrastructure are more limited than in urban areas. They are faced with inadequate welfare, educational and child protection services. As the extended family arrangement has faced fragmentation by economic constraints and migration, urbanisation, and the breakdown in parenting skills and family organisation (especially among the younger generation of parents) many children are raising themselves and have only material objects as the main evidence of parental life.

Culturally, children are still seen as a parent's 'old age pension'. Increasingly, children and youth are expected to earn their keep and to supplement family incomes. Most working children are employed in rural agriculture. In urban centres they are a large part of the informal sector. Their growing numbers can be seen on the streets – peddling a variety of goods or wiping wind-shields. Employment, underemployment and low wages mean that more children number among the poor. So, more children are living in poor housing, in overcrowded conditions with violence and with limited community support networks.

Added to these ills, is the fact that children are rarely consulted before major changes are made in their lives. This often leaves them feeling abandoned, bereft and angry, feelings that are often acted out in anti-social ways. The net effect has been declining educational attainment and skills, a growth in unemployment and increased incidence of youth involvement in crime and violence. Young males aged 15–29 are currently the main offenders in violent crimes.[11]

The disabled face even greater social and income poverty than other groups. They have lower levels of education (75 per cent have primary-level education only) and experience high levels of unemployment, especially among women (only about 14 per cent of the disabled are employed). Many have very precarious livelihoods and are dependent on care-givers whom they might outlive. Since there are no subsidised attendant care services, many parents/caregivers are unable to work outside of the home because care-giving, particularly for the severely disabled, is a full-time occupation. This adds to the financial vulnerability of the whole family.

The mentally ill are the most vulnerable. For example, in July 1999, there was the case of the abduction of homeless and mentally ill people from the streets of Montego Bay, the second city and major tourist centre, and the severe and fatal beating by members of the security forces of a young, mentally ill man in Kingston in September indicate the extent of vulnerability of this group. Five to ten per cent of the population (approximately 125,000–250,000 people) has some form of mental illness. In 1996, only 7,526 people were treated. The majority are unable to afford private psychiatric care, they depend on a public mental health-care system which provides few acute care facilities, no crisis response services, few mental health officers to handle community-based follow-up (mental health officers have a case load of some 500 patients to 1 officer) and very little in rehabilitative services.

Poverty exacerbates vulnerability and social alienation

Vulnerability, asymmetries of power and access to resources become even more stark when one considers the realities of life among the poor. Poverty here refers to more than a lack of adequate income to meet basic needs as the results of recent studies indicate. Studies using techniques of participatory rapid appraisal have been carried out in urban and peri-urban communities with people considered poor, marginalised and/or 'vulnerable'.[12] There has been remarkable similarity in the perceptions/ identification of problems – their causes and solutions, priorities and prescriptions which have been articulated by residents of the communities studied.

In the subject's identification of the main problems they face, recurring themes have been:

i. **Employment:** particularly among youth, due to lack of skills, unwillingness to work for 'little and nothing' and limitations to movement and marketability due to stigmas attached to communities
ii. **Violence:** also referred to as the 'war' which stems from idleness, political tribalism, gang turfism, drugs, prevalence of guns and ammunition, and violence being a non-formal route to achieving and maintaining 'respect'
iii. **Loss of freedom:** of movement, interaction and choice due to violence and the stigmas attached to communities
iv. **Politicians:** as both benefactors (based on favoritism) and as contributors to the problems of guns, drugs and violence
v. **Churches:** their waning influence in social development
vi. **A decline in physical infrastructure:** buildings are not maintained due to absentee landlords and sanitation is poor
vii. **Decline in 'community spirit':** violence has a greater impact
viii. **Decline in parental guidance:** parents have less influence on and control over youth
ix. **Police abuses:** police are often feared and resented because of abuse of power and privilege and acts of brutality

In outlining these problems, youth, women, men, and the elderly, elaborate on intricate webs of cause and effect. What constitutes 'poverty' is expressed in much broader terms and based on different indices than official income-related descriptions, and a distinction is made between income poverty and poverty of the spirit. This is captured in the statement 'Me poor but me no poverty'.[13]

Some Signs of Social Disintegration

Violence and crime

One of the main expressions of people's feelings of disconnection from and lack of tolerance and responsibility for one another is by violence and crime in various forms. Jamaicans have become a more 'violent' people – in how we drive, in our verbal interactions and even in how we express pleasure (for example the gun/fire cracker salute at stage shows and dances, and the popular slang for sex – 'slam', 'agony'). Violence and crime have a damaging effect on the whole society.

A great many people have learned to expect violence from those whose sworn duty is to protect them. They expect and suffer violence as the main means of problem-solving, discipline and correction in families and schools. 'Violence and crime greatly increase the vulnerability of households, businesses, and community life,' as Moser (1996)[14] notes.

In a case study of one urban community, researchers note that:

... the levels of violence and insecurity in the area not only stigmatise people when they go for jobs but have meant that taxi drivers will not come into the area, credit companies say their staff are afraid to go in and such basics as garbage collection are suspended when periodic violence erupts. All the community pays for the violence created in the area'.[15]

In Levy's report the many ways in which violence impacts on people's lives are illustrated by residents of one community in the following way:[16]

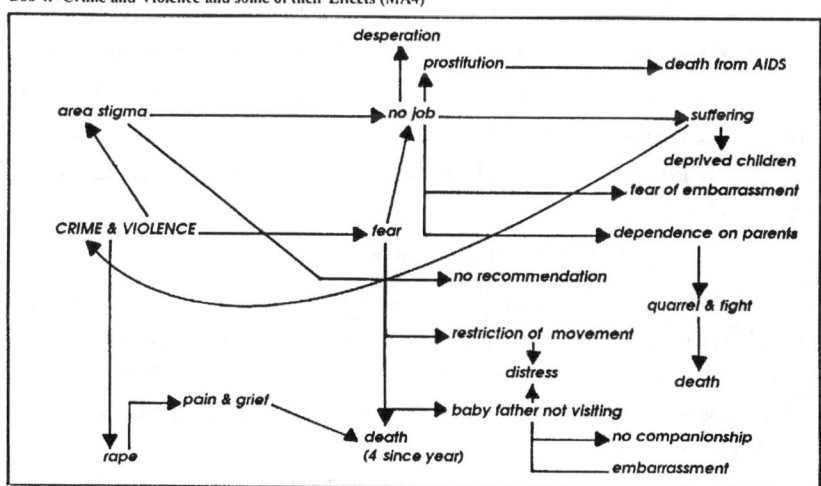

Box 4. Crime and Violence and some of their Effects (MA4)

Such far-reaching impacts are based on the fact that there are wide ranging types of violent situations:

Inner-city residents distinguish many kinds of violence each with its agents, motives, methods, frequency, target groups and effects . . . their lists include political violence, drug violence, gang violence, rape, domestic violence, contract war, power violence, pickney war (violence between adults whose children are fighting), woman war, matey violence (violence between women over men) . . . murder, wounding, theft, child abuse and more.[17]

Fear is a common experience across the different groups in the society – fear of rape, of being robbed, of early death, of domestic violence. Levy notes that the 'climate of pervasive and crippling fear gripping sections of communities or sets of people within them, generally or at certain times, cannot be exaggerated.'[18]

The responses to the high levels of violence and crime in Jamaica include, among middle and upper level income groups, an increased attention to making homes secure through burglar bars, electronic security systems, security guards, guard dogs and ownership of firearms. Social interaction between the different income groups has been severely curtailed as low income communities are avoided. Outward migration is also a solution for many.

In violence-prone inner city communities, responses include the bearing of arms. Young men readily access guns and knives and women carry an assortment of weapons such as ice picks, knives and acid. Community dons provide protection, as do road blocks which are intended to keep intruders out. Silence about crimes witnessed is a major part of keeping alive – in many communities the 'informer' (and his or her family) faces severe consequences. Many flee communities, going to live with family in rural areas or in other parts of the urban areas. For those with no relatives or friends to turn to, capturing land and squatting become the alternative as the following case illustrates. Norma, who lives in a squatter community recalled why she moved to the area:

'It isn't that I wanted to live up here but I just couldn't take the war no more, I lived in fear. Every night I would spread the bed so it would look like nobody was sleeping in the house. Me and the children would squeeze under the bed. One night after the bad boys passed through and broke a couple of windows and shot up the place I decided that I had to leave the area.'

The following morning, Norma decided to find somewhere to live. A friend told her of a place in Papine where some people were squatting. She took a bus to Highlight View (then called Mud Town) and the next day she moved with the children into the friend's house. Several weeks later she marked off a piece of land and started to construct her one-room apartment (Source: Report, 'Highlight view: Twenty Years of Development', Construction Resource and Development Centre [CRDC], Kingston, 1998).

Squatting

Another factor contributing to vulnerability and which further undermines social cohesion is limited access to housing, shelter, and land tenure. As Norma's case illustrates, many resort to squatting as a means of affording shelter. The high costs and limited availability of land or housing in the formal sector has resulted in a burgeoning of informal settlements. The informal sector now accounts for over 50 per cent of housing units. The 1996 Habitat report indicates that for the period 1987–1993 the average annual production of housing units (in the formal sector) was 4,338 compared with 16,000 new households formed each year. The net number of units produced per 1000 population was five (Source: UNCHS Report, *'Towards A Shelter Policy and Strategy For Jamaica'*, 1997).

Squatting is not easy. It often means living with the constant threat of ejection by land owners, loss of possessions and materials and sites are often physically perilous – on the banks of gullies, on steep slopes or in flood plains. Part of the logic of squatting as a survival strategy is that informal, low or sometimes sporadic incomes give rise to a need to keep overheads (rent, utility bills) down, especially since these are regular payments. With squatting, what income is available becomes free for use on other things, such as further income-generating activities or incremental building. Squatting is a very vexed issue in society however, and responses by land owners have sparked a number of demonstrations and violent confrontations in recent times.

Survival in the Current Context

The foregoing demonstrates that the macroeconomic, political and social framework of society undermine rather than facilitate and sustain human development, equity and social integration. Over the past thirty years, the environment in which the majority of Jamaicans have lived has become more threatening to people's well-being – physically, emotionally and psychologically.

As a consequence the range and scope of individuals' responses and survival strategies have increased. In response to their vulnerability and insecurity, people devise various survival mechanisms and strategies which, though beneficial to the group or individuals using them, often have a negative impact on the wider society, diminishing the quality of life for all and adding to a general insecurity in the nation. What emerges can be a vicious cycle of mutually reinforcing cause and effect which impedes individual, national, and community development.

Some State Responses

Successive governments have shown an awareness of the negative impact which macroeconomic policies such as structural adjustment, have had on specific groups in society. This awareness is demonstrated by various state interventions including welfare programmes and a targeted social safety net addressing the needs of groups such as pregnant and breast-feeding women and young children. Some of the policies and programmes implemented by the state within the last ten years are summarised below:

Some Current State Interventions

State policies and initiatives	Programmes
Creation of an enabling environment	Constitutional, local government and labour market reform; The Public Sector Modernisation Programme; health sector reform; The Reform of Secondary Education (ROSE) and reform of primary school curricula
National Poverty Eradication policy	The National Poverty Eradication Programme: promoting integration and collaboration of government services/agencies; partnerships between government agencies, private sector, NGOs, CBOs and donor/lending

	agencies; environmental sustainability and community empowerment.
	The Jamaica Social Investment Fund provides communities with resources to improve physical, social and economic conditions. The Integrated Community Development Programme carried out by the Social Development Commission focuses on building local institutions/groups' capacity to develop and implement projects.
Expansion of the productive sector/productive employment, National Industrial Policy (NIP)	Training programmes: Skills 2000, the Special Training and Employment Programme (STEP), National Youth Service, the National Vocational Qualification of Jamaica (NVQ-J) for occupational certification, The Human Employment and Resource Training Trust/National Training Agency (HEART/NTA) National Council on Technical and Vocational Education and Training (NCTVET).
	Micro-enterprise development: The Micro Investment Development Agency Ltd (MIDA) provides wholesale credit to approved lending agencies, and technical services to the micro-business sector.
Social integration, equity and social development; national policies on youth, elderly and disabled; The Commission on Gender and Social Equity	The National Plan of Action for Children; the Domestic Violence Act; gender neutral amendments to laws related to sexual offenses; The Food Stamp Programme; Drugs for the Elderly programme; National Health Insurance Plan.

It is important to note that among the interventions in education and for poverty eradication are programmes funded in significant part by loans from international agencies such as the World Bank and the Inter-American Development Bank. In such cases the interventions can at best only represent a deferral of the problem to the time of our future generations.

As the role of the state in the provision of basic social services and amenities has declined there has been a considerable growth in private voluntary, NGOs and CBOs which have been filling the gap. Jamaica has a long history of voluntarism and philanthropy. Currently there are over two thousand civil society groups which rely primarily on volunteers to provide a wide range of services.

These services include education and training, housing/shelter, environmental protection and conservation, legal aid, conflict/dispute resolution, counselling, crisis intervention (for example rape or domestic violence), micro-credit and technical assistance for small business development, health, public education and advocacy. There are NGOs which provide services to all the vulnerable groups in the society – children and youth, seniors, the disabled and mentally ill, the homeless, women and girls, and young males.

Most of the civil society groups are faced with challenges to their own survival. These include dwindling sources of funding, especially as many have been dependent on foreign aid agencies, a number of which are pulling out of Jamaica in particular or the Caribbean in general and redirecting aid to countries considered less developed. Many groups also lack proper management systems and personnel and have poor quality leadership.

Survival Strategies among some Specific Groups

The middle class

With retrenchment in the public and private sectors, and high levels of inflation eroding real wages and purchasing power, the middle classes have been faced with a reduction in their standard of living. Among those employed in the private sector, job prerequisites such as health insurance, a company car, or concessionary loans go a long way in helping them to maintain their accustomed lifestyle. Recent private sector failures, for example in the financial sector, have pulled such safety nets from beneath the feet of many in the middle class. Consequently, many in the middle class are now faced with poverty due to loss of investments in entities in the financial sector, from an inability to save to meet contingencies, and from prolonged unemployment following redundancy, among other factors.

One study carried out by Lynette Brown in 1994 in one urban community of 'a typical cross section of the national middle class' examined the 'strategies used for dealing with structural adjustment' and found that many people were 'struggling to maintain their accustomed lifestyle'. The main strategies which Brown found to be employed were:

i. Self-employment.
ii. Cuts in consumption (such as some purchases, entertainment, dispensing with domestic help, more conservative budgets for shopping, suspended home expansion/improvement plans).
iii. Greater reliance on family in rural areas and abroad for some foods or other consumer items.
iv. Shifting from liquid assets to long term investments, certificates of deposit and land.
v. Lower standards of housing among the more educated and those employed in the public sector in particular as costs for traditional middle-class housing has become too expensive.

Small farmers

In relation to the small farming sector, Newman and le Franc[19] in their examination of the impact of structural adjustment outlined the following policy and programme changes which have impacted most:

i. The divestment of government lands, productive assets and some marketing and management services in the sector.
ii. Market liberalisation via the reduction of controls on the marketing of major export crops through the export marketing organisations, and the introduction of 'efficient pricing policies'.
iii. The gradual elimination of any tariff barriers that may have provided protection to domestic producers from agricultural imports.
iv. The gradual elimination of monopoly import procurement by the Jamaica Commodity Trading Co
v. The gradual elimination of generalised food subsidies.

In addition to these changes, there was also the elimination of subsidies on production inputs for example, fertilisers; reorganisation and rationalisation of the agricultural credit banks; increased involvement of commercial banks in the disbursement of credit, and a substantial increase in loan interest rates to bring them closer to market rates.

From case studies in one fairly typical small farming community Newman and Le Franc identified the following strategies for coping and surviving among the farmers:

i. Incremental building of houses.
ii. Farming as a safety net to supplement income from other occupations
iii. Utilisation of 'idle' land for cash crops.
iv. Keeping livestock as an investment; for example layers and broilers (chickens) are a source of continuous income and fowl supplements diet.
v. Out-migration from villages particularly of the young. This has implications for the older people left behind and their ability to cope with economic hardships. It also implies a likelihood of there being 'a vibrant two-way communication (and aid) process'.
vi. Off-farm occupations to generate incomes to invest in the farm. Those with least land to cultivate depend more on secondary occupations, particularly those occupations requiring no formal training given their lower educational attainment.
vii. Mixed cropping, inter-cropping and interplanting, which increase the total production of the land. A wide variety of crops are grown for both consumption and sale.
viii. Planting of tree crops which take less physical energy to care for and so reduce dependence on hired labour. Also tree crops are permanent and are considered a legacy for the next generation, as well as being an 'old age pension'.
ix. Farmers seek markets independently and negotiate better prices.
x. Various forms of land tenure: freehold (whether bought or inherited), family land, rent, lease, settlement land, caretaking, land given, land captured.

Women and Men: Gender Differentials

Gender differentials which exist in employment, levels of income, representation in leadership and participation in decision-making also exist in the nature and range of survival strategies which men and women are able to employ. Males, particularly young males, have a wider array of legal and illegal options open to them through which to access and command resources.

Gender socialisation, and society's consequent expectations of women, mean that for survival women primarily utilise informal networks of friends and family from which reciprocal aid and mutual assistance can be had. Transactional male-female relationships in which women depend on male partners for money and material goods in exchange for sex, domestic chores and child bearing, traditional occupations such as working as domestics and garment factory workers, higglering and sidewalk vending.

The following table illustrates the difference in range and type of strategies for income-generation among men and women in one urban community (Source, *They Cry Respect! Urban Violence And Poverty In Jamaica*, Horace Levy, 1996, p 20).

In different studies carried out in urban, inner-city communities and using techniques of Participatory Rapid Appraisal[20] reference is made to women's dependence on men, especially among women who are unemployed. Levy reports that 'women are expected to depend on men as a major source of their survival even though they are also respected for working and earning a good income'.[21] In the same community a male 'must be tough, so he turns to a gun'. Consequently, Levy notes 'The link between unemployment and crime

MEN		WOMEN	
Frequency	Income Source	Frequency	Income Source
10 (most frequent)	Exchange US$	10	Garment factory
9	Pickpockets	3	Hotel work
7	Factory work	7	Dressmaking
5	Electrician	10	Domestic help
3	Masonry	4	Ganja sale
1	Tailoring	5	Straw vending
5	Woodwork	8	Men
6	Baking	7	Higglering
2	Operate sound system	2	Prostitution
6	Ganja sale	6	Hairdressing
4	Hotel work		
8	Straw vending		
3	Barbering		

and violence refers above all to men'.[22] This point is substantiated by data from the correctional services which indicate that as at November 1998 there were 3129 males and 161 females in prison. There were 250 wards of the state in juvenile institutions, the majority of whom were males.

The Poor and Vulnerable

The range of short term coping and longer-term survival strategies which a large percentage of the population employs is extensive. Moral codes have changed to allow for greater possibilities for action aimed at enabling survival in a hostile socio-economic and physical environment. The strategies serve to both maintain as well as undermine community and social relations and the country's economic development. Some of the strategies being used are summarised below.

Type of asset/Response	Some responses/Survival strategies
Labour/Income-generating activities	**Low skilled jobs:** day work (household and gardening) and casual labour; **Vending:** petty vending, itinerant trading (there is increased reliance on child labour as children help parents with stalls or hustle on the streets), recycling/resale – people visit dump sites or homes to collect items for resale **Own-account businesses:** home-based shops and sale of ice, sweets, and other small goods; small manufacturing (wood work, grill work), community-based personal services (barbering/hairdressing, shoe repair, dress-making, tailoring), child care, basic nursery schools, backyard industries (making of bricks, pots, batteries) **Vice:** drug dealing, particularly marijuana, cocaine and crack; prostitution, extortion (many stores, construction

	sites and market vendors are forced to pay community 'dons' to ensure unmolested operations), gambling (formal lottery and horse racing, informal community gambling) **Begging:** people beg for money, clothes, and food. Tricksters abound with well rehearsed stories, entirely fabricated. Children are often sent out to beg or are kept with adults who beg because they increase the sympathy factor. **Theft:** pickpocketing, petty theft, robbery. **Informal savings scheme:** called 'partner' in Jamaica. **Music:** becoming a DJ or singer following sound systems.
Housing/ Household economies/Family relations.	**Use of housing/land:** for income earning through subletting and small businesses; varied household formations – intergenerational and multi-relational. **Aid from family:** relatives abroad provide opportunities for travel/migration; send remittances (which are a significant factor in the formal economy) clothes or food. There is a strong 'barrel culture'; rural relatives are a source of food and child-rearing support.
Social and economic infrastructure	**Legal and illegal access to state and NGO services/programmes:** many people access state and charitable agencies' support (since there is limited tracking, some people access more than one of the same type of services); many households have illegal connection to electric-

ity and water supplies thus they avoid utility rates, some people also sell the service to neighbours); there is also illegal use of telephone lines for making local and overseas calls. Deals made with corrupt public and private sector officials enable access to goods and services for personal use or sale (licenses, passports, visas), roads are sometimes blocked and a 'toll' collected by young men carrying out repairs. Demonstrations are now a frequently used method of getting prompt attention and action from public or private officials/agencies.

Social capital/Establishing socioeconomic support groups

Unofficial community soldiers: provide personal and community security, community 'godfather/godparents' provide financial and other assistance. This person might be a 'don' or some other more financially well off member of the community.

Sports clubs and teams: minimise violence and provide recreation and earnings, street dances and shows offer entertainment and income earning activities; mutual aid societies such as burial schemes which provide members with assistance with costs of funerals etc are among the older socio-cultural traditions. In recent times barrels of clothes are received and shared in the community for funerals and other occasions. In 'corner'groups young people, especially young males, share money, food, laughter, grief and protection.

What Can Be Done?

Learn from past initiatives

Earlier, reference was made to the approaches taken by Jamaica Welfare from the 1930s to 1940s. If it sounds like such a long time ago that that process could not be relevant in these more sophisticated and modern times, a reading of the book *Working Together For Development* edited by Norman Girvan[23] indicates otherwise. There are a number of lessons which can be learned from that process which are relevant for application today. Four such lessons and related questions for consideration are:

1. **Alliances among people of different classes/social backgrounds and racial/ethnic origins:** Jamaica Welfare was a process by which people from different social/economic and racial backgrounds worked together with mutual respect, united around the common ideal of 'building a new Jamaica'. Could such alliances be forged and galvanised into a national movement today as well?

2. **A human development fund paid for by the private sector:** The funding to establish Jamaica Welfare was negotiated for from the multinational companies in the Banana industry following a dispute which these companies had with the Jamaica Banana Producers Association. The funds negotiated for by Norman Manley were for the specific purpose of cultural and human development. Dare we make similar demands of the local and multinational companies doing business in Jamaica today?

3. **Community development is more than community buildings:** Between 1937 and 1940 the one area of focus of Jamaica Welfare was on building community centres. By 1940 internal debate raged about the efficacy of this approach. In 1941, the Board accepted Girvan's recommendation for adopting what was called a 'better village' later 'better community' approach. This approach took the felt needs and existing leadership of the community as points of departure. It emphasised the stimulation of self-help and community organisation leading eventually to a community association or community council, and the provision of external support as a complement to, not a substitute for, local effort (p 11).

    Can we today muster the confidence to 'listen to the people' and follow their lead in determining needs and priorities? Can we have a goal of decentralising power to the extent that both government and non-government agencies function to enable and complement community decision-making and management?

4. **Government support should not be synonymous with partisan support or government control:** World War II brought the export of bananas to an end and thus ended the funding from the banana companies. Funding was assumed by the British government through the Colonial Development and Welfare (CD&W) funds. With this shift, Jamaica Welfare went from being an entirely non-government organisation to having, in 1943, government appointees on the board. The organisation continued to see dramatic expansion in its programmes.

Then, in 1948 CD&W funding ended, the Jamaican government assumed full funding responsibility, and Norman Manley resigned to make way for a government-appointed chairman. In 1961 Girvan, who had been away for three years, returned as executive chairman of what was then the Jamaica Social Welfare Commission on the invitation of Norman Manley.

He immediately noticed how much had changed. Addressing the staff of the Commission in 1961, he expressed dismay at the breakdown of 'national consensus and togetherness' asking, 'Where have we gone astray?' and remarking that, 'People with scruples can very successfully build up organisations which in due time are taken over by unscrupulous leaders' (p 18–19). Norman Girvan notes that by the 1960s and 1970s the organisation 'was to become more explicitly a tool of government policy and of the party in power' (p 19). It had major changes made to its structure and programme and was renamed the Social Development Commission in 1965 by then minister of development and welfare, Edward Seaga. Can we today resolve to break this cycle?

Document and learn from current initiatives by communities

There are many initiatives devised by people in communities across Jamaica which are examples of hope for the future and which demonstrate, as Nettleford says, the 'richness of the people's intellect and collective imagination, and which 'can be seen as an alternative driving force for development . . .'

Case 1: The 'Rodney Raiders' miniature park and community vegetable garden

The Rodney Raiders ('corner' crew) miniature park and community vegetable garden was created on a derelict site. They Raiders explained how they did it:

The mobilisation was not really difficult. Mobilisation was the easy part. Nearly all the youth know each other, so you go up the road and pass it around that we are going to do something. We go from yard to yard. If a person really can't support by giving his or her labour, them assist financially. The older people willingly give because they see the productiveness of the youth. They give moral support. That counts for a lot.

We contemplated to have the farm, a park, raise fish or chicken, a play area. The majority decided we'd go for the park. We raise money by playing domino, charge people $2.00 per game. Within a week we raised $700 or $800, and every weekend we do that again. We get KRC to send a tractor to level the land. We put money together and give the tractor man something extra so he do the work good and not leave it half-way.

At our meeting we assigned people to design the park. Anything they could come up with together – that's the design we can work with. So they come up with the design and we make it out and stick with it right up to now. It's not yet completed – there's a fish pond and the children's play area still to come. But each area we designed is really appreciated. You find that every little youth takes part and can go inside the park and say 'me plant that tree' or 'me laid those bricks'. You have to be flexible – you can't make it too hard and fast. People have their own ideas – maybe move the trees around a bit – but we still have the park getting together and looking good. You have to allow people to be flexible, let them think for themselves. But you still have one main agenda and one main aim.

Those youths see their labour, what it has done, and each takes pride when someone passes by and says ' That park is pretty, man'. And that alone kind of builds him up inside. We find that we get more people all the time, because people are seeing an end product. they feel competent and they feel nice . . . (Source: 'Jones Town: A Case Study', Kingston Restoration Company (KRC); May 1996)

Case 2: The truth and reconciliation process working in Bennet Land, Kingston

Bennett Land is a community with a high level of poverty. Unemployment is high. Nutrition, sanitation, literacy, training opportunities, employment and viable livelihoods are among the major needs of the residents. They have combined individual effort with assistance from an NGO – the S-Corner Clinic and Community Development Organisation – to provide for their needs.

For years, the community was beset by gang-related violence and crime. Young men earned income by illegal means, for example, from 'forced tax' – collecting 'protection' money from local businesses – and from robbing buses plying the route. There were gangs which went to war at the slightest provocation. Many atrocities were committed: arson, murder, permanent maiming and disfigurement, and rape.

Representatives of the community, especially women, the church, school and NGOs, especially the S-Corner clinic, made various attempts to get the warring gangs to cease fire. Eventually, the young men themselves grew tired of the cycle of death. Through a long process of negotiations (based on carefully worked-out terms) peace was eventually called, leaders arose among them, and the process was taken by these leaders in the direction of systematic dialogue within the community. This dialogue involved all age groups, men and women. One requirement was a process of admitting/confessing wrongs done to one another, followed by apology and action to repair breaches and rebuild the community. The community agreed on a code of conduct for its members. Street and community committees which include former gang members were established, a 'child watch' programme was begun, conflicts were mediated to reduce crime, a sports programme was established, as were income-generating projects with former warring gang members (a chicken-rearing project is doing well). Residents now enjoy a renewed freedom of movement and association and local tradesmen are seeing improvement in their businesses. Bennet Land has come a far way in a relatively short time. The area has had very little external assistance, however, which has undoubtedly slowed the process down and might ultimately jeopardise its sustainability.

Implement new, important international conventions for social, economic and environmental justice and development.

In March 1995, Jamaica became a signatory to the Declaration and Programme Of Action of the World Summit for Social Development. Among the commitments that were signed were pledges to:

eradicate absolute poverty promote social integration based on the enhancement of all human rights, achieve equality and equity between women and men and create an economic, political, social, cultural and legal environment that will enable people to achieve social development.[24]

The Government of Jamaica is also a signatory to Agenda 21, arising out of the UN Conference on the Environment; the Beijing Platform For Action from the Fourth World Conference on Women, as well as the Convention on the Elimination of all forms of Discrimination Against Women (CEDAW); and the International Conference on Population and Development, among others. It is also a signatory to CARICOM plans of action arising from these conferences and there are many national plans of action which are yet to be implemented. One such plan which needs to be carried out is for the establishment of a Commission on Gender and Social Equity.

The forgoing discussion illustrates how much of a challenge achieving those commitments and plans will be. However if fundamental changes in Jamaica's political, economic and social structures are made – constitutional change and a significant overhaul of laws – they may be possible.

A Suggested Way Forward

Moving forward might be helped by a process involving the three Rs:
- revelation: a process of, and for, truth-telling
- restitution/reconciliation: righting wrongs and historical disadvantages through appropriate social policies and equitable distribution of resources as well as of sacrifices for the national good
- reconstruction of a Jamaica to which all citizens can feel a sense of belonging, a sense of being 'counted' and where access, contributions and benefits are equitably divided.

The words of Girvan senior are an appropriate thought with which to end:

What of the future? All over the world people are asking themselves what they can do to find a way out; people are dreaming, planning and talking about a Better Order. We in Jamaica have our full share of responsibility both for conditions that exist today and those that will exist tomorrow. There is no time for delay . . .[25]

Notes

1. See DTM Girvan, *Working Together For Development*, compiled and edited by Norman Girvan, (Institute of Jamaica Publications, 1993), p. 6
2. Girvan, 1993, p. 1
3. See Girvan, 1993, pp. 406–407

4. See Patricia Anderson & Michael Witter, 'Crisis, Adjustment And Social Change – A Case Study Of Jamaica' in Consequences Of Structural Adjustment – A Review of the Jamaican Experience, Elsie Le Franc, ed. (Canoe Press, UWI, 1994)
5. Ibid.
6. See Anderson & Witter, 'Crisis, Adjustment And Social Change – A Case Study of Jamaica', p.21
7. See Atherton Martin's introduction to *Hope and Disillusion; The CBI In Jamaica – A Case Study*, (Joan French, Association of Development Agencies, 1990)
8. Henry-Lee Aldrie, et al, preliminary findings, An Examination of the Socio-economic Conditions and Coping Strategies of Workers in Selected Occupations Which Have a Minimum Wage *(Policy Development Unit, Planning Institute of Jamaica, 1998)*
9. Robert Chambers, Vulnerability, Coping and Policy (Sussex IDS Bulletin, Vol. 20, No. 2, 1989)
10. Carrie Higinbotham, *Women, Kinship Networks and Change: The Effects of Socio-economic and Structural Changes in Woodside* (St Mary: Independent study project, School for International Training, Kingston, 1996)
11. See *Economic and Social Survey of Jamaica* (ESSJ), 1996, p. 23.6
12. 'They Cry Respect: Urban violence and Poverty In Jamaica', Compiled by Horace Levy (Centre for Population, Community and Social Change, UWI, 1996); and Primary Data, Action Research Project, Jamaica Social Investment Fund, 1998
13. Levy, 1996, p.28
14. Caroline Moser, 'Urban Poverty And Violence – Consolidation or Erosion Of social Capital?', presented at the Second Annual World Bank Conference on Development in Latin America and the Caribbean, Bogota, Colombia, 1996
15. Implementation Strategy for Jones Town, Kingston Restoration Company and Overseas Development Agency (ODA) Consultancy Team, 1996, in A Review of Formal and Informal Survival Strategies at the Community Level (Trevor Spence, Canadian High Commission, 1998)
16. Levy, 1996, p.9
17. Ibid
18. Ibid, p.12
19. Margaret Newman & Elsie Le Franc, *'The Small Farm Sub-Sector : Is There Life After Structural Adjustment?',* in Consequences Of Structural Adjustment – A Review of the Jamaican Experience, Elsie le Franc, ed. (Canoe Press, UWI, 1994)
20. See Levy, *'They Cry Respect – Urban Violence And poverty in Jamaica'* (1996); and see forthcoming report on the Jamaica Social Investment Fund's Action Research Project
21. See Levy, 1996, p. 22
22. Ibid
23. DTM Girvan, Norman Girvan, ed., *Working Together For Development* (Kingston, Jamaica: Institute of Jamaica Publications Ltd., 1993)
24. The Copenhagen Declaration and Programme of Action; World Summit For Social Development 1995; p. vii
25. Girvan, 1993, p. 102

Part 6
Caribbean Thought and the Political Process

22 | TREVOR MUNROE

Caribbean Thought and the Political Process

Many of the challenges of the new millenium to the political process of the CARICOM states were already present in the last decade of the twentieth century. The decade opened with an attempted armed insurrection in Trinidad and Tobago in July 1990, during which the prime minister and members of parliament were held hostage, and closed in April 1999 with a nationwide social protest in Jamaica, which resulted in 9 deaths (7 people were fatally shot by the police); 14 security personnel injured; 6 attacks on police stations; over 110 instances of looting and arson; 16 vehicles of the security forces damaged; and 34 instances of shooting at the police – all in the space of three days. The overall damage to the economy and, in particular, to the tourism sector was estimated at hundreds of millions of dollars. Subsequent to these protests, the administration was forced to modify its stance on the fuel price increase which sparked the protests. Opinion polls confirmed that two thirds of the electorate supported the protests and a majority believed that the government had lost the moral authority to rule. In Trinidad and Tobago, surveys subsequent to the July 1990 insurrection sound little sympathy for the government of the then Prime Minister Robinson.

July 1990 in Trinidad and Tobago, and April 1999 in Jamaica, were but two, albeit the two most extreme, episodes challenging the legitimacy and the effectiveness of the political processes in the region. One other bears mention – the credible implication of the leadership of both the government and opposition parties in St Kitts in the illicit narcotics trade. Interlinked with these incidents, are some of the enormous challenges which we shall have to address in the new millenium. I would list these as follows:-

1. Halting growing voter de-alignment and citizen alienation from formal politics, reflected in downturns in electoral participation, fall-off in support for political parties and party leaders (see Table 1, Regional Electoral Turnout, 1950s–1990s).
2. Dealing more effectively with corruption in the political process affecting both the public and the private sectors. (A recent survey revealed that a significant majority of Jamaicans regarded corruption as the number one problem facing Jamaica's democracy.)
3. Halting the decline in social capital and reconfiguring relations of trust
4. Reducing the degree to which processes of transnational governance – at the local, regional, hemispheric and global levels – are distant, non-responsive and unaccountable to the people
5. Generating new approaches to leadership appropriate to the new conditions at the turn of the century

These challenges are undoubtedly urgent and unquestionably have their Caribbean (indeed island by island, territorial) peculiarities. But, we would do

TABLE 1
Commonwealth Caribbean: Average Electoral Turnout 1950s–1990s

Country	1950s	1960s	1970s	1980s	1990s
Antigua/Barbuda	64 (2)	48 (2)	86 (2)	67 (3)	63 (2)
Montserrat	–	47 (2)	77 (3)	73 (2)	67 (1)
St Kitts/Nevis	–	68 (2)	80 (2)	73 (3)	66 (1)
Dominica	74 (3)	79 (2)	79 (2)	77 (2)	65 (2)
Grenada	69 (3)	68 (3)	74 (2)	86 (1)	62 (3)
St Lucia	55 (3)	52 (2)	76 (2)	64 (3)	63 (1)
St Vincent/Grenadines	67 (3)	81 (3)	67.5 (3)	81 (2)	66.5 (2)
Barbados	62 (2)	70 (2)	78 (2)	74 (2)	60 (2)
Jamaica	66 (2)	77.5 (2)	82 (2)	83 (2)	66 (2)
Belize	–	72.5 (2)	80 (2)	74 (2)	72 (1)
Trinidad and Tobago	75 (2)	77 (2)	56 (1)	61 (2)	66 (1)
Averages	66 (20)	68 (24)	76 (23)	74 (24)	65 (17)

(Parentheses indicate number of elections on which the average is based. The percentages are rounded)

Source: Emmanuel (1993) and reports on General Elections

ourselves a disservice, to say nothing of diagnosis and prescription, if we did not recognise the following:

1. Entering the twenty-first century and beyond, the political process in the Caribbean remains, on all recognised comparative measures of democracy, among the most democratic regions in the world. (See the Freedom House Index, Table 2, where 1 indicates the highest degree of freedom and 7 the lowest. All Caribbean states except for Antigua ranked between 1 and 2.5, placing them in the category of free states.)

TABLE 2
Freedom House Index
(The first number in each box indicates score re: political rights; the second re: civil liberties)

Country	1978	89-90	90-91	91-92	92-93	93-94	94-95	95-96
Antigua (-) [4]	2,2 [F]	2,3	3,2	3,3	3,3	4,3	4,3	4,3 (6)
Bahamas (+) [4]	1,2 [F]	2,3	2,3	2,3	1,2	1,2	1,2	1,2 (2)
Barbados (0) [1]	1,1 [F]	1,1	1,1	1,1	1,1	1,1	1,1	1,1 (1)
Belize (+) [2]	1,2 [F]	1,2	1,2	1,1	1,1	1,1	1,1	1,1 (1)
Dominica (+) [2]	2,3 [F]	2,1	2,1	2,1	2,1	2,1	2,1	1,1 (1)
Dom Repub (-) [4]	2,2 [F]	1,3	2,3	2,3	2,3	3,3	4,3	4,3 (6)
Grenada (+) [3]	2,3 [F]	2,2	2,2	1,2	1,2	1,2	1,2	1,2 (2)
Guyana (+) [6]	4,3 [P.F.]	5,4	5,4	5,4	3,3	2,2	2,2	2,2 (3)
Haiti (+) [7]	7,6 [N.F.]	7,5	4,4	7,7	7,7	7,7	5,5	5,5 (7)
Jamaica (-) [3]	2,3 [F]	2,2	2,2	2,2	2,2	2,3	2,3	2,3 (4)
St Kitts (-) [1]	2,3 [F]	1,1	1,1	1,1	1,1	1,1	2,2	1,2 (2)
St Lucia (0) [2]	2,3 [F]	1,2	1,2	1,2	1,2	1,2	1,2	1,2 (2)
St Vincent (0) [2]	2,2 [F]	1,2	1,2	1,2	1,2	1,1	2,1	2,1 (2)
Suriname (0) [5]	2,2 [F]	3,3	6,4	4,4	3,3	3,3	3,3	3,3 (5)
Trin &Tob (-) [1]	2,2 [F]	1,1	1,1	1,1	1,1	1,1	1,2	1,2 (2)

Source: *Freedom in the World: The Annual Survey of Political Rights & Civil Liberties* (Freedom House, various years)

(0) = 4; (-) = 5 (+) = 6; P.F. = partly free; N.F. = not free; F. = free

1. [1989-90 covers the year 1989, and so on]
2. (-), (+), (0) indicate whether the particular country declined, improved or remained the same in its scores on the Freedom House Index between 1989/90 and 1995/96.
3. [ ] The number in the square brackets indicates the ranking in 1978 of the particular country among the states named on the Freedom House Index: ( ) indicates the ranking in 1995/96.

FIGURE 1
Parliamentary Elections: Differences betwen regions over time 1945–97

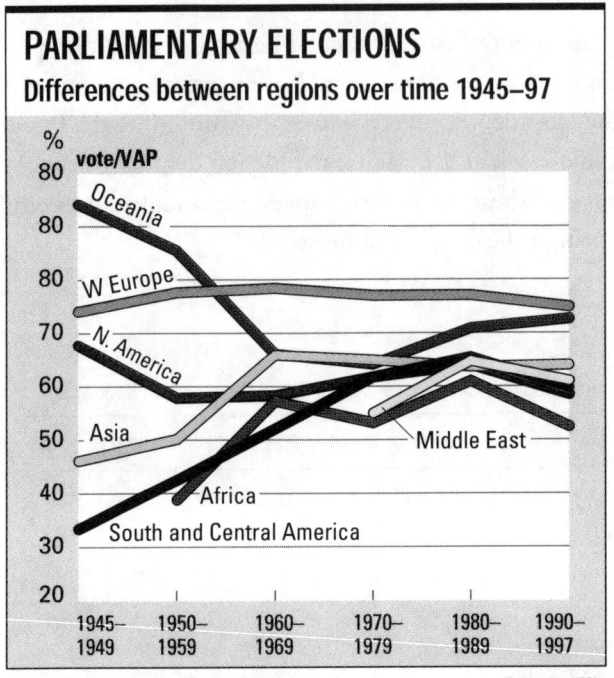

Source: 'Voter Turnout from 1945 to 1997: A Global Report on Political Participation, International Institute for Democracy & Electoral Assistance', Varberg 1997, p. 24

2. In all major regions of the world (Western Europe, North America, Middle East, Asia, South and Central America), voter turn-out has been falling since the 1980s (see Figure 1).
3. In most democratic states for which there is data, while democratic values remain strong, there is a definite loss of confidence in politicians and a loss of faith in established political and government institutions (see Figures 2 and 3). This trend cuts across high, middle and low income countries and should warn us against any simplistic reduction of political crisis to economic stagnation or non-performance. Conversely, it should guard us against the view that all we need to do, difficult as that may be, is to get the economy right and the politics will follow. Exclusively economy-centred diagnosis and prescriptions are simplistic and therefore flawed. The US economy is enjoying unprecedented prosperity, yet trust in the presidency, Congress and in government as a whole, continues to fall. The crisis facing

FIGURE 2
Losing Faith: Confidence in Political Institutions*, %

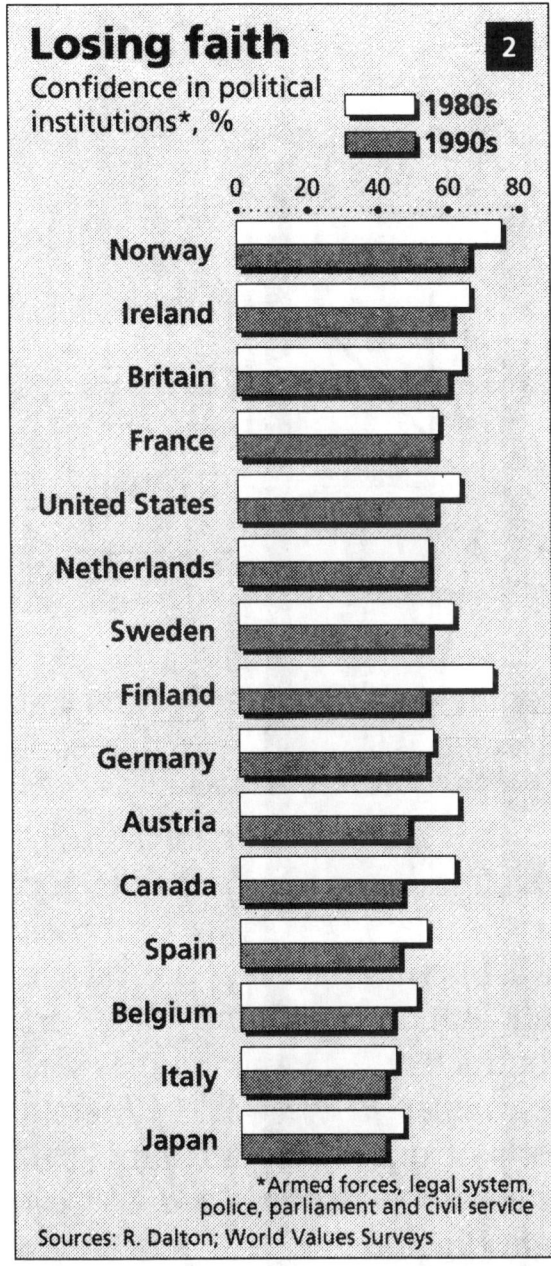

Source: *The Economist*, July 17, 1999

FIGURE 3 Losing Faith: Confidence in Political Institutions*, %

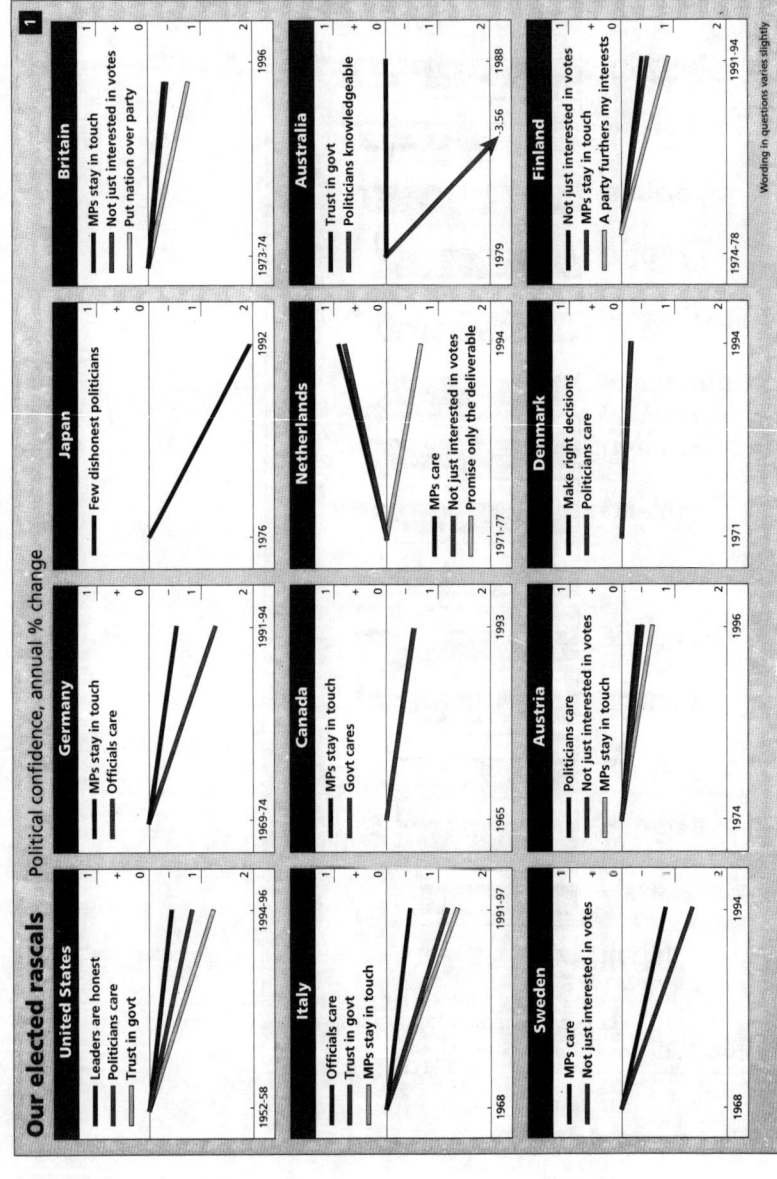

Source: *The Economist*, July 17, 1999

the Caribbean political process, and indeed, politics globally, whilst having an economic dimension, is not only, or even primarily, economic.

What, then, are some of the other fundamental underlying factors which we must grasp if we are to properly prepare to successfully meet the challenges now upon us? I shall only mention one: There is a fundamental mismatch between politics (parties, unions, legislatures, executives, electoral systems, leadership) evolved out of and designed for early and mid-twentieth century agrarian/industrial systems (developed and developing) on the one hand, and the new end-of-century citizen formed in the information age; a participant, to varying degrees, in processes of globalisation and in increasingly knowledge-based economies.

In the Caribbean context this means that a political process essentially formed in the 1950s cannot, unless it undergoes fundamental transformation, be functional for a growing segment of the people in the twenty-first century and beyond, all the more so when there is economic stagnation, but even when there is economic growth.

The simple but critical fact is that the typical Caribbean person of the year 2000 is relatively young, urbanised, educated, informed, and exposed to modernity and post-modernity in all its manifestations. Take one simple indicator: The amount of time which the average Caribbean citizen spent on international telephone calls in 1995 was 25 times the average for developing countries, almost seven times the global average and, most surprisingly, 80 per cent higher than the industrialised states (see Table 3). This is no longer the old-time cane cutter, small farmer, or even civil service clerk! The needs and capabilities of this person are fundamentally different from the needs and capabilities of his parents and grandparents: typically rural, relatively uninformed, uneducated, unexposed, unconfident, for better or worse, living in a relatively protected environment.

The needs and capabilities of this Caribbean of the 1950s and 1960s, even into the 1970s, made for a considerable degree of congruence between this person and political processes that were essentially paternalistic, ultimately becoming clientelistic and tribalistic. Take the fundamental issue of leadership. The political process so evolved, became so structured that all a citizen was required to do, and perhaps, relatively speaking, all he was capable of doing was to 'leave it up to the leader' – whether the leader was charismatic, managerialist, or technocratic.

TABLE 3
Country Access to Information and Communicaton, 1995

Country	Radios Per 1000	TVs Per 1000	Telephone Per 1000 People [1996]	Intl Calls mins Per person	Cell Phones Per 1000	Internet Per 1000 People [1998]	PCs Per people
Barbados	900	287	370	123	18	5.4	57
Antigua	439	409	423	–	–	3.7	–
Bahamas	735	233	315	–	–	2.0	–
Trinidad & Tobago	505	318	168	45	4	3.1	19.2
Dominica	634	141	264	–	–	1.2	–
St Kitts & Nevis	668	–	382	196	–	0.2	–
Grenada	598	158	243	82	4	0.1	–
St Vincent	670	234	171	–	–	0.0	–
St Lucia	765	301	235	76	6	0.2	–
Jamaica	438	306	142	22	18	0.7	–
Guyana	494	42	60	24	1.5	0.1	–
Belize	587	167	133	27	6	2.3	28
Caribbean {Average]	619	320	242	74	8	1.58	27.2
All developing Countries {Average]	185	145	39	3	3.6	0.5	6.5
Industrial Countries [Average]	1005	524	414	41.6	61	18	156
World [Average]	364	226	122	10.9	16.8	4.8	48.6

Source: Adapted from *Human Development Reports*, 1998, pp.166–167; 1999, pp. 53–56
In 1996 – outgoing traffic per subscriber per minute was as follows: Jamaica 183; T&T 277; UK 148; US 113; Costa Rica 113 – [1998 World Development Indicators, World Bank pp. 290–292

Not so the end-of-century Caribbean person. He or she requires and can enrich what Owen Arthur has called 'a new form of governance'. For him, what Prime Minister announced at the opening of this conference, is absolutely true: 'Old hierarchical ways of managing must give way.' The question then must be, on what principles must the 'new form of governance be constructed?' How is the old to give way?

I suggest the following principles. The foundation for their application is the preservation, rather than the negation of existing political rights and civil liberties.

1. Transparency, rather than secrecy: Freedom of information and access to documentation must replace Official Secrets Acts. Reports should be posted on the internet (in July 1997, Jamaica hosted 1.4 internet users per 10,000 and Trinidad and Tobago 3.2 per 10,000).
2. Accountability, rather than autonomy: What this requires is the establishment of performance standards for public officials, and of rights of recall of elected representatives (as proposed in the Grenada Constitution Commission in 1986 and the Stone Committee Report in Jamaica, 1991). Those in authority should have a duty to report to their constituencies. Interactive media (TV and radio talk shows) should be used constructively, for example, ministers should be required to spend a given number hours each week on pre-designated and rotated talk shows.
3. Participation, rather than passivity: This would include citizen education and involvement/oversight in anti-corruption agencies, contract award systems, redress of abuses by police and other authorities. Systems of people's initiatives (as proposed in the Barbados Constitutional Review Commission, 1998) should be installed. The twenty-first century is going to be the age of the referendum. In the 1960s, referenda averaged less than eight per year, globally; whilst the first half of the 1990s, saw up to two each month. Civil society and NGOs must also put their houses in order in terms of participatory structures and culture.
4. Consensualism, leading to partnership, rather than majoritarianism leading to adversarialism. Networking, trust-building across parties, unions, class, colour, ethnic groups, and inner-city gangs are fundamental preconditions. Mixed rather than pure electoral systems; meaningful and effective consultation with political oppositions, civil society and the private sector up to and including power-sharing arrangements.
5. Regionalism and globalism, rather than insularity: This requires the involvement of the private sector and civil society in all aspects of regional and global relations. For example, involvement in negotiations/preparations for negotiations with International Governmental Organisations, multi-lateral

agencies and Trans-National Corporations. New ways must be devised to involve the diaspora in national and transnational political processes. Take note of the fact that Caribbean people are among the most globalised in the world.

6. A new influence-based, rather than authority-driven, leadership is required.

Perhaps above all else, such leadership must encourage a following which is informed, educated, active, diverse, independent, self-directed, and self-organised in ways that are largely incompatible with charismatic, managerialist, authoritarian or paternalistic leadership. In this sense, Joseph Rost is right when he comments that in 'the post-industrial model', the word 'followers' has a new meaning: 'Followers are active agents in the leadership relationship, not passive recipients of the leader's influence.' Moreover, leadership must be consciously consensual, seeking to build bridges and negotiate compromises, rather than majoritarian in orientation and insensitive to minorities. In so doing, leadership of the new type cannot neglect the empowerment of the majority whilst seeking to power-share with minorities – whether political or ethnic – not only as a temporary expedient but as an enduring appreciation of their permanent place and valued contribution to society. This is never an easy endeavor (as the course of the negotiated settlements and continuing challenges in South Africa and Ireland graphically illustrate) but it is especially complex in Jamaica. At the minimum, such leadership has to develop an attitude of respect for 'the other sides', resist recrimination and victimisation, promote meaningful dialogue and continuing consultation in crafting and sustaining institutions which facilitate majority upliftment and, at the same time, minority partnership. (Trevor Munroe, *Renewing Democracy*, pp 111–112)

My own experience at sectoral level partnership building suggests that we can make the necessary changes at the national and regional levels (for example Bauxite/Alumina 'Memorandum Of Understanding', 1995-1999). The Caribbean contribution to the politics of the twentieth century has been a substantial one:

1. The philosophy and immense organisational work of Marcus Garvey contributed significantly to the reentry of non-European peoples and people of African descent as major players on the world stage, and ultimately, the birth of new states and countries. (Garvey's movement spread over some 37 countries, and his organisation had 3 million members.)

2. The universalisation of political rights – the first black country to win universal adult suffrage was Jamaica, in 1944.
3. The development of popular culture as a force for progress (Marley, Berlin Wall, Apartheid)
4. Consolidation of democratic systems in ethnically and culturally diverse societies.

In much the same way as we helped to transform the politics of the twentieth century, from political dependence to independence, we can transform the twenty-first century from a liberalised globalisation serving primarily the minority of mankind, to a regulated, managed globalisation with much potential benefit for the majority: *If we move beyond talk and begin to act now.*

23 | SELWYN RYAN

Caribbean Political Thought, From Westminster to Philadelphia

With the possible exception of Rastafarianism, Caribbean political thought, as opposed to Caribbean political analysis, has not distinguished itself by its originality. Most of what has been articulated has been a literal transference to the Caribbean environment of the grand theories that were fashionable in the UK, continental Europe, or the USA or adaptations thereof. Every 'ism' or current of thought which emerged in the various metropoles found their echo in the writings of our political intellectuals, and in the various political parties and social movements which have appeared on the Caribbean landscape. Over the decades we have had Caribbean versions of conversatism, liberalism, socialism, Fabianism, Marxism, welfare democracy, Marxism-Leninism, Stalinism, Trotskyism, nationalism, pan-Africanism, Fidelism, pluralism, civil rights, black power, dependence, feminism, Afro-centrism, populism, imperialism, vanguardism, multiculturalism, neo-liberalism, globalism, Maoism, the name but a few of those 'isms' that have had their high priests and disciples in the region.

This view about the absence of indigenous theorising is of course neither unique nor new. Many have said it before, none more eloquently than Lloyd Best when he remarked in an essay that,

> owing to the facts of power, the easiest way for the intellectual elites of the so-called new states to acquire legitimacy abroad (they have not yet acquired it at home) is for them, at best, to show technical competence in the methods and procedures of what is in their own habitat, western scientism and western propaganda. At worst, if they cannot acquire the competence, they must have the *paquotille*, the trinketry of western science. (*'Independent Thought'*,1966, p 26)

In their search for legitimacy and respectability at home, Caribbean intellectuals and political activists fought bitterly and schismatically to show that they were more faithful and better schooled exponents of one ism or another. In this regard, they were much less innovative than their Latin American, African, and Asian (including the Chinese) counterparts who, let us admit, had a more traditional social base upon which to experiment with alternative strategies of action. Located in the West as the Caribbean was, our intellectuals and politicians perhaps felt that what was applicable to the geographically adjacent metropoles was equally so in the ex-colonies, the size and openness of which led many to think that exotic options were not sustainable in either cultural or geo-strategic terms.

To say this is not to disparage Caribbean intellectuals and political elites. We are all familiar with the work of CLR James, Marcus Garvey, Sylvester Williams, George Padmore, Eric Williams, Walter Rodney, MG Smith, Carl Stone, Havelock Brewster, Gordon Lewis, Michael Manley, William Demas, Clive Thomas, Arthur Lewis, Orlando Patterson, George Beckford, Norman Girvan, Patrick Emanuel, and Trevor Munroe to name but a few of those whose writings and speeches have had a significant influence on political thinking and public policy-making in the Caribbean. We are also familiar with the work of Lloyd Best and the New World Group, of Tapia in Trinidad and Tobago, and of New Beginning in both Trinidad and Tobago and Jamaica, all of which sought to develop alternative political paradigms to those that were then prevailing. And we have of course a new crop of political analysts and thinkers who have begun to make an impact.

When I was asked to present a paper on the subject of 'Caribbean Political Thought and the Political Process', my plan was to attempt a retrospective of the ideas of some of our university-based intellectuals and then see whether they had anything to offer us as we move into the twenty-first century. In the end, I decided that it would be more relevant to our purpose to focus on the 'thought' of those who are, or who have been, actively involved in political action as conventionally understood, bearing in mind that many of these people were the university-based intellectuals of yesterday, or their students. In deciding to do this, I was mindful of the view of Lloyd Best that, for the intellectual, 'thought is action'. If this is so, as I believe it to be, the converse is also true: action is thought in practice. As Keynes reminded us, political practitioners are invariably acting, whether consciously or unconsciously, on the basis of some system of thought borrowed from intellectuals either living or dead.

My decision to focus on the 'thought' of our political practitioners was informed by another consideration – the mandate given to us by the organisers of the conference to generate ideas and recommendations that could serve to shape policy in the region in the twenty-first century. In an attempt to fulfill this mandate, I have decided to do five things:

1. Review very broadly our post-war experience with the political paradigms which we borrowed from Westminster to determine the extent to which the model is sustainable in the contemporary environment.
2. Determine whether we should continue to structure our political system along Westminster lines or whether we should restructure it along more consociational lines.
3. If the former, what modifications are called for?

If the latter, what steps do we need to take to ensure that we do not end up with a paradigm that replaces probable state collapse with certain collapse?

Quite apart from whatever system we adopt, what roles do we advocate for the political opposition and for civil society in the next millennium?

The Post-Colonial Experience

Whether positioned on the 'right' or 'left' of the ideological spectrum, Caribbean political thought was invariably of the populist variety. This was so whether the parties followed a Marxist-Leninist line, with its prescriptions about a vanguard party, or a mass democratic party with a welfarist or labourist flavour – the one which characterised so many of the parties which emerged in the 1950s and 1960s. All of the latter accepted as given the prescriptive notions that informed the Westminster model. Most of those on the left also felt that they had no option but to participate in Westminster-type elections even if their ultimate ideological ambition was to change it in its essentials. That model in fact seemed to be the only game in town.

The view which prevailed throughout the Caribbean, with but few exceptions, was that the wishes of the majority as expressed through voting in competitive elections should prevail. As Michael Manley (1974, p 30) explained:

It is the Jamaican instinct in the Jamaican personality to argue, to be disputatious, to listen to contending views and eventually to say 'let us take a vote', or as the worker would put it: 'majority must carry'. Others formulate it as: 'majority must rule'. And to understand a people it is best to listen and discover what come naturally to them. The democratic process comes naturally to the Jamaican people. Therefore, arguments about one-party states as against multi-party states begin with the supreme disadvantage or irrelevance in the Jamaican situation, because the one-party state is unthinkable to the Jamaican.

Very few constitutions provided for a qualitative majority except where entrenched clauses in the constitution were concerned. One exception to this generalisation occurred in Trinidad and Tobago where Dr Eric Williams, the founder of the People's National Movement (PNM), argued that it was necessary to depart from strict majoritarianism in the case of Trinidad and Tobago. Williams' argument was that in a multi-racial society such as Trinidad and Tobago's, economic, religious, and other vested interests should not only be given some say in running the country, but should be given effective and symbolic representation in a nominated chamber. As he put it, 'The nominated system is so essential that if it did not exist, it would be necessary to invent it.' William was Madisonian in his approach to constitutional engineering. To quote him:

Checks and balances [are] necessary in a democratic society. Such checks and balances are doubly necessary when, as is always possible, one party might sweep the polls and find itself without effective opposition in the elected house, as has happened with Bradshaw in St Kitts, Bird in Antigua, Gairy in Grenada, Nkrumah in the Gold Coast and Muñoz Marin in Puerto Rico. To make assurance doubly sure, the delaying power of twelve months enjoyed by the House of Lords in Britain should be extended to twenty-four months in Trinidad as the system is new and as we have only a limited experience of democratic process. That experience dates back only thirty-two years, a short time in the life of man and an insignificant period in the life of a country.

Williams argued that it was critical to create a system in which all interests of race, creed and economics would feel secure. 'The last apology or excuse for colonisation will have been removed when Caribbean democracy can prove that minority rights are quite safer in its hands.' (Williams, 1957, p 60).

The Williams' record showed, however, that while in power, the PNM was as intolerant of opposition and as exclusionary as most other leaders and parties in the Caribbean. Those who opposed what Williams sought to do or what he considered national were either accused of being 'recalcitrant,' 'obscurantist,' 'reactionary', 'massas' or dismissed with some such term of abuse. The pattern was the same in all the other territories. Premiers and prime ministers were intolerant of abuse to opposition in whatever form it reared its head. The winners were entitled to take all the power and all the resources available. As Arthur Lewis complained in respect of the Eastern Caribbean:

> ... in a small island of 50,000 to 100,000 people, dominated by a single political party, it is very difficult to prevent political abuse. Everybody depends on the government for something, however small, so most are reluctant to offend it. The civil servants live in fear; the police avoid unpleasantness; the trade unions are tied to the party; the newspaper depends on government advertisements; and so on. This is true even if the political leaders are absolutely honest. In cases where they are also corrupt, and playing with the public funds, the situation becomes intolerable. (cited in Blackman, 1989, p 6)

Part of the problem was that all of the governments which came to power in the post-depression post-war world believed that they had a mission to create a brave new Jerusalem in which want, unemployment, landlessness, poverty and disease were eliminated. This was a course true of the developed, as well as the so called 'newly developing' world. In the case of the Caribbean, the feeling was that the *raison d'être* of the state was to complete the emancipation agenda which had been left unfinished by the colonial state. The view expressed in Ghana by Kwame Nkrumah, that one merely had to seek the political kingdom for all else to be added, was shared by most Caribbean leaders who believed that socialism and nationalism were magical keys that would in time unlock the doors that had shut out the people of the Caribbean from realising their potential.

Michael Manley, for example, argued that after 300 years of slavery, politics in Jamaica had to be transformative rather than merely adjustive. In Manley's view, 'Jamaica society [was] disfigured by inequities that go too deep for tinkering . . . Nothing less than transformation can provide answers to the dilemmas within which we are currently trapped' (Manley, 1974, p 23). That vision was also shared by Eric Williams. Whether out of intellectual conviction or out of an awareness that it was dysfunctional in the context of Trinidad society, Williams rejected the utopian socialist tradition, and opted instead for a programme designed to create jobs by seeking to attract foreign investment for an import substitution industrialisation programme. He was confident that an energetic scientifically oriented puritanical elite leading a highly disciplined political party such as he conceived the PNM to be, could mobilise the energies of the entire population, regardless of race or class. As he put it, 'It is not a question of race, religion or colour; it is not a question of labour, or capital. It is a question of jobs, schools, houses, water. It calls for the united effort of the entire "population". It was bootstrap political economy, Puerto Rico style.' Much the same could be said of the political strategies of the political leaderships in Barbados and the island states of the Eastern Caribbean. It is generally agreed, however, that notwithstanding the many glaring flaws and abuses such as those to which Arthur Lewis referred above, the states of the anglophone Caribbean were more successful in making Westminster institutions work than were states in other parts of the world to which they were also transplanted.

The question now being anxiously asked by many has to do with the extent to which these achievements can be sustained, given the powerful forces that are now serving to undermine and subvert them. Is the 'historically favourable political culture' which was inherited together with a sophisticated complex of liberal democratic institutions sufficiently well entrenched to withstand the hurricane-like social storms that are roaring throughout the region? Is there sufficient democratic renewal taking place to compensate for the diminution in the stock of social capital that is rapidly taking place, or is the decline of democracy secular and irreversible? Many are of the view that liberal democracy is in grave danger in the anglophone Caribbean and that unless drastic steps are taken to bolster and renew the democratic character and institutional capability of the political and social systems of the island states in the region, they will be lumped with other states that are negatively classified along the governance continuum.

Several proposals have been made as to what should be done to reduce the democratic deficits and ameliorate the political crises which characterise Caribbean democracy. The suggestions range from those which we may define as minimalist and which aim to strengthen the regulatory machinery of the states while retaining the basic Westminster architecture, to proposals that are more far reaching and which seek to replace that model with structures and processes that are more American and more consensual.

Minimalist Formulations

Among the first group are the following which are drawn from across the Caribbean are the following:

a) Limit the number of consecutive terms that a given political leader can remain in power as is the case in the US and Latin America. It is believed that frequent elite circulation would help to strengthen groups in civil society and force political elites to share resources more equitably and to be more accountable. It may, however, serve to encourage new incumbents to grab as much as they can as soon as they come to power as is the case in Mexico and elsewhere in Latin America.

b) Provide the office of the ombudsman, currently found in many Caribbean states, with the material and other resources needed to enable him to monitor administrative abuse and to intervene more effectively to minimise it.

c) Establish or, where they already exist, empower financial oversight committees in parliament to engender transparency and accountability.

d) Establish, or where they exist, empower parliamentary committees to monitor the activities of state-owned enterprises and statutory corporations.

e) Establish oversight committees which would seek to ensure that rules for free and fair elections are adhered to. International and regional observers should be routinely invited to monitor electoral processes prior to, during, and following elections.

f) Privatise state-owned media, where it exists, to make it compete. This is particularly important regarding electronic media.

g) Depoliticise the public service and find ways to balance the loyalty needs of the ruling party with the autonomy required by the public service to enable it to function professionally.

h) Strengthen local government bodies to encourage greater public participation, accountability, and generally to empower civil society. De-emphasise the centrality of party in local government elections and resource allocations. Adequate funding should be provided to allow local bodies to function autonomously.

i) Improve standards of internal party democracy to enable grassroots elements to have more say in policy identification and implementation. This may also help to restrain the predatory behaviour of maximum leaders which has reduced popular control and popular input to empty rituals.

j) Establish or empower integrity commissions to monitor and report on the cumulative activities of elected officials and certain categories of officers in the employ of the state.
k) Establish structures to monitor the award of government contracts to foreign and local investors or agencies, such as the Office of the Contractor General in Jamaica.
l) Limit the number of parliamentarians who could be appointed to the executive to 40 or 50 per cent of the membership of parliament to strengthen the role of backbenchers and, by extension, the powers of parliamentary oversight committees in relation to the executive.
m) Introduce an element of proportional representation in the upper house to even out the swings and distortions which often occur in electoral systems. One might also try 'topping up' formulas such as the 'best loser' system used in Mauritius to compensate for the under representation of small parties that is a product of the zero-sum, first-past-the-post-system.
n) Give the head of state a greater role in the appointment of officials to sensitive national offices and regulatory institutions.
o) Appoint an independent council with full powers to investigate executive wrongdoing.
p) Resolve to call on directors of state enterprises, statutory bodies and members of commissions to resign or offer to resign as a matter of course following the coming to power of a new regime. Allow them to serve out their terms of office and replace them, if necessary, as those expire. The limited nature of the professional resource base in most islands is too limited to sustain the indiscriminate haemorrhaging of talent which this policy encourages.
q) Design electoral systems such as the alternative vote which would encourage candidates for electoral office to make non-partisan rather than partisan appeals, such as occur in the first-past-the-post-system.
r) In the interests of political morality, integrity, and party stability, a candidate who faces the electorate as a representative of a political party and who does not support the policies of the party when elected, should be made to vacate his/her seat and contest a by-election if he/she wishes to remain in office. In default of resignation, the party should be entitled to expel him and tender his undated letter of resignation or other authorising document (which he should sign prior to accepting nomination) to the presiding

officer of the body to which he/she was elected. Parties should not be used as 'flags of convenience'. Proposals have also been made that delinquent MPs should be recallable.

The Problems of Securing Accountability and Control

Many of the minimalist reforms suggested have been tried in one island state or another with mixed or indifferent results. Quite apart from the cost of implementing some of these proposals, there is also the question as to whether they can work as intended in the anglophone Caribbean. One of the problems faced by Caribbean states in securing accountability along the lines itemised above is that the size of most parliaments and their human resource capacities do not allow certain conventional mechanisms of control to be utilised effectively. In larger political systems, it is possible to put in place elaborate committee systems or other preventative measures to monitor and scrutinise government budgets and prevent the occurrence of certain kinds of social diseases. It is even the norm in some countries to have parliamentary committees chaired by backbenchers or members of rival parties. Such arrangements do not work well in small states either because parliaments meet too infrequently, or because the opposition or backbench elements are too small and weak to provide the manpower and expertise needed to staff such committees. In many countries, all members of the ruling party are in the cabinet. As such, the cabinet becomes the *de facto* legislature. Party loyalty and party discipline also mean that legislators invariably support the executive on such committees since they wish to avoid scoring 'own goals' which embarrass their party.

The Dominica Constitution Review Commission (1999, p 21) makes similar observations:

Size of itself affects the dynamics of government. In small states, almost all the members of the party can be given some office as minister, parliamentary secretary or chairman of a statutory corporation. The only critical voices in the Parliament will be those of the opposition which inevitably carry little weight. All of this strengthens the power of the Prime Minister in relation to the House.

The small size of parliament also means that prime ministers are limited in their ability to reshuffle cabinet ministers or call for the resignation of ministers who embarrass the government. In large parliaments, the prime minister can bring in competent backbenchers to replace ministerial incumbents. In small parliaments, this option is not normally available unless an appointment is made via the senate where such an institution exists, and constitutional arrangements allow.

Arend Lijphart (1990, pp 326–327) has argued that the small size of Caribbean parliaments weakens losing political parties, not only by allocating a disproportionately small *percentage* of seats to them, but also a small *number* of seats. 'In almost two-thirds of the elections (63 per cent), the second party won only two or fewer seats, and it won three or more in only slightly more than one-third of the elections (37 per cent).' Lijphart notes that when third parties contest, it takes only the winning of 1 or 2 more seats for the minority to become the plurality or majority. Given this and other reasons, 'We see a high frequency of deviation from the Westminster ideal of a strong majority party that governs but is watched and criticised by a vigorous opposition party. It is extremely difficult if not impossible to conduct such an effective opposition with only one or two seats in the legislature.' Lijphart argues that in order to improve the electoral chances of second parties, and the effectiveness of parliamentary opposition, the size of some Caribbean parliaments needs to be doubled.

While it is conceivable that some of the difficulties identified above might be overcome by increasing the size of Caribbean parliaments or by the introduction of mechanisms which strengthen the regulatory capacity of the state, the reality is that political and group competition in small states is invariably fierce and personalised. Those who wish to remain within the narrow elite circle or to benefit from state patronage either for themselves or firms which they own or represent, are generally disinclined to challenge a potentially punitive officialdom. The difficulty is exacerbated in plural or dual societies such as those in Guyana or Trinidad and Tobago where the government has its centre of gravity in one community and opposition parties in others. The problem of loyalty in such cases becomes not merely one of the loyalty to party or leader, but also to community. Critics remain silent out of concern that they might be viewed as *namakharams,* a term used by Hindus to describe those who betray their kin or ethnic group. Such inhibitions affect individuals in the private sector as well as those in the public sector.

Societies that are small are also generally characterised by the narrowness of their resource base. There are few free floating material assets. In order to secure a share of the small resource pie, interest groups, real or potential, feel compelled to forge links with and become clients to those who are in a position to allocate valued resources. Clientelism has in fact served to transform the workings of the Westminster parliamentary system in the anglophone Caribbean (Stone, 1989; Edie, 1994). Those who are under the 'clientele' umbrella are either suborned to stay mute, at least in public, or do so in the hope of being incorporated or shaded by the political banyan tree.

Maximalist Formulations

Jamaica

Proposals for more radical constitutional and electoral changes have been forthcoming from Trinidad and Tobago, Guyana, Jamaica and the East Caribbean. In the eighties, and more particularly the mid-nineties, there was a significant debate in Jamaica as to what ought to be done with respect to changing the structure of government to address some of the critical problems of governance which were being experienced. The basic questions revolved around the issue of retention or replacement of the 'monarchy' as head of state and the retention or replacement of the Westminster model with a presidential type system or some other hybrid form. There was general agreement among the parties that a president should replace the British Queen as head of state. In his final speech to the Jamaican parliament, Michael Manley spoke for many when he argued that it was time to repatriate the symbols of Jamaican sovereignty and in so doing, break the psychological link between the Jamaican people and the British Crown. Only so would people come to accept that they were responsible for their destiny. Manley admitted that a symbolic break would not in itself be sufficient to solve the problem, but, 'If you want to solve the problem, start there' (Manley, 1992).

There was, however, little agreement amongst the three parties and the intelligentsia as to what the new structure of government should look like. The Jamaica Labour Party (JLP) and the more conservative intelligentsia preferred to retain the Westminster edifice, and argued for its strengthening by the addition of a range of select committees which would monitor and scrutinise the work of the executive. They wanted 'drastic' but not 'radical' reform. In their view, the problem in Jamaica was that the Westminster system was never fully implemented. As Professor Rex Nettleford explained (1994, pp 4–15),

'The Westminster system has a life of its own which must be fully understood and adapted after being imitated.' In the model, properly imitated, the opposition must oppose the government, but must not do so at the expense of good governance and continuity. To quote Nettleford further:

Rewriting the Jamaican constitution merely (by borrowing) from here, thither and yon will not do the trick. An understanding of the principles underlying the system we now run and others which attract us, is an inescapable necessity for any effective constitutional reform.

Professor Gladstone Mills (1997) also advised the retention of the Westminster architecture and heritage, but would introduce radical improvements to enable greater control of the executive by parliament. Michael Manley likewise expressed reservations about replacing the Westminster model with the American model. As he said in his final speech to parliament in 1992:

I advise against proposals that are being advanced in some quarters which are based on the United States constitution. That constitution reflects the type of mix of basic principles and special historical realities which make all constitutions unique reflections of each society.

Manley was in fact repeating arguments about the relationship between culture and political change which he had articulated in his seminal work, *The Politics of Change*. One of the basic arguments of this retentionist school was that the Westminster model encourages cooperation between the executive and legislative branches, and reduces the likelihood of gridlock, and in other ways is conducive to party discipline, political stability and effective policy implementation.

The JLP has also opted for a non-executive president as head of state who did not represent any political party. In terms of parliament, it opted for changes which would give MPs more opportunity to sponsor private bills and motions. It also agreed that there should be more select committees which would be chaired by opposition MPs but which would have a majority of government MPs. In terms of the senate, the JLP position was that it should be a non-elective body.

The JLP opposed proportional representation, arguing that it would lead to coalitional government and instability. The JLP admitted that the Westminster model and the first-past-the-post- system had built-in defects, but believed that the baby should not be thrown out with the bath water. The JLP also agreed with Manley that the Westminster system fits the Jamaican political history and culture. As the political leader of the JLP, Mr Edward Seaga (1995) put it, 'The inescapable bottom line is the nature of the political culture. The political system, to be effective, must function within this cultural framework, not outside of it.' Mr Seaga also believed that Jamaicans were not overly preoccupied with the constitutional issue. 'They are much too busy worrying about where their next meal is coming from to be interested in such esoteric matters as the rules by which they are governed.'

The People's National Party leadership, under PJ Patterson, Manley's successor, plumped for the executive presidential model in which the president functioned as the symbol of national unity. The PNP's proposals broadly mirrored the American model, though with some important exceptions. Among them was the proposal that the membership of the senate would be determined by the results of elections to the house of representatives and would be based on proportional representation, provided parties get at least five percent of the popular vote. As in the American system, policies advocated by the president must obtain legislative approval following committee scrutiny. The legislature was also to be empowered to formulate policies and programmes, though these may be vetoed by the president who is impeachable.

The argument given by the PNP was that the proposed system grounds the office of the presidency in the Jamaican people, while providing important checks and balances to prevent political abuse. Critics of the model, however, argued that it concentrated too much power in the hands of the executive. In the PNP formula, the president would have more power than the prime minister since he would be directly elected and would have a mandate which would be constitutionally superior to that of his cabinet. It is, however, not clear why this should in fact be so, since under the current system, elections in Jamaica are virtual leadership plebiscites. People vote to decide who should control Jamaica House.

A closely related formula was that recommended by the National Democratic Movement (NDM), a breakaway faction from the JLP. The NDM would retain a prime minister, but the latter would be elected directly by the people on a fixed date, and would be limited to two five-year terms. Elections to the legislature and senate (the latter on the basis of PR) would be held separately from those for the prime minister, also on a fixed date. The NDM claims that this would force a rupture in the patronage link between the prime minister and parliament, especially since parliamentarians would not be eligible to become ministers. This would enable MPs to focus on their roles as representatives of their constituency and as scrutinisers of the executive branch.

The NDM model provided for the president to veto proposals coming from the legislature, but would allow the latter to override the president's veto by a two-thirds majority as obtains in the American system. In the view of the NDM, their system would undermine the 'winner take all' character of the present system, allowing MPs to view their position in parliament as independent of the patronage of the prime minister. The NDM package also provided for the speaker of the house and the president of the senate to be elected by their respective houses independently of the prime minister, and for important offices of state to be filled independently of the wishes of the prime minister at the cabinet. Officers such as the commissioner of police, and members of the service commissions would be filled by a two-thirds majority of both houses of parliament.

In response to criticisms that policy and other kinds of disputes between an executive prime minister and a legislature elected at separate times could lead to deadlock, the NDM argued that deadlock could have positive outcomes in that it would force compromise and consensus, even if the two institutions were controlled by different parties. As the NDM (1995) also hoped:

Such cooperation and consensus will help to break down the barriers of tribal politics, while the veto power on either side should reduce the likelihood of the Prime Minister making arbitrary or capricious decisions; this should rebound to the country's credit, for, in some instances, gridlock can serve as a positive force to check abuses of power on the part of the Prime Minister (and the Cabinet). In addition, in cases of genuine disagreement between the Prime Minister and the Parliament, the over-ride provisions will provide clear guidance for the resolution of the disagreement.

Bruce Golding, the NDM leader (1995), argued that it is the concentration of power in the Westminster paradigm which lay at the root of the problem of political tribalism in Jamaica. As he moaned:

The enormous concentration of power . . . at the centre (is) at the heart of the (problem). That enormous concentration leads to and enormous fight for control of that power. There is no joy in being in opposition, you know. When you are in opposition, you control nothing!

Golding disagreed with Manley and Seaga that the executive model was alien to Jamaican culture. In his view, the reverse is the truth. The Westminster model presumes a culture that no longer prevails in Jamaica.

There were elements within the PNP who disagreed with the proposals being advanced by their leaders. Indeed, according to the Stone Committee Report (1990, p 36), 80 per cent of the MPs of both parties were opposed to the presidential model. In part, this was due to the fact that under that system (at least in its extreme form), they would not be able to hold ministerial office but would instead be required to serve as full time constituency representatives. They claim that if MPs were excluded from holding ministerial portfolios, the quality of person aspiring to office as an MP would decline, even if better salaries were to be paid.

The Stone Committee was itself divided on the issue, as was the public. Stone himself endorsed it on several grounds. In his view, the main justification was that it would allow MPs to work full time in their constituencies rather than part time as was the case at present. All 60 MPs would be available to check and control the executive and serve as watchdogs of the people. They would also be expected to serve the entire constituency rather than only those who had elected them. Stone also recommended that in order to establish broader citizen contact with MPs, constituency offices, which were separate and distinct from party offices, should be established and made accessible to all. Funds provided by the state to MPs were also to be expended in a non-partisan manner. Such changes were required if people were to regain confidence in the parliamentary system.

Guyana and Trinidad

In Guyana and Trinidad and Tobago, both of which are ethnically heterogeneous societies, there have been calls for 'power sharing' or even 'rotational power sharing' in the context of 'compound' governments of national unity. The prime minister of Trinidad and Tobago expressed the view that the only way to deal holistically and meaningfully with the problems of alienation and justice for all ethnic groups was to abandon the Westminster model altogether and experiment with a more consensual formula. As Mr Panday declared in 1988:

... the Westminster model has proved inadequate to meet the hopes and aspirations of our people as a developing nation; we must (therefore) strive for genuine constitutional reform. We must create a political system that is more relevant to the nature of the society at this given juncture. (Ryan, 1996, p. 554)

There are many who agreed with Mr Panday that the Westminster paradigm was not suitable for ethnically plural societies such as those to be found in Trinidad, Guyana and other plural 'third world' countries. Sir Arthur Lewis (1965, p 55), for example, argued that in such societies, a 'consociational' rather than a 'majoritarian' model was more appropriate. As Lewis wrote:

> Britain and France are class societies, and their institutions and conventions are designed to cope with this fact. West Africa is not a class society; its problem is that it is a plural society. What is good for a class society is bad for a plural society. Hence to create good political institutions in West Africa one has to think their problem through from the foundations up . . . men who stand for elections represent groups with different interests, ideas and characteristics, and the real contest is between these groups. To exclude the losing groups from participation in decision-making clearly violates the primary meaning of democracy.

Lewis argued that the democratic problem in a plural society is to create institutions which allow all the groups to participate in decision-making since, only thus, would they feel that they are full members of the nation. Lewis was of the view that the Caribbean people have been brainwashed into believing that coalitions and other features of consensual democracies are bad. As such they may need much 'un-brainwashing' to grasp their problems in true perspective. Basically, the consociational or 'concurrent majority' model argues that what affects all must be approved by all. This is particularly important in multi-ethnic states where no group has an effective as opposed to a mere numerical majority, and as such is unable to govern meaningfully on non-routine matters *without* the active involvement or concurrence of other critical interests *without* having to use coercion.

This school of thought argues that strict majoritarianism is a principle of exclusion and that one needs a multiple or overlapping mandate rather than a uni-layered mandate for plural societies if representative government on a sustainable basis is to be achieved. To borrow a term from James Madison, what one needs to create is a 'compound republic'. In such societies, ethnicity has to be formally recognised and even integrated into the electoral and in some contexts, the bureaucratic and constitutional system. One of the most articulate advocates of the consociational model, Arend Lijphart (1984, 1990), argues that 'The real choice of plural societies is not between the British (majoritarian) model and the consociational model, but between consociational democracy and no democracy at all.'

Interestingly, both the Peoples National Movement (PNM) in Trinidad and Tobago and the Peoples National Congress (PNC) in Guyana have come out against the concept of power sharing in a national unity government. There must, they both argue, be someone 'to tell the Emperor that he has no clothes'. Someone has to hold the executive to account and be ready to form an alternative government. That is the role of the official opposition. In the view of the PNM and the PNC leadership, the Westminster multi-party system 'is still the best' in spite of all its acknowledged faults. These Westminster fundamentalist views were, however, articulated while these parties either held the reins of power as in Trinidad and Tobago or, as was the case of Guyana, hoped to regain it.

Given the ethnic heterogeneity of the population of Trinidad and Tobago and Guyana, and given that communal consciousness is likely to increase in the years immediately ahead, whatever might occur in the distant future, a strong case could be made that the political system ought to be restructured to take account of this social reality. Several attempts have been made in the past in both countries to forge pre-electoral multi-ethnic fronts or coalitions, but these failed because one group or another had come to feel that the balance of forces in the coalition did not accurately reflect their political strength, or that sufficient expression was not given to their desire to occupy more prominent positions. The various coalitional efforts thus collapsed under challenge from constituent units for larger shares of the material resource. The inability of the leadership elements to manage the ethnic tensions that inevitably arise in coalitional politics creatively and with political sense as to what the limits were, was also a contributing factor (Ryan, 1989).

Notwithstanding these failures, demands continue to be made for power-sharing or for the creation of a 'party or parties'. Clive Thomas (1998) spoke for many Afro-Guyanese when he observed that despite claims about cross over voting, the 1992 and 1997 elections were ethnic censuses. Given the demographics of Guyana, free and fair elections would thus exclude Afro-Guyanese from a meaningful share of political power, perhaps permanently, something which most Afro-Guyanese regard as totally unacceptable. To avoid the political instability that this structural problem invites, Guyana had to find a constitutional formula that would permit power to be shared. As Thomas wrote:

In so far as the legal and constitutional framework promotes political competition based on 'winner-takes-all' results, this exacerbates the insider/outsider dynamic and heightens the feelings of insecurity among the losing groups. When, as in Guyana, the Constitution also concentrates immense power in an Executive President and representation in the Parliament is not based on local constituencies and/or communities, the situation becomes even more difficult. Constitutional reform therefore offers a way forward in seeking to modify the excesses of political competition based on racial affiliation.

In Thomas' view, there was also need to promote national consensus among all the major political forces and key social partners over the main lines of economic strategy.

Such a strategy can contribute not only towards protecting the national interest in relation to foreign investments, but also allow issues of equity, racial security, social balance, democratisation, participatory development and the flowering of civic society to emerge as alternatives to mutually self-destructive racial competition.

In the light of unhappy post-independence political experience with 'winner take all politics' in Guyana and Trinidad and Tobago, the time may well have come for both societies to re-examine the Westminster political paradigm and consider experimenting with consociational formulas such as those suggested by Lewis, Lijphart and others. These take various forms. The most familiar is of course the pre-election coalition best exemplified by the United Front (UF), the United Labour Front (ULF) and The National Alliance for Reconstruction (NAR) in Trinidad and Tobago and the Peoples Political Party (PPP/CIVIC) and Working Peoples' Alliance in Guyana. As indicated above, those have not been successful so far.

There is debate as to whether in this model, the affiliating parties should erase their institutional identities and merge or whether they should retain their identities. The experience of the PPP in Guyana in the fifties and the NAR in Trinidad and Tobago in the eighties and nineties do not give much reason to be optimistic about how the umbrella party system would work. Institutions do matter. They circumscribe options. Realism thus suggest that the parties should maintain their organisational integrity and principles such as they are, and campaign as discrete units, working out arrangements where possible to facilitate governance. The electoral outcome would determine who leads the coalition formally. Post-election governing coalitions should be structured either by an agreement to consult and arrive at consensus on key policy issues or by a *concordat* that would bring representatives of significant parties or groupings formally into the cabinet. Both strategies should be attempted, as in the case of Germany or Mauritius. In essence, a case is being made here for a decision-making system in which accredited standard bearers of all or most of the major ethnic groups and policy orientations would be visibly and genuinely represented and allowed to have a say. The arrangement might not work given the absence of trust which currently exists between the major parties in the two countries. But it should not be rejected as being impossible to achieve.

There is, of course, the possibility that if the experiment fails, the fall-out from the attempted 'cure' might be worse than the disease. But given the increased communal competitiveness that now prevails, and the poisonous rhetoric that has come to characterise public political discourse, the risk of experimenting further with a more consensual paradigm seems to be well worth taking, notwithstanding the refusal of the current leaders of the PNM in Trinidad and Tobago and the PNC in Guyana to consider any basic modification of the Westminster model.

One should, however, concede that in countries where national unity governments have been tried, the experience has not always been encouraging. Examples which come to mind are Israel and Suriname. In the latter case, what one often had in place was an 'elite cartel' in which corruption was rampant. The various coalitions which were attempted were often characterised by contradictoriness or *immobilisme* in terms of policy, and agreement on desirable change was hard to secure. Party granulation (there were some 19 parties or groupings in Suriname National Assembly in 1999) and coalitional instability are also characteristic of the system. On many occasions, groups or individuals pulled out of complex coalitions or defected to other alliances when their demands for certain ministries or policy considerations were not met. Parties in the governing coalition often failed to agree on who should be appointed to ministries or foreign embassies. They also tended to regard the ministries which they held as their own bailiwicks with little concern for coordination and coherence. The interest of the group took precedence over that of the nation.

The arrangement likewise encouraged 'out elites' to outbid 'apostates' within the governing coalition in the hope of replacing them electorally or otherwise. As Rabushka and Shepsle (1972, p 83) note:

... ambitious politicians not included in the multi-ethnic coalition have incentives to generate demand for communal rather than national issues ... Second ... communal politicians can defeat candidates of the multi-ethnic coalition, whose position on the ethnic issue is ambiguous by taking extreme positions ... In short, communally based political entrepreneurs seek to increase the salience of communal issues and then to outbid the ambiguous multi-coalition.

In spite of efforts to stabilise Surinamese politics by the use of consociational formulas, the country experienced two military coups, seven years of military dictatorship, widespread guerrilla activity, and one minority government since it achieved independence in 1975 (Dew 1996). The system also gave rise to significant difficulties in the choosing of presidents and the maintenance of governments. *Koehandel* (cow-trading) thus became endemic. It is the case, however, that all the major parties in Suriname now seek to be multi-ethnic and that governing coalitions also strive to be inclusive. The political system is corrupt and disorderly, but the fundamental cleavages are not as ethnically based as they once were. Indeed, parties which were once based on a monolithic ethnic identity have now splintered into a multiplicity of parties based on economic, religious or some other interest. Indians are now represented in six political parties.

It may be that the countries in the Caribbean would achieve more consensus if they identified mechanisms through which *functional* unity could be achieved in critical areas of the policy menu. There are a number of industries and activities which are central to the economic survival of the countries in the Caribbean – tourism, energy, bauxite – where a measure of multi-party consensus should be sought. Decisions as to which national assets are to be sold and to whom, and the ballpark prices for which they should be hypothecated, should also be treated as borderless or cross-party, rather than partisan, issues. Agreements on these issues may not be easy to achieve, but the effort is worth making. This approach may serve to avoid the 'tit for tat' syndrome which tends to characterise politics in the region.

Civil Society

Some reform minded elements in Caribbean society are looking to 'civil society' and other non-state actors to provide the energy and vision needed to reconstruct Caribbean democracy. 'Civil society' is seen somewhat sentimentally as the 'midwife' which would bring into being the new society which would leaven, humanise and democratise the authoritarian political cultures of the region and which would contain, if not eliminate, completely the private violence that is all too evident in so many of its twilight zones. There is indeed an articulated teleology abroad that sees this civilising process as being not only desirable, but inevitable in the long march towards 'progress'.

Not everyone agrees however with this optimistic diagnosis. In fact, there are three competing scenarios as to what is likely to happen to Caribbean society as it moves into the new millenium. There is the view which we might describe as 'dogmatic utopianism' which sees the ultimate triumph of 'people power' as ineluctable. This view, which fetishes 'civil society', is partly informed by what happened in Eastern Europe, the Philippines, and elsewhere during the 1980s when spontaneous popular mass movements overthrew autocratic regimes and 'blew down' the Berlin Wall. It is also informed by the associational revolution which is taking place in many northern and southern countries where thousands of NGOs and other organised advocacy groups are aggressively campaigning for change, and are successfully forcing national governments, international agencies and global regimes to take heed of their demands for greater economic, political, social and environmental sensitivity and accountability. This view sees the movement to 'civilise' the state and use it for people centered social ends as unstoppable, even if some admit that there might be short term reversals. As Allan Atkison bragged in 1998 in relation to the United States, 'When collapses of any kind occur, society will be there to pick up the pieces and rebuild. When transformation occurs, civil society will undoubtedly have hatched it. It's all but inevitable: democracy will give birth to sustainability and civil society will save the world.' (Cited in Swift, 1999, pp 67–68)

One defining characteristic of this 'new politics of civility' is that the term 'civil society' is used loosely to define only those 'authentic' elements which work for what are considered progressive and just causes. As John Keane complains (1996, p 10), there is little recognition that civil society, past and present, has been plagued by tendencies towards cruelty that openly contradict the *idealtypisch* concept of civil society as a haven of openness, non-violence, solidarity and justice. In sum, 'civil society' contains elements of 'uncivility' – terrorists, cronies, racketeers, political adventurers, warlords – as well as groups committed to democracy and social justice. These conflicting forces or tendencies cohabit the same space, sometimes peacefully, sometimes violently.

The second perspective we might label 'dogmatic pessimist'. It holds that Caribbean societies are haemorrhaging economically and socially, dying a slow convulsive death. Those who articulate this metaphysic of decline point to what is happening to the politics and economies of the Caribbean, particularly those in Jamaica, Guyana and the 'banana states'; to the corruption that is becoming pervasive in places like Trinidad and Tobago, Antigua, Guyana and Jamaica; to the growth of decentralised anomic violence everywhere in the region, but particularly in Jamaica and Guyana; and to the boldness with which narco-elites intimidate and suborn state officialdom. What is said to be mushrooming, is not 'civil society,' but 'uncivil society'. Perhaps to put it more correctly, what one is witnessing is dialectical tension between competing forces within Caribbean civil society, with the dice seemingly being loaded in favour of the forces of incivility rather than with those which are striving to rebuild the collapsing walls of political and social civility.

Those who take this pessimistic perspective seem to share the view of the Comte de Mirabeau (1756, p 176) that there is no law which ordains unlimited secular progress. Instead, there is an 'iron law' which leads to a cyclical reversion to barbarism and decadence after eras of wealth and civility. Civilisations and nations collapse just as certainly as they rise. According to this view, the modern world, and the Caribbean as part of that world, is slowly 'going back to the dawn' (Kaplan, 1996) or at least to the patterns of violent uncivil behaviour that was characteristic of the Middle Ages in Europe, patterns which, the modern state, once seen as part of civil society, was supposed to have eliminated (Eco, 1986, pp 73-85). The ease with which the means of violence can be obtained has also stacked the cards against those elements in civil society seeking to civilise it.

A similar view was articulated by Francis Fukuyama in his recent book, the *Great Disruption*. As he writes:

There seems to be two processes working in parallel. In the political and economic sphere, history appears to be progressive and directional, and at the end of the twentieth century has culminated in liberal democracy as the only viable alternative for technologically advanced societies. In the social and moral sphere, however, history appears to be cyclical, with social order ebbing and flowing over the space of multiple generations. There is nothing that guarantees that there will be upturns in the cycle. (1999, p 282)

The third perspective we might label 'creative pessimism' or 'democratic realism'. While this perspective is equally gloomy, its 'moroseness' or morbidity is not unrelieved. It argues that the ontological perspectives of the utopians, the pessimists, and the cyclical declinists are ahistorical. Moreover, they underestimate the power of human resolve to turn what seems like certain defeat into victories, given new conjunctures or institutional developments. As Keane (1999, p 111) observed in a commentary on the Mirabeau's perspective:

The metaphysic of decline and renewal has obstructive policy implications, since it implies that little or nothing can be done to stem the floods of violence that periodically sweep away the protective walls of civility that maintain peace among citizens. More plausible are those mesolevel theories that seek to account for the eruptions of violence by tracing them to the specific institutional structures of civil society.

What this third perspective argues is that while the forces of barbarism seem poised to overwhelm Caribbean society, they will not prevail in the end, since their very existence serves to fertilise and give renewed life to those democratic forces and structures that are deeply embedded in Caribbean society and which are struggling to create the right conjunctures which will facilitate their reflowering. It further argues that the positive counter forces in Caribbean civil society are not acting in isolation anymore than are the uncivil forces. The belief here is that the progressive forces in Caribbean society, aided by its associates in global civil society, will ultimately remoralise and get the better of, if not comprehensively defeat, the negative forces in that society.

At the end of an exercise of this sort, readers are entitled to ask the author whether specific recommendations are being advanced for improving the system of governance in the region. While much of what has been said seems to suggest that incremental changes are unlikely to yield much given the constraints identified above, it is nevertheless our view that there are a number of measures that are worthy of consideration. Some of them involve expenditure that may be burdensome for the units. Others may have consequences that are not politically cost effective. There is no formula that can be applied to all cases. In politics, one size does not fit all; culture, structure and conjuncture are all relevant. The following are my own tentative suggestions as to what reforms might be undertaken to improve standards of governance in the region:

1. Increase membership of lower houses of parliaments to a minimum of 24. This would make it possible for monitoring committees to be adequately manned, provided, of course, that the size of the executive is not correspondingly enlarged. A larger backbench should also mean that more parliamentarians are available to service their constituencies effectively.
2. Discourage the adoption executive presidential models, as suggested by the PNP and the NDM in Jamaica. The Westminister model has its flaws and needs to be revised to allow for greater consociationalism, both in terms of election arrangements and policy formulation. The German model, which mixes proportional representatives with the first-past-the-post system, should be seriously considered. The Alternative Preference System, which induces vote pooling and preference swapping, should also be looked at.
3. Limit the number of terms anyone can serve as prime minister to two. This may affect the electability of parties, but on balance the provision is worthy of support.
4. Retain the principle of civil service neutrality but provide for greater use of special advisers to ministers. There are difficulties with the relationships between permanent secretaries and these advisers, but on balance, this is to be preferred to politicising the public service fully.
5. Abandon the wholesale firing of permanent secretaries or chief executives of state corporations following changes of administrations.
6. Allow chairmen, directors of state corporations and holders of national offices to serve out their terms except where there is clear evidence that this would not be in the public interest. There should be no presumption that resignation or even offers to resign is the normal thing to do. It is certainly not a 'Westminster' convention.
7. Give local government bodies greater autonomy and more financial resources to undertake community determined development activity, provided they are also given the manpower to effectively manage these resources.
8. De-emphasize party politics at local government level, since it invariably serves to paralyse rather than encourage local community activity.
9. Maintain a CARICOM presence as routine during all general elections held in the region. While the body would not have the power to reverse any outcome, its presence and its report may well serve to discourage

electoral malpractice, and empower those who are seeking to ensure that elections are free and fair at *all* stages of the electoral process.
10. Create citizens' protection bureaus which would serve as guardians when citizens' rights and freedoms are being abused by the state. The bureaux should be given power to compel compliance with its decisions and in appropriate cases, make recommendations to the appropriate constitutional or statutory body.
11. Fix election dates to discourage parties from behaving as though elections are always imminent.
12. Implement the provisions of the CARICOM Charter for Civil Society and encourage and empower those groups within civil society that are working to deepen and improve the functioning of Caribbean democracy.

References

Dominquez, Jorge, et al, *Democracy in the Caribbean* (Baltimore: John's Hopkins, 1993)
Dominica Constitution Review Commission, *The Commonwealth of Dominica*, 1999. Chairman, Hon Telford Georges
Eco, Umberto, Living in the New Middle Ages' in *Faith in Fakes, Essays*, (London, 1986)
Edie, Carlene, ed, *Democracy in the Caribbean Myths and Realities*, Westport Praeger, 1994
Fukuyama, Francis, *The Great Disruption* (Illinois: The Free Press, 1999)
Golding, Bruce, Address to National Democratic Movement Conference, Kingston, 1996.
Kaplan, Robert, *The Ends of the Earth: A Journey to the Frontiers of Anarchy* (New York: Vintage Books, 1996)
Keane, John, *Reflections on Violence* (London: Verso, 1996)
Lewis, Arthur, *Politics in West Africa* (Oxford: Oxford University Press: 1969)
Lijphart, Arend, 'Size, Pluralism, and the Westminster Model of Democracy: Implications for the Eastern Caribbean' in Heine, Jorge, *A Revolution Betrayed* (University of Pittsburgh Press, 1990)
Manley, Michael, Final Speech in Parliament, March 26, 1992 (Kingston: Gordon House Parliamentary Library
Mills, GE, 'Democracy and Democratisation: Global and Caribbean Perspectives on Reform and Research', *Social and Economic Studies*, Vol 46, No 1, March, 1997
National Democratic Movement, General Policy Document No 1, Kingston, Jamaica, 1995
Nettleford, Rex, 'Political Leadership in the Commonwealth Caribbean: Responsibilities, Options and Challenges at the End of the Century', *Caribbean Contemporary Affairs*, No 1, UWI Press, 1994
Rabushka, Alvin and Shepsle, Kenneth, *Politics in Plural Societies: A Theory of Democratic Instability*, (Merril, Columbus, 1972)

Ryan, Selwyn, *The Disillusioned Electorate*, Imprint, Trinidad, 1989

Stone, Carl, 'Power, Policy and Politics in Independent Jamaica' in Nettleford, Rex, ed, *Jamaica in Independence* (London: Heinemann Caribbean, 1989)

Swift, Jamie, *Civil Society in Question* (Toronto: South Asia Partnership, 1999)

Thomas, Clive, 'Exception and Rule: Racial Constructs and Dynamics of the African Diaspora Experience', mimeo; paper presented at Conference on Diaspora Studies University of California, Berkeley, 1998

24 | LLOYD BEST

Independent Thought, Policy Process

Wise Words

1. Dudley Seers

Universities almost generate irrelevance. In the social sciences an additional cause is the pressure (even if potential) from educational bureaucracies and governments, which usually have their own interest in current problems not being explored deeply and may well find that theory inherited from the past suits their purposes very well.

The theoretical equipment of the new generation of third world economists and political leaders 'was twice removed from reality – it reflected the doctrines developed for *other* countries in response to *earlier* events.' (*The Cultural Lag in Economics*)

2. Havelock Brewster

The main protagonists for Caribbean integration have always stressed enlarged size as its principal rationale and some, like Arthur Lewis, have also made much of 'good government' as its justification. However, size as represented by CARICOM would fail our test of the first best. And the good government argument simply does not hold water, when one considers the dismal record of many large countries. Small size can indeed be an advantage for good government.

I believe the best, the unique, most lasting rationale for Caribbean Community is cultural identity and kinship. This has even greater relevance these days when there seems to be a strong, world-wide tendency toward racial and cultural affinity, even if it is combined with the pragmatic pursuit of economic opportunities. In such a world, shrinking but exclusive, West Indians are even more isolated than before, stranded as they are, between an unknown, introverted Latin south; a familiar, unwelcoming, Anglo-Saxon north; and a very distant, mysterious east and west. (Adlith Brown Lecture)

3. Gruzinski

Colonisation of imagery – that is, inculcating ways of seeing, feeling, and conceiving reality – has been a crucial expression of the westernisation of the New World in general.

The invasion spawned a series of fractal societies in the Caribbean, in Mexico, and then in the Andes . . . new and chaotic environments in which social relations and cultural roles were exposed to short circuits of all sorts and to incessant turbulence; open and latent conflicts; virtual civil wars; clash and scattering of factions; precariousness and intermittence of solidarity; sudden shifts in alliances; brutal juxtaposition of two parent societies; diversity in ethnic and religious components, so many of which were uprooted; the predominance of improvisation (*The Colonisation of Indigenous Imagery*)

4. CLR James

It was only long years after that I understood the limitation on spirit, vision, and self-respect which was imposed on us by the fact that our masters, our curriculum, our code of morals, *everything* began from the basis that Britain was the source of all light and leading, and our business was to admire, wonder, imitate, learn; our criterion of success was to have succeeded in approaching that distant ideal – to attain it was, of course, impossible. Both masters and boys accepted it as in the very nature of things. (*Beyond A Boundary*)

We of the Caribbean are a people more than any other people constructed by history, and therefore any attempt not only to analyse but to carry out political or social activity, in connection with ourselves and in relation to other peoples, any such attempt has got to begin and constantly to bear in mind how we came into being, where we have reached, who we are and what we are. We were brought from Africa and thrown into highly developed modern industry and a highly developed modern language. We had to master them or die. We have lived. ('The West Indian Intellectual', in JJ Thomas, *Froudacity*)

5. Edward Said

A confused and limiting notion of priority allows that only the original proponents of an idea can understand and use it. But the history of all cultures is the history of cultural borrowings. Cultures are not impermeable; just as Western science borrowed from the Arabs, they had borrowed from India and Greece. Culture is never just a matter of ownership, of borrowing and lending with absolute debtors and creditors, but rather of appropriations, common experiences, and interdependencies of all kinds among different cultures. (*Culture and Imperialism*)

6. Edouard Glissant

The notion of Caribbean unity is a form of cultural self-discovery. It fixes us in the truth of our existence, it forms part of the struggle for self-liberation. It is a concept that cannot be managed for us by others; Caribbean unity cannot be guided by remote control. (*Caribbean Discourse*)

7. Antonio Benitez-Rojo

The almost arithmetical constant in the Caribbean is never a matter of subtracting, but always of adding, for the Caribbean discourse carries . . . a myth or a desire for social, cultural and psychic integration to compensate for the fragmentation and provisionality of the collective being. The literature of the Caribbean seeks to differentiate itself from the European not by excluding cultural components that influenced its formation but, on the contrary, by moving toward the creation of an ethnologically promiscuous text that might allow a reading of the varied and dense polyphony of Caribbean society's characteristic codes. (*The Repeating Island*)

The State of Business

When I saw who was involved in this conference, I had a great sense of exhilaration. I was truly delighted at the prospect of seeing so many old friends, collaborators, and colleagues held in high esteem, remembered with great affection. Among them are some I first knew as students here a long time ago, but whom I have no hesitation now in acclaiming as masters. They include Dr Meeks and professor of public policy, Dr Denis Benn, whose *Growth and*

Development of Political Ideas in the Caribbean is a pioneering work of exceptional merit, one which has redeemed the promise of this august institution.

My heart is glad but I miss Beckford and I miss Augier from the programme. I am also a little disappointed that the agenda is so full. We can hardly afford to miss such an opportunity to talk especially when, as vehicle of thought, talk is more than ever for us the most productive form of action.

What I see is a state of under-fulfillment so excessive and so abiding, it is past dangerous: it is revolutionary, at least in some places. I hesitate to call it crisis because the condition is endemic – though not to be confused with our immanent disarray, and tantalising unpredictability, fertile for creativity, the essence of Caribbean Creole civilisation – where none has the ancestral right to the seascape but where, nevertheless, all and sundry are required to inherit the patrimony.

I hesitate to call our condition a crisis, because, in some elusive and ineffable way, we are all aware of the peril. And a crisis is crisis only when the principals are effectively innocent. The moment you discern the condition, it should precipitate you into action, first into thought and theories of action, arising organically out of the materials and experiences of the condition itself. If that is not the response, as has famously and tragically not been our case, we pass to an altogether different order of challenge, one which transcends mere management intervention, mere reformulation of strategy and policy, mere dallying with symptoms which surface as issues of implementation – or even as imperatives of strategic planning, as normally understood.

Such a predicament, to my mind, compels a therapeutic initiative, by which I mean a healing of the self, individual and collective. My diagnostic is tending towards a certain pathology. I think we do discern the predicament and, in a curious, active way, we become feverishly grounded, mired in the minutiae and protocols of inaction.

I am suggesting remission is not only urgent but possible, if only because we have for the first time seen the possibility of a leader of our own making in this cradle institution. And yet, though the way forward needs to be straight, it is not straightforward. What it involves is a candid and studied attempt to penetrate the issues of being and knowing, specific to a people within specific coordinates of space and time – which is to say, of culture and psychology. Perhaps because of the space in the firmament which they occupy as validating elites, such frank talk can begin only with high priests such as are assembled here this weekend – for once in a lifetime. I hope this does not turn out to have been an opportunity missed.

We in the Caribbean face a double problem; first the chronic unviability of states, territories and islands – at whatever level of effective integration – and second, in the endemic illegitimacy of the political regime, whatever the colour of its ideology, and by whatever route it would have come to be installed.

There seem to be certain system properties which limit the impact of intelligence, industry, and initial integrity, all of which are present in abundance and, in my experience, keep on ratooning and coming back. These properties will continue to block and inhibit – until such time as the fragments are assembled whole, as Kamau Brathwaite has put it, in a radically different way.

What, then, is the substance of the diagnostic? Why is there this profound sense of stasis? At the crossover to the twentieth century, we had the crisis of the modified plantation economy in the new international order, the need for imperial preference, the pronouncements of the 1898 Royal 'Sugar' Commission on the pattern of production and on the form of tenure and of business organisation. At the crossover to the twenty-first century, we face the same economy only minimally further modified, the need for new 'transitional mechanisms' offering a reduced ration of non-reciprocity, and the West Indies 'Royal' Commission.

The prime minister of Barbados here presented a superbly lucid taking-of-stock, and an enticing vision of what might be done to introduce a new way of doing business. But how are we to prepare ourselves with the political preconditions, as distinct from the protocols and legal preconditions, or the strategic initiatives for concepts such as the single market and economy advocated by Demas, or the West Indies Union proposed by Brewster? This is the question which scared me, when I heard Owen Arthur.

How do we intend to persuade the multitude, in a fragmented region in which the common island homeland is the principal basis of ethnic solidarity? How are we to reach the people, especially in Jamaica, where the public is no longer listening, and is wary of anything that looks like the promised land, with or without Joshua? Do we not need a precise and rigorous accounting for stewardship and for past endeavours, now gone and largely barren? After the promise of the last awakening, how in hell did it get this way? Ms Narcisse has spoken of a crisis of enormous proportions. But who or what is responsible?

Slavery, indenture and colonialism? Capitalism and/or communism? External shocks, deteriorating terms of trade? The lending institutions? It does not seem to me that answers can be escaped or withheld for very much longer. Or there will be hell to pay.

Elements of a Diagnostic

We need a diagnostic which would make sense of the facts in all the countries at the same time and raise the enquiry above local peculiarities and individuals. If the whole region is in trouble, it can't be that all the leaders are wicked or crooked or unaccountably incompetent. But even if they were, would that not be all the more reason to look at the much larger picture? If everybody is incompetent, then nobody is.

Such a transcendent offering must somehow stand the test of popular scrutiny. It has to rise above mere interested polemic to reconcile the competing claims of anecdotal evidence, the kind all people – including scientists and calypsonians – see as difficult to dismiss. I therefore hazard the following observations.

It is 60 years since emancipation from below was finally clinched for us all by organised labour, arising initially in 1935, in St Kitts. It is 55 years since adult suffrage (1944) shifted the centre of gravity from labour agitation on the streets and in the fields to popular participation in parliamentary elections involving political parties, inevitably headed by the educated elites. It is 50 years since the UWI was launched as the agency to breed these elites at home, in the process opening opportunity to a multitude of people and offering a career to the talented. It is almost 40 years since independence for Jamaica and Trinidad and Tobago opened the floodgates, not only of opportunity but also of responsibility, including that responsibility for past mistakes which goes with becoming the inheritor of the patrimony. From this standpoint, independence was a much more decisive threshold than even emancipation or arrival (by which is meant our initial transplantation from other continents, and introduction into America, under conditions essentially unfree, though in different degrees).

Because of this pervasive 'unfreedom', independence has been perhaps the most important of our thresholds. But there is another and more immediate reason for its primacy: the twentieth century is less the age of technological, economic and business expansion and more the age of the collapse of empire, beginning with the Ottoman, culminating with the Soviet. The honing of the ideology of globalisation at the end of the century is ominous; it sounds suspiciously like a response and, for the coming millennium, seems already to have placed recolonisation at the top of the policy agenda.

At our peril do we fail to see the second half of the twentieth century as a defining moment. Is it an opportunity which the educated elites of the West Indies may already have missed? Were we not caught with an obsolete strategy of playing dead to 'ketch corbeau alive'? Are we not still playing the coloniser in order to acquire a fitness to rule, as Norman Manley put it, perceiving the imperative of the nineteenth century? Are we not still making – ourselves enthusiastically available to be processed by the imperial school into becoming the true believers in the development industry, the transfer of technology and ideology too, with its limitation of spirit, in the way that CLR James notes, and for which Wilson Harris has long ago prescribed?

I think this a beguiling, bewitching hypothesis. Does it not possess all the elements of high tragedy in this particular sense? That, perhaps, the source of our undoing lies precisely with those instruments we found necessary to our triumphs in an earlier incarnation, after emancipation. However the delay in the transfer of power occasioned by World War II, after the compelling upheaval of the 1930s, may well have been instrumental in fossilising the vision of the leadership. I know the awe in which we hold Norman Manley, Eric Williams and Arthur Lewis, and properly so. But looking back, and being duly careful not to misjudge by the canons of a later generation, can we say that any of them even came close to discerning the imperatives of full democratic participation in the post-Independence Caribbean and the models it implied for economics and business?

What did it imply for schooling and education, and university campus education in particular? Though a boy, I was there when it was all happening and my intuition told me no. We may not wish to face it, but we have not been producing the people – and I would hazard the view that some of our best people are precisely the challenge. Have we been breeding too many innovators? Or too many *apparatchiks*? Admittedly, the arts and humanities have performed differently. Right from the start, the error may have been to think the main requirement was money to train more people to staff Independence. We find ourselves today still incurring huge overhead costs to install new amenities for learning. But unless and until we unravel the epistemological issue, might we not find ourselves trying to produce entrepreneurs and managers by substituting faculties of management for faculties of economics and social science and then the management faculties by institutes of business?

The near economic and political calamity we have had in the region has only confirmed by experience what instinct should first have alerted us to. (Had we still such a sixth sense, what with all the science, rigour and reputable output on which we are hooked at the expense of empirical observation of what is on the ground and then the long hard, intellectual speculation without flash or easy victory.) One speaks this way not in indictment or demonology but in explanation. One feels it fits the facts, in regard to a truly superior quality cadre in charge of the transition, distinguished for its lucidity, integrity, industry, intelligence and commitment, but which can have produced the results it has above and beyond the individual endowment and the personal presence.

As James has put it, not without irony, because it is as much the limitation as the opportunity, we are a modern people; we were taken from Africa and thrown into modern industry and a modern language. We had to develop a mastery or die; and we have lived. As Walcott has added, there was no question of reverting to a leonine ancestral past, back to green beginnings. And yet, as Glissant demands, we need a new grammar of feeling to escape from the homogeneising sameness of the West, an imaginative history to counter the empiricism, linear and totalising. Harris for his part favours and counsels a new philosophy of history. He chides Williams and even James for their obsession with overwhelming British historians and imperial history. But it is James himself who invokes the philosopher to insist on an emphatic response that facts must be topped by ideas permitting us to appropriate any situation by endowing it with figurative meaning beyond the real.

We have always needed to break out of that barracoon, with its perception that the issue is small size and open economy, that what we need are manufactures and wider markets, industrialisation by invitation and free trade areas, science and technology, research and development, and the whole unholy inheritance of second-hand, third-rate, import-substitution cliches. This includes Marxism, to which we have added too little for my liking, so eager are we to be victims, creatures of migrating capital and expanding business, fashioned in our own image. And now the new mercantilism of the self-avowed neo-liberals, without shame presuming to sell us globalisation, as if we, more than any other people, could not recognise it when sleeping, with its level playing fields and soaring inequities.

The *encomienda*, servitude, slavery, indenture and the constraints of the colonial condition drove us directly back unto ourselves, from the start. We were required to invent new elements. First, the limbo (making space where there was none). Second, the *mas* (playing oneself or the other, as required, in any number of incarnations, all the while wearing one's art, one's identity, upon one's person). Third, the calypso (double entendre, always meaning at least two things). Finally, the pan (making music wherever one goes, with whatever one finds). This is of course metaphor, applicable *mutatis mutandis* to any island and, from the experience of Trinidad and Tobago (the extreme case of the Caribbean condition), defined by the following properties:

i) A civilisation built on transplanted peoples, introduced by absentee investors not as settlers or proprietors with a claim to the patrimony, but as proletarians, free of the means of production and needing desperately to inherit the seascape

ii) The dislocated personality with multiple identity

iii) The segmented society, rent by cleavage

iv) Communities reconstituted on any available ethnic basis, be it race, colour, class, island homeland, religion, language, or whatever is capable of being the surrogate for kinship. These communities therefore permit rapid, indeed automatic, political mobilisation, thereby averting the need for consultation or explicit communication (ideal for a political system dominated by government from above and having no organised, open and effective politics below, if the latter is taken to mean permanent, private, capacity for public purpose)

v) Of course, the central process in which all of this is enmeshed is what Glissant, in the words of Dash, sees as an intricate breaching, an infinite wandering across cultures where triumphs are momentary; the prevailing forces are adaptation, metissage, Creolisation and, in Trinidad, douglarisation.

What the Caribbean has always needed is to put the humanities out in front and to organise ourselves to sell the cultural, intellectual and artistic services which, in the first instance, we have produced for our own satisfaction. The

Rastas have shown this to be eminently feasible by what they have done with their locks and their reggae. To make this possible, alas, at certain critical, defining moments, we needed to validate a certain subversive political and intellectual tradition. Not only did this not happen; it could not have happened. Our predicament lay in this sad fact: the only people and leaders, by the fact of culture and tradition, who enjoyed the legitimacy to open the door to subversion, to creativity and to theoretical and philosophical innovation as a basis for praxis, were precisely those luminaries whose dazzling successes on the coloniser's ground had long since served to staunch their intuition, curb their imagination, cut them off from their own obeisance, distort their estimates both of what was necessary and what was possible for us. This remains the tragedy of our condition, especially in the University, but also because the majority of people cannot be acquitted of complicity.

Especially between emancipation and independence, the Afro-Saxon strategy of operating European culture and practising European institutions in America was entirely legitimate and wholly indispensable, given the balance of forces and the unequal conditions. It was not that the elites struck out on their own, but that the whole tradition of advancing the claims of our brightest and best to enter the portals of hope and glory had its grounding in the schools and the church, embraced by the multitude. To the extent that left and right are different, the posture of the one, which demonises the middle classes and glorifies the masses, is as inadequate a representation of reality as the stance of the other, which denounces radical resistance and celebrates incorporation.

To my mind, the recommendations are very simple. More than anything else, we need thought and a relevant university system. We need independent, innovating thought to meet new reality. It has never been otherwise, but we were in such a hurry, so pragmatic, so populist, and, in spite of ourselves, so secure in the imperial paradigm, that what we have established is mainly a polytechnic catchment for the graduate school system of the North Atlantic countries. Odd as it may seem, it is not the main business of the University to supply practical recommendations of any kind to anybody, crucial as those recommendations might be for our survival and viability. If the University devoted itself to its work of providing theory, including relevant theory of action, why should practical proposals pose a problem? But I am not persuaded that the University has ever done its work.

In terms of the specifics, perhaps we should convert the Institute of International Relations at St Augustine into an autonomous, multi-lingual, multi-national, extra-disciplinary graduate school, involving all the CARIFORUM countries. Such an agency would, of course, have a capability for carrying out systematic and wide-ranging policy studies, making use of student interns and focussing on the Atlantic crucible. Its main concern would necessarily have to be the articulation of a moral philosophy – in the old sense – starting from history as well as social, cultural and physical geography to arrive at an ontology, an epistemology and a hermeneutic. In the end, there is nothing so practical or compelling for finding creative composure, in the Walcott sense, as reverting to being, knowing and the reinterpretation of self, with the aid of both myth and reasoned history.

Bibliography

Benitez-Rojo, Antonio, *The Repeating Island, The Caribbean and the Postmodern Perspective* (London: Duke University Press, 1992)
Benn, Denis, *The growth and development of political ideas in the Caribbean 1774–1983*, ISER, UWI, Kingston, 1987
Brathwaite, Edward, *Contradictory Omens, Cultural Diversity and Integration in the Caribbean* (Mona: Savacou Publications, 1974)
Brathwaite, Edward, *Caribbean Man in Space and Time, A Bibliographical and Conceptual Sketch* (Mona: Savacou Publications, 1974)
Brewster, Havelock, 'The Caribbean Community in a Changing International Environment, Towards the Next Century', eighth Adlith Brown Memorial Lecture, 1992
Emmanuel, Patrick, *Elections and Party Systems* (Bridgetown: Caribbean Development Research Services, 1992)
Emmanuel, Patrick, *Governance and Democracy in the Commonwealth Caribbean: an Introduction* (ISER, UWI, Cave Hill, 1993)
Glissant, Edouard, *Carribean Discourse* (Charlottesville: University Press of Virginia, Caraf Books, 1989)
Hennessy, Alistair, *Intellectuals in the Twentieth Century Caribbean*, vols I and II (London: Macmillan, 1992)
Gruzinski, *Colonisation and the War of Images in Colonial and Modern Mexico*, International Social Science Journal, November 1992, 'The Americas 1492–1992: Multiplicity of Historical Paths and Determinants of Development'
Harris, Wilson, *History, Fable and Myth in the Caribbean and Guianas*
James, CLR, *Beyond A Boundary*, paperback edition (London: Stanley Paul, 1969)
James, CLR, 'The West Indian Intellectual', Introduction to Thomas, JJ, *Froudacity* (Port of Spain: New Beacon Books, 1969)

Lewis, Sir Arthur, Collected Papers (Mona: UWI Press, 1999)
Lewis, Arthur, *Labour In the West Indies: The Birth of a Workers' Movement*, afterword by Susan Craig, (London: New Beacon, 1977)
Said, Edward, *Culture and Imperialism* (New York: Vintage Books, Random House, 1994)
Sherlock, Philip and Nettleford, Rex, *The University of the West Indies: A Caribbean Response to the Challenge of Change* (London: Macmillan, 1960)
Sankatsing, Glenn, *Caribbean Social Science, An Assessment*, UNESCO's Regional Unit for the Social and Human Sciences for Latin America and the Caribbean, Caracas, 1960
Seers, Dudley, *The Cultural Lag in Economics*, IDS, University of Sussex, August 1978
Smith, MG, *Culture, Race and Class in the Commonwealth Caribbean*, Dept of Extra-Mural Studies, UWI, Mona, 1984
Stone, Carl, *Democracy and Clientelism in Jamaica* (New Brunswick and London, 1980)
Williams, Eric, *Education In The British West Indies* (New York: University Place Bookshop, 1968)

25 | DAVID PANTON

The Politics of Principled Proactive Pragmatism

I have a confession to make. It is something I don't admit to often, but I feel comfortable sharing it now. My confession is that I have spent much of my formative years in academia – not as a lecturer or a professor like my fellow panelists, but as a student. Although a lengthy academic sojourn is nothing to be ashamed of, I must confess in addition that in those years, I have been somewhat 'less than focused' in my studies. By 'less than focused', I mean that I have not studied in one area, but have studied instead in various fields including law, business, politics, and economics. I view my lengthy academic sojourn as a wonderful exploration of ideas in a wide and diverse range of subject matters. My parents take a different view, however. They view my academic journey as youthful indecision, an inexplicable fear of the working world, and a wide and diverse range of means to avoid bankruptcy in order to finance that education.

I should also add that while my parents are pleased with my studies in law and business, they are less 'enamoured' with my studies in politics and economics. I once overheard my father tell my mother that law improved my ability to argue and business improved by ability to make money – to repay them, I suspect. On the other hand, he pointed out that all politics and economics qualified me to do was to babble on incoherently and passionately about issues that nobody either understood or cared about. I should add that he was not speaking from a position of ignorance, because he is himself an economist by training.

I now hope to avoid my father's worst fears and I plan to focus on issues that we as a people in the Caribbean do, or at least should, care about passionately, and that we do, or at least should, all understand well. The question that I would like to address is what kind of leadership do we need in the Caribbean for the twenty-first century? What should the twenty-first century Caribbean leader look like? I focus on leadership because it is leaders who must define, or at the very least express and communicate, the vision and the strategy for ensuring success in whatever endeavour we as a people collectively set out to do.

In examining what our future leaders should look like, we must first focus on what factors are expected to affect or influence the Caribbean most in the twenty-first century, many of which have already begun to have an impact. In examining where we are going, or where we need to go, we must first focus on where we are coming from and where we are today. We must therefore examine the contextual environment. Numerous scholars and commentators have identified significant trends that affect our lives and which are expected to have the greatest impact on our lives in the twenty-first century. I will focus on the three variables that I believe will have the most impact in the new millenium. Importantly, these three variables are all interrelated – each has contributed to, and has been affected by, the others.

The first variable is the end of the cold war and the claimed triumph of capitalism as the dominant economic and social model. Capitalism has emerged triumphant at the very least by force and by will, if not by inherent moral authority or widespread acceptance. Ideology, therefore, and in particular *ideological extremism*, has waning influence in the world. The second variable is the rise in the pervasiveness and rapidity of technology. Numerous scholars have written about the importance of technology in changing the way we act and interact. The rise of the internet in particular – which did not exist until the early 1990s – has given rise to a widespread increase in the exchange of knowledge and information. The third variable is the rise in the pervasiveness and rapidity of what I shall call 'global liberalisation'. By global liberalisation, I mean the increasing removal of barriers to movements across national borders. This movement has focused on three main variables: information and ideas, goods and services (led by the World Trade Organisation), and labour and capital.

There are several implications of these variables and the subsequent contextual environment. The first is the decline in the ability and power of the state to effect change. In the 1970s and 1980s, Caribbean states could use the ideological trump card to enhance their global status and to extract financial and other kinds of support from wealthier nations. These ideological advantages have largely disappeared in the 1990s, however, and thus Caribbean states must find other means to secure support from wealthier and more powerful countries. The increased global liberalisation has also reduced the power of the state to control the flow of goods, services, and, in particular, capital. The increasing difficulty in implementing controls has reduced substantially the arsenal of tools available to Caribbean countries. The second implication is the increased power of global conglomerates. Although multinationals have wielded significant power in Caribbean countries since the 1940s and 1950s, the kind of power they wield today is different. Whereas, in the past, governments expressed concern about what multinationals did (regarding the environment and transfers of capital, for example), today governments are more concerned about what multinationals do not do: invest. Caribbean countries are increasingly competing to attract foreign investors to their shores and thus global conglomerates are able to extract costly concessions and incentives from these countries. The third implication is the increase in the expectations and demands of the citizenry. Because of the increased education and information that Caribbean people have about 'best practices' in other nations, citizens have become increasingly aware of what policies and practices are available – and have become more vocal in their demands to see them implemented in the region. Caribbean people want greater responsiveness, transparency, and results from their governments.

In short, Caribbean governments today are caught between the proverbial rock and a hard place. On one hand, they are facing greater pressure and demands from the people: to act better and quicker and do more than ever before. On the other hand, the governments' ability to respond and the options available are greatly reduced. The reduction of options is made even more stark when we recognise that most Caribbean countries have very high debt burdens that severely limits the ability of countries to effect discretionary spending, particularly on capital development projects. It is therefore clear that Caribbean countries face more pressure today than they did in the past. The question is, how do Caribbean leaders deal with the overwhelming pressures placed on them, without the adequate resources or ability to control which they possessed in the past? This is the context that we face and which forms the backdrop for an approach to leadership and the political order that I call 'the politics of principled proactive pragmatism'. I shall now outline in broad strokes the fundamentals of this particular political approach.

The Politics of Principled Proactive Pragmatism

Perhaps the best place to begin is with a definition. The current governor of California, Gray Davis, explained at his inauguration that he planned to 'govern neither from the right nor the left, but from the center; propelled not by ideology, but by common sense'. Although this statement is not particularly new or profound, it in many ways encapsulates one of the core premises of principled proactive pragmatism – that decisions should be made not by reference to any ideological or hardline position, but by whether the decision makes common sense.

For example, the principled proactive pragmatist (PPP) attempts to remove too much ideological baggage about whether assets are owned by locals or foreigners, or about whether the government or the private sector should be doing things. It is based on the premise that things need to be done and those who have the greatest resources and best incentives should be the ones to do those things. To be more specific, this approach involves a shift in both the *criteria* leaders use to evaluate policies and practices, and in the general *orientation* and *focus* of those leaders with regard to those policies.

In evaluating the criteria for evaluating policies and practices of reform, the PPP asks three fundamental questions. First, does the proposed policy ensure the long term survival of the country? Second, does the proposed policy benefit the majority of people in the country? Third, does the proposed policy harm any groups in society? If so, does this harm outweigh the benefit to the majority? If not, what strategies are being designed to minimise the harm to those groups? The PPP conducts an extensive cost-benefit analysis that is detailed and fact-based. After conducting that analysis, the PPP designs an implementation strategy designed to maximise the benefits and minimises the costs.

But the PPP is not merely a cold technocrat concerned only with minimising costs and maximising benefits, the PPP also acts in a principled manner. The critical issue is what principles are important to the PPP. These principles should be associated with the method in which action is conducted and the manner in which the PPP relates to colleagues and others. I focus on six principles that are not exhaustive, but which should form the PPP's principle 'core' – that of ACTION:

Analysis and Debate
Cooperation and Unity
Transparency and Accountability
Integrity and Honesty
Organisation and Structure
National Interest First

These principles are focused first on placing the national interest above narrow political or personal interests: nationalistic concerns must always be paramount to the PPP. Second, the principles are focused on acting in a manner that is above reproach and that involves operating with integrity, decency, and honesty. Third, the principles are focused on acting in a transparent, accountable manner with sufficient openness to minimise even the perception of corruption. Fourth, the principles are focused on acting thoughtfully and deliberately using careful analysis and debate. Fifth, the principles are centred around establishing an effective organisation and structure to supplant the cult of personality that has dominated Caribbean politics for decades. Sixth, the principles involve a cooperative and inclusive approach that values working closely with other parties to devise solutions rather than engaging in unnecessary conflict or destructive activity. Importantly, the acronym for the six key principles spell the word 'action' because all the principles are rendered essentially meaningless unless they are acted upon and put into action in a consistent, credible manner.

In terms of orientation and focus, the PPP involves taking a proactive, results-oriented approach. The PPP is more interested in generating results than reports, action than apathy, effective implementation over empty ideals, and creative solutions over cumbersome statements. Proactive refers to a systematic, analytic, action-oriented approach to making decisions.

The PPP seeks to balance participation and delegation with personal involvement in decision-making. The PPP is a micro-strategist, involved in micro-decisions and possessing the abilities to make an effective contribution. Importantly, however, the PPP also recognises his or her limitations and actively seeks to recruit the talents and involvement of others who can also make effective communications. Ultimately, the PPP recognises that accountability is important and that someone must eventually take responsibility for all actions. As such, the PPP is involved with decisions and actions at all levels, including the micro-level.

The PPP is also a political reformist, committed to perpetually reforming and improving infrastructure. British prime minister Tony Blair, a classic PPP, recently argued that Britain needed to 'fight the forces of conservatism'. The PPP is constantly fighting those resistant to change – the PPP is constantly thinking of and devising methods to improve the political and constitutional process so as to improve representation of the people.

Third, the PPP is a globalist and an integrationist. Although the PPP is primarily a nationalist, focused on putting the interests of the nation and its citizens above other concerns, this is not the same as parochialism or short-sightedness. While committed to enhancing national concerns, the PPP also recognises that these concerns are enhanced and improved when the nation learns from and works with other nations. The PPP thus acquires substantial information about other nations and maintains close relationships with leaders and civil servants in those nations.

In the Caribbean, the PPP is an economic integrationist, committed to bringing the economies of the Caribbean together. With just under six million people and a total GDP of less than US$25 billion, the English-speaking Caribbean is becoming increasingly irrelevant and vulnerable from a global perspective. The only way forward for Caribbean economies is to put our markets together and to forge alliances with the leading world blocs such as NAFTA, the EU, and APEC. The PPP recognises this imperative and seeks to overcome the cultural and political obstacles associated with this needed integration. Importantly, the PPP is relatively ambivalent on the issue of political integration. Although economic integration brings clear economic and social advantages, the advantages of political integration are less clear and tend to point to a further erosion of state power which has certain negative consequences.

Finally, the PPP is a knowledge and information enthusiast. The most powerful and valuable commodity in the world today is information. The most powerful 'finished good', which uses information as its primary ingredient, is vision. The PPP labours in an unending journey to improve the knowledge base personally as well as for the citizenry. The PPP believes that expanding the opportunity for citizens to become more educated and improving the delivery of education are critical to ensuring national competitive advantages in the new century. The PPP is thus committed to substantially improving the amount and quality of information delivery both personally and for the nation as a whole.

In many ways, we in the Caribbean are charting new territory as we enter the new century. We are entering a frightening period filled with unprecedented change and unlimited opportunities. We seriously face the potential of having the world pass us by. These new challenges require fortitude, courage, and a commitment to succeed. More specifically, we need in the Caribbean principled, proactive, pragmatists who are committed to micro-strategy, political reform, economic integration, and to the improved knowledge base of the Caribbean people.

Part 7
The Caribbean in the International System

26 | RICHARD L BERNAL

The Caribbean in the International System:
Outlook for the First Twenty Years of the Twenty-first Century

Small states, which are also small, vulnerable, developing economies, are particularly influenced and affected by events and trends in the global arena. How these countries react to and influence these developments will be a critical determinant in their economic, social and political development. The Caribbean (that is, CARICOM), as a collection of small states/economies will confront profound external changes which will have far-reaching and long term implications.

This paper examines the changes in the international system and how CARICOM will cope with these developments in the first 20 years of the twenty-first century. Part A reviews the recent global developments and trends and projects these in the period 2000–2020. The implications of these trends are analysed in Part B. The main ingredients of a CARICOM response are outlined in Part C.

Recent and Projected Developments and Trends

There are three principal developments, namely

Globalisation

Globalisation, a multi-dimensional process in which national barriers to the international flow of goods, services, capital, money and information are being increasingly reduced or eliminated is well advanced and is in many respects irreversible.[1] Globalisation is not merely acceleration in the process of the internationalisation of capitalism or the market,[2] it is an epochal shift in capitalism, affecting every aspect of human existence.[3]

During the period 1950 to 1994, the volume of world trade grew at a rate of 1.6 times faster than that of world production, ranging from a low of 1.2 times during the 1970s to a high of 2.8 times in the 1990s. Over this 45-year period, the value of world output increased by a factor of five, while the value of world trade in goods multiplied by a factor of 14.[4] The WTO calculates that the ratio of world trade in goods and services to output increased from 15 to 22 per cent between 1974 and 1994 and estimates that it increased from 7 to 15 per cent over the period 1950 to 1974 – it has more than tripled since 1950. In recent years, international trade and capital flows have grown at a faster rate than world GDP.[5] During 1983-93, there was a 71 per cent increase in the volume of world merchandise exports, double the 35 per cent growth in world output.[6]

The transition from an atomised world economy of nation states to a seamless global economy is taking place via an intermediary phase of the planned and/or market driven regional integration of national economies into trade blocs. Globalisation is creating larger units, both corporate entities, such as multinational corporations, and the coalescing of national economies through regional integration to form regional trade blocs.[7] Trade blocs are a fundamental aspect of the world economy, both in terms of the share of world trade they encompass and the number of countries that participate in them. In 1995, 51 reciprocal, GATT-notified regional trade agreements were in force and accounted for 50 percent of world trade.[8] A 1992 survey listed 23 preferential trade arrangements, encompassing 119 countries and accounting for approximately 82 per cent of international trade in goods.[9] Most of these arrangements seem to be moving toward becoming trade blocs, and they accounted for two-thirds of world trade in 1992.[10] Intra-regional trade has grown rapidly throughout the world since the late 1940s and now accounts for one half of world trade, accounting for almost 70 per cent of trade in Western Europe.[11]

The advance of globalisation involves production and consumption on a global scale. The fusion of computer technology with telecommunications makes it possible for firms to relocate an ever-widening range of operations and functions to wherever cost-competitive labour, assets and infrastructure are available. The new technologies make it feasible to standardise, routinise and coordinate activities that previously were subject to the friction of space and therefore regarded as non-tradable. They also enable such activities to be turned into 'real-time' activities.

The increasing globalisation of consumer demand and economic transactions and activities have been facilitated and in some instances impelled by rapid development of new technologies of communications, informatics and manufacturing. New technologies have reduced transaction time, eliminated geography and distance, reduced the importance of economies of scale and created an environment of 24-hour trading. The new developments in information processing, and telecommunications propel globalisation by eliminating the costs resulting from distance, the importance of location and the advantages of large size. Technological developments have been a major catalyst stimulating global competition. Even goods and services, which are produced and exchanged within national boundaries, have to meet global standards, cost and tastes. Essentially, there is only one market and that is the world market. Management guru Peter F Drucker explains that, 'Every business must become globally competitive, even if it manufactures and sells only within a local or regional market. The competition is not local anymore – in fact it knows no boundaries. Every company has to become transnational in the way it is run.'[12]

The globalisation of production and consumption will be accelerated by the rapid growth of electronic commerce (e-commerce). This new global phenomenon entails business conducted on the internet and other network based data inter-change systems. E-commerce has and will fundamentally affect the way economic activities are conducted in financial services, telecommunications, entertainment and various other services. Internet access and use is likely to grow rapidly. Electronic commerce is predicted to involve $300 billion by the end of the year 2000.[13] By 2003, the internet could account for two per cent of all commercial transactions.[14] (In 1997, there were about 100 million internet users; this number is projected to increase to 300 million by 2001). It was estimated that in 1998 on-line commerce revenues amounted to $12 billion.[15]

There has been enormous growth of non-material economic activity on a global scale, much of it beyond the ambit and competence of national and international regulations. This is most pronounced in the expansion of services, electronic commerce and financial flow. The average annual growth in trade in commercial services between 1980 and 1993 was 7.7 per cent, compared to 4.9 per cent for merchandise trade. The overall share of services in total trade amounted to 22.2 percent in 1993, up from 17 per cent in 1980, and in the early 1990s service industries accounted for 50 to 60 per cent of total foreign direct investment flows.[16] Furthermore, services account for 61 per cent of GDP in industrialised countries and between 35 and 51 per cent of GDP in developing countries.[17]

Financial flows have become disembedded from the real economy, with much of the global financial flows being unrelated to production, trade and investment. This has been compounded by emergence of global financial markets as governments have liberalised their national financial system. There has been a dramatic shift from a financial structure, which was based in national economies with some transnational links to a predominantly global system in which some residual local differences in markets, institutions, and regulations persist.[18] The magnitude of the flows have dwarfed the resources of central banks and have reduced considerably the capacity of even the industrialised countries to control these flows.[19] The significant increase in short term financial flows and reduced regulatory capacity of governments has been a growing vulnerability to the disruptions, which result from instability of short term funds.

Three broad categories of work are emerging with increasing divergence in remuneration leading to pronounced labour market segmentation and skewed income distribution. The three types of work are routine production, in-person services and symbolic-analytic services. The symbolic-analysts, also referred to as knowledge workers, concentrate on problem solving and strategic brokering by manipulating symbols which generate the highest value added[20] and compete in a global labour market with high international mobility. Routine producers and in-person servers are immobile internationally, but given the mobility of capital, technology and management, their wages are influenced by lower wages in developing countries and labour saving technological innovation. By the year 2000, approximately 70 per cent of all jobs in Europe and the USA will require cerebral rather than manual skills. One-half of these so-called brain skill jobs require personnel with university level education or the equivalent professional qualifications.[21]

Collapse of the Cold War Political Architecture

The nature and conduct of international relations has changed profoundly during the last two decades. The post-World War II political architecture collapsed with the end of the cold war, leaving the United States as the single super power. The implosion of the Soviet Union, the fragmentation of Eastern Europe, the rise of the newly industrialised economies in Asia and Latin America and the intensifying tri-polar economic and political rivalry with Japan and the EU [22] have combined to change the dynamics of international affairs. For example, traditional enemies like the Soviet Union have been replaced by a group of countries, including Russia, desperately in need of economic assistance. Further, communism has been disbanded in Eastern Europe ushering in need democracies with market economies and former allies in Europe and Japan have become formidable economic competitors. Despite an inward-looking mood,[23] the United States has persisted in attempts to fulfill the role of hegemony albeit while experiencing a decline in power relative to its status at the end of World War II. This situation has been described as the 'impotence of omnipotence'.[24]

At present and in the immediate future, international relations will be more complex because of diversity and proliferation of political actors, the evolution of governance in response to the erosion of the sovereignty of the nation state, and the need for new forms of management of the global economy and cultural milieu characterised by a dialectic of homogenising and centripetal, sub-national influences.

The end of the cold war has coincided with the spread of nuclear capability to a number of regional powers, rogue states such as North Korea and poor neighbouring states with traditional antipathies such as India and Pakistan. In addition, the former Soviet Union's nuclear arsenal is now under the control of states which are not politically stable. The prospect of the spread of nuclear capability to other countries such as Iraq is of great concern to the international community. Admittedly, part of the expression of misgivings from the traditional nuclear powers is partly racist and motivated by a desire to monopolise this capability while assuring the rest of the world that they are the only 'responsible' governments. An even more dangerous development is the emergence of terrorism utilising military technologies which are potentially devastating, easily affordable and extremely difficult to detect. Sophisticated weaponry and explosives are utilised by drug traffickers, in some cases exceeding the capability of government security forces.

a) Increased Diffusion and Complexity

A global convergence of economic, technological and ideological forces which drive the process of globalisation is shifting power away from governments toward multilateral institutions and a small number of multi-nationals, corporations and financial institutions [25] who increasingly wield economic and political influence. Concomitant with the globalisation of economic process proceeding rapidly at the economic level, there is a tendency for the nation-state to fragment, particularly where there are long-standing religious, racial, tribal and ethnic differences. Some have gone as far as to proclaim the demise of the nation state, [26] certainly in an economic sense but also increasingly as a viable political actor. This seems premature, as the nation state has not been superseded by any political formation, however sovereignty in all its dimensions has been constrained considerably by economic interdependence.[27]

The legal and illegal [28] migration of people from economically depressed areas to areas where jobs and higher wages are available is likely to be more pronounced in the next two decades. Growth rates persist at high levels in developing countries, while these economies produce a limited number of new jobs - most of which have low wages. This will be a major economic problem and political issues in the United States, the EU and Canada. The developed countries cannot be oases of affluence in a sea of poverty, but will face an increasing number of migrants, creating a under-class or a low strata among the working class, which is racially, culturally and linguistically different from the rest of the society. Migration will profoundly change the US, socially, culturally and politically as the melting pot of assimilation wilts under cultural chauvinism, ethnic assertiveness [29] and a generalised nihilism. Diversified, developed countries will witness the emergence of domestic constituencies with sympathies and applications to other countries or cultures. Although the English-speaking Caribbean is too small to figure prominently by virtue of numbers, it could benefit from broad social impacts of migrant communities and their influence on US foreign and immigration policy.[30] Legal immigrants from Mexico, Central America and the Spanish-speaking Caribbean account for one third of the total immigrant population and more than half of undocumented immigrants. They tend to concentrate in Florida, New York, Texas and California.[31]

The demographic shifts in industrialised countries will dramatically shift the age structure of their population.[32] The total fertility rate in the developed countries has fallen to 1.6, which is already 25 per cent beneath the rate necessary to replace the population generation to generation. At present, 14 per cent of the population in developed countries is over 65 but by 2030 this will have increased to 25 to 30 per cent. As the age structure shifts, the labour force as a share of population will decline. For example, in Japan during the next decade the number of workers under age 30 will decline by 25 per cent. This will create an enormous demand for young workers and these will have to come from developing countries where population structures have a high component of people under age 30. This could be a favourable development for densely populated Caribbean countries, especially those experiencing high rates of unemployment, particularly among the young. Ironically, migrants may contribute more to Caribbean economies than if they had remained in the region, because of their substantial remittances.[33]

Displaced people, both those dislocated within their own countries and those who flee to other countries, are likely to be a burgeoning problem of global dimensions. In the early 1990s the estimated figure was 43 million – 18 million refugees and 25 million internally displaced.[34] As artificial nation states fragment under the mounting centrifugal forces of ethnic pogroms, genocide, communal strife, violence of civil wars, religious conflict, famine and natural disasters, the magnitude of this human tragedy will mount. The systematic response to these types of disasters by the international community is yet to be defined. This problem could face the Caribbean, as was demonstrated by Cuban and Haitian boat people and the cataclysmic events in Montserrat. Part of the problem is that the end of the cold war has obliterated the rationale for the prosperous and peaceful countries to intervene in poor and unsafe countries or regions. What is left as a basis for action is compassion and moral outrage. The problem is that the tensions and nascent nature of what Michael Ignatieff refers to as 'an ethnic of universal moral obligation among strangers' and 'a politics that takes the world rather than the nation as its political space and takes the human species itself rather than specific citizenship, racial, religious, or ethnic group as its objective, as its object.'[35]

Migration is at the center of the tension between the denationalisation of national economies and the re-nationalising of national politics, which is a prominent feature of globalisation.[36] Sassen points out that immigration policy is 'now shaped for forces ranging from economic globalisation to international agreements on human rights, and it is made and implemented within settings ranging from national and local legislatures and judiciaries to supra-national organisations.'[37]

b) Governance

The emergence of an increasingly globalised and integrated world economy and community raises the question of its management and governance. The post-World War II economy was atomistic, consisting of national economies managed by the Bretton Woods institutions (the IMF and World Bank) and by the GATT. This system reflected the existing polarisation of the cold war and the hegemony of the United States. The delinking of the United States dollar from the gold standard in August 1971 marked the end of this institutional structure for global management. The end of the cold war and the relative decline of US dominance have left an increasingly globalised and interdependent world economy without hegemony to ensure decision-making and to enforce the rules. The decline of US hegemony [38] has caused a shift towards cooperation, which recognises the present tripolar [39] economic configuration and requires a consensual decision-making process. A global architecture of rules must increasingly replace power-based international decision-making. However, while a multilateral system of rules and institutions such as the IMF, World Bank, WTO and the UN has been established, a genuinely democratic decision-making process is not even in its embryonic stage.

Globalisation will require increased international cooperation on worldwide issues, such as sustainable development. This will necessitate a trade-off between national sovereignty and multi-lateralism. National governments will not willingly relinquish management of national and international phenomena, but governments will have less control over the design and implementation of national and international economic policy. Policies will therefore have to be much more closely calibrated and flexible.

The end of the cold war has ushered in a period of ideological entropy but it would be wrong to mistake this conjuncture as Francis Fukuyama's eurocentric and euphoric 'end of history' – the end of mankind's ideological evolution and the universalisation of Western liberal democracy.[40] The subsidence of ideological conflict does not condemn mankind to vicious and unrelenting struggle between irreconcilable civilisations as Huntington suggests.[41] While democracy has become pandemic in the last 10–15 years it is fragile, beset by internal fratricidal social, ethnic and political disputes and anti-libertarian external pressures of globalisation and resurgent parochial hatreds and prejudices. Benjamin Barber has characterised these as opposing tendencies which paradoxically produce a corrosive effect on the nation state and its democratic institutions.[42] While this is a real danger, it does not portent an era of unmitigated chaos anticipated by Zbigniew Brzezinski's *Out of Control*, Daniel Patrick Moynihan's *Pandemonium* and Robert Kaplan's *The Coming Anarchy*.[43]

The nature of international politics has changed significantly because of the political influence of multi-national corporations, both within the nation state and at the multilateral level, and the emergence of 'civil society', in particular non-governmental organisations (NGOs). These NGOs have been particularly influential on environmental issues, reform of social institutions and gender issues. They have expanded their reach to the international arena and now their views while not always welcomed or invited, must be taken into account. For example, at the World Trade Organisation, NGOs from developed countries in particular have pressed the environmental and labour issues. They have developed extensive international networks such as the NGO statement on the Multilateral Agreements on Investment endorsed by 565 organisations in 68 countries.[44] In recognition of their demands for involvement, the Free Trade Area of the Americas (FTAA) has included in its institutional structure a consultative group of civil society – a first for trade negotiations.

c) Cultural Dialectic

The rapid and profound technological changes which have occurred in recent years have ushered in a new era in world economy, which is distinguished by a comprehensive globalisation of all spheres. Advances in electronic data interchange, establishment of systems for the computer-controlled trans-shipment and clearance of goods, improved voice and data communication networks, automated banking and international telemarketing have defined the nature of international relations. Global society and international politics have been transformed by developments in telecommunications technology, which have revolutionised the speed and conduct of all aspects of global interaction – economic, social and political. The instant global availability of information via satellite, computers and telecommunications technology has the potential to change, irrevocably, all aspects of human life.

Technological developments in telecommunications, computerisation, and informatics have eliminated the barriers of distance and time, resulting in the reconstitution of the world into a single social space.[45] Globalisation at the cultural level is reflected in the emergence of 'global consciousness', manifested as a social matrix of people all over the world, unified through mass communication, who think in global terms. Today we have social relations and even organised community relations regardless of space – regardless of the territory that we share. This has enormous consequences not only for the role of the nation state as a territorially bounded community, but also for the organisation of economic production on a cross-border basis. It permits the emergence of 'imagined' communities, cultures and even systems of authority and social control that traverse borders.

Increasing Disparities

In the last 25 years the global economy has witnessed increased disparities. The three most prominent trends are the widening gap in the standard of living between developed countries and developing and least developed countries, growing corporate concentration around a small number of multi-national corporations and the concentration of wealth and power in the 'Triad' – the United States, Japan and the European Union.

a) Widening Development Gap

A prominent feature of globalisation is the widening gap between developed countries and the majority of developing countries. This is reflected in differences in income levels and other indicators of human well-being. The share of the poorest 20 per cent of the world's population in global income is 1.1 per cent, down from 1.4 per cent in 1991 and 2.3 per cent in 1960. The ratio of the income of the top 20 per cent to that of the poorest 20 percent rose from 30-1 in 1960 to 61-1 in 1991 – and was at 84-1 in 1995.[46]

The decline in the value of unskilled labour to production and labour-saving technological innovations has had a deleterious effect on employment in developing countries. The process of globalisation is highly uneven in the world economy and is associated with (although causality cannot be definitely established) an increasing gap between the rich and the poor. The concentration of private foreign investment among the OECD countries and the profound marginalisation of Africa are the most dramatic examples. According to the Human Development Report, global poverty is not being reduced. Indeed, of the 4.4 billion people in developing countries, most are poor. Nearly three-fifths lack basic sanitation, a third have no access to clean water, a quarter do not have adequate housing, a fifth have no access to modern health services and about 20 per cent do not have enough dietary energy and protein. Almost 3 billion people – half the world's population – live on less than $2 dollars a day. [47]

Prospects are not good for closing the gap. The disparities in growth are not likely to be reduced while 92 per cent of foreign direct investment is received by only 28 per cent of the world's population.[48] This is compounded by the fact that direct foreign investment in developing countries is highly concentrated. During the first half of the 1990s, nine of the 147 developing countries received 90 per cent of all direct investment flows.[49]

b) Economic Concentration

The concentration of economic activity is taking place in the form of corporate concentration and the growing share of the triad countries in the global economy. Multinational corporations (MNCs) now account for about a third of world output and two-thirds of world trade. A quarter of world trade is intra-firm transactions taking place within multinational corporations.50 UNCTAD estimates that the foreign affiliates of transnational corporations produce a quarter of world output. They had sales of 11,000 billion in 1998, which far exceeds world exports of 7,000 billion.[51] They also account for half of world trade in manufactured goods and 80 per cent of the world's land cultivated for export crops.[52] Their prominence is such that Greider regards the MNC as being at the center of what he calls 'the manic logic of global capitalism.'[53] The most prominent feature of corporate concentration in recent years has been mergers and acquisitions. The total value of mergers and acquisitions in 1998 was $2.5 trillion, an increase of 54 per cent over 1997 and up by 613 per cent from $0.4 trillion in 1992.[54] While the number of mergers per annum has fluctuated over the last decade, nine of the ten largest mergers occurred during the past year. Mergers will widen the disparity in size, so no Latin American or Caribbean firm was in the 1,000 largest companies in the world.[55] By mid-September 1999, cross-border mergers and acquisitions amounted to 1.3 times higher than the total for 1998.[56]

The triad of the US, Japan and the EU dominate the global economy and is the home base of the largest multinational corporations. In 1996, 85 of the top 100 MNCs were headquartered in the triad in 1990 with the United States, Japan, the United Kingdom, France and Germany alone accounted for three-quarters of the entries in both years. Their dominance is evident in the number of firms, foreign assets, foreign sales and foreign employment. The world's 500 largest industrial corporations account for 25 per cent of the world's economic output.[57] The top 300 transnationals, excluding financial institutions, own some 25 per cent of the world's productive assets.[58] The combined assets of the world's fifty largest commercial banks amount to nearly 60 per cent of *The Economist*'s estimate of a $20 trillion global stock of productive capital.[59]

c) Increasing Heterogeneity of National Economies

International economic strategies and foreign relations policies in the cold war era were firmly rooted in a tri-sector conceptual model which consisted of the 'First World' (developed capitalist countries), the 'Second World' (communist countries) and the 'Third World' (developing countries). Since the collapse of the Berlin Wall, the so-called second world has contracted significantly with the democratisation of Eastern Europe and the Soviet Union. The first world has become more integrated economically but has drifted apart, while Europe and Japan have caught up economically while evolving different types of capitalism. The famous western alliance epitomised by NATO is no longer operating under US suzerainty. The term 'Third World' no longer has any meaning due to the wide diversity among developing countries. For example, GNP per capita ranges from just over US$100 in countries such as Burundi, Ethiopia and Haiti to more than US$4,000 per year in countries such as Korea, Argentina, Brazil and Chile. Countries vary from the newly industrialised nations of Asia to those dependent largely on the export of primary products and unprocessed raw materials such as agriculture, which accounts for more than 50 per cent of GDP in Cambodia, the Central African Republic, the Congo and Myanmar.[60]

Implications

The implications of the profound changes which are likely to take place in the next twenty years are primarily the loss of special consideration by developed countries – the United States and the United Kingdom in particular – and the increased complexity of international relations.

Loss of Special Consideration

The strategic importance of the English-speaking Caribbean to the United States and Europe has declined in recent years. This is a reflection of the fact that the region is no longer a supplier of critical raw materials which are either scarce or not as cheaply available from other regions, and the end of the cold war. The principal exports of agricultural products and raw materials from the region – such as sugar, bananas and bauxite – are no longer vital to US and EU interests. All of these are readily available from other regions and, in the case of sugar and bananas, at lower prices. Security concerns have changed dramatically in the post cold war era, and the priorities are the Middle East, rogue states such as Iraq and North Korea, economic competition from Asia and the rehabilitation of the Soviet Union and Eastern Europe. Consequently, less attention is being given to Latin America, and the Caribbean, other than Cuba and Africa. Dame Eugenia Charles warned that, 'In a political sense the Caribbean in relation to the US has lost its strategic importance. But in a very real sense the Caribbean remains the frontier for domestic peace and stability in US.'[61]

This decline in strategic importance has resulted in the loss of special consideration for the small states of the region. This is evident in the attempts to progressively reduce and eventually eliminate preferential bilateral trade arrangements and reduced foreign aid allocated to the region. Preferential trade arrangements for developing countries are likely to be progressively reduced. Developed countries no longer feel obliged to provide special treatment to developing countries, especially those that have minute markets, lack essential raw materials, and have limited strategic importance. Future trade arrangements will be based on reciprocity, given the present global emphasis on free trade. Developing countries must be prepared to adapt to the elimination or erosion of preferential trade regimes, such as the Lomé Convention and the Caribbean and Canada Trade Agreement (CARIBCAN). The EU Commission responsible for the Lomé Convention has declared its intention to conduct a radical reappraisal of the convention that could involve the gradual elimination of preferential tariffs.

Another indicator of the decline in importance of the ESC to the US and EU is the steady reduction in foreign aid. Aid from the US to Jamaica declined from US$116m in 1984 to US$32m in 1994, a fall of 72 per cent. Over the same period US aid to Barbados declined by 98 per cent, to Grenada by 99 per cent and to Trinidad and Tobago by 99 per cent.[62] Aid from Canada has plummeted in spite of the so-called 'special relationship' with the ESC.[63] Official development assistance to Jamaica dropped from US$117 per capita in 1990 to US$20 in 1997.[64] This has occurred at a time when aid to all developing countries has been reduced by OECD countries, no doubt reflecting a reallocation in favour of the transitional economies of Eastern Europe. Official development assistance peaked at $69 billion, reflecting the unwarranted parsimony of the OECD countries. Foreign aid as a share of GNP has dropped to 0.2 per cent with the decline being especially pronounced in the United States, so that by 1997, aid was only 0.08 per cent of GNP.[65] This decline is paralleled by the reduction in concessional loans from bilateral aid agencies, such as the elimination by the US of the 936 funds programme.[66]

Economic and security motives will be elements of future US and EU policies toward the Caribbean as they give expression to the continuity of their interests in the region and, to a lesser extent, reflect an awareness of its problems and potential.[67] However, the cold war has ended, and this has virtually eliminated concerns about the threat of Communism. While US concerns about the vulnerability of the region to communism have diminished, there are residual concerns about migration and the prevalence of drug trafficking. Nevertheless, the Caribbean is not viewed as an area which can pose problems on the scale of illegal Mexican immigrants or Colombia as a source of narcotics. This perspective is compounded by a perception that the region is not poor but it is relatively 'well off' in terms of GDP per capita compared to other developing countries. This is already reflected in reduced allocations of development assistance to these countries. The English-speaking Caribbean is not viewed as a crisis area or 'flashpoint'[68] nor is it big enough to warrant ongoing surveillance. Put bluntly the English-speaking Caribbean is too democratic, too stable and not big or poor enough.

There is a tendency for large developed countries to focus on a few so-called emerging markets among the developing countries and these tend to be the largest developing countries, such as India, Mexico and Brazil. This focus diverts attention from small, developing countries. In fact, it has been suggested that the focus for US policy should be on the ten largest emerging markets.[69] The perception that a few big emerging markets constitutes the next concentric ring of development was formalised at the 1999 IMF World Bank Annual Meeting, which established the G20. The new forum comprises the G7 and 11 other large economies, mainly emerging market countries.[70]

Increased Complexity of International Relations

While the foreign policy of Caribbean states will be formulated in a way which recognizes the continuing preeminence of Europe and North America, there will be diversification. Payne and Sutton describe the dilemma of these two enduring relationships as working themselves out in different time frames. Europe represents the legacy of the past, North America holds the prospect of the future.[71] The economic and political configuration of the world will change in a way which will lead to the emergence of new 'regional powers'. These include Brazil,[72] Korea, India and South Africa.

Among the issues that are likely to become more prominent and more complicated is the question of security. While the threat of US military intervention is an ever present danger, security issues will increasingly involve drug trafficking [73] and money laundering; illicit arms trafficking and the link to terrorism, crime and violence; and trans-border shipment of nuclear and hazardous wastes through the sea and airspace of small island states. Such problems are of course not unique to small island states in the Caribbean. However, because of their extremely small size these states suffer the consequences to a much greater extent than would normally be associated with these problems. In addition, the geographical location of the small island states of the Caribbean make them a natural transit corridor for a range of materials, including illicit drugs and arms, and therefore these small island states are vulnerable to considerable movement of dangerous goods through this area.

Arms shipments are of particular concern as they now pose a major security challenge which directly threatens the social and political fabric of small island states because they stimulate violence, and are associated with the illicit drug trade, which now assumes such enormous size and involves so much money that it is difficult for small island states to withstand the pressure. Small states are particularly vulnerable because of the very limited capability for air and sea defense. These states are not able to match the enormous resources that are involved in drug trafficking and the associated traffic in arms. In addition, the traffic in drugs involves introducing and spreading the use of drugs in these small societies which is associated with crime, violence and corruption.

In addition, the fact that small island states in the Caribbean are located close to major production points of drugs and are also major markets for drugs, encourages drug smuggling and the multi-national drug trafficking groups to relocate to small island states. Efforts to combat drug smuggling have proven to be an expensive exercise, diverting substantial resources from social investment, such as education and health, in small island states. In addition, the police and military capability in small island states is very limited, particularly in equipment such as ships and airplanes. This makes it difficult, despite the strong commitment of governments in this area, to struggle against drug trafficking and firearms, and makes it difficult to translate that will into effective action.

New issues are likely to confront the foreign policy machinery of Caribbean countries, such as biodiversity, epidemics, soil erosion, exhaustion of fish stocks.[74] Also international relations will involve encounters with new configurations – trade blocs, non-governmental organisations and new multilateral governance arrangements. The nature of conflict could broaden to include terrorism, international crime and resource use, including the seabed. Conventional war between countries has been replaced by what has been described as 'low-intensity conflict' in which the factions are not national crimes but tribal, ethnic and religious rivals. In this type of war, traditional distinctions are blurred, including those between civilian and soldier terrorism and war, and military action and violent crime.[75] Demographic shifts and rapid population growth in developing countries could lead to altercations over scarce resources like arable land and water. An estimated 95 per cent of global population growth between now and 2050 will occur in developing countries.[76] Even projections based on favorable assumptions about growth in developing countries and world agricultural output indicate that food insecurity and widespread malnutrition will persist in 2020 and beyond.[77]

Response

The world is not changing, it has changed. The dismantling of preferential trade arrangements such as the WTO ruling on bananas,[78] indicate that fundamental changes which profoundly affect the Caribbean have already occurred. Several significant developments are already taking place at an ever-increasing speed and the Caribbean must respond proactively and creatively. Three important aspects of the response are:

Strategic Global Repositioning

Strategic global repositioning (SGR)[79] is a process of repositioning a country in the global economy and world affairs by implementing a strategic medium- to long term plan formulated from continuous dialogue of the public sector, private sector, academic community and the social sector. It involves proactive structural and institutional transformation (not adjustment) focussed on improvement and diversification of exports and international economic and political relations. Achieving SGR requires changes in both internal and external relations. The external relations are of paramount importance because of the highly open and vulnerable nature of these small, developing economies.

Structural adjustment and economic transformation begin with a change of mind, outlook and attitude. The prerequisite for such change is a recognition of the need for new ideas and a willingness to abandon the traditional mindset. This will be incumbent on governments in the region as well as the business sector. An integral part of strategic global repositioning will be export diversification encompassing the development of new exports, such as informatics, as well as improving competitiveness and productivity in existing export sectors like bauxite. Some foreign exchange earning sectors will have to undertake a continual process of adjusting their product mix to shifting demands such as increased travel by older and retired people. Traditional export commodities such as sugar and bananas may not be viable and face the alternative of being phased out or being used as inputs in higher valued added goods such as rum.

The experience of Antigua's transition from an economy based on sugar to one in which tourism is the core activity is encouraging. This is a very real prospect for economies heavily dependent on the export of bananas, for example St Lucia, St Vincent and Dominica.

Part of the crisis of the Caribbean is intellectual. Too many academics and policy-makers are caught in a time warp using old paradigms and traditional policies to deal with difficult new problems in a changed reality. This attempt to put new wine into old bottles is doomed to fail, and the theology of orthodoxy must be challenged. It is not the Washington consensus that is the problem; it is the Caribbean consensus. New situations require new solutions, which can only be derived from new ideas.

The only certainty in tomorrow's world economy is change and change at an exponential rate, which makes speed decision-making and implementation an essential aspect of life in the future.[80] The ability to discern changes, to adopt and adapt to new technology,[81] and to reorganise rapidly will ultimately determine one's capacity to respond. Firms, governments, and individuals must become accustomed to a lack of permanence and recognise that it presents challenges and opportunities. The countries which achieve economic development practice 'proactive adjustment', by adjusting rapidly in anticipation of global changes in demand and technology. Defensive and reactive adjustment, which aims to preserve uncompetitive industries and retain aspects of production is self-defeating. In the short run, reactive adjustment reduces the competitiveness of exports and increases the prices of domestic goods. In the long run, entrepreneurs will find ways to import cheaper alternatives and will relocate inefficient production to other countries in order to retain international competitiveness.

Today, in a very real sense, there is only one market – the global market – from which no country is isolated. Since all firms in small economies are small by global standards, their survival even in national markets will increasingly depend on strategic corporate alliances and 'constellations'.[82] Companies have to be flexible, responsive, competitive, innovative, efficient, and customer-focused. The traditional hierarchical and pyramid-shaped organisation of corporations is too cumbersome and slow to respond effectively. This has prompted a process of 'reengineering',[83] which entails the fundamental rethinking and radical design of business processes to achieve dramatic improvements in critical, contemporary measures of performance, such as cost, quality, service and speed.[84] Strategic corporate alliances and the fragmentation of transnational production processes into separate stages currently undertaken in different countries [85] have made it possible for networks of small firms to overcome their size limitations and compete effectively against large corporations. [86] Small firms can ensure their survival and profitability in the global economy by specialising in a single aspect of production or distribution; capitalising on specific market niches; specialising in 'flexible' manufacturing, and concentrating on economies of speed, which are now more important than economies of scale. [87]

New Paradigm of Small State International Relations

The issue of small states in international relations is not new, indeed there is a well-established literature on the subject in general [88] and regarding the Caribbean in particular.[89] However, changes in circumstances changes sufficiently warrant a reexamination of the subject.

Given the far-reaching changes in the global economic and political environment which are likely to occur in the near future, there is a need for a 'new paradigm of small state international relations'. Especially significant is the increasing heterogeneity of developing countries which undercuts the fundamental tenet of 'third world cooperation' which has been central to a pragmatic foreign policy of the small states of the Caribbean.[90] Developing country heterogeneity makes it more complex to build, maintain and effectively operate alliances such as the Group of 77.

Small Size as a Basis for Strategic Alliances

Disparities in size is one of the fundamental and contentious issues in a globalised world. These disparities occur among countries and among business entities. The former reveals a large potential coalition of 87 countries with a population of less than five million. The number of countries and states in the world has increased significantly in recent decades; in particular, there has been a proliferation of small countries and states. At the time of the first World War, there were 62 independent countries; by 1946 that number had risen to 74; currently, there are 193. Most of these are small states. Indeed, 35 countries have less than 500,000 people, 58 have under 2.5 million people, and 87 have a population of less than five million.[91] The number of small states could increase in number as large states fragment, due to political turmoil (the Soviet Union), ethnic differences (the former Yugoslavia) and separatist movements (East Timor). The possibilities are alarming, given religious differences (Kashmir), cultural divergences (the Basque Provinces, Quebec) [92] and the tribal differences which threaten the arbitrary boundaries of the nation state in Africa (Sudan, Somalia and Nigeria).[93]

The majority of countries are small, and the issue of 'smallness' must be addressed by the global community both at the political and economic levels. It is particularly important in international groupings that include both large and small states. For example, the Commonwealth maintains a Ministerial Group on Small States, and the Free Trade Area of the Americas includes a Consultative Group on Smaller Economies.[94]

It is firms, not countries, that conduct international trade, including a substantial amount of intra-firm transfers. Nationally-owned firms from small countries are small both by global standards and by comparison with firms in large economies, and multinational corporations owned by or based in large countries. Except for a few sectors where economies of scale are not a significant factor, size makes a significant difference in a firm's ability to survive and compete in the global marketplace. Small firms are at a disadvantage because they cannot realise economies of scale, are not attractive business partners, and cannot spend significant funds on marketing intelligence and research and development.[95] There is a huge difference between the top companies in the United States and the top companies in the English-speaking Caribbean. For example, Wal-Mart, the largest employer in the United States, has a staff complement of 675,000, while the Caribbean's top employer, Lascelles Demercado (Jamaica) employs 6,800. The total sales of General Motors are 328 times larger than that of Neal & Massey (Trinidad and Tobago).[96]

Differences in size, both national and corporate, can be the basis for new strategic alliances cemented by the commonality of the disadvantages of small size. Small economies are aggregations of small firms by global standards and are natural allies with firms in developing countries and small businesses in developed countries. This new transnational strategic alliance of firms and farms goes beyond the limits of the old north-south and south-south axes. It has the advantage of providing for the first time an internal constituency in the developed countries.

Reinventing Regionalism

Regionalism is essential for groups of small states and small economies but must be reinvented. Policy-makers in the region need to undertake a rigorous, critical re-evaluation of the operation of CARICOM and reassess the economical and political feasibility of certain long-standing ideas. These ossified ideas include a single currency, a regional airline and political federation. The repeated incantation of these sacred cows is a form of collective escapism. The region must confront uncomfortable issues such as the growing diversity of perspectives on regionalism and different strategies of national development, and their compatibility with existing concepts and structures of regionalism. The objective of regionalism should be the creation of a seamless regional economic space conducive to globally competitive economic activities where nationality of ownership is not a consideration. Market-driven corporate integration should take precedence over government-induced market integration. The process must be flexible, accommodating different development strategies and different speeds of integration.

There is diversity within CARICOM as Trinidad consolidates its industrialisation. Jamaica, Barbados and the Bahamas become advanced, diversified service providers, the OEC expand tourism and Belize, Guyana and Suriname increase commodity production. This divergence could lead to heterogeneity in policy perspectives. Instances have already occurred and portent such possibilities, for example Prime Minister Panday of Trinidad and Tobago suggested that while it was ideal for CARICOM to enter NAFTA as a group, it was not ready and Trinidad and Tobago and Jamaica should go ahead in seeking membership in NAFTA.[97] He also questioned the efficacy of regional integration saying, 'CARICOM has not really succeeded as a trading bloc a lot of things that they agree upon unanimously, [but] there's nothing they implement unanimously.'[98] This situation requires 'flexible integration' which allows groups of member countries to integrate beyond to core agreement.[99]

There is an urgent need to overcome the phobia of widening CARICOM to include relatively larger countries such as Cuba and the Dominican Republic. The region must put aside xenophobic nationalism to allow a re-dimensioning of regionalism to include corporate integration, freedom of movement of skilled professionals and widening of CARICOM while simultaneously deepening economic integration. The case for widening as a priority[100] is based on the fact that merging 14 or 15 micro-economies does not increase the regional market to a size sufficient to achieve the benefits of economic integration such as economies of scale. The dilemma of widening versus deepening is illustrated in The West Indian Commission's aptly titled report, *Time for Action*, which states:

> ... the widening of CARICOM's relations into the entire Caribbean must be an essential part of the way forward. But we believe it would be a mistake to see that process of widening simply in terms of enlarging CARICOM's membership. There are important factors to be balanced. On the economic side, we have to feel our way in enlarging the CARICOM market so that we make progress in that direction without being lost within our own widened Community.[101]

A long-standing idea for widening is the inclusion of the small states of Central America with the Dominican Republic or Belize as an interlocutor or bridging state between Central America and the Caribbean.[102] The most significant change could be Cuba's admission to CARICOM, an event that will transform the economic size and political weight of the region.

Small countries will never be able to match the financial resources of large, developed countries. In 1997 industrial countries deployed an average of six to eight officials to follow WTO proceedings in Geneva, but developing countries were only able to post an average of 3.5, with many of the least developed having no representative.[103] Caribbean countries have had to grapple with these problems in the negotiations.[104] Cooperation and coordination has been a well-established practice through the CARICOM Secretariat and was recently improved by the establishment of the Regional Negotiating Machinery (RNM). The need for cooperation also derives from external developments in which lending agencies treat CARICOM countries as a group. Aid may have to be accessed by regional rather than purely national basis as aid delivery systems respond to disenchantment with country-focused assistance and increasingly tackle transnational problems such as the environment. Possible new approaches include delivery via common-pool mechanisms and spending on international public goods, the benefits of which are shared by several countries.[105]

c) Nation Without Borders

In the next twenty years the Caribbean must conduct its international relations on the foundation of the Caribbean not as nation states only in the physical sense, but as a nation without borders. In today's modern global economy, communications by e-mail, telephone, facsimile and satellite make it possible for countries and their citizens abroad to be linked instantly, comprehensibly and continuously. This effectively abolishes the disabilities of physical distance and allows geographically dispersed nations to function as networked economies and societies. The implications are that Caribbean nations are much larger than the Caribbean nation state, allowing access to a much larger pool of human resources, finance and contacts. In addition, these constituencies can be more informed and mobilised for nation building, as sources of investment, and export markets. They also can play an enhanced role in influencing the foreign policy of their host countries, in particular the United Kingdom, Canada and the United States.

Making the paradigm operational

The Caribbean states have demonstrated a capacity to exert influence on international events through concerted, collaborative diplomacy, such as the dialogue on the New International Economic Order.[106] Small states, such as those of the Caribbean, should eschew spreading their limited resources on a broad foreign policy agenda. Instead, small states should concentrate on select priority issues, a strategy which is aptly described by Bryan as 'niche diplomacy'.[107] These issues include law of the sea, the environment and small, developing economies. Small states can increase their influence in international affairs by focusing on a few issues of particular significance to them. For example, small island states are particularly vulnerable to environmental degradation,[108] a global environmental problem that is capable of solution by implementing the objectives and policies of Agenda 21,[109] a programme which has already been endorsed by the global community. This will require what Ramphal calls 'enlightened change' – inclusive, collective, democratic, internationally cooperative modes of decision-making, possibly within a strengthened United Nations system.[110]

An important determinant of how effective the small states of the Caribbean will be in international relations is the quality of their foreign service. The ossified structure, antiquated procedures and outdated thinking will have to be changed. Frankly, it will be necessary to close down the mid-twentieth century foreign service and retire the 'traditional diplomat'. The twenty-first century foreign service must set goals related to strategic global repositioning and the new realities; employ specialised human resources; use the most modern technology and management systems; revamp global deployment of missions to reflect new priorities; and improve coordination of national agencies involved in external relations. Of course some of these issues such as internal national coordination, are long-standing problems which have persisted from the inception of foreign ministries.[111]

Given the highly open structure of Caribbean economies, meditating the encounter with the global marketplace should be the priority for foreign policy. This does not mean abandoning the traditional, broad-based politically-oriented foreign policy objectives. It does, however, require the development of a foreign service which has a higher complement of officers trained in economics, business and law – skills which should be preferred to history, languages and the arts. The need for this shift in human resource skills is also dictated by the adverse changes in the international arena which make the 'diplomacy of mendicancy' increasingly difficult. The foreign ministries will have to become more involved in commercial and financial negotiations and draw on expertise from the private sector.[112] The negotiations faced by small Caribbean countries will be more complex than ever, involving negotiations with multinational corporations [113] and complicated and interrelated trade negotiations.[114]

The changes that will be necessary are possible because, as a region, the English-speaking Caribbean has shown an exceptional ability to adapt and innovate as the region's history demonstrates beyond doubt. At the political level it will require vision, leadership and will.

The views expressed in this paper are those of the author and not those of the Government of Jamaica.

Notes

1. John Gray, False Down, *The Delusions of Global Capitalism* (London: Granta, 1998), p. 206
2. A Glyn and B Sutcliffe, 'Global but leaderless? The new capitalist order', in R Miliband and L Panitch, eds., *The New World Order: The Socialist Register* (London: Merlin Press, 1992), pp. 76–95; Paul Hirst and Grahame Thompson, *Globalisation in*

Question (London: Polity Press, 1996); and Paul Sweezy 'More or Less on Globalisation', *Monthly Review*, Vol. 49, No. 4 (1997), p. 1–4

3. Roger Burbach and William I Robinson, 'The Fin de Siècle Debate: Globalisation as Epochal Shift', *Science and Society*, Vol. 63, No. 1 (Spring 1999), pp. 10-39
4. Peter Dicken, *Global Shift: Transforming the World Economy* (London: Guilford Press, 3rd edn., 1998), p. 24
5. Peter Dicken, *Global Shift: The Internationalisation of Economic Activity* (London: Guildford Press, 1992), p. 16
6. Ernest H Preeg, *Trade Policy Ahead: Three Tracks and One Question* (Washington DC: Center for Strategic and International Studies, 1995), pp. 6–7
7. Richard L Bernal, *Trade Blocks: A Regionally Specific Phenomenon, or Global Trend?* (Washington, DC: Walter Sterling Surrey Memorial Series, National Planning Association, September 1997)
8. 'Regionalism and the World Trading System' (Geneva: World Trade Organisation, 1995), p. 25; and 'Reflections on Regionalism', Report of the Study Group on International Trade (Washington: Carnegie Endowment for International Peace, 1997)
9. Norman Fieleke, 'One Trading World, or Many: The Issue of Regional Trading Blocs', Federal Reserve Bank of Boston, *New England Economic Review* (May/June 1992), p. 3
10. Ibid., p. 13
11. Hege Northeim, Karl-Michael Finger, and Kym Anderson, 'Trends in the Regionalisation of World Trade, 1928 to 1990', in Kym Anderson and Richard Backhurst, eds., *Regional Integration and the Global Trading System* (New York: St Martin's Press, 1993), pp. 436–486; and World Trade Organisation, Annual Report 1996, Vol. II (Geneva: World Trade Organisation, 1996), p. 23
12. Peter F Drucker, 'Beyond the Information Revolution', *The Atlantic Monthly*, October 1999, p. 51
13. 'Electronic Commerce and the Role of the WTO' (Geneva: World Trade Organisation, 1998), p. 1
14. 'Electronic Commerce and the Role of the WTO', op. cit., p. 10
15. Tim R. Furey, 'Why Profits Still Elude E-Commerce', The Journal of Commerce, January 21, 1999
16. *World Bank: Global Economic Prospects and the Developing Countries* (Washington DC: World Bank, 1995 edn.), pp. 47–48
17. *Liberalising International Transactions in Services: A Handbook* (New York and Washington DC: United Nations Conference on Trade and Development Program on Transnational Corporations and the World Bank, 1993), pp. 6–7
18. J Stopford and Susan Strange, *Rival States, Rival Firms* (Cambridge: Cambridge University Press, 1991), pp. 40–41
19. Gregory J Millman, *The Vandals Crown: How Rebel Currency Leaders Overthrew the World's Central Banks* (New York: The Free Press, 1995)

20. Robert B Reich, *The Work of Nations* (New York: Alfred A Knopf, 1991)
21. Charles Handy, *The Age of Unreason* (Boston: Harvard Business School, 1989), p. 32
22. Lester Thurow, *Head to Head: The Coming Economic Battle Among Japan, Europe and America* (New York: William Marrow & Co., 1992)
23. Charles Kauathammer, 'The Lonely Superpower', *The New Republic*, July 29, 1991, pp. 23–27; Patrick J Buchanan, 'Now That Red is Dead, Come Home America', *Washington Post*, September 8, 1991; Alan Tondson, 'What is the National Interest?', *The Atlantic Monthly*, July 1991, pp. 35–81; and Zbigniew Brzezinski, 'Selective Global Commitment', *Foreign Affairs*, Vol. 70, No. 4 (Fall 1991), pp. 1–20
24. John Lewis Gaddis, *The Long Peace* (Oxford: Oxford University Press, 1987)
25. Susan Strange, *The Retreat of the State: The Diffusion of Power in the World Economy* (Cambridge: Cambridge University Press, 1996); and David C Korten, *When Corporations Rule the World* (Hartford: Kumarian Press and San Francisco: Barrett-Kochler, 1995)
26. Kenichi Ohmae, *The End of the Nation State* (New York: Free Press, 1995)
27. Walter B Wriston, *The Twilight of Sovereignty* (New York: Charles Scribner & Sons, 1992)
28. Nigel Francis, *The New Untouchables: Immigration and the New Worker* (London and New York: IB Tauris & Co., 1995)
29. Arthur Schlesinger, Jr., *The Disuniting of America: Reflections on a Multicultural Society* (New York: WW Norton & Co., 1992)
30. Christopher Mitchell, ed., *Western Hemisphere Immigration and United States Foreign Policy* (Pennsylvania: Pennsylvania State University Press, 1992)
31. John Isbister, *The Immigration Debate: Remaking America* (Kumarian Press, Inc., 1996), pp. 61–91
32. Peter G Peterson, *Gray Dawn: How the Coming Age Wave Will Transform America and the World* (New York: Times Books, 1999)
33. Ransford W Palmer, *Pilgrims From The Sun: West Indian Migration to America* (New York: Twyne Publishers, 1995); and Deborah Waller Meyers, *Migrant Remittances to Latin America: Reviewing the Literature* (Inter-American Dialogue & Tomas Rivera Policy Institute, 1998)
34. Francis M Deng, *Protecting the Disposed: A Challenge for the International Community* (Washington DC: Brookings Institution, 1993)
35. Michael Ignatieff, *The Warrior's Honour: Ethnic War and the Modern Conscience* (New York: Henry Holt and Company, Inc., 1997), pp. 20–21
36. Saskia Sassen, *Losing Control? Sovereignty in an Age of Globalisation* (New York: Columbia University Press, 1996), pp. 59–99
37. Ibid, p. 98
38. There is a debate over whether US hegemony has declined and whether this decline is absolute or relative. See Paul Kennedy, *The Rise and Fall of Great Powers* (New York: Vintage Books, 1987); Henry R Nau, *The Myth of Americas Decline* (Oxford: Oxford University Press, 1990); Joseph S Nye, *Bound to Lead: The Changing Nature of*

American Power (New York: Basic Books, 1990); and Donald W White, *The American Century: The Rise and Decline of the United States as a World Power* (New Haven: Yale University Press, 1996)

39. Lester Thurow, *Head to Head: The Coming Economic Battle Among Japan, Europe and America* (New York: William Morrow Co., 1992), pp. 203–218; Kenichi Ohmae, *Triad Power: The Coming Shape of Global Competition* (New York: Free Press, 1985); and Lester C Thurow, *The Future of Capitalism* (New York: William Morrow and Co., 1996), ch. 7
40. Francis Fukayama, *The End of History and the Last Man* (New York: Free Press, 1992)
41. Robert A Pastor, ed., *A Century's Journey: How the Great Powers Shape the World* (New York: Basic Books, 1999), p. 10
42. Benjamin R Barber, *Jihad vs. McWorld* (New York: Times Books, 1995)
43. Zbignew Brzezinski, *Out of Control: Global Turmoil on the Eve of the Twenty-first Century* (New York: Scribner, 1993); Daniel Patrick Moynihan, *Pandemonium: Ethnicity in International Politics* (Oxford: Oxford University Press, 1993); Robert Kaplan, 'The Coming Anarchy', *Atlantic Monthly*, February, 1994, pp. 44–76; and Robert Harvey, *The Return of the Strong: The Drift to Global Disorder* (London: Macmillan, 1995)
44. Andrew Jackson and Matthew Sanger, eds., *Dismantling Democracy: The Multilateral Agreement on Investment and Its Impact* (Ontario: Canadian Centre for Policy Alternatives and James Lorimer & Co., 1990), pp. 319–337
45. Ankie Hoogvelt, *Globalisation and the Post-colonial World: The New Political Economy of Development* (Baltimore: Johns Hopkins University Press, 1997), p. xiv
46. United Nations Development Program, Human Development Report, 1997 (Oxford University Press, 1997)
47. Human Development Report 1998, (New York: Oxford University Press, for the United Nations Development Program, 1998)
48. Paul Hirst and Grahame Thompson, *Globalisation in Question* (London: Polity Press, 1996), p. 68
49. World Bank, Global Economic Prospects and the Developing Countries (Oxford: Oxford University Press, 1997)
50. United Nations Conference on Trade and Development (UNCTAD), World Investment Report, 1994 (Geneva: UNCTAD, 1994)
51. Op. cit.
52. John Stopford and Susan Strange, op.cit., p. 15
53. William Greider, *One World, Ready or Not: The Manic Logic of Global Capitalism* (New York: Simon and Schuster, 1997), pp. 20–26 and 55–223
54. Paul M Sherer, 'The Lesson From Chrysler, Citicorp and Mobil: No Companies Nowadays Are Too Big to Merge', *The Wall Street Journal*, January 4, 1999
55. 'The Business Week Global 1000: Country by Country', *Business Week*, July 13, 1998, pp. 59–77

56. Frances Williams, 'Mergers may lift foreign direct investment to more than 800 billion', *Financial Times*, September 28, 1999
57. David C Korten, *When Corporations Rule the World* (Hartford: Kumarian Press, Inc. and San Francisco: Berrett-Koehler, 1995), p. 221
58. 'A Survey of Multinationals: Everybody's Favourite Monsters', *The Economist*, March 27, 1993
59. Korten, op.cit.
60. *Entering the Twenty-first Century*, World Development Report (Washington DC: World Bank, 1999), *passim*.
61. Anthony P Maingot, *The United States and the Caribbean* (London: Macmillan Press, 1994), p. 11
62. Richard L Bernal, 'US Foreign Assistance and Sustainable Growth in Jamaica', in Hearings before the House Committee on Appropriations Subcommittee on Foreign Operations, Export Financing and Related Agencies, April 24, 1997 (Washington DC: US Government Printing Office, 1997), pp. 682–693
63. Richard L Bernal and Winsome Leslie, 'Canadian Economic Aid to the CARICOM Countries: An Assessment', in Jerry Haar and Anthony Bryan, eds., *Canadian-Caribbean Relations in Transition: Trade, Sustainable Development and Security* (New York: Macmillan, 1999), pp. 190–209
64. Op.cit.
65. *Assessing Aid: What Works, What Doesn't and Why* (Washington DC: World Bank, 1998), p. 7
66. Richard Bernal and Steve Lamar, 'Caribbean Basin Economic Development and the Section 936 Tax Credit', North-South Agenda Paper, No. 22 (Miami: North-South Center, University of Miami, December 1996)
67. Bill Clinton, 'We must also reach out to the small market economies of the Caribbean Basin to ensure that they too, are part of our efforts to expand trade and prosperity.' Remarks of the President-elect to the Annual Conference on Trade, Investment and Development in the Caribbean Basin, Miami, Florida, December 2, 1992.
68. Robin Wright and Doyle McManus, *Flashpoints: Promise and Peril in a New World* (New York: Alfred A. Knopf, 1991)
69. Jeffrey E Garten, *The Big Ten: The Big Emerging Markets and How They Will Change Our Lives* (New York: Basic Books, 1997)
70. Alan Beattie, 'New forum to supplement G7 work', *The Financial Times*, September 27, 1999
71. Anthony Payne and Paul Sutton, 'The Commonwealth Caribbean in the New World Order: Between Europe and North America?', *Journal of Inter-American Studies and World Affairs*, Vol. 34, No. 4 (1992), pp. 71–72
72. Bertha K Becker and Claudio A. Egler, *Brazil: A New Regional Power in the World Economy* (Cambridge: Cambridge University Press, 1992)
73. Ivelaw Lloyd Griffith, *Drugs and Security in the Caribbean: Under Siege* (Pennsylvania: The Pennsylvania State University, 1997)

74. Michael J Mazarr, *Global Trends 2005: An Owner's Manual for the Next Decade* (New York: St Martin's Press, 1999), pp. 53-55
75. Marten Van Creveld, *The Transformation of War* (New York: Free Press, 1991)
76. John W Sewell and Kevin M Morrison, 'We' ll be 9 Billion Soon, So Start Getting Ready', *International Herald Tribune*, October 30–31, 1999
77. Per Pinstrip-Andersen, Rajul Pandya – Lorch and Mark W Rose-Grant, *World Food Prospects: Critical Issues for the Early Twenty-first Century* (Washington DC: International Food Policy Research Institute, October 1999)
78. Richard L Bernal, 'WTO Banana Case: Friendly Fire Hits Caribbean', *The Journal of Commerce*, April 24, 1997 and 'Banana Trade Vital to Caribbean', *The Journal of Commerce*, February 3, 1999
79. Richard L Bernal, *Strategic Global Repositioning and the Future Economic Development of Jamaica*, North South Agenda Paper No. 18 (Miami: North South Centre, University of Miami, May 1996) *and Strategic Global Repositioning: The Imperative for Change* (University of the West Indies, Mona, Jamaica, forthcoming)
80. Alvin and Heidi Toffler, *Creating a New Civilisation: The Politics of the Third Wave* (Atlanta: Turner Publishing, 1995), p. 47
81. Hilbourne A Watson, ed., *The Caribbean in the Global Political Economy* (Boulder: Lynne Rienner, 1994), pp. 67-90
82. Benjamin Gomes-Casseres, *The Alliance Revolution: The New Shape of Business Rivalry* (Cambridge: Harvard University Press, 1996), pp. 3, and 35–38
83. Empirical studies of the United States show that re-engineering coupled with computerisation have resulted in enormous increases in efficiency, productivity, and returns on investment. See 'The Technology Payoff', *Business Week*, June 14, 1993, pp. 57–68
84. Michael Hammer and James Champy, *Re-engineering the Corporation* (New York: Harper Collins, 1993), p. 32
85. Robert C Feenstra, 'Integration of Trade and Disintegration of Production in the Global Economy', *Journal of Economic Perspectives*, Vol. 12, No. 4 (1998), pp. 31–50; and Paul Krugman, 'Growing World Trade: Causes and Consequences', Brookings Papers on Economic Activity, No. 1 (1995), pp. 327–377
86. Joseph L Badaraco, Jr., *The Knowledge Link: How Firms Compete through Strategic Alliances* (Boston: Harvard Business School Press, 1991); and Martin K Starr, *Global Corporate Alliances and the Competitive Edge* (New York: Quorum Books, 1991)
87. Small firms taking advantage of market niches are discussed by Tamir Agmon and Richard L Drobnick, eds., *Small Firms in Global Competition* (New York: Oxford University Press, 1994)
88. Georges A Fauriol, *Foreign Policy Behaviour of Caribbean States: Guyana, Haiti and Jamaica* (Lanham: University Press of America, 1984)
89. Vaughan A Lewis, ed., *Size Self-Determination and International Relations: The Caribbean* (Jamaica: Institute of Social and Economic Research, 1976), pp. 307–339;

and Anthony Bryan, J Edward Greene and Timothy M Shaw, *Peace, Development and Security in the Caribbean* (London: Macmillan Press, 1990)
90. For a lucid and cogent exposition, see Michael Manley, *Jamaica's Struggle in the Periphery* (London: Third World Media Ltd./Writers and Readers Publishing Cooperative Society, 1982), pp. 59–71
91. 'Small but Perfectly Formed', *The Economist*, January 3, 1998, p. 65
92. Lasing Lamont, *Breakup: The Coming End of Canada and the Stakes for America* (New York: W.W. Norton, 1994)
93. Basil Davidson, *The Black Man's Burden: Africa and the Curse of the Nation State* (New York: Times Books, 1992)
94. Richard Bernal, 'The Integration of Small Economies in the Free Trade Area of the Americas', CSIS, Policy Paper on the Americas, Vol. IX, Study No. 1 (Washington DC: Center for Strategic and International Studies, February 2, 1998)
95. William E Nothdurft, *Going Global: How Europe Helps Small Firms Export* (Washington DC: Brookings Institution, 1992)
96. Richard L Bernal, *The Integration of Small Economies in the Free Trade Area of the Americas*, CSIS Policy Papers on the Americas, February 2, 1998
97. 'T&T, J'ca must go ahead with NAFTA bid – Panday', *The Daily Gleaner*, July 18, 1994
98. Ibid.
99. *Flexible Integration: Towards a More Effective and Democratic Europe* (London: Centre for Economic Policy Research, 1995), pp. 11–14
100. 'CARICOM: Externally Vulnerable Regional Economic Integration' in Roberto Bouzas and Jaime Ros, eds., *Economic Integration in the Western Hemisphere* (Nôtre Dame: University of Notre Dame, 1994), pp. 171–202; David Lewis, 'Caribbean Regional Cooperation and Strategic Alliances' in Winston Dookeran, ed., *Choices and Change: Reflections on the Caribbean* (Washington DC: Inter-American Development Bank, 1996), p. 41–61; and David Lewis, 'Intra-Caribbean Relations: A Review and Projections' in Anthony Bryan, *The Caribbean: New Dynamics in Trade and Political Economy* (Miami: North-South Centre, University of Miami, 1996), pp. 75–108
101. *Time of Action: The Report of the West Indian Commission* (Black Rock, Barbados: West Indian Commission, 1992), pp. 445–46
102. DO Mills and VA Lewis, *Caribbean/Latin American Relations* (Port of Spain: Economic Commission for Latin America, Sub-regional Office for the Caribbean, CEPAL/CARIB 82/16, November 2, 1982), p. 50; and Bernard Vega, *Estudio de las implicasciones de la incorporacion de la Comunidad del Caribe* (Santo Domingo: Fondo para el Anance de las Ciencias Sociales, Editora Taller, 1978)
103. Entering the Twenty-first Century: World Development Report 1999/2000 (Washington DC: World Bank, 1999), pp. 55 and 57
104. Richard Bernal, 'Caribbean States and the FTAA: Adequacy of Preparation, Participation and Negotiating Structures', in Anthony Gonzales, ed., *Small Caribbean States*

and the Challenge of International Trade Negotiations (Port of Spain: Institute of International Relations, University of the West Indies, St Augustine, 1998), pp. 76–103

105. Ravi Kanbur and Todd Sandler with Kevin M Morris, *The Future of Development Assistance: Common Pools and International Public Goods* (Washington, DC: Overseas Development Council, 1999)

106. Denis Benn, 'The Commonwealth Caribbean and the New International Economic Order', in Anthony Payne and Paul Sutton, eds., *Dependency Under Challenge, The Political Economy of the Commonwealth Caribbean* (Manchester: Manchester University Press, 1984), pp. 259–280

107. Anthony T Bryan, 'Diplomacy and Small States in Today's World: A Caribbean Commentary', 12th Lecture, Dr Eric Williams Memorial Lecture Series (Port of Spain: Central Bank of Trinidad and Tobago, May, 1998)

108. Dennis Pantin, *The Economics of Sustainable Development in Small Caribbean Islands* (University of the West Indies Centre for Environment and Development, 1994)

109. Daniel Sitarz, ed., *Agenda 21: The Earth Summit Strategy To Save Our Planet* (Boulder: Earthpress, 1994)

110. Shridath Ramphal, *Our Country, The Planet: Forging a Partnership for Survival* (London: Lime Tree, 1992)

111. Basil A Ince, 'The Administration of Foreign Affairs in a Very Small Developing Country: The Case of Trinidad' in Vaughan A Lewis, ed., *Size, Self-Determination and International Relations: The Caribbean* (Jamaica: Institute of Social and Economic Research, 1976), pp. 307-339

112. Patrick H. Rousseau, *Negotiating Change: Pat Rosseau and the Bauxite Negotiations, 1974-7* (Kingston: Heinemann, 1987)

113. Carlton Davis, 'Jamaica in the World Aluminium Industry', Vol. II, 1974-1988, Bauxite Levy Negotiations (Kingston: Jamaica Bauxite Institute, 1995)

114. Richard L Bernal, 'The Compatibility of Caribbean Membership in Lomé, NAFTA and GATT', *Social and Economic Studies*, Vol. 43, No. 2 (June 1994), pp. 139–147

27 | VAUGHAN A LEWIS

Looking from the Inside Outwards:
The Caribbean in the International System after 2000

This paper, pointing as is does to the next millennium, is, in part, necessarily speculative. It attempts to look at the present position of the Caribbean states in the global system and its subsystems, to examine how they have sought to deal with some of the challenges being posed to them from trends emanating from the global system, to speculate on some of the challenges that are likely to arise in the first years of the new millennium, to look at the capacity of the Caribbean states for adequate response, and finally to see how the combination of challenge and response will position the Caribbean states as the millennium proceeds.

Characteristics of Current Caribbean States' Orientations

We start with the present position of the Caribbean states, since the future will in part be conditioned by past and current domestic responses to international system change. The Caribbean to which we refer will include the member states of the Caribbean Community and the remaining countries of the Greater Antilles. We recognise the countries of Central America as falling, in certain definitions and contexts, within what is called the Caribbean Basin, but do not take them as the direct subject of our analysis, though as we proceed, certain interconnections will be discussed.

When (commencing in 1962) the so-called Commonwealth Caribbean states came to sovereign independence, it seems a general assumption was that the international framework of their existence would remain more or less as it was, with the USA gradually assuming a greater influence in their transactions than before. A further assumption was one of continuing empathy from the major poles of the western international arena (particularly the US and the UK). The Cuban challenge to hemispheric norms about necessary alliances and modes of economic development was recognised, but not generally accepted by governments as applicable to their circumstances.

The shock emanating from the political and economic pole closest to these states, the UK, when it announced its desire to join the European Community in 1963, with its implications for the protectionist arrangements from the country's major agricultural commodities, registered momentarily. But circumstances, including a general British acceptance that the Caribbean states could obtain 'bankable assurances'(the phrase of the then Jamaican minister of trade) for continuing protection, and then the French rejection of the British application, permitted a return more or less to business as usual. Little by way of deliberate analysis of the change implications of a wrenching of the states as economic entities from their British moorings was subsequently undertaken.

At the onset of independence, certain of the states had recognised that domestic relationships and geopolitical location implied the development of new international relationships. Trinidad and Tobago and Guyana, with their ethnic mixes of relatively equal proportions, quickly saw the necessity for establishing close diplomatic relations with India and the large African countries. But this could be seen as largely cosmetic (though admittedly cosmetics do have a purpose) in the sense that the relationships were intended to give a degree of 'social comfort' to the extant ethnic groupings. For coupled with the new emphasis on recognition and exploitation of the ethnic heritage of the populations went an insistence by the ruling regimes that their new national independence (and therefore national identity) had to be autochthonous – deriving its inspiration from domestic history – and that loyalties could not, as it were, be bifurcated between the national state and the countries of ethnic origin.

Dr Eric Williams' famous phrase, 'No Mother India, no Mother Africa', can be taken as representative of the general sentiment of the ruling regimes with mixed populations. In Jamaica, with its largely African population, stronger sentimental allegiances to the African continent could be shown, and the resonance of the visit of Haile Selassie to the country gave an early indication of what might be called the 'reserves of Africanist and black racial sentiment' in a country with strong minority influences on its socioeconomic make-up and its political orientation. Barbados, with its peculiar racial inheritance, sought to minimise such aspects in the conduct of its political relationships, but as more recent circumstances have indicated, genuflections have had to be made in their direction.

The particular geopolitical location of Guyana, and later of an independent Belize, indicated also the necessity for states like these to take particular cognisance of the orientations of their neighbours, and to undertake pre-emptive diplomatic alliances of both a bilateral and multilateral nature to secure themselves against temptations to predatory activities.

Even Trinidad was haunted by the unsettled nature of its maritime boundaries with the much larger Venezuela – in 1962 a state only recently experiencing a renewed regime of democratic rule. Dr Eric Williams' on-again-off-again conduct of relations with Venezuela, and his popularisation of alleged Venezuelan inclinations to domination, are evidence of the unstable character of a relationship which, as we have written elsewhere, had been veiled by British diplomatic protection.

The temporary post-independence phase of apparent stability has, of course been rudely interrupted by a series of shocks that have continued to affect Caribbean international economic relations. The progressive evolution of the European Union from acceptance of Britain, through the single market, the Maastricht accords and the Amsterdam Treaty, have found the Caribbean states unprepared for adaptation to new circumstances.

Ad hoc arrangements, as instanced in the regional negotiating team assembled for the 1975 Lomé Agreement and the Regional Negotiating Machinery of the present time, have indicated that the Caribbean states had sought to make no provision for a viable permanent structure for ensuring external adaptation. And this is no more evident than in the fact that in the present circumstances the basic institutional structure is supported in large measure by resources from outside the region – even from countries with whom the Caribbean is negotiating and with whom they may have differences of perspective on the desired outcomes of the negotiations.

This matter of dependence on external resources for the provision of the basic institutional structure for collective negotiation is in some degree a reflection of the difficulties which Caribbean states have had, and apparently continue to have, in extracting resources from their national economic systems on a continuing and predictable basis for the external requirements of the region. The early decision of, for example, the European Community states, to ensure this aspect as a means of underpinning the bureaucratic structure of the EU, has not been followed by the Caribbean states, as they continue to treat collective external obligations as separate from domestic obligations.

This casts extreme doubt on the committment of the Caribbean Community, for example, to effectively pursue its international relations, and can lead to a diplomatic openness which must surely be undesirable. It is instructive that the first initiatives in forging closer institutional relationships between the Caribbean Community and the Greater Antilles states of the Dominican Republic and Haiti – the evolution from CARICOM to CARIFORUM – were underpinned largely by the European Union with whom we are now in difficult and complex negotiations indicating differing perspectives on possible outcomes.

The thirty-seventh year since the independence of the first of the CARICOM states also finds little evolution in relationships of cohesiveness, certainly since the transition from CARIFTA to CARICOM. No state has evolved in strength on a sufficiently consistent basis to be able to have acted as a 'pivotal state' in the construction and sustenance of the regional integration system, or as a pole either on a cooperative or competitive basis for giving impulses to cooperation. On the other hand the shocks administered to the national economic systems, and consequently to the regional economic system by periodic recessions (externally and domestically inspired) particularly in the late 1970s and 1980s, have made difficult, and even reversed tendencies towards cooperation based on reciprocal arrangements assuming equality of competences and capabilities among the states.

This has led, in effect, to unilateralist orientations in attempts at reactions and adaptations to changes in the states' relevant international environments. Most notable in this regard was what appeared to many states to be the sudden decisions of both Trinidad and Jamaica in the mid-1990s to seek individual accession to NAFTA in the wake of Mexico's adherence to that system, and indications from the United States that she was willing to entertain applications for membership from other states in the hemisphere.

That the United States proved unable to sustain this offer allowed the developing anomie among other CARICOM states to be minimised. But the unilateralist orientation in the face of rapidly changing international trade and production trends, though now somewhat muted by, again, changes in external circumstances (including the swift American switch from NAFTA to a collectivist FTAA approach), can still be said to constitute a significant characteristic of state behaviour at the present time. And it raises the question of the real extent of regional cohesion regarding the external environment, in spite of the forced necessity at the present time to arrange diplomatic coherence for current negotiations.

Two other characteristics of current Caribbean state and regional relations are worth noting. First is the difficulty which some of the leading states have had for over twenty years or so now, in evolving coherent domestic policies in response to the shocks induced by the commodities crises of the 1970s and 1980s with their consequent recessions and debt crises. These difficulties have been accompanied by increasing social disequilibrium in some states, creating in turn instability in the policy responses of the political regimes.

In these domestic environments, governments would appear to have either resorted to extreme populist measures in an effort to exert control and induce stability; or they have succumbed to subordination to particular socioeconomic interest groups within the states which desire particular economic policy orientations. The result has been an apparent loss of autonomy by governments as steering institutions, and their inability to ensure sufficient medium-term stability of the countries' social systems as a whole, as a basis for providing predictability to their decision-making, either domestic or external. In that respect, such governments have come to be viewed by relevant leading states in the external environment and by relevant international institutions, as not dependable.

The second characteristic relates to a trend towards unbalanced growth as countries have lurched from one policy orientation to another, or as recessions have forced reduced domestic production, consequent reduced domestic demand, unemployment and social alienation. This has been reinforced in some countries by demographic disequilibrium, a longer term trend. Patricia Anderson has discussed this latter phenomenon in the CARICOM area drawing attention to the implications for, among others, a country like Jamaica. And Preeg has discussed perhaps the most serious case, that of Haiti.[1]

Both of these strengthen trends favouring governmental options towards populist policies or towards policies deliberately biased towards one social grouping over others, in governments' efforts to maintain political domination.

Characteristics of the Present/Emerging International System

The most discussed current characteristic of the present and emerging international system, particularly in its economic aspects but with derivative implications for other spheres, is obviously that of globalisation. A particular effect of this phenomenon is said to be the speed with which countries are integrated into sets of transactions affected by particular dynamic processes, such that the effects on their behaviour or evolution can be said to be systemic in nature. The phenomenon is said in particular to reduce the traditionally isolating effects of time and space – negating the significance of distance for the functioning of economic processes and for economic decision-making.

Some analysts have pointed out that many countries, in terms of the participation of their populations, cannot be said to be substantially a part of the globalisation process. But this can hardly be argued of the Caribbean area, being in its origins as a production and trading location a creation of a particular international economic system - that of mercantilism. In this regard the Caribbean countries have always tended to be subordinated to, and feel the effects of, the economic shocks emanating from their particular metropole-dominated economic systems; and policy-makers have come to appreciate the extent to which the parameters of their decision-making have been dependent on the dynamism/stagnation of their international environment.

Policy-makers have also appreciated the extent to which their economies, as both small and extremely open sub-systems, have lacked 'internal depth' which, when combined with the minimal and weak nature of the instruments available to them for adaptation, allow little leeway for rapid adaptation. Such internal depth would normally display itself in a reasonably large or diversified economic space and/or in a degree of policy control of certain key domestic variables which could allow them to influence the timing of implementation of adaptive decisions.[2]

It is in this regard that Caribbean policy makers have tended to depend on the empathy of 'external others' for supporting the means of riding out structural economic shocks, seeking to an extraordinary extent goodwill or 'bankable assurances' from these others. This largely remains the situation today.

Threats from the International System

First is the foreboding loss of the preferential system leading to the diminishing relevance for national income of the traditional economic staples. It should be noted too that even some of the newer staples have become of diminishing relevance, either because of competition from other sources or of technological changes in the particular industries. Economic analysts from a country like Taiwan have demonstrated how, as openings for agricultural commodity exports to the United States closed or diminished due to competition or deliberate American protectionism, they were forced to introduce and export new types of such commodities. They have shown that this is a continuous process, requiring the technical capability and structures for innovation.

In large measure, the Caribbean countries have not attempted to deal with the diminished relevance of their staples, this leading to periodic crises, the latest of which is the threat from the new European arrangements and the WTO system to the staples like bananas, and agro-industrial activities like rum.

The region is therefore in another phase of seeking empathy and goodwill for stays of execution so to speak, while the diplomatic initiatives prompted by this search are not publicly complemented by indications of active attempts at innovation. To foreigners, this must seem like yet another rearguard action characteristic of similar attempts over the last few hundred years. But as even major countries now seek new economic directions and struggle with the creation of new institutional forms for ensuring appropriate domestic policies and external arrangements, the traditional goodwill on which the Caribbean has depended is likely to become itself a diminishing asset.

The harsh attitude of the US government, its Congress and its political parties on the banana issue is instructive. And the British government is unlikely to continue to mortgage its diplomatic assets for long, particularly in the US, on the altar of Caribbean traditional staples, particularly in the present and coming struggles for economic markets over which the new 'legal litigation', rather than 'democracy-based', WTO regime is the adjudicator. Secondly, with the demise of the cold war, its disappearance having, as is now often remarked, removed the American perception of a security threat in the Caribbean Basin, Caribbean states are the objects of a certain loss of 'security protection' which had absolved many of them from substantially meeting the admittedly heavy costs of appropriate structures for this.

One result of this cold war demise aspect is that, although the United States has sought to initiate new proposals for developing a coherent Caribbean Basin economic system (as part of its proposed hemispheric arrangements), a complementary holistic security system, to meet new challenges designed from the point of view of mutual interest and reciprocal obligations, particularly those of narcotics movement has not been suggested, either by the United States or by Caribbean policy-makers. Instead, ad hoc American gifts to Caribbean regimes continue to be largely the pattern of what is called 'security assistance'.

Now some may well dispute the need for any such holistic security system, given the excessive weight of the United States and its inclination to take a 'command approach' to such issues, which the Caribbean countries are too small and weak to influence. Others may argue that such initiatives should take place within the ambit of a more balanced OAS set of arrangements, or as a strictly indigenous Caribbean venture on the basis of which multilateral assistance might be sought.

The stark reality, however, is that over the last two decades, as Caribbean states have perceived new emerging security threats to the region as a collectivity, a degree of lethargy in policy-making in this sphere too, has been apparent to observers. The anxiety induced by the attempted coup in Trinidad and Tobago in 1990 led to a CARICOM heads of government decision that a conclusion should be quickly reached that would extend or reformulate the existing OECS/Barbados Regional Security System to cover the region as a whole. Little has transpired since, as the claims of sovereignty have taken precedence, or it is argued, the region is to multifaceted to be subordinated to such a regime.

But the threat to national, and therefore collective, security that has emerged in the 1990s in which an increasing external injection of pollutants has been apparent, gives cause for concern into the new millenium. First, the Caribbean land and sea space is increasingly ravaged by the narcotics pollutant as the cycles of control and expansion occur in the neighbouring South American states. This in turn has led to an American definition of a new security threat in the emergence of money laundering in the region of funds acquired from the trade, and now from funds emanating from the former Soviet geographic space.

In addition, the United States has itself created a new a new national security threat for many of the Caribbean states, by its wanton expulsion of criminal elements long removed from the places of their birth and, as has been said, well-trained in the modern American technologies of crime, back to their native Caribbean lands; this being done with minimal consultation until the onset of vociferous protests from Caribbean states. This phenomenon is likely to continue, leading, paradoxically, to a new dependence on the United States for the wherewithal with which Caribbean states can control the new bandits on their home ground.

Taking a wider international perspective on the fate of small countries like those of the Caribbean, we might note that in spite of the well-known vulnerability of such entities, there are points of view that suggest that in spite of the negative effects of the dynamism of the globalisation process, and the unipolar character of the contemporary (and for the foreseeable future) global system, the possibilities for viable activities by small states may not be as limited as the analysis of threats indicates. One such analyst, a Singaporean diplomatic practitioner, has suggested that, 'The space for political and economic action on the part of small states was limited during the cold war, but with its end small states now have greater flexibility in pursuing their interests.' From his perspective, 'Times of great change offer small states the greatest flexibility in formulating their own foreign policies as well as the greatest opportunity in helping shape the international order'.[3]

The source of the analysis tempers our inclination to assess it as over-optimistic, since as has been said of Singapore, it too has been 'an international creation for the purposes of trade...' though concomitant with this it has been noted that 'Singapore's development relied on a combination of external free trade and strong internal economic control,' and that:

The Singapore model carries the lesson – perhaps in its most emphatic form – that an extensive role for the government can be combined with free trade, and that *laissez-faire* (absence of government intervention) and laissez-passer (free trade) are distinct concepts . . . *Interventionism in Singapore aimed to adapt the domestic economy to the international requirements of the international economy*'[4] (my emphasis)

The interconnections between domestic arrangements and the possibilities for successful intervention in the international environment is what is worthy of note here. Along with the reminder that vulnerability is a continuing aspect of small state existence to be taken as a given of both analysis and policy, the lesson for the Caribbean is that circumstances will favour those countries demonstrating a commitment to continual policy adaptation and to structures (national and collective) which are sufficiently sustained, over time, to allow such adaptation to be systematically implemented.

The International System and Possible Configurations of the Caribbean

Certain analysts, including those of the so-called Plantation Economy School in the Caribbean (basing themselves substantially on the work of Wagley), have long brought to our attention a Plantation America definition of Caribbean economy[5] that reminds us of the dynamism of the mercantilist system and the rising and falling poles of economic strength in the region which it induced.

It therefore should be no surprise that, depending on the relative strengths of countries within and outside the area, definitions and political configurations of the region should be proposed, or should be sought to be imposed, by the dominant or pivotal states of the time; and that the weaker elements largely subscribe to such configurations. We discuss some of these configurations below:

1. The likely passing of the era of preferentialism in the course of the earlier part of the new millennium, along with the global struggle for economic rearrangement of the world in accordance with globalisation and liberalisation trends, is known to have already led to geopolitical designs implying a repositioning of the Caribbean in its immediate environment.

In recent times, the Mexican adherence to NAFTA has given force to those who have taken the view that a *'Hemispherisation' of the New World area*, based on economic arrangements, is necessary for the continued sustenance of the area as a whole and of its leading poles. Hence the development of initiatives like the Enterprise of the Americas of the Bush administration and the FTAA of the Clinton administration.

Protagonists of this view in the United States are well aware that countries like Brazil and Argentina have substantial trade with the countries of the European Union, but also assert that the dynamism of the American economy and now of NAFTA will draw them into more closely integrated relationships. Their view is given strength by the turn, following Mexico, of a country like

Argentina from a tradition of isolationism and muted antagonism to the United States, towards closer economic and diplomatic (alliance) relationships, to the extent that a president of Peronist origins should propose the 'dollarisation' of the Argentinian monetary system.

They have noted too, the pretensions of a country like Brazil to seek to arrange more balanced relationships between the major South American countries, Europe and the United States; but the partial countervailing of such sentiments by the increasing influence of US economic policy-makers, and that of the international financial institutions, in the resolution of the difficult and sudden financial crisis that befell Brazil in the wake of the Asian and Russian crises.[6]

It is fair to say that while certain Caribbean states (Jamaica and Trinidad and Tobago) seemed to wish to take the initiative and position themselves for entry into NAFTA, seeing this as a logical move following the anticipated effects of NAFTA on the Caribbean Basin Initiative, and the failure of American administrations to fast-track CBI-NAFTA parity legislation, those Caribbean states must have perceived the implications of their adherence to NAFTA for the viability of the Caribbean Community and Common Market. And we should note in this connection the assertions of Brewster,[7] made partly in response to the recommendations of the West Indian Commission Report, that the economic integration/development provisions of the Treaty of Chaguaramas were now a dead letter in the light of new developments in the trade and production relationships of the international economy.

Finally, states like Trinidad and Tobago, desiring to ensure predictable access for their industrial exports to the North American market after its initial failures of the 1970s/80s, exports which in effect compete with Mexican natural-gas based exports; or like Jamaica which wished to secure the gains for its low-cost labour exports which it had developed in the early phase of the CBI, would favour an economic reconfiguration of the economic arrangements of the Caribbean Common Market which facilitated NAFTA entry. The succession of NAFTA by the FTAA will hardly have dimmed these perspectives, and we can expect the reactive diplomacy in which the Caribbean is now engaged in relation to the FTAA to eventually reflect this orientation into the new millennium.

The inclination of Caribbean states towards some arrangement of 'hemispherisation', essentially unilaterally introduced by the United States (acting as the pivotal state), is in one sense enhanced by a factor of demography – the extensive migration of Caribbean people, including medium- and highly-skilled ones, to the North American continent – continuing a tradition of the early twentieth century, but this time involving an upgraded human skill content largely provided from the financial resources of the Caribbean countries themselves.

In this respect, what may appear as somewhat cynical characterisations of the 'Floridisation of the Caribbean' reflect a certain reality, in which middle and professional class Caribbean persons in North America are likely to influence Caribbean policy-making towards integration with the continent – a welding of Middle and North America so to speak, so that movement and income generation can be derived from one single, large economic space.

2. A question arising for the future is how the Caribbean Community's *traditional relations with Europe*, having been pushed in new directions by the European Union, will evolve, and whether they can have a continuing content from which the Caribbean can benefit, permitting the much desired geographical diversification.

The present European inclination would appear to suggest a relationship with an almost Caribbean Basin-wide configuration (involving Central American states), in consonance with Europe's desire to strengthen economic relations with the larger states of the South America. This would surely be the implication of the REPA proposals, either as immediate (post 2005) or medium term solutions to their relationships with the Caribbean. (REPA also suggests a regionalisation of the 'large' continent of Africa.)

Such a strategy would recognise the Caribbean as an integral part of the hemisphere, not of the ACP arrangement and relationships, and has been recently given academic voice in the suggestion for a characterisation of the area as 'Caribbean America'.[8] And it is not negated by the fact that certain European countries wish for an indefinite period to retain 'sovereign footholds' in the region, through the dependencies which now come under their jurisdiction – for material, diplomatic or psychological reasons.

It should also be said that the failure of the CARICOM region to consolidate itself as a homogenous diplomatic arena and single economic space during the 1980s and 1990s, while the Europeans were struggling with a similar concern, has not enhanced the CARICOM cry for an identifiable role as an element of a post-2005 ACP diplomatic-economic configuration. For the Europeans would most likely have surmised that a CARICOM consolidation could have led to a consolidated system involving all the Greater Antilles (following on the European CARIFORUM initiative), with European support, and with connections to the Central American states.

Caribbean diplomacy, from its still weak collective orientation however, is probably incapable of calling back what might now be called 'this yesterday's possible configuration' and taking it into the new millennium.

3. We have made reference, in discussing the present state of the Caribbean's location in international relations, to early post-independence awareness of the significance of ethnic heritage and its relationship to nation-building – *the relationship between geography and ethnicity*. In recent years this is an issue that has tended to reinvigorate itself as, in states like Trinidad and Tobago and Guyana, demographic growth has given an increasing sharpness to electoral competition among the main ethnic groupings; and emphasis is placed on the potency of ethnic heritage as a motivator of mobility and of reaffirmation of what might be called 'original identity'. This has been reinforced by the technological trends influencing communications processes and the transmission of real and immediate, rather than second-hand and dated, images of events and belief systems from the countries of ethnic origin.

What this would appear to be doing is to give rise to processes of legitimising the existence of multiple identities within the single state, these functioning in some degree as countervailing forces to the notion of nationality deriving firstly from the specific geographic location of the Caribbean states great distances away from the 'ethnic metropoles' of their inhabitants; secondly, from the social matrix created by the necessary coexistence of ethnic groupings involved in meeting the demands of metropolitan economic activity; and thirdly, from a 'culture' deriving from their social interaction in the specific Caribbean geographic space.

While some of these attempts at legitimising multiple identities can be exaggerated by people's artifices, groupings or institutions seeking political dominion by the manipulation of any symbols at their disposal, it would seem useful to consider this competitive relationship between geopolitical location and geo-economics on the one hand, and attraction of social groups to the identity symbols of ethnic metropoles, as having a bearing on the configuration of what is currently called the Caribbean Community. There could well be, in time, the development of a counter view that the historical definition of the Caribbean giving rise to that version of 'community' can be contested as not reflecting new ethnic identity realities.

4. This leads us into another possible impulse towards changing configurations – one deriving from what might be called *the influence of regional geopolitics*. It is obvious today that this is beginning to have some significance in the configuration of international relations of, for example, the African continent.

In respect of the Caribbean, we alluded earlier to the anxieties raised in Guyana and Belize and in some measure in Trinidad and Tobago in their immediate post-independence years, by what were believed to be predatory interests in areas allocated to them via the colonial inheritance. The same phenomenon characterised the independence of Suriname, though to a lesser extent.

Arrangements of a temporary but renewable character, some arrived at autochthonously, some arrived at through diplomatic and/or material assistance from regional neighbours or major powers, have resulted in a muting of the claims originally made. But we do need to note that persistent domestic instability in any of these Caribbean states will be liable to reinvigorate the concerns of their larger neighbours who assert the existence of stable systems contiguous to their borders as a condition of their own national security, and for the non-occurrence of opportunities for intervention by other countries or forces there.

The limited populations of countries like Guyana, Belize and Suriname combined with restricted capabilities for quick and effective intervention in distant regions, puts them at a disadvantage in responding to contests of perception about the salience of local instability as a threat to security, between themselves and their larger neighbours. In some degree, while undertaking continuing diplomatic initiatives as, for example, in the case of Trinidad and Tobago's maritime delimitation difficulties with Venezuela, Caribbean countries will depend partly on their neighbours' observance of norms of non-intervention in the hemisphere in respect of boundary disputes, and partly on the maintenance of domestic coherence.

The problem, as a longer term one, might from a Caribbean perspective be posed as ensuring the taking of measures to inhibit the occurrence of what might be called the limiting case: contiguous large state intervention and dominion or condominium over contested areas of a CARICOM state which would change the character of the state system in the Caribbean Basin, or more properly put, the Association of Caribbean States (ACS) area. The extent to which therefore the ACS can develop as a diplomatic umbrella with accepted norms of behaviour in the early years of the new millenium is a critical question. But posing the question in this way also takes us back to our earlier allusion to the future salience/relevance for Caribbean geopolitics of the OAS system, with the predominant power as one of its members.

Trends into the Future

Faced with a possible loss of markets for traditional commodities, a delay on the part of the United States in providing NAFTA-parity that would allow them to hold their own in producing some non-traditional products, and a certain loss of interest on the part of the United States in support for infrastructural development, Caribbean states might well be said to face an era of isolation and benign neglect in the immediate future – apparently having no substantial assets to take to the new emerging bargaining tables of international production and trade or of security organisation.

Secondly, as the new millenium approaches, Caribbean states find themselves challenged by processes that stand to dissolve the traditional and defining regional boundaries that they have partly inherited and partly constructed for themselves. These boundaries have been essentially based on cultural homogeneity criteria, but external definitions of economic relationships have also been critical. Hence the original phrase used to define the area in the post-independence era: the Commonwealth Caribbean. What is being challenged by both economic and political forces is an assumption of unique relationships that might have allowed the member states of the area to arrange and achieve recognition for their own diplomatic-economic zone (community) and, therefore, a geopolitical identity.

It is in recognition of the need to achieve this, in conjunction with growing awareness of a changing external environment rapidly challenging any reality of unique defining relationships, that has led the Caribbean Community to seek to redefine boundaries by creating a broader geoeconomic space for future action. Hence the establishment of an Association of Caribbean States – a mechanism for finding within the immediate geographical environment assets or attributes that might enhance their bargaining power and their collective international identity. Prior to this of course, as we have previously observed, the states felt constrained to include Haiti and the Dominican Republic within a wider institutional space – the CARIFORUM – in order to ensure that such leverage or bargaining capacity that they possessed in relation to the European Union was not lost.

That the ground was shifting under this conception even while the ACS was being formalised has, we can be certain, not been lost on Caribbean policy-makers. Though both Venezuela and Colombia for example, have been inclined to devise new free trade arrangements with the Caribbean Community, the attraction to them, even as members of the Andean Pact, of developments in the MERCOSUR region would seem to provide a competing set of negotiating priorities. And on the other hand the preoccupation of Mexico with formalising its NAFTA arrangements seems to give this a clear priority over its membership of the ACS.

Further, the challenge posed by the proposal for an FTAA is essentially a challenge based on a presumption that subregional groupings need, even if they continue to exist, to harmonise their arrangements in such a way that the wider hemispheric system takes precedence over their particular arrangements. One question that arises from these considerations for the Caribbean as it seeks to organise an ACS, is whether a sufficient number of incentives for cooperation would exist within this defined area (when compared with other possibilities) to allow the development of a meaningful space, or whether this stratagem has been in effect superseded by subsequent developments.

In examining this issue further we might look at the comparative activities of the countries of Central America which, attempting to avoid the marginalisation implicit in the hemispheric developments, have sought to treat Mexico as a regional pivotal state, and negotiate with that country a kind of second-order access to the NAFTA privileges through a number of free trade agreements. These agreements would, however, seem to be undertaken largely on a bilateral basis, even though there are efforts in train to reinvigorate the Central American integration system.

The Caribbean/CARIFORUM area does not possess any such pivotal state, though it could be thought that Canada's membership of the Commonwealth, and more particularly of the CARIBCAN arrangement, and her membership of NAFTA, might suggest an avenue for achieving a similar objective. This might seem farfetched. But the issue is posed in this way to dramatise the notion that on the brink of the millenium, the Caribbean states face a situation of being 'small states alone' with no firm alliances that might point a way towards meaningful arrangements or enhancing their small size (their reduced systemic size as the preferential system, in particular, dissolves and the multinational corporation systems into which they were integrated change and become, from their perspective, more fragile). It is for this reason that a strong temptation might develop, on the part of one or other regional state, as time goes on, to 'break ranks' from any notion of a regional or community system, in the search for future economic growth. Unilateral attachments and connections might then become the norm. In this scenario, the notion of a Caribbean identity within the Americas would practically cease to exist. There might exist a 'Caribbean America', but not a 'Caribbean Community in the Americas'.

This pessimistic scenario faces us in part because, one might hypothesise, the Caribbean region has, in attempting over the years to devise 'community', failed to approach the development of any system of regional governance – the development of a regime composed of a set of norms, rules and regulations that give predictability to decision-making. This is of course, one of the hallmarks of the European Union. And even the NAFTA arrangement has provisions for precise responses to breaches of norms and rules, and the participant members have recognised that non-economic aspects of the relationship (for example, migration and narcotics movements) have a bearing on the strictly economic process and therefore need to be subordinated to regulatory regimes. (In addition an emerging structure of parliamentary accountability is beginning to give the system its required legitimacy.) This notion of governance has tended to be resisted in the Caribbean region, as a result of strongly held notions of sovereignty over difference spheres of government, even as in many of the larger states of the region it is difficult, after the ravages of recession, to identify meaningful areas of autonomy in decision-making.

With the establishment of systems of governance come also systems of accountability, the basis for 'community' gaining 'legitimacy'. This is, for example, evident in the emerging structure of parliamentary accountability in the EU system. But this too has been absent from the Caribbean system; though it must be recognised that the current attempt at integration of diverse political cultures into the system (Haiti, Dominican Republic, subsequently Cuba), makes the establishment of institutions of accountability and consultation even more necessary. The failure of the Association of Caribbean Parliamentarians to evolve, even while Caribbean states have subscribed to joint arrangements of this kind within the ACP-EU framework, is illustrative of the problem. And it has given the EU the opportunity to assert the necessity for this as a bargaining weapon in the current Lomé negotiations.

It is the intention of the Caribbean political directorate that some notion of Caribbean community should continue to exist, then a priority for elaboration as the new millenium approaches is the form of regime governance that might be developed. Further, the notion of regional governance would seem to have a longer term application to wider geographical spaces in which the Caribbean might be involved. As we have observed elsewhere, the nature of the Caribbean Sea as a gateway both northwards and southwards, implies for its preservation(conservation) a regime of governance that extends beyond the Caribbean member-states, since it requires the competences of neighbouring states and the major metropoles with jurisdiction in the area.

It is imperative that Caribbean member-states themselves begin (as they appear to be starting to do within the ACS framework) to development an appropriate regime that can draw the support of other relevant states. Secondly, the major migrations from the Caribbean to the North America during the last twenty years ago, are spawning networks of relationships between the two areas. The most disadvantageous has been the expulsion of criminals back to the region, which has taken place unilaterally, and without any effective regime in place for the preservation of the security of the receiving countries. Migration is treated as a set of unilateral activities, rather than as a system of relationships and structures for achieving mobility. But the movement of people and their assets across the two regions (as against the movement of criminals) will have an increasingly positive economic significance as time goes on, and it is important that an acceptable regime be developed to monitor and regulate the networks that evolve.

Conclusion

In the years following their independence the small states of the Caribbean inherited the language and practice of the metropole from which they were spawned, these emphasising notions of the need to demonstrate sovereignty in political and economic affairs. This led them, as indeed it did the UK in its relations with an integrating continent, to adopt an extremely cautious approach to regional integration, emphasising continually that the main instruments of policy should only be cautiously merged or harmonised with partner states. This was no more evident than in areas, for example, like monetary policy, free movement of capital and labour, and in the area of regional security.

The harsh years of recession have demonstrated that many of the policy tools thought useful for independent action were less than productive. But the slow pace of movement towards a Caribbean single economic space suggests that there is still reluctance to adopt alternative approaches to the use of, in particular, economic instruments. The traditions of the metropolitan 'closed system' approach to development die hard.

As these countries enter the new millenium, it will be important for them to shed such traditions and adopt, as a philosophical posture, an 'open systems' approach to development: a recognition that as subsystems of a larger system, the policy instruments apparently available to the closed system model are not useful to them. They will have to adopt the approach that adaptation to the larger systems in which they exist is a continuing necessity; that the creation of larger economic spaces, uninhibited by legislative impediments deriving from the traditional sovereignty model, will be a characteristic of emerging economic organisation; and that if they are unable to harmonise policy approaches with neighbours in their smaller subsystems, pivotal states or larger systems in their wider environment will submerge their pretended autonomy in the interests of environmental efficiency – whether in the fields of production and trade, monetary policy or security stability.

The small states of the Caribbean will have to assess the question of whether, such has been the slow pace of the stratagems of regional integration that they have pursued, new forces and trends in the international environment have made, or are rapidly making them, irrelevant. At the same time, they will have to consider how their Caribbean social identity is to be preserved – the Caribbean as a cosmopolitan node in the Americas, utilising for development the connections that derive from the ethnic heritage of its peoples, and the supposed advantages of its proximity to the economic moving force of the globe – in the face of new forces of economic development which either tend to absorb or to marginalise.

In other words, is there going to be in the emerging years of the new millennium, even as we seek to adapt to the wider economic and technological forces of our systemic environment, opportunity for organising a mode and institutions of governance and legitimacy that provide for the maintenance of an identifiable collective social identity in the archipelago of Middle America? This is the substantial question for the year 2000.

By way of some minimal recommendations as we move towards consideration of such questions, this paper would propose the following:

1. A change of philosophy or attitude – a rejection of retained metropolitan mental constructs pertaining to the uses of sovereignty and, in consequence, a continual consideration of the question of cession of elements of state sovereignty in favour of a new regime (or new regimes) of regional governance appropriate to the present and the demands of the future, such cession to be done on a purely pragmatic basis.

2. Working towards the establishment of an appropriate regional regime of governance that will also form the basis for Caribbean states collectively engaging on an identifiable and legitimate basis with wider relevant systems in our international environment. Specifically this would imply (in particular as far as the legitimacy aspect is concerned) the reinvigoration and reformulation of the Association of Caribbean Community Parliamentarians (ACCP), as a basis for accountability to, and legitimacy for, decision-making of regional import or character. The ACCP should have incorporated into it a system of congressional-type committees involving the participation not simply of parliamentarians, but expert witnesses and non-governmental and interest groups of the societies. This should match a similar arrangement reorganising the select committees of the House of Representatives (Assembly) at the national level. The present regional arrangements do not have sufficient public legitimacy to permit them to proceed further. Additionally, the regime of regional governance should involve the networking of the functions of the Caribbean Community Secretariat and the Regional Negotiating Machinery.

3. The establishment of a country (governmental) division of labour in respect of the regional relations with significant Third countries and institutions – to be based on states having significant ethnic, geopolitcal and economic interests with the particular countries or institutions, and the appropriate

capabilities. For the smaller states of the region in particular, with limited capabilities for external representation, this would be an essential element of their diplomacy.

4. The reestablishment of arrangements for policy studies with a regional focus at the University of the West Indies and the University of Guyana in this era of increasing nationalisation of the structures of the university system in the region – paradoxically at a time when the interests of the member countries are becoming increasing internationalised.

Notes

1. See Patricia Anderson, 'The Demographic Basis of Social Instability in the Caribbean of the Eighties', in JE Greene, A. Bryan and TM Shaw, eds., *Peace, Development and Security in the Caribbean: Perspectives to the Year 2000* (New York: St Martin's Press, 1990); and Ernest Preeg, *The Haitian Dilemma: A Case Study in Demographics, Development and US Foreign Policy* (CSIS, Washnigton DC, 1996)
2. Note, for example, the policy actions of Malaysia taken to extricate itself from the effects of the Asian financial crisis. But see also, WG Huff, *The Economic Growth of Singapore: Trade and Development in the Twentieth Century* (Cambridge: Cambridge University Press, 1994)
3. See for a brief summary, L Best and K Levitt, 'Character of Caribbean Economy', in G Beckford, ed., *Caribbean Economy: Dependence and Backwardness* (Mona, Jamaica, ISER, 1975), and for a general discussion, Eric St Cyr, *The Theory of Caribbean Economy: Its Origins and Current Status* (Trinidad: UWI, Institute of International Relations, 1983)
4. See Mark Hong, 'Small States in the United Nations', *International Social Science Journal*, No. 144, 1995
5. Huff, ibid, pp. 24, 31 and 37. Huff also specifically observes that the specific circumstances of Singapore's development do not make it an appropriate model for other countries.
6. Though some analysts argue that the crisis emanates in large measure from the strategy of Brazilian economy policy, with its continual fiscal disequilibrium, and could be foreseen.
7. Havelock Brewster, *The Caribbean Community in a Changing International Environment: Towards the Next Century* (ISER, UWI)
8. Anthony Payne, 'The New Politics of 'Caribbean America', *Third World Quarterly*, Vol 19, No. 2, 1998

28 | ANTHONY T BRYAN

Caribbean International Relations:
A Retrospect and Outlook for a New Millennium

For most of the twentieth century, the international relations of the wider Caribbean region can be characterised as circumstances of limited complexity in a predictable world environment. The key elements in the relations were the historical links with Europe, and the region's geopolitical relevance to the United States, the preeminent military power in the Americas. But the international relations of the Caribbean have never been constrained to relations among states. Various actors, international, regional, local, state and non-state, have interacted on issues and have sought in various ways to shape the conduct and norms of the region's international affairs.

By the beginning of the 1990s, radical changes taking place outside the Caribbean had changed the comfortable and predictable world in which Caribbean international relations had been set and to which Caribbean diplomacy had become accustomed. The bipolar political structure of world politics that arose after World War II has collapsed. The old assumptions, the seemingly immutable structures and intellectual constructs which underpinned the functioning of the international system since the end of the second World War have been shattered and swept away by the tidal wave of far-reaching changes, political and economic, taking place in many areas of the globe. The international community has found itself thrust abruptly into the post-cold war era.

As the world enters the new millennium, trade liberalisation and the globalisation of economic production are destroying barriers to commerce between nations and ushering in a new global community dominated by the explosive revolution in information technology. The trends and characteristics of the emerging international order suggest a disturbing fluidity and uncertainty about the future, brought about by rapid and often unpredictable changes. Regional conflicts now have their origins in purely local conditions and their resolution is less amenable to the coaxing of major powers; economic issues are now preeminent over international political matters; and objectives such as democracy, good governance, economic integration and free trade, sustainable development, preservation of the environment, global climate change, drug trafficking, and cyberspace crimes, have risen to the top of the global agenda. The Caribbean region, like much of the developing world, is caught up in the tide of these profound transformations that reflect the replacement of one international system by another.

The Past and the Present

Despite the rapid global changes, some features in the Caribbean's international relations remain constant. Today, as in the past, both the United States and Europe claim the right to mold the international and the domestic circumstances of the region. This time the battles are mainly economic and are being waged in the World Trade Organisation over the future of preferences for Caribbean bananas, sugar and rum in the expanded markets of the European Union as well as controversy in the OECD and the EU about the overseas financial services offered in certain Caribbean jurisdictions. The economic survival of Cuba is also caught up in the battle between the United States and the world over the extra-territoriality of the US in enforcing its embargo against the largest Caribbean island. Today as in the past, non-state actors such as international drug traffickers, and offshore money launderers (the modern day pirates), use their financial, political, and military power to advance their illegal cross-border activities. Today, as in the past, many non-Caribbean countries such as France, The Netherlands, Russia, and Japan have significant political and economic interests in the region. However, today, unlike the past, relatively autonomous multinational institutions such as the IMF, the World Bank, and the Inter-American Development Bank, provide considerable economic assistance to the region and exercise sometimes disproportionate political and economic influence on governments. Moreover, although threats to the sovereignty and security of Caribbean states have been constant, in the last decades of the twentieth century global television and cyberspace have broken free of the constraints of national boundaries and challenged the sine qua non of governments, namely the ability to govern decisively within their own borders. There are unprecedented clashes both internationally and within states over the governance of virtually every human activity from free speech to press freedom, crime and punishment, privacy, and investment regulation. In essence, the international environment in the Caribbean is polycentric, as various external state and non-state actors pursue their own competitive interests. Much like 'the powers and the pirates' of centuries past, today's actors are contributing to changes in the international environment of the lands and peoples of the Caribbean Sea.[1]

Mainstream theoretical perspectives on realism and pluralism, as well as the literature on democracy, socialism, non-alignment, fragmentation, multilateralism, unilateralism, bilateralism, and regionalism, have served as mantras at various times over the last three decades to partly explain the ideologies, practices, and customs associated with Caribbean international relations and foreign policy behaviour. However, the dominant international relations perspective that has been shared by all Caribbean countries is their vulnerability as small states in the international system. Asymmetry remains central to the region's relations with its Latin American neighbors, North America, Europe, and Asia.

At the turn of the century, as these small states try to overcome their vulnerabilities and take responsibility for their future in the emerging global system, an array of rapid changes during the 1990s have made possible a new range of issues, rules, and activities in the international arena. The traditional paradigms and theoretical analyses of international relations from both global and regional perspectives are being brought into question.

The major political and economic challenges facing the Caribbean in the twenty-first century, have been discussed in several recent general studies and a productive dialogue among scholars and policy makers has ensued. Similarly, discussions on the state of security, always a major concern for the Caribbean region, have gone through an interesting evolution in the post-cold war period: namely, the emphasis on the strong links between the range of development concerns and security concerns.[2] Today, the vulnerability of Caribbean states has increased; and the challenges to economic security, as well as its political consequences, are receiving additional emphasis in the effort to define the architecture of the region's international relations at century's end. In exploring the current dynamic, this paper looks at the political economy and the security dimensions of the contemporary international relations of the Caribbean. It also identifies some of the tangible and intangible elements of the new diplomacy of those relations, as well as some trends that will demand action in the early years of the twenty-first century.

Trends in the Political Economy of the Caribbean

Though faced with rapid changes in the global system, most Caribbean countries have been able to survive the end of the twentieth century as middle-income and democratic countries. The English-speaking Caribbean countries in particular, have been exemplary in their practice of democracy and political stability. Others such as Suriname and Haiti are trying to nurture new democratic regimes. Economically, the region has followed the neo-liberal reform rule book and implemented policies mandated by the IMF, the World Bank, and regional funding agencies. They have trimmed fiscal deficits, privatised state owned commercial enterprises that were losing money and liberalised their trading regimes. Only Cuba continues to labour under a deliberate ideological model that does not encourage political democracy, while its economy mirrors some version of 'a la carte capitalism' in the face of a persistent US embargo. Recent economic reforms have encouraged direct foreign investment in certain sectors of the Cuban economy and permitted the evolution of a small merchant class within the margins of the state-managed economy.[3]

The structural adjustment and reforms carried out by several Caribbean countries since the mid-1980s were not willingly implemented nor sustained by domestic political constituencies. For the most part, such changes in the macroeconomic environment were mandated by international financial or donor institutions and implemented by reform-minded governments or by governments that saw no alternative. Such adjustment has been a challenge for small, open Caribbean economies which are vulnerable to large external shocks and find it difficult to carry sufficient reserves, maintain adequate borrowing capacity, and encourage proper exchange rate policies.

In general, the present transition in the political economy of the Caribbean region is full of uncertainties. Some politicians have portrayed liberalisation and privatisation policies as growth-inducing policies when in effect they are not. Undertaking such reforms encounters resistance and costs. Also individual countries are starting to question the immediate costs of the hemispheric and global momentum toward free trade because in some countries trade liberalisation, far from leading to greater exports, is provoking macroeconomic disequilibrium and an increase in unemployment.

In general, global economic turmoil in Latin America and Russia since 1995 has raised concerns about the capacity of many countries to achieve long term growth without recurrent crises. Inequality in the distribution of income and wealth is a potent global phenomenon, and concerns for alleviating poverty and income equality have not been fully integrated into proposals for growth. Many of the Caribbean's smaller economies are heavily dependent upon one (or a few) traditional export commodities for which world prices are not likely to rise. Increased crime, diminishing social support services, and dramatic increases in the poverty index, visible even in relatively prosperous societies such as Trinidad and Tobago, the Dominican Republic and Barbados, constitute major negative impacts of the reforms. In many Caribbean countries, the much heralded free-market economic reforms have produced their own immediate Waterloo – benefits for a few, uncertainty for the many, and the further impoverishment of the masses through the fiscal inability of governments to maintain essential social services and infrastructure. Much more has to be done domestically, and with the assistance of international donors, to compensate the losers.

Caribbean Democracy and Governance

Certain issues of governance have emerged with the changes in political economy. Strengthening democracy is one of the major items on the immediate agenda. There is widespread official and public perception in the region that economic vulnerability is at the core of Caribbean insecurity. Instability will increase if the economic pillars that support democratic regimes are eroded. Similarly, Caribbean democracy and internal security are also vulnerable to the illegal drug trade, the corruption of law enforcement officials, and domestic insurrection. In some states, such as Trinidad and Tobago, Guyana, Jamaica, and Haiti, ethnic and class tensions may worsen if economic circumstances deteriorate and political factions further exploit delicate situations. While the countries of the Commonwealth Caribbean maintain some of the hemisphere's strongest traditions of parliamentary democracy, even the much heralded Westminster model of parliamentary government is susceptible to authoritarian dispensation in the deliberate weakening of traditional safeguards and rules. It is difficult to be complacent about the future of democracy even in the English-speaking Caribbean countries. Troubling trends apparent since the 1980s have included: declining voter turn-out, particularly among the youth; and sharp declines in public interest in parliamentary proceedings could eventually strengthen the emergence of cabinet dictatorships, single-party rule, or perpetuate the financial and organisational advantages of dominant parties. Similarly, failure to invest regularly, because of budgetary constraints or lack of foreign assistance, in institutions such as the legal system and mechanisms for public security is placing severe strains on democratic governance.[4]

A concurrent trend is the inability of the state, during circumstances of considerable downsizing and economic liberalisation, to deliver levels of welfare and social services similar to the last three decades. There is pressure upon governments to provide economic support and to deliver social services more rapidly and efficiently even while their capacity to do so is severely diminished. The managerial capacity of the state in some countries needs to be rebuilt in order to deliver public services and to confront the challenges created by a competitive market economy. Public tolerance for further sacrifice is also diminishing as the tasks of dismantling or restructuring state enterprises and financial systems continue. While at the end of the twentieth century the inflation rates and fiscal deficits contained in most Caribbean countries and growth rates are respectable, the economic foundations are shaky. Revenues from privatisation sales and reductions in basic government services are not formulas for sustainable growth. Given the domestic costs, both political and economic, even preparing for global enterprise competitiveness is a real challenge for most countries of the Caribbean.

Within the political fabric, declining access to scarce economic largesse, spectacles of corruption in government; abuses of political power; and the use of declining public funds to reward the ruling party faithful have severely weakened traditional political parties in the Caribbean. Many have also lost their historical and ideological differences. But Caribbean electorates are demanding more accountability and clearer economic programs from their leaders, who seem increasingly like pragmatic technocrats. This change is driven by public anger at failing economies, rising social ills, and endemic corruption with attendant tensions and dysfunctions in society.[5]

In sum, trends in Caribbean governance and the democratic tradition, namely: dramatic shifts in social and class structure; declining political participation; frustration with the parliamentary system of politics; changes in leadership; conversion to neo-liberal economic policies by political parties which have traditionally represented labour; and changing relationships between labour, business and government; will have an impact on the political economy of the region in the twenty-first century.

Globalisation

When the cold war ended a decade ago, the fundamental shifts in the international system since that time have highlighted a series of trends that were already developing before its end. 'Globalisation' is the term most often used to describe these trends in the growing integration of economies worldwide through increases in trade, investment flows, and technology transfer. In recent years, this process has been facilitated by rapid advances in communications and information technology, as well as by an international policy environment which emphasises trade liberalisation, privatisation, and deregulation of financial markets. In general terms, its main elements are the spread of economic activities at a global level, and the political and cultural adjustments that accompany that expansion. The economic activities relate to the freer movement of goods, capital, services, people, skills, and knowledge across geographic borders. Fostered by rapid technological change, and characterised by a dilution of the control of national governments, globalisation has earned ideological connotations.

The present period of globalisation received strong impetus from the Bretton Woods institutions created in the early post-war period, in particular the General Agreement on Tariffs and Trade (GATT). The various rounds of the GATT – culminating with the Uruguay Round, which ended in 1994 – have accomplished a vast reduction in tariff rates, particularly in manufacturing. Finally, while advances in communications and information technology have facilitated the globalisation process, the demise of most socialist economic models and failure of inward-looking economic policies in the developing world also contributed to the globalisation process by discrediting alternative world views.

Supporters of globalisation emphasise the welfare benefits associated with increased specialisation and trade, such as lower import prices and increased flow of capital and technology across countries. Also cited are the more efficient allocation of savings and the structural changes in economies, both of which permit faster growth. Critics of globalisation argue that unrestricted trade and capital mobility result in low-wage regions attracting industries away from high-wage areas, thus lowering living standards in the latter. Some also argue that global financial markets undermine the ability of sovereign nations to carry out independent economic policy, while poor nations are further marginalised from the more positive aspects of the globalisation process. The political implications of this process for the Caribbean are important.[6]

Globalisation of the Caribbean's political economy is not a late twentieth-century phenomenon; it always has been a companion of production specialisation, from the sugar plantations of the past to the tourist enclaves of today. Since the late fifteenth century, the Caribbean has been integrated into the world economy through trade and investment. Throughout its history, the Caribbean as a region has had to respond to cyclical fluctuations in the international economy and to adjust its political and economic relationships to challenges in the international economic environment. More often than not, these have involved strategies to compensate the region for the disadvantages of small size and the legacies of exploitation in the colonial past. In this historical process, the economic systems of Caribbean countries have benefited from a series of special preferential trade and financial arrangements designed to underwrite their survival and viability.

What is different today is the increased international vulnerability of the Caribbean's political economy. The post-colonial era of 'special relationships' is coming to an end, and the development assistance policies of the former colonial powers now are based on their assessments of the real needs of developing countries rather than on geopolitical, cultural, emotional, or traditional ties. The Caribbean is once again the focus of political battles over international trade, with the outcome to be decided in Washington, Brussels, and at the WTO in Geneva.

At century's end, Caribbean countries are experiencing excruciating demands on their trading regimes and negotiating capabilities. Negotiations with the EU for a post-Lomé IV arrangement, and the negotiating process for the FTAA have commenced. Discussions on regional trade arrangements and negotiations of further extensions to trade liberalisation following from the completion of the Uruguay Round of the GATT are taking place under the auspices of the WTO. The trade challenges facing the Caribbean region are diverse, including the problem of finding ways for small, fragmented economies in the western hemisphere to survive in an increasingly competitive, global trading environment. More precisely, Caribbean states have to determine how they can participate in the FTAA and in the eventual full reciprocal trade arrangements with Europe. In this context, the integration of the Caribbean nation of Cuba into the regional and global economy on terms acceptable to its people remains as one of the most problematic items facing its neighbors, as well as Europe and North America.

The position taken by industrialised countries in the Uruguay Round, in conjunction with the increasing momentum in Europe away from preferential arrangements and in the direction of trade reciprocity for developing countries, is a challenge for the Caribbean. So also is the implementation of the North American Free Trade Agreement (NAFTA), which has greatly reduced the value of US and Canadian trade and tariff preferences under the CBI and CARIBCAN, respectively. The Soviet Union has disappeared, and so have its subsidies to Cuba. Most Caribbean countries are highly dependent on North America and Europe as markets for their exports and have reason to be concerned about general changes that will make nonsense of the existing system of preferences and significantly alter their access to these markets.

In general, at the dawn of a new millennium, the challenges confronting the Caribbean with respect to trade with Europe and the Americas are essentially similar: the future of existing regimes of significant preferences, the need to plan for the long term without such preferences, and the development of a strategy to meet the transition. Given the division of the world into a number of large trading blocs, growth in the economies of the Caribbean will depend to a large extent on participation in or access to these trade arrangements. A Caribbean strategy for participation is evolving which anticipates regional negotiation for simultaneous access to as many global, regional, and bilateral trade pacts as possible, rather than having to choose between them.

Economic Integration and Free Trade

The trade policy commitments and challenges faced by the Caribbean countries are numerous and stem from multilateral, regional, and hemispheric trade liberalisation initiatives, as well as national policy differences among this group of states that are diverse in size, population, and resources. The process of integration has advanced most rapidly in CARICOM since its formation in 1975. The theories and strategies for Caribbean integration have evolved over time. But within the context of second generation regional integration theories and smaller economies' agendas, new integration prerogatives and prescriptions for wider Caribbean regionalism have emerged.

The history of the regional integration movement in the Caribbean has been cyclical. Each attempt at regional integration has met with surges of excitement and optimism, sobriety, a sense of failure, disenchantment, then renewed optimism, and another cycle. The cycles have been characterised by periodic querying of the concept of integration itself. The fundamental premise for the idea of regional integration in the Caribbean has been the promotion of economic development. Integration has been advanced primarily as a means of accelerating the industrialisation of the countries' primary-product economies and societies and achieving their desired goals of economic development. The nature of the relationship between integration and economic development has been altered over the years, as thinking has changed on the processes of economic development and integration (today's concept of 'open regionalism' is an example), but the relationship itself has never strayed far from the fundamental premise. The key institutions in the development of Caribbean integration – the Federation of the West Indies (1958–1962), CARIFTA, and CARICOM – reflect this process.

Historically, Caribbean theories about integration have moved through several phases since the 1950s: from industrialisation by invitation, to regional import substitution, through structuralism and dependency, centre-periphery models, and the neo-functionalist theory of 'integration by stealth'. In their early works on regional economic integration, the thinking of Caribbean social scientists corresponds to that of the Latin Americans, although the former works developed fairly independently and out of economic circumstances similar to those in Latin America. Subsequently, the influence of the Latin American schools of thought on Caribbean economic theory became more visible.[7] By the time governments in the Caribbean were ready to establish the proposed free trade institution CARIFTA (despite warnings from university economists regarding the inadequacy of its institutional structure), there was substantial pride in the fact that the strongest impetus for regional cooperation had come from economic theorists, social scientists, politicians, and business persons representative of several Caribbean countries. Moreover, the academic thrust and accompanying theoretical constructs had been directed mainly from the Institute of Social and Economic Research at the University of the West Indies. This Caribbean ethos must be viewed as an important stage in a region very much concerned with exercising autonomy in thought and action. This time there were no exogenous institutional or governmental actors openly directing the establishment of CARIFTA, as had been the case with the Federation. By the time CARICOM was established, most Caribbean leaders and bureaucrats were persuaded that deliberate and incremental progress toward regional integration was a practical course. In the history of CARICOM, this added intellectual understanding of the superior bargaining strength that comes from regional cooperation and the benefits of participating as a bloc in the global economy has emerged as a strong pivot in the movement for Caribbean regional integration, and in the region's conduct of its international relations.[8]

Collectively, while the contributions of Caribbean theorists were remarkable, the matching of theory and practice in the CARICOM integration experience has been less than distinguished. By mid-1999, CARICOM's membership comprised 13 English-speaking countries of the Commonwealth Caribbean, plus Suriname and Haiti.[9] Unlike the Federation, CARICOM has been able to survive. However, like the Federation and CARIFTA, ongoing national rivalries and regional economic difficulties have characterised CARICOM and have threatened the viability of the regional integration movement over the past 25 years.

Generally, CARICOM has done well with respect to both foreign policy coordination and functional cooperation. No other regional integration group in the western hemisphere has demonstrated such a vocal commitment to coordination of foreign policy, despite some notable fragmentation, as in the varied national responses to the US intervention in Grenada in 1983 and the signing of separate bilateral 'ship rider agreements' with the United States in 1997 and 1998. Functional collaboration efforts have also resulted in a number of very successful regional institutions of CARICOM.[10] However, progress toward true regional economic integration has been slow. The success stories in the area of functional cooperation have not been repeated in the area of economic integration. From a broad perspective, the CARICOM economic integration strategy has not advanced dramatically because the process has been a means to an end but not an end in itself. Individual states have always been ready to defect, in deed if not in word, from second-best arrangements, while the reality of uneven costs and benefits has inhibited the deepening of integrationist ventures.

At century's end, in order to hasten the integration process and establish the CARICOM Single Market and Economy (CSM&E), the organisation is undergoing a comprehensive reform process, highlighted by the planned implementation of a series of protocols that revise the founding Treaty of Chaguaramas. Protocols dealing with institutional reforms, service sector liberalisation, industrial policy, agricultural policy, trade policy, as well as protocols on disadvantaged countries, regions, and sectors; transportation policy; competition policy; and dispute settlement are scheduled for ratification by the year 2000.

Regional integration in its present form in CARICOM still has severe limitations because a conglomeration of small economies still yields a mass that, in many respects, is inadequate to ensure development and transformation. While size constraints are important, it is also clear that the declared ambitious integration goals have not always been followed up by timely or practical action. Many factors are responsible: waning political will, changes in integration strategy, failure to implement national adjustment programs, and technical obstacles to the implementation and enforcement of common policies. However, the current phenomenon of globalisation, with both its benefits and its ominous downside for small nations, fortifies the need to widen the scope and membership of the Caribbean Community and to move toward a more outward-looking integration agenda.

At the turn of the century, across the Caribbean region, there is genuine concern about the challenges and opportunities presented by the FTAA and the successor Lomé agreement, and the consensus is that some of these small, fragile economies will not be able to compete internationally or to survive the wave of globalisation. But while the regional market is too small, fragile, and vulnerable, in global terms, it is still a base that could be improved upon with strategic global repositioning.[11] The prevailing argument among the region's economists is that 'widening' the regional integration movement would be more in line with current integration realities in the global economy. Consequently, traditional, narrow definitions of the Caribbean are being abandoned and replaced by a 'wider' Caribbean vision, and 'second-generation' regional integration theories are starting to be formulated for the region. What is the nature of the new Caribbean regionalism? In the early twenty-first century how broadly will the Caribbean be defined?

Redefining the Caribbean

On July 24, 1994, a major step toward implementing a wider Caribbean vision was taken when the convention establishing the Association of Caribbean States (ACS) was signed in Cartegena, Colombia. The proposal for the creation of the ACS had been put forward by the heads of government of CARICOM in October 1992. The idea itself had its origins in the document, *Time for Action: The Report of the West Indian Commission*, which recommended that CARICOM 'bridge the divide between its Member States and the rest of the Caribbean and Latin America' through functional cooperation and economic integration.[12] The ACS vision encompasses countries with different geographic, demographic, and economic ideals and development levels and also different historical, cultural, and linguistic backgrounds. It offers a new regional configuration that provides a framework for closer political, economic, and functional cooperation in the wider Caribbean. There are 37 signatories to the convention. Twenty-five of them are independent states eligible for full membership, and the other 12 are non-independent states eligible for associate status. The ACS membership includes all countries in the Caribbean Sea (regardless of their constitutional status), the rim-land countries of Central America, as well as Colombia, Venezuela, and Mexico. As of mid-1999, all of the countries eligible for full membership had ratified the convention.

The broad objectives of the ACS as enshrined in the convention are 1) strengthening of the regional cooperation and integration process, with a view to creating an enhanced economic space in the region; 2) preserving the environmental integrity of the Caribbean Sea, which is regarded as the common patrimony of the peoples of the region; and 3) promoting the sustainable development of the Caribbean region. The ACS is seen primarily as an 'integration grouping' and a consensus-building political entity, with a role in the advancement of trade liberalisation and regional integration. Yet the ACS has the potential to become the world's fourth-largest regional grouping (three-fourths the size of South America's MERCOSUR). The ACS countries currently have a population of 216 million, an accumulated GDP of US$506 billion, and approximately US$180 billion in merchandise trade.[13] Clearly, the prospect of increased intra-regional trade and investment is a strong catalyst for the ACS and one of the motives for a renewed look at regional integration as means of facilitating broader Caribbean insertion into the global economy.

Not surprisingly, many regional policymakers regard the ACS as a very ambitious attempt to integrate a region that has been characterised by its heterogeneity as well as by great disparities in economic size and power. But the ACS represents an important space for consolidating a complex web of bilateral and subregional processes and for the smaller economies of the Caribbean region to forge alliances, unify their policies, and build negotiating power in the wider hemispheric free trade process.

While the potential of the ACS is apparent, the concern is whether it can define, seize, and effectively occupy its own policy space. Its real challenge is to become an effective vehicle for regionalism and not merely another piece of idle machinery. More important, in the context of regional integration theory in the Caribbean, the ACS represents a 'second generation' approach to the integration prerogative. Its objective is multifaceted, and its approach to regional integration is hybrid. Its agenda is pragmatic. The most intensive efforts of the ACS secretariat are directed toward the issues of regional transportation and sustainable tourism, as well as science, technology, health, education, and culture, where success is likely. In essence, the ACS is not an integration process per se, but an 'attempt to strengthen the region's negotiating position in regional diplomacy.'[14]

The Caribbean and the Emerging FTAA Process

Caribbean countries now face a steep adjustment curve in preparation for the FTAA. Decades of protectionist policies must be eliminated if they are to mitigate the shocks that domestic market-opening will have on their economies or benefit from the opportunities that global market opening will eventually confer. Consequently, several factors will affect the participation of Caribbean countries in the FTAA.

With the FTAA, Caribbean countries would have greater access to Latin American markets. Apart from Trinidad and Tobago, CARICOM countries conduct very little business in Latin America. The FTAA would also provide greater and more stable and predictable access to the US market for small Caribbean countries, as they have a greater need for secure market access and stable and transparent trade rules in order to trade effectively. The FTAA is also likely to reduce uncertainty in the regulations governing the trade in goods and services and produce clearly defined mechanisms for dispute settlement.[15] Further, for a small country facing the risk of domestic policy reversals, establishing regional economic policy in the framework of a multilateral arrangement can have the benefit of increasing domestic policy consistency. Trade liberalisation, which has been resisted in some Caribbean countries, could, therefore, be reinforced or accelerated as a result of participation in the FTAA. So, for the medium to long term, the FTAA holds the potential for promoting increased economic growth in the Caribbean region.

Conversely, there are both political and economic fears expressed by smaller, less developed economies in the hemisphere, concerning their integration into larger economic areas. On the *political* side, nations fear the loss of sovereignty implied by any international commitment having domestic repercussions. Smaller nations fear this the most because they are acutely conscious of their weak bargaining power. This is especially true in the Caribbean context. However, realistically, in light of the changing global dynamics and the increasing globalisation of the world economy, it can be argued that such short term losses would occur anyway for all countries participating in the hemispheric integration process. On the *economic* side, small countries are mainly concerned with the exposure of their domestic industries to foreign competition and with the costs of adjustment to the widened market. For CARICOM countries and many of the small economies of Latin America, the costs of transition to a wider, open, and reciprocal hemispheric market are a serious concern. While the FTAA will probably accentuate these trends, the real issue facing the smaller economies of the Caribbean is how to secure, if possible, sufficient bargaining power to influence the provision of transitional arrangements that would provide some protection from the deep shocks of the FTAA process. So far, the trade dynamic in the western hemisphere has not been very accommodating to the smaller economies.

In a scenario where NAFTA membership and NAFTA parity remain elusive and any possibility of securing special concessions for small economies within the FTAA is subject to negotiation on a case-by-case basis during the period

1998 to 2005, the challenges for Caribbean states appear overwhelming. CARICOM's response to the specific concern about limited bargaining power is the decision to conduct its member country negotiations on the basis of a regional group approach, even though the strategy involves some loss of sovereignty for individual countries. CARICOM has turned over its own external trade relations to the RNM established in February 1997 in order to enhance the coordination and execution of its own external relations with the FTAA and the EU. The RNM has since been working with the CARICOM Secretariat and other organs and member states of the community to develop a coordinated and cohesive strategy to prepare CARICOM countries for their entry into the FTAA.[16] For CARICOM, clearly the main issue is the identification of concrete measures to meet the needs of its small, fragile economies, given the level of adjustment needed and the great disparities in size and development of the economies participating in the FTAA process.

As formal negotiations for the establishment of the FTAA by January 2005 progress, the Central American and Caribbean countries are accelerating their trade relations with each other. The proposed creation of a Caribbean-Central American Free Trade Area is consistent with the FTAA process and part of a trend where principal subregional groupings are also establishing trade agreements among themselves in order to strengthen their bargaining positions during the negotiations. In the long term, however, the 'new regionalism' paradigm for the Caribbean will also depend on implementing other, very challenging regional objectives. These would include the liberalisation and harmonisation of investment regimes, the convergence of regulatory frameworks to match global best practices, the promotion of free trade in goods and services throughout the region, the fostering of competition in the transport and telecommunications sectors, the enhancement of convergence in macroeconomic policies, the promotion of continued institutional reforms in order to face the hemispheric integration challenge, and the preparation for effective participation in trade negotiations and the capacity to implement resulting agreements.

The FTAA initiative is already testing the limited human, financial, and technical resources of CARICOM by placing heavy demands on its trading regimes and negotiating capabilities. The FTAA process has spawned a multitude of meetings involving trade ministers, vice-ministers, and several technical working groups, which have severely taxed the resources of CARICOM. In addition, CARICOM, the Dominican Republic, and Haiti are simultaneously involved in negotiations with the EU for a post-Lomé arrangement. This means that into the early years of the twenty-first century, the region has to undertake complex negotiations in parallel but in different time frames, with each impacting on the other.

Europe, the Caribbean and the Lomé Convention

The principle of partnership that underpins the series of Lomé Conventions is one of the distinguishing features of EU cooperation with the African-Caribbean-Pacific grouping as it has evolved since 1975. The Lomé Convention comprises a succession of comprehensive agreements covering aid and trade, based on the principle of non-reciprocity. Since the inception of Lomé I in 1975, the European community has enlarged, with consequent effects on the shape of Lomé policy. The current Lomé IV Convention includes specific sections ranging from environmental to cultural and social cooperation, but the trade and financial aspects are the most important to ACP members.

Since the negotiation of Lomé IV in 1989, the Lomé partnership has come under increasing pressure as a result of several factors. The new GATT arrangement as finalised in the Uruguay Round has ushered in a climate of trade liberalisation spearheaded by the WTO. At the same time, there is a widespread sense of 'aid fatigue', due in part to disillusionment from recognising that the aid has not worked. Those opposed to further aid point to the development success concentrated in Asia despite a lack of European assistance to that region. In addition, the demise of both the Eastern European bloc and the Soviet Union has caused a change of focus and perspective in Europe. An expanded post-cold war EU is starting to favor its new partners in Eastern Europe and the Mediterranean.

Since 1992, the EU's move toward a more global development cooperation policy has placed significant pressure on Lomé's present exclusive membership structure of ACP countries, which is seen to be inconsistent with the new directions in EU development cooperation policy. The EU has not abandoned its ACP partners, and supports the concerns of the vulnerability and special status of small island states. But the geopolitical and historical justification for EU-ACP relations since 1975 has disappeared. After the expiration of the present convention in 2000, there is a commitment by the EU to employ stricter conditions in an effort to foster trade and investment so that sustainable development is achieved without substantial European aid. The broad framework of cooperation after 2000 includes the move toward region-specific arrangements, an emphasis on decentralised cooperation with the identification of new private sector partners, efficiency in the use of aid resources, the incorporation of respect for human rights, and demands for the consolidation of good governance and democratic principles as essential elements of cooperation. As Europe restructures from many trading partners into one and the Lomé Convention becomes but one of a varied group of relationships that the EU maintains with developing and other countries, more fundamental shifts are likely.

Europe is a major trading area for Caribbean countries. The Lomé Convention is a vital agreement for the 12 independent CARICOM countries, the Dominican Republic, Haiti, and Suriname. Through it, duty-free access to the markets of the European community is critical for the region's producers of sugar, bananas, and rum. The regional cooperation programme functions through a special body, CARIFORUM (comprising the Caribbean members of the Convention), which maintains a formal relationship with the EU through the Lomé Convention. Because of its relatively high per capita income, the Caribbean's focus on the Convention has been its trade instruments. The Caribbean countries that are beneficiaries of the Lomé Convention have grown accustomed to a strongly concessionaire trade environment, guaranteed by treaty obligation.

Although the Lomé agreements have served to protect traditional exports, the trade results have been uninspiring. They have not benefited the Caribbean countries in terms of stimulating export expansion. Export diversification, either by sector or by product, is still marginal. The European Union accounts for some 17 per cent of CARICOM trade and has been running a trade surplus with the Caribbean in recent years. Protection of traditional export staples, such as bananas, sugar, and rum, was central to the Caribbean region's motives for entering into the Lomé agreements. The arrangements guaranteed the region reasonable market access for these products and an assured flow of export earnings. For the sugar and banana protocols, ACP Caribbean countries also benefit from a relatively generous EU price for their exports because of the Common Agricultural Policy. Yet trade liberalisation has put the benefits of higher prices and the guaranteed access of the protocols at risk, while the pressure of the WTO and major trading partners (both within and outside Europe) also threatens their very existence. For example, in the final year of the twentieth century, as the US and the EU battle in the WTO over the legality of continued preferences for Caribbean bananas in the EU market, the importance of the issue for the Caribbean seems to have been subsumed.

The dispute between the US and the EU over bananas is caught up in their long term battle over agriculture. The current banana protocol will come to an end in 2000 in any case, and the EU will be forced to put a regime in place, which may not be enough to support the viability of the banana industry in the Caribbean. Until now the Windward Islands have been isolated from low cost Latin American banana producers. The Caribbean countries may have the moral high ground in the current dispute, but after 2000 they will have to face the possible demise of a non-competitive industry.[17]

Facing Choices and Change in New International Economic Relations

In general, the countries of the Caribbean are struggling toward greater progress on economic and trade policy reform in the region. But any regional strategy must take into account the specific economic characteristics of its member countries. They are small economies in terms of territory, population size, and GDP. They are also open economies; their external transactions are large relative to their total economic output. Openness renders them extremely vulnerable to external shocks, such as fluctuations in international commodity prices or policy changes abroad. Vulnerability is compounded by the region's narrow export base, and most countries depend for their export earnings on a small number of natural resource products or tourism. The generous preferential market access for their exports to the EU and North America is in danger of being eroded or phased out in the coming years. Export diversification has been limited and insufficient for generating satisfactory growth rates. Dependence on trade taxes for government revenue is also common among the majority of CARICOM countries; thus, particularly in the Organisation of Eastern Caribbean States (OECS) economies, the pursuit of any trade liberalisation initiatives affects national fiscal accounts disproportionately.

On the positive side, Caribbean countries share location advantages, such as proximity to the US market and strategic location on the main trading routes between the Americas and Europe. Geographic location brings advantages for the further development of tourism services though there is also a disadvantage to the island members in terms of high infrastructure and transportation costs. Such characteristics have important implications for the design of a regional strategy for the Caribbean. The lack of a sizable regional market, for example, indicates that the Caribbean approach to integration must, by definition, differ from that of MERCOSUR or other large integration areas. But the region's high level of trade openness also dictates that successful interaction with the world economy and the promotion of long term, *sustainable*, export-led growth should be key elements in the development strategy.

Despite a number of common features, Caribbean economies are also different in terms of natural endowment, economic output, and relative wealth. In the case of CARICOM, three countries, Trinidad and Tobago, Jamaica, and Barbados, together account for almost 80 per cent of the Common Market's total GDP and more than two-thirds of its merchandise exports. At the other extreme are the six small island states of the OECS, which together account for just one-tenth of CARICOM's total GDP and only 7 per cent of its exports. Greater integration of the Caribbean economies is hampered by deficiencies in intra-regional transport infrastructure, with high costs and low reliability of delivery being the major impediments to the development of intra-regional and extra-regional trade.

Similarly, while the Caribbean Community has a long tradition of regional cooperation and integration, the results have not always matched its ambitious goals. Avowed cooperation, combined with lack of institutional capacity, has often sown the seeds of potential conflict. Disparities in resources and capabilities, as well as the compulsion of the leadership, particularly in the smallest or least powerful members of the group to guard jealously the political sovereignty of the national entities, have often undermined multilateral initiatives. As new attempts are made to widen the Caribbean or to craft a new regionalism with an increase in the number of states, policymakers will have to create formal and informal mechanisms to compensate for differing capabilities and resolve conflicts that are prompted by sovereign national interests.

The structuralism, neo-structuralism, and dependency theories that provided the intellectual foundations for the Caribbean integration movement in the past are today no longer relevant. The economic integration strategy that was nurtured by these theories may have been accurate for the times, but as the twentieth century draws to a close there is still a gap between the intellectual paradigm and contemporary political and economic realities.

Now pleading for the luxury of uniqueness or special needs because of smaller economies status is no longer a realistic option for the Caribbean. The assumption that small Caribbean economies cannot compete in international markets is not necessarily valid. Some small economies can dominate specific niche markets such as tourism in the case of many Caribbean countries and certain energy-based or petrochemical industries in the case of Trinidad and Tobago. Highly educated and skilled labour resources in the region can compete with many other areas of the world. However, strategic alliances and collaboration with government, business, and civil society in other countries in the wider Caribbean are necessary in order to realise the full potential. The new regionalism in the Caribbean also highlights a more profound process. In the opinion of one Caribbean economist, the countries are now more willing to explore the options of multiple integration schemes simultaneously, as they approach the consolidation of hemispheric integration by the year 2005.[18]

In the Caribbean, integration emerged as a response to overcoming the development constraints of small size. The new regionalism is an accelerated response to the new dynamics of globalisation. The missing element in the new regionalism is the corporate integration of national companies, which outgrow their markets and accelerate the flow of goods and services, capital, and finance throughout the region. Corporate integration is the stimulus that will push Caribbean regionalism into the new age.[19] In essence, the acceptance of globalisation, corporate integration, and the hemispheric trade momentum requires a management process and a strategy by small countries to reassess the dynamics of regionalism in a much broader context than was originally conceived by many Caribbean theorists. In the Caribbean context of political economy, the colonial past is no longer the emotional road map for the integration of the region. The new regionalism in the Caribbean is one that reflects a paradigm shift in integration theory and practice, from a vertical perspective (North America and Europe) toward a horizontal relationship between the countries of the wider Caribbean and Latin America.

Caribbean Security

The topic of small state security was one of the major concerns of Caribbean scholars during the 1970s and 1980s while the cold war was still germane. The topic had both domestic and international facets. Its major themes (geopolitics, militarisation, external intervention, subregional imperialism, domestic and regional instability, peace and development) were eventually categorised under the broader rubric of 'vulnerability'.[20] The threats to economic security, identified during the cold war era involved 'action that can have the effect of undermining a state's economic welfare and which, additionally, can also be used as an instrument of political interference.'[21] The argument was framed in the prevailing economic and development models of the period (which included protected domestic and regional markets, bilateral and multilateral concessionary aid, commodity price stabilisation) and did not foresee the challenges which would emerge as a result of the completion of structural adjustment, the process of liberalisation of the global economy, and the implementation of new trading blocs.

While the liberalisation of economies and the evolving financial markets in the Caribbean may be a welcome and legitimate development, there is an enormous 'downside' to the process of trade and financial liberalisation. Without effective controls and safeguards the economies of small states are susceptible to a range of new vulnerabilities. Clearly, corruption at all levels is a very disturbing trend. No region of the world has a greater concentration of offshore secrecy financial havens than the Caribbean. Given the globalisation of finance and investment, the importance of these centres for the economies of small island states there is understandable. But their use by organised crime and money launderers has dangerous implications for Caribbean countries. Neither traditional theories of political relations, distinct cultural characteristics, nor poverty can fully explain the money-laundering phenomenon. The Caribbean islands with some of the largest offshore financial centres (Caymans, British Virgin Islands, Turks and Caicos, Anguilla) are the most European of all in constitutional linkages, culture, law, and business traditions. They are not destitute, and they benefit from transfers from the metropolis. Their economic activity takes place across a spectrum of businesses that is both legitimate and illegitimate.[22]

However, the social, economic and political impact of the 'money laundering' phenomenon is *not* restricted to major financial or offshore centres or to the reputation of some countries for confidentiality laws. Powerful countries with extra-territorial reach in such matters have the potential to attack the financial sector of small countries that permit such activities. Already by mid-1999 the OECD, a conglomeration of the world's wealthiest states, had unilaterally devised international standards to combat 'harmful tax competition' directed against 47 countries (15 of them from the Caribbean) with offshore financial services and nominal corporation taxes which it claims are causing capital flight and injury to the tax regimes in OECD countries. The establishment of such criteria has moved the governments of the Caribbean to open a dialogue with the OECD and to formulate joint approaches to maintain acceptable international regulatory standards, implement international best standards and practices, and to eliminate opportunities for money laundering using offshore financial institutions. As the Caribbean moves toward free trade and common markets, anti-laundering measures become more necessary. There is legislation in place in many Caribbean countries for asset confiscation and other measures – but the record of implementation is unsatisfactory at best.[23] There are terrible costs to society, polity and economy associated with inaction in this circumstance. The spectacle of business monopolies controlled by criminal elements can constrain investment and competitiveness in a country; while massive infusions of illegal funds into the economy can have an adverse effect through the artificial inflation of prices.

An even greater threat to Caribbean democratic institutions derives from the apparent increasing synergy between government officials and organised crime-including the drug cartels. For Caribbean countries the distinctions between the legal economy and the informal economy lies more in their 'legal' character than in the 'economic' nature of activities. The legitimate global financial community does not take kindly to countries that knowingly facilitate laundering. There is little incentive for foreign direct investment if criminals dominate the commercial sector.

Increasingly, the major contributor to corruption and criminality in the region is the illegal drug trafficking trade. Some Eastern Caribbean countries on the northern tier of South America have now become key trans-shipment routes for South American cocaine into US and European markets.[24] Most Caribbean countries cooperate with the United States in counter-narcotics efforts. Some US anti-drug action appeared to push extraterritorial jurisdiction too far and provoked government and public hostility in some Caribbean countries where the US is criticised for having little regard for national sovereignty. A case in point is the United States Maritime and Overflight (Ship Riders) Agreement that is intended to stem the intra-regional flow of drugs. The agreement permits land and sea patrols by US Coast Guard and Navy vessels, maritime searches, seizures and arrests by US law enforcement authorities within the national boundaries of Caribbean countries. It also allows US aircraft to over-fly Caribbean countries and order suspect aircraft to land there. By the end of 1998 most Caribbean countries had signed some version of the agreement, but its ability to have any impact at all remains to be seen. The transnational nature of the drug trade is difficult to combat. Narcotics trafficking is unlikely to stop in the near term given the demand in the developed countries, the ease of electronic money laundering, offshore bank secrecy, a network of official protection enjoyed by traffickers, and the 'corporate' structure of the drug trade. A new policy may be required, one that chases the money rather than the drugs, and one that is directed more to demand reduction in the metropoles.

Drug trafficking and the production of illegal narcotics constitute a security problem; but they are also symptoms of profound economic crisis and poverty. The failure of economic development strategies, and the lack of viable economic alternatives, have made the illegal narcotics business the most profitable sector of the Caribbean's informal economy. One important goal in the international fight against drugs should be to support democratic institutions and to combat efforts by drug cartels or other organised criminal groups to corrupt and to penetrate democratic governments. Victory in the struggle against drugs is unlikely until those running the criminal organisations and cartels are put out of business. Otherwise seized drugs and lost revenues are simply the cost of doing business. Given the region's limited resources, the drug trade will not be halted any time soon. In the meantime, corruption and violence will probably increase even more, and valuable national and regional resources will be diverted from infrastructure, education and health care to fighting the illegal drug scourge.[25]

Migration and international economic interdependence, and the economic, trade, and foreign investment consequences of migration (for both the sending and receiving societies), have also emerged as a major security issue in the international relations of the Caribbean. The flood of Haitian and Cuban refugees to the US in the 1980s and 1990s illustrates the extent of the problem. Political issues aside, Haiti is an extreme example of Caribbean demographics. Under current conditions, the land can no longer adequately support its population. Many of Haiti's economic problems stem largely from an environmental crisis (the degradation of natural resources) made worse by the uncertainty of politics, development planning and inadequate distribution and delivery systems. The depletion of resources is a fundamental cause of conflict and human misery and national policies must make sustainable development a priority.

Haiti and Cuba, for other reasons, may be extreme scenarios of migration and refugees propelled by combinations of political and economic circumstances. However, migration, legal or illegal, will continue as a safety valve for economic dislocation in the Caribbean. But the resulting movement of human talent does not necessarily present a doomsday scenario for either the Caribbean or receiving countries such as the United States. The remittances and investments sent by productive Caribbean emigrants should be regarded as part of a larger transborder contribution to long term economic growth, peace, and security in the hemisphere. In fact, migration is an item on the international development agenda. Cross-border networks, and linkages between diaspora and home societies, will continue to sustain trans-border migration flows. In spite of frequent anti-immigration fervour the United States, and other developed nations, stand to benefit economically from the immigration flows.[26]

The environment and sustainable development are also important security issues for the Caribbean. They are in fact critical to the economic survival of many countries. The environment is at the centre of the tourism industry, the principal source of revenue for many countries and coordination in the tourism sector inevitably implies coordination in the area of the environment. The urgency for effective disaster emergency response, storm hazard assessment and impact monitoring, disaster preparedness and prevention, relevant insurance, environmental health and population relocation are some of the urgent matters which dictate consensus and collaboration at the regional and international levels. At another level, the rapid industrialisation of an important Caribbean country, Trinidad and Tobago, provides a case study in the inherent risk for environmental disaster in a small country. Trinidad and Tobago is a hydrocarbon-based economy, and by 1999 it had become the major energy-based economy in the Caribbean. Its large new investments in heavy manufacturing activities include sugar refining, oil refining, the production of ammonia, methanol, urea, direct-reduced iron, steel, and cement. Trinidad and Tobago's developing industrialised economy is due primarily to its vast resources of relatively cheap natural gas. It is estimated that in the year 2000, there will be over 3,100 industrial establishments. The necessary associated environmental planning for industrialisation of this magnitude still lags. A lack of environmental consciousness and awareness in every stratum of society has resulted in a large majority of industries discharging unmonitored, untreated quantities of waste into the environment and the Caribbean Sea. In reality, Caribbean governments will need to overcome their ambivalence on environmental issues. Governments, in collaboration with the private sector, international donor agencies, and NGOs as advocates, must develop regional strategies and set up effective mechanisms and infrastructure to regulate and enforce appropriate laws.[27]

Finally, from a security perspective, the Caribbean can be described as the only region in the world with a relatively small population which harbours such a diversity of political, as well as administrative and institutional systems in a small geographical space. If local or regional imperatives for collaboration do not prevail, international and hemispheric circumstances will dictate other responses.

Multilateral intervention by the United States and United Nations forces in October 1994 to restore political freedoms in Haiti serves as an example of how the internal abuse of democracy and justice in one country can impact on, not only its own economic and entire developmental ethos, but on the stability and security of the region. The concerted and measured diplomatic and military response of CARICOM and other Caribbean nations to these events subsequently had an impact on both the hemispheric body (the OAS) and on the United Nations. The situation was sufficiently serious to solicit widespread international collaboration. But it was only as a 'regional' collective that the Caribbean could play its part in any significant way.

A new international role for Caribbean nations will take into account their participation in multilateral missions. Caribbean people have participated in election observer missions, and the region's police and defense forces have been involved in international monitoring and security missions. CARICOM countries, with their traditions of parliamentary democracy, and well-established professionalism in civil services and police and military forces, are well poised to play active roles as trainers and observers in the international promotion of democracy worldwide. Such roles are subject to the economic limitations placed on small states. But with financial support from the UN or the OAS, Caribbean nations could become more actively involved in addressing international problems. A multilateral Caribbean impact on the promotion and enhancement of good governance, democracy, human rights and justice in the region would seem to be a requisite for the twenty-first century.

The New Diplomacy

In the course of the twentieth century, diplomacy has undergone enormous changes. But the last decades of the century have borne witness to even more profound transformations. The diplomatic sanctuary of sovereignty, which protected countries against interference in their internal affairs by other states or international bodies, has begun to erode. Diplomatic activities often take place outside the traditional framework of conference rooms. Information technology and cyberspace are overcoming distance and facilitating continuous contact with all segments of a country's own diplomatic establishment as well as with international institutions. But at the same time the flow of communication over the Internet so far has largely defeated national, regional and even worldwide efforts to exercise sovereign control.

The major political factor influencing diplomacy is the relative decline of the role of national governments. Today governments face severe competition in diplomatic activities from other actors in civil society: private sectors, religious groups, immigrants, media, NGOs and other elements. They demand that their interests be taken into account and that they have some voice in the making of foreign policy. Similarly, legislative branches of countries are themselves contributing to this evolution in diplomacy. The parliamentarians of the world have set up a structure of global and international interaction and are claiming a role in diplomatic meetings, which was traditionally reserved for the executive arm of government. Individual countries, however big and powerful, can no longer handle global problems by themselves. They have to be tackled by the international community as a whole.

The media's involvement and influence on the public in international affairs has led to strong displays of public diplomacy. Public pressure groups or vested interests can influence governments to follow or abandon certain courses of action, often in disregard of international commitments or true national interests. In many instances, the appropriateness of external policies of the government is publicly questioned in the media.

Professional diplomacy itself is undergoing considerable change with respect to methodology and mechanisms. In several Caribbean countries, the need to maintain costly diplomatic missions and consular posts has been questioned, even though the element of personal diplomacy would be difficult to replace as a mechanism for bilateral relations. In the multilateral field fruitless ideological and political confrontations are giving way to cooperative interaction aimed at actually dealing with the problems at hand. Neither individual countries nor international institutions can afford the endless conferences and meetings of yesteryear. This has led to an increasingly informal approach to discussions, with few formal meetings. The preparatory role of international secretariats and the importance of interaction with them through permanent missions (or over the internet) is constantly growing, and it is now possible to expedite complex issues in less time.

NGOs, pressure-groups and lobbies of all kinds now surround bilateral as well as multilateral events and insist on being heard and consulted. External involvement in internal issues and conflicts also increasingly relies on specialised and also non-governmental institutions. The International Red Cross delegates and others in the humanitarian field are playing important roles as intermediaries and even negotiators in conflict resolution.

At the level of foreign ministries, new communications technology allows the diplomat to be in continuous contact with home base. Information technology also contributes to networking since all missions and posts abroad can constantly interact by having access to each other's files and to the databases of the foreign ministry and all other ministries, and government agencies which conduct or influence foreign policy both at preparatory and decision-making levels. Most administrative work, accounts and consular matters can be handled at home base. In the future such networks may well be extended to include the private sector and non-governmental bodies which have a stake in external relations. Similarly, networking could go beyond national establishments to include members of regional groups such as CARICOM, with resulting enhancement of their capacity and efficiency. Fortunately for small countries, international institutions are providing access to their libraries and documentation facilities available to member countries over the internet.

In the twenty-first century the new diplomacy will become even more important, and will evolve in ways that we cannot yet imagine. It is important for those involved in the study, teaching, and practice of diplomacy in small countries to fully exploit the potential provided by the new tools of diplomacy. The Caribbean must be a part of this momentum.

Conclusion: The Way Forward

The global economic environment is in a state of rapid transition. The new dispensation in both the developing and developed world is the opening up of national and regional economies to market forces. Profound transformations in the relations between state, civil society and economy are accompanying the process. In this vaguely Darwinian scenario, concepts of nationhood are being challenged by international integration, and national governments and politicians are hard pressed to demonstrate proper administrative capacity over this implicit surrender of sovereignty. The Caribbean countries have to cope with these new dynamics. There are no precise road maps, no easy solutions-only operational principles.

Integration into the global economy is the best route for Caribbean countries. Economic marginalisation would be a disaster. In addition, Caribbean countries have to turn their attention to forging economic development strategies that go well beyond the current global euphoria with liberalisation and privatisation. In undertaking this task, CARICOM countries in particular have an advantage in respect to human capital. High literacy rates and excellent records of primary and secondary school enrollment must now be bolstered by proper policies to raise educational quality in technologies, management and finance which are crucial ingredients for competition in the emerging global economy.

The challenges are complex but they all lead to eventual global interaction. Caribbean countries need to reposition their economies to take advantage of the transitions in the global economy. Preliminary studies suggest that many Caribbean countries could have a comparative advantage in the trade in services sector: primarily the provision of health care, biotechnology, tourism, education, finance, retirement and the information-processing industry. But they need to move quickly to develop niches and move beyond the stage of simply exporting manufactured goods. Services rather than the export of manufactured goods are increasing more rapidly as a component of international trade. This repositioning should not mean abandoning traditional sectors of the economy, such as manufacturing or agriculture. Rather it should include, if possible, the reform and strengthening of these sectors for global competitiveness.[28]

The public and private sectors in the Caribbean will have to work in tandem to secure capital, technology, and marketing through joint ventures and strategic corporate alliances. Similarly, every effort will have to be made to repatriate or engage the talent of Caribbean human resources in the diaspora. The forward-looking planners should already anticipate that the Caribbean's demography has expanded to include significant financial, intellectual and market sectors among Caribbean peoples in Florida, New York, Toronto, London and many other European and Latin American capitals.

If there are lessons to be learned from recent experience in Caribbean diplomacy, they are as follows. First, in the race to global liberalisation and free trade, the interests of the small states and smaller economies must be constantly and convincingly expressed. The Caribbean still has friends in Europe and the United States who understand the importance of establishing a special place in the world for small island states. Second, inter-European politics or EU-US negotiations will have a strong bearing on the Caribbean relationship with both regions and Caribbean states should be prepared to influence them accordingly. Third, the Caribbean must be proactive about future objectives and not simply try to defend the status quo or hold onto traditional and supposedly 'safe' diplomatic postures. Fourth, the Caribbean must approach its future relations with Europe and the Americas on the basis of an integrated *regional* strategy.

But there is also a diplomatic challenge for the twenty-first century. As one Caribbean scholar has suggested, the operating system for the diplomacy of Caribbean countries should be a policy of 'concentric diplomacy'. This is an operating system of diplomacy that seeks to provide the region with an effective strategy to reconcile its relationships with a number of economic and trading groups. At a practical level the real challenge faced by the strategy of 'concentric diplomacy' would be a consolidation of regional initiatives and the reconciliation of CARICOM obligations with new opportunities deriving from a series of concentric economic and trade linkages with the wider Caribbean, Latin America, the hemispheric system, the European Union, and ultimately the emerging global economic community. The pursuit of such diplomacy requires a creative partnership between government and private sector in the context of a liberalised economic system that relies on increased private sector dynamics and market forces. Government would provide the broad policy, regulatory and supportive framework.[29]

There is no reason why small states of the Caribbean cannot find ways to position themselves on the international stage and claim some of the diplomatic spotlight for themselves. The prerequisite for such 'niche diplomacy' would be a precise correlation of basic national and international interests. The active involvement of civil society, NGOs and public opinion would be important to ensure that a national or regional 'brand name' diplomacy will have intellectual substance, and political continuity from one political administration to another. Some precise areas for niche diplomacy for the Caribbean would be in the areas of tourism, the environment, ocean policy, energy diplomacy, financial services, regulatory diplomacy, and emphasis on a rules-based international order. These are areas in which Caribbean countries have a large stake. In 'niche diplomacy' a country's, or region's, foreign policy can be proactive, and occupy secure and influential places on the international scene, by emphasising national or regional distinctiveness and by concentrating limited resources on certain specific objectives.[30]

In sum, as this paper has tried to point out, there is a strong link between development concerns and security issues in international relations. Policies that enhance economic development show distributive justice, encourage the rule of law, protect fundamental human rights and foster the growth of democratic institutions are also items on the international relations agenda. Most importantly, the governments and people of the Caribbean have to devise new strategies to cope with a new international relations environment that demands proactive and hard reciprocal bargaining and a rejection of the siege mentality of the past.

Notes

1. For a detailed discussion of change and continuity in the architecture of Caribbean international relations, see Jorge Domingues, 'The Powers, the Pirates, and International Norms and Institutions in the American Mediterranean', in Joseph S Tulchin,

Andres Serbin and Rafael Hernandes, *Cuba and the Caribbean: Regional Issues and Trends in the Post-Cold war Era* (Washington, DC.: The Woodrow Wilson International Center for Scholars, 1998), pp. 3–19

2. See Andres Serbin, *Sunset Over the Islands: The Caribbean in an Age of Global and Regional Challenges* (New York: St Martin's Press, 1998); Georges A Fauriol and G. Philip Hughes, eds., *US -Caribbean Relations into the Twenty-first Century* (Washington, DC: CSIS Americas Program, 1995); Policy Paper on the Americas, Vol. VI, Study 4; Domíngues, Jorge, 'The Caribbean in A New International Context: Are Freedom and Peace a Threat to its Security?', in Anthony T Bryan, ed., *The Caribbean: New Dynamics in Trade and Political Economy* (New Brunswick, NJ: Transaction Publishers/ North South Centre, 1995); Anthony T Bryan, *The Caribbean: New Dimensions in Trade and Political Economy* (New Brunswick, NJ: Transactions Publishers/ North South Center, 1995); Anthony P Maingot, 'Trends in US-Caribbean Relations', *The Annals of the American Academy of Political and Social Science* Vol. 533 (May 1994); Hilbourne A. Watson, ed., *The Caribbean in the Global Political Economy* (Boulder and London: Lynne Rienner Publishers, 1994); H Michael Erisman, *Pursuing Post-dependency Politics: South- South Relations in the Caribbean* (Boulder and London: Lynne Rienner Publishers, 1992); Andrés Serbin and Anthony T Bryan, eds., 1991, *El Caribe Hacia el 2000* (Caracas: Editorial Nueva Sociedad, 1991).

3. On Cuba's regional relations, see Joseph S Tulchin, Andres Serbin and Rafael Hernandes, eds., *Cuba and the Caribbean: Regional Issues and Trends in the Post-Cold war Era* (Wilmington, Delaware: The Latin American Program at the Woodrow Wilson International Center for Scholars, 1997).

4. See Douglas W Payne, *Storm Watch: Democracy in the Western Hemisphere into the Next Century*, Policy Papers on the Americas Vol. IX, Study 3 (Washington, DC.: Center for Strategic and International Studies, 1993); and Patrick Emmanuel, *Governance and Democracy in the Commonwealth Caribbean: An Introduction* (Cave Hill, Barbados: Institute for Social and Economic Research, 1993).

5. See Ivelaw L Griffith and Betty N Sedoc-Dahlberg, eds., *Democracy and Human Rights in the Caribbean* (New York: Westview Press, 1997); and Trevor Munroe, 'Democracy and Drugs in the Caribbean: Some Policy Perspectives', MS paper presented at the Conference on International Narco-Trafficking on the Economy of Caribbean States (Institute of International Relations/ University of the West Indies, Trinidad, January 19–21, 1997).

6. For contemporary insights on the globalisation phenomenon, see the essays in Thomas Klak, ed., *Globalisation and Neoliberalism: The Caribbean Context* (Lanham, Boulder, New York, Oxford: Rowman & Littlefield Publishers, Inc. 1998); and Felipe Aguero and Jeffrey Stark, eds., *Fault Lines of Democracy in Post-Transition Latin America* (North South Center Press, University of Miami, 1998).

7. For discussions on the symbiosis between the Caribbean and Latin American schools of thought, see Anthony T Bryan, 'The CARICOM and Latin American Integration

Experiences: Observations on Theoretical Origins and Comparative Performance', in *Ten Years of CARICOM* (Washington, DC: Inter-American Development Bank, 1984), pp. 71-94; and Norman Girvan, 'The Development of Dependency Economics in the Caribbean and Latin America: Review and Comparison', in *Social and Economic Studies*, 1973, pp. 22.1.

8. A detailed discussion of the contributions of Caribbean scholars and practitioners to integration theory is found in Anthony T Bryan and Roget V Bryan, *The New Face of Regionalism in the Caribbean: The Western Hemisphere Dynamic*, North South Agenda Paper 35 (Coral Gables, Florida: North South Center at the University of Miami, 1999).

9. Suriname and Haiti are the only new members accepted in the recent history of the Community. The Bahamas was not one of the original members of CARICOM. It first had observer status and finally became a member of the Community in July 1983.

10. These institutions include the Caribbean Examinations Council (CXC), Caribbean Meteorological Organisation (CMO), Council of Legal Education, Caribbean Development bank (CDB), and the University of the West Indies.

11. For recent discussions of the small-state trading dilemma in the Caribbean, see Anthony T Bryan, 'Toward 2000: The Caribbean Confronts Changing Trends in International Trade', in *Caribbean Affairs* (1998), pp. 8.1; Richard L Bernal, 'The Integration of Small Economies in the Free Trade Area of the Americas', *Policy Papers on the Americas*, p. 9.1 (Washington, DC: Center for Strategic and International Studies, 1998); Henry S Gill, 'CARICOM and Hemispheric Trade Liberalisation', in *Integrating the Hemisphere: Perspectives from Latin America and the Caribbean*, eds. Ana Julia Jatar and Sidney Weintraub (Washington, DC: Inter-American Dialogue, 1997); Norman Girvan and Miguel Ceara Hatton, *CARICOM, Central America and the Free Trade Agreement of the Americas* (Kingston, Jamaica: Friedrich Ebert Stiftung, 1998); and Richard L Bernal, *Strategic Global Repositioning and Future Economic Development in Jamaica*, North-South Agenda Paper 18 (Coral Gables, Florida: North-South Centre at the University of Miami, 1996).

12. See *Time for Action: The Report of the West Indian Commission, 1992* (Black Rock, Barbados, 1992). The Report (592 printed pages) was the result of a three-year consultation with Commonwealth Caribbean people (including governments, the private sector, NGOs, and civil society in general) in the region, the United Kingdom, and North America.

13. Miguel Ceara Hatton, 'The Role of the Association of Caribbean States in Promoting Economic Integration within the Greater Caribbean', February 1998, ACS Secretariat, unpublished manuscript; and Henry S Gill, *The Association of Caribbean States: Prospects for a Quantum Leap?*, North-South Agenda Paper 11 (Coral Gables, Florida: North-South Centre at the University of Miami, 1995)

14. See Winston C Dookeran, 'Crosscurrents in Caribbean Policy Analysis', in *Choices and Change: Reflections on the Caribbean*, ed. Winston C Dookeran (Washington, DC:

The Inter-American Development Bank, 1996), p. 9. In the ACS trade context, Cuba poses a dilemma. It is a member of the ACS and has economic links with CARICOM countries. But it is *not* a member of the FTAA process and has been largely isolated from the hemispheric economic movement. For Cuba, the ACS represents the opportunity to break its regional isolation and to reincorporate itself into the hemispheric community. While the ACS as a body has welcomed the inclusion of Cuba, its inclusion raises some questions regarding the larger FTAA process, especially with the United States.

15. See 'Factors Affecting the Participation of Caribbean Countries in the Free Trade Area of the Americas', 1995, LC/CAR/G.459 (Port of Spain, Trinidad: UN/ECLAC Sub-regional Office).
16. The RNM consists of CARICOM members and the Dominican Republic. The latter and CARICOM will negotiate with the EU on a post-Lomé agreement as part of CARIFORUM. However, the Dominican Republic will *not* be part of the RNM for the FTAA negotiations. It has elected to be part of the Central American group for those negotiations. There is also some indication that the Central American countries are hoping to negotiate an FTA with the United States in anticipation of the FTAA.
17. For a detailed history of the banana issue see Paul Sutton, 'The Banana Regime of the European Union, the Caribbean, and Latin America', *Journal of Interamerican Studies and World Affairs*, 39, 2 (1997), pp. 5–36.
18. Ceara-Hatton (1998), p. 30. See also Miguel Ceara-Hatton (1998) *'Hacia la integración del gran caribe: Una respuesta a la globalisación'*, unpublished manuscript.
19. This dynamic between globalisation and corporate integration is analysed by Richard L Bernal, *Trade Blocs: A Regionally Specific Phenomenon or a Global Trend?*, National Policy Association Report No. 287 (Washington, D.C.: National Policy Association, 1997).
20. See Anthony T Bryan, J Edward Greene and Timothy M. Shaw, eds., *Peace, Development and Security in the Caribbean* (London: Macmillan, 1990); Colin Clarke and Anthony Payne, eds., *Politics, Security and Development in Small States* (London: Allen and Unwin, 1987); Humberto Garcia-Muñiz, *Boots, Boots, Boots: Intervention, Regional Security and Militarisation in the Eastern Caribbean* (Rio Piedras, Puerto Rico: University of Puerto Rico, 1986); Sheila Harden, ed., *Small is Dangerous: Micro-States in a Macro World* (New York: St Martins, 1985); Commonwealth Secretariat, *Vulnerability: Small States in the Global Society* (London, 1985). For a review of the scholarship see Ivelaw L Griffith, 'Caribbean Security: Retrospect and Prospect', *Latin American Research Review*, Vol. 30, No. 2 (1995), pp. 3–32.
21. Commonwealth Secretariat, *Vulnerability: Small States*, p. 23 and pp. 112–113.
22. See Anthony P Maingot, 'Bucking the Trend: Offshore Secrecy Centres and the Role of Government', *CARICOM PERSPECTIVES*, Issue No: 66 (June 1996). pp. 32–37.
23. For a discussion of the OECD measures see Bruce Sagaris, 'OECD Report on Harmful Tax Competition: Strategic Implications for Caribbean Offshore Jurisdictions', Tax

Notes International (November 1998). On money laundering counter-measures see Ivelaw L Griffith, 'The Money Laundering Dilemma in the Caribbean', *Cuaderno de Trabajo*, No. 4 septiembre de 1995 (Rio Piedras, Puerto Rico: Institute of Caribbean Studies).

24. The scope of the drug-trafficking trade in the Caribbean is discussed in the following: Ivelaw Lloyd Griffith *Drugs and Security in the Caribbean: Sovereignty Under Siege* (University Park: Pennsylvania State University Press, 1997); David A Andelman, 'The Economics of the Drug Trade', *US/Latin Trade: The Magasine of Trade and Investment in the Americas*, Vol. 3, No: 9 (September 1995), pp. 42–49; Cathy Booth, 'Caribbean Blizzard', *Time*, February 26, 1996; Klaus de Albuquerque, 'Drugs in the Caribbean: A Five Part Series', *Caribbean Week* (Barbados), various issues January–March, 1996.

25. See Ivelaw L Griffith and Trevor Munroe, 'Drugs and Democracy in the Caribbean', *The Journal of Commonwealth and Comparative Politics*, Vol. XXXIII, No. 3 (November 1995), pp. 357–376.

26. On the various dimension of this topic see Max J Castro, ed., *Free Markets, Open Societies, Closed Borders? Trends in International Migration and Immigration Policies in the Americas* (Coral Gables, Florida: North South Center Press at the University of Miami, 1999).

27. See Erik Blommestein, Barbara Boland, Trevor Harker, Swinburne Lestrade, and Judith Towle, 'Sustainable Development and Small Island States of the Caribbean', in George A Maul, ed., *Small Islands: Marine Science and Sustainable Development* (Washington, DC: American Geophysical Union, 1996).

28. World Bank, 'Caribbean Region: Coping with Changes in the External Environment', LAC 1281, April 1994.

29. See Denis Benn, 'Global and Regional Trends: Impact on Caribbean Development', in *Caribbean Public Policy: Regional, Cultural, and Socioeconomic Issues for the Twenty-first Century*, eds. Jacqueline Anne Braveboy-Wagner and Dennis J Gayle (Boulder, Colorado: Westview Press, 1997), pp. 15–25.

30. On niche diplomacy see Alan K Henrikson, 'Diplomacy and Small States in Today's World', The Dr Eric Williams Memorial Lecture Series, 12th Lecture, Central Bank of Trinidad and Tobago, 1998; and Andrew F Cooper, ed., *Niche Diplomacy: Middle Powers After the Cold war* (London: Macmillan Press, Ltd., 1997).

29 | HILBOURNE A WATSON

Global Neo-liberalism, The Third Technological Revolution, and Global 2000:
A Perspective on Issues Affecting the Caribbean on the Eve of the Twenty-first Century

The Caribbean moves into the twenty-first century in a world caught in the cauldron of new forms of violence, much of which is the violence conditioned by the political economy of the property relations of global capitalism. Capitalist property, property rights and social relations transgress the disciplinary boundaries in the social sciences. Capitalist property and property rights are 'like a seed that germinates in each discipline and spreads roots in all of them connecting them' in such a way that 'property rights *and the forms of violence associated therewith* neatly frame the relations between the state system and global capitalism' (Burch 1998: 8, 15, the italics are mine). Capitalist property relations frame the context for this project.

I will develop several arguments with the centrality of property in the means of production and property rights and relations in mind.[1] First, under globalisation, which I see as capitalism in the age of electronics, neo-liberalism is a subsidiary within capitalist restructuring, but capitalism is the central issue. Second, national states and sovereign autonomy are best conceived as expressions of particular capitalist social relations of production. Third, technology and money as capital converge in particular relationships to class power in the world, for example, in reconfiguring the monopoly power held by the West in five key areas (see Amin 1997). Fourth, the techno-industrial and biotechnological transitions (around nanotechnology) in the revolution in science and technology are transforming the nature and character of work, intensifying human dumping and aggravating the decomposition of national societies. Fifth, the dominant institutions such as the World Trade Organisation (WTO), the International Monetary Fund (IMF), the World Bank, and key agencies of the US state function as surrogates for a global state and ruling class. Their strategy is to try to usher in the 'autocracy of private capital' as part of the plan for running the world like a market. Lastly, crushing the insubordination of labour and disarming the working classes around the world is an integral part of the strategy for ushering in capital's autocracy. Monetarist policies are central to the strategy for crushing the insubordination of labour, which is not a foregone conclusion.

I do not see neo-liberalism as a problem-solving strategy for resolving the current crisis[2] around the dominance of money in the global accumulation process. Rather, neo-liberalism involves a set of crisis-management mechanisms, which reflect the economic and political dominance of money as capital in the global market economy. In setting about to run the world like a market, neo-liberals have been trying to convince the world that capital and the market have a natural right to define the interests and direct the lives of global humanity. In reality, the market economy is a political space that requires specific politics for money to assert its brazenness as the abstract form of the social power of capital, the dominant form of power relations and the abstract identity of labour in global capitalism (Bonefeld and Holloway 1995: 2).[3] As matters stand, 'short term transitional measures are already taking on the characteristics of a highly volatile permanent emergency' (Marazzi 1995: 78; Amin 1997; Cummings 1998: 72).

Procedurally, I challenge methodological individualism: I treat the inside and outside of national states as a co-constituting and constituted complex totality. There are no rigid boundaries between the national and international spheres. I do not separate national states (political autonomy) from the international system (capital accumulation). National states are already in the international system, so much so that they do not have the liberty to be outside the system. Mainstream approaches to international relations and international political economy treat human nature and the nature of the world as inherently selfish, aggressive, competitive and given to primordial anarchical tendencies. Such academic and policy prejudices privilege the sovereignty of violence, which aids and abets the projects of big power chauvinism.

I start with the social construction of nature and argue that the human history of nature is the space-time context of human conscious action, for the production of power in history is a function of human agency. I review the cold war project to support my contention about the role of power in history. I argue that the United Nations model of sovereign autonomy took shape within the cold war project, which deepened the separation between the political autonomy of national states and the global process of capital accumulation. Then I discuss capitalist property and property relations – the basis of the modern international system – in order to clarify the nature of the state and its embedment in the social relations of production. I see states as 'differentiated forms of capitalist social relations', and I argue that states use sovereignty foremost to mediate complex capitalist property relations.

My discussion of global neo-liberalism covers key changes in the configuration of national states and capital accumulation under the dominance of money as capital, an argument that unfolds around a discussion of glocalisation and globalisation. Then I focus on the 'new agendas' of the World Bank, the IMF and the Organisation for Economic Cooperation and Development (OECD) for inaugurating the 'autocracy of private capital' to run the world like a market. Mindful of the role of United States imperialism[3] in the post-Soviet era, I discuss the restructuring of the US national security strategy, generally, and with reference to the Organisation of American States Resolution 1080 of 1991, which I see as part of a broader strategy for redefining collective security in the western hemisphere in the era of post-Keynesian militarism. Then I discuss the transition from silicon-based microchip technology to nanotechnology and the restructuring the techno-industrial information base of the market economy. This analysis facilitates the transition into my discussion of 'global 2000' and some of the myriad contradictions and civilisation shifts world labour and culture will encounter in the coming decades.

Finally, I discuss two cases of Jamaica and Cuba, asking questions about the impact of monetarisation and the heterogeneous division of labour in the western hemisphere on Jamaica's prospects for becoming what Bernal (1996) calls a 'western hemisphere technopole'. For Cuba, I examine the implications of monetarisation and convergence for socialist power. I draw out a number of conclusions from the analysis to inform recommendations, which Caribbean states might consider.

The Social Construction of Nature, Power, Markets and Capital Accumulation

Klaus Eder (1996) revisits the Enlightenment representations of the relationship between nature, history, culture and reason through the concept of the 'human history of nature' to inform his thesis on 'the social construction of nature'. Eder argues that the real history of nature is the 'human history of nature' and stresses that nature, culture, reason, the economy and the market are social constructs. He questions the assertion that the market is an extension of the development of pure reason that miraculously informs the pursuit of individual self-interest. The nature and role of power in the production of history (Trouillot 1995) confirms that given structures of power and accumulation are not natural. Politics and power guide the hand of property and markets. The fundamental capitalist process is inherently contradictory, a fact which confirms that 'anarchy is the characteristic social form of capitalist modernity'. (Rosenberg 1994: 125.)

Eder notes that "modern myths of creation describe a more or less fictitious transition from the state of nature to society, which becomes possible by a contract concluded among the participants . . ." (1996: 96). In the liberal imaginary science, reason, law, technology, money, production and private capital accumulation constitute a unity of sorts, from which human labour and labour power are externalised and submerged in the tracks of the market and price value! The Protestant spirit and the Protestant work ethic also normalise exploitation and private accumulation by making them into extensions of a timeless nature located beyond history, politics and power, and anchoring them in a psychology of egotism and asceticism. The rationalisation lies in a rhetoric of an 'other-worldly deferred gratification', which negates "the realistic recognition of the necessary conditions of survival . . . and . . . the right to subsistence for all . . ." (Mies 1997: 17).

As ideology, neo-liberalism rationalises the business of equating civil society with competition (market) subjects. Neo-liberals insist that the transfer of resources from the state to private hands empowers private interests over the state and creates a stronger civil society and a healthier democratic ethos. This notion that privatisation and democracy go hand in hand, encourages the transfer of assets from the public space to the private arenas to the benefit of mostly corporate privilege (Derlugian 1996: 163). The neo-liberal strategy is to shift the machinery of control upward and outward to the global level, with corporate forces and multilateral institutions playing a seemingly more impersonal role beyond popular accountability. National states and many civil institutions are deeply implicated in facilitating the upward and outward shift, for as Polanyi observed, 'free markets could never have come into being merely by allowing things to take their course laissez faire itself was enforced by the state' (Polanyi 1944 quoted in Overbeek 1995: 216). Substantively, the market is a complex site of conflict and struggle where power guides the hand of production, distribution, surplus value extraction and capital accumulation to mediate the subordination of labour.

Therefore, the boundaries of personal freedom, market freedom and social freedom are not coterminous: money as capital does not engender 'freedom in general', for money at once expresses the social power of capital and the abstract identity of labour, and together with law, money conditions the social nature of freedom in bourgeois society (see Giarini 1995: 99). Under the capitalist division of labour the majority of workers worldwide reproduce themselves as cheap unskilled and semi-skilled labour to produce a variety of cheap commodities for export. Global capital accumulation necessitates such a division of labour under which the workers and peasants in the neocolonial zones produce but do not consume much of their protein which they export 'to Europe in the form of animal feed to produce milk seas, butter mountains, etc.' (Mies 1997: 17). Neoclassical economists call it comparative advantage – a rational response to market forces – but create the impression of removing morality from market capitalism. In fact, the moral economy of capitalism has to invent a false dichotomy between human history and nature to help normalise poverty, which is the condition for capital accumulation. In fact, seeds of moral scruple have no room to blossom in the heavy underbrush of the free market (Lapham 1998: 24–25)

The Newtonian-Cartesian synthesis met the ideological needs of the evolving capitalist market economy and society partly by engendering methodological individualism, which come to life through the separation of the individual from society; the state from economy, society, and the market; and the knowing subject from subjectivity. The separation of coercion from the economic sphere and the relocation of coercion in the politico-juridical sphere are integral parts of the process (Tilly 1990: 54-55). With capitalism and the Enlightenment morality was retired to the 'private' sphere of the feminine 'moral gender' for certain women to patrol the boundaries of appropriate moral conduct, outside the male-dominated 'rational' sphere of the state, politics, market, and private capital accumulation. The new state emerged as the reconstructed 'total patriarch' and the bourgeoisie as the new ruling class, which has a way of appearing to leave its class identity at home, so to speak.

The capitalist commodification of labour power has been a violent process in which 'the autonomy of women's bodies, their productive capacity to maintain life through work, their sexuality, and procreation' (Mies 1997: 18) have been further compromised. One site of 'capital accumulation (has taken place) at the level of women's bodies on a global scale, from household reproduction to export manufacturing and the tourism and sex industries' (Cabezas 1998: 86). Historically, violence has been built into the sexual division of labour and its corollary, the 'breadwinner-housewife-model'. State control over women's sexuality and fertility has been constructed on a foundation of violence (Tilly 1990: 50). Religion is pertinent here, considering that all the world's major religious structures have been built on assumptions about and attitudes towards women that are not in fact compatible with the demand for the full equality of women . . . because all the world's religious institutions have been centrally concerned with the control of sexuality . . . (Walerstein 1996: 242). The control of female sexuality is tied to broader issues like the control of women's bodies, reproduction, resources, the separation of so-called domestic household work from the market economy, and the labour process. In neoclassical economics commodity value is determined by price and the interdependence between market price and non-market determined economic processes is a function of capital accumulation priorities, which condition the production of the power relations and truth regimes about what constitutes productive and nonproductive work. (Waring 1997: 31, 36)[4]

Neo-liberals want to intensify this process, partly by making all states more independent of popular pressures for democratic accountability and social welfare that are implied in the United Nations Universal Declaration of Human Rights (UNUDHR) (Clarke and Barlow 1997). Article 55 of the UN Charter linked the creation of conditions of stability and well-being which is necessary for peaceful and friendly relations among nations, based on respect for the principles of equal rights and self-determination of peoples to the promotion of higher standards of living, full employment, and conditions of economic and social progress and development.

The UN historic pledge of commitment could not be sustained under capitalism and so it has been undermined to the point where neo-liberal politicians, businessmen and some labour groups now ridicule full employment strategies 'as a leftover from an era of statism or the welfare states' (Simai 1995: 240; Cox 1992: 145) The construction of liberal democracy has rested largely on the subordination of labour to capital. It is inevitable that the primary protective functions of Caribbean security forces[5] will revolve around protecting the lives, property and other interests of transnational capitalist forces.

The capitalist strata in the G7 countries control or monopolise five key areas of resources, namely science, technology, finance, raw materials and their substitutes, and weapons of mass destruction (Amin 1997). The near monopoly over the production of weapons of mass destruction cradles the system of private capital accumulation and protects the system of capitalist private property rights around the world. The global majority lives under the political blackmail of a global minority to produce for export to feed capital accumulation. In contrast, the bulk of those who produce exchange value have to struggle to obtain basic food, water, shelter, clothing, sanitation, medicine and protection. Poverty and inequality are the condition of capital accumulation.[6] The cold war project reorganised the conditions for the normalisation of poverty in the world (see Landau 1988: 33).

The Cold War Project: Restructuring National States and the Global Economy

The postwar world order rested on the pillars of the cold war project, neo-Fordism, military-industrial Keynesianism, Sovietism, and modernisation in the third world (Amin 1997). Those pillars supported the 'institutional vectors' of the interstate system, world production, the world labour force, world human welfare, the social cohesion of states, and the structures of knowledge (see Hopkins and Wallerstein et al 1996). In part, the post-1960s transition of the postwar world order has been marked by the erosion of United States hegemony, the acceleration of the third technological revolution (TTR), the disintegration of the 'Bandung Project' of nonalignment, the rise of neo-liberalism to spearhead global restructuring under the aegis of money, the triadic restructuring of hegemony, and the transition to post-Keynesian militarism. The restructuring of the cold war has coincided in some ways with the collapse of the Soviet Union.

The cold war project was a key component in the restructuring of the postwar capitalist world-system. I am sympathetic to Robert Cox's contention that the cold war Project 'has not ended', considering that the 'structures of cold war power continue to exist in the West . . . Manichean mental frameworks preserve the cold war form while searching for new content' (1996: 34). Much of the cold war scaffolding and architecture of anti-working class strategies remain in place around militarism, national security, capitalist dominance, anti-Communism, and third world subordination. Hence my argument that the cold war project is being restructured as opposed to having ended: at no point was the cold war delimited by east-west military or ideological competition. Rather, the east-west conflict was one part of the cold war project.

Ideological assertions about the end of history, the ascendancy of 'geoeconomics' over geopolitics and the idea that there is no alternative to capitalism are matters of faith not fact. Social democracy and Keynesianism assumed that national 'planned development' was compatible with the requirements of capital accumulation on a world scale, but the global market economy is not reducible to an assemblage of autonomous national economies. National states are particular forms of global capitalist relations, and the main functions of sovereignty include processing and mediating capitalist property relations, protecting private property and facilitating the expansion of the global bases for reproducing capital and expanding capitalism. The political power base of national states does not correspond to a definitive economic space called an autonomous national economy, nor are national states equally equipped with the economic, political, financial, technological, coercive and other means to process the social relations of capitalism. It is more useful to speak of forms or types of national states than to assume there is one form of state in the interstate system.

National States, Sovereign Autonomy and Property Relations

The state may represent itself as sovereign and as the guardian of the general interest of society; this is largely an illusion. Though it may exercise power and subdue both groups and individuals to its will, the state in the context of a capitalist society expresses the will of private property as the highest political and moral reality. The sovereign state is in one sense the 'official expression of civil society', yet it reflects the unhampered development of bourgeois society, or the free movement of private interests... (Camilleri 1990: 19)

Sovereign autonomy speaks to class ruled states within the system of global capitalism. Camilleri's account takes the matter of the nature of the state beyond functionalist representations of the state's roles in domestic and international affairs, in relation to sovereign autonomy. In liberal ideology the dominant forms of private interests are individualised and pulverised, particularly the capitalist forces. Liberalism creates a false dichotomy between dialectically interconnected structure and agency. The liberal habit of reducing members of civil society to market-defined competition subjects produces the effect of privileging capitalist class interests and equating private property in the means of production with the general interests of society. Capitalist private property becomes the foundation of the highest form of personal freedom, individual rights and democracy. Liberalism builds a 'world of walls around civil society, which it holds together through the medium of democratic repressive tolerance. But civil society is an expression of dense, congealed complexities of social relations that are masked in the fog of the market.

Liberals mask the state's 'role as protector of the socially and economically dominant class' (Camilleri 1990: 19) in its legal political independence. But to understand the social and political nature of the modern state it is necessary to locate the state and sovereignty deep within capitalist property relations. The fact is that the modern national state is a particular form of bourgeois property relations, in terms of fixed (territorial) property and mobile property that have conditioned the making of the modern international system (Burch 1998; Holloway 1995; Rosenberg 1994)

The explicitly military, political and administrative functions of the state reflect its coercive monopolisation and normalisation of those specialisations in the social division of labour. The concept of the 'autonomous' state refers to the political independence or separation of the state in law, but cannot remove the state from the social relations of production. The state and the so-called 'non-political' civil society of 'sovereign subjects' are structurally interdependent. The state emerges from society, rises above society, dominates society and feeds off of society. Liberal ideology meanders through the crevices of logical positivism and structural-functionalism, along the way fetishising the separation of the unsegmentable and genuflecting to the reflection of that rather 'crude form of Anglo-Saxon idolatry' the free market (Lapham 1998: 32).

Civil society does not and cannot exist outside the social relations of which it is an integral part. It comes already as contradictory class society that is held together by the state. More concretely, civil society, the state, and capital are linked as integral parts of the social relations of production, which the state mediates. As class society civil society is political society! The relationship between the state and civil society is marked by differentiation within the dialectical whole of the political sphere (Rosenberg 1994: 88) rather than by absolute separation. In the reduction of society to competition (market) subjects of rational calculus the link between money and labour would appear to be eliminated (Bonefeld 1995a: 203). Another way this link can appear to be broken is through the alienation of philosophy and the production of an academic cacophony that equates private accumulation with national purpose. But the fact is that the sociality of labour is based on the historical concept that the socialisation of individuals takes place through work, which makes labour indispensable for socialisation. Bourgeois society socialises labour through work, not for the socialisation of civil society as such, but for its marketisation to facilitate private accumulation of capital. This is at once the most transparent and opaque manifestation of capitalism.

Ideologically, national purpose can be used to package projects of capital accumulation with power buried in the tracks of purpose, but without capital ever losing its central position within the project itself (Trouillot 1995: 128). Citizenship, democracy and virtue are derived through private property, as private property is the moral/civic principle for the good life, in relation to political participation.[7] Inequality underscores the significance of private property, and property rights have grounded 'authority and justice'. Property structures individuals, rights, and social relations. This, then, is the *sine qua non* for getting to civil society (Burch 1998: 27–28) as class society.

The state created the national public and shaped it into a national entity around the state's collective identity. The modern state also invented the nation's traditions on populist axes that cut across class, gender, race, and ethnicity. National holidays, flags, anthems, monuments, war memorials, parades, exhibitions, and other creations make national distinctiveness into an invented tradition that is used to differentiate a given nation from all others. Precisely when the production of power is most closely associated with the production of the nation, its honor, identity and purpose, power and class seem most distant, almost invisible (Trouillot 1995: 124, 127).

Substantively, the state possesses a dual collective identity in relation to civil society, standing as 'separation-in-unity' and 'unity-in-separation' (Reuten and Williams 1989). In the first instance, the state is the sovereign body standing above all else; in the second instance the state mirrors the collective national personality of aggregated (but individualised) sovereign subjects. In liberal ideology the primacy of each isolated subject is never transcended by any collective social identity. Marx's account of the nature and process of economistic alienation under capitalism traces, registers, and isolates the 'inner connections' of phenomena to mark the defining moment of his dialectical methodology. In Marx's materialist methodology externality and structure are 'replaced by dialectical categories of process and contradictory internal relationships' (Burnham 1995: 96).

Rosenberg argues, using Marx, that the "establishment of the political state and the dissolution of civil society into independent individuals – whose relations with one another depend on law, just as the relations of men in the system of estates and guilds depended on privilege – is accompanied by one and the same act (1994: 69) Marx analysed the concrete ways in which surplus labour is pumped out of the labouring population under capitalism. He stressed that the separation of coercion from the economic instance (economy) and its relocation within the state (political instance) simultaneously reveals and masks the concrete forms of institutionalised political subjection, which is determined by the structure of social, economic, and political privilege and domination (Marx [1894], 1981: 927, see Burnham 1995: 97).

At best, liberal pluralism hides subjection and appropriation behind the backs of the 'sovereign' subjects who miraculously inhabit states with a pristine democratic nature, after the fashion of Montesquieu (see Manent 1994), states that are somehow not disposed to sacrifice the sovereign subjecthood of citizens. Such a belief borders on faith not fact! In reality, liberalism invents an inhospitable environment that is fit only for 'subjects without subjectivity'. Castoriadis defends the social nature of individuals and their individuality in the following terms:

the social side of the social fabrication of the individual concerns the whole complex of institutions in which the human being is steeped as soon as it is born and, socialised in a determinate manner. The effective validity of the institutions is thus ensured first and foremost, by the process, which makes a social individual out of the screaming little monster. The latter can only become an individual if it internalises the institutions of society (1991: 148, 149)

The formal separation of economics from politics is the model that gave us state autonomy, and state autonomy informs the formal separation of coercion from the economy, the site where the subjection of the direct producer is canceled in logic and law, but not in fact. In reality, subjection is at once restructured and reconfigured in the 'structured inequality of the labour contract within the privatised realm of production where it is maintained via the direct material dependence of a free (propertyless) and untied labour force' (Rosenberg 1994: 84).

Under capitalism and the bourgeois revolution(s) the model of universal freedom – the abstract universality – gave certain men the freedom to transform might into right and right into law. This laid the basis for normalising the coercive and political means to command and transform the existing means of production into capital and to appropriate the surplus labour of direct producers. The state is structurally embedded in the global social relations of production; as such the state's coordinates are at once national and global. As the 'mode of existence of class relations' the nature of the form of the state changes. Therefore, neither the state nor class relations turn out to be fixed entities. Fluidity is a feature of the state-class process. The state is not a fixed object: it is the relations of domination of this fluid order of class relations that the state protects. The world order is grounded in the domination of labour, which is indispensable for the reproduction of the capitalist world (Burnham 1995: 95, 98). This can be seen in the changing relationship between states and their cities and regions around capital accumulation.

Contesting Neo-liberal Ideology: The Dialectic of Globalisation and Glocalisation

By the late 1960s and into the early 1970s the pillars of the postwar hegemonic order had begun to disintegrate.[8] We cannot hope to comprehend 'geopolitical systems and processes until their analysis is integrated into that of the wider social structures which constitute them' (Rosenberg 1994: 93). In order to grasp the dynamic process of restructuring it is necessary to pay close attention to all aspects of the spatial relations between states, regions, cities and social classes. Just about all of the room that was left for national planned development under military Keynesianism has been exhausted to the degree that much 'that was hidden from view by the welfare state capitalism of the postwar period has ... become obvious: principally, the power of money and ... the inherently global nature of power relations' (Bonefeld and Holloway 1995: 2).

According to Brenner,

"Since the 1970s ... state-centric geography has been profoundly reconfigured as a direct outgrowth of the global crisis of Fordist-Keynesian development model. The crisis of Fordism was expressed in a specifically geographical form, above all in the contradiction between the national scale of state regulation and the globalising thrust of postwar capital accumulation. The scales on which the Fordist-Keynesian socio-spatial order was organised – national regulation of the wage relation; international regulation of currency and trade – have been radically reconfigured ..."

By extension,

" ... the deregulation of financial markets and the global credit system since the collapse of the Bretton Woods system undermined the viability of state-level demand management and monetary policies, the increasing globalisation of production, competition and financial flows has diminished the ability of territorial states to insulate themselves from the world economy. The intensification of global interspatial competition among cities and regions has also compromised national industrial policies and forced regional and local states to assume increasingly direct roles in promoting capital accumulation on sub-national scales' (1998: 14; see Burnham 1995: 110).

Ankie Hoogvelt explores the impact of information technology and the intensification of money flows upon states and national decomposition:

The speed with which money can move across national borders removes the need to anchor it firmly in (national social relationships). Globalisation makes national solidarity (as expressed in transfer payments to the old, sick, the unemployed and the lower income groups) dysfunctional. This process is being sharpened by recent deregulation in the core countries which encourages the globalisation of small private investors and undercuts the last remaining vestiges of national social solidarity. (1997: 130)

Brenner argues that the 'denationalisation of the most elemental territorial building bloc of the postwar geoeconomic and geopolitical order – the ... national economy' has been the main 'geographical consequence of these deeply intertwined politico-economic shifts' (1998: 14). The new information technology strengthens the connections in the arteries of real production and trade, and squeezes workers and peasants all over the world for their last drop of surplus in a manner that makes invisible . . . the innumerable threads that lead to the pension funds, the share prices and the bank accounts in the core of the world system. (Hoogvelt 1997: 68)

Global city-formation points to a re-scaling of states and territory from the inside-out and from the outside-in, leading to the glocalisation of territorial states in relation to the intensification of capital accumulation. Glocalisation highlights the rearticulation of the state's political and territorial base, while globalisation depicts the shift in the capital accumulation processes. The TTR, which expresses capital's quest to conquer space by time, also intensifies the growing 'territorial non-coincidence' and 'scalar disjuncture' of interconnected global and local processes. Global cities are key centres of capital deployment and accumulation and they play a critical role in the re-scaling of the institutional power base of states and the socioeconomic role states play in the restructuring process. The 'place-based and territorial preconditions for accelerated capital circulation are being constructed on multiple spatial scales' (Brenner 1998: 3). As pivot points for attracting capital, global cities dramatise the discontinuity and the profound socio-political and cultural contradictions within national states. Money as capital has become the primary bearer of power relations, 'as the very stuff of conflict' (Bonefeld and Holloway 1995: 3).

Brenner's interpretation provides a better sense of how neo-liberal restructuring has 'compromised national industrial policies and forced regional and local states to assume increasingly direct roles in promoting capital accumulation on sub-national scales' with cross-border linkages (see also Tabak 1996: 115). His argument also highlights the intensification of the international socialisation of production, which is a matter of space-time compression. In Latin America, for example, financial liberalisation and structural adjustment policies accelerate the net transfer of resources to the US and contribute to the emergence of 'a new class of Latin billionaires who increasingly dominate politics and the economy and are major partners with US banks and multinationals.' The integration of the top echelons of the bourgeoisie into global capital contrasts with 'the growth of an impoverished labour force faced with declining state social expenditures, chronically low paid employment, and landless peasants deprived of influence in politics and economy.' (Veltmeyer, Petras and Vieux 1997: 121–22)

In the age of electronics there is a deepening of the transnational character of production, the widening of the scope of the world market, and the intensification of heterogeneity and disparity in the cost and remuneration of labour power. The neo-liberal strategy applies pressure from the outside via institutions like the IMF and from the inside by rolling back the economic and social borders of the state. Neo-liberals promote free production and trade zones across the global economy and support the liberalisation of the tax laws and foreign investment rules of all states (Clarke and Barlow 1997). Their idea for lean government rests on lowering the tax burden for capital, while circumscribing civil liberties, human rights, and the power of trade unions and expanding the coercive power of the state (Teeple 1995: 75–127).

Many states have adopted or expanded a number of indirect taxes like sales, lottery, consumption, social security, gambling, and value-added taxes (VATs), in conjunction with the rolling back of the economic and social borders of the state, in the process further lowering the standard of living of workers and peasants. By the end of 1996, about 23 Latin American and Caribbean states had adopted VAT (IDB 1997: 25). With respect to the national debt, state 'indebtedness contains much of the secret of capital's control over the state, as creditor over debtor' (Teeple 1995: 99; Tilly 1990: 86). In pursuit of the autocracy of private capital, neo-liberals favor lean governments and weak civil society to undermine the historical insubordination of labour and strengthen the exercise of political power by capital through the market.

New World Bank, IMF, the OECD's 'New Constitutionalism' and Neo-liberal Market Democracy: Mechanisms for Running the World Like a Market

The World Bank and the IMF have designed a more invasive strategy to impose market discipline of the masses of workers and peasants around the globe and to lock in new rules of corporate privilege. The New World Bank[9] is supervising the cultivation of neo-liberal states that are

> ... crucial to the reproduction and institutionalisation of a particular form of global market order. Such a form of state is needed ... to institutionalise market forces, support economic liberalisation, promote public-private partnerships in service provision, enforce contracts and prevent corruption. The World Bank sees the context for such changes as a world-wide market revolution that creates new obligations for the state. (Gill 1998: 9)

The World Bank's approach stresses both 'coercive and consensual' mechanisms that emphasise 'a more formally democratic world order in which the pressure for recognition and representation is significant . . .' The Bank also advocates a 'hierarchical system of representation in which the key economic and strategic areas of policy are separated from democratic participation and accountability'. Actually, the Bank is working to offset 'limitations imposed by mass democracy in the economic realm by restricting democratic participation to safely channeled areas.' (Gill 1998: 4)

The Bank's SAPs, the IMF's conditionalities, and the WTO's authority – as reflected in the new rules for Trade-Related Intellectual Property (TRIPS), Trade-Related Investment Measures (TRIMS), the General Agreement on Trade-in-Services[10] (GATS) – and the MAI proposals strengthen the legal and juridical basis of capitalist property rights on a global scale (Watson 1998b). The TTR expands the technical basis for strengthening the WTO's authority and the power of corporate capital, partly through the medium of intellectual property rights. The strategy is to broaden and intensify the foundations of capitalist property, property rights, rules, regulations, institutions, and property income.

Gill uses the concept of the 'new constitutionalism' to refer to a set of arrangements and a process through which OECD states and multilateral institutions like the Bank and the IMF have been locking in new rules, policies and arrangements under G7 mandates for restructuring the market economy. The objective is to strengthen investor confidence in the public policies of national states. Investors demand sound macroeconomic policies built on the protection of private property rights and free mobility of capital. They insist on state policies to promote low taxes and price stability to rein in inflation. The challenge to the state is in how to guarantee investor privilege and confidence in a 'democratic' culture where political realignments and governments change over time (Gill 1998). The key tactic has been to accelerate the integration of key aspects of national public policies into the global movement of capital, a process that aggravates the decomposition and restructuring of national states and their societies.

Politically, the 'new constitutionalism' means the ongoing subordination of liberal democracy and public policy in the interest of investors. As key aspects of public policies become more integrated into the global movement of capital the investor becomes more and more like the sovereign political subject of the market. Investors are demanding the most favorable investment climate – low taxes, low inflation, financial liberalisation, abandonment of capital and exchange controls, reduction of tariff rates, transparency of the budgetary process, abandonment of full employment as a public policy mandate, insulation of finance ministries and central banks from political determination, and constitutionally binding provisions – to make it illegal for states to succumb to popular demands for controls on capital (Gill 1998).

The new constitutionalism is about broadening the power of the market via the abstract power of money. Working from Burnham's thesis that 'national states are best theorised as differentiated forms of global capitalist relations' (1995: 103-04, 105), it follows that globalisation does not mean the disappearance of states. States already have different capabilities and capacities as 'differentiated forms of global capitalist relations'. In the neo-liberal dispensation, states are more active in strengthening business interests and privatising certain public roles. Gill (1998) argues that the World Bank is actively working to preempt a second Polanyi-style 'double movement' or counteraction of resistance from oppositional social and political forces to rollback neo-liberalism.

Global neo-liberalism represents markets as universal and capital accumulation as endless. The actual arrangements for capital accumulation by owners of corporate capital require monopolistic and oligopolistic conditions that engender and reinforce structural inequality (see Hopkins and Wallerstein 1996: 4; UNDP 1998: 37). By theorising national states as 'differentiated forms of global capitalist relations' it is possible to discern, depending on the combination of social and political forces that control national states, that states will tend to adopt policies that reproduce the heterogeneity and inequality which characterise the world labour force. The relations of domination are reproduced in the reproduction of the world's labour force, and class exploitation and inequality are necessary to secure high profitability and capital accumulation.

Restructuring the United States National Security Strategy: OAS Resolution 1080 and the Neo-liberal Project

Restructuring the United States National Security Strategy

We have about 50 per cent of the world's wealth but only 3.6 per cent of its population . . . In this situation, we cannot fail to be the object of envy and resentment. Our real task is to devise a pattern of relationships, which will permit us to maintain this position of disparity . . . We should cease to talk about vague and unreal objectives such as human rights, the raising of living standards, and democratisation . . . The day is not far off when we are going to have to deal in straight power concepts . . . It is better to have a strong regime in power than a liberal government if it is indulgent and relaxed and penetrated by Communists. (George Kennan February 1948; quoted in Landau 1988: 33)

George Kennan was instrumental in the framing of the American cold war doctrine and strategy. The above statement is explicit about how the US came to see the relationship between liberal democracy, imperialism, sovereignty, economic and social inequality and the class and labour questions in the world. Under the cold war project in the third world national security concerns took clear precedence over democracy. Where liberal democracy embraced the rule of law through the abstract universality, engendering ordinary people with a public civic personality (through the rule of law), it worked systematically to normalise the subordination of ordinary workers to capital at the point of production. Military-industrial Keynesianism defined the proper context for conducting the new global geopolitics and monopolising the lion's share of global surplus value. American hegemony was built partly on strengthening the subordination of national (sovereign) autonomy to the imperatives of the global movement of capital.

More recently, Washington has been revamping its global security strategy. President Clinton's strategy is to use America's leadership to harness global social forces to secure America's interests and values. He says:

We can, and must use America's leadership to harness global political forces of integration, reshape existing security, economic and political structures and build new ones that help create the conditions necessary for our interests and values to thrive. Our responsibility is to build the world of tomorrow by embarking on a period of construction constructing international frameworks, institutions and understanding to guide America and the world far into the next century. (*National Security Strategy for A New Century*)

Clinton defined his primary national security responsibility as follows:

Protecting the security of our nation – our people, our territory and our way of life – is my foremost mission and constitutional duty. As we enter the twenty-first century, we have an unprecedented opportunity to make our nation safer and more prosperous. Our military might is unparalleled; a dynamic global economy offers increasing opportunities for American jobs and American investments; and the community of democratic nations is growing, enhancing the prospects for political stability, peaceful conflict resolution and greater hope for the people of the world. (National Security Strategy 1997: 1)

Clinton makes it clear that the role of the American state is to serve the interests of American capital in the global arena. His main mission is 'to tear down trade barriers abroad to create jobs at home' and 'secure and enforce agreements that enable Americans to compete in foreign markets'. Since over ninety-five percent of the world's consumers live outside the United States, exporting becomes mandatory to 'sustain economic growth at home'. Clinton wants to make it incumbent on the world to 'expand export opportunities for US workers, farmers and companies.' (NSS 1997: 2, 15, 17)

Clinton reminds the LAC states and their workers and peasants of their economic contributions to America's national security strategy: 'Latin America has become the second fastest growing economic region in the world, and by 2010, our exports to Latin America and Canada will likely exceed those to Europe and Japan combined' (NSS 1997: 18). The trade component of the US security strategy stresses 'open regionalism'[12] to maintain the western hemisphere as America's home grown competitive son which is built on a heterogeneous division of labour that reproduces structural inequality in the western hemisphere (Watson 1998b).[13]

The American national security doctrine masks the sovereignty of violence principle by depublicising and naturalising violence and domination to foster the impression that the international system is inherently anarchical and to separate capitalism from its historical anarchical nature. National states grew up on foundations of territorial and extraterritorial violence, which played a key role in how the state achieved monopoly over the means of violence. The history of capitalism is replete with evidence of violence being deployed in defense of private property. The market economy masks domination in the transformation of society into an agglomeration of individualised market subjects. The effects work through a number of separations, including especially the formal separation of politics from economics, national states from the international system and international politics from international economics.[14] Yet we cannot hope to understand sovereignty by starting from sovereignty itself. The US supervised the construction of the United Nations model of sovereign independence, on the strategy of widening the gap between national autonomy (sovereignty) and economic independence (capital accumulation) (Rosenberg 1994). The foundations of that strategy have their antecedents in American foreign policy in the western hemisphere in the century before cold war (Watson 1998c). The strategy has been updated to suit post-Soviet times.

OAS Resolution 1080 and Neo-liberal Subordination

The neo-liberal doctrine of free trade and open regionalism identifies the rules, principles, and ideology for yoking the Caribbean to America's revamped global security strategy. The post-Soviet basis of America's global security strategy can be traced to the Organisation of American States (OAS) Resolution 1080 of 1991, known as the Santiago Commitment. Resolution 1080 updates the Rio Treaty (1947) which girded the cold war strategy in the western hemisphere. Resolution 1080 commits the OAS and its member states to defend against 'threats' to state sovereignty, democracy and capitalism 'in any American republic' (Bloomfield 1998: 126). It also provides a *de jure* confirmation for a *de facto* reality, namely that a certain degree of spatial economic integration has already been achieved between the US, Canada and the LAC region.

Resolution 1080 reconfigures the basis of reciprocal collective security by making it incumbent on LAC states to use sovereignty to process and protect global capitalism in more transparent ways. This form of collective security sets the tone for placing sovereignty and democracy under global capitalist jurisdiction as part of the restructuring of hegemony. In economic terms corporate capital would appear to have eclipsed the state as sovereign entity, with parliaments and civil society subsumed under markets. For the Caribbean the restructuring of hegemony extends to dismantling what is left of neo-mercantilism in terms of protected markets and special preferential market access. The main lesson is the deepening of the separation between formal sovereign autonomy and economic independence. This strategy is also taking its toll on states like Japan and Korea (see Cummings 1998: 71).

Democracy becomes market democracy of capital: the capital accumulation imperatives of the twenty-first century require states to demystify their true nature within the social relations of production. In effect, collective security means security foremost for all the circuits of capital and what is left of the empire of western civilisation (see Lapham 1998: 23). Thus Resolution 1080 is part of the neo-liberal strategy for locking in reforms in the LAC countries. However, while Resolution 1080 is specific to the LAC countries, it has to be subsumed under the MAI proposals for strengthening the rights of capital. It clarifies provisions for strengthening the role and power of transnational capital in the internal processes of national states (see Clarke and Barlow 1997).

The MAI framework offers a close study of the intensification of globalisation. The dominant transnational corporate interests are shaping the WTO's global agenda, and the MAI is designed specifically to project and lock in the corporate agenda as the global agenda. Resolution 1080 and the MAI converge around the protection of sovereignty, democracy and free markets. Both would require states to establish and follow uniform investment rules, policies and standards. National priorities would have to be brought into line with the interests of transnational capital and national priorities could not be defined at variance with the investment interests of a foreign company.

Expropriation with compensation would no longer be acceptable. An expropriated company would have the right to sue a state for revenues anticipated but unearned (Clarke and Barlow 1997). The Multilateral Agreement on Investment (MAI) underscores American constitutionalism in matters of the rights of capital and seeks to project the underlying principles to the global level. The restructuring of hegemony carries a number of underlying subtleties for building a new global constitutional consensus grounded in American private property norms. Resolution 1080 articulates the western hemisphere component of the global security strategy to suit post-Soviet times. Neo-liberalism is also engendering adjustments in regionalism and integration.

Neo-liberalism, Regionalism and the New Integration Strategy

Burnham's contends that 'national states provide both the domestic political underpinning for the mobility of capital and offer rudimentary institutional schemes aimed at securing international property rights as a basis for the continued expansion of capital' (1995: 103–4). The neo-liberal strategy is to make the role of the state more transparent than before, partly by reconfiguring the class relations in third world countries and undermining economic nationalism to make palatable the nationalisation of the external debt held by those states and to reproduce them as complementary production sites.

Most third world external debt was incurred by private capital but must now be repaid out of the surplus extracted from the working population. Managing the debt crisis has engendered strategies such as debt-equity swaps, privatisation, further bank lending, official loans, export credits and other instruments that have aggravated the denationalisation of the ownership of third world resources, and support the global expansion of capital. The aggressive strategy of the Clinton administration in forcing open third world financial markets on behalf of the financial services industry in the US (Kristof and Sanger 1999) points to the role of politics in guiding the hand of the market.

The MAI strategy of the OECD for imposing neo-liberalism is also important in this regard. The WTO agenda is constructed by corporate capitalist interests, which are reflected via the MAI project. The Articles of Agreement, under which the Fund was created in the 1940s, are being rewritten for adoption by all states. The OECD has been reformed as the 'OECD Plus', with third world states like Mexico and Korea and eastern and central European states becoming members. The new 'OECD Plus' forum addresses global issues such as 'trade, employment and labour standards, tax on multinational corporations, competition policy, maritime transport, steel trade, and foreign direct investment'. The forum represents 'a flexible mechanism for co-opting the dynamic and emerging capitalist economies of the third world into the political structures of the developed world.' (Ougaard 1999: 56; Burnham 1995: 104)

With respect to the LAC region, Valtonen is skeptical about LAC states embracing the 'bilateral route . . . as such a system with the United States as the hub (it being the only country with free access to the markets of almost all Latin American countries) would . . . enhance United States dominance and hamper the development of intra-Latin American trade' (Ougaard 1999: 180, 186; 178–79). Canada and Mexico would like to see NAFTA operate on a level playing field between them and the US, and they have looked to NAFTA-EU relations to moderate American dominance, but without success. Ougaard sees the American strategy as using the EU-NAFTA forum for rationalising its bilateral negotiations with all other blocs. Valtonen feels Washington wants to keep NAFTA as little institutionalised as possible, as it allows free access to the markets of its neighbors with a minimum of political pressure to harmonise or revoke often contradictory national trade laws, and allow more freedom to operate globally without having to take into account the considerations of the other two NAFTA members. (1999: 181)

American, EU and Japanese protectionism against LAC exports also reinforces structural inequities in production, investment, trade and employment and market heterogeneity in the LAC region. It is true that the pressures from the EU, the WTO, the IMF and the World Bank make it unfeasible for LAC states to pursue 'unilateral economic liberalisation' (Valtonen 1999: 186, 187). However, the reality is that the rulers of economically and politically dominant interests in those states are committed to a division of labour that obviates such an outcome.

Some Features of Productive Forces in the Caribbean

How prepared are Caribbean states, businesses and the broad social strata of workers, small farmers and peasants (where they exist) for the transitions that are being wrought by the technological revolution? Caribbean business culture and practices continue to undergo restructuring, but modern research and development around high technology production or complex engineering, manufacturing or information technology systems is not the norm in the region.[15] The structural composition of business enterprises in the Caribbean has changed in recent times in areas including the sugar, bauxite, oil, banking, tourism, the media, forms of industrial production, and other areas. Restructuring in key industries like bauxite, oil, sugar and tourism has been driven by the global strategies of the transnational corporations (TNCs) which dominate in those areas (see Wade 1995). New transnational alliances have been taking shape between a limited number of businesses in some CARICOM countries and TNCs in North America and Europe (see Blackman Associates 1996; Bernal 1996; Rhodes 1999; Dilla 1999). Foreign companies also dominate in areas like insurance, information services and assembly production. Relatively small family enterprises dominate the local economic and business landscape in the Caribbean.

The technological revolution is posing unusual challenges for the entire region. The new technology continues to reduce 'the proportion of labour cost to total manufacturing' and a growing portion of global labour has become useless to global capital. According to the World Bank, changes in technologies in some sectors have altered the scale of production, weakening the case for offshore production in low labour cost countries, FDI flows *have tended to gravitate* to developing economies with an efficient and dynamic private sector, accompanied by responsive institutions and a highly motivated skilled labour force. (1993c: 32, box 3-3, the italics are mine). Motivation is heavily influenced by the business culture of capital.

The mercantile and commercial activities that predominate in the Caribbean have not been based on strategies for revolutionising the development of the productive powers of industry and labour, as neither capital nor the state has any need for large numbers of highly trained professional and technical workers. The collapse of traditional preferential arrangements poses unusual challenges for Caribbean states, businesses and social classes. The direction of the WTO raises serious concerns for the future of the Windward Islands banana exporters, but the problem is not limited to bananas. In fact, the OECD's MAI project portends a fundamental shift in investment, production and regulatory norms for doing business around the world (see Simai 1995: 236-38; Clarke and Barlow 1997).

The internationalisation of Caribbean working classes has been central to post-war capitalist restructuring in the region and in Europe and North America.[16] The neo-mercantile arrangements reinforced certain weak production structures and certain class and political interests in the private sector and the state. Migration and non-reciprocal preferential market access and other neo-mercantile arrangements have also conditioned Caribbean modernisation strategies. Migration from the Caribbean has had a moderating impact on unemployment, while remittances continue to absorb shocks from poverty.[17] Technological displacement and neo-liberal reforms have already weakened the bases of migration and are forcing organised labour to rethink its strategies. Caribbean governments claim to abide by the labour standards of the International Labour Organisation (ILO), but set up free trade zones to restrict the base of trade unions and undermine the workers rights as identified under the UNUDHR. There are several reasons for this approach. One is political, namely to control the independent movement of workers via trade unions; the other is to mediate contradictions associated with low productivity production and open unemployment. Broadly, these measures have profound impacts on the development of the productive forces. The expansion of the scope of privatisation in the 1990s in several Caribbean Basin countries (IDB 1997: 25–6) has also altered the relationship between the state and many workers.

At the end of the 1980s, in global terms, the Caribbean region had the second lowest average adult illiteracy rate of 16 per cent; the second highest life expectancy at birth of 68 years; the second lowest infant mortality rate of 41 per 1000 (1990); and the fifth in daily caloric intake with 2631 calories per person per day (World Bank 1993b: 52, Table 1V.1).[18] In 1990, about 9.95 million people or a combined average of 55.1 percent of the total population of the Dominican Republic, Guyana, Haiti, Jamaica, and Trinidad and Tobago lived below the poverty line: Guyana (64.8 per cent) and Haiti (75.7 per cent) were above the average, while Trinidad and Tobago (16.2 per cent), Jamaica (42.6 per cent), and the Dominican Republic (44.6 per cent) were below the average. Approximately 34 per cent or 6.1 million of the combined population, which resided in rural areas in these same countries, lived below the poverty line, with Haiti and Jamaica registering the highest concentrations of persons in that category.

Large numbers of people in a number of Caribbean countries lack access to health services, safe water and sanitation (World Bank 1993b: 55, Table 1V.3). In the Caribbean over '40 per cent of households are headed by women. Almost 90 per cent of *female-headed households* (FHH) have only a primary education and about 38 per cent work in the informal sector' (World Bank 1993b: 64; ILO 1993:2; 13, 17–18; the italics are mine). Poverty, deprivation and the oppression of women are linked to the political features of a system based on the patriarchal organisation of society to suit production for private accumulation. Capital and the state exploit women's vulnerability to increase exploitation and raise the rate of profit in the production process. The vulnerability of female employees is aggravated by the restructuring of production in export processing zones (EPZs). FHHs and kinship groups shoulder a rising share of the social cost for reproducing labour power.

Semi-proletarianisation is evident across the Caribbean, for example Haiti's massive pool of expatriate labourers who toil in the Dominican Republic under conditions of involuntary servitude. Many of Haiti's bourgeois and middle strata households have a gargantuan appetite for child labour. In Haiti, more than 100,000 'restaveks' – the children of poor rural families – are 'sold or given to better off families in the towns to work as domestic servants' and 'children as young as six can find themselves in a position of involuntary servitude' (ILO 1993: 17). 'Restaveks' seldom attend school and many of the street children in Port au Prince are runaway 'restaveks' who have to choose between involuntary servitude and the dangers of street life (ILO 1993: 18). The pervasive use of extra-economic coercion against Haitian migrant labourers in the Dominican Republic and large numbers of Haiti's rural and urban people confirm that the separation of coercion from the economy remains incomplete in some Caribbean societies. The use of primitive techniques of surplus extraction also reveals something about the uneven development of the productive forces within the capitalist process in the region.

The use of child labour for surplus extraction in the Caribbean is part of the larger issue of children's rights in relation to adults, family obligations and the state. The crisis in which growing numbers of children and youths find themselves suggests that there is no clear vision for how to invest in the future in terms of the material, intellectual, psycho-social, and educational development of children (see Newman-Williams 1997: xiv). The crisis of children and youth in the Caribbean points to some of the ways in which neo-liberal restructuring aggravates the decomposition of national societies.

The development of modern science and technology policy and practice in the Caribbean remains rudimentary. There are no significant bodies of research scientists, technologists and engineers to constitute a critical mass around the production of important publications, to bolster the formation of an intellectual paradigm. The Caribbean Council for Science and Technology (CCST), the Institute of Applied Science and Technology (IAST), and the Caribbean Agricultural Research and Development Institute (CARDI) and several others are of recent origin (WICR 1992: 255). There are factors other than deficiencies in national and regional coordination, equipment, and understaffing that undermine the achievement of a significant impact by the science and technology institutions. Science and technology are isolated from production proper. The West Indian Commission Report (WICR) stated that 'many operate without links to the productive sector, so that much of the work being carried out is not demand-led' (1992: 256–7). A number of leading Caribbean firms are forming alliances with global companies, which might suggest that they are not sanguine about the prospects of forging effective linkages within the region (see Blackman Associates 1996; Bernal 1996).

Financial liberalisation and structural adjustment policies have accelerated the net transfer of resources from the region to the US. Caribbean states have liberalised their markets, reduced or abolished high tariffs on imports and local production, and adopted liberalisation measures by removing controls on interest rates and credit. But those neo-liberal reforms have done little to improve the economic performance of most Caribbean countries in terms of productivity and quality. Foreign capital predominates; income inequalities are pronounced; inflation takes a severe toll on the masses of workers, small farmers and peasants; job growth is unstable, and education[19] continues to be a problem.

By the middle of the 1990s, economic adjustment and recovery were reflected through exports and investment. In 1996, there was modest improvement in the low savings rate and economic growth. Barbados had a growth rate above 4 per cent, while Jamaica contracted. In 1996, real investment in the Latin America and Caribbean region stood slightly above 20 percent of GDP or 5 per cent below the 1980 high point. The Caribbean declined by 2.6 per cent and most of the countries showed substantial weakness in their investment experience. The Inter-American Development Bank (IDB) observes that the terms of trade cannot be singled out as the sole or main factor (IDB 1997: 9).

In the Caribbean, the experience of Jamaica and the Dominican Republic was instructive. Jamaica has lived through topsy-turvy times in the 1990s, with stabilisation, high inflation and inflation stabilisation, high interest rates, over-extended banks and insurance companies, a costly financial crisis associated with the collapse of a number of financial institutions, and state takeover of a number of institutions and the closure of others. 'As a result of high real interest rates, costs of the financial crisis, the recession, and other fiscal developments, the Jamaican fiscal balance swung from a surplus of nearly 2 per cent of GDP to a deficit of at least 18 per cent' (IDB 1997: 15).

In contrast with Jamaica, the situation in the Dominican Republic stabilised: the economy grew by 7 per cent in 1996, with strong investment in the face of a decline in the terms of trade. In 1996, unemployment rates for Barbados, Jamaica, and the Dominican Republic ranged from 15–20 per cent (IDB 1997: 16, Figure 12). The concentration of wealth at the top contrast with impoverishment, declining state social expenditures, very low remuneration, landlessness among the rural proletariat and peasantry, and a lack of influence in politics and economy. The IDB attributes persistent poverty to the weakness of the recovery, and concludes that there was no improvement in income distribution, as the 'relatively well-off groups of Latin American society appear to have benefited from the recovery of the 1990s somewhat more than the poorest classes' (1997: 17, 18). The neo-liberal perspective of the IDB ignores important facts about the class politics of income distribution (see Veltmeyer, Petras, and Vieux 1997: 121–22).

Technological upgrading to strengthen export competitiveness also results in the destruction of many labour-intensive jobs. In addition, financial liberalisation has accelerated the liquefaction of quantities of fixed capital and the creation of new financial instruments, signaling that there is an insufficiency of profitable opportunities in 'bricks and mortar' (Holloway 1995). The burgeoning of markets for new financial instruments suggests the arrival of a point where

> both domestic and international credit have been increasingly transformed into credit *ex nihilo*, into artificially created money which is no longer based on accumulated surplus value, but on no existing value. The requirement for 'artificial money' to act as a productive force beyond the value embodied in gold reserves is that it must become money as capital, that is, it must become credit which commands alien labour: money must command. (Marazzi 1995: 75)

In part, the US approach to financial liberalisation has involved applying great pressure on governments around the world, from East Asia and Russia to the LAC Region to accommodate the free movement of money capital (see Cummings 1998). Mickey Kantor, former US trade representative and commerce secretary claims the 'United States was insufficiently aware of the kind of chaos that financial liberalisation could provoke.' Laura D'Andrea Tyson, former chairwoman of Clinton's Council of Economic Advisors, acknowledged there was pressure from America's financial services industry (Kristof and Sanger 1999). Kantor's assertion that in the absence of modern banking and legal systems financial liberalisation is like 'building a skyscraper with no foundation' is unsatisfactory. Financial liberalisation and market integration have also benefited certain strata within third world ruling circles, while contributing to the decomposition of their national societies.

Laura D'Andrea Tyson points out that the 'heavy capital flows that had drowned the Asian economies' came not from Asia, but from 'Europe and the United States, from fully developed industrial countries well-equipped with sufficient data and the instruments of democratic oversight.' She stresses that the money strategy was one of greed... stupidity, cowardice... about investors in London and Paris and New York seizing the prey of easy profits and then, when the luck went bad, seeking to transfer their markers to a government about privatising the gains and socialising the losses. (quoted in Lapham 1998: 63–64)

Part of the problem for capital is that the World Bank and IMF cannot guarantee the effectiveness of international credit as a key medium of global socialisation. In fact, this very problem signals that the 'command function' of money is more and more unstable. The dollar, as international currency, is not convertible into gold and 'money as capital... can no longer be converted into effective command over labour' (Marazzi 1995: 74). Jamaica has gone further than most other Caribbean states in embracing the 'Washington Consensus on Latin America' and is paying a heavy price as a result (Blackman 1999; *Jamaica Gleaner*, July 30, 1999). The nationalisation of the private debt, which was incurred by capitalist interests, capital flight, the net transfers of surplus to pay interest on the external debt, the reduction of the tax burden on the elite, and the shift of capital into liquid investments compound the problem for workers, small farmers, and peasants in a number of Caribbean countries. The new departures in the technological revolution are going to aggravate the crisis in the Caribbean.

From Microelectronics Technology to Nanotechnology: Transitions within the Third Technological Revolution

The Third Technological Revolution (TTR) and the Transition from Microelectronics Technology to Nanotechnology

Tapscott (1996: xiv) defines the world of networked intelligence as an 'age of vast new promise and unimaginable opportunity'. Capital sees this world in terms of intensifying the exploitation of labour. Increasingly, labour's strategy is to move the struggle beyond the factory floor to the broader social arenas. Tapscott locates humans at the centre of the revolutionary technological change and helps to de-fetishise the TTR and the tendency to make smart machines autonomous of the social and political process. His argument has much to do with the intensification of the socialisation of production.

Technology and 'machines . . . locomotives, railways, electric telegraphs, self-acting mules, etc . . . are the products of human industry . . . the power of knowledge objectified. The development of fixed capital indicates to what degree general social knowledge has become a direct force of production' (Marx 1971: 706). The base of knowledge is social and is linked to the production and reproduction of material culture. Information has long been a commodity under capitalism. The TTR intensifies the commodification of information in the production of good and services. To say glibly that information empowers individuals is to mask the real nature of information in the intensification of the commodification process. Information technology has been pivotal in the global movement of money. Thus information features in projecting the power of capital. Capital's strategy for conquering space by time necessitates incessant reductions in the turnover time of constant and variable capital. To this end, companies have turned to advanced computers, numerically controlled robots and software applications to facilitate the processing of very large quantities of information and complex data in the production of goods and services. Incessant innovation accelerates the transfer of productive activity from human hands and mind to machines, so as to harness human energy and skills more effectively and intensify the exploitation of labour in production.

Silicon-based technology continues to shrink the size of computers, cell phones and many other high-tech objects, while increasing their computing and processing power. Still, silicon-based microchip technology has begun to reach its limits. A transition to nanotechnology is under way, giving a new twist to shrinking size, increasing power and lowering unit cost. A 'nanometer is a billionth of a meter – about the size of two large atoms – and a hundred of them are still only about the size of a virus.' Nanotechnology is threatening to increase the rate and scale of human redundancy in production. According to a recent issue of *Technology Review (TR)*, in order to maintain the current rate of growth in computing power, microelectronics makers will have to squeeze roughly 18 million transistors on a microprocessor chip by 2003. That means feature sizes will need to be as small as 130 nanometers. This, then, is where you begin to enter the nanoworld and existing technologies begin to fall apart. (102: 2: 44)

There is an impending collision between the worlds of microelectronics and nanoelectronics that seems destined to deconstruct today's conventional silicon-based electronics technologies (Rotman 1999: 49, 53). Successful breakthroughs in nanotechnology could result in the production of hard disks that are capable of storing as much as a trillion bytes. *Technology Review* reports on the progress that is being made toward the development of a new, cheaper, faster 'computer that assembles itself – in a beaker' (Vol. 102: 5: 93-96). There is likely to be a hollowing of nanotech giants that will have the means to remain financially viable research entities in the nanotech world: it costs about $3 billion to start a nanotech fabrication plant (Voss, 1999: 57). A '$10 billion fabrication plant', or "fab", is not far off. By 2010 a fab is likely to cost $30 billion' (*TR*, Vol. 102: 5: 94).

To overcome the financial cost and technical constraints of silicon-based technology that rests on producing perfect or near perfect materials, research is being done to find ways to produce 'nanometer-scaled components cheaply and easily assembled using simple chemistry' in which 'technicians will dip substrates into vats of chemicals. And if the mix is right, wires and switches will chemically assemble themselves from these materials. It would make possible tiny, inexpensive and immensely powerful computers' (*TR*, Vol. 102: 5: 94). If successful, R&D in computers would no longer be based on constantly rising cost of complexity to accommodate perfection and the exponentially rising cost of fabs. A new term, 'architecture defect-tolerant', is gaining currency around a strategy for building 'an entire computer using nothing but chemical processes'. The aim is to make things more cheaply 'that are imperfect but still work perfectly'. Defect-tolerant designs are going to become the norm precisely because 'it's going to become impossible to make such small things perfectly'.

Much is covered over in the statement that there is 'proof that a highly defective system can operate perfectly' (ibid, p. 96). As far as production relations are concerned, the ability to produce faster, smaller, cheaper and more efficient machines points to the deepening of the international socialisation of production, the intensification of exploitation to raise the rate of surplus value, and thereby the inescapable proletarianisation of professional labour. The new assembly line model reaches higher up the ladder of the working population, and many more will be driven down into the surplus population. It is necessary to consider issues of class politics at the intersection of money and technology.

Class Politics of Neo-liberalism and the Technological Revolution

The bulk of the world's economically active population does not own capital in the means of production and the majority of the economic and social civil rights of the global majority are de-ontological by nature. Workers do not have a right to employment or subsistence under capitalism. Depending on the society, some workers may have recourse to legal provisions for safety and health but no social guarantee. Workers have to work for others and reproduce others as the precondition for their own social reproduction. Neo-liberals want to convince people that there is too much dependency on the state, while asserting that the market has 'a natural right to regulate all of the world's societies in their best interests'. Polanyi reminds us that "at all times, and at all levels, the invisible hand was guided and steered by politics and power, and that it always, ended up in concentration of wealth and prosperity for some people in some places, while causing abject misery, poverty and appalling subjugation for a majority of people in most other places". (In Hoogvelt 1997: 15; Thomson 1994: 67)

The impact of technological displacement can be seen in the growing surplus population around the world. A large portion of America's surplus population is reproduced as the excluded urban and rural masses; many from this group are housed in the Prison-Industrial Complex (P-IC). The P-IC war on crime is a thriving business that brings important economic benefits to corporate capital, financiers, real estate and construction magnates, agri-business firms, and consultants (Schlosser 1998). The residents in the P-IC are part of America's domestic free trade zones: prison inmates earn about $0.23 cents per hour producing 'goods for companies like McDonalds, TWA and Starbucks'. According to a recent Department of Justice publication, American prison labour – 'factories with fences' – offers real competitive advantage over labour in offshore assembly sites: 'Inmates represent a readily available and dependable source of entry-level labour that is a cost-effective alternative to work forces found in Mexico, the Caribbean Basin, Southeast Asia, and the Pacific Rim countries' (*Ifco News*, Winter 1999: 1). The P-IC expresses some of the contradictions of globalisation (Schlosser 1998).

In the free market the machines of the TTR execute many 'conceptual, managerial, technical, and administrative functions and coordinate the flow of production, from the extraction of raw materials to the marketing and distribution of final goods and services' (Rifkin 1995: 60). The reproduction of capital requires the subordination of 'the productive power of labour . . . value in production' (Bonefeld 1995: 201; Graham 1995). Labour has a constitutive existence within the concept of capital that is expressed in the social form in, and through, a class-divided social context. Basically, the class relation lies within the existence of the capital relation. The capital relation is not above or outside of class relations. Rather the capital relation exists in and through class relations. The capitalist exploitation of labour does not stand above, but rather in and through class relations (Bonefeld 1995b). Therefore, to understand the real purpose behind the new technology in capitalist production, it is necessary to start with the social relations of production where technology and the technological revolution are grounded. The question of technology is inseparable from the question of labour and its resistance to capital's strategies of accumulation.

The TTR, Labour Productivity and the Future of Work Under Global 2000

The shift in the relation between national state and global capital means a significant change in the forms of global capitalist domination. There is a shift in state power to the world level. Political decisions taken at the level of the national state are now more directly integrated into the global movement of capital the subjection of the national state to the global movement of capital makes more difficult the national decomposition of society . . . In all this, capital appears all-powerful . . . The violent restlessness of capital is the clearest indication of the inadequacy (for capital) of the . . . relations of exploitation, of capital's incapacity to subordinate the power of labour on which it depends. Despite appearances, the restless movement of capital is the clearest indication of the power of the insubordination of labour. (Holloway 1995: 134, 135)

The insubordination of labour contributes to capital's restlessness and unhappiness with the relations of exploitation. Japanese, American, and European R&D enterprises are working on a new generation of 'intelligent machines that can read text, understand complex speech, interpret facial expressions, and even anticipate behavior', to replace the ones that already 'recognise casual speech, carry on meaningful conversations, and even solicit additional information upon which to make decisions, provide recommendations, and answer questions' (Rifkin 1995: 61).

Companies employ thinking machines to compress space-time distances, with a view to making the workerless factory the norm. Capitalists want a work environment free from worker fatigue, work stoppages, lunch breaks, vacation, workmen's compensation, promotions, health benefits, or other labour rights and intrusions from the era of social democracy. Capital wants to cancel labour's invasion of its 'prerogative' to set the working day and working conditions. Capital's quest for the workerless factory is intended to inaugurate the age of the 'management of machines instead of the management of men', the era of 'emancipation from human workers' (Rifkin 1995: 68). Yet labour is the substance of value in the abstract.

Capital has also turned to the rule of money to try to 'overcome the disruptive power of labour which resists an exploitation beyond certain limits and below a certain wage'. But in the rush from bricks and mortar into speculative money, such money becomes 'unemployed because it cannot command labour in the present and seeks . . . to invest in the future exploitation of labour. It seeks redemption in the future' (Bonefeld 1995a: 195). The revolutionary changes that mark the TTR become intelligible when they are situated in their proper relationship with money as a form of capital and as the abstract identity of labour.

The large-scale revolution in world manufacturing, transportation, agriculture, biotechnology, farming and services will transform human culture and civilization. About "half the human beings on the planet still farm the land. Now, new breakthroughs in the information and life sciences threaten to end much of outdoor farming by the middle of the coming century. The technological changes in the production of food are leading to a world without farmers, with untold consequences for the 2.4 billion who rely on the land for their survival". (Rifkin 1995: 109; Simai 1995: 8–27)

Many producers are already using highly sophisticated robots to plant and harvest crops in some countries. Nitrogen fertilizer has been contributing to greater farm yields and falling demand for farm labour.

The mechanisation of animal husbandry contributes to rising productivity of farm animals, due mainly to the introduction of animal-based pharmaceuticals, innovative breeding technologies and specialty feeds (see Mann 1999). Since the 1940s in the US, technological displacement in farming and agriculture abolished many jobs. Coincident with very large increases in agricultural productivity, factors such as overproduction, depressed prices, technological displacement and the inability to meet fixed costs have bankrupted many American family farms. One leading consequence has been a higher concentration of agro-commercial and agro-industrial capital in the hands of large banks and complex agro-industrial companies. The massive gains wrought by the revolution in farming and agriculture return as growing poverty in depressed rural areas across the US.

New agricultural software and farm robotics are key in the restructuring of the productive base of American agro-industry. The effects of many such innovations are already being felt in the Caribbean in areas such as price competitiveness of imported agricultural products from the US and other parts of the North. Farmers are relying on computers to find new strategies for balancing 'acreage targets and profit objectives' with environmental risks. There are computer programmes to help farmers choose the right fertiliser for particular lands with given conditions of moisture and soil. It is anticipated that within two decades just about all areas of American farming will be managed and monitored by computers (Rifkin 1995: 113–14). Farmers and agro-industries are feeding dairy cows with the aid of robotised computer systems that can be programmed to identify each cow, its feeding time, and dietary allotment.

Molecular farming is part of the new norm: gene-splicing technologies are being developed and/or applied to manipulate genes to change the production of plants and animals. Molecular biologists are 'able to add, delete, recombine, inset, stitch, and edit together genetic materials across biological boundaries, creating novel new microorganisms, plant strains and animal breeds that have never before existed in nature' (Rifkin 1995: 118). The idea of the indivisibility of entities has become a historical relic. Virtually all biological boundaries can be transgressed, for life has become 'an assemblage of individual genetic traits.' For one, the American state has embraced the idea that 'living creatures are reducible to the status of manufactured inventions, subject to the same engineering standards and commercial exploitation as inanimate objects' (Rifkin 1995: 118–19; see Mann 1999).

The transition from 'petrochemical-based agriculture to gene-based agriculture' will become the norm in the twenty-first century. Genetic engineers are creating in laboratories new breeds and new varieties of plants, fruit and vegetables which can endure extreme drought, heat, and cold (Mann 1999: 36-43). Genetic engineering is making it possible to produce cows to yield much more milk than today, with prospects for massive overproduction of milk yields. Experiments are being conducted to produce bovine, porcine, and chicken varieties to yield the exact amount of desired fatty tissue. Genetically engineered pigs that mature faster and require much less labour to bring them to market are being produced in countries such as Australia, where cheaper pork and higher technological displacement seem to be moving hand in hand.

The biotechnology revolution is contributing to a transition from farming to 'pharming' (Rifkin 1995: 122), with farming and agriculture moving from outdoor to indoor, 'divorced from land, climate, and changing seasons, long the conditioning agents of agricultural output.' The 'biotechnology revolution is likely to replace land cultivation with labouratory cultures, changing forever the way the world views production of food' (Rifkin 1995: 122-23; Mann 1999), ushering in a new relationship between biotechnology, automation, land and human civilisation.

Madagascar, Reunion, and the Comoros Islands produce close to 100 per cent of the world supply of vanilla, with Madagascar accounting for more than 70 per cent of the total. Biotechnology experiments have resulted in the production of tissue culture techniques for producing vanilla flavor by extracting cell tissue from the vanilla plant. The estimated cost of producing natural vanilla is about $1,200 per pound, compared with cell tissue production at $25 per pound. More than 100,000 farmers in Madagascar, Reunion, and Comoros whose livelihood is still connected to the vanilla bean are at risk. The relevance of the mass production worker to capital and the world is a serious question! The fully automated workerless farm is on the drawing board; the workerless factory is a reality at a certain level.

There is a conservative estimate of 800 million unemployed persons in the world. Very large numbers of mass production workers in global farming, agriculture, manufacturing, services and other industries around the world could be made redundant by the computer and biotechnology revolutions. According to Paul Kennedy, most of the 1.2 billion workers who recently joined the global labour market will earn about US$4 per day, with the effect of depressing the wages of workers in the advanced capitalist countries by about 50 per cent (1996: 28-9). In broader terms, plans to privatise some 87,000 Chinese state enterprises could lead to the scrapping of up to 112 million jobs. At least 26 million of China's state sector employees have lost their jobs so far. China is projected to lose close to 40 million manufacturing jobs[20] in the coming decades due to technological upgrading and displacement, let alone millions in agriculture from the impact of the revolution in agriculture and biotechnology (Mann 1999; see Hoogvelt 1997: 240). China's leaders stress that finding the garden of prosperity by crossing the river of austerity means some workers and peasants must drown in the process (Lapham 1998: 29-30). What is clear is that workers around the world are going to have to fight like never before for jobs and other means of livelihood.

The implications of a revolutionary transition in which much of 'the human workforce is being left behind and will likely never cross over into the new high-tech global economy' (Rifkin 1995: 127) are mind-boggling. Prospects seem dim for the rest of the world 'to absorb the reserve from the rural and informal economies... because global competitiveness... requires techniques of production that make such absorption impossible, and because the safety net of mass immigration is not available' (Amin 1997: ix; Pintasilgo). Some of the key problems are rising poverty, social violence, mass migration, and new forms of international conflict. Labour markets in some regions like the OECD and other parts of Europe are becoming more interconnected, while the countries of the south face growing heterogeneity. Regionalisation strategies like the EU and NAFTA, global sourcing of production by transnational corporations, and migration patterns and flows are important matters to consider in this regard (Simai with Moghadam and Kuddo 1995). National states are not prepared to cope with these developments, though the type of state and the means at its disposal can make a difference. Caribbean states face acute challenges to deal with the fallout.

Jamaica's Global Repositioning Strategy[21]

The western hemisphere does not compare favorably with Europe and Asia, in terms of the degree of trade integration because 'while intra-European and intra-Asian trade constantly increases, intra-regional trade in North America declines and that of Latin America stagnates...' This tendency is also evident in manufactures where, 'while the Americas "disintegrate" exports and imports, Asia integrates exports and... imports, and Europe integrates exports even further (it sells more to itself) but disintegrates imports (buying more and more from Asia).' The United States techno-industrial production base realigns 'the vertical axis of increasing flexibility... in a universally Taylorist industrial paradigm' (Lipietz 1997: 21-22, 29). The US-Caribbean economic relationship is built on the same 'Taylorist . . . paradigm".

Bernal (1996) makes a plausible case for repositioning Jamaica in the global market economy, fully aware that Jamaica will not achieve a competitive edge on the basis of factor advantage and that the leading political parties have compressed the economic policy and ideological space between themselves (see World Bank 1995: 255; *Weekly Gleaner*, January 24-30, 1997: 19). During the 1980s, David Rockefeller led a group of potential foreign investors from the US to Jamaica. The American businessmen lamented the lack of a modern industrial business culture and the 'low propensity and preparedness to engage in joint ventures' with foreign capital (Henke 1997: 8). Edward Seaga's Jamaica Labour Party (JLP) government deepened Jamaica's integration with foreign capital to restructure the country's production-for-export base. Seaga felt that merchants, home market producers, and exporters who drained the state coffers of subsidies could not restructure Jamaica's production base.

Bernal argues that industrialisation 'has not taken place in Jamaica' (1996:7), and since 'services are the fastest growing component of the world economy, the export of services can provide development that has been elusive thus far' (1996:1). Whether in services or in industry the key point is how, when and where one enters. My earlier discussion of the transitions in the TTR and of the future of the global labour force puts this question in its proper context. Service industries like retail, distribution, marketing, finance, insurance, health, tourism, and entertainment are heavily affected by digitisation (see Giriani 1995), which explains why it is vital to look at the restructuring of services in relation to the TTR. Bernal recommends looking 'toward financial services in the new dynamic sectors in the global economy such as microelectronics, biotechnology, telecommunications, robotics, and information' (1996: 7). He urges Jamaica 'to create a technologically advanced and information-based society and . . . keep up with customisation and increased information in such key industries as apparel' (1996: 8). Of course, competitive advantage in services cannot be achieved by promoting and marketing incentives in isolation from a restructuring of the technological and educational infrastructures.

In spite of the fact that the textile and apparel production industries in the US share a complex techno-industrial base with a high degree of R&D, investment capital, and a very cost sensitive business culture, the industry has had to shift mass production to offshore sites in Asia, Latin America and the Caribbean. NAFTA augments Mexico's advantage in semi-skilled labour over the US, a factor that also erodes the position of garment assembly operations in Jamaica and other Caribbean sites. Bernal recommends 'improving human resources' through high quality management, by drawing on the skills, capital, and other resources of overseas Jamaicans, and collabourative labour-management relations, to exploit innovation opportunities and raise productivity. He advises the state and businesses to stress literacy and numeracy in education to reduce the length of the learning experience for workers and raise productivity.

Bernal is sympathetic to 'worker participation in managerial decisions and employee stock ownership programmes' and 'trade union involvement in job creation . . . education, training, and ownership participation' (1996: 9). Neo-liberals are not interested in social strategies to strengthen the economic and social power of labour or the neocolonial state. The international financial institutions link criteria of eligibility for their loans to evidence that states are rolling back their economic and social borders; Caribbean states like Jamaica are aiding and abetting this process.

Based on the assumption that 'capital has no nationality' in the global economy, Bernal recommends 'developing strategic corporate alliances' (1996: 10). But it is not that capital is without nationality, rather what makes nationality seem unimportant is that the capital accumulation process transcends national political borders. Companies form transnational alliances to intensify competition by pooling capital, technology, and scientific knowledge from R&D, to anticipate competition from many different sources. Strategic global alliances thrive on intra-alliance competition in certain industries and markets, for example, the car industry. The pursuit by certain Jamaican companies of strategic alliances with American and British firms in industries such as poultry and eggs, beer, bananas, and telecommunications, and joint ventures in finance indicates that those Jamaican capitalists are not confident about finding the competitive edge at home.

Bernal thinks there are greater possibilities in telecommuting, 'software design, data processing... accounting' and back-office operations. I have noted that back-office work and data processing do not offer good prospects for growth in offshore assembly sites (Watson 1994). In fact, the rapid expansion of capitalism in China, Eastern Europe, and the former USSR has given investors access to a vast supply of skilled and semi-skilled low-wage labour.

Bernal insists that Jamaica's chances of 'becoming an international business centre' stems from the fact that 'the essentials of a stable government, a dynamic market-driven economy, and a highly skilled labour force are already in place' (1996: 12; World Bank 1995: 255–6). Global repositioning is not such a straightforward matter.

It is questionable that recent developments in Jamaica's economic and financial situation will favour the transition that Bernal recommends. He expects financial liberalisation and other market-friendly initiatives to complement the repositioning package, along with joint ventures in tourism-health care services, retirement communities tied to health care services, entertainment (see Robinson 1997: 13) and other measures to integrate health tourism and offshore health care. Bernal anticipates the arrival of multinational hospitals that might help stem 'the loss of medical personnel' and rebuild Jamaica's health care system (1996: 15). The financial and personnel security requirements of such a development would be considerable in Jamaica. The state and/or private companies would have to boost security to support such a transition. Foreigners with financial resources will not retire in Jamaica or seek offshore health care there without a clear certainty about their personal safety. Private security services in the US are growing much faster than public security services due in part to the rise of fortress communities in America's wealthy residential areas. This trend is conditioned by impacts from state restructuring, technological displacement and the increase in violent crime from rising levels of urban poverty in America.

Bernal makes comparisons between Jamaica and India, Mexico, Canada, and East Asian countries, in relation to retirement services, informatics, and information processing, but he does not address the real differences of scale, scope, infrastructure, capital formation, the strong record in venture capitalism, the size of the high income middle strata and the critical mass of entrepreneurs found in those places. Capital from 'Overseas Chinese' fuels considerable venture capital expansion in East Asia, in addition to large capital inflows from Japan, the US, and Europe. Jamaica has no comparable counterpart experience.

Bernal raises the question of what Jamaica might accomplish by repositioning as a 'western hemisphere techno-pole' (1996: 17). He calls for a closer working relationship between the state and private capital. As Rosenberg notes, the separation of the political and the economic indicates precisely the central institutional linkage between the capitalist economy and the nation-state: that is, the legal structure of property rights which removes market relationships from direct political control or contestation and allows the flow of investment capital across national boundaries.

Specifically, the capitalist 'economy is not entirely a nationally constituted instrument ready at the disposal of the state'. Capital helps to shape public policy and capital flows are never reducible to 'instruments of state policy' (Rosenberg 1994: 14).

Bernal's reading of global restructuring understates the complexity and heterogeneity that mark the labour process and the wage labour-capital relation at the global level. The workhorses of the market-restructuring, contingency employment, structural adjustment and the mass of surplus labour from the former USSR, Eastern Europe, China, and beyond – are powerful conditioning factors on which neo-liberalism thrives. Furthermore, CARIBCAN, the Canada-US Free Trade Agreement, and NAFTA incorporate a complex of Taylorist, neo-Fordist and post-Fordist techniques of production and surplus extraction. It is necessary to consider the complex of global labour strategies to get a sense of what Jamaica's repositioning strategy would have to confront. Labour regimes face a systematic destruction of the 'long term contractualisation of the wage labour-capital relationship', the indexing of wages to productivity and profit and the 'vast socialisation of services through the welfare state (that) assured a permanent income for wage labour' (Lipietz 1997: 2, 3; Teeple 1995). As soon as we focus on the prevalence of contingency employment, long term structural unemployment, widespread worker insecurity, the systematic erosion of benefits, and the declining standard of living for many workers worldwide we begin to see that the strategy for the overthrow of the insubordination of labour operates through the discipline of monetarism.

Nor does Bernal pay careful attention to the contradictions of global financial swarming that affect the economy and financial system in Jamaica (see Rose 1997: 3; Watson 1998a). McBain addresses the 'paradoxical coincidence of the growth of financial services and financial institutions . . . amid decline in real economic growth'. McBain suggests that the 'softness of the stock market, and some segments of the real estate and tourism markets . . . led to the collapse of some financial institutions and to loss of confidence in the financial sector' (1997: 131). The president of the Caribbean Development Bank, Sir Neville Nicholls, has noted that 'the de-linking of Jamaica's monetary sector from the real sector of the economy has been central to its current problems and the challenge lies in finding ways to "put an end to that dichotomy"' (*Jamaica Gleaner*, July 30, 1999).

There is room for skepticism about Bernal's appeal to 'nation without borders' to draw overseas Jamaicans with capital back to Jamaica. Leading Jamaican capitalists are looking to linkages with the global market to reproduce their capital just as overseas Jamaicans are being encouraged to return to help develop Jamaica (Rose 1997: 3). The tendency of flight capital is to join the global swarm rather than move into bricks and mortar. Largely, Caribbean people emigrate because of the combination of 'too low a skill level despite extremely low labour costs. In such countries exclusion develops, which is to say that the labour supply is of no interest to capital' (Lipietz 1997: 17; Hoogvelt 1997).

Countries like Jamaica combine dependency and comprador functions in accommodating capital, some of which has exhausted options for profitable production at home. The absence of a well-developed and integrated market in the western hemisphere undermines any prospect for implementing the repositioning strategy that Bernal envisages for Jamaica. The Caribbean is not as important to Japan as Latin America. The US and the WTO are vigorously redirecting the EU's trading relationship with the Caribbean (see *Inside Europe*, No. 21 September 1998). I am skeptical that the combination of the harsh effects of the workhorses of the global market economy and competition from the unlimited reserves of skilled, cheap, 'ultra-flexible' labour from other parts of the world will force the demise of primitive Taylorism any time soon.

The World Bank concludes that Jamaica's ability to attract and keep private capital inflows 'can be sustained as the continuation of the adjustment programme increases the willingness of private investors to make their assets in Jamaica more permanent'. Given Jamaica's 'high debt service on external and domestic debt Jamaica's external financing needs will remain substantial' and the prospects for reducing the debt-service ratios will depend on how it meets three strategic conditions. According to the Bank, if external official support can be obtained primarily in grants and concessional loans, if the government can implement a sound borrowing strategy, and if private capital comes mainly as direct foreign investment or repatriated capital owned by Jamaicans, the debt-service ratios will decline substantially by the late 1990s. (World Bank 1995: 256, 254).

Handa and King (1997: 928-29) do not seem very sanguine about those prospects materializing. A country's trade deficits put pressure on its currency, especially when imports consistently exceed exports: the trade deficit depresses the value of the currency, given that the demand for foreign currency is exacerbated by the cost of imports. Relatively, the value of the foreign currency tends to rise for the importing country as its own currency declines. Countries like Jamaica are in constant trade deficit and they face a potential threat of currency depreciation. They offer significant incentives to attract money to augment the supply of capital, raise productivity and increase output and exports in order to raise the supply of foreign exchange, assuming the money goes into productive activity. Another practice is to raise interest rates to attract money. Jamaica has offered very attractive interest rates on short term inflows of money (*Jamaican Gleaner*, July 30, 1999), without raising productivity and export earnings to pay up when short term money matures. Higher interest rates also raise the cost of doing business, and unless productivity and quality can offset the higher business cost the strategy may be self-defeating,[22] especially where there is reliance on factor advantage to achieve export competitiveness.

There is wrangling between the PSOJ and commercial banks over interest rates. The PSOJ feels lower interest rates would complement the low inflation and exchange rate stability toward stimulating economic growth (*Jamaica Gleaner*, July 30, 1999). Producers say the 'stringent conditions imposed by commercial banks' during the past four years have made the 'liquidity crisis' more burdensome for them. The banking sector retorts that the term productive sector is used too loosely in Jamaica and bankers criticise some in the productive sector of using 'loans for unproductive purposes'. Bankers say they are willing to fund projects that are going to provide jobs and growth, and they encourage borrowers to use loans for the purposes for which the funds were intended and honor their loan obligations.

Three years after the appearance of Bernal's proposals, observers stressed that for Jamaica to encourage investor confidence it would have to improve its inefficient transportation system, reduce crime and violence, introduce banking sector reforms, raise the savings rate, and facilitate the consolidation of financial and non-financial institutions (*Jamaica Gleaner*, July 30, 1999). International lenders to countries like Jamaica take measures to protect their loans with steep interest rates so as to protect 'the integrity of the balance sheet', but at the expense of economic growth in the borrowing country. Should borrowers make cheap credit available to their citizens they can expect the lenders to take away the loans (Lapham 1998: 26). Thinking of Bernal's bold proposals and looking at Jamaica's reality today, there is quite a distance to travel to come close to what he envisages for Jamaica.

Cuba in the Caribbean Crisis: Contradictions of Monetarism or Convergence?

Attempts by the state and capital to make workers and peasants share a greater portion of the cost of reproducing labour power, and the strategy of state retrenchment have forced workers to see conflicts and struggles in increasingly social terms. The eruption of third world worker protests against IMF austerity programmes in recent decades is a case in point (Mars 1996: 6). The ways the state in Caribbean society 'expresses the will of private property as the highest political and moral reality' (Camilleri 1990: 19) has been masked by the politics of populism. It would appear that the Cuban state might be forced in the direction of having to adopt a neo-populist politics of convergence to deal with the predicament in which the country and society are now gripped. In this respect, could it be that 'socialism in one country' has reached a point where the Cuban socialist state is being forced to adapt to neo-liberal capitalism in a world dominated by money capital? If so, might this signal a closer convergence with the rest of the Caribbean and Latin America? Does the Cuban situation provide any particular lessons for our understanding of the nature of states under global capitalism?

Some Features of the Cuban Problematic

Derlugian has argued that the socialist world system 'was at most a geopolitical bloc within the world system and precisely lacked an economic foundation to become a system on its own' (1996: 166). This argument revives the debate on the question of 'socialism in one country'. The financial indebtedness of the COMECON countries to the western banks is a key factor that lends Derlugian's perspective more than a ring of plausibility. The economic and financial links between the West and the COMECON countries were quite strong. For example, the USSR had accumulated large debts to banks in the

West, especially German, French and American institutions to obtain machinery and grain. Moscow had normally settled its foreign accounts with gold payments. The demonetarisation of gold in the 1970s had a strong negative impact the USSR's ability to settle its foreign accounts, which forced Moscow and COMECON to adjust further to the terms and conditions set by their western creditors.

COMECON states adjusted by modernising their production infrastructures to raise labour productivity and extract higher rates of surplus value from their workers. Demonetarisation contributed to growing insolvency, worker resistance to productivity increases, and greater adjustment by those states to the requirements of their western creditors. Worker resistance turned to rebellion in Poland and other countries and forced the USSR to initiate *glasnost* ('openness') and *perestroika* ('reconstruction'). Soviet bloc workers saw the issue in terms of gaining a larger share of the social wage for their own reproduction, rather than giving more to the state to pay the external debt and finance the elimination of jobs. Such a disposition has been part of a pattern in other highly indebted countries (Marazzi 1995: 84), particularly around so-called 'IMF riots' in many neocolonial countries.

Haroldo Dilla (1999) has offered an imaginative analysis of the Cuban situation. He explains how the global motion of capital is conditioning key areas of Cuban national public policy and forcing the restructuring of class relations and the bases of popular power and socialist institutions. Dilla argues that the scope of the changes in Cuba since the late 1980s do not signal 'an adjustment to an existing capitalist mode of operation but a radical restructuring of the political economy, the form of social regulation and cultural-ideological production' (1999: 2). He is also concerned about the implications of the rise of a 'technocratic-entrepreneurial bloc'[23] for the distribution of power and the 'socialist development project itself' (1999: 3).

The collapse of the COMECON system left the Cuba and its entire society in a precarious situation. Between 1986-1990, the economy stagnated and fell into serious decline. By 1993, the GNP had contracted by 40 per cent and Cuba lost about 85 per cent of its traditional and preferential markets and its medium-term and long term lines of credit and technology, and its import capacity fell by two-thirds. To counter these adverse developments Cuba embarked on a vigorous economic liberalisation strategy. The opening to foreign investment began in the late 1980s. In 1992, private property rights in the means of production were recognised and the state decentralised its monopoly in foreign trade. In 1993, the state granted the public permission to hold foreign currency, legalised self-employment in services and transferred significant public agricultural holdings to cooperatives. In 1995, the state legalised the protection of foreign investor rights. The government also adjusted the budget to mop up liquidity by imposing taxes, raising prices and facilitating a free market in food in 1994. In 1996–97 the state reorganised the banking system, modified customs laws, and inaugurated free trade zones (Dilla 1998: 1; Girvan 1999: 7–9).

The new dynamic is one in which the Cuban state and the social power of money are conditioning the allocation of resources, the distribution of meager surplus, reshaping class relations, and subordinating civil society and production processes to employers and private capital accumulation. Dilla notes that capitalist expansion is raising the rate of exploitation across the economy and undermining the standard of living. Gender and trade union issues are surfacing around the class and labour questions (see Girvan 1999: 9). The expansion of private sector employment through EPZs modifies the relationship between the state, labour and capital. The expansion of tourism has fueled the growth of sex work[24] and thrown up new gender dynamics. Many persons have resorted to sex work, partly to compensate for the contraction of the state provisions (Fusco 1998) and to earn foreign exchange as a means of asserting independence and gaining access to commodities. Unemployment is growing, nominal and real wages are declining, job competition between male and female workers is on the rise, and self-employment[25] permeates all the social strata. Such developments point to the reconstruction of the working class and the rising incidence of pragmatism in the face of the erosion of socialist property and power. There is the unavoidable question of the impact of money capital, the market, and individualism on the institutions of socialist power (Dilla 1999: 11).

The tendency to reduce prostitution or sex work to an issue of moral gender removes it from the context of economic reproduction and employment, makes it a matter of pure choice and places a moral stigma and burden on women (see Kempadoo and Doezema 1998). If it is plausible to view gay, lesbian and bisexual activity in Cuba in extreme terms of 'an unspoken revolt against both the socialist emphasis on productive work and the revolution's puritanical morality', it also raises a contradiction for the state. Can the Cuban state permit sexual liberalism on the one hand and expect to regulate the private lives of adult women and men (Fusco 1998: 157, 156)?

Dilla wonders whether the refusal of the bureaucracy to 'share its legitimate competence in matters of social control' might be a function of the state's disposition to 'present to international capital a country in good order, incompatible with the existence of combative autonomous organisations' (1999: 10). In fact, when a government has to adopt a strategy of cheapening the labour of its workers to attract and capture a share of global capital through the medium of tourism, it can't afford to have a working class that is free to make waves which can drive away investors and tourists and put foreign exchange and the rate of capital accumulation at risk. In view of the fact that Cuba's tourist industry has spawned the new 'informal economy' of self-employed people, including sex workers, it would be very difficult for the government to put a lid on sex work, without affecting the main source of foreign exchange and capital accumulation. Clearly, the retrenchment of the state forces people to find alternative ways to reproduce themselves.

Cuba appears to be moving closer to the model of national states as 'differentiated forms of global capitalist relations'.[26] There has been a significant increase in the volume and scale of foreign investment in Cuba, up from 20 foreign investors in 1990 to 260 with 800 operations in 1996. More than 35 countries and US$2 billion are represented in the joint investment ventures. Directors of state enterprises and local and foreign businesses are strategically located to benefit from profit making and social differentiation (Dilla 1999: 5).[27] The state stresses that foreign investment is vital for protecting socialist gains such as free education and health care, and insists that Cuba has successfully incorporated features of capitalism and the market economy while preserving the socialist foundations. But state wages are lower for most Cubans than they were 10 years ago (now about $15 per month) and the state has legalised EPZs. Many Cuban workers are educated and technically proficient. These and the other factors discussed above have contributed to the increase in international business activity in Cuba.[28]

The US Chamber of Commerce has been scouting Cuba for investment opportunities on behalf of American firms and supports the call for the repeal of the trade embargo that keeps American capital out of the Cuban market. CNN Fortune ('Island of Profit', July 28, 1999) reports that 'Cuba is not a country closed to the rest of the world. It's closed only to the United States because of the 37-year-old embargo signed by President Kennedy that prohibits American businesses from trading with Cuba.'[29]

Cuba survived the US embargo and the collapse of the Soviet Union. The US Congress enacted the Cuban Democracy Act of 1992 with the expectation of forcing Cuba to abandon the socialist path. The 1992 law failed to accomplish what the embargo and the Soviet collapse did not achieve. The Cuban Solidarity and Democracy Act of 1996 (Helms-Burton) was designed to secure what the embargo, the Soviet collapse, and the Cuban Democracy Act failed to accomplish. The implications of Helms-Burton for sovereign autonomy fostered large-scale opposition from most member states of the UN to the American strategy of economic warfare against Cuba. The strategy is to bring Cuba into compliance with the terms of OAS Resolution 1080 and Clinton's 'National Security Strategy' to make neo-liberalism more effective in Cuba. Resolution 1080 and the 'National Security Strategy' are key components of the US collective security arrangements for the western hemisphere in post-Soviet times.

The tenacity of the cold war project in American-Cuban relations is evident in Washington's resistance to appeals from foreign governments, congressional republicans and democrats, former secretaries of state Henry Kissinger and Lawrence Eagleberger, and the call by a number of prominent Cuban-Americans for a reexamination of American policy toward Cuba and an end to the economic blockade (Alarcon de Quesada 1999: 2, 22). While Helms-Burton has failed to achieve the goal of strengthening US influence in the foreign policies of other states, including CARICOM states, towards Cuba, it does not mean there is no coincidence of interests between the US and its leading allies with respect to the LAC.[30] The ineffectiveness of the American strategy can be seen from the fact that since the Soviet collapse, foreign investments and especially tourism have soared in Cuba: in 1998, at least 1.4 million tourists visited Cuba and spent $1.8 billion in hard currency. Cuban tourism is estimated to be growing four times faster than that of its Caribbean neighbors.

Cuba's large foreign deficits condition how the state deals with its current international situation. Like other Caribbean countries with weak currencies, Cuba is in the difficult position of having few options in the face of global monetary austerity. In fact, the room states used to have with the instrument of convertible gold has disappeared in contrast with the growth of the multinational centres of power like the IMF that increasingly mediate the affairs of highly indebted countries. Devaluation and state retrenchment leave political parties and trade unions to manage the crisis and mediate restructuring.

Socialism and social democracy have been transformed into a regime of monetarist austerity, within the norms of the class power and rule of money as capital. Says Marazzi, 'monetarism and the policies deriving from it presuppose a relation of class forces completely subordinated to money as capital' (1995: 88, 87). Money lives as 'the most abstract form of capitalist property' and as such is 'the supreme social power through which social reproduction is subordinated to capitalist reproduction' (Clarke 1988: 13–14; see Bonefeld 1995: 203). Cuban socialism has been drawn more decisively into an orbit of credit where 'the stability of credit depends on the capacity of capital to exploit labour effectively' and capital must 'exploit labour effectively because capital has not only to generate surplus value sufficiently to allow accumulation but also to satisfy its creditors' (Bonefeld 1995: 204). In other words, neo-liberalism demands the subordination of 'social reproduction to capitalist reproduction' and this is the decisive point that Cuban socialism has reached.

The traditional conception of nation, national state and self-determination[31] does not sufficiently reflect the nature of states and sovereignty in relation to global capitalism. The relationship between the national and the international is so inextricably linked that the physiognomy of the national is illuminated in the reflection of the international. The cultural particularism of national agency does not define itself in opposition to the global; rather, the particularism of place is mediated through its contradictory unity within the global system. Cuba's anti-imperialist strategy is under stronger pressure from her new role around the global movement of capital, which highlights the limits of socialism in one country (see Girvan 1999: 11). The dialectic of globalisation and glocalisation points to the futility of attempting to segment the national from the international.

There is a clear shift in the relation between the Cuban state and global capital, a shift that signals a major 'change in the forms of global capitalist domination'. Cuban national political decisions 'are now more directly integrated into the global movement of capital', a development that 'makes more difficult the national decomposition of society' and gives the impression that capital has become omnipotent. Holloway reminds us that capital's 'violent restlessness is the clearest indication of the inadequacy (for capital) of the . . . relations of exploitation, of capital's incapacity to subordinate the power of labour on which it depends (1995: 134, 135). Dilla's case for strengthening the popular institutions of socialist power in Cuba (1999: 8-10) to protect the working class and the institutions of socialist power moves the argument beyond national-global dichotomies. These matters cannot be left entirely up to the state.[32]

Conclusion and Recommendations

To view states as differentiated forms of global capitalist relations is to transcend the static state-to-nation, class-to-nation, nation-to-culture and geography mapping that characterises the theories of conventional international relations. Looking at states from this perspective puts Caribbean states squarely within capitalist social relations of production. States are predisposed to make the private interests of capital primary in the determination of public policy, based on the balance of social forces. Class issues matter a great deal, as we can see from the move by states and capital to implement global neo-liberal monetarism to reequip the accumulation base and combat the insubordination of labour. We know that capital is always more or less unhappy with all strategies of accumulation and relations of exploitation. Capital is nervous about strategies that give workers a role in the determining the conditions of their own reproduction.

The core norms of the postwar interstate system stressed self-determination and state sovereignty, froze national borders, reinforced the sovereignty of violence that typifies the national state model, rekindled suspicion between states and reserved disproportionate power for the permanent members of the UN Security Council. Just as the dominant powers and their ruling classes have been extremely suspicious of real participatory democracy, they have also been skeptical about the idea of running the world in an open democratic fashion. One of the major challenges of the coming century will be to move humanity beyond the model that privileges the sovereignty of violence, inequality, and exploitation. In order for the UN principle of 'we the people' to become reality both the sovereignty of violence and the strategy for running the world like a market would have to be overturned. Global peace, stability and genuine human progress are incompatible with the system that separates sovereign autonomy from economic independence. It is impossible to deepen the links between the UNUDHR and democratisation, when full employment has been scuttled and when high unemployment and permanent job loss as a percentage of total unemployment have become the norm.

It is necessary to work for the international abolition of the violence that is built into the gendered sexual division of labour and its corollary, the 'breadwinner-housewife-model'. The abolition of the state's role as 'total patriarch' is also necessary to advance the abolition of national and international violence. This will require ending state control over women's sexuality and fertility. The question of religion is pertinent, as already indicated above.

The Caribbean region is being affected by global transitions in R&D, science and technology, manufacturing, information systems and financial liberalisation and integration. Giving capital the freedom it needs to pursue accumulation for its sake is the preferred model of market democracy, which necessitates rendering most human rights increasingly deontological. Global neo-liberalism subjugates human welfare to capital's imperatives of efficiency. Capitalism in the age of electronics, hot money and monetarism are incompatible with sovereign autonomy: money as capital thumbs its nose at sovereign autonomy! Employment and employment priorities, unemployment, private ownership or state ownership, and technological heterogeneity are global political issues. The ratio of the formal sector to the informal sector has much to do with the politics of restructuring. Industrial countries use protectionism to keep out exports from third world countries, which is also a political matter. The transition from Keynesianism to neo-liberalism for managing the global economy is a matter of political choice around new capital accumulation strategies.

One reason that national territorial sovereignty remains unresolved is that nation states are not ordained to be the ultimate container of global humanity. The transnational 'triadic' restructuring of hegemony deepened with the demise of the USSR. The world is less responsive to American initiatives than in the past. As the US turns increasingly outward in response to the changing structure and composition of capital and other challenges, it becomes increasingly subject to the norms of the market it seeks to direct via the politics of global monetarism.

The Caribbean is becoming more secondary and marginal. The rejection of parity with Mexico under NAFTA coincides with America's aggressive approach to the banana issue. The WTO is the mouthpiece for corporate capital and the American strategy is to dominate the WTO. The US prefers formal rules-based regimes of trade, while masking inequality in the tracks of the market and geopolitical subordination. The IMF is facilitating this strategy on a so-called level playing field 'in conditions of structural inequality and hierarchy' (Cummings 1998: 72). Caribbean states have few choices with or without a WHFTA, so they do what they believe will moderate their marginality. The strategy of offering workers for exploitation involves policies that force down the real wages and standard of living of vast numbers of workers. In the north this occasions periodic outbursts of protectionist, anti-immigration, and racist anti-foreign sentiment among workers, politicians and other xenophobic forces. In the age of electronics, spatial changes are afoot that render geography less important than class.

The Caribbean has to pay closer attention to the move by the EU towards the consolidation of Greater Europe. The EU wants a stronger foothold in greater Europe and Russia to become the centre of a new economic and financial Europe. While Japan exploits its reservations about China and Russia by sticking close to Washington on Asia issues, Tokyo also wants to accelerate the economic pace in the wider East Asian markets, to stem fragmentation and help adjust its own internal crisis. Mexico, Russia, China, and East Asia offer much more to the triad powers in terms of resources, productive and disciplined labour, investment and consumer markets, and military capabilities (Wallerstein 1996: 231–32) than the LAC countries. In economic terms, Latin America is much more important to the triad powers than the Caribbean. Since capital is never comfortable with any given accumulation strategy, states are always at risk of losing favor with investors. States that live by offering their working population as cheap labour for exploitation tend to have serious self-esteem and identity problems that are compounded by their dependency-comprador reality.

Another key issue the Caribbean has to deal with is that of intellectual property and rights. The US has sought to generalise American constitutional norms to inform the new rules and regulations for protecting the intellectual property rights and property income on which capital relies for its own reproduction. Intellectual property rights issues have come to dominate the industries and services that anchor the global political economy. Triad states can be expected to adopt new forms of selective protectionism and other measures that will reinforce technological displacement in the north, semi-proletarianisation in the third world and other consequences that will squeeze third world workers and peasants. Post-Keynesian militarism, the new regionalisation, drugs, the production and proliferation of weapons of mass destruction, and other issues will test America's power in unprecedented ways. How the US deals with these and other problems will affect how it relates to the Caribbean.

Building social cohesion at the intersection between class and nationalism seems incompatible with running states like markets and driving down the standard of living of workers, including hollowing the ranks of the middle strata. As more people become disillusioned about the future, some states are trying to deconstruct national borders. Bernal's theme of 'nation without borders' touches on aspects of a sentiment that is growing in the Caribbean region (see Bryan 1998; Serbin 1998). Other less obvious dynamics are at work in the 'nations unbound' construct. States like Jamaica are looking for new ways to tap into the pension and retirement funds of overseas Jamaican retirees. Jamaica thinks there are ways to gain influence in American foreign policy by getting Jamaican-Americans to become active in appropriate level of politics in large American cities like New York, Washington and Miami. The nation without borders concept raises issues of citizenship, bearing in mind that tensions between globalisation and sovereignty are deepening. Could the nation without borders concept promote a sense of global citizenship identity, and are there civil institutions to forge the identity necessary to engender support for such a project (see Serbin 1998a-b)? There are strategic symbolic and material issues to address in this regard. The national state is being renegotiated: nationalism, ethnicity and citizenship are more like 'continuous plebiscites' than finished products.

Caribbean states have stressed human welfare issues in their foreign policies. The restructuring of the cold war project has moved human welfare matters from the backburner. Issues of the ecosystem, migration, refugees, aids, drugs, deprivation and exclusion, hunger, gender, ethnic violence, violence against women, and homelessness are some of the key human welfare issues of importance to the Caribbean, but those issues have been seconded to capital accumulation imperatives. There is no simple way for Caribbean states to lift their industries and workers out of the rut of low productivity employment and high open unemployment. Economists who defend labour intensive production (low productivity employment with high open unemployment) do not normally have to reproduce themselves in that mode.

The masses of Caribbean workers and small farmers have only marginal influence in the politics of their countries. High productivity workers in the Caribbean are a minority without the clout to shape public policy. The comprador leadership, other local business forces, foreign capital and other fragmented interests are better positioned in relation to the state than are the broad mass of workers. Mercantile and commercial interests have drained the state of subsidies or have exploited protected markets via preferences. They lack the means to fight for a larger share of the world market, so they pushed the state to adopt trade policies that treat small domestic markets as viable home markets. They have played key roles in leading Caribbean states to try to alleviate open unemployment rather than to end low productivity employment. This approach is reflected in the ambivalence of those states toward their workers, which is conditioned by how they help to reproduce global capitalism. Clearly, selling their workers as cheap labour obviates fighting to end low productivity employment.

Historically, states and ruling classes that reproduce themselves in a comprador relationship to the global ruling interests seldom move to develop their resources on their own initiative. They rely on other states and their capitalists to develop those resources, becoming intermediaries in the process. This has been the dominant reality in the Caribbean. Their reliance on others is largely a function of the nature of their states within global capitalism. Their resources, strategic location and other variables are scarcely theirs to manipulate in any important respects. Their geopolitical importance is determined by other powerful states and capitalist interests! At times their key resources like sun, sea and climate may not require much effort to develop them, but as soon as commodification is normalised around those resources, the opportunities are customarily exploited by others. There is no natural law that dictates the coincidence of dependency and comprador status (see Abu-Lughod 19: 310–313). Rather, it is a matter of human agency and class and political interests. Political contingency, economic instability and uncertainty tend to plague states that have to rely on attracting capital, trade, shipping, financiers, and special preferences to survive. The status and achievements of such states are always heavily conditioned by what goes on in the wider world system of which they are a part. The dominance of the US in the Caribbean has conditioned the existence of those states and their societies for many years.

Caribbean states and societies will have to grapple with several other tenacious and protracted issues. The expanding urban informal sector; the erosion of labour protection and social security regimes that account for a fairly small portion of the employed labour force; the absence of a high technology industrial and informational base for incorporating complex technology and complex labour; the changing role of the state and trade unions in labour markets under neo-liberalism, drugs and their effects, ecological problems, and violence.[33] Informality transcends modernisation and can be expected to encompass housing, transportation, sanitation, access to safe potable water, electricity and other areas.[34] Groups trapped in high levels of poverty are forced to appropriate public goods by eating out of the state in order to survive. This is likely to become more pervasive across the Caribbean as part of the process of national decomposition and restructuring.

Notes

1. I have discussed issues such as drugs, sovereignty, and global financialisation in Watson 1998a-b. For Barbados, see Watson 1997.
2. Holloway (1995: 5–6) notes that crisis 'does not simply refer to "hard times", but to turning points. It directs attention to the discontinuities of history, to breaks in the path of development, ruptures in a pattern of movement, variations in the intensity of time.' The proper starting point for analysing capitalist crisis is not the exhaustion of a given capital accumulation strategy. Crisis is rooted in the very nature of the capital relation itself and the accumulation strategy is where the crisis gains expression.
3. Lewis Lapham (1998: 16–17) defines postmodern imperialism as that condition in which 'the lesser nations of the earth become colonies not of governments but of corporations, the law of nations construed as the rule of money, and the world's parliaments intimidated by the force of capital in much the same way that in the eighteenth and nineteenth centuries they had been intimidated by the force of arms.' There is truth and cynicism in Lapham's depiction of imperialism.
4. Says Marilyn Waring: 'In New Zealand, companies dry dung products and sell them in pellitised form for the home gardener. The process is called manufacturing. The results are marketed. The workers are paid. When the rural women of the developing world recycle dung, nothing in the process, the production, or the labour has an economic value' (1997: 31).
5. Serbin offers reasons why the Association of Caribbean States (ACS) Treaty 'does not contain any agreement for cooperation on matters of regional collective security in the traditional sense of the term , or that the dominant discourse in regional security

matters is shifting radically away from strategic military issues to police intelligence matters' (1998: 57). The fact remains that the framework for regional security lies in the Rio treaty of 1947 which is already modified in the OAS Resolution 1080, which also predates the ACS. Clinton's national security strategy for a new century shows where the emphasis lies.

6. In 1998, the leading businesses in the world had corporate assets of around $4 trillion, an amount that was greater than 'the collective net worth of all the member governments of the United Nations' (Lapham 1998: 7). UNDP (1998: 37, Table 1.12) gives the following estimates of the additional annual cost required to achieve universal access to basic social services in all developing countries (figures are in billions of US dollars): basic education $6bn; water/sanitation $9bn; reproductive health for all women $12bn; basic health/nutrition $13bn. Compare these figures with the annual amounts spent on certain products in the USA, Europe and Japan: cosmetics (USA) $8bn; ice cream (Europe) $11bn; perfumes (Europe/USA) $12bn; pet foods (Europe/USA) $17bn; business entertainment (Japan) $35bn; cigarettes (Europe) $50bn; alcohol drinks (Europe) $105bn; narcotics drugs (world) $400bn; and military spending (world) $780bn. We should note that these industries exist in the North because they are key to production of exchange value for capital accumulation purposes and they consume certain inputs from the South.

7. In order to bring about genuine political participation it would be necessary to banish inequality from democracy, get rid of the alienation of unpaid labour, and put an end to alienation.

8. Richard Nixon confirmed this fact shortly after his 1972 Inauguration, when he observed that 'the postwar order of international relations, the configuration of power that emerged from the Second World War' had passed, along with 'the conditions which determined the assumptions and practices of United States foreign policy since 1945' (quoted in Landau 1988: 102).

9. The 1997 World Bank Report, *The State in A Changing World* (Oxford 1997), not only redefines the role of the state in the neo-liberal era but also provides insights into the reinvention of the World Bank itself.

10. National and international agencies (such as the World Bank) rely on national account statistics to assess and appraise the prospects of development programmes. Needs assessments of deserving cases are determined by per capita GDP, but lenders, donors, and investors privilege cases with high growth rates because such cases favor exports, investment, loans, and other business opportunities. Commodification, exploitation, pollution, and dehumanisation become an integral part of statistics that record economic growth. Monetisation for capitalisation actually rules the construction of national account statistics. A country's cash (surplus value) generating capacity linked to its balance of trade and payments profile is what interests lenders and investors, not so much the scope of its productive capacity (see Waring 1997: 32).

11. This point was appreciated by Huntington in the 1970s, when the Trilateral Commission commissioned the study, *The Crisis of Democracy*, which concluded that there was too much democracy in the West (see Huntington et al 1973).
12. According to Serbin (1998: 54; CEPAL 1994: 2), ECLAC defines 'open regionalism' as a process that fosters regional economic interdependence under liberalisation with a view to enhancing economic and export competitiveness of LAC countries. My perspective is that the 'Washington Consensus' on Latin America takes precedence in the working definition of open regionalism.
13. Washington sidelines Canada and Mexico in NAFTA-European Union relations, and treats all the regional groupings in the western hemisphere - the Canada-United States Free Trade Agreement (CUSFTA), MERCOSUR, the Andean Group, and CARICOM – as arrangements for rationalising and reinforcing the heterogeneous division of labour that benefits American capital disproportionately (see Ougard 1999; Valtonen 1999).
14. Billionaire George Soros argues that there 'is something contradictory in banishing the state from the economy while at the same time enshrining it as the ultimate source of authority in international relations' (Soros 1997: 53).
15. See Girvan, 1999: 9, for a discussion of R&D institutions, output and linkages in Cuba. See also Figueros and Plasencia Vidal (1994) on Cuba's R&D and techno-industrial achievements.
16. For the period 1950-1989, the Caribbean Region had a migration balance of -5.586 million; for the same period the Caribbean islands had a migration balance of -5.116 million and *CARICOM countries* had a migration balance of -1.943 million (see UNECLAC 1998: Table 1, p. 23, figures are rounded).
17. See ECLAC 1998: 25-28, Tables 3–6, for data on net remittances (Table 3), net remittances as percentage of GDP (Table 4), ratio of export of goods and services (Table 5), and remittances as ratio of merchandise exports for selected Caribbean countries (Table 6), covering the period 1985-1994.
18. For data on the Human Development Index for Caribbean countries in middle of the 1990s, see UNDP 1998.
19. For relevant information about the array of problems facing secondary and tertiary education in various CARICOM countries see, for example, World Bank 1993a; 1996a; 1996b; 1996c; *Economic and Social Survey of Jamaica* 1988; West Indian Commission Report 1992. Between 1954 and 1988, the University of the West Indies awarded a total of 43,411 First Degrees, Certificates, Diplomas, and Higher Degrees, of which 3.3% were in Agriculture; 23.27% in Arts and General Studies; 13.48% in Education; 6.8% in Engineering; 4.12% in Law; 9.43% in Medical Sciences; 15.53% in the Natural Sciences; and 23.92% in the Social Sciences (World Bank 1993a: 164, Table 7.5). In the age of incessant innovation it is very difficult for any state to be definitive about mapping a long term development strategy, partly because it is very hard to be certain about the nature and quantity of jobs that might become available.

The high technology production process suggests that states are at a loss to map accumulation programmes that satisfy capital. The UWI faces a daunting task providing education and training for the 21st century in an environment where global capital accumulation strategies increasingly define the parameters of development.

20. At the 1998 World Economic Summit in Davos, Switzerland, a Chinese delegate remarked to Lewis Lapham, editor of *Harper's Magazine* that Chinese have moved from zero cellular phones and pagers four years ago to 20 million cellular phones and 40 million pagers today. The Chinese delegate also remarked, 'in China we're spending $750 billion for infrastructures, but in the last two months we laid off one million railroad workers. You could say that our lack of democracy is a blessing. In Europe or America there would be arguments' (Lapham 1998: 8).

21. This section draws on an unpublished version of Watson, 1998a.

22. Sir Neville Nicholls, president of the Caribbean Development Bank, says Jamaica will need about US$4 billion over the coming 10 years to lower unemployment to around 10% of the official labour force. He noted that while premium interest rates serve to attract capital inflows, there is 'no justification for why that premium should be so high as to render those same inflows useless for productive investment.' He stressed the need to improve education and skills, protect the environment and improve social equity (*Jamaica Gleaner*, July 30, 1999).

23. Dilla says the size of the Cuban working class has shrunk and the economically active population declined by 16 % between 1988–1996. The state sector has contracted and self-employment has expanded. Real wages have fallen dramatically and exploitation of workers has risen across the economic spectrum (1999: 6). Unemployment is being normalised due to state retrenchment, technological displacement and the expansion of production for profit, more broadly. The Cuban state allocates about 60% of the budget to public health, social security, education, and the role of the state in key areas to moderate the contradictions of economic liberalisation.

24. In Cuba, *Jineterismo* is the business of Cubans exchanging 'a range of services, including sex, for money from foreigners'. Cuba has come to be identified in certain European magazines as the 'sex tourist paradise'. Of course, Cuba is not peculiar in this regard among Caribbean and other third world countries. Jamaica's sex workers are said to be mainly male. This might also be the norm in Barbados. Sex work is rampant in parts of Asia and it has grown rapidly in Eastern Europe after the collapse of the Soviet empire (Fusco 1998: 152–57, *passim*). Sex workers are active in several other Caribbean countries like Jamaica, Barbados, and Antigua.

25. In addition to *jineteros* and *jineteras*, many of Cuba's new self-employed vendors, cab drivers, beauticians and other petty traders were once economists, architects, engineers and such (Fusco 1998: 162). This shift in the composition of the working class leads Fusco to remark that a society where sex work is the best paying job for women or men is a society in crisis (1998: 166, 159).

26. Girvan (1999: 9) says Cuba used the 'Special Period' to redesign the system to meet national survival and for the 'reinsertion into the global market economy, drawing on the strong participatory ethos and practices that have been features of the Cuban revolutionary process'. Dilla argues that national survival and revolutionary institutions have been compromised by reinsertion.
27. According to Dilla, Cuban National Bank figures reveal that 77.8% of total savings were held in 41 % of bank accounts in 1994; 83.7% of savings were in 43% of bank accounts in 1995, 84.7% in 12.8% of accounts in 1996, and 43.8% of savings were in 2.7% of savings accounts in 1996 (1999: 6). Private accumulation is also taking place in agriculture and certain areas of self-employment.
28. A Canadian capitalist with $400 million in investments in Cuban tourism says he expects his investment 'to pay off with a 10-year, 600% return' (CNN Fortune, 'Island of Profit', July 28, 1999 – 8pm, ET).
29. There are exemptions in the embargo that allow certain businesses such as telecommunication companies like AT&T, religious and humanitarian bodies, sporting events, entertainers, artists and news organisations like CNN to operate in Cuba (CNN Fortune, 'Island of Profit', July 28, 1999 – 8pm, ET).
30. Katada argues that while Japanese aid to Latin America and the Caribbean during 1971–91 benefited Japan's economic and political interests, Japan has collaborated with the US to maintain and strengthen American 'power and dominance especially in political and security issues', thereby improving the 'US-Japanese relationship' and contributing to making 'US hegemony in Latin America more stable and long-lasting than otherwise' (1997: 931).
31. Cuba's position is that the revolution has deep roots that antedate the cold war and 1959. Cuba sees 1959 as the culmination of a long process of autonomous struggle (see Girvan 1999: 10).
32. Dilla's perspective contrasts with Ricardo Alarcon's on the Cuban miracle and socialist power and democracy (see also Girvan 1999: 10).
33. Buendía says: 'If informality is the politics of the urban poor, and social security is the politics of the organised working class, protectionism is . . . the politics of many Latin American economic elites' (1995: 77). Thus informality, social security and protectionism have constituted a key political factor, but neo-liberal restructuring has been transforming the reality and the weights of the three component parts.
34. See Buendía, 1995: 72–73.

Bibliography

Abu-Lughod, Janet, *Before European Hegemony* (New York: Oxford University Press, 1989)
Alarcon de Quesada, Ricardo, President of the National Assembly of People's Power of Cuba, Presentation on the United States Policy against Cuba. Havana, Cuba, January 8, 1999.

A National Security Doctrine for A New Century (Washington DC: The White House, May 1997)

Alleyne, Mark, 'The Global Context of Regional Imperatives of Telecommunications Policies in the States of CARICOM' in *21st Century Policy Review* (Vol. 1, No. 2, Winter 1994)

Amin, Samir, *Re-reading the Postwar Period* (New York: Monthly Review Press, 1994)

Capitalism in the Age of Globalisation (London: Zed Books, 1997)

Association of Caribbean States, Constitutive Agreement of the Association of Caribbean States, Cartagena de Indias, July 24, 1994.

Bernal, Richard, *Strategic Global Repositioning and Future Economic Development in Jamaica*, The North-South Centre Agenda Papers, Number 18 (Florida: University of Miami: North-South Centre Press, 1996)

Blackman Associates, *Comprehensive review of CARICOM Investment Climate*, commissioned by the Caribbean Community Secretariat (February 1996)

Blackman, Sir Courtney, 'Financial Globalisation: A Small State Perspective', Address to the Eastern Caribbean Institute of Banking, Basseterre, St Kitts, March 24, 1999

Bloomfield, Richard J, 'Security in the Greater Caribbean: What Role for Collective Security Mechanisms?' in *From Pirates to Drug Lords: The Post-Cold War Caribbean Security Environment*, Michael Desch, Jorge Dominguez, and Andres Serbin, eds. (Albany: SUNY Press, 1998)

Bonefeld, Werner, 'Money, Equality and Exploitation: An Interpretation of Marx's Treatment of Money' in *Global Capital, National State and the Politics of Money*, Werner Bonefeld and John Holloway, eds. (New York: St Martin's Press, 1995a)

Bonefeld, Werner, 'Capital as Subject and the Existence of Labour' in *Emancipating Marx: Open Marxism 3*, Werner Bonefeld, Richard Gunn, John Holloway and Kosmas Psychopedis, eds. (London: Pluto Press, 1995b)

Bonefeld, Werner and Holloway, John, 'Introduction: The Politics of Money' *in Global Capital, National State and the Politics of Money*, Werner Bonefeld and John Holloway, eds. (New York: St Martin's Press, 1995)

Brenner, Neil, "Global Cities, Local States: Global City Formation and State Territorial Restructuring in Contemporary Europe", in Review of International Political Economys: 1 Spring, 1998: 1–37

Bryan, Anthony (1998) 'The State of the Region: Trends Affecting the Future of Caribbean Security' in *From Pirates to Drug Lords: The Post-Cold War Caribbean Security Environment*, MC Desch, Jorge Dominguez and A Serbin, eds. (Albany: SUNY Press, 1998)

Buendía, Hernando Gómez, 'The Politics and Economics of Global Employment: A Perspective from Latin America' in *Global Employment: An International Investigation into the Future of Work, Volume One*, Mihaly Simai, Valentine Moghadam and Arvo Kuddo, eds. (London: Zed Press Zed Books for the United Nations University World Institute for Development Economics Research, 1995)

Burch, Kurt, 'Property' in *The Making of the International System* (Boulder: Lynne Rienner Publishers, 1998)

Burnham, Peter 'Capital, Crisis and the International State System' in *Global Capital, National State and the Politics of Money*, Werner Bonefeld and John Holloway, eds. (New York: St Martin's Press, 1995)

Cabezas, Amalía Lucia, 'Discourses of Prostitution: The Case of Cuba' in *Global Sex Workers: Rights, Resistance, and Redefinition*, Kamala Kempadoo and Jo Doezema, eds. (New York: Routledge, 1998)

Camilleri, J. (1990) 'Rethinking Sovereignty in a Shrinking, Fragmented World' in *Contending Sovereignties: Redefining Political Community*, RBJ Walker and Saul Mendlovitz, eds.(Boulder: Lynne Rienner Publishers, 1990)

Castoriadis, Cornelius, *Philosophy, Politics, Autonomy: Essays in Political Philosophy*, David Ames, ed.(Curtis, New York: Oxford University Press, 1991)

Clarke, S, *Keynesianism, Monetarism, and the Crisis of the State* (Aldershot: Edward Elgar, 1988)

Clarke, Tony and Barlow, Maud, *The Multilateral Agreement on Investment and the Threat to Canadian Sovereignty* (Toronto: Stoddard Publishing Company, 1997)

Cox, Robert, *Production, Power and World Order: Social Forces in the Making of History* (New York: Columbia University Press, 1987)

Cox, Robert, 'Towards a Post-Hegemonic Conceptualisation of World Order: Reflections on the Relevancy of Ibn Khaldun' in *Governance Without Government: Order and Change in World Politics*, J Rosenau and E Czempiel, eds. (Cambridge: Cambridge University Press, 1987)

Cox, Robert W. with Timothy J. Sinclair, Approaches to World Order, Cambridge University Press, Cambridge, 1996

Cummings, Bruce, 'The Korean Crisis and the End of "Late" Development' in *New Left Review* (Number 231, September/October 1998: 43–72)

Das, Udaibir S, and Gobind, N Ganga, 'A Retrospect and Prospect on the Reform of the Financial Sector in Guyana' in *Social and Economic Studies* (46: 2&3: 93–129)

Dilla, Haroldo, 'Comrades and Investors: The Uncertain Transition in Cuba' in *The Socialist Register 1999*, Leo Panitch, ed. (London: The Merlin Press)

Eder, Klaus, The Social Construction of Nature, Sage Publications, Beverly Hills, CA, 1996

Figueros, Miguel A and Sergio Plasencia Vidal, 'The Cuban Economy in the 1990s: Problems and Prospects' in *The Caribbean in the Global Political Economy*, Hilbourne A Watson, ed. (Boulder: Lynne Rienner Publishers, 1994)

Fusco, Coco, 'Hustling for Dollars: Jineterismo in Cuba' in *Global Sex Workers: Rights, Resistance, and Redefinition*, Kamala Kempadoo and Jo Doezema, eds. (New York: Routledge, 1998)

Economic and Social Survey of Jamaica, Kingston 1988

Giarini, Orio, 'The Future of Work: Redefining Productive Work' *in Global Employment an International Investigation into the Future of Work, Volume I*, Mihaly Simai, Valentine Moghadam and Arvo Kuddo, eds.(London: Zed Books for the United Nations University World Institute for Development Economics Research, 1995)

Gill, Stephen, 'Problematising the Question of Globalisation', Lecture delivered by Stephen Gill, Professor of Political Science, York University, Toronto, Canada at Bucknell University Langone Centre. Sponsored by the Social Colloquium Series Programme, March 8, 1998

Graham, Laurie, *On the Line at Subaru-Isuzu: The Japanese Model and the American Worker* (Ithaca: ILR Press, imprint of Cornell University Press, 1995)

Henke, Holger (1997) "Towards an Ontology of Caribbean Existence" in Social Epistemology, Vol. II, No. 1, January-March, pp. 39–58

Hoogvelt, Ankie, *Globalisation and the Postcolonial World* (Baltimore: Johns Hopkins University Press, 1997)

Hopkins, Terence and Wallerstein, Immanuel, 'Is There a Crisis?' in *The Age of Transition: Trajectory of the World System 1945-2025* by T Hopkins and I Wallerstein, et al. (London: Zed Books, 1996)

Holloway, John, 'Global Capital and the National State' *in Global Capital, National State and the Politics of Money*, Werner Bonefeld and John Holloway, eds. (New York: St Martin's Press, 1995)

Ifco News, The Interreligious Foundation for Community Organisation, Inc., Winter 1999: 1

Inside Europe, No. 21, September 1998 (A Caribbean Council for Europe (CCE) Weekly Newsletter on Developments within the EU Affecting the Caribbean and the ACP)

Inter-American Development Bank, 'Economic and Social Progress in Latin America, 1997 in Report: *Latin America after a Decade of Reforms*, distributed by Johns Hopkins University Press for the Inter-American Development Bank, 1997

International Labour Office, World Labour Report (Geneva: ILO, 1993)

Jamaica Gleaner, 'Moses Challenges Banks to Lower Interest Rates', July 29, 1999

Jamaica Gleaner, 'Meeting Financing Needs in the New Millenium', July 30, 1999

Jamaica Gleaner, 'US$4b Needed for Unemployment in Jamaica', July 30, 1999

Katada, Saori N, 'Two Aid Hegemons: Japanese-US Interaction and Allocation to Latin America and the Caribbean', *World Development*, Vol. 25, No. 6: 931-45, 1997

Kempadoo, Kamala and Jo Doezema, eds., *Global Sex Workers: Rights, Resistance, and Redefinition* (New York: Routledge, 1998)

Kennedy, Paul, 'The Global Gales Ahead' in *The New Statesman and Society*, May 3, 1996: 28–9

Kristof, Nicholas and Sanger, David, 'How US wooed Asia to let Cash Flow In' in 'Global Contagion: A Narrative', second of four articles (*New York Times International*, February 16, 1999)

Landau, Saul, *The Dangerous Doctrine* (Boulder: Westview Press, 1998)

Lapham, Lewis, *The Agony of Mammon: The Imperial Global Economy Explains Itself to the Membership in Davos, Switzerland* (New York: Verso Books, 1998)

Lee (1996)

Lipietz, Alain, 'The Post-Fordist World: Labour Relations, International Hierarchy and Global' *in Review of International Political Economy* (4: 1: 1–41, Spring, 1997)

Manent, Pierre, *An Intellectual History of Liberalism*, translated by Rebecca Balinski (Princeton: Princeton University Press, 1994)

Mann, Charles C, 'Biotech Goes Wild' in *Technology Review*, Vol. 102, no. 4: 36–43, July/August, 1999

Marazzi, Christian, 'Money in the World Crisis: The New Basis of Capitalist Power' in *Global Capital, National State and the Politics of Money*, edited by Werner Bonefeld and John Holloway (New York: St Martin's Press, 1995)

Mars, Perry, 'Political Conflicts and Democratic Change in the English-Speaking Caribbean' in *Transition*, Issue 25, June, pp. 1–18, 1996

Marx, Karl, *The Grundrisse*, translated with an introduction by Martin Nicolaus (Harmondsworth: Penguin, 1971)

Marx, Karl, *Das Kapital, Volume III* (1894) (London: Pelican, 1981)

McBain, Helen, 'Factors Influencing the Growth of Financial Services in Jamaica' in *Social and Economic Studies* (46: 2&3: 113–67, 1997)

Mies, Maria, 'Do we need a 'New Moral Economy?' in *Canadian Woman's Studies/Les Cahiers De La Femme*, Vol. 17, No. 2, Spring 1997, pp. 12–20

Newman-Williams, Preface of *Poverty, Empowerment and Social Development in the Caribbean*, Norman Girvan, ed. (Kingston, Jamaica: Canoe Press, University of the West Indies, 1997)

Ougaard, Morten, 'NAFTA, the EU and Deficient Global Institutionality' in *Economic Integration in NAFTA and the EU: Deficient Institutionality*, Kirsten Appendini and Sven Bislev, eds. (New York: St Martin's Press, 1999)

Overbeek, HW, 'Globalisation and the Restructuring of the European Labour Market: The Role of Migration' in *Global Employment an International Investigation into the Future of Work*, Mihaly Simai with Valentine Moghadam and Arvo Kuddo, eds.(London: Zed Books for the United Nations University World Institute for Development Economics Research, 1995)

Pintasilgo, Maria De Lourdes, 'Unemployment: A Threat to a Humane Society', Foreword in *Global Employment: An Investigation into the Future of Work*, Volume I, Mihaly Simai with Valentine Moghadam and Arvo Kuddo, eds. (London: Zed Books for the United Nations University World Institute for Development Economics Research, 1995)

Reifer, Thomas and Sadler, Jamie, 'The Interstate System' in *The Age of Transition: Trajectory of the World System 1945–2025*, Terrence Hopkins, Immanuel Wallerstein, et al. (London: Zed Books, 1996)

Reuteen, Geert and Michael Williams, Value – Form and the State: The Tendencies of Accumulation and the Determination of Economic Policy in Capitalist Society, Routledge, London, 1998

Rhodes, Leara, *Transfer of Media Management Models: US to the Caribbean* (Athens, Georgia: University of Georgia, 1999)

Robinson, John, 'Reggae Music too Risky for Banks', *The Weekly Gleaner* (N.A.), January 24-30, 1997: 13

Rose, Garth, 'Return of Confidence in Jas Financial System', *The Weekly Gleaner* (N.A.) January 24-30, 1997: 3

Rosenau, James and Czempiel, E, eds., *Governance without Government: Order and Change in World Politics* (Cambridge: Cambridge University Press, 1992)

Rosenberg, Justin, *The Empire of Civil Society: A Critique of the Realist Theory of International Relations* (London: Verso Books, 1994)

Rotman, David, 'Will the Real Nano Tech Please Stand Up' in *Technology Review* (Vol. 102: 2:53, 1999)

Schlosser, Eric, 'The Prison Industrial Complex', *The Atlantic Monthly*, December 1998

Serbin, Andres, *Sunset over the Islands: The Caribbean in an Age of Global and Regional Challenges*, Warwick University Caribbean Studies (London: Macmillan Education Ltd., 1998)

Serbin, Andres, 'Globalisation, Regionalisation, and Civil Society in the Greater Caribbean' in *From Pirates to Drug Lords: The Post-Cold war Caribbean Security Environment*, MC Desch, Jorge Dominguez and A Serbin (Albany: SUNY Press, 1998)

Simai, Mihaly, with Valentine Moghadam and Arvo Kuddo, eds., *Global EmploymentL an International Investigation into the Future of Work*, Vol. I (London: Zed Books for the United Nations University World Institute for Development Economics Research, 1995)

Simai, Mihaly, 'Employment and the Internationalisation of the Labour Markets' in Mihály Simai, Valentine Moghadam and Arvo Kuddo, eds., as above

Soros, George "The Capitalist Threat" in *The Atlantic Monthly*, February, 1997: 45–48 (1997)

Soros, George "Towards a Global Open Society" in *The Atlantic Monthly*, January, 1998: 20–22, 32 (1998)

Sudhanshu, Handa and King, Damien, 'Structural Adjustment Policies, Income Distribution and Poverty: A Review of the Jamaican Experience' in *World Development*, Vol. 25, No. 6: 9, 15–29, 1997

Tabak, Faruk, 'The World Labour Force' in Terence Hopkins, and Immanuel Wallerstein, et al, *The Age of Transition: Trajectory of the World System 1945-2025* (London: Zed Books, 1996)

Tapscott, Don, *The Digital Economy: Promise and Peril in the Age of Networked Intelligence* (New York: McGraw-Hill, 1996)

Teeple, Gary, *Globalisation and the Decline of Social Reform* (Toronto: Garamond Press, 1995)

Thomson, Janice, *Mercenaries, Pirates and Sovereigns: State-Building and Extraterritorial Violence in Early Modern Europe* (Princeton: Princeton University Press, 1994)

Tilly, Charles, *Coercion, Capital and European States AD 990-1992* (Boston: Blackwell, 1990)

Trouillot, Michel-Rolph, *Silencing The Past*, Beacon Press, Boston, 1995

United Nations Development Programme (UNDP), *Human Development Report 1998*, published for the UNDP (New York: Oxford University Press, 1998)

United Nations' Economic Commission for Latin America and the Caribbean, Subregional Headquarters for the Caribbean, Caribbean Development and Cooperation Committee, *The Contribution of Remittances to Social and Economic Development in the Caribbean*, General LC/CAR/G.543 (Port of Spain, Trinidad and Tobago, 1998)

Valtonen, Pekka, 'The Challenges of Regionalism: Unbalanced Integration in the Americas' in *Economic Integration in NAFTA and the EU: Deficient Institutionality*, Kirsten Appendini and Sven Bislev, eds. (New York: St Martin's Press, 1999)

Veltmeyer, Henry, Petras, James and Mieux, Steve, *Neo-liberalism and Class Conflict in Latin America: A Comparative Perspective on the Political Economy of Structural Adjustment* (London: Macmillan Press, 1997)

Voss, David, 'Chips Go Nano' in *Technology Review* (102: 2:57, 1999)

Waring, Marilyn, 'The Invisibility of Women's Work: The Economics of Local and Global "Bullshit"' in *Canadian Woman Studies/Les Cahiers De La Femme*, Vol 17, Spring 1997, pp. 31-37

Watson, Hilbourne A, 'The United States-Canada Free Trade Agreement, Semiconductors, and a Case Study from Barbados' in *The Caribbean in the Global Political Economy*, Hilbourne A Watson, ed. (Boulder: Lynne Rienner Publishers, 1994)

'Global Change: Restructuring the Enterprise Culture and Power in Contemporary Barbados' in *Journal of Eastern Caribbean Studies*, Vol. 22, No. 3, September 1997: 1-47

'The Globalisation of Finance: Role and Status of the Caribbean' in *Beyond Law*, Vol. 6, No. 20, 1998a, special issue on Integration and National Sovereignty in the Caribbean.

'The "Shiprider Solution" Agreement and "Post-Cold War" Imperialism: Beyond the Ontologies of State and Sovereignty in the Caribbean', paper delivered at the Caribbean Studies Association Annual Conference, St Johns, Antigua, May 24-29, 1998b

'Guyana, Jamaica and the Cold War Project: The Transformation of the British West Indian Labour Movement and the CARICOM Labour Movement into Agents of Cold War Globalisation', paper delivered at the Conference on 'Labour and Politics in the Caribbean: The Contributions of Cheddi Jagan and Michael Manley' (Wayne State University, Detroit, MI, April 17, 1998c)

'The Caribbean in Modernity: Explorations on State, Nation, Citizenship, Ethnicity and Gender', paper delivered at the Caribbean Studies Association Annual 24th International Conference, Panama City, Panama, May 24-29, 1999

West Indian Commission, 'Time for Action: The Report of the West Indian Commission' (Wildey, St Michael, Barbados: Cole's Printery, 1992)

World Bank, 'Caribbean Region: Current Economic Situation, Regional Issues and Capital Flows, A World Bank Country Study (Washington, DC: The World Bank, 1993a)

World Bank, 'Global Economic Prospects and the Developing Countries' (Washington DC: World Bank, 1993b)

World Bank, 'Trends in Developing Economies' (Washington DC: The World Bank, 1995)

World Bank, 'Caribbean Countries: Public Sector Modernisation in the Caribbean', Report Number 15185-CRG (Washington, DC: The World Bank, 1996a)

World Bank, 'Caribbean Countries: Prospects for Services Exports from the English-Speaking Caribbean', Report Number 15301-CRG (Washington DC: The World Bank, 1996b)

World Bank, 'Caribbean Countries: Poverty Reduction and Human Resource Development in the Caribbean', Report Number 154342-LAC (Washington DC: The World Bank, 1996c)

Yuval-Davis, Nira, *Gender and Nation* (London: Sage Publications Ltd., 1997)

30 | CEDRIC GRANT

An Experiment In Supra – National Governance:
The Caribbean Regional Negotiating Machinery

A Conceptual Overview

A commonplace proposition in the literature on integration is that the adoption of supra-regional institutions becomes progressively necessary as regional arrangements aim at 'deep' integration through either a custom union, a common market, or a single market and economy. In the form of 'spillovers' that could lead ultimately to political integration, these institutions bind the phases of integration that have already been achieved, and facilitate the pursuit of the next. There is, however, the contention that the occurrence of supra – national institutions within regional arrangements makes it difficult for each participating country to retain its national economic goals, and its power over policies for pursing them while maintaining the ability to participate in decisions that transcend national boundaries. Tensions therefore exist between the assertion of national sovereignty that allows for domestic policies with minimal inter-territorial effects and the superimposing requirements of regionalism. In short, the federalists and functionalists' expectations about the ascendancy of supra-national organizations are not always consistent with the heavily statist orientation of most regional arrangements. The inconsistency was so pronounced that integration theory was proclaimed 'obsolete' in the 1970s as a means of understanding European integration.

Although it is the best example of deepening regional integration, the European Union (EU) took almost four decades to initiate dialogue about a single market. The national instinct is so marked that in the agricultural sector, the EU has become an instrument for extending national protection to the region.[1] This national impulse also contributed significantly to the doubts that the European Monetary Union (EMU) would have commenced as scheduled in January 1999. Standing in the way of Europe's experiment in creating a common currency was the rising pressure from national interest groups on their respective nations to pay greater attention to their slowing economy and rising unemployment. Britain is reluctant to cede control of its monetary policies to the EMU and many British people cannot conceive of life without the British pound. As the country prepares for a referendum on joining the EMU, the nationalists or realists have made a proposal to seek treaty changes to allow countries to opt out of new European legislation. This proposal is considered to be more modest than a previous one to use treaty changes to devolve regional powers to member states, and to block further centralization of decision making.[2]

In the case of regionalism among the less developed countries, the literature has focussed on their integration into the world trading system. The emphasis is on their response to the issues – services, trade-related investment measures, and intellectual property – that the Uruguay Round that ended in late 1993, addressed. It also extends to the three current high profile issues, those of competition policy, labor standards, and trade and environment, that are likely to be on the agenda of any future round of global negotiations. The literature focuses on the adoption by these countries of common institutions principally when the more economically powerful countries and such developing countries bring together their very different institutions in integration arrangements, as in the case of the North American Free Trade Area (NAFTA). Generally, the studies closely follow the commitment to policies that are desirable, especially those that combine economic openness and effective civil and political institutions. There is, however, a paucity of work on the implications of the effects of the interaction between these smaller countries and the common institutions or supra-national organizations which they create to solidify the integration among themselves.

In addition to the focuss on the integration of south – south arrangements into the world economy, there are at least three reasons for the limited work on the emergence and the creation of common institutions within developing countries. First, the views as expressed in the works of Faezed Forountan and others were dismissive of the first generation of integration efforts that occurred in the 1960s in Latin America and Africa in terms of either their administrative capacities, compensation schemes, the share of intra-regional trade in total exports or, more basically, adherence to the treaties sanctioning these arrangements. These theorists also envision little future for the current and second generation of of integration among developing countries. W Max Cohen stated that it is far better for Argentina and Brazil to pursue vigorously their repective integration into the world market than for either of them to concentrate on the market of the other which their regional arrangement, MERCUSOR, encourages.

A second reason for the inattention to common institutions is that few of them existed. Developing countries did not conceive their regional cooperation as a means of political unification. They embraced the newer dependency theory, a particularly Latin American contribution to the political economy of development. This theory focused on economic integration through a strategy of import substitution as a means of industalization and in an effort to end the developing countries exclusive orientation towards the north.

The third reason for the paucity of work and a variant of the second is that the colonial experiment in political and economic union failed or stalled. The East African Economic Community whose beginning in the 1960s had engendered expectations that were higher than similar initiatives in Africa and Latin America ended in the mid 1970s over the distibution of the benefits derived from the arrangement.

Among academics and public policy officials in various developing regions there is an awareness that regionalism has an added focus on coordination at the institutional level and on the creation of common institutions. In 1997, the secretary of the Organization of American States claimed that the Andean community has little to gain by remaining 'part customs union and part free trade area', the result of the failure of some member states to subscribe to one aspect of the customs union or another. The Secretary General was, however, encouraged that all the states supported the creation of an Andean political identity that would strengthen the impact of their collective decisions. In the same year, an academic, Lehlohonolo Tlou, wrote in a similar vein on the Southern African Development Community (SADC). He argued that the challenge for SADC is to transform itself from a loose form of cooperation (the coordination conference – SADCC) to higher levels of integration (a community – SADC). He also posited the view that SADC will need to resolve the question of state sovereignty, if the community is to succeed.

The experiences of these two economic groupings confirm that the crux of integration endeavors is the balance between sovereignty and supranationality. As in the case of the EU, the challenge that this balance poses becomes more pronounced within regional arrangements among developing countries, as their internal dynamics and/or external influences require them to create collective decision making processes, that is, common or politcised institutions to which governments delegate decision making authority.

This study represents an initial attempt to focus on the creation of a supranational institution within regional grouping of developing countries. It examines the Caribbean Common Market and Community's (CARICOM) experiment in the supra – national governance of the negotiations between its member states and their trading partners and of those in the World Trade Organization (WTO). CARICOM evolved from the Caribbean Free Trade Area (CARIFTA) and was codified in the Treaty of Chaguaramus (the Treaty) in 1973. It is currently preparing to move to a single market and economy. In February 1997, CARICOM heads of government established the Caribbean Regional Negotiating Machinery (RNM) to enhance the coordination and the execution of the region's external negotiations. These leaders have entrusted the RNM with the responsibility to develop the strategy for, and to lead various negotiations in which the CARICOM states are engaged.

Neither the concept of supranationality or regional governance, nor the idea of a negotiating machinery was new. The study therefore begins with an examination of the region's political conception of supra-nationality, and its use of the concept as a guide to external negotiations. The study then discusses those ideas that shed light on the main factors at work in the establishment and elaboration of the role of the RNM. Thereafter, it focuses on two other issues that predated the RNM. One is executive efficiency, that is, the capacity of the CARICOM Secretariat (CCS) to undertake the region's external negotiations. The second issue is that of the external influences on the establishment of the RNM. The study then turns its attention to the RNM in terms of the elaboration of the concept of regional governance and the structure, which the development of the concept has eventuated. It does so with particular reference to the process of regional policy formation and the relationship between the RNM and the other key actors in the negotiating process, the CCS and the member states. A subsequent section of this study discusses the performance of the RNM. Some concluding remarks identify several lessons that could inform efforts in the future to establish or restructure supranational arrangements in the region.

Political Conception of Supra-national Governance

CARICOM's integrationist concept has been influenced greatly by the disastrous attempt to establish a political federation in the 1950s. The Community founding fathers had learnt that any conscious derogation of national sovereignty of member states was to be avoided. Among the consequences of the Community's efforts to establish a balance between sovereignty and integration are reliance on mechanisms of unanimity and consensus to reach decisions, and keeping formal community institutions to a minimum. In 1986, Bernard St John, then the prime minister of Barbados, stated that even if this strategy had led to delays in the implementation of agreed programs 'any attempt to advance on a less universal basis [would contradict] the need for each member to balance Community interests against its own perception of national interest'.[4]

William Demas who was a former CCS secretary general and president of the Caribbean Development Bank, an influential WIC member, and, more generally, the doyen of Caribbean integration, looked at the balance between sovereignty and regionalism from the regional perspective. In 1990, Demas noted that the Caribbean community functioned "with no Organs or Institutions with supranational powers and with no sanctions either on member states or legal or natural persons for not implementing the Treaty or decisions of the Community's Organs or Institutions".[5] He urged that consideration be given to a stronger set of mechanisms on the ground that "[t]o some extent, there must be an element of supranationality in successful integration, as experience has shown".[6] In the absence of this element, the purely economic integration or common market part of CARICOM "has not performed too well"[7] and is the least successful of the three areas of community activity, the other two being common services and functional cooperation, and foreign policy coordination.

A reason for the under achievement of the common market is the identification of intra-regional trade as the main focus of the regional integration process. To some extent, the future of CARICOM would be more linked to the development of trade in intermediate goods for the integration of production. As this integration is pursued, monetary integration would follow and the need for supranational institutions would become more self-evident. The pressures of international competitiveness for export markets, however, often crowd out this regional agenda for the deepening of integration among developing countries.

In the area of functional cooperation, the establishment of the Assembly of Caribbean Community Parliamentarians (ACCP), a deliberative body, the adoption of a CARICOM Charter of Civil Society, and the proposed CARICOM Supreme Court are developments in the direction of Institutions with supranational powers. For many member states, however, the main purpose of joint action is to enhance and maintain national sovereignty. Indeed, Demas cited one of the CARICOM leaders, John Compton, then prime minister of St Lucia, as often stating that 'CARICOM is a shield' for the individual West Indian countries vis-a-vis outside countries or groupings.[8] The provision of a sense of direction to the national economies is considered to be secondary.

This avoidance of the regionalising of national prerogatives has been the guiding or organising principle in the conduct of external economic negotiations. Combined action has been ad hoc. In 1991, CARICOM leaders took the first step in developing an agreed strategy and in establishing objectives and priorities. They created an interlocutory group and named the prime minister of Jamaica its coordinator for the purpose of refining the region's position and entering into negotiations with the United States (US) for an agreement between the US and CARICOM concerning a US/CARICOM Trade and Investment Council.[9] Two years later, CARICOM leaders upgraded this arrangement by establishing the Prime Ministerial Sub-Committee on External Negotiations (PMSC). Its task was to develop a strategy for the conduct of the external economic and trade relations of the Community, which would provide a framework for quick response to short term issues, while preserving the integrity and effectiveness of the Community's long term interest and viability. The PMSC was supported, in the form of a technical advisory group, by technical representation from various regional entities involved in external relations.[10]

Between the years in which the interlocutory group and the PMSC were established, CARICOM leaders appointed a Working Group of Experts

(WGE) comprised of senior officials of the member governments to identify elements of an overall strategy for international economic and trade negotiations in which the region must engage.[11] One of the elements that the WGE identified was the organisational arrangement for the preparation for, and execution of, negotiations at the technical and the political levels. The expert group noted that CARICOM basically had employed two approaches to major negotiations. In the run up to the United Nations Conference on the Environment and Development (UNCED) in 1992, CARICOM experimented with the team approach based on expertise made available by individual member states.[12] CARICOM also used the ad hoc technical group approach in developing its technical position for the Caribbean Basin Initiative (CBI) and the Enterprise for the Americas Initiative in 1983 and 1991, respectively.[13] The WGE recommended that the UNCED approach be more systematically used. In the case of the ad hoc technical group approach, the WGE observed that the group might be too large, and the availability of individuals identified by their governments was not always assured.[14]

The WGE therefore proposed a structure whose elements were three-fold. One element was a small team of top level negotiators to develop the required negotiating strategy and tactics for a particular issue or center. Another was an ad-hoc technical advisory group comprised of representatives drawn from the public and the private sectors of member states, diplomatic missions at key centers depending on the issues, the CCS, and other regional institutions. The third element was the diplomatic representatives who were to function as embassy groups. Continuous negotiations were to be arranged around them with the support of delegations from the region.[15] The inclusion of this element as an integral part of the region's strategy was intended to give formal recognition to a principle which CARICOM applied in the negotiations for the Lomé Conventions as a member of the African Caribbean Pacific Group (ACP) of countries, and in the Fourth Preparatory Committee Meeting for UNCED. In 1993 the PMSC used the WGE report as the basis for formulating a short term plan of action for priority attention as well as a longer term overall strategy for the conduct of the region's external economic relations. However, it did not embrace the proposed negotiating structure. The CARICOM leaders' search for the appropriate negotiating machinery was not at an end.

Independent Proposals for Supra-national Governance

The Proposed Caribbean Commission

In 1989, CARICOM leaders established the West Indian Commission (WIC) as an independent body under the chairmanship of Sir Shridath Ramphal, a venerable integrationist, to formulate proposals for advancing the objectives and goals of the treaty. The WIC proposed the establishment of a Caribbean Commission that it described as:

> A small but high level authority in CARICOM working at the interface between political decisions and practical actions; a Commission with confidence to initiate proposals, update consensus, mobilize action and secure implementation of CARICOM decisions in an expeditious and informal manner.[6]

This last function, the facilitation of the implementation of Community decisions, was a central element of the rationale for the Commission, and the most innovative and controversial recommendation. The Commission was to be "appropriately empowered to implement CARICOM'S decisions"[17] and to be exclusively accountable to the heads of government. It was to be composed of three commissioners appointed by the heads of government and also of the secretary general of the CCS in an ex-officio capacity. In support of its judgment that "implementation called for political action,"[18] the members were to be seasoned public and political figures.

The Commission was to be provided with an autonomous, automatic source of income from customs revenues and a small secretariat of its own. This secretariat was to function as a unit of the CCS and provide service to the Commission under the authority of the CCS secretary general. The option of creating an independent administrative machinery with separate lines of authority, and a rigid distinction between the Commission and CARICOM institutions and organs did not appeal to the WIC. It concluded that this route would not contribute to the minimisation of costs and maximisation of the use of resources.

In making its case for the Commission, the WIC argued that as an administrative organ, the CCS did not fit the bill. Its bureaucratic character imposed limitations on its capacity and readiness to act promptly and decisively when problems arose. Likewise, as a bureaucracy the CCS was restricted in its means of ensuring that member states implement and abide by decisions to which they have subscribed, including those pertaining to international negotiations. The WIC did not consider a change in the character of the CCS from a bureaucracy to an executive authority comprised of persons of political stature to be the best way forward for the CCS and therefore the purpose to which its strengthening should be dedicated.[19]

In defining the respective roles of the Commission and the CCS, the WIC recommended that only the former would initiate proposals and ultimately place them before the Community organs and the conference of heads of government. The CCS role was to be limited to assisting the Commission in developing its proposals. It was also to retain its function of servicing CARICOM meetings.

The limited role, which the WIC proposal assigned to the CCS, could have been interpreted as constituting the first step in its steady marginalisation. For in leaving the structure of the Commission to evolve and in giving the commissioners a hand in shaping the authority and functioning of the Commission, the WIC had proposed a creeping executive authority. The participation of the CCS secretary general in the work of the Commission was unlikely to be seen by the CCS as sufficiently allaying its concern that its responsibilities and those of the Commission would overlap, and that the latter body would eventually outflank it. Attitudinal problems seemed destined to arise, and a climate of institutional cordiality difficult to develop and maintain.

Another problematic issue created by the WIC proposal was the implementation of CARICOM decisions. Although the WIC proposed the introduction of an enforcement mechanism, it placed considerable store on the political powers and stature of the commissioners to secure cooperation at the national level. Havelock Brewester, Guyana's ambassador in Brussels and then a United Nations (UN) official, however, queried the realism and feasibility of the commissioners' powers to secure implementation at the national level. He also posed the issue of the credibility of former political leaders or other prominent personalities being both acceptable to the incumbent heads of state and able to exercise their implementing powers successfully.[20] In any case, acceptability was not automatic, for relationships are often determined by the political culture in which they are conducted. Partisanship in many member states is so rife and pervasive that the acceptance of ex-political leaders is vulnerable to shifts in the domestic political environment.

Brewester had inferentially referred to the fundamental problem of the surrender of national sovereignty. This issue seemed to inform the reaction of some of the prime ministers to the proposal. Patrick Manning, the prime minister of Trinidad and Tobago, although a proponent of the idea, noted that "the recommendation for a new Caribbean Commission as an executive arm of the integration movement has, in particular, served as a lightning rod for anxiety and opposition."[21] While defending the proposal, Lester Bird, the prime minister of Antigua and Barbuda, stated more pointedly, that the WIC did not intend the Caribbean Commission to be a "law unto itself". He further contended that "neither control nor authority will pass from the hands of the current Heads of Government".[22]

However, the relationship between the Commission on the one hand and the national governments and the CCS on the other was never put to the test since the heads of government did not establish the Commission. They favored a bureau of heads comprised of rotating members – the current, the outgoing, and incoming chairmen – and the secretary general in his executive capacity- to undertake the same functions that the WIC had assigned to the Caribbean Commission. It is interesting to note, however, that the ultimate RNM structure, as described later in this study, embraces many characteristics of the proposed Caribbean Commission. Further, the idea of a standing machinery to secure the implementation of CARICOM decisions is resilient. As recently as 1996, the prime minister of Antigua and Barbuda posited the view that CARICOM should "return to the concept of a Caribbean Commission as proposed by the West Indian Commission".[23]

Proposed Negotiating Arrangements

In its progress report in July 1991, the WIC identified regional mobilisation as one of six issues that called for immediate action. The WIC also stated that, unaided, the human and financial resources at the disposal of the CCS did not allow it to quicken the pace of regional preparedness for international negotiations. It therefore recommended that:

... the expertise available at the CARICOM Secretariat be supplemented by a facility that enables those carrying the main responsibility at the political level to draw as required on the technical skills available in the region but scattered throughout it. Additional resources will be required for this purpose, but they were modest when compared with the magnitude of the issues and the urgency of the need for the region to protect and advance its vital interest.[24]

The idea of experts constituting a regional reservoir of skills to be differentiated from those within the CCS, separately financed, and interfacing directly with the political directorate contained the seeds of an external negotiating arrangement. Indeed, the WIC envisioned CARICOM acquiring "a single negotiating posture and a single voice for international negotiations vital to [the region's] common interests".[25]

In a 1994 essay on the importance of negotiation preparedness, Sir Alister McIntyre, the then vice chancellor of the University of the West Indies (UWI), who had been the vice chairman of the WIC, brought the concept of an interpositioning authority with a wide berth and political muscle into sharp relief. He elevated the WIC proposal for a facility from which the political directorate could draw technical skills as the negotiating process warranted to a "negotiating team" which would develop "an ethos and identity of its own with group loyalty to the aims and strategies that have been worked out by all the members".[26]

A former CCS secretary general and a member of the advisory group to the PMSC, Sir Alister brought to his essay an institutional memory as well as a quasi-political perspective. He observed that despite CARICOM's impressive negotiating record, experience showed that the structure was in need of improvement in a number of respects. One was the lack of transparency of the preparation for negotiations in individual countries. Another was the unevenness of preparation and representational capacity among the countries. The third was the failure to transmit to the regional level important information received in national capitals on major issues or to do so in a timely fashion. The fourth was the limited interface between the regional negotiating teams and the CCS on the one hand, and persons involved in the negotiations at the national level on the other, which was reflected in the delay in transmitting information. The fifth was the reliance on information from a single source, including diplomatic dispatches, and difficulties of ascertaining and verifying its reliability.[27]

These shortcomings were accentuated by the tendency, at both the national and regional levels, to involve heads of government and ministers too early in the negotiating process and to expose them to relatively junior officials steeped in details. In Sir Alister's view, the participation of the political leadership should be reserved for the resolution of major sticking points and negotiations at comparable levels with the other side. Sir Alister also argued that CARICOM should continually involve a wide range of social partners – the private sector, representatives of non-governmental organizations, and members of the academic community – in both the preparatory process and the negotiations. This arrangement had greater merit than adherence to the prevailing tendency of limiting their participation on a "very selective [and] on call" basis.[28] This inclusiveness would also extend routinely to public officials who were involved in previous negotiations, especially those who were retired, so that continuity could be maintained and their institutional memory utilised to CARICOM's good advantage.

Sir Alister did not limit his analysis and recommendations to the institutional and organizational aspects of the preparatory process but extended them to the quality of the substantive preparation of the negotiating strategy. Negotiating briefs were often analytically flawed and almost exclusively couched in economic terms with inadequate consideration of their political and social dimensions. This, he observed, ultimately led to narrow perspectives and inappropriate timing of the negotiating initiatives because insufficient attention was paid to the political calendar in the prospective countries. Furthermore, CARICOM negotiators embarked on negotiations without sufficient knowledge of the comparative experiences of other countries negotiating the same issues, and about the strengths, weaknesses, and predilections of the key actors involved in the negotiations.[29]

Sir Alister considered the negotiations perspective to be not only narrow but also short term. He suggested the establishment of machinery for foreign policy planning where trends could be highlighted and issues identified within a medium to long term horizon, together with options for dealing with such issues. In the absence of this compass, the region's approach to negotiations has tended to be reactive rather than pro-active with the other side defining the agenda, which limits the governments' leverage and room for maneuvering.[30]

Sir Alister provided yet another clue to the deficiencies in preparatory negotiations when he observed that there was an absence of an integrative approach to the economic prospectus and development strategies in the region, which could apply *mutatis mutandes* to particular negotiations.[31] He therefore proposed that the CCS should be asked to undertake the task of thinking through the fundamentals of a negotiating strategy based on the varied national economic agendas.

It is clear that Sir Alister's analysis and recommendations, especially his proposed interpositioning authority representing the region in external negotiations, and acting as a buffer between the political leadership and public officials, were as instructive of the national governments' outlook on regional governance as their negative response to the proposed Caribbean Commission. Brewester captured this outlook in his observation that, notwithstanding their periodic reiteration of their commitment to the goals of CARICOM,

[I]ndividual states actually behave as if economic development and political independence would be best secured through individual state efforts. Derogation from and delays in implementing CARICOM regimes and in furthering accepted regional objectives and commitments are some of the manifestations of this approach.[32]

Executive Efficiency

Of the several institutions, organs, and agencies, the CCS is the flagship of the Caribbean integration movement. It is therefore regarded as the main repository of the Community's collective wisdom and experience, and has been extensively examined. The foregoing analysis noted that the CCS was assessed as either unsuited for a supra-national role in the resolution of the perennial problem of implementing CARICOM decisions in the member states or as simply underperforming. Nonetheless, with every step taken to improve the negotiating arrangements, the scope and volume of the CCS responsibilities were progressively enlarged. The responsibilities that the PMSC assigned to it were multiple. These included identifying and examining issues in relation to the region's external relations, providing support for the work of the PMSC and its advisory working groups and the special negotiating teams, mobilizing resources for the execution of programs and maintaining a direct link with the CARICOM group of ambassadors in the various capitals. In addition to discharging these responsibilities, the CCS was not inhibited from taking initiatives and presenting proposals to the PMSC which were beyond its statutory functions, in the same way as it promoted activities aimed at facilitating the achievement of other CARICOM objectives.[33]

In 1990, the CCS received the attention of the CARICOM review team (CRT), that CARICOM leaders appointed under the chairmanship of Gladstone Mills, professor at UWI, to undertake a comprehensive review of CARICOM programs, institutions and organizations.[34] The CRT identified several ways in which the CCS could be reconstructed. It proposed that the CCS be empowered and its secretary general be encouraged to formulate recommendations, deliver opinions on matters dealt with in the treaty, and resolve differences when they arose among member states.[35] For this purpose, the CRT proposed that the CCS be better staffed, equipped, financed, and placed in a better position to offer satisfying careers to a core of suitably qualified and motivated personnel. The CRT acknowledged, however, that the feasibility of recruiting and retaining experienced personnel from certain member states even for relatively short periods depended on the host government of the CARICOM headquarters, Guyana, to provide the appropriate physical environment, including suitable office accommodation.[36] This deficiency had periodically prompted suggestions that the CCS either be relocated, decentralised, or its reliance on consultants throughout the region be increased.

The CRT report provided considerable impetus to two sets of decisions in 1993. One was the establishment of new institutional structures of the Community, some features of which represented a radical departure from those established by the treaty. One of the new features was the designation in each member state, of a minister with responsibility for CARICOM affairs, who collectively would constitute the Caribbean Community Council of Ministers. This new Council would replace the Common Market Council of Ministers as the second highest organ of the Community. Another was the creation of three councils: (1) the Council for Trade and Economic Cooperation (COTED), (2) the Council for Foreign and Community Relations (CFCR), and (3) the Council for Human and Social Development (CHSD). The third new feature, and perhaps the most important, was the conferring of executive powers on the secretary general of the Community.[37] The empowerment was intended to enable the CCS to transform itself from a primary 'reactive administrative mode' to a more pro-active catalytic executive machinery capable of providing greater foresight, leadership, and implementation assistance in an accelerated process of deepening and widening the integration movement.[38]

The other decision was the development of the secretariat's strategic and restructuring plan. A revamped organisational structure within the CCS provided for three directorates that corresponded to the three newly established ministerial councils. It also created three assistant secretary generals, one each to be responsible for the directorates.[39]

Despite these boosts to the CCS capacity to function more effectively, a fundamental question remained unanswered. It was whether these changes were sufficient for the CCS to overcome the constraining milieu in which it was required to function, an environment that was largely derived from the member states' aversion to strong regional mechanisms and their preference for a statist oriented integration arrangement. As will be seen later, this question remained pertinent to the analysis of the interaction between the RNM and some of the other actors in the negotiation.

External Influences on the Establishment of the RNM

Prior to CARICOM adopting a negotiating strategy in 1993, rapid changes in the international environment that required a regional response were occurring, and in particular, with respect to the global and regional trade negotiations. These presented opportunities to CARICOM countries for improving their arrangements for pursuing collective negotiations and policies. Two major negotiations were on the immediate horizon. One was for the future relations with the EU after Lomé IV expires in 2000. The other was for the creation of the Free Trade Areas of the Americas (FTAA) which the Summit of the Americas mandated in 1994. Allied to this negotiation was one on the non-economic issues of the Summit. Beyond these regional negotiations, and as significant as any of these, were also those within the WTO and a possible round of global trade negotiations. These three major negotiations have overshadowed two long standing issues within the hemisphere: the lobbying for the enhancement of CBI to NAFTA parity which US politics has held hostage; and the expansion of CARICOM trade relations in the Caribbean and elsewhere in Latin America.

The preparatory discussions for the FTAA suggested that CARICOM's interest in retaining the preferential treatment of past international arrangements for as long as possible as well as special and differential treatment for small economies, which constituted the foundation of the regional economy, was being ignored. Likewise, there was limited acceptance of CARICOM's argument that like developing countries in other groupings, it needed development assistance to expand its embrace of market forces. There were other premonitions of danger to CARICOM economies. The WTO has been unsupportive of the maintenance of the preferential access of CARICOM bananas to the EU market. It ruled in 1997 that the enabling framework agreement, which unified the EU banana policy in 1993 and maintained the special Lomé banana arrangement, was discriminatory and incompatible with its rules. A spirited CARICOM campaign against the ruling did not deter the US, which initially brought the complaint against the EU on behalf of US companies that operate in Latin America, from aggressively extending its challenge to the revised banana regime that the EU had developed to replace the outlawed arrangement.[40]

The US pledged assistance to mitigate the effects of the WTO ruling and to improve and broaden the base of CARICOM's export competitiveness.[41] Nonetheless, CARICOM countries remained apprehensive as they interpreted US actions as opening new doors in its relationship with them while closing those on CARICOM's relationship with Europe. This zero-sum approach was at variance with the CARICOM strategy of keeping both the European and the hemispheric doors open in its effort to maintain and expand trade concessions while developing arrangements to facilitate the transition to more free market competition.

Although ad hoc, the banana issue dramatically demonstrated the interlinkage between the negotiations in which CARICOM was engaged and the need for it to develop a holistic approach to negotiations that were upcoming. Indeed, the two major regional negotiations and those within the WTO constitute a single agenda for CARICOM in the sense that its trade formula, which allows for preferential arrangements to recede – not prematurely, but as regional conditions for reciprocity in trade become more conducive – is common to all of them. Consensus that is favorable to CARICOM interests in one negotiation could offer positive spin-offs in other fora.

From the standpoint of refining the negotiating strategy that had evolved since the PMSC was established in 1993, the negotiations seemed manageable. From several other perspectives, however, the negotiations promised to be a massive and unprecedented undertaking that was capable of overwhelming the existing machinery unless it was reinforced. First, the negotiations were multifarious, highly complex, and separate. The FTAA and the post Lomé negotiations were also formidable because they were scheduled to run simultaneously over a seven year period. Although either one of these negotiations could proceed on a faster track, neither of them had a prior claim on the region's resources in terms of their respective importance to the Caribbean economy. Altogether, the need for CARICOM to refine the negotiating strategy and to move forward on both the FTAA and the post Lomé fronts with equal commitment and vigor and without moderating its efforts to expand its trade relations within the Caribbean Basin gave rise to the idea of the RNM that would enhance the CCS capacity to drive the negotiating process.

The Establishment and Elaboration of the RNM

(a) Original Concept and Structure

In a memorandum, 'Measures to Enhance the Coordination and Execution of External Negotiations', which he presented directly to the CARICOM Summit in July 1996, Edwin Carrington, the CCS secretary general, conceptually continued to regard the PMSC and the CCS, the political and administrative components respectively of the existing negotiating machinery, as the core elements of a revised and more expanded arrangement. The concept placed the RNM unmistakably within the CCS domain and endowed it with a limited life coterminous with the pursuit of the cluster of negotiations to be conducted over the anticipated seven years. The RNM was to be represented as a project to facilitate the securing of operational funds independent of the normal arrangements for financing the Community organs and structures. The CCS envisioned that benefits from the experience acquired by the RNM would accrue to the building of institutional capacity in member states through their systematic involvement in RNM activities. Beyond the seven year period when the group of negotiations would cease to maintain its level of intensity and the special circumstances would disappear, the RNM, as a project, cannot be justified.

In keeping with several guiding principles which the heads of government had provided in their comments on its measures, the CCS revised proposals allowed for greater inclusiveness of the social partners – the private sector, labor, non-governmental organisations, regional experts and academic policy experts.[42] These proposals also provided for greater interaction between the RNM on the one hand and the COTED and the CFCR on the other. A third ministerial council, which was responsible for finance and planning, was also associated with the RNM.

As the political element specifically charged by the heads of government to direct the external negotiations, the PMSC remained at the apex, but in an enhanced form. While it retained its existing core membership, participation in its sessions became open-ended. The change had the obvious advantage of allowing interested heads of government to be effectively involved in the negotiation process. Another change was the reconstitution of the PMSC technical advisory group. This group was restyled as the policy advisory group to distinguish it from the consultative advisory group, which was a new element of the PMSC. Essentially comprised of the chairpersons of COTED, the CFCR and the ministerial council responsible for finance and planning, regional representatives of the private sector and other social partners as well as a representative from the ACCP, the consultative advisory group addressed the issue of greater inclusiveness of the negotiating process. As the CCS secretary general observed, the PMSC had "agreed to establish a negotiating team" not only "to design a strategy to participate in the forthcoming negotiations," but also to facilitate through this coordinated approach "broad consensus building among all the principal actors of the Region [in order for them] to have a more structured interface with the extra-regional community".[43]

One of the priorities that the CCS had identified was contracting a body of people exclusively dedicated in a variety of positions to drive the negotiating process. The foremost new element was that of a full-time chief negotiator (CN).[44] The person was to be accorded ambassadorial rank and recruited from among prominent political figures with the requisite negotiating skills and experience, technical competence, and a substantive grasp of the issues involved in the negotiations. Allied with the CN would be a full time chief coordinator and a technical advisor.[45]

The CN was authorised to consult with the PMSC for the purpose of eliciting its advice and directions. The CN was to serve in his ex-officio capacity as a member of the PMSC consultative advisory group, as was the CN's principal lieutenant, the chief coordinator. The CN was not to be a member of the more influential sub-group, the policy advisory group: the terms of reference merely allowed the CN to consult with the members of this body. Finally and most importantly, the CN was to report to the PMSC not directly but through the CCS. While these arrangements reflected the RNM's basic role as an integral arm of the CCS, they were not intended to proscribe its operations.

Another new element that was intended to reinforce the CCS negotiating capacity was the establishment of four specialised negotiating working groups (NWG), one each for the broad negotiating areas which constituted the RNM's principal remit – Lomé, the FTAA, the Summit of the Americas Non-Economic Issues, and the WTO.[46] The NWGs represented another forum for the social partners to connect with the negotiating process. These non-state actors, together with officials of the governments of the member states and representatives of the CCS, the secretariat of the organization of Eastern Caribbean States (OECS), and other regional institutions, were to comprise the membership of the NWGs. The NWGs were to be responsible for the preparation of technical reports which were to be referred through the CCS and the PMSC policy advisory group to the PMSC for approval. The CCS structure provided for no formal link between the CN and the NWGs. It was assumed, however, that as an integral arm of the CCS, the CN would be involved in the work of the NWGs. The comfort level of these NWGs was to be significantly aided by the support of personnel in the key embassies, including participation in special meetings, in keeping with previous practice within the CCS.

Two elements of the RNM were created within the CCS. One was a special technical unit comprised of technical secretaries to assist in the work of each of the four NWGs, and more generally, to provide the highly specialised technical analyses and advice which the complex negotiations were certain to entail. These four technical secretaries were also to be at the disposal of other elements of the RNM.[47]

The other element within the CCS was the assistant secretary general for regional trade and economic Integration who was to function as CCS coordinator. The assistant secretary general was to supervise the work of the technical secretaries, coordinate more generally the work of the NWGs, and develop a close working relationship with the CN and the chief coordinator.[48]

Taken together, the new elements presented a picture of the RNM as a composite body, under the canopy and coordinating responsibility of the CCS. It appeared to be a fully developed structure that captured all aspects of the negotiating process, most notably the input of the national governments and the participation of the private sector, labor, and the other social partners. The purpose of this structure was to manage the negotiating process, including the finance that was to consist of a basic contribution from member states and international resources, to facilitate the technical work to be undertaken. Mobilising these resources was a major challenge that the PMSC had recognized when the prime minister of Barbados, Owen Arthur, accepted the responsibility for coordinating the efforts to obtain the support of donor agencies and governments.[49] The CCS also conceived its coordinating role as a filter of the proposals of the CN and those of the deliberative groups into the ministerial stream of decision making.

(b) Establishment of the RNM

The revised proposals were routed through the two sub-prime ministerial committees, the PMSC and the bureau,[50] before the heads of government adopted them at their inter-sessional meeting in February 1997.[51] In endorsing the proposals, the PMSC

> . . . agreed that in order to have a cohesive regional position for these complex talks and varied negotiations, some of which have already been initiated, there needs to be established a machinery which will maximize the Region's chances of success, by harnessing all of its talents to successfully undertake this process.[52]

The CCS structure assumed that the RNM headquarters would in principle be located in the region, and more specifically, in the member state from which the CN would be recruited. In the run-up to the heads of government inter-sessional meeting that decided to establish the RNM, Bernard St John, who, in addition to being a former prime minister of Barbados was a practicing trade lawyer, appeared to be the choice for the assignment of CN.[53] In anticipation of the acceptance of the structure as proposed, the appointment of Bernard St John, and of Barbados constituting the headquarters of the RNM, the CCS secretary general proceeded to identify and appoint the chief coordinator, Bishnodat Persaud, a Caribbean specialist in international and economic development. He also appointed a lead technical adviser, Arnold McIntrye, a Caribbean economist. Both of these appointees were located in Barbados. The secretary general further enhanced the capacity of the RNM by appointing another technical adviser, Maurice Odle, a Caribbean economist and then a UN official, who was located in the CCS.

Interest in the appointment of the CN was stimulated when the prime minister of Antigua and Barbuda disclosed to the media that he held a point of view that was different from that of the prime minister of Barbados on the preferment.[54] The prime minister of Barbados curtailed the debate on the appointment by withdrawing his nominee. The search for a CN continued, and was terminated when the heads of government unanimously decided to invite Sir Shridath to undertake the assignment.[55] They also authorised the Chairman of the PMSC, the prime minister of Jamaica, Percival Patterson, to convey the request and pursue detailed arrangements with Sir Shridath. The Heads also authorised the PMSC to make any necessary modifications to operationalise the RNM.[56]

The decision to establish the RNM was taken at the CARICOM level. Recognising, however, that the Dominican Republic and Haiti were part of the Caribbean membership of the ACP Group, CARICOM invited these two countries to participate in the work of the RNM as it related to the post Lomé IV negotiation.[57] Together, CARICOM, the Dominican Republic and Haiti constitute Cariforum, which was established for the purpose of coordinating the allocation and undertaking the monitoring of regional resources that the EU directs to them under the Lomé Convention.

Cuba has also been included in the RNM and, as an observer, in Cariforum and the ACP group. Its entry into these groupings derives from its interest in participating in the ACP-EU process and from its view that its deepening relationship with CARICOM during the last decade is its best chance of achieving its objectives. The RNM observed that acceptance of Cuba within Cariforum was not without need for careful strategic thinking in relation to Cuba's trade relations in traditional Caribbean product areas like rum and sugar. Nonetheless, the RNM concluded that as with tourism, the Caribbean as a whole would probably be stronger in the post Lomé IV negotiations with Cuba inside the tent.[58]

(c) RNM Modifications

Consistent with the expectation that the location of the CN and the base of the RNM would be the same, England, where Sir Shridath resides, rather than a CARICOM member state, became a base; "only a small part of the RNM"[59] but an important part nonetheless. The chief coordinator, who was appointed before the CN and was located in Barbados in anticipation of the appointment of a resident Barbadian as CN, was moved to England. Barbados became a sub-base following the establishment of the technical unit under the charge of the lead technical adviser. The CN's technical adviser, who like the chief coordinator was appointed in advance of the CN, was stationed at the CCS as previously planned. Another notable change that was made in the structure of the RNM was the upgrading of the rank of the CN from ambassador to minister.

Because it resulted in the establishment of two bases across two regions of the world, the choice of CN brought into question the criteria for determining the location of the RNM headquarters. It is to be noted though that the choice of location was consistent with proposals which the WIC had made on the diaspora's commitment to the integration process and its potential to contribute to it. More specifically, the proposals called for the establishment of a 'Skills Bank' [in the diaspora] and the identification and location of professional skills and technical expertise which could be harnessed by the region on terms and conditions mutually advantageous to both donor and recipient".[60]

The shift in location of the RNM headquarters also highlighted a dilemma in the resolution of management problems in the region. Is the existing institution to be rectified, discarded where feasible in favor of a new one, or superseded by an additional layer? In his address to the heads of government conference in July 1999, the prime minister of Barbados recognized this dilemma. He stated:

Faced with a ticking clock on three crucial negotiation processes, we responded by establishing the Regional Negotiating Machinery. The fact that we have superimposed a new structure on an old system addressed only the urgent present need. It does not absolve us of the responsibility to revitalize the Secretariat of the Community, nor to guard against the need for such ad hoc solutions in the future.[61]

Yet another change in the structure of the RNM was the establishment of a high level advisory group (HLAG) of which Sir Alister was appointed its chairman. The group occupied 'a rather special place in this [RNM] structure'[62] and was appointed by Sir Alister in consultation with the PMSC. It was provided with the authority 'to draw into the process, as it needs skills and talents and experience from any quarter'[63] and to function as an independent advisory body to the RNM. It is also one of the organs through which the requisite technical studies would be channeled to the PMSC. In the evolution of the HLAG, its chairman was restyled chief technical adviser of a newly established technical studies unit in 1998. This reconstituted element has rendered the HLAG non-functional and has resulted in the establishment of a RNM sub-base in Jamaica.

(d) RNM Leadership

In bringing the Sir Shridath and Sir Alister as a team once more, CARICOM leaders had placed the RNM in the hands of two of three persons with whom the CARICOM model of integration is principally associated[64] (the third person being William Demas). In addition to their major intellectual contribution to regional unity, Sir Shridath and Sir Alister's distinguished careers have been deeply involved in the regional movement. As early as 1956, Sir Shridath was present in a minor capacity at the meeting of West Indian leaders that decided the site of the federal capital. Sir Shridath became the solicitor general of the West Indies Federation, and later, as minister of foreign affairs and attorney general of Guyana, he participated in the creation of the integration movement, and played a more significant and instrumental role in the establishment of the ACP Group, the forging of the ACP countries position in their negotiation of the first Lomé Convention with the European Community and the conduct of the actual ACP-EU negotiations.

The period during which Sir Alister served as secretary general of the CCS covered the Lomé negotiation and the evolution of the CARIFTA into CARICOM. Sir Shridath and Sir Alister had returned to the region from a long tenure with international organizations, the Commonwealth Secretariat and the UN respectively, with their personal stock and public policy experience enhanced. Furthermore, they shared years not only as chairman and vice chairman of the WIC, but also as officials of UWI – Sir Shridath as chancellor and Sir Alister as vice chancellor – for a period that spanned the WIC and the establishment of the RNM.

A familiar and influential figure in various substantive capacities at heads of government meetings for over forty years, Sir Shridath is viewed by prime ministers as one among them. It is a measure of the region's political leaders' easy relationship with Sir Alister that they considered him the preferred Grenadian to lead the provisional government of Grenada following the military invasion of that country in 1983.

The upgrading of the CN's status and the addition of the chief technical adviser of the technical studies unit were a portent of the inclusion of elements of supranationality in the RNM; a utilisation of the ideas that had informed the WIC proposals on the establishment, authority and functioning of the Caribbean Commission as well as Sir Alister's proposals on the need for a negotiating team with its own ethos. As the principal authors of the WIC report, Sir Shridath and Sir Alister had rejected the concept of a prefabricated entity in suggesting that the elaboration of the structure of the Caribbean Commission should await the appointment of the commissioners. Under Sir Shridath's leadership, the RNM was therefore resolved to play a pivotal role in formulating the negotiating strategy, and to possess a relatively radical quality.

(e) Elaboration of the RNM: From Reinforcement to Empowerment

In their mandate to the CN, the CARICOM leaders conveyed their decision to invest the RNM with elements of supra-nationality or regional governance. The mandate required the CN to undertake the following responsibilities:

- within the policy guidelines established by the conference or the Prime Ministerial Sub-Committee on External Negotiation, the chief negotiator will:
- develop an overall plan from a management perspective, of the various negotiations in which the region will be involved to the end of 1999 and execute the plan with the approval of the Prime Ministerial sub-committee;
- lead the region's negotiating team and be the main spokesperson in the conduct of the negotiation, especially those at the decision making level;
- develop or fine tune the strategy for the various negotiations within the time table identified for the particular area;
- maintain regular contact with sectoral negotiators and work with them in the identification of issues and the development of appropriate responses."[65]

Although mandated to cover the full range of negotiations, the RNM focused on the four priority areas that had been initially identified: Lomé, the FTAA, the Non-Economic Issues of the Summit of the Americas, and the WTO. The negotiations towards free trade agreements with the wider Caribbean, notably the Dominican Republic, the Andean Community, and the Central American Common Market countries, remained the CCS responsibility.

Apparently, as a reiteration of the WIC ideas on a Caribbean Commission, the revised concept of the RNM entailed detaching it from the CCS, reconstructing it as a free standing entity, placing it under the control of the CN, making the CN answerable to the PMSC and the heads of governments only, providing the RNM with a separate source of financing to give effect to its autonomy, and limiting the RNM's reliance on the CCS to logistic and administrative support – all elements of supra-nationality. An additional element was the creation of an independent administrative machinery. This separate machinery was the only change that was a reversal of the WIC ideas on the Caribbean Commission. As discussed earlier, the WIC proposal had catered for a secretariat within the CCS and that was under its control. It had eschewed a separate administrative arrangement in the interest of cost and a smooth working relationship between the Caribbean Commission and the CCS.

Secured in its mandate, fortified in the support of the prime ministers and with the enthusiasm of a new organisation, the RNM and its CN vigorously proceeded to further define their mandate and to continue to mould the new arrangement. With respect to developing a cohesive, organic approach to the negotiations that had frequently eluded CARICOM endeavors, Sir Shridath stated:

[W]e cannot be a Single Market and each go our separate ways in negotiations with Europe or the Americas. In particular, we must not abandon CARICOM in separately pursuing prospects of joining other groupings, that however enticing at a national level, may turn out to be illusory or minimalist. CARICOM is our bedrock; it is on that we build our external economic relations. It is on that regional position that we must negotiate.[66]

Perhaps in taking the view that a unified approach to the negotiation was an imperative which CARICOM should obey, the CN was expressing the hope that the heads of government would not decide as they did in 1994 in relation to access to NAFTA,[67] that some members may seek to conclude trade agreements ahead of others, a decision that was likely to severely fracture CARICOM. The CN's concern was not only pertinent but also prescient. In November 1998, more than one year after he had belabored the need for unity of action, some private sector interest groups in Trinidad and Tobago responded to a free trade negotiation impasse between CARICOM and the Dominican Republic by suggesting that the country should either take a leadership role in CARICOM when negotiating the FTAA or consider breaking away from the group to negotiate on its own.[68] The CN obviously viewed the role of the RNM in terms of rendering unnecessary the exercise of the latter option.

The merits of a unified approach to the negotiations were one of several basic propositions as he termed them, advanced by Sir Shridath.[69] Another proposition, which was two-fold, concerned the balance between sovereignty and regional governance. In the first place, Sir Shridath effectively disabused the notion that either the concept of the RNM or the existence of the CN foreclosed the Cariforum group of countries from occupying more than one place at the negotiating table. On the contrary, both regional and national interests dictated a multiple and diverse presence integrated by a regional strategy.

The second aspect of the proposition was that there was no place for a cacophony of sounds at the table. In their varied negotiating roles, every one – heads of government, ministers, officials – should be speaking "from an agreed regional brief, to an agreed regional position".[70] Waxing on the theme of unison and the pivotal role of the RNM, the CN contended that the Caribbean cannot "afford the luxury of separate texts, of separate ideas, of separate conclusions"[71] when it was engaged in the negotiations. Using an ecclesiastical analogy, the CN said everyone must "sing from the same hymn sheet. That is at the heart of the concept of a regional Negotiating Strategy. The RNM's consultation . . . are essentially about composing that hymn sheet"[72]

A third proposition implicit in the region's unified approach to its engagement with its trade partners was that the negotiations themselves would be multifaceted and inter-linked. The negotiations were not about choosing between Europe and the Americas, but keeping open to CARICOM all of the many windows of entry into the wider world. The CN considered this proposition the region's most fundamental economic strategic approach to the several negotiations.[73]

The CN's final proposition was that solidarity beyond the region was vital to the strengthening of the regional negotiating position. This was especially the case in relation to the negotiations with Europe since there were hints that ACP solidarity was not necessarily a European priority. More importantly, the CN believed that the collective ACP machinery was old and in need of modernisation and that an intense political structure was necessary to spearhead the ACP-EU negotiations.

As evidenced in the discussion of many of these issues earlier in this study, there was considerable awareness of the CN's general principles. His statements, however, suggested a variation, probably more in terms of emphasis than substance, on CARICOM's policy of placing the retention of trade preferences and special treatment in the foreground of the region's negotiating strategy. The CN was appreciative of the strategy of striving to slow the erosion of preferences and to minimise the costs of adjustment. Indeed, early in his tenure the CN decried the US position on the EU banana regime and assailed the WTO ruling on it. After he posed the rhetorical question: "Is the WTO going to be in trade the rod of chastisement the IMF was in finance – an instrument in the hands of the strong to be used against the poor?", the CN stated, "Benign neglect is one thing, deliberate action to destroy the fragile economies of West Indian Islands is another as are global processes which elevate the claims of unvarnished doctrine above those of human security".[74]

At the same time, the CN seemed more emphatic than many CARICOM leaders in recognizing reciprocity as an "imperative"[75] and in adopting a more pro-active approach to maximize the benefits of adjustment as the most important part of the composite way of thinking. As he stated:

That environment [preferential] will change. We may win time to adjust to that change; but we have to be prepared in our minds for a world in which our markets will be open increasingly to competition and not only at the level of goods but also of investment and services . . . Indeed, transitional arrangements will prove ineffectual by way of preparation for change unless we embrace the imperatives of change itself . . . What I am saying is that we cannot expect to derive the full potential from these negotiations unless here at the local level we prepare for the new kind of world they will usher in. We have to begin these preparations now.[76]

More instructive than the propositions was the primacy of the role of the RNM that emerged from the CN's message. While the RNM was to be the director of the "the choir",[77] there was a major issue still to be determined. It was the implications of the primacy of the RNM's role as it relates to the relationship between the RNM and two other sets of actors in the negotiating process. One was the CCS which had overarching responsibility for the RNM under the original RNM structure and whose secretary general had begun to implement the structure by assuming the primacy of his role, prior to the appointment of the CN. The other actors were the representatives of the member states accustomed to the primacy of national governance in the integration arrangement.

Operationalisation of the RNM

(a) The Start Up

By the time the RNM presented its first progress report on its operationalisation that had begun in April 1997, to the heads of government meeting in July 1997 the machinery had covered considerable ground and made substantial progress. As a start to the process of helping to develop the regional strategy, the CN prepared a discussion paper entitled 'Approaches to the Development of a Strategy and Position for the Caribbean' with the assistance of the chief coordinator and the high level advisory group.[78] As the RNM had correctly hoped, the conference endorsed the document as a basis for consultation towards the development of a regional negotiating strategy.

To ensure that the work of the RNM was inclusive, the CN travelled extensively in the region to encourage the national advisory committees on external negotiations that had been established in Barbados, Jamaica, and in Trinidad and Tobago, and to urge other countries to follow these examples. These committees were added as an element to the RNM following the CN's appointment. Their value was intended to be three – fold. First, they would allow the member states to press their priority interests on the attention of the RNM. Second, they would provide an opportunity for consultations with the local private sector, which is qualitatively important to the formulation of national proposals. Third, the committees would contribute to the evolution of the regional strategy at the regional level.[79] As Sir Shridath put it, the complementary work at the level of member states would result in "streams of policy proposals feeding into the regional strategy".[80]

Funding that was so critical to the start-up of the RNM, and in the more long term to the costly negotiating process, also occupied the attention of the RNM. The CN was generally regarded as being emphatic on the member states assuming the main responsibility for the cost of the RNM, thereby demonstrating the strength of their commitment. The CN also appealed for an 'exceptional act of generosity from the business community.'[81] Finally, the RNM seized every available opportunity to highlight and promote its principles and goals, both internationally and within the region.

(b) Interaction between the RNM and the CCS

It is instructive that the discussion paper was produced without the assistance of either the NWGs that were charged with preparing the technical briefs for the RNM or the CCS that was responsible for coordinating these studies. This omission contributed to the perception that the CCS had been and would continue to be sidelined by the RNM strategy, notwithstanding that a joint meeting of the four NWGs reviewed the discussion paper subsequent to the heads of government meeting.[82]

It was difficult for the CCS to reconcile itself to the new concept of the RNM and to the decision of the heads of government to reverse their initial determination on the control of the RNM. Furthermore, the RNM was not obliged to provide the CCS with assurance of a substantive role, given the prime ministers' confidence in Sir Shridath and also given the WIC proposal for the Caribbean Commission in which Sir Shridath had viewed the CCS in minimalist terms. Indeed, the analysis of the WIC proposal for the limited role of the CCS in the work of the Caribbean Commission, and of Sir Alister's proposal on the region's negotiating preparedness, had prepared the region not only for an uneasy relationship between the RNM and the CCS but also for the RNM's complete separation from the CCS that occurred, except for its reliance on the latter for logistic and administrative support. This final outcome was once more reminiscent of Sir Alister's contention that the aim should be to develop a negotiating team with a culture and a personality of its own.

It should also be recalled that in his proposal on national preparedness, Sir Alister commented on the quality of negotiating briefs, and the limited resources available to the CCS and national ministries for undertaking such work, as detracting from a fully effective CCS negotiating machinery. It is not surprising, therefore, that under its revised structure, the RNM would attempt to monitor quality and resources with respect to the work produced, and that the responsibility for the conduct of technical studies and the associated training workshops and seminars would be transferred to the technical studies unit.

The bypassing of the NWGs by the RNM proved to be the prelude to the disbanding of the NWGs through which the CCS could have exercised considerable leverage on the negotiating process. In place of the NWG for the FTAA, the RNM established a college of negotiators. A lead representative and an alternate were appointed for each of the nine subject areas of the FTAA negotiating process and the three technical committees – electronic commerce, small economies, and civil society – that are not part of the formal negotiating process but interact with it. In an attempt to include as many significant social partners as is feasible in the negotiating process, some of the lead representatives are from the private sector and the UWI. An overarching functionary, the dean of college, was also named.

Given the awkward relationship between the CCS and the RNM, it is interesting to note that the recent negotiation impasse between CARICOM and the Dominican Republic over a free trade agreement may seem to justify the separation of the RNM from the CCS. The Dominican Republic suspended the negotiations because, in contrast to its very short list of items, CARICOM proposed a very extensive list of products to be excluded from tariff cuts. Its extensive list of reservations also included more than two hundred products for which it was willing to provide gradual tariff cuts.[83]

CARICOM, and in particular the CCS, whose ranks spearheaded the negotiations, had suffered a set back. The stumble placed the CCS on the defensive in sharp contrast to the RNM's offensive posture with respect to its preparation and conduct of those negotiations for which it is responsible. It also raised the issue of culpability regarding the extent to which, as was noted earlier, the CCS is hamstrung by inflexible mandates. Ian Boxhill, a UWI academic, has suggested more emphatically that it would be a mistake to fault the CCS for CARICOM's miscalculations. In his view, the CCS negotiators were entrusted with a negotiating machinery that was 'cumbersome and with little power to make decisions on their own.'[84]

The breakdown of the negotiations may conceivably have an impact on the RNM negotiating strategy, since a protracted negotiating process could slow aspirations of solidarity. This consideration probably contributed to the CARICOM leaders' decision in July 1999, to interpose the RNM in the CARICOM – Dominican Republic negotiations. The decision assigned the RNM, together with the CCS and the OECS Secretariat, to examine the CARICOM list of products that were not granted duty free treatment initially in the negotiations with a view to reducing them to acceptable levels. Furthermore another decision requested the RNM to analyse the capacity of CARICOM to grant reciprocity in free trade agreements and to design a strategy for trade negotiations involving reciprocity.

The ultimate transfer of responsibility for the management of the financial resources of the RNM from the CCS to the government of Barbados completed the RNM's separation from the CCS: its final act, to be free of the CCS bureaucratic culture. This change seemed a logical outcome of the decision for the CN to be answerable only to the prime ministers. Furthermore, its appeal to the regional private sector representatives to contribute to the costly negotiating process, indicated that the RNM was probably prepared, as the need arose, to be its own fund-raiser.

(c) The Interaction between the RNM and the National Negotiating Actors

The introduction of elements of supra – national governance into the RNM created a difficult relationship between the RNM and two groups of national actors. One was the senior government officials who were accustomed to being routinely involved in regional trade and development negotiations and undoubtedly expected to play a prominent role in the NWGs. The RNM's policy of recruitment of experts 'from any quarter' did not guarantee these officials' automatic participation in the negotiations. For example, in the case of the college of negotiators, the CN identified only five of the twelve lead representatives from national governments. The CN envisioned that the other government officials would occupy the table as representatives of their governments.[85] But they do so essentially as monitors of the negotiations. While they also assist with the negotiations, these government officials cannot intervene in the negotiations without the permission of the lead representatives, thereby ensuring adherence to the regional position. Nonetheless, it has tended to marginalise or subsume the role of government officials in the RNM process and to dilute their status. Another outcome of this marginalisation is a shared perspective between the CCS officials and those of member-states on the form that the structure and functioning of the RNM is evolving.

The ministers are the second group of national actors who may have also been marginalised by the RNM structure and modus operandi. Sir Shridath had observed that:

"it is generally agreed that to make the COTED role effective we [CARICOM leaders and the RNM] need to develop special COTED sessions attended at official and Ministerial level, creatively designed to involve officials and Ministers actually associated with the negotiations".[86]

Despite the intended outcome of this view, recognition of COTED's role seemed to be undermined by the arrangement for the RNM to report directly to the PMSC. The arrangement encourages the short-circuiting of discussions and the routing of RNM documents, especially when the pace of the negotiations places a premium on time. It therefore endangers the role of the COTED through which the ministers are involved in the decision making process. The CN's ministerial rank does not add to the comfort level of the ministers' relations with the RNM. The interaction between the RNM and the ministers could be viewed in terms of either a problem of ministerial adjustment to the new dispensation of regional governance or the need for more intense and structured RNM consultations.

These many awkward relationships often arise when the political or, in this case the negotiating space, is reconfigured upon the introduction of a new institutional actor or the ascension of an existing one. This is especially so when the new entrant to the space, the RNM in this case, in its resolve to quickly and effectively push the process forward, adopts independently of its sponsor, the CCS, an alternative paradigm which is radical and/or calls for fundamental changes in existing structures and mechanisms. An analysis in terms of notions of contest for turf that veer towards the adversarial is, however, inadequate. If contest was the primary issue then a solution could be found in the development of a constructive and cooperative relationship that depends on a sensitive appreciation of each actor for the mandate, roles, objectives and capabilities of the other and an understanding of the content, and the dynamics of it in which they function. As Rashleigh Jackson, a former minister of foreign affairs of Guyana, observed, in the case of the relationship between Governments and non governmental organizations (NGOs), "this process can be facilitated by an understanding of respective capacities and rights, a practice of dialogue and open communication and willingness to use beneficially the experience gained from effective cooperation".[87]

A more comprehensive analysis reveals several underlying problems, some of which are related to the balance between sovereignty and integration. One of these is the heads of government approach to the establishment of the appropriate negotiating machinery. While the negotiating machinery cannot be final, fixed and unresponsive to changes in the region's external economic relations, the Heads have been groping for the appropriate arrangement. This is evident in their delay in embracing the idea of a distinctive negotiating group that the WGE had mooted in 1993. Furthermore, the Heads did not act on their own decision taken in 1990, to appoint a commissioner to facilitate and expedite the timely implementation of all the actions in their Grand Anse Declaration in 1989. These actions included the set out of a work program and specific initiatives over the ensuing four years to deepen the integration process in response to the challenges and opportunities presented by the changes in the global economy. Illustrative of this contention also is the relative ease with which the CARICOM leaders reversed themselves on the concept and structure of the RNM, and empowered the CN without apparently considering the implications of the change for the relationship between the RNM and the other actors in the negotiation process.

The change from one concept and structure of the RNM to another also suggests a measure of indecisiveness and uncertainty on the part of CARICOM leaders towards the nature and role of the CCS. As was observed earlier, two major commissions of inquiry, the WIC and the CRT, reached opposing conclusions on the issue of enhancing the role of the CCS beyond those functions specified in the treaty. The conferring of executive authority on the secretary general in accordance with the recommendation of the CRT report, did not necessarily result in a new phase in the evolution of the CCS. The CARICOM leaders have maintained a stance that veers towards the minimalist position which, in the view of the prime minister of Barbados, existed from the inception of the Community. In calling for a strengthened CCS to move the integration process forward in line with contemporary realities he stated:

"[I]n 25 years, we have not seen it fit to equip the Caribbean Secretariat with the minimum institutional capacity required to execute the elaborate mandates and sometime idealistic time tables which we set. The CARICOM Secretariat that can truly serve our interest in the 21st century must function in a modern, accessible and technologically advanced environment. It must have human and financial resources commensurate with the heavy load of responsibilities we continue to entrust to it. It must have an in house capacity for strategic analysis to support decision-making in a dynamic environment.[88]

After noting that '[t]hese things are not in place' he concluded that '[t]he dithering about their creation must stop'.[89]

Another basic problem relates to the small size of most of the member states, the differential levels of their economies and the long-standing focus of the regional integration process on trade facilitation. When a matter is deemed politically important the politicians become deeply engaged in order to apprise themselves of developments. This is the reason prime ministers in many of the CARICOM states tend to retain the finance and perhaps less so the foreign affairs portfolios. By the same token, ministers of trade and of economic development will not readily overcome the tendency to be involved too early in the negotiation process, notwithstanding Sir Alister's contention in his essay that premature ministerial intervention could complicate the negotiation process. Nor would the ministers acquiesce readily to a preponderant or burgeoning RNM role.

The problem of automatic and uncoordinated state or national efforts is linked to these aspects of the political culture and the importance of these matters to the very survival of the political regimes. For Trinidad and Tobago the preferential access to the Lomé market is of little importance to its economic prospects. On the other hand, for the Windward Islands nothing matters more than this market, not even the national indicative program or the financial package that the EU provides. This market is also important to Guyana. None of these dependent states, except perhaps Guyana, is willing to be far from the fireplace with so much at stake. They would grudgingly support the transfer of authority to the RNM to take care of the ember. Strong national interests are also more evident in bilateral negotiations as the recent suspension of the negotiations between CARICOM and the Dominican Republic demonstrated in late 1998 over CARICOM's very extensive list of products to be excluded from tariff cuts. It is important to note also that the extent of the dependence on the different markets, US as against the EU, as instruments of trade as opposed to cash, also varies from country to country.

The outcome of the nature of the national political economies is the reluctance to subsume national interests in joint efforts in trade and economic negotiations. This behavior is unlikely to be overcome in the absence of an effective regional mechanism to compensate losers in an integration process that is still to shift its emphasis away from merely facilitating trade and allow for the vigorous introduction of the elements of the single market and economy that is being incrementally established. Stated differently, the behavior would persist once the equitable distribution of the gains from integration is not forthcoming or guaranteed. In short, the nature of the integration process ensures that tensions between the RNM and the national ministers will continue to persist. A more constructive relationship between these two actors therefore would only be attenuating.

These problems that arise from national – supranational transactions are not peculiar to the CARICOM experiment with them. They surfaced thirty years ago in an analysis of integration based on the European experience at the time. Leon N Lindberg, the analyst, concluded that the capacity of a collective decision making system to function effectively, and maintain or increase its level of diffuse support or general legitimacy depended on the frequency of the interactions between supranational authority structures on the one hand and national authority structures on the other. Among the reasons that he provided for the importance of this interaction were:

- supranational institutions do not have, nor are they likely to develop sufficient authority, skills or personnel to develop and implement policy without constant and close collaboration with national level institutions. Problem recognition, decisions, and application are activities implying a long- term relationship between the two.
- the impact of cleavage based on nationality is lessened by representative structures such as the councils, permanent representatives, etc, which engage the representatives of governments in decision making.
- the more intense and sustained are transactions, the more likely is it that norms of conflict resolution will develop, thus facilitating bargaining and joint problem solving.
- for most members of the mass public, support is and will continue to be mediated through the national authorities and elites. Hence continued support for and participation in systems structures on the part of national authorities and elites is important.

(d) The RNM and the Post Lomé IV Negotiation Process

As opposed to the preparatory process, during the negotiation process the interaction between ministers and the RNM seems less susceptible to the tensions between the assertion of national sovereignty and the requirements of regional governance, and therefore to notions about displacement or emasculation in the actual negotiations. The structure of the post Lomé – negotiation process sustains the primacy of the ministers' role. Because it is the most structured and institutionalised negotiating arrangement in the annals of north-south cooperation, the Lomé process is highly illustrative of not only the primacy of ministers with whom the negotiating process "starts and ends on each side"[90] but also the awkwardness of the relationship between the RNM on the one hand and ministers and other negotiating actors on the other.

ACP – EU negotiations are highly structured and complicated for a variety of reasons. They are complicated because there are very many issues and states involved: some fourteen very broad areas of cooperation and, since South Africa's accession, seventy-one ACP and fifteen EU states. Secondly, there is much at stake for the majority of ACP states and for that reason a veto still resides with the states' representatives, the ministers and ambassadors. Limited power has only been relinquished in favor of the negotiators. Thirdly, there are cross cutting interests that often transcend regional solidarity.

The structure of negotiations is modeled on that of the EU except that the ACP Secretariat does not have the executive power of the Commission. But in all other respects the ACP structure mirrors that of the EU. First, negotiations take place at three levels, the ministerial, the ambassadorial/ commission and the technical (ACP Secretariat/EU Commission). Inputs to the negotiations can be effected at each level with varying degrees of effectiveness – through the working groups and sub-committees that report to the committee of ambassadors; the plenary of the committee of ambassadors; or the Bureau of the Council of Ministers on which six regional Ministerial representatives and their advisers sit. The latter Bureau is, for the purposes of overseeing the negotiations, enlarged to include the four ministerial negotiators and their eight alternatives. The plenary of the council of ministers and the ACP Secretariat may receive inputs directly.[91]

Obviously, the RNM's most effective and influential point of entry into the negotiating process is the ACP ministerial bureau even though the advisers are not accepted as a formal part of the structure, and their appointment and funding are matters for the respective regions. But its appeal to the RNM is limited since it is not one of the hives of negotiating activities. It merely overviews the arrangements of the negotiating process, and in that regard, its most important role is to resolve inter-regional problems, including disputes.

Another drawback that the structure presents to the RNM is that each of the four negotiators for the ACP represents the entire ACP group rather than a region and is responsible for a number of defined subjects rather than geographical areas. Furthermore, while each spokesperson is a minister, it is the full ACP council of ministers that approves the final positions and decisions.[92] The same applies to the ambassadorial spokesperson who negotiates when the council is not in session. The arrangement poses additional problems of insertion into the process for the RNM, a region/specific advisory body. It is the plenary that approves changes in the positions within the mandate, and in that forum national and regional perspectives more readily find their way into the collective ACP positions.

The other points of entry are more hidebound. At the ambassadorial level the interaction between the RNM and the Cariforum Ambassadors is not continuous. The RNM's participation in the work of these diplomatic representatives is essentially confined to technical support in the form of position papers. But RNM submissions have been few, and some of them are very general in nature. This may be partly attributable to the hurried assembling of resource persons available to the RNM for preparing papers, a phenomenon that is associated with research endeavors in their nascent years and with consultancies. It may also be due to notions of hierarchy, which would regard the committee of ambassadors as too junior a level for the RNM to substantively engage. However, the most critical contributory factor to the limited interaction between the RNM and the ambassadors is the extent of the ACP Ambassadors involvement in the actual negotiations. Carl Grenidge, the deputy secretary-general of the ACP Secretariat has observed that the ambassadors' role as negotiators has been "less than normal",[93] the probable result of "an evolving regional preference for a restricted role for Ambassadors".[94] For their part, the ambassadors have extended a measured embrace to a negotiating agency that does not have a *locus standi* in the negotiations or a veritable base in Brussels, and whose relationship with their kindred national actors in the region is awkward.

CARICOM leaders' efforts to open the ACP-EU ministerial doors for the RNM have acquired little traction. A two-fold CARICOM proposal for the negotiations to be guided regionally and for them to be supervised by the Bureau, that should be enlarged, as well as by advisers, was rejected at the ACP ministerial meeting in Barbados in 1998. The African ministers considered the attempt to vary the ACP ministerial mechanism that is subject rather than region specific and to restructure it around regional non-ministerial representation to be at variance with the integration of regions and the cohesion of the ACP group.[95] They also took the view that it was odd to call for greater political oversight while seeking to entrust responsibility to non-elected representatives. Furthermore, they perceived the CARICOM initiative as an attempt to enlarge the scope of the Caribbean influence by widening the decision making forum to take on board a special strength of the region, in the form of the leadership qualities of the CN who is very regionally focused and who has no political mandate. Another CARICOM initiative, which was to transfer the responsibility of the committee of ambassadors to the ministerial bureau and more specifically to a ministerial spokesperson advised by regional teams, met a similar fate at a meeting of the Bureau in January, 1999.

The attempts to increase the responsibilities of the ministerial bureau and to enhance the role of the advisers in it reflected the high premium which CARICOM leaders and the RNM attached to the political dimensions of the post Lomé IV negotiations. In the first place, the heads of government impressed on the other ACP Heads "the importance of developing effective ACP machinery involving more direct leadership from Capitals and some of the best technical and professional support that the ACP countries could assemble".[96] Secondly, Sir Shridath was able to take opportunity of his chairmanship of the Swedish-based Board of the International Institute for Democracy and Electoral Assistance (IDEA) to present the CARICOM perspective to the Europeans at a conference in Stockholm. The CN contended that the negotiating styles that informed the renegotiations of the Lomé Conventions from II to IV were inappropriate to the post Lomé IV negotiations and that the two negotiating sides should consider adopting a negotiating mode similar to that of the original Lomé convention. He observed that while "technical discussions were, of course, a prominent feature" [of the first convention] "the essential negotiations were about matters of principle and policy".[97] Sir Shridath

> believe[d] profoundly that if genuine progress is to be made in the current negotiations for the post – Lomé IV arrangements ... those negotiations themselves must develop a larger role for political encounter – a larger role for ministers, a role which acknowledges that these [negotiating] issues [that are being projected] are of a political nature which cannot be subsumed in a technocratic process [and which] will not lend themselves to such a subliminal process.[98]

In CARICOM's and more specifically the RNM's judgement, detailed negotiations will not proceed very far and fast unless there is first political agreement on what the trade negotiations are about and the options to be considered.

Despite the difference between CARICOM and other elements of the ACP group over the former's proposal to restructure the negotiating arrangements within the group, CARICOM leaders recognise other developments as encouraging. They have considered as hopeful and a move in the direction of their negotiating arrangement, the decision of their African counterpart to establish an Advisory Panel of Experts, under the ageis of the Organisation of African Unity (OAU), as an independent back up to the African delegations in the post-Lomé and WTO negotiations. The OAU Group of Experts and the RNM seem to have a common perspective on the validity of technical inputs. The two groups have met in the WTO context to fashion a set of ACP concerns relative to the third ministerial meeting that is to be held in Seattle in December, 1999. Analogous to this OAU development, the ACP Ministerial Council has agreed to invite a Group of Experts drawn from the ACP regions to advise on alternative trade agreements. This decision offers scope to the RNM to enlarge its participation in the post Lomé process and an opportunity for the RNM and the Cariforum Ambassadors to close the gap in their relationship, since the Group of Experts would function under the purview of the committee of ambassadors. The committee, however, need not engage the group of experts in any substantive dialogue in its consideration of the reports. Ironically, this is an arrangement that the RNM sought to avoid in the first instance by having experts, including the RNM, attached to each member of the ministerial bureau.

The scope for the RNM to deepen its insertion through its team of experts in the negotiation process is, however, unlikely to materialise in the sense that CARICOM envisages. This is because in sharp contrast to the RNM, the African Group of Experts is entrusted with limited powers. Their mandate does not go beyond their ministers. Nor is it roving or permissive. Furthermore, it is the committee of ambassadors or council of ministers that determines the scope of the Group of Experts' contribution and involvement.

The challenge to the RNM is to obtain permission to address the meetings directly which is the exact opposite to the situation in the FTAA process where officials of CARICOM member states must seek the approval of the RNM lead representatives to speak. In the ACP context, the CN ministerial rank is of little consequence. However, the CN's ideas have weight in the development of ACP positions and could conceivably contribute to the realisation of any ambition on the part of CARICOM to provide leadership to the ACP group as it did in the early 1970s when Sir Shridath was also involved as the foreign affairs minister of Guyana. But once the negotiations begin, the CN's ability to convert a CARICOM position into an ACP position, and still more into an ACP–EU one, is limited. This is because the CN is not currently recognised at the ACP negotiating table.

Another cause for frustration is the limited scope available to the ACP Secretariat to vary either the complex ACP or the ACP–EU arrangements to accommodate the CARICOM unorthodox representational arrangement. In the membership driven post – Lomé process, the CN would be required to don a national garb in order to be eligible to intervene in debates. Domestic political considerations, however, are not likely to favor the governments of the member states sharing their seats with the CN. Compounding this problem, is the reverting of issues, once a ministerial round of negotiations is concluded, to capitals and also to the Cariforum Ambassadors to continue the negotiations.

The intractability of the problem suggests that CARICOM leaders are faced with three choices. They could persevere with their efforts to change the ACP-EU *ancien regime*. Another choice would be to revisit, in the absence of the ACP – EU machinery yielding to CARICOM representation, the concept and structure of the RNM as these relate to the post Lomé IV process. The third choice is more specific and limited. It is for CARICOM to make greater use of the services of the Cariforum Ambassadors *a la* the FTAA since they are the sole conduit from CARICOM to the ACP. These Ambassadors would not be able to negotiate, but on the basis of shared responsibility, they would represent CARICOM's reference points on the issues assigned to them. This arrangement would hold for the CARICOM Group of Ambassadors in relation to the WTO in Geneva where CARICOM countries are less represented, the issues to be addressed are more extensive, the entry of the RNM is still new, and the lessons of Brussels could be more readily heeded.

(e) The FTAA Negotiation Process

The FTAA process provides greater scope for the RNM to influence the negotiations. This process allows states or subregional integration groups to be the negotiators, as CARICOM member states have elected to do. Accordingly, the RNM's involvement in the work of the negotiating groups is direct. The dean of its college of negotiators, Richard Bernal, the Jamaican ambassador in

Washington, DC and the chairman of the working group on small economies in the preparatory FTAA negotiation process is the chairman of the consultative group on smaller economies whose task it is to ensure that the interest of small economies is recognised in the negotiating groups.

The negotiating arrangement has, however, encountered a problem. This is the availability of some of the lead representatives and alternates to attend the meetings and prepare reports of the group as required by the RNM. This problem which arises from recruiting some of the lead representatives from outside the governments and the CCS and with calendars that conflict with the RNM's could have been foreseen, moreso as it is not new. As was observed earlier, the WGE report noted that when identified by their governments, some individuals were not able to participate in negotiation process as effectively as possible due to regular commitments and inadequate technical and financial support. The challenge to the RNM is to restructure the arrangement without undermining the principle of inclusion of civil society in the negotiating process.

Another and perhaps greater challenge lies ahead for the RNM in these negotiations. It arises from Cuba's inclusion in the RNM. While the EU policy of engagement towards Cuba has facilitated the RNM's embrace of Cuba in the context of Cariforum – EU relations, a similar enabling environment for CARICOM-Cuba relations does not exist within the FTAA negotiating process. Still pursuing a policy of isolation and punitive action towards Cuba, the US was instrumental in Cuba's exclusion from the Summit of Americas and consequently from the FTAA process. In the event that the US perceives the RNM as a Trojan horse for Cuba's integration aspirations in the hemisphere, the prospects of its punitive response and of it adopting a less favorable attitude towards CARICOM's vital interest in the FTAA negotiations are real. At the same time, the countervailing influence, including the disposition of the international community towards Cuba and domestic pressure in the US for a reversal of its policy, suggests that instead of open hostility, the US relationship with CARICOM in the FTAA negotiations would be nuanced.

(f) The WTO Negotiations Process

In contrast to the Lomé and FTAA negotiations, those in the WTO have occupied a back seat partly because the RNM appears to be still searching for the appropriate modus operandi, moreso, as the WTO does not acknowledge regional groupings in its negotiating structure. Nonetheless, the WTO dimension has pressed itself on the RNM attention since the post Lomé IV negotiations will be highly cognisant of the issue of WTO compatibility, while the FTAA negotiations, as envisioned by the US, is likely to result in free trade rules that extend beyond those of the WTO. Furthermore, as the Third ministerial WTO meeting began to approach, the RNM increased its attention to the WTO. This is reflected in its submission of a 'Blue Book' on this issue to the heads of government in July 1999.

RNM Performance

It is appropriate to base the discussion of the RNM's performance on the four terms of reference given to the CN: develop a plan of the various negotiations and execute it; lead the negotiating team and be the leading spokesperson for the conduct of the negotiations; develop the negotiating strategy; and involve the sectoral negotiators.

(a) Plan of Action

The RNM has placed considerable emphasis on the development of a program of policy studies, and associated training workshops and seminars hitherto administered by the CCS. The studies are aimed at strengthening the technical capabilities of the RNM. They are carried out by regional and international consultants and for the most part being undertaken without the benefit of the CCS institutional memory. Similarly, the resource persons available to the RNM are often not close to the substance or locale of the negotiations. The reports, therefore, run the risk of being insufficiently focused, of lacking vital information, and of their quality being impaired. Perhaps in taking cognisance of Sir Alister's disappointment with the quality of the studies that emanated from the CCS, the RNM may have swung the pendulum too far to the experts' side. In the case of the training activities, these are aimed at strengthening the negotiating capabilities of CARICOM member states. Training would occur in the various fields of international trade negotiations, especially the new trade – related areas such as competition policy, services and investment, and dispute settlement.

Operationally, the RNM has concentrated on the utilisation of information technology rather than building a conventional bureaucratic infrastructure. It has installed a Caribbean Trade Network linking its three major offices with the CCS, the OECS Secretariat and the Eastern Caribbean Currency Board. The RNM also plans a second stage of the network that will involve the linking of the CARICOM Ministries of Trade. Those CARICOM states that lack the resources to participate in the negotiations and that have been deprived of the CCS traditional role of briefing them on developments as a result of the marginalisation of this organ would be less at a disadvantage.

The RNM has launched a CARICOM Trade Project (CTP) and appointed a communication director at the Barbados base.[99] The CTP is intended to boost the Technical Studies Programme and enhance the RNM's ability to mount training programs and to recruit 'call down' technical expertise to assist in the preparation and conduct of the negotiations. The RNM also plans to formulate and implement a communication and partnership strategy whereby a mechanism would be fashioned for ongoing participation of stakeholder groups.[100] To operationalise this strategy, the RNM would utilise information technology. This capability would at once offset the spread of the RNM bases across continents and islands, cater to the needs of the CARICOM member states as they define their individual and collective positions through the RNM, and establish a two-way information flow between the RNM and its stakeholders.

The RNM's preference for the governments to be its main source of funding has given way to a less discriminate approach. The bulk of support is received from the donor community and the largest contribution has come from a member state, the United Kingdom, of the other post Lomé negotiating party. The donor agencies that the RNM has approached for financial resources, except the United Kingdom, are the same ones that the CCS has traditionally tapped. These agencies are therefore constrained to fathom the differences between the CCS and the RNM and to make a choice. In any case in view of the RNM's political clout, the appeal to the same sources is certain to have an adverse effect on the CCS extra budgetary funds and ultimately on its regular funds to discharge its manifold and mounting mandates having regard to the region's governments new and separate financial obligations to the RNM. The difficulties that the CCS may experience in mobilising financial resources for its negotiating endeavors would add to reservations concerning its suitability as a negotiating entity. These doubts could result in the transfer of more of its responsibility for negotiations of trade and economic agreements with countries and groups of countries in the hemisphere.

Despite the decision to fuse the scattered RNM offices and cost centers, their efficacy remains an issue. While the offices in England and Jamaica are each under the charge of one of the two principal RNM functionaries and the office in Barbados has been strengthened by the appointment of a leading Caribbean expert and diplomat, Henry Gill, as the team leader of the CTP, two of the major negotiating centers, Brussels and Washington, exist as outposts and are undermanned. In the other major center, Geneva, an RNM presence is non-existent. The status of these three centers has highlighted questions about the criteria for locating offices and deploying skills within the RNM.

(b) The CN as Leader of the Negotiating Team and as Leading Spokesperson

As the foregoing discussion indicated, this term of reference presents the CN with his greatest challenge in relation to the Lomé negotiations and perhaps also those in the WTO. The mandate revealed CARICOM's limited appreciation of the format and procedures of the intergovernmental negotiations in Brussels.

The RNM priorities have been dictated to some extent by the timetable of the separate negotiations. The focus has been on the post Lomé IV and the FTAA negotiations in that order, a reflection of the Lomé negotiations proceeding on a faster track than the FTAA.

The primary focus on Lomé is also perhaps the result of the involvement of the principal RNM actors in one substantive capacity or another in earlier Lomé negotiations. Adverting to his association with the pioneering years of ACP–EU cooperation, Sir Shridath stated that he was "a founding father", a "part of that ancestry [that] is a reality that continues as factor into the future" and of which he is "proud".[101] Although bereft of a *locus standi,* the CN has been visible in Brussels and has been in the forefront of CARICOM's efforts to advance the region's interest in the two rounds of the ACP–EU ministerial negotiations that have been concluded. Within the ACP, the CN has also been prominently associated with CARICOM's efforts to allay concerns about its motives in opposing the EU plan for regional free trade areas, while actively participating in the FTAA negotiations, and while also its member states have requested the US to list them as eligible for negotiations with NAFTA. To the extent that Africa is developing an appreciation of CARICOM's seeming contradictory stance, the RNM should share in the credit. It would obviously remain engaged in this matter in the event that all suspicion has not been put to rest.

Beyond trade, there are other issues on the post-Lomé negotiating agenda. They are: political and institutional matters; investment, private sector development and other development strategies; and, instruments and management of financial cooperation. In all of these areas the EU had put forward radical proposals for change. For CARICOM, the issues offered opportunities for bold and dynamic initiatives that could be customised to the needs of a new Caribbean. The RNM showed an interest in the EU's notion of 'good governance' and in opposing that negotiating party's intention to use breaches of it to suspend cooperation under the new treaty. There is, however, little indication that the RNM had been deeply engaged in the other three issue-areas. Similarly, the RNM's contribution to the negotiations on the Non-Economic Issues of the Summit of the Americas appeared to be limited. It may be that the RNM, still relatively in the early stages of its development, lacks the financial resources and expertise to be more involved in these issues. In other words, rather than spreading its resources thinly, it has adopted a studied strategy to focus on securing trade agreements favorable to CARICOM.

(c) Develop the Negotiating Strategy

As in the case of the strategy and position for the WTO negotiations, the RNM's development and refinement of those for the post Lomé and the FTAA negotiations are embodied in separate 'Blue Books' which were the hallmark of the RNM's endeavors in the start-up phase. These latter two studies have been extrapolated and elaborated in 'Red' and 'Green' Books dealing with each of the two negotiations. With the CCS withdrawn, the relevant ministers and agencies of the member states essentially by-passed, the NWGs discontinued, and the COTED minimally involved, these two substantive and policy submissions were the outcome of little broad-based consultations before they were forwarded to the PMSC. Although this sub-committee is open-ended, many Heads do not attend. It is therefore difficult for ministers and their agencies to closely follow the formulation of the regional strategy and position. CARICOM leaders, however, on the recommendation of the RNM, referred the subsequent WTO 'Blue Book' to a High Level Reflection Group, trade officials, and COTED for examination. This interaction between the RNM and the national actors is recognition that the RNM was established as a project with a finite existence. Its impermanence necessitates national involvement in the negotiation process since this would be of immense benefit to the member states in the post negotiation and implementation phase.

The decision to accord a more substantive role to Ministers and national technical experts in the development of regional positions and possibly in their articulation as necessary is open to several interpretations. One view is that it disproves the muted institutional charges that the CARICOM leaders' confidence in the RNM is unqualified. The second view is that the heads of government have become sensitive to these charges and are reacting less defensively to them. Another view is that these leaders' action reflects once more their groping for the most appropriate arrangement for formulating regional policies on external negotiations. Whatever is the validity of these perspectives, there is a closing of the gap between the RNM and the other actors in the negotiation process. This trend allows the RNM to benefit from inputs from as many stakeholders as possible, and in turn to place its considerable capacities at the disposal of the other negotiating actors.

(d) Involvement of Sectoral Negotiators

With the RNM's high profile, the varied and multifaceted negotiations in which the region is involved have attracted the attention of one of the major elements of the civil society, the private sector. Two Caribbean companies have responded substantially to the CN's financial appeal made at the start-up stage of the RNM to the business community. On the other hand, the RNM's promised involvement of the other social partners, for example, labor and the NGOs have not materialised.

The capacity of the RNM to make the negotiating process more inclusive is, however, dependent upon the political culture within the member states and in the region as a whole. Except in very few of these states, notably Barbados, the incorporation of inputs of non-state actors into the methodology of governance has been slow. Since this member state leads in inclusiveness, its prime minister was preeminently qualified, in a comment on the nine protocols that are to amend the treaty and usher in the single market and economy, to rhetorically pose the question: 'Are our politicians, who do not regularly attend CARICOM meetings, familiar with the Protocols? What about our private sectors? Our unions? Our people?'[102] He had posed these questions as he 'prepare[d] to interact directly in the changes in CARICOM with Barbadians as a whole'[103] since he saw 'these things as [his] national responsibility. The people must know and care about what we are doing'.[104]

At the regional level the record of inclusiveness is also mixed. Illustrations of the involvement of NGOs in the negotiation process abound. They could be drawn especially from UNCED in 1992, the subsequent conference on Small Island Developing States, and other UN thematic conferences. Similarly, a feature of the conference of the heads of government is a dialogue between the CARICOM leaders and the social partners – the private sector and the labor movement.

The practice of involving the region's social partners has, however, developed without the benefit of a consistent policy. A watershed in the relationship between governments and NGOs that could have led to the emergence of such a policy was established in 1991. This was the Regional Economic Conference in which the social partners – private sector, labor, the church, the media and the universities – not only participated actively in the deliberation but also were integrally involved in the preparation for it. All sides judged the conference a success, and the heads of government also pledged their commitment to a process of dialogue and consultation among social partners and urged that efforts towards broad-based cooperation in the region be maintained. A second conference was to be held but it is long in coming. The creation of the ACCP inclusive of the social partners and the adoption of a Charter of Civil Society are redeeming developments.

The absence of a more enabling environment regionally and its uneven spread nationally present the RNM with a formidable challenge in promoting sustainable national mechanisms for the participation of civil society, especially the private sector and labor. As part of its response to this challenge the RNM has decided to undertake a study on 'Preparing the Caribbean for a FTAA' which would point the way to greater awareness and the development of a broad-based client support in civil society.

In any case, success in involving the non-state sectors might not be uniform depending on the negotiations in which the RNM is engaged. Within the previous Lomé process, the private sector, and in particular the commodity groups, have been very effective in taking their concerns directly to the ACP. They may not therefore be easily persuaded to modify this procedure and experience. However, the bleak future of the Commodity Protocols in the post Lomé arrangements, that the WTO ruling on the banana regime signified, summons the entire region to collaborative action.

Conclusions: Lessons for the Future

This study has examined an experiment in supra-nationality in the context of a region engaged in efforts to deepen its integration process. The initial experiment was inauspicious. The ill-fated West Indian Federation has had a chastening effect on efforts to embark once more on integration, building on earlier experiences of functional cooperation in a variety of areas. At the core of this cautious approach is the reluctance of CARICOM member states to countenance supranational or regional governance. It is for this reason that CARICOM member states did not adopt the WIC proposal for a Caribbean Commission, and that, as recently as 1994, ideas of a regional negotiating team, advanced by a leading integrationist, did not resonate. The establishment of the RNM was more a hurried response to external influences, in particular the three crucial negotiations that were either underway or imminent, than a facilitator of the growth of the internal dynamics of integration.

Located within the framework of the CCS, the RNM eschewed all elements of supra-nationality until it was reconceptualised, restructured, and became, in effect, the embodiment of the proposed Caribbean Commission. The change disrupted the equilibrium that existed between sovereignty and regionalism. The implications of this change for the ability of the negotiating actors within member states to balance regional interests against their own perception of national interests quickly informed the relationship between the RNM and the national actors. So did the removal of the RNM from within the framework of the CCS. The experience of other integration groupings that possess common institutions, notably the EU, suggests that however awkward the balance between sovereignty and integration may be, the move, once started, towards a stronger set of mechanisms for the making and implementation of regional decisions is irreversible.

The imminent introduction of the single market and economy reinforces the unilinear direction of the deepening of CARICOM. The CARICOM leaders' decision to involve the RNM in the CARICOM – Dominican Republic negotiations has a similar effect. The need for an enhanced appreciation of the irreversibility of the journey towards supranationality, however arduous and agonising the deepening process, is one lesson that could be drawn from this study. The fact that the previous experiment in political union does not commend a return to this deepest form of integration is no reason for discounting the lesson.

The manner in which the change in the concept and structure of the RNM was elaborated represented a failure or unwillingness of the Heads to think through the structural/political implications of the ad hoc arrangements they were making, as could be inferred from the comments of the prime minister of Barbados on the RNM and the CCS. The basic issue that seems to be inadequately addressed is the manner in which the procedures and mechanisms of the RNM reporting to the PMSC would actually work, if the CCS were not interposed. The need for a rationalisation of the RNM decision making process and for a more inclusive approach to its work is another lesson that emerges from this study. A final lesson is that the acceleration of the pace of deepening the integration movement, and making the bureaucratic, managerial and economic developmental foundation more secure are necessary for the achievements of supra-national arrangements to be sustainable and for them to benefit the cause to be served.

Notes

1. Jaime De Melo and Arvind Panagariya (eds.), *New Dimensions in Regional Integration*, Cambridge University Press, 1992. p.9
2. *The Economist*, October 16th – 22nd, 1999, London. p.58.
3. Robert Z. Lawrence, Dani Rodrik, and John Whalley, *Emerging Agenda for Global Trade: High Stakes for Developing Countries*, Overseas Development Council, Washington, DC. 1996. pp.101, and Dani Rodrik, *The New Global Economy and Developing Countries: Making Openness Work*, Overseas Development Council, Washington, DC. 1999. pp.168.
4. Address by Honourable Bernard St John, Prime Minister of Barbados and Chairman of CARICOM Heads of Government in James Porter (ed.), *Development and Regional Co-operation in the CARICOM Area*, Commonwealth Institute, London. p.5.
5. William G. Demas, *Towards West Indian Survival*, Occasional Paper No.1, The West Indian Commission Secretariat, Barbados 1990. p.40.

6. Ibid. p.46.
7. Ibid. p.41.
8. Ibid. p.42.
9. *Annual Report of the Secretary General 1991*. Caribbean Community, CARICOM Secretariat, Georgetown 1992. p.32.
10. *Annual Report of the Secretary General 1993*. Caribbean Community, CARICOM Secretariat, Georgetown 1994. p.7.
11. *Report of Working Group of Experts on Strategy for International Economic and Trade Negotiations 1993*. CARICOM Secretariat, Georgetown. May 1990. p.25.
12. Ibid. p.30.
13. Ibid. p.31.
14. Ibid.
15. Ibid. p.33.
16. Shridath Ramphal, 'Time to Act: The Time for Decision is Now'. *Caribbean Affairs*. October-December 1992. Vol.5. No.4. p.70.
17. *WIC Report*. p.476.
18. Ibid. p.475.
19. Ibid. p.475.
20. Havelock Brewester, 'The Report of the West Indian Commission, Time for Action – Critique and Agenda for Further Work'. *Caribbean Affairs*. January–March 1993. Vol.6. No.1. p.70.
21. Patrick Manning, 'Compromise and Conciliation: The Way Forward'. *Caribbean Affairs*. October - December 1992. Vol..5. No.4. 1992. p.62.
22. *Statement by Hon. Lester B. Bird, Prime Minister of Antigua and Barbuda to Seventeenth Meeting of the Conference of Heads of Government of the Community on Wednesday, 6 July, 1996 in Barbados*. CARICOM Secretariat, Georgetown. p.4.
23. Ibid. p.6.
24. *Towards a Vision of the Future: Progress Report on the Work of the Independent West Indian Commission*. The West Indian Commission Secretariat, Black Rock, St Michael, Barbados 1991. p.53. (Hereinafter the WIC Progress Report)
25. The Report of The West Indian Commission, *Time for Action*, Black Rock, Barbados 1992. p.15.
26. Alister McIntyre, 'The Importance of Negotiation Preparedness: Reflections on the Caribbean Experience'. *Caribbean Dialogue*, ISER Vol.1. No.1. July/August 1994. p.2.
27. Ibid. p.2–3.
28. Ibid. p.7.
29. Ibid. p.3.
30. Ibid.
31. Ibid. p.4.

32. Havelock R. Brewester, *The Caribbean Community in a Changing International Environment: Towards the Next Century*. Eighth Adlith Brown memorial Lecture. Institute of Social and Economic Research, UWI. p. 2. (Hereinafter Brewester Adlith Brown Lecture).
33. *Report on Review of Regional Programmes and Organizations of the Caribbean Community*. CARICOM Secretariat, Georgetown. p. 25. (Hereinafter CRT Report)
34. Ibid. 121pp.
35. Ibid. p.22.
36. Ibid. p.23.
37. *Secretary General Report*. 1993. p. 6–7.
38. Ibid. p.4–5.
39. *Secretary General Report*. p. 58.
40. David Jessop, 'The US is Set on Retaliation'. *Stabroek News*. December 6, 1998. p.11.
41. *Caribbean/United States Summit: Partnership for Prosperity and Security in the Caribbean*. Bridgetown, Barbados. 10 May, 1997. 30pp.
42. Sir Shridath Ramphal, *The West Indian Society – A Recipe for Strength and Growth*. Opening Address on the Seventeenth Caribbean Insurance Conference on Securing Our Future. Bridgetown, Barbados. 2 June, 1997. p . 7. (Hereinafter Ramphal CIC Address).
43. *Annual Report of the Secretary General 1996*. CARICOM Secretariat, Georgetown. p.68.
44. 'Key Decision on Regional Negotiating Team this Week'. *Stabroek News*. February 17, 1997. p.5.
45. Ibid.
46. Ibid.
47. 'CARICOM Bureau Heads on Preparatory Meetings, for Today in Barbados'. *Stabroek News*. May 7, 1997. p. 11. (Hereinafter *Stabroek News*. May 1997).
48. Ibid.
49. *Stabroek News*. February 17, 1997. p. 5. See also *Ramphal CIC Address*. p .8.
50. *Ramphal CIC Address*. p. 8.
51. *Communiqué Issued on the Conclusion of the Eighth Inter-Sessional Meeting of the Conference of Heads of Government of the Caribbean Community*. 20–21 February, 1997. CARICOM Secretariat, Georgetown. p. 12.
52. Cited in *Ramphal CIC Address*. p. 7.
53. *Stabroek News*. February 17, 1997. p. 5.
54. *Remarks by Hon. Lester Bird, Prime Minister of Antigua and Barbuda at the Eighth Inter-Sessional Meeting of Heads of Government of the Caribbean Community*. 20–21 February, 1997. CARICOM Secretariat, Georgetown. p.1.
55. *Communiqué, Eighth Inter-Sessional Meeting*. CARICOM Secretariat, Georgetown. 26 February, 1997. p. 12.
56. *Ramphal CIC Address*. p. 7.

57. *Ramphal CIC Address.* 2nd June, 1997. p.7.
58. *Ramphal Heads of Government Address.* 1–2 July, 1998. p.2-3.
59. Sir Shridath Ramphal, The Regional Negotiating Machinery, Remarks at the 18th Caribbean heads of Government Meeting, Montego Bay, Jamaica. 1 July, 1997. p.1. (Hereinafter Ramphal Caribbean Heads Remarks). p.1.
60. *WIC Report.* p.415.
61. *From Chaguaramus to Port of Spain.* Address by The Rt. Hon. Owen Arthur, Prime Minister of Barbados at the Opening Ceremony of the Twentieth Meeting of the Conference of Heads of Government of the Caribbean Community (CARICOM). Port of Spain, Trinidad and Tobago. July 4, 1999. p.4. (Hereinafter P.M. Arthur Statement July 1999).
62. Sir Shridath Ramphal, Keynote Address at the Ninth Annual Private Sector Conference of the Caribbean Association of Industry and Commerce. Kingston, Jamaica. 26 June, 1997. p.8. (Hereinafter Ramphal CAIC Address).
63. Ibid.
64. *Brewester, Adlith Brown Lecture.* p.2.
65. *Ramphal CIC Address.* p.8.
66. Ibid.
67. Final Report on the North American Free Trade Agreement: The Implications for the CARICOM Region and a Proposed Response G.S.R Associates, Port of Spain, Trinidad and Tobago. 1995. p.1.
68. Ian Boxhill, 'Trade, the D.R and CARICOM'. *The Gleaner.* 1 December, 1998. p. A4.
69. *Ramphal CIC Address.* p.10-11.
70. Sir Shridath Ramphal, *The Negotiations: Process and Preparation.* Presentation on Free Trade of the Americas (FTAA) Seminar: Bahamas Public and Private Sector. Nassau, Bahamas. 6 March, 1998. p.3.
71. *Ramphal's CIC Address.* p.10.
72. Ramphal Bahamas Presentation. p.3.
73. *Ramphal CIC Address.* 2 June, 1997. p.11.
74. 'Sir Shridath takes Crack at WTO. *Stabroek News.* May 20, 1997. p5.
75. *Ramphal Bahamas Presentation.* 6 March, 1998. p.2.
76. Ibid.
77. *Ramphal Heads of Government Address.* July, 1997. p.4.
78. Ibid. p.3.
79. *Ramphal CAIC Address*, 1997. p.9.
80. Ibid.
81. Ibid.
82. *Ramphal Heads of Government Address.* 1 July, 1997. p.4.
83. Boxhill. *op.cit.* p. A4.
84. Ibid.
85. *Ramphal CIC Address.* 2 June, 1997. p.10.

86. *Ramphal Heads of Government Remarks.* 1–2 July, 1998. p.4.
87. Rashleigh Jackson, *CARICOM Integration: The Role of Non-Governmental Organisations (NGOs).* Public Affairs Consulting Enterprise. Georgetown, Guyana. 1997. p.3.
88. *PM Arthur Chaguaramus Statement.* July 4, 1999. p.3-4.
89. Ibid. p. 4.
90. Carl Grenidge, *General Overview of Convention. Post Lomé IV Negotiations and Update on Process and Meetings So Far Held.* Paper presented to the SADAC Regional Workshop on Negotiations on Post Lomé IV. Harare, Zimbabwe. 10–11 May, 1998. p.5.
91. Ibid.
92. Ibid.
93. Ibid.
94. Ibid.
95. *Draft Summary Record of the 67th Session of the ACP Council of Ministers* held on 5 and 6 May, 1998 in Bridgetown, Barbados. ACP/25/98. Brussels. 7 July, 1998.
96. *Ramphal's Heads of Government Address.* 1–2 July, 1998. p.2.
97. Sir Shridath Ramphal, *Dialogue For Democratic Development: A partnership Approach Political Dialogue In the Context Of The ACP-EU Relations.* Stockholm. 23 November 1998. p. 3. (Hereinafter Ramphal Stockholm Address).
98. Ibid. p. 3.
99. *Caribbean Regional Negotiating Machinery: CARICOM Trade Project* (CTP). "David E. Lewis" delewis @erols. com.
100. Ibid.
101. *Ramphal Stockholm Address.* 23 November 1998. p. 3.
102. *PM Arthur Chaguaramus Statement.* July 4, 1999. p.4.
103. Ibid.
104. Ibid.

31 | ORLANDO PATTERSON

Reflections on the Caribbean Diaspora and its Policy Implications

The West Indian islands have produced a culture of migration like no other in the world. Migration over the centuries has become a means of exploitation and of liberation; an economic and political resource as well as a cultural pattern. As soon as people had the opportunity, they left to seek their fortunes, or to spend them, elsewhere. The first to leave were the poor whites who had come as indentured servants during the seventeenth century. Those who survived the tropical diseases, the hard life and the cheap rum, soon fled to the mainland colonies of America, especially to the Carolinas, or else joined pirate bands in Tortuga and became buccaneers.

Not long after, those European planters who were successful in sugar departed as soon as they had made their fortunes and became absentee owners. By the second half of the eighteenth century, most of their descendants had never laid eyes on the region. As soon as slavery was abolished Afro-Jamaicans joined the migratory pattern. After 'pulling foot' internally from the plantation to the hills where they established peasant systems, they started to pull foot externally.

There have been four great waves of migration of Jamaicans and other West Indian peoples since then. One was the migration to Central America during the nineteenth century. Jamaicans and other West Indians were the core of the labour force that dug the Panama canal, and by the end of the nineteenth century over 50,000 had moved there. Most stayed behind and later spread out over the isthmus to work as clerks and labourers on the large plantations.

Today, nearly all the English-speaking pockets of peoples in Central America hail from Jamaica and the other islands.

Two of the four great waves of migration have been to the United States – the second wave, which overlapped with that to Central America and indeed was partly fed by it, and which lasted from the 1830s to 1923, and the fourth and present wave which began in the mid-Sixties and is still in progress. By the end of the nineteenth century more than 95,000 migrants had left for America, mainly from Jamaica. This wave escalated during the first three decades of the twentieth century, when 290,000 left, but it was severely curtailed by the racist immigration law of 1924. During the next thirty years an average of fewer than 2,000 annually were allowed into the United States. This first wave of migrants to America defined the American image of Jamaicans and other West Indians in the country, and General Colin Powell is its ultimate success story. These early immigrants came mainly from lower-middle and solidly working-class backgrounds. Powell's parents fit this pattern: his father was working class, and his mother's high-school background would have placed her firmly in the middle class at a time when less than 2 per cent of Jamaicans had such an education.

The second great wave to America started in the mid-Sixties. The Hart-Cellar Immigration Reform Act of 1965 came in the nick of time for West Indian migratory culture. Only three years earlier Britain had closed its doors to the wave of mainly working-class migrants. The pent-up migratory force, fueled by the failure of the economies of the islands to solve their unemployment problems, broke on America right after. By the late Sixties, Jamaica alone was sending more than 10,000 people per annum. Between 1960 and 1993 a total of 845,588 had arrived from the West Indies, 57 percent from Jamaica. By 1999 a shade under one million had migrated legally to America. We can safely add another quarter to a third of a million illegal migrants to that figure.

Jamaicans of this second wave to America have a more complex origin. They come mainly from the two extremes of the island's talent pool: the most able and the least able. Upwardly mobile lower middle class people now find greater opportunities in the island, or did until recently. Many of the most talented Jamaicans, however, find that the island is too small to meet their professional ambitions. At the same time, cheaper transportation, easier immigration laws and high unemployment, have led to a mass movement of poor and often unskilled people.

The first wave of migrants to America found a very different society from the present wave. The earlier group found a highly segregated industrial society. More educated than native Afro-Americans and more at ease with white people, they not only found good jobs but soon came to occupy a very influential middle-man role in New York politics. West Indian politicians became, in effect, the race leaders of New York both in radical politics, most famously with Marcus Garvey, and in traditional machine politics. It was West Indians, mainly Jamaicans, who cracked the racist walls around Tammany Hall and came to represent mainstream American politics for blacks, men such as J Raymond Jones, the first black to lead the Tammany machine; Bertram Baker, New York's first black state assemblyman; and MacDonald 'Mac' Holder, Brooklyn's pre-eminent power broker for over half a century. They were also quite successful in business and culture. West Indians owned the leading Afro-American newspaper in New York, and writers such as Claude McKay were leading lights in the Harlem Renaissance. Today, the twin traditions of radical and mainstream politics continues in the persons of Louis Farrakhan and Colin Powell, the first person of African ancestry who had a realistic shot at becoming president of the United States.

How large is the West Indian population in the US? This is not as easy a question as might first appear due partly to the way the US census collects its ancestry data, and partly to the large number of illegal migrants from the region. A conservative recent estimate suggests that in 1990 at least 6 per cent of the black population – approximately 2 million persons – were of non-Hispanic Caribbean origin, of whom 86 per cent were foreign born.[1] We can reasonably add another third of a million people to this figure to account for illegal immigrants. This high ratio of foreign to native born is typical of the post-Sixties wave of migrants. It stands in sharp contrast with the earlier wave, among whom over 50 per cent were, like Colin Powell, American born.

About two thirds of West Indians in America are from the anglophone West Indies, Jamaicans being by far the single largest group (29 per cent). Haitians now rank second (19 per cent); and Hispanic blacks third (16 per cent). Because they are among the most highly concentrated populations in the United States, West Indians represent a major component of the Black population in states such as New York, New Jersey and Massachusetts. Almost half of all blacks from the Caribbean live in New York, making up 30 percent of the state's black population. The second largest group, some 17 per cent, lives in Florida; 7 per cent live in New England, mainly Massachusetts, where they make up nearly a third of the state's black population. In all, over 80 per cent live in the New England, Middle Atlantic and South Atlantic regions. These demographic facts are important in any consideration of how the island states might exploit their presence for their own political and economic ends.

Since the 1960s, just when they increased in numbers, the West Indians lost their grip on urban politics even though they still maintain a national presence in the form of people such as Powell and Farrakhan. Basically, with the civil rights movement, Afro-Americans booted them out of their middleman role and established their own political leadership. West Indian leaders have subsequently shifted to traditional ethnic politics, attempting to mobilise the growing West Indian population instead of the old strategy of leading on behalf of Afro-Americans. This new ethnic strategy has not been very successful so far although it is too early to say whether or not it will be successful in the long term.

The main reason for their political failures is the fact that the current pattern of migration takes place within a new international context that obviates the need for ethnic politics. This is what I have called the emerging West Atlantic system, and it is thoroughly enmeshing the fate of the Caribbean with that of the United States.[2] It is itself merely one part of America's transformation into a global, post-industrial system. The West Atlantic system is a circular flow of social, demographic and economic forces embracing the Caribbean archipelago and the eastern US as well as Canada. The flow of American capital, technology and mass culture to the islands, far from promoting self-sustained national development, as was once innocently hoped, has thoroughly disrupted their traditional economies and cultures and is, in fact, the main reason for the current mass migration to America. It is seriously to be questioned whether Caribbean economies are viable as separate national entities. Not only are most of them too small, but the proximity and overwhelming economic and social presence of America means that the tastes and income of their middle and elite classes are determined by the most advanced post-industrial economy in the world. The gross discrepancy between income and development levels will always undermine attempts at catching up.

These problematic developments, however, present their own opportunities. And West Indians have been quick to see and exploit them. In the migratory process, they have created a wholly new set of human communities;

genuinely transnational social systems that exist equally in both the US and the Caribbean. West Indian culture, especially that of Jamaica, can no longer be identified exclusively with the islands. Instead, it is post-national, found partly in New York, partly in Florida and to a lesser extent in Toronto. (It also partly exists in Britain, which I discuss briefly below.) People move freely between these different locations while remaining within the transnational community, and they move at all levels. Jamaican and other West Indian elites are endlessly mobile, with homes and bank accounts all over the West Atlantic, and the West Indian masses are easily the most travelled lower classes on earth. Peasant higglers and hawkers who only a decade ago bartered yams and sweet potatoes now think nothing of pooling their resources, chartering a plane and flying off to Florida, Panama or Hong Kong to buy their merchandise.

What this means is that ordinary Jamaicans and other West Indians are way ahead of their leaders who continue to hold to the traditional model of the nation state. Jamaican migrants, and those who may live here but consider Brooklyn or Fort Lauderdale as much home as Kingston or Spanish Town, have seen the coming global economy as clear as the waters of Negril and, molded by historical insecurity into masters of survival, they have positioned themselves a step ahead of the game.

Before coming to discuss some ways in which Jamaican leaders might take advantage of this post-national diaspora system, let me complete my discussion of that system by briefly looking at those in Britain. Between 1955 and 1962 thousands of Jamaicans and other West Indians migrated to Britain. Today there is an emerging third generation of them. The outcome of this flow is a population that, in 1991, amounted to 518,500 persons according to the British census. In addition there were 184,000 persons of mixed racial ancestry, the vast majority being West Indian-English mixtures. We can safely put the present Caribbean-identified population at about three-quarters of a million people.

There are two important things to note about this part of the diaspora. First, it has often been remarked that they are not as successful as their US counterpart. This is hardly surprising, given the fact that unlike the first wave of migrants to the US most of those who went to Britain came from the working and lower classes. They also found very different opportunities from those found by the earlier wave of migrants to the US. The fact that there was not a large native black population, as in the US, was certainly important. In many ways the British migrants are more like the post-Sixties wave of migrants to the US.

The second distinctive feature of the British-Caribbean population is that, in spite of their economic and civil rights problems, especially with the British police, they are physically assimilating at a remarkable rate. According to the 1991 census, 40 per cent of all Caribbean men in the UK and 20 per cent of women between the ages of 16 and 34 were in unions with an English partner. Even more striking, however, is the marital behavior of the second generation. Over half of all men *and* women who are partnered are living with, or married to, a white English person. This has led to the rapid growth of the mixed population. More significant is the fact that this mixed group largely identifies itself as simply British. The net effect of this is that the Caribbean-identified British population is actually declining. It reached a peak of 590,000 in 1976 and has declined thereafter. Thus, there was a 14 per cent decline between 1981 and 1991. At this rate of miscegenation and identity loss, I predict that in about 40 years or so the Jamaican and other West Indian populations will nearly disappear, absorbed into the native British population.

Partly for this reason, but also due to the very different context that Britain presents, I will confine my remaining remarks about policy possibilities to what I have called the West Atlantic diaspora system. This system presents Caribbean leaders, political and entrepreneurial, with enormous opportunities that are not being exploited. First, let us look at the political possibilities. To understand what these are one must say something about what has happened to American foreign policy since the end of the cold war. There are four distinctive features of present American foreign policy which, from an American perspective, is pretty awful but presents opportunities for enterprising countries fortunate enough to have large numbers of their people resident there.

The first is that American foreign policy is now largely driven by very local, sometimes even parochial, concerns. The cold war gave American foreign policy tremendous focus and an international orientation, whatever one may think about actual practices. That focus disappeared with the end of the cold war. Instead we find that today Congress has come to play a major role in foreign policy decisions and this reflects the very local concerns of American politics. As the late Tip O'Neill, my own former congressman, once famously remarked, all politics is local. To give some examples: America's delinquency in not paying its UN membership fee is largely due to the fact that several congressmen object to UN family-planning practices. Congressman Christopher Smith of New Jersey has one obsessive local concern, to fight abortion practices wherever they exist, and this very domestic concern, strongly supported by his Catholic constituents has led him to block US payments of its UN bill. Another example was the recent refusal of Congress to give President Clinton the 'fast track' authority to negotiate treaties which he requested. The rejection was based entirely on domestic conflicts between the president and congressmen driven by very local constituency concerns.

Closely related to this is the second major feature of current American foreign policy – it is the fact that American ethnic groups play a significant role in determining major foreign policy decisions, especially those relating to their homeland countries. As a *US News* edition recently headlined: 'The ship of state is more likely to be tugged by *US* ethnic groups than by foreign policy'. Here are some examples: the pro-Israeli lobby almost completely determines *US* foreign policy in the Middle East and no one even tries to deny it anymore. The Cuban-American lobby largely determines American foreign policy toward Cuba. So powerful is this little group that America risks alienating even its NATO allies in order to placate it. This was evident in the Helms-Burton Act which sought to punish European allies who traded with Cuba. This was driven completely by the Cuban lobby. The Irish-American lobby explains why America was willing to annoy its major ally, Britain, and allowed Gerry Adams, the Sinn Fein leader, to visit the US. The small Armenian lobby explains why the US chose to support Armenia against Azerbaijan, in spite of the fact that the latter's vast oil resources would suggest that it is in US interest to either support them or not take sides.

The third thing to note is that success is not automatic – there are ethnic groups such as the Arabs who have not had much clout. The Arab case is of special relevance to the West Indies since the main reason for their failure to exercise influence is the fact that they are divided into many nationalities and have not been able to coordinate. At the same time, the Polish experience should give heart to little states like Jamaica. It demonstrates that one does not need a huge operation or a lot of money to have a major impact. According to the *Chicago Tribune*, the Polish-American lobby in Washington is a mom and pop operation led by Casimir Lenard and his wife. These two have organised the Polish lobby so very effectively for 30 years, that many people attribute the speed with which Poland was accepted into NATO and the European community to them. Persistent, incremental action and a very savvy organisation that knows where to get the best bang for its buck by selecting the right congressmen and the right local issues is what counts in the long run.

A fourth factor, however, is also critical; it is the degree to which the ethnic communities in question are concentrated, especially in critical states that are decisive in America's voting system. Thus the Cuban concentration in Florida has been as important as their numbers, which are not all that large, in determining their enormous influence. Florida is a vital swing state in American presidential politics.

These four factors immediately suggest the opportunities that might be seized by astute Caribbean leaders. As I noted earlier, the West Indian population is not only significant in number, but is concentrated in several crucial states, most notably New York and increasingly Florida. West Indians also have a historical head start over other groups, given their long tradition of engagement in American politics. It is time that Caribbean leaders start playing the ethnic lobbying game. The resources are there. And if they do not know how to go about it, there are literally scores of consulting firms ready and able to set them up in this business. And as the case of little Armenia shows, one does not have to be a big country to play it.

Let me move, finally, to the economic opportunities that the West Atlantic diaspora offers. My basic position is that we have to stop thinking economically in national terms. To repeat, we live in a post-national world. The nation state may still be important for political and emotional reasons, but economically it is all but dead; and culturally ordinary Jamaicans have already decided that it is irrelevant. What are the possibilities?

First, there is the opportunity offered by our closeness to America and its ageing population. Remember how we used to emphasise proximity in the old days of economic planning and how this turned out to be a dud? Well, that is so mainly if one is concentrating on the production of goods. The East Asian advantage is such that it easily overrides distance. Not so with services, something which we already know from our tourist industry. However, we can extend this considerably. Here are some examples of directions in which we can move.

As the American population ages the need for nursing homes and other services to the aged increases. There are now some 17,000 nursing homes in

America, and there is general unhappiness with them. Many people find them prohibitively expensive and their services unsatisfactory. At the same time, many of these homes are going bankrupt. The main problem, the experts all agree, is the desperate shortage of qualified workers. There is an oversupply of beds but an undersupply of staff not only in the standard nursing homes, but in the rapidly expanding home health care, hospice, adult day-care and assisted living arrangements.

I suggest that we should start to think of ways in which we could meet these needs both here in the Caribbean and in the US itself. A few attempts have been made, but on a small scale and not very impressively. Our experience with the tourist industry has already given us an edge in planning to meet these needs. I conceive of a large network of such homes here in the islands. Distance is hardly a problem. Jamaica is less than an hour and a half from Florida and only three and half hours from New York. Many Americans travel five to six hours or sometimes have to take a plane for an even longer trip to visit their aged relatives. I also think that the assisted living programmes which are extremely popular with wealthier Americans, are a natural for us. When you think about it, these are simply hotels with lots of good nurses and a resident doctor.

A second way in which we can take advantage of the West Atlantic diaspora is to start thinking in terms of training people to work in America. In the Sixties and Seventies such a view would be condemned on the grounds that it contributes to the brain drain. But have you noticed that countries like India, with among the highest numbers of professionals migrating, no longer complain? Why? Because India quietly discovered that the remittances sent home by its graduates not only paid for their entire education within a couple years, but constituted a major source of foreign revenues. Further, a significant minority of those who work abroad return to start up firms in India, drawing on their experiences in the diaspora. All this should have been obvious to us here in the Caribbean long ago, given our long tradition of migration and the importance of remittances and skilled returnees for our economies.

And yet, one still hears people talking about the brain drain here. Instead of complaining about the nurses leaving, I suggest that we follow their lead and start turning out hundreds more nurses – enough to supply both local demand and that of America. Indeed, it would make sense to shift resources from producing doctors to graduating more nurses. America now has a surplus of doctors according to the American Medical Association. At the same time, there is a desperate shortage of nurses there. However, equally important in this mode of planning is the fact that nurses tend to maintain stronger ties with their home countries than doctors and tend in the long run to send back far more in remittances.

Mention of the training of nurses brings me to another opportunity offered by the diaspora. There is now a crisis in American public education, especially for Afro-Americans. West Indians in America are often caught up in this educational mess because they tend to live in communities with or near Afro-Americans. Many would favour sending their children back home to boarding schools for their secondary education. Indeed, what I see emerging is a pattern of transnational life in which diaspora West Indians spend their childhood and senior years in the islands. Enterprising educational entrepreneurs could seize this opportunity to establish large numbers of private educational institutions which would provide services not only for diaspora parents but the local middle class as well.

Finally, I suggest that we leap-frog the industrialisation process – which is a lost cause anyway since we can never compete with the Asian industrial countries in this area – and move straight into the high-tech, post-industrial world. This is exactly what India is doing (and they, like us, also missed out on industrialisation) with the rapid growth of a high-technology sector based on its large number of programmers. India made good use of its diaspora high-tech migrants in developing this sector back home. A number of those who succeeded in America have returned home and used their contacts with the diaspora community to develop Indian versions of Silicon Valley. Local entrepreneurs might want to emulate this Indian pattern. Note, however, that most of these suggestions make one fundamental assumption: that we invest heavily in education. Barbados and Trinidad have recognised the importance of this and are forging ahead, even though they already have good records in this area. Jamaica, sadly, is falling behind in this vital area.

I was asked to speculate about the future of the Caribbean and it is in this spirit that I offer these suggestions. They are based on several certainties about the present and near future: that we live in a world that is increasingly global, post-industrial and post-national. One of the interesting things about West Indian history – a point often made by the late George Beckford – is the way in which ordinary West Indians have tended to act ahead of their leaders in coming to terms with the changing times. Today we see this happening again. The Jamaican proletariat, in their construction of reggae, have created one of the world's truly global cultural products. West Indian migrants have plunged into the post-industrial world of North America and can be found at all levels of this economic system. And West Indians have been among the first to create a wholly new social type: the transnational community which straddles borders in a post-national disregard for the nation-state. The region's leadership, however, is still thinking and planning in insular, industrial and nationalistic terms. It's catch-up time again, fellows.

Notes

1. These estimates are based on unpublished work by the Dutch sociologist Matthijs Kalmijn.
2. See Orlando Patterson, 'The Emerging West Atlantic System', in William Alonso, ed., *Population in an Interacting World* (Cambridge: Harvard University Press, 1987), pp. 227–260

Part 8

The Caribbean and the Creative Imagination

32 | KENNETH RAMCHAND

The Lost Literature of the West Indies

This paper begins with some reflections on works of the creative imagination and focuses on the capacity of such art to engender cultural self-knowledge, cultural confidence, and regional self-affirmation. The second movement points to 'the lost literature' of the West Indies with proposals for retrieval of what is secreted in scattered places and for minimising the loss and non-recognition of current output. The next section argues that our artists seem to have more outreach than our intellectuals, and it illustrate how uniquely and effectively works of the West Indian creative imagination analyse social, cultural and political issues. In the last part of the discussion it will be argued that most of the West Indian literature that is not physically lost is still lost to our societies, and suggestions are put forward about how to improve both transmission and the quality of reception.

The Lost Literature of the West Indies

The Creative Imagination

The imagination is creative already. It expresses itself in literature, music, dance, song, story, painting, carving, sculpture, and in many other forms when the need for self-expression has to have an outlet. One indulges in the redundancy of 'creative imagination', however, in order to insist that there are specific acts and procedures of the imagination and certain seasons when that faculty is engaged in a conscious, disciplined and consistent effort to make artistically shaped entities. It has to be insisted upon that the knowledge these fabrications give us about ourselves, our society, our landscape and the community of man to which we belong is a special kind of knowledge, the specialness deriving in large part from the way the knowledge enters the work of art and from the way it comes to us. Art comes out of unusual states of being, and it has its own ways of knowing and telling. Its particular virtue lies in its power to work through our senses and to make us think with our feelings. It depends upon the integrity of the union between reason and emotion.

I want to feel free to use the term 'art' to cover the full range of works of the creative imagination. It follows from what I have been saying that not all self-expression is art. The artist may claim to be motivated by a personal need for self-expression but what comes out is not art if it does not speak to and of other people. Nor is it art just because there is sincerity or intensity of feeling, or because some half-creating observer finds form and pattern in someone else's half-baked production. If raw expression or imperfect expression were art, the half-naked man wining on the pavement outside Hi-Lo would be a fine dancer, not an untuned spirit, and the cry of pain in the verses of a young woman whose husband has just died would have been poetry rather than a cry of pain. If raw expression or imperfect impression were art we wouldn't need the word 'art'.

On the other hand, we have always known what Euro-American critical theory is now rediscovering: people are unlikely to pay attention to any art that makes the mistake of thinking that artistic form exists for its own sake. Form is the servant of content. But it is content with a difference. The content of a work of art is of minor significance if it merely confirms what social scientists and historians have already told us. The content of a work of art turns out to be more than familiar content because of the way art comes about and because of the way it expresses itself.

Art begins when the need for self-expression drives the artist, whether he knows it or not, to find a form or vehicle that takes the self beyond itself, from what it already knows and knows only too well to what it doesn't know it knows. The writer's scrupulous and disciplined approach to language and style, his search for the appropriate form, is part of the process and adventure of discovering and clarifying what he/she feels and wants to say. I am afraid it follows from this that there can be no shortcuts, no Cole's notes, no question of 'getting the gist' of a novel or poem. What is required is attentive reading and a willingness to enter into the work and experience the things that the writer is writing about. A novel or a poem or a short story can have no effective meaning for someone who does not read it in this experimental way.

Art brings the special and revolutionary knowledge that it alone can bring because the artist, who is usually without formal academic training and without the urge to political power, operates outside the paradigms, frames of reference and consciously-held ideologies of social scientists, politicians and others with an avowed or secret interest. A similar liberation from the known and the familiar and from the pressure of palpable designs is brought to the reader who has the self-assurance and tolerance, or the patience and the training to submit provisionally to the work of art.

The artistic process that I have been sketching takes place, of course, in a cultural context which influences it and which it influences. This is what makes art meaningful in the first instance, and it is the ground that allows us to propose that whatever else art may be called upon to do it can promote self-knowledge and help to create cultural confidence. But what is cultural confidence? The term is not an easy one. It shows itself in the attitudes and behaviours of individuals and groups in a society or in the society as a whole. These signs are difficult to read in countries with histories like ours and the hazards multiply in periods like the present when it is not only economies that are being subjected to global conscription. Culture, including and especially popular culture, is once more taking on a mimic character with the infected media exposing members round the clock to a selection of the most banal and conservative items from the dominant American culture.

Where our culture manages to resist full-blown mimicry, it still runs the risk, aggravated by a tourist-hungry state, of either turning itself out as another minstrel show or packaging itself as a cultural product to be sold for foreign currency. The show is only show – acts of bravado or theatre, acts of chauvinism or conceit - projecting an image out of touch with how a people actually work and play, and how they stay on terms with their gods.

If cultural confidence is neither display nor chauvinism, what is it, and what is it good for? Here is a tentative formulation: cultural confidence is knowing who you are and why you are in the midst of all the convulsions that are changing your life. It is a difficult knowledge to achieve ('To find the true self is still arduous') and it can never be fixed or final. The outcomes of post-independence education, politics and economics suggest that a more serious look has to be taken at the possibilities inherent in the works of the creative imagination. Here is how the task is set out by Jamaica Kincaid, a writer from Antigua. She is writing about people in a small place:

> They go back and forth, exchanging places, and their status from day to day depends on all sorts of internal shadings and internal colourings, and the forces that manipulate these internal shadings are kept deliberately mysterious and unknown. And might not knowing why they are the way they are, why they do the things they do, why they live the way they live, why the things that happened to them happened, lead these people to a different relationship with the world, a more demanding relationship, a relationship in which they are not victims all the time of every bad idea that flits across the mind of the world? I look at this place (Antigua), I look at these people (Antiguans), and I cannot tell whether I was brought up by, and so come from, children, eternal innocents, or artists who have not yet found eminence in a world too stupid to understand, or lunatics who have made their own lunatic asylum, or an exquisite combination of all three.[1]

Knowing who you are and why you are in a dynamic and provisional way makes it easy for you to be open to, and selective about, influences from outside yourself. At the same time, it makes it very difficult for those who want to tell you what you should be. This applies to countries threatened by structural adjustment programs, and to individuals in contact with governments and bureaucracies.

How does a society with a history of enslavement indenture and colonialism get to know itself? In spite of one man one vote, and in spite of political independence in the 1960s, the process of liberation and self-discovery that should have picked up speed and taken on added dimensions after the Act of Emancipation has led neither to the creation of a just and equal society, nor to the evolution of a people with a national purpose.

How can our societies complete their recovery from the effects of the first colonial relationship when, even before they began the work they were being licensed to do with universal suffrage in the 1940s, another colonising agent was literally setting up the bases that were to open us up to the invasion of our living rooms by aliens, the heaping upon us of the debris of a communications revolution that created a global village in which we, and people like us are the mindless villagers? To mention only one of the consequences: the domination by foreign television programmes has not only affected values, it has contributed to the underdevelopment of local programming and production skills, and has put popular culture to tests that may be too difficult for the next forgetting generation.

Global imperialism comes not as single spies but in battalions. To count overseas remittances in cash and material objects in barrels as contributions to island economies[2] is, in the first place, to accept the conditions that produced the modern transfer by which the formerly absentee landlords now live it up in the islands while an émigré labour force toils in the cold metropolis. But it is also to acquiesce in the establishment of certain habits of consumption that would make impossible the change in lifestyle that is the only deep solution to our problems. In all these ways we need to address the old and continuing split in our societies between person and place, and between culture and agriculture.

What hope of cultural confidence can there be for a society that slouched into Independence after the death of Federation only to see its new beginning, its youth and freedom, captured by middle-class politicians trained to think to eat to drink to drive and to travel first class as their colonisers did, and free to do so once they remain committed to financial systems and categories they had no say in setting up and no voice in influencing? An integrated regional voice may allow some minor negotiated concessions in selected areas but the matter is too internalised and structuring for such plasters to have any effect.

The time has come for us to conclude that our independence is compromised and vulnerable and it is so because we go through series after series of external motions and development plans without having discovered or seized the inner country whose fundamental reality the creative imagination is never tired of intimating. What we need, in brief, is a complete revamping of the system of education in the region in the light of our own answers to the questions 'What is education?' and 'What is education for?' Somewhere in the new dispensation there will have to be made, philosophically, a living connection between education and the creative arts; and this will be reflected in a commitment to use the creative arts as a means in the delivery of education.

What is called for in the first place is a series of measures designed to raise the level of consciousness and the degree of self-knowledge through the entire population and in the whole Caribbean region. The system of education in the region should ensure that every person is at least trilingual for ordinary communication and for accessing the rich literatures of our region; and the school curriculum in each set of territories should include exchange visits to the others to enhance familiarity and to facilitate language acquisition.

Governments are flinging money at education, and there is encouraging talk of secondary school places for everybody, but education means something more than just providing school places for everybody. It means liberating ourselves from the controls and persuasions that came built-in with the existing system. It means refusing to take the economist's view in which 'education' is replaced by 'human resource development', and in which people are reduced to being economic resources to be developed or exploited rather than human beings needing space and time for fulfillment. It means recognising that the socialisation process and a sense of being part of the environment are fundamental to the personal development of the child and that school subjects are not so much 'subjects' at this stage as experiences to be lived and discovered in the school.

It means debunking the practices and objectives that many of our bureaucrats and administrators slavishly follow, and embarking upon the construction of a system and a curriculum of our own, taking into account our particular means and needs and making use of all the legacies available to us. The new curriculum would forge a fruitful relationship between education in science and technology and education in the creative arts. A far-reaching aspect would be its encouragement of proper nutrition and exercise which would reduce the pressure upon medical services and perhaps help to develop a lifestyle in closer relationship to the physical environment and the products of this environment.

It means abolishing competitive exams for secondary school places and with them the books, teaching practices and curricula these have spawned; and after that there will need to be clear recognition of the difference between the educational task of providing for a wide range of learning experiences in the schools and the administrative one of devising a way of assessing aptitudes for the different kinds of secondary schools that must be set up.

It means recreating the teaching material used in our schools especially at the primary and secondary levels where there is a crying need to re-make the textbook. The first step would be to revise content, and attitudes to content, in the light of readings of history, culture and society and the human capacities of our people emerging from the work of our scholars and artists. The second and more visionary step would be to modify the very notion of the book which must now carry built-in couplings with the computer, film, theatre and performance, painting and drawing, musical expression and other student activity. The new book must come in a format that permits additions and deletions with the same ease and flexibility that word processing allows us to alter the manuscripts we create.

In our countries education means starting all over again with the primary schools and developing a system that recognises the need to offset the disadvantages caused by poverty and the absence of a home life whether through poverty or from the fact that in many households where both parents work the child is deprived of both educational help and emotional sustenance. In practice this may involve not setting up early childhood care and education centres separate from the primary schools but lowering the compulsory age and beginning primary school at age four, involving adults in the community as adjuncts to the teachers. The primary school would have to be designed according to our particular needs and would therefore have to serve curriculum requirements and physically create a sense of home.

Investment in the kind of education being suggested here may well turn out to pay back with interest when we try to imagine the effects it would have in preventing sickness, reducing crime and aberrant behaviours, and in lessening the need for the building of prisons and unsuccessful corrective institutions.

My main focus is the creative imagination in the literary arts but the creative imagination needs to operate in all the systems by which we seek to order and remake our societies.

The Lost Literature of the West Indies

A great deal of our written literature is lost in the newspapers, magazines, pamphlets, other ephemeral publications and books printed in the United Kingdom or in the West Indian islands in the eighteenth, nineteenth and early twentieth centuries. Some of it is secreted in the form of digressions, diversions and asides in the histories, journals, travel books, missionary accounts, church records, plantation papers and official documents of the eighteenth and nineteenth centuries. The Histories by Long (1774) and Edwards (1793) and M Lewis's *Journal of a West India Proprietor* (1834) contain passages descriptive of landscape and the social lives of Africans and Europeans as well as transcriptions of folk tales, songs and conversations that are deserving of inclusion in the corpus of West Indian Literature. Rare and unrecognised books include:

Emmanuel Appadoca or Blighted Life (1854) by the distinguished Trinidadian lawyer of mixed race Michel Maxwell Philip; *Selections from the Miscellaneous Posthumous Writings of [the Jamaican] Phillip Cohen Labatt* (1855) containing 'Curgy's Funeral or the Old Time Busha' a story of anancy being out-nancied, the first of our fictions to incorporate anancy qualities in the characters and apparently not knowing it is doing so. The Scotsman EL *Joseph's Warner Arundell: the Adventures of a Creole* (1838) belongs to the literature, as does Charles Rampini's *Letters from Jamaica* (1873) which contains an excellent version of 'Annancy and the Tiger' and in which the author from Scotland shows a remarkable memory for Jamaica talk in the love letters reproduced or invented in his book.

By the 1920s nearly all the newspapers in all the islands had come around to having a literary section or a literary page. In all the islands, these newspapers are our prime source for tracing the history of theatre and performance. In Trinidad, Sam Selvon began editing a weekly supplement for *the Trinidad Guardian* right after the Second World War, with short story and poetry competitions and regular book-reviewing. Writers like Edgar Mittelholzer, Errol Hill, Harold Telemaque, Cecil Gray and Selvon himself headed a wide cast. Selvon's stories and essays in this publication have been collected in an important volume *Foreday Morning* (1989) which shows the importance of the newspaper outlet in the development of the career of one major writer.

After the First World War a number of short-lived magazines and newspapers had sprouted in Trinidad including the organs associated with writers who became known as 'The Beacon Group'.[3] Even before that, at the turn of the century, literary and debating societies sprang up in all the islands and some of them had their own little magazine. Judging from the contents of surviving Trinidad examples there was healthy rivalry with fierce disputes about standards among the clubs. With respect to newspapers we note that an editor of the *Jamaica Gleaner*, Tom Redcam used the resources of the newspaper to set up The All Jamaica Library which published six novellas between 1903 and 1909. The same newspaper serialised HG De Lisser's *Jane's Career* in 1912 before it was published in book form. Given the fact that about the only thing that is read universally and regularly in the islands is the newspaper, the serial publication of novels and collections of short stories today might be one of the most effective ways of encouraging authorship and cultivating a reading public.

The Indian Koh-I-Noor, edited by an Indian merchant and devoted to the interests of Indians in Trinidad started in 1898, and in 1904 the Presbyterian Church began publishing its newsletter The Trinidad Presbyterian. Among the newspapers and magazines that were coming out in Trinidad at the end of the First World War were some that were owned, edited, and written for by people of Indian origin living in Trinidad. These business or middle-class 'Indian' publications were signs that class formation was well advanced among the former indentures, but they still give a good sense of the life of the Indians in the island as a whole. show the embattled emergence of Indians as nationals of Trinidad and they bring the literary and cultural aspirations of people of Indian origin into the light. They included *The Indian Koh-I-Noor Gazette* (1898–1899); *The East Indian Herald* (1919–1924, irregular); *The Patriot* (c.1921–1925); *East Indian Weekly* (1928–1932); *The West Indian Magnate* (1932-193?); *The Spectator* (1948-196?); *The Observer* (1940-); and *The Sentinel* (1946-195?). There were many East Indian literary and debating societies, a literary magazine called *The Minerva Review* (1941-44); and a compendium published in 1945, *The Indian Centenary Review: One Hundred Years of Progress 1845–1945*.

Recent work on these organs help us to understand a neglected side of West Indian Literature and make the emergence of Sam Selvon, Ismith Khan and VS Naipaul seem much less out of the blue than they are taken to be. The career of the late Patrick Chokolingo, a person of Indian origin who emerged as an outstanding journalist and as a Trinidadian person before anything else in the non-Indian newspapers (usually called 'the national newspapers'), is significant for an understanding of Trinidad culture and society, and so is the career of Seepersad Naipaul (1906-1953) who contributed to all the 'Indian' publications as well as to *The Trinidad Guardian* and its associated *Evening News* . Seepersad eventually self-published a small collection of stories *Gurudeva and Other Indian Tales* (1943) which was praised for showing the unknown half of Trinidad and which had a profound influence on the career of VS Naipaul.

In Trinidad the gradual retrieval of some of the lost literature has brought new insights into the making of modern Trinidad as well as of the making of the literature of Trinidad. It has also contributed to our understanding of the impact of the shorter literary forms particularly the short story on the development of the West Indian novel since nearly all of the West Indian novelists of the 1950s and 1960s were first practitioners of the short story.

What is true of Trinidad from the 1920s is true of the other islands. But the role of the newspapers and the various magazines in the development of literature in the islands and in the establishment of the short story as the most indigenised of the inherited literary forms has still not been properly measured. The time has surely come for teams to be set up in all the islands to list all the newspapers, to collect what can be collected, from overseas sources, and to read with a view to selecting items for reprinting as a part of our literary history and cultural heritage.

As for our early oral literature we have to recognise that what has been recorded or collected might be only a fraction of what existed. We cannot be sure that the calypso or reggae or dance hall that comes to our attention is the full sum of what is being produced. One obvious consequence of the incompleteness of the inventory is that while our generalisations about the oral literature or popular culture as a whole are unlikely to be far off the mark, there may be unrecognised items of high quality some of which will fit into the trends but some of which may well be pointing in new directions. It follows from all this that there could be important missing elements in our analysis of the penetration of imposed literary forms by living and functional popular traditions and vice versa.

Nobody needs to be persuaded about my last category of lost literature. In the modern period, the islands have only incomplete information about one another's literary productions. It is difficult for a reader in Trinidad for example to know what is being written in Jamaica, how the books may be obtained and who are the new authors. One of the casualties of this situation is the late Harold Sonny Ladoo of Trinidad whose brilliant and promising novels[4] have still not come into dialogue with the work of his contemporaries or the new generation.

The regional projects indicated for retrieving what is lost and preventing loss of current material are:

i. Island inventories of printed material from the earliest period
ii. Catalogues of relevant printed material located in other countries
iii. Descriptive accounts of printers and printing in each island
iv. Microfilming/ scanning of all newspapers and perishable printed material
v. A system of registration in association with the copyright organisations in each island of all oral productions and performances with scripts attached
vii. Annotated annual bibliographies of written works in each island
vii. Circulation of all lists to other islands

These projects will cost money and take time but they are basic. The main burden of this paper, however, is a problem that is at least as important as the problem of retrieval, discovery and preservation.

Artists as Intellectuals

There is a strong tradition of indigenous thinking and a formidable line of committed intellectuals in the English-speaking Caribbean from JJ Thomas through CLRJames, George Beckford, George Lamming, Lloyd Best and Walter Rodney. The legacy is more compelling and radical if we take the Latin American and French Caribbean traditions into account. Such Caribbean thought, however, has little currency as thought or as part of a way of seeing the world. It remains locked away from ordinary people, and it hardly influences political and economic policy. Over 80 per cent of the Humanities undergraduates I have taught in the last fifteen years are not familiar with the work of even two of the following: Cesaire, Fanon, Glissant, Freyre, Marti, Paz, James, Beckford, Rodney, Nettleford, Best.

There is enough material and enough of an intellectual tradition for a wide dialogue to begin about the nature of intellectual life, the role of intellectuals, and what we must do to create a rational and critically alert population. But apart from George Lamming nobody seems to be interested in thinking about the role of the intellectual (and the treason of the intellectuals) in our society. The society's lack of interest in thinking is symbolised by the fact that after fifty years there is still no department of philosophy at any campus of the University of the West Indies, no attempt to teach philosophy as it is taught at other universities or to seek to innovate a philosophical tradition, including the Amerindians and including the traditions of all the people who came. One of the decisions of this conference might usefully be to invest immediately in the creation of departments of philosophy and intellectual history at all three campuses of the University of the West Indies offering honours programmes but also devising compulsory courses to be taken by students in all faculties.

The peculiarities in our intellectual situation, meanwhile, have brought it about that it is the artist who seems to be performing not only the role of philosopher but also that of the traditional intellectual offering insights into and possible solutions to problems in our society. Some of the writers cover major issues like 'national identity', 'unity', 'integration' and so on. and

African/Indian relationships in Guyana and Trinidad. Some write about the problematic relationship between the leader and the mass. They write about religion, sports and culture, as mediums for authentic self-expression against the kind of self-expression imposed upon us by the foreign influenced media. They write about the need to form our own language.

Others focus on poverty, violence, and post-independence problems exacerbated by a heavy reliance upon imported commodities and by abject failures in productivity. They make satirical attacks on the international lending agencies, on the whoring after foreign investors and the corrupt deals between these investors and local capitalists associated with political parties. As early as 1979. Derek Walcott's poem 'The Star-Apple Kingdom' saw this:

> One morning the Caribbean was cut up
> by seven prime ministers who bought the sea in bolts –
> one thousand miles of aquamarine with lace trimmings ,
> one million yards of lime-coloured silk,
> one mile of violet, leagues of cerulean satin-
> who sold it at a mark-up to the conglomerates,
> the same conglomerates who had rented the waterspouts
> for ninety-nine years in exchange for fifty ships
> who retailed it in turn to the ministers
> with only one bank account, who then resold it
> in ads for the Caribbean Economic Community,
> till everyone owned a little piece of the sea
> from which some made saris, some made bandannas;
> the rest was offered on trays to white cruise ships
> taller than the post office; then the dogfights
> began in the cabinets as to who had first sold
> the archipelago for this chain-store of islands

Can there be a more devastating indictment of the corruptions of post-independence politics and the new enslavements and resentments being sown by the encouragement of servant industries than this chastening explanation of the bases of tourism by the ferociously reasonable voice in Jamaica Kincaid's *A Small Place* (1988)?

That the native does not like the tourist is not hard to explain. For every native of every place is a potential tourist, and every tourist is a native of somewhere. Every native everywhere lives a life of overwhelming and crushing banality and boredom and desperation and depression, and every deed, good and bad, is an attempt to forget this. Every native would like to find a way out, every native would like a rest, every native would like a tour. But some natives – most natives in the world – cannot go anywhere. They are too poor. They are too poor to go anywhere. They are too poor to escape the realities of their lives; and they are too poor to live properly in the place where they live, which is the very place that you, the tourist want to go – so when the natives see you the tourist, they envy you, they envy your ability to leave your own banality and boredom, they envy your ability to turn their own banality and boredom into a source of pleasure for yourself.

After reading *A Small Place* would anybody want to award the order of CARICOM to any of the taloned creatures of Antigua? Has there been a more moving expression of the break-up of traditional family structures, the effects of emigration to the city or to foreign, the motivations of urban youth violence, the loss of sanctity, and the gaps between generations than Olive Senior's 'Country of the One-Eyed God'? [5]

And how about this poem by the late Jamaican poet Tony McNeil which links the Columban invasion with cross and the sword to the tourist invaders of our time planting their flags in the form of umbrellas. Against the twentieth century takeover of the land by prowlers with cash ('the cats') the dispossessed person in the poem can only assert his attunement with what is un-buyable and elemental in his island:

I
The wind is crisp and carries
a tang of the sea. The flowers
burn richly against the grass.
The grass itself shines and is precious.
II
Ahead, the sky and the ocean
Merge in a stain of blue. On the beach
Yesterday, lolloping tourists
Were posting umbrellas like crosses.
III
This morning I chose to stay home
To watch the cats and think of
Columbus. And the grass is precious
Merely because it belongs to us.

The poem was written in 1975[6] and the threat it registered is even more menacing in 1999. It is incidentally a fine example of how an artist makes a statement and how the discourse in literary texts differs instrumentally from the discourse of a social scientist.

'What is not lost is still lost'

The social relevance of West Indian writing is easy enough to illustrate. But one cannot avoid a most distressing proposition. Most of the literature of the West Indies is lost because too many readers do not know how to read literature and too many go to literature for extractable content and without the time or the inclination to experience or enter the world the writer has created – which is why they are quite happy to take the word of a critic who tells them what the book says and why it is important to the society. If literature is lost in these fundamental senses, it cannot carry out the necessary work of raising the consciousness of individuals, it will have no hot line to the individual, and the archival work and the bibliographic responsibilities being recommended towards retrieval of the past and registration of what is current would add up to just so many soulless scholarly and cataloguing chores.

Most of the literature of the West Indies is lost because hardly anyone ever reads it; there are few occasions or opportunities for the mass to experience it; it has had no practical effect on socioeconomic policy or political behaviour; where it is read, particularly by social scientists, it is not engaged with as if it has new or different perspectives, but is treated merely as supplementary material; and nowhere in public discourse is there any acknowledgement of the power of literature to bring into the social equation our capacity for feeling.

This last seems to me to be crucial in a society like ours that has been brutalised, and that could only survive by seeming to lose the capacity to feel. But the political, economic and sociocultural crises of our period seem to suggest that the time has come to exhume this buried capacity. What I mean is conveyed in dramatic terms in Earl Lovelace's *The Dragon Can't Dance* (1976). A change is coming over Aldrick, the main character who has been content to hint at his potential and dangerousness by playing dragon on the designated days, and who has been an 'aristocrat' in the group's traditional philosophy of non-possession which translates into not showing humane feelings, not being touched by anything, not being committed to anything or anybody, and not participating in any way in an economic order whose agenda is seen as corrupting and exploitative.

When he approaches the girl Sylvia on carnival day she is still hurting over his earlier rejection of her and she takes a bitter pleasure out of telling him that she has a man of her own now. On Ash Wednesday morning, the morning after carnival, Aldrick wakes up with Sylvia's dismissing phrase in his head and new light in his eyes:

All his life he had managed in such ways to disconnect himself from things which he couldn't escape and which threatened to define him in a way in which he didn't want to be defined, and go on untouched, untouched by things that should have touched him, hurt him, burned him. And that was why this hurting over Sylvia, even though he explained it to himself as love – love? – confused him. He had reached home last night with the phrase 'I have my man' hammering in his brain, hammering at his whole self, torturing him so that if he had been able to he would have cried, if he could have felt the extent of feeling that it called forth, he would have been happy to let himself be soaked by the pain. And he had said to himself in anguish: 'I have to learn to feel.'

Aldrick looks at the shacks around him and tells himself at last in so many words that he had never embraced this place as home, like his Uncle Freddie who had behaved as if real life would begin later and who died with his old house falling around him and not a flower planted, nor a fence mended:

She have her man. He couldn't laugh at that. No, sir. But this morning he felt humble before his own feelings, and not so afraid of them. He wanted to call them to him, to feel them. He felt a great distance from himself, as if he had been living elsewhere from himself, and he thought that he would like to try to come home to himself; and even though it sounded like some kind of treason, he felt that at least it was the only way he could begin to be true to even the promise of the dragon to which he felt bound in some way beyond reason, beyond explanation, and which he felt had its own truth.

This is not an isolated episode. Its authoritativeness as one of the main messages in the novel comes from the centrality of Aldrick and from Lovelace's use of the omniscient author convention to trace all the windings of the war between Aldrick's accustomed way of thinking and the waves of feeling that began form in the deep long before the first actual conversation with Sylvia. Lovelace's novel is a good exemplification of the dictum that a work of literature wants to smuggle new thoughts into consciousness through the feelings, making you feel before it makes you think, or making you feel at such intensity that feeling is thought.

In an address of 1956,[7] George Lamming speaks of three distinct but related worlds to which the creative writer bears some sort of responsibility. The second of these worlds is 'the world of social relations', his experiences in 'the particular world he happens to be living in'. The third is 'the world to which he is condemned by the fact of his spirit the world of human beings'. These two worlds are familiar enough and distorted enough, no more so than in the coloniser's formulation that urges the reality of the universal and the spuriousness of the local.

But they are renewed and they take on a more problematic and empowered identity because of the connections Lamming insists must exist between them and between them and the first of the writer's worlds which he describes as 'the world of the private and hidden self, a world which turns quietly, sometimes turbulently within one man, and which might be known by others only after that man has spoken.' The urgencies of day to day living keep intruding on that world of private and solitary concerns but Lamming insists that it must not be sacrificed to the immediate neighbourhood however bonding shared experience or misfortune may be. To Lamming, this private world is the writer's 'one priceless possession' and his 'initial capital', it is the point from which everything else proceeds, and it is responsible for his relation to words, for his attempts to find a language to express all the things that go 'pop, pop, pop in your head'.

Twenty-six years later on a visit to Carriacou in 1982[8] Lamming explained the difference between the language of his novels and the language of his speeches. The speeches are given in 'a language of statements'. The statements are directed to the mind. But they are structured in such a way 'that makes the mind feel'. The language of novels on the other hand is 'directed to an area of feeling and with the specific intention of making the feeling think'. In the same address he places emphasis on the need for school curriculums to include 'the education of the feeling', then he places education of the feelings 'at the heart of the struggle for liberation', and finally delivers this unpolitical and profoundly political dictum:

The work of art, be it theatre, music, novel, or poem is not seen primarily by the artist as a call to revolution, or a call to anything else, nor as a celebration of victory. Artistic expression can do those things and in particular situations may regard or must regard this function as a priority. But the central and seminal value of the creative imagination is that it functions as a humanising and civilising force in a process of struggle. It offers an experience through which feeling is educated. Through which feeling is deepened. Through which feeling can increase its capacity to accommodate a great variety of knowledge.

This statement about artistic value and function is also an invitation to make the reading of literature an experiencing of literature (see again, p 2, para 3) to which all other things may then be convincingly and effectively added.

Notes

1. Jamaica Kincaid, *A Small Place* (New York: Farrar Straus Giroux, 1988), pp. 56–57
2. When this opinion was put in private conversation to the economist who had been doing such counting at the Conference on the Caribbean in the 21st Century (UWI, Mona Campus September 3–5, 1999) he did not seem to think it necessary to change his tone while registering the facts.
3. For the Beacon Group and related activities see Kenneth Ramchand, *The West Indian Novel and its Background* (London: Faber and Faber, 1970), pp. 63–74
4. Ladoo's novels are *No Pain Like This Body* (Toronto: Anansi Toronto, 1972) and *Yesterdays* (1974) by the same publisher
5. Olive Senior, *Summer Lightning* (London: Longman1986), pp. 16–25
6. Tony McNeil, *Residue* (Kingston: Savacou Publications, 1975), p. 11
7. George Lamming, 'The Negro Writer and his World' in *Caribbean Quarterly* (Vol. 5, No. 2, February 1958)
8. George Lamming 'A Visit to Carraicou' in *Conversations*, R Drayton and Andaiye, eds. (London: Karia Press, 1992), pp. 22–31

33 | IAN McDONALD

Caribbean Creative Achievement:
Preserving the Record/Extending the Influence

I am taking Caribbean Creative Achievement as something given to us as a sort of extraordinary birthright, a godsend. In a famous conversation I had with Viv Richards, CLR James at one point asked a rhetorical question: 'What is it about these tiny island in the Caribbean where cricketers seem to grow on trees? They drop like ripe fruit and give us such pleasure. We produce the most amazing batsmen and bowlers with very little effort'.

CLR could, and probably sometimes did, as easily have substituted for cricketers, writers and artists and makers of music in that statement.

Who can doubt that the West Indian nation in relation to its tiny population and completely insignificant economic and military might has been disproportionately blessed by the fruits of our extraordinary range of creative men and women?

In my own little corner in Georgetown, immersed in the day to day, rather workaday, business world of trying to safeguard and strengthen the sugar industry, for years just around another corner I could meet extraordinary, world class imaginations like those of Martin Carter and Denis Williams and the visionary artist Philip Moore, to mention just three of many, and be inspired by their views of the world and our tumultuous times. And I am sure my experience is no different to that of all of us throughout the length and breadth of the West Indies.

So I will not dwell long on the fact of Caribbean creative achievement. I consider these achievements to be world-class at the least in literature, music, art, cricket in particular, and sport as a whole, and in that astonishing popular spectacle which is Trinidad carnival.

I make no special plea for drastically stepped up official action in the new millennium, or steeply increased funding, or emergency measures, to stimulate, induce and bolster our creative imaginations or our creative efforts. The genius of West Indians will find its way. We have done something right in cultivating the ground where our roots have been put down and I strongly believe that the trees of our cultural creations will continue to flourish.

My theme is something different and it is an area in which in the new millennium we do indeed need immensely more focused official attention and largely increased public funding. This is in preserving the record of our creative achievements and its subsidiary area of extending the influence of these achievements.

We are certainly not world-class, indeed, I fear we may in general be distressingly inferior in the effort and time and resources and money we put into preserving the record of our world class creators and the fruits of their endeavours. For instance, at the very basic level of establishing and maintaining really well organised and comprehensive national archives, how far from world-class are we in most, if not all, instances around the region? Alarmingly far I suggest. Resources for maintaining and extending archives may well be among the lowest of low budgetary priorities. When last did a prime minister summon an aide and ask him what plans we have in place to keep the archives in good repair? When last did a prime minister lecture one of his cabinet meetings on the importance of well-kept archives, which represent, after all, the historical soul, the continuity of the creative spirit of any nation?

And may I ask what progress we have made when thinking about two institutions which I would have thought in the new millennium must sooner or later be established if we are truly to create a West Indian nation – a West Indian National Library and a West Indian Dictionary of National Biography continually updated and amplified?

Such institutions no doubt exist in individual countries but we need to think of how we can begin to build a West Indian National Library, if not a West Indian National Archive, and we need to record the lives of our great and our medium-great and even our merely distinguished achievers in a form which makes them routinely recognisable around the region.

I want now simply to proceed by anecdote to illustrate my theme that we are sadly neglecting how we preserve the world of our creative achievements. Are we, for instance, doing enough to preserve the world of the creative and special contribution of our original peoples? I draw attention to the chapter of the West Indian Commission on this subject. At the most fundamental of all levels, are we even preserving the record of their various languages? I think of Richard William's moving poem *To the Etruscan Poets*, as I think of the passing forever of those slowly dying Amer-indian languages.

> Dream fluently, still brothers who when young
> took with your mother's milk, the mother tongue,
> to which pure matrix, joining world and mind,
> you strove to leave some line of verse behind
> like a fresh track across a field of snow
> not reckoning that all could melt and go.

Let me cite the case of Martin Carter. Those who know his work have little doubt that he is one of the great poets. So many of his poems are rare, as Randall Jarrell said, rare as a meteor landing in your garden. In other countries whole industries of remembrance and scholarship have built up around poets of infinitely less worth than Martin Carter. Very little scholarship or remembrance or even the most elementary infrastructure of distribution has built up so far around Martin Carter's great poems. For most young West Indians these poems are and seem likely to remain secrets. UNESCO is funding a Spanish translation of the poems. That is good, but what it means is that soon Martin Carter's poems will be better known in Latin America than they are in the West Indies. That is strange. When lately I asked at our radio station for recordings of Martin reading his own poems, I found they had lost or at least mislaid the tapes. How sad all this is!

My final symbolic example of how we neglect our own concerns cricket where our creative achievement has been supreme in the world and which will remain world-class as long as we continue to care at all for that great art and craft.

When I was in London a year or two ago, I visited the booksellers Hatchards and I found on their shelves a wonderful history of the Yorkshire cricket club, more than 400 pages long, lavishly illustrated. Compare that with the fact there is not even a slim booklet on the Georgetown Cricket Club (GCC) at Bourda, though the GCC is considerably older than the Yorkshire Cricket Club (it will be celebrating its 150th anniversary in a few years), and certainly more significant in the history of cricket. Our great game, one of our true and deep imaginative possessions and the oldest cricket club in the West Indies, and we do not even have a short history of it. For me it symbolises the state of neglect in which we keep the record of our achievements and our creations.

This conference is focused on how to master the extraordinary challenges of the future. It is right that it should. But, of course, always and soon the future becomes the past. Therefore I think this conference should find some time and some space in its proceedings to consider how the past is to be reflected as true and whole as possible in the annals we preserve for the generations coming on.

34 | JEAN SMALL

Fostering the Creative Imagination

This conference is about dissonance: using dissonant factors to come up with original strategies to solve a problem. It is about space. With conditions that support the implementation of the creative imagination. It is about business. It is about funding.

In the context of the theme of this conference on the Caribbean and the creative imagination in the twenty-first century, the subject of the creative imagination is not limited to the work of the creative artist. I discovered when I started putting together some thoughts for this paper that we are not talking about inspiration or the muse or how to choreograph a dance or paint, but we are really talking about 'brio'. About business. We are talking about the central place of the creative imagination in a successful business venture whether it be ensuring the life of an artistic group, managing an arts institution, running a university, governing a country or finding ways to bring the fragments of the islands that we are in the Caribbean to make a viable economic whole. We are talking about the factors that must be put in place to allow the creative imagination to have full reign. We need either economists who can tell us how to put the creative imagination to work or persons who have spent their lives researching the creative process.

So, I am really out of my depth here and we begin by making the traditional error of asking the creative artist to speak about the future of the creative imagination in the twenty-first century. The creative artist does not know how the creative act takes place until it has taken place. It is the unknowable until it is known. We have known for too a long time that the artist is a notoriously bad manager. After seven years of running the Philip Sherlock Centre, I am just learning that it is meaningless to say, 'I want to do something creative', but rather 'I need to be empowered with creative marketing strategies', because the body of the arts is another system of communication, and creativity is one of the most important elements of effective marketing communications. There is no artist who creates and does not want to communicate his creative work to others. Some definitions of the creative imagination are: 'connecting the seemingly unconnected', 'making the complicated simple', 'trusting your instinct' or again, 'going into the wilderness of your intuition'. I would take the first – 'connecting the seemingly unconnected'.

I believe that the process of thinking creatively can be learnt, that a series of systems, techniques and thinking tools can be designed to help anyone think more creatively provided that they learn and develop their basic skills. I believe that creative thinking and problem solving should be integrated into every subject area in the schools' curriculum. It has to start very early in the education process if we want to see change at the level of human everyday existence, in family life and in the country in general.

Let us take for example the types of examination questions that are set. Many questions ask for a regurgitation of information rather than an application of learnt information to a new situation. CXC is trying to do something about that and all the teachers are finding it hard. A system of assessing the self or situation at the end of the day or at the end of a process and finding solutions to small problems is the beginning of problem solving and creative thinking. The Ministry of Education must supervise this and reintroduce the system of inspection of schools and teachers at regular intervals. I taught at Immaculate Conception High School for twenty years and not once did anyone come from the Ministry of Education to see what I was doing. I am not sure that the computer and all the new technology fosters thinking. It provides easy access to information but it does not educate and it certainly does not teach us humanity and right now, certainly in Jamaica, what we need is to turn out more humane individuals. I intuitively feel that the more our people are exposed to creative ways of solving problems the less domestic violence there would be.

Two articles I read recently in the *Daily Gleaner* brought forcibly to mind the link between financial health and artistic creativity. In the *Sunday Gleaner* of August 29, the headline The Disappearance of Green Gables (p. 7E) reports that, one of the most prolific roots player promoters, Mr. Balfour Anderson has been forced to leave the Green Gables theatre which he occupied for 12 years for being delinquent in paying the rental of the venue. Among the reasons he gave for his delinquency is that the venue had become less popular since the government implemented the one-way system along Cargill Avenue (where the complex is situated).

The other article was in the *Outlook* magazine of the same paper on the same date, titled 'A Bajan Celebration', which told of Square One, the Barbados band which is backed by the national purse. The government has apparently grasped and embraced what other islands have only given lip-service to – the fact that 'music is a resource as valuable as white sand beaches and sunshine', said the article. I quote the minister of education herself who said,

The branding of products and services have made our tastes universal. The only thing that distinguishes us are those things rooted in our culture – how we have been raised traditionally and how we have been taught to sing and dance. It is the essence of our culture which will determine whether persons will go to Barbados, the Pacific, or remain in Europe. We must develop this resource, while at the same time making sure it reflects us as a people. We have put the legislative, fiscal and promotional framework in place because many of our artists do not have the wherewithal to launch themselves. We need to facilitate their expression.

The article explains that a very vibrant National Cultural Foundation works jointly with Barbados Tourism Authority and the minister of education and Culture to promote the island's seven annual musical festivals. Both of these accounts are testimonies to the importance of sound financial backing, government backing, partnerships and management in the form of permanent staffing.

The Bajan government is also throwing its weight behind overseas events. In Suriname the government pays a creative artist a stipend to share his expertise with the cultural groups of the country. I do not know of another country in the region that does that. Here in Jamaica most of the artistic groups are run by individuals or private companies and funding is acquired through sponsorship. Sponsors are now few and far between and the present economic doldrums of the country does not allow even those few sponsors to give assistance. Artistic groups are now opting for sponsorship in the form of benefit shows which works out profitably for both parties. I understand that of the 95 shows that the Pantomime performed this year, 47 were benefit shows. At the

Philip Sherlock Centre, when a major production which was in financial doldrums because of escalating costs during the production was being staged for the Fiftieth Anniversary of the university (the director asked for elements that assured quality), the University refused to provide financial assistance and the performance, which was a brilliant creative work, had to be closed prematurely. Were it not for Professor Nettleford, who understands the frustration that the creative artist faces when his creative imagination cannot be expressed, the production would not have even played for the one weekend that it did.

The University Singers have excelled because they have the expertise of a musical director and an artistic director paid by the university. Otherwise, it generally is a depressing landscape for the arts. Our most talented directors don't want to even try to go through the hassle of putting on a production without proper funding. Companies start and die for lack of funds and proper management and so we have grassroots plays being performed in small non-traditional spaces or what I call middle-class roots plays that are either bawdy or very humourous which manage to exist. Tastes have obviously changed with the times and there is no Arts Foundation in the Caribbean that can give financial assistance to entities that want to explore the classics of the Caribbean or elsewhere. A recent excellent production of *The Father* by Strindberg (even though not a Caribbean play) could not attract packed houses even though the highly respected first lady of Jamaican theatre was a member of the cast. It was just not the right taste for current audiences.

In the 1999 Winter Report of the Ford Foundation the point is clearly made. And I must thank Professor Nettleford for this. Everybody needs a Rex who sends them the right sorts of articles to read. 'Financial health,' the article said, 'enhances creativity by freeing arts organisations from depressing, restricting and time-consuming spirals of crisis management'. The hungry poet in the attic is not the image of the artist today. Everyone wants to be paid. There is only one company I know of which has managed to get its artists to perform voluntarily for 37 years, and it is my opinion that the commitment is because it is a national company and because of the charisma of the leader of that company who has a very efficient working team. The Ford Foundation started supporting arts stabilisation in the 1960s. This is not a mere hand-out, but a grant contingent on organisations hitting financial benchmarks and balancing their budgets year after year. They provide assistance with managerial and financial skills so that strategic financial planning and reporting become ingrained habits.

This is the way we ought to go in the Caribbean. Investment companies should marry their business skills and their money to the arts in order to make the arts a viable economic source. This will also ensure quality work. The government must stop asking why there are no local programmes on the local TV stations when they have no policy or structure or funding for fostering the production of educational and entertainment programmes with a local cultural input. They must provide teams of consultants with expertise in arts management, accounting, marketing and computing to develop the arts for local and foreign consumption. It is time that we recognise the value and financial viability of CD Roms on different aspects of Caribbean culture. We have the talent. What the Caribbean needs is training in the management of the arts and creating the conditions that foster artistic enterprise over the long term. On the side, I would like to say that my son went to Berklee, Boston last year and when he got there he called me and said, 'Mummy ,this place has 105 practice rooms all equipped with all the electronic stuff. I can write a piece compose and arrange in one day. In Jamaica we have three practice rooms and you can't get the key!' We have the talent. 'The farmer cannot make the germ develop and sprout from the seed; he can only supply the nurturing conditions which will permit the seed to develop its own potentialities'.

Michael Fairbanks, that eminent speaker who visited Jamaica some time ago, looked at the economic pattern in Jamaica and came to the conclusion that we are still thinking the old way and doing all the wrong things. Like depending on sand, sea and beach because it seemingly is a low-cost export product. This type of thinking based on the notion of 'absolute advantage' made sense as long as international markets were relatively undeveloped. With the impact of global trade and the mobility of capital and skilled labour as well as the role of technology in lowering costs and improving quality, this kind of thinking will become even less adequate in the face of global competitive pressures. Mia Motley, minister of education and culture in Barbados is right in recognising that all nations differ in their endowments and will gain advantage by packaging and processing those factors efficiently. The new idea of 'comparative advantage' is based on the theory of producing goods more efficiently for export and importing goods that we cannot efficiently produce. There is quite a running export of Jamaican theatre to England and the United

States. Very little, I think, to the other Caribbean islands. Governments must protect and subsidise these products to sustain comparative advantages. Trinidad should have an international workshop on the pan every year and while we are waiting to decide what to do Japan is asking us if we play reggae too. With the low cost of transportation, boundaries and borders are disappearing, therefore knowledge and innovative approaches to productivity will determine the winners and the losers. Economists are promoting x-efficiency, that is, more efficient utilisation of the individual components of productivity such as training. We talk about human resources. Human resources is what people have and what can be trained. It is not just people. It is training workers. It is providing the necessary machinery. In the centre we have one 486 computer. We're not even on line yet. We just don't have the machinery to work efficiently, and allocate efficiency (such as improving the mix of inputs or determining how certain resources can substitute other resources).

I have read that one explanation of the growth in Japanese productivity is because of their 'organisational knowledge creation'. It seems to me that one of the solutions for success in the Caribbean in the twenty-first century is the concept of clustering in just about every sphere, and free movement of professionals. The concept of clustering is an economic one that I can't go into very deeply, but we can see that we already have clusters of nations, we have different races and cultures and skills. I think we need to cluster these in the Caribbean and use them for effective management.

When I was in Australia, the Ministry of Education took charge of professionals and if a school was in a bad condition they would take a professional and send him to that school to help upgrade that school. If I understand the meaning of 'movement of professionals' in the Caribbean, we ought to be sending the right people to the right places to have overall improvement in the Caribbean.

What are the factor conditions present in a country and how can they be upgraded? How sophisticated is the demand of the local consumer and what signals do they give for the global market? What related businesses exist that can give support to the process of innovation? How high is the rivalry and the competitive advantage and what conditions exist to encourage healthy competition? I don't think anything new is going to happen in the Caribbean in the twenty-first century unless governments adopt a new thinking about the place and the importance of culture and provide the budget for the creative imagination to flow. Governments should come together and establish a Caribbean Arts Foundation that provides the money and a financial advisor to monitor the implementation of the grants.

The vision I had for the Philip Sherlock Centre was to integrate the Caribbean through the arts; but to move artists and creative works around the region. But that takes money, plain and simple. We have managed to cause some movement, very often personally standing some of the cost, just so that it could happen. I did a play recently and everybody said it was a great performance, but do you know how I did it? Because I want to act I had to put up thirty-eight thousand dollars out of my pocket so that we could start. We had to pay twenty thousand dollars for the royalties before we could start and that was only for nine performances. Because I was dying to act! Ladies and gentlemen I am talking to you about *pain*. Pain to do the work that we want to do.

We need a Caribbean publishing house that will publish creative works. The University Press does not publish creative works. I have asked them to publish my plays and they said they do not publish that! And yet our fate rests on publication. We say that we are recognising the work of creative artists, yet they do not publish our works. Our work is not considered to be 'academic'. We have to find the money to publish through the Canoe Press or self-publish like some of my colleagues here. Not all of us can afford to do that. We need to develop creative writers. Most of our writers live abroad where they become part of the landscape and can more easily get their work published. We need to develop creative writers. Our courses at the Centre do not attract large numbers because when they have written a good piece of work, they want to have it published. We do not have the possibility of publishing, so they do not come back! They want to be published.

Playwriting has not taken on because a play does not really exist until someone decides to stage it. It takes too long to be known and to see your work performed on stage, so they do not opt to do playwriting. We ought to be doing creative writing across the region. I would like to see novels written across the region with individuals making their input. If only we were *on line*. I have written up proposals for teaching directing as a distance teaching course and it was not accepted as vitally important. This summer we offered our skills to St Vincent, which was very anxious to have our courses, but because we did not have the money to go there to do it for them the project could not be carried out. We are not lacking in creative imagination. What we are lacking is a culture in which we share and collaborate creatively. Instead we hide information from each other and set up unhealthy rivalries. I understand that some artists were sent from Jamaica to participate in the first Rat Island workshop, but when they returned they did not share their newly gained knowledge with us. So we get little or nothing done.

Whether we want to admit it or not there is still gender-bias in the workplace. The men are still the driving forces. The men meet and talk to each other and support each other. They make decisions outside of the office, at the bar or wherever. We hear about them after. Consider how many women are deans of faculties and how many are the real heads of a department. What we are lacking is the technology. We are in the technological age but we do not have the technology. I have just returned from the Universal Studios in Hollywood where they asked me if I wanted to see a flood and they pressed a button and the flood came rushing down on me and then I was asked if I wanted to see an earthquake and a whole set collapsed and immediately after was back in place. In Scotland I saw a staged production where the stage opened and the actors jumped in and swam. What I was seeing was the power of money. We are a far way from all that. At the present moment all I want is an air-conditioning unit, a front curtain for the theatre and a leaking roof to be repaired.

But let's say that in the twentyfirst century we still don't have the money to support the creative imagination, what we will have to do is go back to basics, start thinking and be creative. And this is not new to us. We have been doing this for a long time. I would just like one year with a little money to do something! I remember that when Sistren Collective had no money, they did their most creative work because they had to think how to use whatever they had. Their work then was the most powerful in metaphor and image as I have not seen since. I have read recently that the form of theatre which has the most impact in the Netherlands now is the monologue – the one person on stage. This can be powerful theatre and we have the literature in the Caribbean which can be used as source material.

In France the mode that is predicted for theatre in the twenty-first century is the puppet. This form of communication can be very creative and low cost and if we do not get a publishing house we may very well have to equip ourselves with the software to self publish. One thing of which I am quite sure is that the creative mind will survive. It may be frustrated but it will survive.

35 | GORDON ROHLEHR

Change and Prophecy in the Trinidad and Tobago Calypso Towards the Twenty-first Century

Between 1997 and 1999, I have participated in four conferences that have sought to assess the chances for survival of the Caribbean region in the face of globalisation, the information revolution, technological change and the increasing economic, political and cultural hegemony that is being exercised by various agglomerations of international capital. My role at these conferences has been to make projections about how Caribbean cultural identities might be expected to cope with such enormous forces of change and erosion, as are evident towards the end of the twentieth century and show every likelihood of intensifying in the twenty-first. This paper is an attempt, not so much at predicting the future, but of documenting how a popular art-form such as the calypso has behaved in the face of both the localised or microcosmic and the global or macrocosmic aspects of change.

Calypsonians have been deeply concerned with change and the future and some of their at times sober, at times bizarre, prognostications make interesting reading alongside the ominous projections of the social scientists and the more engaging speculations of the scientists and technologists. Consider, for example, the Mighty Spoiler's *World of Tomorrow* or *What the Scientist Say* (1954); or his *Money in the Bank* (1959) or what is perhaps, his most famous calypso *Reincarnation* or *The Bed Bug* (1954). In *World of Tomorrow*, Spoiler's visionary scientist has predicted since the mid-Fifties, that virtual electronic cohabitation – something that late-night soft-porn TV has only just imagined – will become a commonplace reality in the world of tomorrow:

> The scientist say, so help me bless
> People will make children by wireless
> You quite up the road, your wife there alone
> And allyuh could make children on the telephone.

Spoiler's scientist offers the possibility of controlled conception to women rebelling against the fixed roles of home-maker and child-bearer that the patriarchy has imposed on them. All the woman would need to do in the world of tomorrow is to hang up the phone on horny husband, outside man or prospective lover as soon as the conversation becomes too hot. The fact that Spoiler's scientist turns out to be an escapee from the madhouse should cause us little bother. Many genuine prophets and geniuses have been mistaken for madmen, and vice versa. We will, in fact, see this illustrated by David Rudder in his *Madman's Rant* (1996).

Spoiler's *Money in the Bank* (1959) might also be read as a prophetic parable about the problems that globalisation poses the micro-state. In this calypso, the protagonist inherits a small amount of money from his deceased cousin in Toco, a remote village on Trinidad's north-eastern peninsula, which he deposits in the bank. This act of localised economic independence simply exposes him to the perils of the world of high finance, because important rich people smother his tiny deposit with their big money, and he can no longer gain access to his money, buried as it is at the bottom of the vault. Whenever he tries to make a withdrawal he is told:

> Ah have to wait again just a couple years
> In order to get out mine, they have to take off theirs

In this parable of the neo-colonial absurd, the investment of the small man is smothered and absorbed by the weight of big bucks until he grows frantic in his efforts to retrieve some modicum of his financial independence:

> I pull so much strings, I pull cable wire
> To see if they could move mih money from centre
> Stand up by the bank sometimes for a fortnight
> Wetting in the rain, drying in the sunlight

He becomes frustrated, then, not because he has no money, but because his money is now so entangled in the vast machinery of an alienating system that he is too small to challenge or control, that he cannot put it in motion to work for him. What Spoiler's protagonist endures on an individual microcosmic basis – humiliation, anguish, desperation, madness and bitter resignation to a life of penury – has been on the macrocosmic level the fate of small nations caught in the trammels of international capital. Stalin's *Cry of the Caribbean* (1992) and Rudder's *Banana Death Song* (1998) provide a grim contemporary update on the situation of economic powerlessness that Spoiler explored with such rare, wry laughter four decades ago.

Spoiler's *The Bedbug* or *Reincarnation* (1954) provides us with what our 'one-book' minister of education in Trinidad would term a 'para-diggim' for how small states need to function in a world dominated by the big, the fat and the rich. Like *Money in the Bank*, *The Bedbug* functions on the microcosmic level of the individual confronted by larger forces. Both calypsos are about smallness; but whereas *Money in the Bank* presents the small man as victim crushed by big capital, *The Bedbug* portrays him as trickster, living pragmatically and surreptitiously – as the political scientists at these millenium conferences have been recommending we little people should live – in the cracks of the system, from which he emerges when hungry to make quick sharp incisions in the juicy backsides of the big, the fat and the rich. There is, of course, a danger in living in the niches of the system that neither Spoiler nor the political scientists have been stressing, which is this. The last thing that vampires like to lose is blood, however small the quantity, and the bedbug who attempts, however unobtrusively, to suck the blood of an equally parasitic system will, if detected, die the death of kerosene and insecticide.

Essentially, calypsos are texts of survivalism and millenium economists, sociologists and political scientists whose careful horizons are today limited to the mean pragmatics of survivalism, might learn much from a study of such attitudes as are engrained in calypso. Stripped of his comic mask, the calypsonian articulates a desperate philosophy of survivalism. Consider Shadow's *Survival* (1991) and *Poverty Is Hell* (1994) or Johnny King's *Nature's Plan* (1984) in which he portrays the small person (or race or nation) in the grip of dominant forces that work resolutely towards his extinction.

> Ah weak but I'm holding on
> In order to stay around
> In a life terribly imbalanced
> For it is Nature's way
> Until Judgement Day
> Weakness ain't got a chance.
> Playing strong cause ah realise

The price little ones must pay
To keep the big ones in paradise
Is torment and misery all day

Chorus
Destruction of the weak
Is Nature's plan
The humble and the meek
Must understand
This day of the strongman
Is the Devil's heyday
Today will bite the ground
When the Master play

According to the social Darwinian logic of *Nature's Plan*, only the strong will survive. Little people – particularly black people who emerge as subject later in the calypso – are not strong. Logically, then, they ought not to have survived the inexorable efforts of Nature. So what possibilities for action does King offer to whom he calls the humble, the weak, 'the little ones'? The only possibility is one of holding on, of long-suffering endurance to the end. This end is not a moment in history so much as one of divine intervention and reversal of fortunes. Nature and someone called the Master will put an end to 'Today'; that is this present system of the tyranny of strength, might and inequity over humility, weakness and powerlessness. The Master's play, his intervention in the card game of human existence, will put an end to the 'wild play', the irresponsible exercise of power to dominate and suppress. (A similar idea exists in Explainer's *Tables Turning*, 1980).

Darwinian nature thus becomes entangled with the medieval Wheel of Fortune and the Greek *deus ex machina* as the little ones seek refuge in a doctrine of karmic reversal and retribution. There is no perspective of active rebellion here. That went out with the Seventies in Trinidad and was crushed in the Eighties in Grenada. What replaces it is earnest hope in divine justice; desperate faith in the power of the cosmos to correct social imbalance and firm resolve to 'hold on' until divine purpose works itself out.

Calypsonians function as prophets in this universe where social class relations seem to be fixed and frozen in the unequal contestation of little versus big, weak versus strong, powerless versus powerful. There are several dimensions to the role of prophet, most of which may be illustrated from the world of calypso. The prophet is usually a wise man or wise woman who has been gifted with vision. King Austin, singing 'Joker' Devine's words in *Progress* (1979), begins each stanza with the words 'I see' to illustrate his role as prophet illuminating the ironies of change.

The prophet is the sometimes anointed, sometimes self-appointed keeper of the values of a community, a people or a nation. Prophecy is a calling, a vocation, something that the prophet feels impelled to do. Calypsonians often define their roles and responsibilities. Sometimes they claim to be the eyes of society, at other times they function as defenders of the freedom of the citizen; or they function as an opposition party that serves all constituencies (Stalin: *Nah Ease Up*,1990); or they preserve and hand down what is wholesome in the traditions of the past (Chalkdust *Calypso Versus Soca*, 1978). They sing against oppression and for their peoples' liberation (Valentino *Liberation*, 1973); Stalin *Nothing Ent Strange* (1975); Watchman *Rise Up My People*, 1996). They function as warners, exhorters and at the same time bring hope and encouragement (Stalin *Sing for the Land* (1985), *Look on the Bright Side* (1991); *We Can Make It if We Try* (1988); Sparrow *We Can Make It Easy If We Try*, 1991).

From even that brief listing of calypsonians' mission statements, it may be seen that both vision and intention vary from singer to singer. Calypsonian/prophets generally have a clear insight into the present. They tend to focus on areas of moral and spiritual decay and to monitor the threat to or collapse of values and the transgressions of both the people and their leaders. There are several hundreds of calypsos that have done this over the century. Atilla alone sang over fifty, while contemporary singers such as Chalkdust and Stalin must each be nearing one hundred socially conscious songs. Cro Cro, Sugar Aloes, Watchman, Gypsy, and Shortpants are all dedicated monitors of social and political behaviour, as are Sparrow, Shadow, Kitchener and Valentino.

Calypsonians who perceive collapse tend, after the fashion of prophets, to predict disaster. During the Seventies, one of these, a law student then and state prosecutor since, used to call himself 'The Prophet of Sisyphus'. Denunciation, doom-saying, the calling down of curses on the heads of the corrupt : these are some of the rhetorical modes of the prophet. Delamo at one point even adopts the mode of address of the biblical prophet to condemn the corrupt leadership of his country: 'Woe unto you, leaders of my land.'

The calypsonian/prophet is, nevertheless, a praise-singer, the voice that acclaims virtuous behaviour, that calls down blessings on the head of the righteous, that bestows healing on the poor and afflicted and affirms the power and the glory. Rudder's *Dedication* (1987) and what are now hundreds of calypsos celebrating the steelband; patriotic songs; calypsos expressing appreciation for outstanding performance in politics, sport and scholarship, are a corpus of praise-songs which counterpoint the generally gloomier calypsos whose subjects are crime, social and moral decay.

A rather special type of prophet is the prophet of the Apocalypse. Such a prophet usually claims to have been given in a dream or state of rapture, a vision or message of disintegration brought on by some final act of cosmic violence that is read as divine retribution, or by a slow but inevitable process of collapse as termites inhabit and undermine the moral and social structure. Delamo's *Apocalypse* (1981) is the best example in calypso of this type of prophecy. The recipient of the apocalyptic message becomes himself a messenger, prophet and illuminator of the future.

The biblical Apocalypse (Revelation) also contains a counter-vision of a new heaven and a new earth, suggesting that the time of destruction – the Age of Kali in Hinduism – is only one phase on a Wheel of Time, and may even be a rite of terrible passage into the new age. Only the righteous, however, can complete the rite and cross over the river. The job and mission of the prophet is to oversee the nurturing of such righteousness among the people, by warning and reminding them constantly of the judgement that lies at the end of their existence. (Note that on occasion, as frequently with Shadow, judgement is reduced to a personalised revenge against past oppressors, such as *King From Hell*, 1975; *Judgement Day*, 1982; *Jump Judges*, 1977. Stalin's *Bun Dem*, 1987 fuses personal with cosmic revenge against the oppressors of Africans at home and abroad.)

Prophets tend to emerge and abound during eras of uncertainty and transition, in the space between the closure of one cycle of time and the beginning of another. The last five decades of the twentieth century have been a time of rapid and unprecedented social, political, economic, technological and cultural change in which several micro and macro-cycles have come into being and passed out of existence. Some of these eras have been the era from the Franchise (1946) to the end of Federation (1962); the era/cycle from Independence (1962) to the death of Eric Williams (1981). One might date the beginning of this cycle in 1956, the year of the first PNM electoral victory. The third phase is the post-Williams phase (1981) to the present (1999). Each of these cycles had its definitive central moment. 1956 was the distinguishing moment for the 1946-1962 cycle. The Black Power upheaval of 1970 was both the central and the decentring moment of the 1962 to 1981 cycle, while the third phase (1981 to present) had as its traumatic centre the Muslimeen uprising of 1990.

These micro-cycles, each with its moments of solidarity and crisis, are all contained within the wider circle of the twentieth century. The first era, 1946-1962, was one of relative hope. It was a time of tremendous ferment characterised in the calypso world by the waning of the Old Guard of Executor, Beginner, Growler, Tiger, Lion, Atilla and Invader, which closed a calypso cycle that had started in 1901 with the emergence of Executor. The objectives for which Atilla fought were those of freedom to vote, freedom of conscience, honesty in the conduct of public affairs and nationalism. Like Lion and Beginner, he supported the idea of Federation which in that era was understood to be the only pathway to full independence.

The aspirations of the Old Guard were nominally fulfilled when Universal Adult Suffrage was granted in 1946, meaningful party politics emerged over the next decade and the Federation was inaugurated in 1958. The rapid dissolution of the West Indian Federation between 1961 and 1962 was a terrible disappointment, though the surprising acquisition of Independence seemed more than adequate compensation at the time. The idea of regional unity would, nonetheless, be explored in scores of calypsos over three decades of Independence. It would emerge as the ongoing and complex crisis in Caribbean affairs kept shifting its geographical location from Guyana (19620-1964) to Trinidad (1970) to Jamaica whose intestinal violence had become politicised in the Sixties and formed in the Seventies a new norm of uncivil society. Then there was Grenada in the early 1980s, Trinidad again in 1990 and the banana producing Windwards and Leewards in the later 1990s.

The second phase, 1956–1981, was in its first decade dominated by the sound of Sparrow's assertive voice. It was a period of nationalist consolidation under the Williams PNM and despite a number of sharply critical calypsos such as Sparrow's *Get to Hell Outa Here* (1965), Blakie's *The Doctor Ent Deh* (1965) and Leveller's *How to Curb Delinquency* (1966), most calypsonians were, during the 1956-1966 period, more concerned with legitimising the

Doctor's benevolent dictatorship than criticising its failures. After 1968, though, a querulous prophet emerged in the person of Chalkdust, whose mission seemed to involve a relentless identification of the holes in the armour of the PNM.

Chalkdust ushered in the Black Power era with calypsos such as *Reply to the Ministry* (1968), *Message to Doctor Solomon* (1969) and *Massa Day Must Done* (1970) whose very title, in its ironic echoing of Williams's famous 'Massa Day Done' address of 1961, signalled the disillusion of a younger generation with Williams's performance as a nationalist leader. The theme of *Massa Day Must Done* was the persistence of racial and colour discrimination in all areas of Trinbagonian existence: that is, in employment practices, in the area of social services, in how the economy was being administered and in the machinations of the Law. The ruling party which had from its foundation pledged to fight against discrimination had, after three terms in office, simply consolidated alternative structures of privilege, patronage and discrimination. Chalkdust, after the style of Williams, documented his accusations with a wealth of illustrations and initiated what one might call the calypso-essay.

The impact of calypsos like *Massa Day Must Done* and Young Creole's Chalkdust-composed *Behind the Bridge* (1970), was felt among older PNM loyalists such as Bomber, whose calypsos had supported many a PNM Buy Local competition during the 1960s. Bomber's *Political Wonder* (1970), intended as a praise-song for Williams of the old adulatory type, was, however, resonant with omen. Its choruses kept asking how Williams would die and what would be his legacy. Would he die like the great world leaders of his generation from Churchill to Nehru, Cipriani to Norman Manley? Would be he remembered as 'Founder, Builder, Lover of our nation?' Would he die like Gandhi, Kennedy, Martin Luther King all of whom had been assassinated in the cause of democratic freedom and civil rights? Whence, one wonders, only six weeks before the 1970 State of Emergency and Army Mutiny, did this intuition of assassination come? Williams was as vibrant and as arrogantly self-confident as ever, yet the calypsonian-prophet had dreamed, had sensed the end of his cycle and was talking about his prospects of being remembered favourably by a people whom the calypsonian Valentino would, sixteen years later in *De Roaring Seventies* (1986) define as having 'this funny way of forgetting.'

After 1970, even calypsonians who had optimistically celebrated Independence and young nationhood in the Sixties, began to see in the repressive and recriminatory measures of the state omens of a new and fast-advancing era of austerity and autocracy. Sparrow's *Sedition* (1972) was a outcry against the muzzling of dissent, while Kitchener's *No Freedom* of the same year, prophesied that 'the vengeance of Moko' would surely fall on a country where union leaders and other dissenting spokespeople for the working-class, were being arrested at gunpoint and jailed indefinitely without charges being laid or a hearing of any kind. By 1975, in *Dis Place Nice* Valentino of a younger generation, was predicting revolutionary change, fighting and fire to come, even as the banks recorded mega-profits and the erstwhile empty Treasury overflowed with billions of oil dollars. Stalin in *Run Something* (1976) demanded his 'piece o' de action' 'before all finish and the Yankees go'. The younger calypsonian-prophets of the mid-Seventies had absolutely no faith that the hot-house wealth of the oil-boom years would be equitably, honestly or wisely distributed.

The accumulated strain of such phenomena as Independence, the Black Power revolt and its repressive aftermath, the delirium of the oil-boom years (1974–1981) and the death of Eric Williams (1981) after twenty-five years of stable though troubled government, was reflected in the mood of doom and gloom that entered many calypsos of the Eighties. 'Entered' is, perhaps, an inaccurate word here, since there had been a succession of pessimistic calypsos throughout the seventies, a decade redolent with the smell of corruption. It is, therefore, more correct to say that the Eighties continued and intensified the pessimism of the Seventies, a decade that ended with several calypsos which measured the bitter paradox that in spite of the windfall of oil dollars, Trinidad was no nearer to a solution of any of her age-old social problems.

Shorty's *Money Is No Problem* (1979) tabulates some of these: shortage of hospital beds; bad roads despite a self-renewing lake of pitch; phones that don't work; inadequate water distribution; deteriorating human relations; and the remoteness of the political directorate from the masses even as the almighty Corporation Sole was pledging Spoiler's meagre pittance in his bid to become a player in the hard and unequal game of international finance. Stalin's *Breakdown Party* (1980) violently condemned the combination of laziness, complacency and false luxuriousness that seemed to have overtaken national lifestyles during that just-ended decade of patronage and clientelism, when the system of state-controlled discrimination that Chalkdust had denounced ten years earlier in *Massa Day Must Done* (1970) had matured into a lifestyle.

Sensing the horror of what had taken place, Penguin employed the metaphor of the Jouvert morning Jab Jab (*The Devil*, 1980), to portray the diabolic patterns of social and political processes. There were:

> Devils in business
> In halls of justice
> In pot guts old men
> Who seduce girl children

There were also suave devils in parliament masked as political leaders, and violent devils in the police service masked as officers of the law, pledged to protect and serve the citizenry. Penguin concluded that all such devils could only exist because society, itself diabolical, had permitted them to survive. 1980 was remarkable, not only for its ominous contemplation and cataloguing of change but for its deeply sad and angry recognition that an era or cycle of time was drawing to its close.

Next year, 1981, Chalkdust in *Bring the Ayatollah* began his calypso with the words 'So Eric Williams will be leaving' and proposed that he be replaced by an even more dreadful dictator whose big-stick approach to leadership alone could restore all that had broken down in the latter years when Williams either lost control of or had grown indifferent to the processes of efficient administration. Relator in *Take a Rest* (1980) attributed the breakdown of things to a regime that had been in office too long – a point of view that Blakie had expressed four years earlier in *Twenty Years Is Too Long* (1976). According to Relator:

> It is useless trying to blame
> A horse that is tired and almost lame

Out of sheer compassion, he recommended that the electorate send the PNM and its leader on holiday 'before the man drop down dead on the work'. One year later this prophecy, intuition or warning came to pass when Williams died after a session in Parliament. There was great uncertainty as to how he had died and dismay when the crowd who had gathered to pay homage, learned that they would not see his face. Confusion, a sense of void and a cloud of pessimism came over those who had supported the PNM purely on the trust that they had placed in Williams's character. Now they were being forced to contemplate whether the systems he had initiated and consolidated would survive his passing.

Delamo's *Apocalypse* (1981) focused on the scandal of the Caroni Racing Complex on which an estimated 240 million Trinidad dollars had been spent to no visible end. Most of the money had been expropriated to seed major real estate investments in places like Panama and Canada. Bursting at the end of the Seventies, the Racing Complex scandal epitomised the corruption that had overtaken that decade, even as it became the gateway into the hysteria, dislocation and economic collapse of the Eighties. From it Delamo elicited the metaphor of apocalypse which, though latent in certain of the prophetic calypsos of the seventies, had not been openly employed in any of them.

In *Apocalypse*, true to the biblical prototype, the bard receives his vision through a series of dream-images and is schooled in their interpretation by the 'Most High'. He thus becomes transformed into a messenger whose mission is the illumination of society through a revelation of its encoded future. Here the vision is of four horsemen of the Caroni Racing Complex, Trinidad versions of the four horsemen of the biblical Apocalypse: War, Pestilence, Famine and Death. Delamo's first, second and third horses are coloured like the national flag of Trinidad and Tobago, white, red and black. They also seem to represent the broad colour/class/racial complex of caucasian (white) mulatto, *mestizo*, mixed races and Indo-Trinidadian (red) and Afro-Trinidadian (Black), all of whom will be overtaken by the last horse: a mangy, grey and headless horse ridden by a skeleton around a race track that has suddenly metamorphosed into the Lapeyrouse Cemetery.

The white horse, still vibrant and strong, and ridden by a jockey who bears a bow and wears a crown, seems to represent vestiges of an old colonial order of privilege which have remained alive and well after nearly two decades of nominal independence. The French Creole elite in Trinidad were, on the mere strength of their whiteness, endowed with substantial lands by the Cedula of 1783. On the basis of such entitlement they consolidated social and economic power for two centuries. The Franchise and Independence have meant little more to this class than a bugbear of having to negotiate with whatever regime happens to be in power. By 1981, the old PNM had worked out its arrangement with this group.

The white horse laughs sneeringly at the working class, boasting of its 'connections in a big political party' and flashing the balisier symbol of the once anti-elitist, anti-imperialist PNM scornfully at its rear end. The white horse also mocks at the efforts of the underclass to take the lead in the unequal horse race towards power.

> Ah see a horse laughing kee, kee, kee
> He say in this country is he spending we money
> He say that if wishes were horses beggars would ride
> So the Complex is for beggars to ride and fall and break their backside

If the white horse represents the entrenchment of an ancient order of aristocrats (the bow could be the emblem of a lodge such as the Foresters), the second horse, the red one, represents the growing corruption of the coloured middle class whose position as buffer between the old elite and the black majority, gives them a vested interest in preserving the status quo. Delamo illustrates their corruption by citing the cases of two of the 'red' ministers – one half-Irish and half-Syrian, the other Indian – whose visible assets seem vastly to exceed their legitimate earnings. The true evil of this red rider, however, lies in the fact that while he presides over graft and the expropriation of national public revenue, and while he seals a profitable alliance with the fraternity of kings of the old status quo, he is also correspondingly vicious towards and violently repressive of the protesting poor, whom he threatens with his sword of unending disrespect and brute force.

The red horse boasts that it is better housed than the poor (the Racing Complex was being designed to have air-conditioned stables), and accepts this social arrangement as part of the natural and divine order of things:

> He say from the beginning the horse come before the buggy
> So build a home for the horse and leave the people in box-board shanty

Occupying a complacent yet insecure middle space, the red horse will be a bastion against any sort of social equity or genuinely democratic reform.

The third horse is black. His rider bears a scale which should signify fair distribution or equal justice, articles in the manifesto of the ruling and supposedly Afro-based PNM since its inception. The degradation of the party's ideals is seen in the emptying-out or reversal of language and sign. So the scale signifies the very opposite of what it should: it means 'a shortage of materials and labour' brought about by the disproportionate amounts of these (materials and labour) that have been wasted on an elitist-oriented project such as the Horse Racing Complex. (The recognisable parallel situation in these days of the formation of the UNC oligarchy of new and old moneys has been that of the $US 60 million spent on building a set for the Miss Universe competition of 1999.)

The black horse too has learnt to laugh in the faces of the masses who have elected him to power:

> Ah see a horse laughing kee, kee, kee
> He say in this country he have more weight than me
> He say if you ride a cockhorse to Banbury Cross
> You stupid! You riding the horse though you can't see
> The horse is your boss

Here the black parliamentarian mocks at the electorate who really believe that by voting for a representative from their own race, they have ridden triumphantly to power, but have not yet grasped the truth that they have simply substituted one boss for another. He spurns the masses for having mistaken him for a 'cockhorse', something that any child can ride, someone that can easily be controlled. He views them as stupid not to understand that once elected, the cockhorse has now been invested with the power to lord it over the electorate. As boss, he seals his profitable peace with the moneyed elite and abandons the poor, the teachers, the then ill-paid judiciary, the workers and artists, the people of Tobago whose refusal to support the PNM since Robinson's departure from that party in 1970 is rewarded by a decade of contemptuous neglect.

The sick laughter of the black horse is too much for the dreamer to bear. Assuming his role of prophet, he cries out against this betrayal: 'Woe unto you! Oh leaders of my land'. He becomes, like Isaiah, the voice of the poor and downtrodden; the squatter whose home is torn down by the protective services of army and police; the common man whose trust and faith in 'cockhorse' leaders has just been termed stupidity. He then reveals his final images, a headless mangy grey horse that laughs at the Racing Authority, and its skeleton jockey. The decapitated horse is, quite literally, a champion in the local derby of the Seventies that was named 'Beheaded'. Unbeatable at home, Beheaded was a sad disappointment abroad. Decoded, the headless horse is the leaderless state on its directionless gallop through the cemetery. Its greyness suggests the loss of colour, purpose and identity that has overwhelmed the nation, whose proud colours of white, red and black are now consumed, erased and swallowed up by this pale horse of Death.

Williams did indeed die, and though George Chambers tried his best to tighten the reins, Delamo's representation of the nation as a headless and diseased nag hopelessly outclassed and running last in the race of thoroughbred countries, seemed to have come true. Scores of calypsos now chronicled each year's crop of scandals, measuring the symptoms of disintegration. Two of these were Explainer's *The Country Sick* (1981) and *Burn Dem Jah* (1981). The second one, indeed, a general call for divine retribution against kidnappers, murderers, abusers of power, intellect and position, and corrupt ministers of government, would in 1987 find its echo in Stalin's more famous *Bun Dem*.

Chalkdust's *Ram the Magician* (1984), *Port of Spain Gone Insane* (1986), *Rum Mania* (1985); Valentino's *Trini Gone Through in Consciousness* (1984) and *The Roaring Seventies* (1986); Commentator's *Dragon Slayer* (1990) and *The Satellite Robber;* Sparrow's *Sam P* (1984) and *Prophet of Doom* (1983); Gypsy's *The Sinking Ship* (1986); Delamo's *Sodom and Gommorah* (1982) and *Armageddon* (1985) and Rudder's *Madness* (1987) though all radically different from each other, shared one quality: they all spoke of a nation that had lost direction and was falling apart. Deple's *Vote Dem Out* (1986) out-Chalkdusted Chalkdust in its long catalogue of the deficiencies of the dying Chambers' regime, and its refrain 'Let us put our country together again' struck a responding chord in the hearts of the electorate.

The mid-decade success of the NAR seemed for the briefest moment to be a sign of new day, the new heaven and the new earth that the best prophets knew to be on the farther side of Armageddon. The charismatic rhetoric of the NAR's arrival certainly proclaimed this faith. The ONR's politics was one of 'conscience'. Robinson, the prime minister, was 'God's Messenger'. The post-election day of prayer and thanksgiving, the symbolic and massive clean-up of the nation's decades of secret garbage suggested goodwill, the possibility of inter-racial harmony and national renewal. Yet nothing was more shocking than the speed with which the spirit of uncertainty and the atmosphere of doom reasserted themselves. By February 1987, no more than two months after NAR's landslide victory, public servants who had been deprived of their cost of living allowance by the first NAR Budget, appropriated the venom of Black Stalin's *Bun Dem* to consign the new regime and its leader to retributive hellfire.

Watchman in *Airborne One* (1989) presented a variation on the allegorical dream-vision, which was the shape that apocalyptic narratives traditionally assumed. In *Airborne One* the divine source of vision is a police helicopter which used to relay reports to radio stations every morning on the movement of traffic along the nation's clogged highways. The narrator keeps in close contact with the pilot, who provides him with a panoramic view of the political landscape and predicts early elections, the rejection of Bhoe Tewarie and Brinsley Samaroo by the Caroni electorate and the defeat of the NAR:

> Ah see Robbie with a hoe
> Helping the Shadow
> To plant peas up in Tobago

The air in 1988 was already heavy with omen as the ruling party split into its constituent and querulous factions. Cro Cro's *Three Bo Rats* (1988) partly predicted, partly chronicled this disintegration, while Black Stalin, veteran of earlier heart-breaking experiences of fracture – the Black Power movement of the Seventies and Grenada of the early 1980s – sang a brave anthem of hope, *We Can Make It If We Try* (1988) for the nation in what he termed 'its darkest hour.' Calypsonians hostile to the NAR regime (a considerable number) and those who, like Stalin were sympathetic to what the NAR had had the potential of becoming – a multi-ethnic, multi-class, national party – were both unified on one score: there were dark times ahead. One group, by far the larger, sang in welcome of an apocalypse they had predicted, while another very small group of bards sang to avert a catastrophe that they too had intuited. Protector in *We Talking Change* (1988), expressed deep disappointment at the failure of the society to make the slogan of 'One Love' real on either the individual or the collective planes. As far as he was concerned, nothing had really changed: at least not for the better.

Sugar Aloes in *Public Advice* (1989) attributed all the woes of the nation to 'a pact' that he said the prime minister had signed with evil forces, which involved the removal of a weathercock and the installing of a dragon as the weather-vane atop the House of Parliament. Prophecy deteriorated into hysteria as the calypsonians as readers of signs, created a counter-rhetoric to the charismatic discourse that had accompanied the NAR's accession to power. Chris 'Tambu' Herbert, bandsinger turned calypsonian and triple roadmarch winner (1988, 1989 and 1990) depicted mankind as being faced with absolute and mutually exclusive choices:

> The world is doomed to disaster
> If they don't obey the instruction of the Father

> Hear me heaven's children
> We are walking in the wrong direction
> Creating a ball of confusion with creation
> Hear me heaven's children
>
> *Chorus*
> Do you want pain and sorrow
> Or do you want a brighter tomorrow
> I want to know
> I want to know
> Do you want fire and brimstone
> To burn up all of your bones
> You know the answer
> You know the answer

What Do You Want (1990) was not a calypso. It typified the other music that was in Tambu's head, a music that was the diametrical opposite of the breakneck hot 'kaisoca' that had become his trademark. This other music was addressed, not to the gyrating rhythm-possessed bacchants of what David Rudder was later in the decade to term 'the holy temple of soca', but to mankind, the world in general; to heaven's children who had abandoned the path of righteousness. Tambu's language in this other music was that of the prophet of the Apocalypse urging a mankind 'blinded by power, greed and luxury' to 'avoid the abomination of all nations'. In the context of the Trinidad of 1990, Tambu's song was a particular warning (in a manner similar to Rudder's *Fire in the Laager*, 1990, which, though it spoke to the South African struggle was easily transferable to the Trinidad situation).

Tambu's *The Cry* of the same year was an even more pointed and desperate appeal:

> This is a cry coming from my heart
> Where is the love? Why are we so apart?
> Every time I look around
> I see war, hate and hunger.

Besides these, he also saw children caught up in drug abuse, violence and crime, and the 'useless pain' caused by racism and colour prejudice. As with *What Do You Want*, *The Cry* was meant to be a response to a general world-situation; but Tambu's vision was clearly based on what he was seeing every day in his own country. The cloud of doom that overhung the nation in 1990 was read by Sugar Aloes as a sign of the coming Apocalypse (*Sign of the End of Times*, 1990).

Calypsonians of the Nineties have reacted to change in various ways. Chalkdust, for example, shares Protector's view in *We Talking Change* (1988), that what is proffered as change has been mere rhetoric and illusion, in a society caught up in cyclic movement back to old modes of being and doing, even as it purports to be journeying into the future. 'Trinidad ain't change,' sang Chalkdust in 1992, 'The whole place just rearrange'. The new political arrangements are the old ones in disguise. This analysis recurs in Too Much Parties (1998) where Chalkdust observes an essential sameness of PNM and UNC as racially-based parties that, driven by the same pragmatism, compete for the same clutter of floor-crossing, frog-hopping supporters, and make the same peace with the old oligarchy of 'dem French Creoles in Maraval and St Clair'.

Cro Cro, on the other hand, is shocked at the rapidity with which change occurs. In *Look How Man Does Change* (1998) he observes the duplicity of politicians who, now that they are in government, speak and act in ways that are the diametric opposite to how they had always spoken and acted while in opposition. Cro Cro also ridicules Chalkdust whose roles as anti-establishment critic and director of culture seemed to be in grave conflict with each other. Chalkdust, Cro Cro argued, had changed from a calypsonian who had remorselessly probed the cracks and flaws in the social and political establishment, to a pro-establishment figurehead unable to defend calypsonians' rights against moves to censor the art-form and isolate the most effective critics of the regime.

The larger issue here involved the vexed question of authenticity of voice in an era when all political parties had either lost, or not yet established legitimacy. Nobody's proclaimed word had any meaning or truth beyond the necessary histrionics of the moment. The gaps between what a person in authority really believed and what he said, and between what he said and what he did or was likely to do, had widened disastrously since the time of Eric Williams. The consequent devaluation of official political discourse affected all other categories of discourse including that of protest calypsonians who had begun to vie fiercely among themselves over the issue of whose was the most authentic voice speaking in defence of the public interest.

In 1977, Tobago Crusoe placed second in the Calypso Monarch competition. One of the calypsos he sang was entitled *Change* and grew out of the great uncertainty that then existed in Trinidad and Tobago, as more and more people began to sense the exhaustion of Eric Williams's PNM, its inability to inspire the nation, and the closure of its cycle of authority. Beneath Tobago Crusoe's *Change*, one could feel alarm at the new coalition of opposition forces – workers in sugar and oil, the unemployed, the urban disaffected and the small cadre of Marxist intellectuals – that had consolidated to form the ULF out of the shambles of dead Bhadase Maraj's DLP and Robinson's half-dead ACDC. *Change* was meant to be a warning to disaffected PNM supporters to re-examine their options and be clear in their minds whether they really desired the kind of change that the society seemed to be getting.

Calypsos of the Eighties and Nineties have simply continued this strain of pessimistic skepticism about change. In the process, they have with deep apprehension measured the erosion of old existences, the dissolution of old solidarities and the reconfiguration of old coalitions. Calypsos that have thus measured change have assumed various guises, one of which has been nostalgia for a dead or dying past. Chalkdust's *De Spirit Gone* (1978), Relator's *Country Life* ( ), Chalkdust's *It Ain't Have No Man Again* (1985) and his *Stickman's Lament* (1993); Nappy Mayers's *Bring Back the Old Time Days* (1990); Rudder's *De Long Time Band* (1993); Shorty's *Gone Are the Days* (1979) or Boyie Mitchell's *Real Ole Time Ting* (1999) – are just a few of the calypsos that have lamented the passage of old forms, values, life-styles, old-time folksiness, neighbourliness, self-respect, politeness, discipline, whose disappearance has left the older generation with a sense of void or anomie; of things being emptied out, or falling apart.

Another guise which rejection of change has assumed, has been that of doubt about the doctrine of progress. This doubt may be directly expressed, as in King Austin's *Progress* (1979) or those calypsos that questioned the nation's great expansion in material development during the years of the oil-boom wealth, such as Shorty's *Money Ain't No Problem* or Stalin's *Money* (1980). Concern for the youth and pessimism about the future have intensified since Sparrow sang *No Future* in the early Seventies. Shortpants's *Lost Generation* (1986) became Ella Andall's equally *Lost Generation* (1996) as Valentino's *Trinis* who had 'gone through in consciousness' by the mid-Eighties bequeathed to their children Duke's No Role Models (1979) and Watchman's *No Heroes Again* (1990). Such leaders as have emerged since Williams's death have either, according to Gypsy, incompetently steered the ship of state straight into a hurricane (*The Sinking Ship*, 1986) or, to change the metaphor, driven the maxi-taxi drunkenly and endangering the lives of people on the street before coming to a halt before a rum shop called Club 88 (Chalkdust, *Chauffeur Wanted*, 1989). Employing the same image as Chalkdust, Luta sarcastically comments on the equally deficient leadership of Manning's 1991-1995 government (*Good Driving*, 1994). Since 1996, Panday has been receiving his share of the fire.

The fierce critique of all post-Williams regimes has been part of an unconscious rejection or fear of change. If a cycle closed with the death of Williams, it has not been replaced by any new sense of confident venturing forth. Williams's death coincided with the end of the oil-boom and the forced adoption by all succeeding administrations of IMF-imposed policies such as 'downsizing', devaluation, divestment of state-owned enterprises, disempowerment of the once radical labour movement and the general departure from old-style welfare state type policies. Calypsonians during the NAR years (1986- 1991) transmitted the negative reactions of the population to post-recession economic strategies meant to erase forever the memory of the old-time days.

Since then, a new orthodoxy has emerged which requires the promotion of private enterprise, the attraction of foreign investment, the divestment of even (of mainly) profitable state-owned enterprises, the re-education of a new elite for an impending age of rapid technological change, and the improved and intensified policing of the country to make it a safe place for local and foreign investment. This new orthodoxy – strikingly similar as it turns out to strategies adopted in the post-1945 era – has made inevitable the partnership of successive governments with the private sector, and has reduced the role of the state as honest broker between what Panday used to call 'the parasitic oligarchy' and the masses. It has also made necessary a preoccupation of the new oligarchy of ruling party and private sector (so fiercely criticised at its inception by Delamo's *Apocalypse* and Valentino's *Dis Place Nice*) with manipulating the images that the country projects to the potential investor or tourist. This has in turn determined state policy not only in regard to the print and electronic media, but towards all categories of popular social and political discourse.

This explains the current attempts by the UNC government to control the Press and to censor calypsos by open threat and covert legislation. Both the new political and business oligarchies have promoted the notion of positive news reporting; reporting, that is, which will remove from the front page the murders, rapes, robberies, demonstrations and all other such indices of social disorder, and hide them within the body of the newspaper, while highlighting the positive achievements of the society. Since 1990, calypsonians have been encouraged to sing nation-building songs, and successive governments have promoted slogans such as 'One Love', 'Rainbow Country', 'Let Us Go Down the Road Together' and 'National Unity'. But given the general devaluation of rhetoric and the widening of the credibility gap into an unbridgeable chasm, it is no surprise that post-1990 calypsonians have interpreted any attempt by the state even to suggest what they should sing, as an attempt at censorship and a threat to democratic freedom. The media too have found it difficult to conceal social horror despite the entreaties, cajolings, threats and downright abuse that issue periodically from the seat of power.

Thus, although there are substantial numbers of patriotic, positive and optimistic songs – most of which receive little airplay on the nation's fifteen radio stations – there has developed a parallel genre of brutally realistic calypsos and a tendency to dismantle and expose the hypocrisy of slogans issuing from what is perceived as neo-oligarchic and still parasitic officialdom. Perhaps the singer who best typifies this tendency of calypsos towards both transcendent optimism and pessimistic realism has been David Rudder. He has also been calypso's most articulate and intuitive prophet and high priest.

Like Sparrow, Kitchener and Shadow in their different ways, Rudder stands at the point of intersection between the axis of tradition and that of change. Drawing his symbolism and inspiration from the deep well of Orisha, he regards his music as a doorway to what he calls 'the other side', and himself as an Eshu or Legba figure (he does walk with a limp), a keeper of the door and opener of the barrier. This message has been consistent throughout his career in which music has been the catalyst to celebration, memory, solace, catharsis, frenzy, creative or destructive energy, released libido, praise, thanksgiving, community, healing, lamentation and self-surrender in worship of the source of all life. Calypsos such as *Calypso Music, The Hammer, Dedication, One More Mr Officer, Permission to Mash up the Place, Madness, Outta Hand, Song for a Lonely Soul, Hallelujah, The Long Time Band* and *High Mas* are, collectively, adequate illustrations of all the themes mentioned above.

Rudder's emergence as prophet and praise-singer signals the fruition of a century-long quest by calypso for reconciliation with its origins in the sacred.

The unity of secular and sacred existed in many traditional African societies and was part of what was lost or obscured in the New World encounter between African systems of thought, belief and performance and Manichean Christian, particularly Calvinist Protestant, modes of perception. Along with Rudder, Calypso Rose, Superblue, Andre Tanker and Ella Andall stand at the point of intersection or transgression between sacred and secular.

This has evoked harsh denunciation from one influential Pentecostalist pastor. In 1998, some clergymen felt that Rudder's *High Mas* was a devilish blow aimed at the most sacred ritual of the Catholic Church. Many, however, did not. The response to *High Mas* was in some respects, reminiscent of the ambivalent response in 1995 to Peter Minshall's use of the praise-word 'Hallelujah' for the name of his masquerade band. Two hundred and sixty odd Pentecostal clergymen spoke out against Minshall, whose theme-song was sung by Rudder (*Hallelujah,* 1995). The music which Rudder offers up each year in praise, is accepted by some as a conduit or corridor of descent into suppressed and censored regions of identity, and condemned by others as a sign of the arrival of the Antichrist, the apocalyptic dawning of the last days.

While this pentecostal vigilance is being directed against transgressive singers and masqueraders, there has also been steady transgression from the ranks of the holy into the realms of the secular. This has been most evident in the emergence of Gospelypso over the last two decades. Gospelypso appropriates the rhythms, melodies and narrative power of calypso for the purpose of homiletic instruction. Its aim is both aggressive and subversive: that of penetrating the secular ethos of calypso and carnival towards a goal of social transformation through the winning of more souls for Christ. More conservative fundamentalists, however, believe that the subversion will take place from the other direction: the world will overwhelm and transform those wavering saints who compromise with it.

Gospelypso, nevertheless, has earned its niche among the myriad hybrid musical forms – Soca Parang, Chutney Soca, Ragga Soca, Rapso, alternative music – that coexist, each with its public, in Trinidad and Tobago. In 1999 there were two songs in the Gospelypso mode among the secular fare offered nightly in the tents. The harsh social critic Sugar Aloes rigged like a priest of some sort, sang at Dimanche Gras about *The Power of Prayer*. One also notes the growing tendency for some religious groups to stage their March for Christ during the Carnival season, and the existence of a religious group that actually brings out a band and plays mas – high mas, one guesses. So part of the landscape of change involves the steady erasure of boundaries between polar opposites, a process that parallels the steady transgression across lines of ethnicity in processes of increasing hybridisation.

David Rudder, as we have observed, is the high priest of this process in which the sacred and the secular, the different ethoses, transcendent optimism and pessimistic realism, the pain and the jokes are being steadily unified. In this respect, his mode of prophecy has taken him through and beyond the darkly ominous *1990* and the apocalyptic despair of *Hosay* (1991) towards the transcendent vision of *High Mas* (1998) and the *Ganges and the Nile* (1999). This essay will end with an examination of his apocalyptic trilogy of Rapso chants: *Another Day in Paradise* (1995), *The Madman's Rant* (1996) and *The Savagery* (1998).

Another Day in Paradise, the second item of Rudder's *Lyrics Man* CD (1996) is the beginning of a journey through the Trinidad and Tobago landscape that will take the listener to some strange, frenzied places until it arrives at the exaltation of *Hallelujah*. *Another Day in Paradise* begins with a statement of Rudder's own ambivalence towards a country that its acerbic novelist, VS Naipaul used as a model for his fictional island of Isabella, the land of the 'mimic men', a place that knowing no other pattern of socio-political performance, alternates habitually between playacting and disorder. In Rudder's version 'You run from the pain but the jokes pull you back again'. Pain and laughter, then, are the absolutes of this world, fusing often in the Nineties, as the realms of sacred and secular have fused, to produce painful laughter and grotesque, dark comedy.

It is a land, as Rudder reminds us, whose national anthem begins with the word 'forged'; a land of slogans and cliches, of counterfeit ideals, where the founding words of the 'Father of the Nation' are emptied of meaning and the old professional class of doctors and lawyers have betrayed their contract with the young nation and bartered their souls to the gorgons of violence, illegal practice and materialism. Yet in this sad, harsh jeremiad where the best of the past is ignored and allowed to die, while the worst of the present determines the future, and the self-righteous voice of 'the lord of the swine', Morgan Job, controls prophetic process, Rudder ends with a quest for the difficult positives necessary in this age of disintegration. Parents are given a profound and complex weight of responsibility in an age when the battle is simultaneously against the internal corruption of the nation and 'the fables on the cable, that Nike psychology' imposed from outside on a far too receptive neo-colony.

The children are offered the option of 'making' themselves; that is, they are given responsibility for self-definition, self-construction and identity which the narrator says is the only way they will achieve control over their circumstances. Indeed, even such control is threatened by the powerful pressure of external forces:

> But in this land of the wandering soul
> Children, making yourself is the only one you control
> 'In spite of' is the key to the light
> Your fight going to be all right, hold tight

Affirmation, hard won, is affirmation 'in spite of' all the negative forces that besiege choice. Rudder exhorts his 'children', his pastoral flock, to 'believe in [themselves]'. Such self-definition, self-realisation and self-affirmation as he recommends, go beyond the platitudes of both conventional religion and nationalist politics which, indeed, *Another Day in Paradise* deconstructs, holds up to harsh laughter and discards from the first lines.

Disclosing the shambles of the world that Eric Williams sought to construct, *Another Day in Paradise* also marks the failure of society to construct a viable alternative, and intuits the demise of the Manning regime. Gypsy indeed, had in *The Party's Over* (1994) foretold the collapse of the 'new PNM'. Now Rudder's voice takes up the same line of prophecy. His *The Madman's Rant* paints an even grimmer picture than *Another Day in Paradise*. The most obvious point about this apocalyptic chant is that the poet/prophet derives his message not from an angel as in Delamo's *Sodom and Gomorrah,* or through a dream as in Valentino's *Ethiopia Shall Rise Again,* or Delamo's *Apocalypse,* but from a lunatic whose voice seems to be the most appropriate one to comment on politics and social change in what is now 'a strange land.'

Rudder's Madman seems coldly sane as he juxtaposes several of the absurdities of the 1995 elections campaign. His spiel consists of slogans culled from the various political party manifestos, whose hollowness, untruth and absurdity assail both the intelligence and the sanity of the average consciousness. *The Madman's Rant* holds the key to one's understanding of why more people – a huge 36 per cent of the electorate – chose not to vote at all rather than to vote for either the PNM or the UNC. The major emotion generated by the 1995 elections was disgust. The magnificent Madman hears only a blur of voices, each of whose faceless source is indistinguishable from the other. Each false and unfulfillable promise is located in a context of brutal reality that unmasks its emptiness. In each of these two couplets, for example, the second line unmasks and undermines the first:

> 1. Somebody promising jobs for all
> While some renting gun to make other people bawl
>
> 2. But somebody promising human rights
> While somebody promising to put out your lights.

The Madman's Rant falls into two large stanzas, both of which move from the empty illusion of promises towards the lived reality of violence, murder and the wastage of young lives caught up in the grandest illusion of them all: that crime can provide a short-cut to the good life of – oh pathos! – Nike shoes, gold teeth often inserted at the expense of real ones, and a pocket full of hundred dollar bills ('blue blue silk').

> The mortuary is filled with little Trinidad boys
> A bullet start to wine and put an end to their joy
> Now they lying cold for their mamma to mourn
> Their Nikes gone and their gold teeth pawned
> You see, they want their pocket filled with blue blue silk
> They want their statues drinking full cream milk
> So now a tag on their toe is their ticket to hell
> But look where we reach, well, well, well, well, well

Two points need to be made here. The first is that these dead 'Trinidad boys', caught up in an empty materialistic existence and dying for what has been marketed to them as metropolitan style, vogue and fashion, are actually representative of the shallowness, crassness and immaturity of all classes and sectors of the society itself. The second point concerns the placement of that curious line: 'They want their statues drinking full cream milk' in the middle of a description of the urban gangster scenario. During 1995, the news (or rumour) broke that Hindu murtis in India and overseas had begun to drink milk. The ones in Trinidad, clearly indigenised by the 150th year since Indian arrival, showed a clear preference for Nestlé's Full Cream Milk. Both the milk-drinking murtis and the 150th anniversary of Indian arrival served as rallying points for the consolidation of Hindu identity and the Indian ethnic vote that, with a little help from Tobago NAR and two PNM defectors, resulted in the accession to power of the UNC and the first Indo-Trinidadian prime minister of Trinidad and Tobago.

Rudder, by locating these milk-drinking stone objects in the context of banditry, violence and internecine murder stereotypically associated with black urban youth, is reminding his audience that Trinidad, south of the Caroni has emerged as a major hub and venue in the murder and narcotics industries. The politicians who had so successfully exploited faith and superstition towards the political consolidation and mobilisation of the ethnic Indian community, were much less sanguine in their efforts to confront the problem of organised crime that had infested their constituencies and transformed lifestyles throughout the length and breadth of the nation.

In stanza two, the Natural Law Party, in a manner that somewhat resembles the scientific 'projectors' in Jonathan Swift's *Flying Island of Laputa*, provides an example of the disconnection of well-meaning, well-bred and well-fed yuppies from the grounded realities of everyday life. These shiny-eyed philosophers literally live up in the air:

> Somebody promising natural law
> Just fly like a yogi and end all the war
> Seek inner peace and end all the pain

The futility and escapism of this group are emblematic of the emptiness of their particular class and its irrelevance to political process in contemporary Trinidad and Tobago. But at a deeper level the Natural Law Party is richly illustrative of the carnivalesque fantasy and near insanity of the political process itself, which accommodates milk-drinking statues, yogic high fliers, candle-toting Baptists chanting down the ONR in Woodford Square in 1981, and a young minister of Manning's recently elected New PNM government, officiating in the midnight exorcism at the Red House in 1991 when the rusty 'dragon' weather-cock was removed and a duck or dove or corbeau installed in its place.

Rudder's *Madman* is sufficiently perceptive to recognise that naivete, foolishness and knavery often keep close company. The yogic fliers are comical, not malicious. Yet, as with the milk-drinking murtis, they are located in the vicinity of strange company. The fools are followed by the knaves. So:

> Somebody promise to run all the bread
> Somebody pushing a *world-class* head
> Somebody clean out the weed real fast
> But somebody letting the cocaine pass

No names are called, no faces identified in this gallery of rogues; though 'world-class' had been Manning's unsuccessful attempt at a consciousness-raising, self-esteem – engendering slogan. The line 'Somebody pushing a world-class head' can mean that somebody is displaying the qualities of a world-class trickster. Or it could mean 'Somebody's head is high with some mind-expanding, mind-blowing drug'. Hence the references to marijuana and cocaine in the next two lines.

According to the Madman's insane analysis, both major parties and their leaders exploit the desperation of their followers in a situation where to lead means automatically to deceive, and winning elections demands a display of one's power to offer patronage, 'to run all the bread', to hosts of demanding clients. Rudder's Madman, though he calls no names by his juxtaposition of the various anonymous 'somebodies', invites speculation that, say, the same persons advocating human rights may be the ones organising assassinations; the same ones uprooting locally grown marijuana plants may be importing cocaine for the international drug cartel. Absolutely no politician can be taken at face value, least of all those sudden advocates of the doctrine of 'national unity', who before the elections exploited ethnic distress in order to consolidate the racial vote. It is with a focus on this category of political hypocrite that the song ends:

Somebody going to end all the talk about race
But they can't tell we that with a straight, straight face

Calypsonians' immediate reactions to the new régime were ambivalent, ranging from bitter rejection and feelings of having been betrayed by the black ethnic electorate (Cro Cro, *Black Man All Yuh Look for Dat*; Sugar Aloes, *The Facts*) to joyful approval (Valentino, *Time to Love Again*). Brother Marvin (*Jahaji Bhai, Unity*) and Delamo (*Stay Together, Trinbago*) both felt that patriotism should transcend ethnic rivalry and separation. Both harangued the Afro-Trinidadian community to accept the new regime, even as triumphant Indo-Trinis decorated walls in their areas with the slogan 'Indian Time Now'. Watchman saw in the new government, a tendency to avoid responsibility by blaming previous governments for everything that needed to be set right. His rejoinder was to point out the myriad imperfections which the new regime shared with the old, including some of the same personnel. Chalkdust in *National Unity* (1996) dismissed UNC claims that that party had brought unity to the nation. Such unity as did indeed exist had, according to Chalkdust, been created by the people themselves, through several decades of interface and intercourse across the multiple barriers of ethnicity. Chalkdust recognised the need for the people to be wiser than their leaders, and affirm whatever had brought them together rather than what had marked their difference from each other.

The year before (1995), Rudder had in *Hallelujah* also advised the people that they would have to generate from within themselves, the healing consciousness that alone could redeem the nation from the politicians' depredations. Rudder as prophet and high priest was more directly affirmative than Chalkdust in his articulation of the message:

> Now I'm stepping out with my mighty crew
> And everybody know what to do
> Spread out, children, spread out
> Now we'll show the whole world a form
> That in spite of what's going on
> We can come together, love one another,
>   brother and sister
> Everybody chanting

The major difference between the two songs lies in the fact that Chalkdust as satirist is compelled to set up and be conscious of the spectre that he seeks to negate. In this case, that spectre is the figure of Panday and his new rhetoric of 'national unity'. Rudder in *Hallelujah* (1995) and *The Ganges and the Nile* (1999) has leapt beyond the spectre. In the latter song, the politicians as 'mind-benders' who promote 'hidden agendas' are acknowledged as a wearisome and sad feature of the landscape, beyond whose machinations the two rivers of people flowing into each other must move in power, glory, style and affirmation.

This vision of transcendence may be termed Rudder's prophetic version of the biblical 'new heaven and new earth', which in his now substantial oeuvre is always related to the power of music to transport reveller and devotee, secular and sanctified celebrant, to 'the other side'. Time and again in his journey through the landscape, Rudder has arrived at these spots of joyous transcendence where the vision of apocalyptic disintegration is suspended and the dream of reconciliation entertained. Reality, however, is never far away. So the serene joy of *Hallelujah* (1995) is followed by the Madman's bewildered encounter with people and politics far madder than he; and the exaltation of

High Mas (1998) is counterpointed by the harsh scatological laughter of *The Savagery* of the same year.

The Savagery (1998) is the climax of Rudder's trilogy of Rapso-styled commentaries on politics and society, beginning with *Another Day in Paradise* (1995) and continuing with *The Madman's Rant* (1996). If the Madman was commenting on the murtis drinking full-cream milk to signal the holiness of a Hindu accession to power, *The Savagery* identifies the piles of 'gobar' (Hindi for cow dung) that Rudder sees as having been typical of the UNC years and leadership style. Gobar, according to one Hindu columnist who was reacting to the symbolism of Rudder's calypso, is sacred to the culture; and indeed it may be so. Gobar has been the end result of all that milk-drinking of 1995. 'Look!' exclaims Rudder's narrating persona, 'The bull just purged in the yard.'

Scatology is a branch of medical science that involves diagnosis by means of faeces. *The Savagery* is Rabelaisian, Pantagruelling stuff with a vengeance; the substance of Swift's Laputa or of the environment of his hairy foul-mouthed Yahoos. We have moved from 'the land of the mimic men,' that is from VS Naipaul's territory 'where [we] run from the pain though the laughs pull [us] back again,' through the 'strange land' of the Madman and the mysterious duo of Occah and Motilal. We have, in other words, gone beyond Naipaul whose laughter is not sufficiently dark or mad for him to serve as our muse or guide through this strange, unnamed and unnamable land. Even the stricken wounded ('I've been hit') Madman will not suffice in this new world where word and deed are both 'gobar'.

The voice inviting the hapless visitor to 'step right up', employs the traditional cry of the circus tout or the Ringmaster, shepherding potential customers towards the ticket booth and advertising the pleasures of the big top.

What a scent! What a scent!
The smell of the summer of our discontent

Appropriating and adapting Shakespeare's phrase from *Richard III*, 'the winter of our discontent,' Rudder's Ringmaster reminds us that we have no winter here. What exists between the warring ethnicities here can better be described as heat, heavily saturated with the fragrance of faeces. After this scornful dismissal of public discourse in the 1990's, the Ringmaster warms to his rap by extending the parody of Shakespeare: 'To do or not to do, poppy, that is the quest.' Rudder sees the nation and its leaders caught between action and stasis, will and its absence, mired and asphyxiated in the gobar that someone's sacred bull has deposited on the land. The Ringmaster invites us in – after we have bought our tickets – to see the national show entitled *The Savagery, the Savagery.*

The phrase 'the savagery, the savagery' is an echo from Conrad's *Heart of Darkness*. Early in that novel the narrator, Marlow, imagines the predicament of a Roman administrator who has been sent out into the colonies, perhaps as punishment, and finds himself posted somewhere up the River Thames, out in the bush, far away from the centre of civilisation, feeling that 'the savagery, the utter savagery, had closed round him.' The predominant images in the novel at this point are those of the swamp, the wilderness, 'disease, exile and death, death skulking in the air, in the water, in the bush.' The impact of this strange land, now identified as a place of disease, exile and death, on the hapless stranger unlucky enough to be lured into its snare, is one of simultaneous attraction and repulsion: 'The fascination of the abomination – you know. Imagine the growing regrets the longing to escape, the powerless disgust, the surrender, the hate.' In this scenario, Marlow the narrator says, only the industrious, those involved in some creative form of work, stand a chance of surviving unscathed.

Rudder's allusions to *Richard III*, *Hamlet* and *Heart of Darkness* throw considerable light on how he represents Trinidad and Tobago society towards the end of the twentieth century. He seems to be saying that his nation has degenerated into: (1) a sinister circus upon whose stage crippled clowns perform a cruel tragic farce: (2) a dark, decadent, stinking swamp polluted by gobar of every variety, in which the spirit sickens and dies: (3) a wilderness whose administrators, stricken with paralysis, waver between action and stasis ('to do or not to do') and (4) a place that can engulf one and reduce one to regret, futile struggle, self-disgust, abject surrender and hate.

It may be argued that calypsonians, rooted in and tied to the vernacular tradition, don't read and apply literature with the sort of closeness that is suggested by my reading of *The Savagery*. Maybe. But Rudder's calypso *Heaven* (1995), which is a meditation on Rwanda and Kigali with their genocidal tribal war of Hutus and Tutsis, and their hundreds of bloated African corpses polluting the rivers, ends with Kurtz's last words in *Heart of Darkness*: 'the horror, the horror'. Since then, Rudder has been intensely aware of the essentially tribal nature of the ongoing confrontation between Afro-Trinbagonians and Indo-Trinbagonians, and of the genocidal possibilities inherent in such fierce, blind inter-ethnic rivalry. *Heaven* concludes:

> Foolish men will declare, it can't happen here
> Don't you know tribal war is one dark emotion away?
> Oh the horror, the horror

That ending is both a cry of despair, shame, pain and guilt at the genocide taking place in an Africa that Rudder describes as a 'human abattoir' and 'a river of horror' and a warning to Trinidad to guard against the complacency of believing that genocide is impossible in 'Paradise'.

Heaven, in fact, provides the gloomiest context imaginable for Rudder's *Another day in Paradise* and *The Ballad of Hulsie X*, songs that follow it on the 1995 *Lyrics Man* CD. Rudder viewed Hulsie Bhaggan's racialisation of the issue of rape in 1993/94 as an act that could easily have opened the floodgates to a tide of inter-racial violence in Trinidad. Bhaggan, for her part, had described the rapes of Indian women by masked and armed assailants in the genocidal imagery of the then current Bosnia/Herzegovina crisis as 'ethnic cleansing'. Rudder, comparing Rwanda with Auschwitz, Yugoslavia and Pol Pot's Cambodia, fears for complacent Trinidad.

Yet the CD which begins with *Heaven* ends with *Hallelujah*, and the one three years later (1998) which begins with *The Savagery* ends with *High Mas*; both compilations illustrating (as Minshall's masquerades have frequently done) the two contrasting faces of Apocalypse. Rudder's meditations towards the end of the twentieth and the beginning of the twenty-first centuries – *1990, The Power and the Glory, Heaven, The Day of the Warlord, One Caribbean, Legacy, Hallelujah, Haiti, High Mas* and *The Ganges and the Nile* among others, are characterised by this constant interplay of darkness and light.

One sees the same ambivalent counterpoint of hopes and fears in how other calypsonians have approached the phenomenon of change with its trauma of endings and beginnings, closures and openings. Current hope is that new political régimes will be more aware of people's needs and more conscious of their own responsibility to act in the public interest than previous ones; that Trinidad and Tobago society will become more coherent, less antagonistic, more harmonious, less divided, more creative, less negative and destructive.

of exchanging one parasitic oligarchy for another, one set of hypocritical slogans for another, one style of predation for another.

The nearly two decades since Williams's death have generated scores of calypsos expressing both current fears and current hopes. The society is simultaneously an apprehensive and a self-confident place as it stumbles or leaps into the twenty-first century. On the one hand there are the troubled songs such as Gypsy's *Somebody Thiefing the Soul of the Nation* (1999) or his ominous prediction that as bad as the 1990's have been, the nation is likely to look back nostalgically on this decade as 'the last of the better days' (*The Last of the Better Days*, (1999)). Black Stalin in *Ah Smelling It* (1999), sniffs at a repressive autocracy in the making. Lady B in *No Baggage* (1999) is apprehensive that the twenty-first century will inherit the same 'baggage' of racism, genocide, inequity and inhumanity as has burdened the twentieth. Singing Sandra's *Song for Healing* (1999), while it tells about the need to heal the nation, spends more time tabulating the many diseases for which some universal cure is being sought. These include: 'blood and human sacrifice,' 'daily tales of horror, rape and rampant torture, brutal murders and manslaughter,' racism, tribalism, mimicry, mamaguism. Sugar Aloes in *The Power of Prayer* (1999) presents a picture of overwhelming oppression whose weight the ordinary folk survive only through constant prayer and inexhaustible faith. The point about such a calypso is that, like Delamo's *Armageddon* (1984), it places the solution of society's problems outside of politics or government. Normal social problems have assumed an existential dimension and thus require more than human effort for their solution.

On the other hand, the last five years of the nineties have seen several songs of hope. Apart from Rudder's *Hallelujah, High Mas* and *The Ganges and the Nile*, there have been the various songs on the theme of unity by Brother Marvin (*Unity, 1996* and *Kuimba: Sing of Unity, 1997*); Delamo (*Stay Together Trinbago, 1996*); Gypsy *(Unity,* 1998) Shirlaine Hendrickson (*Unity*, 1999); Kurt Allen *(Unity: Come Together,* 1997; *The Last Call,* 1995); Kitchener (*Unity,* 1993); Chalkdust (*National Unity,* 1996); Valentino (*It's Time to Love Again,* 1996); Trini (*A Nation's Pride,* 1999); Chinese Laundry (*Colours,* 1996); Atlantik (*Together as One,* 1999). There has also been the belief that most of the society's problems are soluble if both the leaders and their followers adopt the proper attitudes of tolerance and patriotism. There are many calypsos that express confidence in the culture, but many that feel that not sufficient is being done to preserve, teach and pass on the culture to the nation's youth.

As we have seen, calypsonians have maintained their severe scrutiny of politicians, leadership styles, and the government's performance in areas such as crime prevention or containment, social services, budgetary allocation, job creation and the rooting out of corruption. Such scrutiny, a normal feature of calypsos in all eras, has been read since 1995 as the unfair rejection by African-ancestored singers of an Indian-based government. The obvious resentment of the prime minister at how he and his 'government of national unity' have been represented in post-1995 calypsos, and the rhetoric of threat and insult with which he has answered media criticism and popular dissent have led some calypsonians to the conclusion that fundamental human rights and freedoms are being threatened.

This feeling is not new. Calypsonians have faced censorship in the past and have either openly defied the censors or found ways of masking their attack that have made for subtler and more interesting calypsos. The bards of the 1990s have displayed the same range of responses as their forebears, meeting covert or overt threats with anything from the mocking laughter of Pink Panther's *I Apologise* (1999) to the retaliatory violence of Watchman's *Price of Democracy* (1999), from the elaborate masking of Chalkdust to the scathing directness of Cro Cro or Sugar Aloes. Meeting threat with threat, Watchman in *The Price of Democracy* admonishes his 'do-them-first' prime minister that popular dissent can never be fully stifled. When it is censored in one form it will simply assume another less manageable shape. Dissent via calypsonians' subversive laughter, Watchman argues, is a small price to pay for democracy, in a world where bloody wars are still being fought in the name of liberty, freedom of choice and conscience. A leader who threatens to retaliate against the people's laughter, may well prove a greater war than he might be looking for.

Sugar Aloes (*Ah Ready to Go,* 1998 and *This Stage is Mine,* 1999); Cro Cro (*Support Social Commentary Calypso,* 1996) and Luta (*Pack Your Bag,* 1998) meet what they perceive as a threat to freedom of speech with increased militancy of attack. No quarter is being given on either side. It is therefore easy to predict that the issues of the twenty-first century will be much the same as those of the dying twentieth. Governments, sensitive about their public image, seeking praise for their achievements and censoring criticism of their shortcomings, will try to increase repressive control on popular freedom. The poet Derek Walcott, reviewing two decades of the post-Independence PNM predicted through the eyes of his narrator, the calypsonian Spoiler that:

> The time could come, it can't be very long
> When they will jail calypso for picong,
> For first comes television, then the press,
> All in the name of Civic Righteousness.
>
> (Derek Walcott, 'The Spoiler's Return')

Such were the omens at the end of the 1970s; at the end, that is, of the Eric Williams cycle. Today, at the end of the millenium, the omens have not significantly changed. Calypsonians as prophets, peoples' voices and protectors of hard-won liberties, continue to work towards the liberation of space for the voice, room on the 'stage' or in the new nation's circus, for the performance of people's freedom.

36 | BERNADETTE PERSAUD

Art, Comrade, Makes Nothing Happen Here

I am extremely pleased to be asked to contribute this article on the role/achievements/contribution of art over the last 27 years in order to add to the deliberations and the re-evaluation of options for the Caribbean to meet the new global environment But, first of all, let me confess that despite our undoubted achievements in the realm of what is traditionally called the Fine Arts, I do not know that as artists we have had a role, far less a role in the Regional Integration Movement, or, that we made any contribution other than what a few gentlemen, representing the dominant intellectual culture, have been telling us so eloquently over the years. In fact, since the early decades of the anti-colonial struggle, Fanon, Césaire, Garvey and others definitively grounded the region's nationalist culture in an aesthetic of Negritude and an ideology of race and vague idealistic socialist values. In the following decades, despite the growing body of opinion, which increasingly displayed an accommodation to the debates on Indigenism and Créolité, nothing substantively new was added to the post-colonial discourse. What Rex Nettleford, in 1989, called the 'cultural imperative'[1] was essentially the restating of the old mandate prescribed by the forerunners of the nationalist culture, which gave the artist an inflated sense of his importance and role as a guerilla and warrior in the decolonisation struggle; and which by implication positioned him in the vanguard of the quest for national/regional cultural identity.

Handmaiden of the Revolution

Looking back, however, from this particular vantage point, here in Guyana – a 'post-socialist' location – it is entirely understandable that in the heady euphoria of the Fifties and Sixties, following the Independence celebrations, regionally and around the world – India, Pakistan, Ghana, Nigeria, Jamaica – it did seem possible to build the new Jerusalem – and Art, a good handmaiden could make something happen; there was Fidel, in Cuba, rebuilding the brave new world in alliance with a revolutionary propagandist art; and adding to the revolutionary excitement, Wilfredo Lam, Picasso's protégé and the Caribbean's first internationally acclaimed artist, was in 1966, painting *The Third World* for the presidential palace in Havana, in a grand gesture of solidarity with the revolution. By the mid-Seventies, Cuba's cultural policy, shaped in the shadow of an hegemonic super-power, was spelling out unequivocally, 'Artistic creation is free as long as its content does not oppose the Revolution; forms of expression are free.'

Thus, under the socialist revolution in Cuba, art became subject to censorship, while at the same time, its role in nation-building, its intellectual power, its ability to transform the individual and collective consciousness – its political functions – were officially acknowledged and promoted in ways no other territory in the Caribbean could compare. Despite periods of vexatious censorship and defections, for most artists it remained as Fidel Castro prescribed, 'Within the Revolution, everything, outside the Revolution, nothing'.

But in Guyana, did the revolution happen or did it not happen? In Guyana, even before the Fifties, the young Cheddi Jagan and his band of militant comrades were beginning to transform the colonial political scene, holding high the scarlet banner. But, in the world at large, the iron-curtain was descending, the cold war brewing. But, for the comrades, it was bliss in that heroic dawn to be alive and part of the world-wide struggle for Independence/Freedom/Swaraj/Uhuru. And for a time the people's poet marched hand in hand with them, the rhythms of his poetry pounding in every heartbeat:

> Comrade, the world is loud with songs of freedom
> Mankind is breeding heroes every day
> On high the scarlet banner flies aloft
> Below the earth re-echoes liberty. [2]

And so for that brief exhilarating moment in history, it did seem that a potent conjunction of poetry and politics could indeed change the world.

Well, we are much wiser now, and we know now that art, as Auden[3] said of poetry, 'makes nothing happen' – especially in our part of the world. In retrospect, we see that the building of a more just and equitable social order was over before it even got started.

As early as 1953, British naval and military forces were despatched to prevent a 'communist takeover in the then British Guiana, its leaders jailed and its Constitution suspended.

. . . to the applause of such regional comrades as Grantley Adams, Alexander Bustamante and Norman Manley, who felt'it was reckless and stupid of the PPP Government to put communist ideology before the good of the people.[4]

By the end of the Fifties the Nationalist Movement was broken and the country irrevocably split into ethnic camps. Independence was granted in 1966 only after what the western imperial powers considered the more moderate socialist party, led by Forbes Burnham, was manoeuvered into power. The stage was thus set for the emergence of the most repressive authoritarian régime in the anglophone Caribbean.

It is against this background that we must look at what unfolded in the realm of art during those decades when Guyana was, supposedly, like Cuba in the throes of its own socialist revolution.

The Role of Art under 'Socialism'

In the mid-Seventies, at about the same time when Cuba was incorporating its cultural policy into its Constitution, attempts were made in Guyana to re-educate artists on 'the role of the artist in a socialist society: the profound difference in the role of the artist in a Capitalist society and the importance of the cultural Revolution in the building of Socialism'. 'Comrades, however you come to define the role of the artist in a Socialist society, he or she cannot be seen as working in any other way than in the interest of the Socialist state.'[6] – for 'Socialist State', read the 'Paramount Party'.

From Denis Williams, the brilliant, much respected artist and director of art at the then Department of Culture, writing in the Carifesta catalogue, 1976, came the proclamation: 'Identity is liberty and liberty is the Revolution'! Williams, however, took pains to point out that -

Socialist art cannot involve a mere doctrinaire picturing of the Revolution . . . for the artists of Guyana the quest for identity is the most revolutionary possibility that exists . . . the problem of identity is strictly the problem of deracine and deculturated immigrants and in facing it the assumptions of bourgeois aesthetics will need to be examined . . .

I suppose, from a regional perspective, this would have been just a stale or wily rehash (in the official jargon of the times) of the old debates of the early nationalist culture – especially in a context where mainstream artists, throughout the region, had decided even before the Seventies, to 'harmonize their options' with 'International' trends, i.e. mainstream western modernism.

Memorabilia

Strangely, despite the socialist rhetoric and its official endorsement, no socialist art of any distinction or conviction came out of the regime's socialist revolution, except, perhaps, Denis Williams' own piece, 'Memorabilia', painted on the walls of the National Cultural Centre.

. . . Memorabilia II (1976) was painted in the first flush of revolutionary excitement, after a trip to Mexico, where he had been fired by the revolutionary art of the great masters, Rivera, Orozco and Siqueiros. It is a distinctive piece of propagandist art which dignifies and legitimizes the 'revolution' under a Regime totally bereft of moral authority.

Ironically, the completed mural was not approved by one of the Comrade Ministers of the Regime, who threatened to take legal action against the artist for deviating from his original proposal, which had been submitted and approved before his trip to Mexico . . .[6]

The political absurdities, ironies and strange contradictions of those times, which defy expression, and even in the present era of 'democracy', can perhaps best be summed up by Martin Carters disillusioned words, 'How utter truth when falsehood is the truth? How welcome dreams, how flee the newest lie?[7]

It is no wonder that many artists joined the exodus of Guyanese, fleeing from themselves, while those who remained, simply buried their heads in the sand, ignored the rhetoric, and did what their counterparts were doing in the rest of the region.

Watamama

Ironically also, it is one of the powerful visual images of the Sixties, sculpted by visionary artist, Phillip Moore, whose work, hailed by Denis Williams as 'the artistic manifesto of the Revolution, which subverts the "Socialist" ethos of the period.' Moore's *Watamama*, a painted, wooden, magical figure taken from Guyanese folklore, becomes a symbol of the emerging independent nation – well endowed and fruitful, carved craftily to lie leaning to the *right*. According to the artist, this magical power-object leans strategically right, so as to propel the country, through its psychic and mystical powers, in the right/righteous/rightist direction, away from godless communism.[8]

... I guess this sublime disregard of the official 'polemics' of the times can perhaps be partially attributed to the fundamental contrariness of the Guyanese artist, or as Denis Williams might have said, as he said of Aubrey Williams, his inability to 'cerebate'.[9]

What must be noted, however, is that a cursory look at the political context of art in socialist Cuba and 'Socialist' Guyana – two of the most untypical of Caribbean states – reveals that the role of art has been seen mainly in terms of its political and cultural imperatives. And this has been the case – generally – in the post-colonial discourse of the region from the beginning of the anti-colonial movement to the present modern/post-modern times. Significantly, despite these pervasive notions about the role of art in the region, as a whole, and despite the strong nationalist sentiments in the aftermath of independence, the nationalist movement in art began losing its momentum as the region's art-practice became increasingly engaged with western modernism.

Modernism

In the long view, the engagement with western modernism, by mainstream artists of the region – including 'Socialist' Guyana – represented a neo-colonial entanglement throughout the decades of the Sixties, Seventies and even the Eighties, in the aesthetic values of the western capitalist powers of Europe and North America. From today's perspective, that is not very surprising, for given the political context in which artists were operating nationalist and socialist debates became increasingly empty and boring in a region which had decided since the Fifties to harmonise its political options with the imperial powers.

"As . . . we all know from the experience of '53 and the bitter decades of racial turmoil and dictatorship that followed . . ."

Modernism, the quintessential 20th century cultural expression of an imperial civilisation, was itself underpinned by an imperial, arrogant notion of universality; it presented itself as an 'International' movement which transcended cultural, national and social boundaries. As such it was essentially in conflict with the nationalist agenda of the, Region's main-stream art – an art burdened with specific political/cultural imperatives, including that missionary quest for an authentic cultural identity.

Modernism's affirmation of the doctrines asserting the autonomy of art, its rejection of audience and communication, its espousal of the idea of progress, individualism and the canons of innovation and change, further positioned it at odds with much of what the region's early nationalist culture had spawned, in its art-practice and debates. It also found itself at odds with those 'minor currents of art – Visionary/ Intuitive/ Primitive/ Outsider/ Folk/ Indigenous/ Roots/ Religious/Ethnic movements – which flowed uncelebrated throughout the region, oblivious or indifferent to western art-historical traditions.[10]

Building Bridges

The resolution of these tensions – the reconciliation between nationalist and modernist (so-called internationalist) trends – became pivotal to the major currents of the region's art-practice. Subsequent developments showed the adoption of a synthetic approach which fused local or indigenous content with modernist techniques and strategies – often resulting in an art which was seen, by the western eye, as derivative and lacking in originality and innovation. This tendency in mainstream art continued well into the Eighties and even in the Nineties in most of the region's backwaters including Guyana at a time when modernism itself, challenged by such movements as feminism and conceptualism – in the Seventies – had already given way to post-modernism.

The Sixties and Seventies, therefore, may be considered a period of transition in which the nationalist, anti-colonialist consciousness became increasingly subsumed and the role and perception of art as a nationalist/regional movement considerably diminished. All roads inevitably led to the art-meccas of New York and the capitals of western Europe. In fact, the building of bridges to the capitals of culture proceeded with such fervor – as in the rest of the third world – it is a wonder that any artist was left in the region.

Needless to say, no sustained or effective bridge-building in the fine arts took place *within* the region, despite the regular, extravagant Carifestas,[11] the rare travelling exhibitions and the existence of such regional institutions as CARICOM and the University of the West Indies. Given this isolation of artists, regionally, throughout the decades of the Seventies, Eighties and to a great extent the Nineties, it is indeed an irony to talk about the role of the artist in the integration process or even in a national context. Besides, the continued allegiance of most of the region's artists to the modernist movement, which embodied an intrinsic disregard for such notions as the role, relevance or function of art, makes even the consideration of such notions, irrelevant and a folly.

... Art, comrade, made nothing happen here – especially in Guyana. As the Cinderella of the Arts – besides a few costly propagandist exercises[12] – it was rarely allowed to play any significant role in the shaping of a truly National, Regional or civilised consciousness. A few privileged artists met one another in the capitals of the West – where the action really was – and where they acknowledged their common interest in learning and assimilating 'relevant, contemporary strategies' or discussed their common predicament, languishing on the margins of the Master Culture.

One of the important factors which undoubtedly pushed artists into relying on the intellectual leadership of the west, was the absence of a relevant historical and theoretical framework in which to locate their art. With the exception of Jamaica, little or no art-historical discourse has emanated from the region over the last three decades. As a matter of fact, with the exception of Jamaica, Barbados and possibly Trinidad, there are no functioning art historians in the region including Guyana. Again with the exception of Jamaica, Barbados and Trinidad no professional art criticism or intellectual culture exists which can adequately interpret or sustain current art practices, in or out of the mainstream.

New Visibility

It is truly a dismal situation for art in most of the Region's backwaters including Guyana ... But I am sad and happy, comrade ...

As we approach the end of the century, Caribbean art seems poised on the threshold of a new exciting visibility – visibility of course in the western art world, not in the region. Let me confess, that for most of us, it remains a sweet and becoming thing to be validated, where it really seems to matter, in the art-capitals of Europe and North America. This is what the 'international' attention we all want amounts to. It is the magnum opus of many mainstream artists from our part of the world: to feel at long last that we are about to enter history.

... Remember, we have no history. The end of the century finds most of us without even a basic text, which documents The history of our own art ...

This interest in the art of the Caribbean, as a whole, is unprecedented. Previous international attention had focused on the Haitian 'Primitive' school and Cuban art, since the Forties, leavin the rest of us in the anglophone Caribbean unnoticed, undiscovered. Now Christopher Colombus is arriving again and again, and we are going down the beaches to greet him with our artistic trinkets. As a result, artists based in the region are now enjoying greater opportunities for international exposure of their work. This contrasts with the predicament of an earlier generation who had to migrate to the centres of western culture in order to gain some grudging recognition.

Post-Modernism

A recent publication by Thames and Hudson, testifies to the growing interest in Caribbean art and to the changing perceptions about its nature and motivation. Perhaps this is as much a result of what has been achieved by artists here in the region and its diaspora, as well as the fact that mainstream western culture has undergone a profound ideological shift with the advent of post-modernism.

Post-modernism espouses a very eclectic, democratic definition of art. It allows for a return to figuration and the use of a wide array of innovative techniques and current technological media. The emergence of movements and trends such as feminism, conceptualism and installation art challenged the very premises of modernist art in the Seventies, initiated a new sense of freedom, and put back on the agenda, social and political concerns and issues of otherness and difference.

As a result, Caribbean art, seen through post-modernist frames of reference has become more politically and culturally nuanced – its essential hybridity, complexity and otherness more obvious. Importantly, for a new generation of artists in the Nineties, the strategic approaches to art-making, in post-modernism, seem particularly appropriate for articulating the peculiar existential condition of Caribbean man – isolated, restless, marginalised, with his own multiple perspectives of reality, more varied than Picasso's.

The work of this avant-garde generation [13] located mainly in Jamaica and, of late, in Barbados and Trinidad, though rooted in the socio-political, cultural and existential dilemmas of the region, fits neatly into a post-modernist theoretical framework.

Now this is where one of the challenges for the new century can perhaps be focused – given the controversies and problematics posed by this avant-garde art. For obviously with the increasing visibility which the new century promises, western readings of the region's post-modernist art could facilitate its incorporation into the art-historical discourse of Europe and North America – albeit as an exotic branch off the main stream of the master culture.

Sour-Sweet Achievement

This is the predicament and sour-sweet achievement of the region's art perhaps best represented by that major contribution to Caribbean art – *Caribbean Art* by Veerie Poupeye, published by Thames and Hudson (1998).
Veerle Poupeye, a Belgian-historian and curator, based in Jamaica, has done a seminal, pioneering survey of the major trends and developments in Caribbean art as a whole – an impossible, heroic task given the linguistic diversity, cultural plurality, surreality and ephemerality of the entire region.

But it is certainly a reflection of a profound failure that even at the regional level we ourselves have failed – at the end of the twentieth century – to write, interpret and evaluate our collective story. Poupeye's insights as a sympathetic outsider though valuable and necessary cannot take the place of an insider mapping the inner landscape of his own territory.

Significantly Poupeye has acknowledged that, 'Caribbean artists have historically had little control over the power-structures that determine their access to the Western Art-world', and this is 'after all what international success amounts to . . .'[14]

Granted the economic impoverishment which has underpinned most of the region's isolated island states, including their cultural infrastructure, it is hardly likely that any signfficant impact will be made on the power structures of the western art-world, in an era of globalisation. Now, unless we can overcome this impoverishment which more specifically underpins the myopia, cultural isolation and failure of Caribbean scholarship to validate and possess its own art, we will continue to depend on sympathetic scholars, like Veerle Poupeye, to facilitate access to the world of western Art. And this, after all, constitutes a mediation of our art by the western/western- trained mind, which merely leaves us with that post-modernist task: to rethink, reconstruct review, revision, reevaluate and redefine what has already been done.

This intellectual subservience to the west also underscores the crucial issue of the role of language – the verbal language itself – which has imprisoned us all, and which continues to be a potent colonizing instrument. One of the central tasks for art-historians and critics within the region which remains undone, at the end of the century, is the critical examination of this exclusive, imperial language which shapes, mediates, evaluates and, ultimately, classifies, marginalises and makes derivative the art which has come out of the Caribbean crucible.[15] The use of this language, incidentally, will be even more inadequate in the critical scrutiny of those 'minor', non-European strands of art – outside of the mainstream – which are also now coming to the fore.

Writing in a mode of language, that could only have come from someone located in a dominant cultural tradition, Timothy Baum in 1993, declared,

Surrealism is the invention of André Breton, and would not have otherwise come into being . . . the need for what this word would come to describe existed. Breton, aware of this void and prepared to open the world's eyes to what existed, undiscovered within this void, invented Surrealism . . .[16]

Over the last three decades, Caribbean scholars in failing to keep pace with the distinctive art which has blossomed in the region, have also inevitably missed these definitive moments when they could have declared like Baum and Breton, that they had invented/named a previously undefined and undiscovered realm in the visual arts of this planet.

I wish to acknowledge my great debt to Veerle Poupeye's *Caribbean Art* which allowed me to for the first time to have an overview of the art of the region.

Notes

1. See Rex Nettleford, 'The Cultural Imperative', *Caribbean Affairs* Vol 2. no. 2, 1989.
2. From 'Poems of Resistance' (1954), 'Let Freedom wake him' Martin Carter, *Selected Poems*, Demerara Publishers, Guyana,1989.
3. W.H. Auden defines here the Modernist notion of poetry:

   For poetry makes nothing happen. It survives
   In the valley of its saying where executives
   Would never want to tamper; it flows south
   From ranches of isolation and the busy griefs
   Raw towns that we believe and die. in; it survives
   A way of happening, a mouth.

4. See *The West on Trial* by Cheddi Jagan, (1972), Berlin, Seven Seas Publishers, p. 130.
5. From an address by Minister of Education and Culture, Vincent Teekah, to a seminar of artists. Published in *Kaie,* official organ of the then Department of Culture (1979) entitled, 'The Importance of the Artist in a Socialist Society'.
6. From an interview with Dr. Denis Williams, 1998.
7. From 'Jail me Quickly',(1964) What can a man do more?, Martin Carter, *Selected Poems*, Demerara Publishers, Guyana,1989.
8. Ironically, it was not until 1992, with the return of electoral democracy and the return to power of Cheddi Jagan's Marxist PPP, that Watama's potent magic apparently began working and Guyana definitely started leaning in a right/Rightist political direction.
9. See Aubrey Williams, monograph published by the Institute of International Visual Arts in association with the Whitechapel Art Gallery, 1996, p. 44.
10. With such notable exceptions as – the Jamaica Intuitives, Philip Moore of Guyana and Caymanian, Gladwyn Bush.
11. Carifesta, the brainchild of L.F.S. Burnham, has focused mainly on the Performing Arts – dance, theatre, music, festival Arts. Its art exhibition programmes, symposia, etc., have made no discernible impact in the Integration Movement, since very few artists were involved.
12. These included the founding of the Burrowes School of Art by Dr. Denis Williams in the mid-seventies, the commissioning of the Timehri Airport Murals by Aubrey Williams, and the commissioning of several National Monuments, including Philip Moore's 1763 Monument at the Square of the Revolution.
13. The avant garde of the Region includes, among others, David Boxer, Petrona Morrison, Margaret Chen, Nicholas Morris, Roberta Stoddart, Charles Campbell, from Jamaica, Joscelyn Gardner, Annalee Davis from Barbados; Christopher Cozier, Irénée Shaw and Suzie Dayal from Trinidad.

14. From *Caribbean Art* by Veerle Poupeye, Thames and Hudson, 1995, p. 20.
15. Invaluable research in this field has been started by Jamaican art-historian Petrine Archer-Straw.
16. From 'Breton's dream a surreal fairytale' by Timothy Baum, New York art dealer and collector in *Australian Review,* March 6–7, 1993,

Conclusion

A review of the content of the volume reveals that it contains a highly sophisticated analysis of the problems confronting the region at the beginning of the tewnty-first century. The analysis identifies the challenges facing the countries of the region at the national, regional and international level. Moreover, it advances a number of practical suggestions that can serve as the basis for the formulation of policies and strategies that could help the governments of the region to respond to the challenges confronting them. As such, it satisfies one of the main objectives of the Conference on the Caribbean in the Twenty-first Century which was in fact designed to elicit not only an analysis of the issues but, more importantly, concrete suggestions on the way forward.

In assessing the various contributions it is useful to highlight a number of major trends and issues which have emerged.

First, there is a growing awareness of the need to adopt a flexible definition of the Caribbean which, in addition to the CARICOM core, permits the possibility of wider forms of co-operation in the region, such as in arrangements being pursued in the context of the Association of Caribbean States (ACS) and even beyond the purely geographical limits of the region in order to encompass transnational relations with the Caribbean diaspora located in various metropolitan centers in North America and the United Kingdom. In this context, Orlando Patterson's analysis of the possibilities of Caribbean societies exploiting political and economic opportunities deriving from the existence of this diaspora offers useful insights for policy formulation in this area.

Secondly, given the formidable challenges which it faces, the Caribbean will need to adopt an innovative and creative approach to the formulation of domestic economic policy which involves a pragmatic understanding of the nature of the relationship between the government and the private sector and also the role and limitations of market forces in the overall development equation. As Prime Minister Arthur reminds us, while markets have their role, they do not deal with fundamentals such as the development of human resources, institutional capacities and the creation of technological assets which constitute the building blocks of development. Consequently, the state has a critical role to play in this area. Moreover, the formulation of economic policy should also take into account the specific characteristics of the region, comprising as it does, a large number of small economies which are susceptible to a number of vulnerabilities deriving from economic as well as environmental factors.

Thirdly, in the context of the inexorable march of the forces of globalisation and liberalisation, it will be important for the region to place special emphasis on the development of a capacity to compete in the global economy, which is increasingly characterised by reciprocity-based relationships, through improved human resources development and the application of increasing levels of technology, designed to improve overall productivity. In this context, efforts should also be made to identify strategic niches which Caribbean countries could exploit for the production and export of new products and services.

Fourthly, the Caribbean will need to forge suitable alliances with other developing countries designed to defend common interests in the ongoing global negotiations on international trade and economic issues taking place in forums such as the WTO in order to ensure that the approach to globalisation and liberalisation serves the interests of the majority of the world's people instead of a privileged minority in the developed countries.

The efforts at this level will be important in sustaining the special negotiations carried out by the Caribbean in the context of the ACP/EU Lome Convention and the FTAA. In this context, it will also be important to ensure that the special needs and circumstances of small economies are given adequate recognition and fully taken into account in the formulation of policies that will govern these cooperation arrangements.

Fifthly, it is increasingly being recognised in the Caribbean region as elsewhere, that effective governance is a critical part of the overall human development equation. It will be important, therefore, for the region to review existing constitutional arrangements and political processes with a view to introducing suitable modifications in governance structures and in the overall political culture in order to ensure an expansion of democracy in terms of the increased decentralisation of decision making and greater popular participation. Selwyn Ryan's analysis regarding the comparative merits of the traditional majoritarian Westminster model of governance, vis-a-vis a consociational approach, with special reference to the political problems facing ethnically plural societies, offers important insights and can therefore serve as a useful starting point for an examination of constitutional change in the region.

Sixthly, in the various papers, special emphasis is placed on the role of the creative imagination in Caribbean societies. Prime Minister Panday and others see this as one of the most valuable assets of the region in its efforts to cope with the challenges of the twenty-first century. The region will therefore need to pay special attention to this area which is at the center of its cultural vitality. Related to this question is the need to cultivate a tradition of intellectual thought in order to contribute to the development of a rational and critically alert population in the region. Kenneth Ramchand's proposal for the creation of departments of philosophy and intellectual history on all of the three campuses of the University of the West Indies is therefore worthy of further consideration.

Underlying much of the analysis in the various chapters of this volume is the increasing recognition of the importance of human resources development as a critical element in the development of the competitive capacity of Caribbean economies in the twenty-first century. Special emphasis will therefore need to be placed on increased levels of skill formation in the society in order to enable the people of the region to function effectively in an increasingly knowledge-based society. The University of the West Indies and other tertiary institutions in the region have a special responsibility to produce the human resources necessary to enable the region to cope with the new and profound challenges which it faces.

It is evident that the challenges facing the Caribbean in the twenty-first century are formidable and daunting. However, the people of the Caribbean who have survived and prospered in the face of the triple imposition of slavery, indenture and colonialism, have the necessary capacity and confidence not only to respond effectively to these challenges but also, in the process, to contribute to the enrichment of our planetary civilisation.

Afterword

REX NETTLEFORD
Vice Chancellor of the University of the West Indies

"The Way Ahead"

I have the unenviable task of trying to find something worthwhile to say, following a number of insightful presentations by an array of distinguished academics and policy makers, including three eminent prime ministers. Given the comprehensive nature of the discussions that have taken place over the past two days, I will not attempt to capture the details of these discussions but will, instead, share with you some broad insights which I believe are relevant to a proper conception of the role and possibilities of the Caribbean in the twenty-first century.

At the 50th anniversary celebrations of the university a year ago, we designated the event 'a celebration of the past and a commitment to chart the future.' We have justly celebrated the past, which is not without its accomplishments, and, as this conference symbolises, we have begun the process of charting the future – a task which we must approach with a sense of urgency, given the profound challenges facing the region as it prepares to enter the twenty-first century.

The Caribbean, which is currently poised between a historical definition of its reality and the possibility of a redefinition of its geographical, linguistic and cultural boundaries, represents a unique coming together of people from different regions of our globe. It is, in a sense, a microcosm of our planetary society and has established itself beyond its purely geographical limits in the form of a diaspora, located in a number of major metropolitan centres. The overseas West Indian aggregations are larger than many of the member states in the region. Moreover, through our remarkable creative diversity – whether in the form of the music of Bob Marley or Sparrow, the cricketing wizardry of a Sobers or a Lara, the athleticism of a Quarrie or an Ottey, the sheer intellectual brilliance of a Lewis or Walcott, or the literary genius of a Brathwaite and a Lamming, not to mention the political activism of Marcus Garvey, Sylvester Williams and CLR James which played a decisive role in the shaping of pan-Africanism, or the pioneering struggle of Grantley Adams, Bustamante and Norman Manley in wresting from former masters political independence for our people, the accomplishments of the region far outstrip the promise suggested by mere size.

And then there is the collective genius of the West Indian people who over time have survived suffering and severance whether in chatteldom, indentureship or colonialism, and have shaped designs for social living which we as legatees have all but squandered resulting in obscenities of crime and violence, a debilitating poverty and chronic unemployment. The post-Emancipation period now looks like a golden era. For people built villages, crafted family structures for nurturing and caring and devised operational and institutional frameworks which prepared them to cope with the changing world that brought self-government and independence. Indeed, the disproportionate contribution made by the small states of the Caribbean to global civilisation warrants further investigation into the unique genius of our societies. Perhaps the secret resides in the interstices of the creative imagination that Gordon Rohlehr, Ken Ramchand, Ian McDonald and Jean Small sought to explore in their presentations.

But while our cultural creativity is central to our unique civilisation, our survival depends on much more. Indeed, it is to be discovered in a complex interplay between political, economic and social forces which include cultural creativity. It is because of an understanding of such complexity that the brightest and the best have managed to emerge with dignity from the cane piece.

At the political level, we need wise and visionary leadership and a vigilant populace to lay the groundwork that will guarantee democratic governance and respect for the rights of individuals in our societies since the freedom of our people is the basis of our modern existence and our creativity and is therefore the bedrock of our future success. Astute political leadership and the existence of a conscious and enlightened population are also critically relevant to the preservation of the social integrity of our societies since it is political leadership built on mutual trust and informed by tolerance that will enable us to overcome the social and ethnic cleavages which have periodically manifested themselves in our societies and which must be dealt with by a process of political inclusion rather than exclusion. In sum, either we swim together or sink individually. And let me assure you – to put it metaphorically – there is enough water in our Caribbean Sea to accommodate the ruins of failed societies. I was pleased therefore to see that the issue of social integration and disintegration was an important feature of the discussions which took place during the conference. The increase in poverty has led us to the sonorous rhetoric of alleviation of landlessness and homelessness exacerbated by rapid urbanisation, of violence and alienation – with aspirations outstripping resources and a consequent deep and piercing anxiety about an uncertain future.

Beyond the political and social spheres, economics continues to occupy a central place in the Caribbean *problematique* since it is in this realm that many meaningful solutions are to be found for the social upliftment of our people by stimulating increased growth and employment through appropriate investment in the productive sector. Since independence we have accomplished much – often in the face of significant social disruptions caused by conflict among classes and races, not to mention the frequent disruptions caused by natural disasters in the form of hurricanes, earthquakes and volcanoes which have visited our region over the years. But there is a great deal yet to be achieved. The challenges facing the region have become more urgent in the context of a rapidly changing global environment that is being inexorably shaped by the process of globalisation and economic liberalisation, which have in turn had a significant impact on our development possibilities. The truth is that the emerging global production and trading arrangements embodied in the Uruguay Round agreements, which are being further refined in the context of the ongoing negotiations carried out within the framework of the World Trade Organization (WTO), have fundamentally altered the environment in which we as a region must function. It will therefore require tremendous creativity on our part to devise strategies aimed at stimulating higher levels of growth and employment at both the national and regional level while also seeking to influence the shape of the emerging global order in keeping with the economic interests of the region.

There is a body of opinion which rests its case on the argument that 'by signing the GATT Uruguay Round and setting up the World Trade Organisation, governments have effectively delegated the task of running their economic affairs to an international bureaucracy that is still more distant from people's lives, indifferent to local concerns, and subservient to the transnational corporations that the global economy has truly been designed to serve.'

This is a view that the Caribbean can ill-afford to ignore without using it to demonise our politicians and the state. What is clearly in our interest are institutional frameworks that are not too distant from the citizenries expected to lend a state or country their loyalty, dedication to service and commitment to sacrifice. This region may well have to go back to basics in the light of the real threat of global hegemonisation and deepen its roots in the specificity of its own realities even while spreading its branches into wider spheres. It is a strategy of survival in an increasingly hostile world that is yet to be seen as part of the *problematique* of Caribbean existence, as it was by so many of our forebears who on attaining legal freedom after 1838 set about making practical sense of self and society in the new dispensation.

All of this will need to be accomplished, admittedly in the context of a profound technological revolution. Developments in microelectronics and biotechnology together with emerging areas such as molecular electronics have radically altered production possibilities and the nature of the global economy. We cannot therefore stand apart from these developments but instead must seek to strengthen our capacity to participate in an increasingly knowledge-based culture by ensuring significant improvements in our human resources and institutional capacities in order to deal with increasingly complex economic challenges, not to mention the application of new techniques in the organisation of production based on the principles of flexible specialisation and cross-functional management arrangements aimed at improving productivity growth and competitiveness. The dire implications for trade unions and their rank and file workers are self-evident. It was therefore most appropriate that the conference should address the topic of science, technology and sustainable development. I would like to believe that the University is playing a pivotal role in the development of our human resources and the necessary institutional capacity that is so vital to our survival in the twenty-first century.

Having said this, it is important to note that, despite its tremendous potential, human capital formation cannot provide a solution on its own but must be accompanied by a conscious policy of investment in the productive sectors, even though the availability of an adequate level of human resources can make an important contribution to the expansion of output and generate improvements in productivity.

In seeking to develop suitable conceptual and methodological approaches for analysing the Caribbean reality, I am conscious of the tendency to counterpose the creative imagination to the historical/social scientific tradition on the ground that the latter has historically been invested with a culture of negativism which has sought to highlight the adverse effects of slavery and social deprivation in Caribbean societies, whereas the former has sought to highlight the accomplishments of the Caribbean people in the face of adverse political, economic and social circumstances. While both perspectives have their merit, there is an obvious need to combine the insights derived from the creative imagination and the historical/social scientific tradition in order to create a more integrated appreciation of the region's rich texture and diversity. In other words, the approaches inherent in the creative imagination and the historical/social scientific tradition are but two aspects of a common Caribbean reality and are therefore mutually reinforcing rather than divisively contradictory. The dialectical nature of this phenomenon is too often missed by academics and policy-determiners alike in the region.

It is also important to begin a process of re-examination of the concepts and categories of analysis that we have traditionally employed in analysing Caribbean societies. We have been far too long the victims of flawed paradigms. Thanks to our ordinary people, the region has been equally a welcome graveyard for such imports. Recently, under the influence of a resurgent neo-liberalism, which is often based on an exaggerated reductionism in terms of its emphasis on the primacy of individual choice, behaviouralism has increasingly shaped our interpretation of the Caribbean reality. The Caribbean faces a profound challenge in seeking to reconcile potentially conflicting tendencies deriving on the one hand, from the need to preserve its historical, geographical and cultural identity and, on the other, from the logic of a global order in search of wider forms of cooperation, albeit with new and profound implications for the preservation of geographical and cultural identities. The solution to this problem lies in the adoption of a strategy aimed at reinforcing a core regional identity while at the same time providing for pragmatic participation in wider forms of regional and extra-regional cooperation.

Given its past achievements, the Caribbean has a historic responsibility to continue to contribute to the creation of a global civilisation that is more humane in nature – a civilisation that justly celebrates the triumph of technology but which at the same time attaches greater importance to the needs of human beings served rather than driven by that technology; a civilisation that is more concerned with social equity than with profits and which also creates an environment that encourages, fosters and facilitates the creativity and flowering of the human spirit. This is the historic task facing the Caribbean which the UWI has rightly acknowledged as a task for itself as well. I would like to believe that the ideas advanced during the conference will enable us to achieve this goal.

It is also fortuitous that the South Summit, bringing together all the developing countries will be held in our region – in Havana in April 2000, thereby providing an historic opportunity to begin a process of reshaping the global environment in a manner that is more consistent with the needs and interests of the two-thirds world, including the countries of the Caribbean. The University of the West Indies has in fact been assisting the Group of 77 in the elaboration of ideas designed to shape a new vision for the south and will in future continue to assist in this effort.

Naturally, the university with its reservoir of intellectual capital stands ready to assist governments and regional institutions in charting the future of the region. Let us therefore proceed together in responding to the historic challenge of shaping our own destiny while at the same time contributing to the creation of an enlightened planetary civilisation imbued with an ethic based on equity and the recognition of the primacy of people as the main beneficiaries of global prosperity.

List of Contributors

Mohammad Ahmad is a Professor of Biotechnology and Director of the Biotechnology Centre, University of the West Indies, Mona, Jamaica. Professor Ahmad has carried out important research into various aspects of biotechnology aimed at improving agricultural production in the Caribbean.

Owen Arthur is the Prime Minister of Barbados.

Richard Bernal is Jamaica's Ambassador to the United States, and Permanent Representative to the Organisation of American States (OAS), based in Washington DC. Ambassador Bernal has served the government of Jamaica in various capacities in the Central Bank and the Planning Institute of Jamaica. He was Chairman of the OAS Working Group on the Enterprise for the Americas Initiative and represented Jamaica at several international conferences. Ambassador Bernal is the author of several studies on economic and financial issues.

Lloyd Best is Executive Director and Editor of the Trinidad and Tobago Review, Port of Spain, Trinidad and Tobago. He is a well known economist and has written a number of path-breaking articles on various aspects of Caribbean development. He is best known for his pioneering work on the concept of 'plantation economy'. Best has also served as a consultant with the United Nations over the years.

Byron Blake is Assistant Secretary General in the Caricom Secretariat located in Georgetown, Guyana in which he has had a long and distinguished career. An economist by training, Mr. Blake is a well known expert on Caribbean affairs, most notably on regional economic integration.

Anthony Bryan is Professor of International Relations and Director of the Caribbean Programme at the Dante B. Fascell North South Centre at the University of Miami. Professor Bryan has been a senior associate at the Carnegie Endowment for International Peace and a Fellow at the Woodrow Wilson Centre of the Smithsonian Institution Washington D.C. He served for a decade as Professor/ Director of the Institute of International Relations at the University of the West Indies, Trinidad and Tobago.

Jessica Byron is a Lecturer in the Department of Government, University of the West Indies, Mona. Her interests are international relations theory and feminism. Dr Byron has written extensively on various aspects of international relations with special reference to the Caribbean.

Edwin Carrington is the Secretary General of the Caribbean Community located in Georgetown, Guyana. He has also served as the Secretary-General of the Africa, Caribbean and Pacific (ACP) Secretariat in Brussels. Dr Carrington is a well known expert on regional integration.

Barrington Chevannes is a Professor and Dean of the Faculty of Social Sciences, University of the West Indies, Mona, Jamaica. He has published widely in local and international journals. He has written monographs and contributed chapters to a number of edited volumes. He is also the author of *"Rastafari: Roots and Ideology."*

Anthony Clayton is ALCAN Professor of Sustainable Development, University of the West Indies, Mona, Jamaica. He is a well known authority on environmental issues.

Omar Davies is the Minister of Finance and Planning in Jamaica. Dr Davies served previously as the Director General of the Planning Institute of Jamaica (PIOJ) and also taught at the University of the West Indies.

Tyrone Ferguson is Senior Lecturer in International Relations at the Institute of International Relations at St. Augustine, Trinidad and Tobago. He is a prolific writer who has published books on the IMF; structural adjustment in Guyana; and the management of Guyana's political economy. Dr Ferguson served as the Director General of the Ministry of Foreign Affairs and also as Head of the Presidential Secretariat in Guyana.

Norman Girvan is the Secretary General of the Association of Caribbean States (ACS) located in Port-of-Spain, Trinidad and Tobago. Prior to taking up his appointment, Dr Girvan served as Professor of Development Studies and Director of the Sir Arthur Lewis Institute of Social and Economic Research, University of the West Indies, Mona. He is a well known economist and author of a number of books on various aspects of the Caribbean economy.

Cedric Grant is Professor of International and Caribbean Affairs, Department of International Affairs and Development at Clark Atlanta University, Atlanta, Georgia. He had previously served as Guyana's Ambassador to the United States, based in Washington DC.

Anthony Johnson is an Opposition Senator in Jamaica and also teaches in the Department of Management Studies of the University of the West Indies, Mona,

Jamaica. Mr Johnson has written a number of books on various aspects of Jamaica's history.

Vaughan Lewis is Professor of International Relations at the Institute of International Relations, St Augustine, Trinidad and Tobago. He is a well known authority on international relations and previously served as Director General of the Organisation of East Caribbean States (OECS) and as Prime Minister of St Lucia.

Ian McDonald is Chief Executive Officer of the Sugar Association of the Caribbean. He is also a poet and novelist who has written extensively on various aspects of Caribbean society. Dr McDonald's periodic articles are published in newspapers throughout the region.

Patricia Mohammed is Head and Senior Lecturer of the Mona Unit, Centre for Gender and Development Studies, University of the West Indies. A well known authority on women's issues, Dr Mohammed has researched and written extensively in the fields of women studies, gender and development and engendering history.

Trevor Munroe is Professor of Government in the Department of Government. He is also an independent Senator in Jamaica. Professor Munroe is an authority on Caribbean politics and society and has published several books on various aspects of governance.

Carol Narcisse is Consultant in Social Policy Development and Analysis in Kingston, Jamaica. She is an authority on community development and has written extensively on social issues in Jamaica and the rest of the Caribbean.

Rex Nettleford is the Vice Chancellor of the University of the West Indies, based in Mona, Jamaica. Professor Nettleford is the founder, artistic director and principal choreographer of Jamaica's National Dance Theatre Company. He is a prolific writer and author of a number of books, including Rastafarianism in Jamaica (with F.R. Augier and M.G. Smith); Manley and the New Jamaica; Dance Jamaica: Self Definition and Artistic Discovery; and the University of the West Indies: A Caribbean Response to the Challenge of Change.

Felipe Noguera is the Chief Executive Officer of the Caribbean Association of Industry and Commerce (CAIC) based in Port-of-Spain, Trinidad and Tobago. He is a graduate of Harvard University, the School of Advanced International Studies and the Fletcher School of Law and Diplomacy. Mr Noguera has published numerous articles on telecommunications and culture. He is a former Secretary General of the Caribbean Association of National Telecommunications Associations (CANTO).

Basdeo Panday is the Prime Minister of The Republic Trinidad and Tobago.

David Panton is the Managing Director of Caribbean Investment Fund based in Kingston, Jamaica. A Rhodes Scholar and graduate of Harvard and Princeton University, he is the author of a book entitled *"Jamaica's Michael Manley: The Great Transformation (1972–1992)"*.

Orlando Patterson is John Cowles Professor of Sociology, Harvard University, USA. He is an internationally recognised scholar and has written extensively on slavery in the Caribbean and race relations in the USA. Professor Patterson previously taught at the University of the West Indies, Mona, Jamaica.

Percival J. Patterson is the Prime Minister of Jamaica.

Bernadette Persaud is an artist who resides in Guyana.

Ralph Premdas is Professor of Public Policy, Department of Behavioural Sciences, University of the West Indies, S. Augustine, Trinidad and Tobago. He has written extensively on social issues in the Caribbean and has received a number of awards for his contribution in this area.

Kenneth Ramchand is Professor of Literature in the Department of English at the University of the West Indies, St Augustine, Trinidad and Tobago. He is a leading scholar on Caribbean Literature and has written extensively on the subject.

Han Reichgelt is Head of the Department of Mathematics and Computer Sciences at the University of the West Indies, Mona, Jamaica. He is a well known authority on information technology and has written a number of papers on the subject.

Gordon Rohlehr is Professor of Literatures in English at the University of the West Indies, St Augustine Campus, Trinidad and Tobago. He is a well known authority on calypso as a musical form and has published several papers and books on the subject.

Havelock Ross-Brewster is Guyana's Permanent Representative to the European Union, based in Brussels. He has written extensively on Caribbean politics and economics with special reference to regional economic integration. Mr Ross-Brewster previously served as a senior official in the UN Conference on Trade and Development in Geneva.

Selwyn Ryan is the Director of the Sir Arthur Lewis Institute of Social and Economic Research (ISER), University of the West Indies, St Augustine, Trinidad and Tobago. He is a prolific writer and has published a number of books on various aspects of governance, economics and race relations in Trinidad and Tobago and in the wider Caribbean.

Verene Shepherd is a Senior Lecturer in the Department of History, University of the West Indies, Mona, Jamaica. She is a well known authority on Caribbean

History and Women's Affairs. Dr Shepherd has published a number of books on these issues.

Jean Small is Head of The Philip Sherlock Centre for the Creative Arts (PSCCA). She is a poet and playwright who has won several awards for her work. She has also played the lead role in a number of theatrical productions. Ms. Small has made a pioneering contribution to the development of art and culture in the Caribbean.

Clive Thomas is the Director of the Institute of Development Studies. University of Guyana. He recently served as the George Beckford Professor of Caribbean Economy, University of the West Indies, Mona, Jamaica. He is a well known economist who has written several books on economic theory and development. He has also served as a consultant to a number of international organisations, including the United Nations.

Hilbourne Watson is Professor of International Relations, Bucknell University, Lewisburg, Pennsylvania, USA. He served previously as Professor and Chairman of the Department of Political Science, Howard University. His speciality is international political economy and political philosophy. He is a former President of the Caribbean Studies Association and has written extensively on various aspects of Caribbean politics and economics.

Index

ACP/EU Lomé Convention, xv, xvi, 481–486

Ahmad, Mohammad; on bio-industrialisation, xxi, 147–153

Antigua; and intra-Caribbean migration, 81–90

Art; in Guyana, 577–583; need for critical evaluation of Caribbean, 583–584; transition from nationalist to modernist trends, 580–581; trends in the Caribbean, 574–584

Arthur, Owen; on economic policy, 12–25; on Washington Consensus, xviii;

Assembly of Caribbean Community Parliamentarians (ACCP), xxvi, 345, 452

Association of Caribbean States (ACS); xvi; establishment and objectives of the, 359–360, 436n; implications of the metropolitan presence in the, 49; trading relationships within the, 50

Barbados; support of Caribbean culture by, 536

Bernal, Richard; analysis of recommendations on Jamaica's global repositioning by, 419–425, on global repositioning of Caribbean, xxiv, 295–325

Best, Lloyd; on inequities of globalisation, xxiv, 274–284

Bilateral investment treaties; 115

Biotechnology; importance of, 148–153

Blake, Byron; on regional integration, xix, 45–52

Bleaching see skin bleaching

Bryan, Anthony; on Caribbean international relations; xxvi, 347–377

Business; restructuring of Caribbean, 404–405

Byron, Jessica; migration in regional integration, xx, 80–90

Calypso; prophecy and social change expressed through, xxviii, 542–574; on cultural integration, 39

Capital controls; need for liberalisation of, 101–102, 111

Capitalism; and labour, 386–388, 406–407, 413–418, 431–432; role of the state under, 389–393

Caribbean see Caribbean region

Caribbean Basin Initiative (CBI); xv, 15, 16

Caribbean Central American Free Trade Area, 362

Caribbean Coalition of Service Industries; need for activation of, 120–121

Caribbean Commission establishment and role of the; 454–456; and the RNM, 463–466, 475–477, 488; responsibilities of the, 459–461

Caribbean democracy see Democracy

Caribbean diaspora; as extension of the Caribbean region, 33–34, 167, 176–177, 343; human resources within the, 35–36; influence of, 343, 508–509; in the UK, 505; in the USA, 501–504, 506–507

Caribbean identity *see* Identity

Caribbean integration *see* Regional integration

Caribbean international relations; the changing nature of, 347–377, 365–370; external influences on, 348; effect of size on, 349–350

Caribbean region; characteristics of, 326–330; defining the, 31–35, 46–48, 161–167, 587; diversity within the, 167–168; ethnicity in the, 338; identity, 164–177; impact of EU on the, 328–329, 337–338; labour issues in the, 434–435; and preferential regime, 331–333, 354–355; redefining the, 340–343, 359–360, 587, 590; response to new international relationships, 327–330; USA relations, 333, 401–402; strategic global repositioning of the, 311–313, 588; issue of size within the, 313–314; security issues relating to the, 333–334;

CARICOM Review Team (CRT); recommendations re CCS, 460–461

Caribbean Sea; management of the, 51–52

Caribbean Single Market and Economy (CSME); 21–23, 41–42

CARIBCAN; xv, 15, 16

CARICOM; capital controls in, 101–102, 111; competitive advantages within, 367; need for concentric diplomacy within, 376–377; Cuba relations, 467; opportunities for integration into global economy, 375–377; economic integration within, 117–122, 366–367; and European Union, 363–365; failures of, 2; fixed exchange rates in, 99–101;and the FTAA process, 360–363; and international financial system, 104–106; and international trade relations, xvi, 41–42, 50, 52, 327–330,354–359, 365–370; limitations in promoting regional integration, 358–359; twentieth century agenda, 3–6, 43–44; role of the RNM within CARICOM, 450–451; sovereignty and regionalism within, 451–452, 477–481; supranational institutions within, 452; USA relations, 329–330, 462–463; vulnerability of states within, 365–370, 432–433, 435–436

CARICOM Charter of Civil Society, 452

CARICOM Single Market and Economy (CSM&E); establishment of the, 358

CARICOM Supreme Court, 452

CARIFORUM, 117–122

CARIFTA; 356–357

Carrington, Edwin; on the challenge of change, 26–28

Chevannes, Barry; on social integration issues, xxii, 179–184

Civil society; and capitalism, 390; defining, 391–392; emergence of the concept of, 303; governance by, 267–270; role of, 175;

Clayton, Anthony; on need for higher education, xxi, 137–146

Coalition efforts; in the Caribbean, 264–267

Code switching: defining; 180–181

Commercial activity *see* Business

Community associations see Non-governmental organisations (NGOs)

Community development; through decentralisation, 169–171; in Jamaica, 205–207, 229–233

Computer programming; opportunities in, 133–135; training in, 136

Concentric diplomacy; system of regional cooperation, xvi

Constitution reform; debate on, 258–272; need for, xiv; recommendations for; 254–256, 271–272

Creative achievements; recoding the Caribbean, 531–533, 591

Creative imagination, xxvii, 4–5, 513–529; fostering the, 534–541, 589

Crime and violence *see also* organized crime; in Jamaica, 216–219

Cuba; art in, 576–580; foreign investment in, 428–430; and globalisation; 425–431; and gender issues in labour force, 427–428, 439n–440n; membership in RNM, 467; and national sovereignty, 430–431; USA relations, 429

Cultural integration, 39

Culture; search for identity through, 515–517

Davies, Omar; on Caribbean economic policy, xx, 93–95

Decentralisation; as a means of community empowerment, 169–175, 589, 591

Demas, William; on balance between sovereignty and regionalism, 451–452

Democracy; decline of Caribbean, 253; threats to Caribbean, 351

Development aid; erosion of, xv, 8, 308; trends in, 185–186, 193–196

Diplomacy; new trends in international, 373–375

Distance education, 137–138, 140–146

Dominican Republic; migrants in Antigua, 83–89

Drug culture; 192–193

E-business; global volume of, 131, 139; phenomenon of, 129–130, 297–298;

Economic conditions; in Jamaica, 209–219; influence of MNCs on Caribbean, 305–306

Economic integration *see also* CSME; 21–23; constraints to, 119–120; failure to achieve, 357–359; and PPP, 291–292; need for, 112–122

Economic performance, 13, 408–409; of the OECS, 14

Economic policies; need for new, xiii, 93–95, 587–588; consequences of regional, 106–109

Education *see also* History education, University education; 114–117; in IT, 135–136

Education policy; fostering culture, 517–519; in promoting regional integration, 2; Environmental sustainability, 151–152, 371–372

Ethnicity; impact on social development, xvii; in the Caribbean, 191–192; influence on Caribbean international relations, 338

European Union, xvi, 3; ACP negotiations, 481–486; impact on Caribbean international economic relations, 328–329, 337–338, 354–355, 461–463; and globalisation, 363–365; as model for a West Indian Union, 40;

Exchange rate policy; macroeconomic management through fixed, 99–101, 109–111

Family land; concept of, 181–182

Family patterns; in Jamaica, 182, 214–215

Feminism; emergence of, 197–199

Ferguson, Tyrone; on social integration issues, xxii, 185–196

Fiscal surplus; need for, 93–94

Foreign aid *see* Development aid

Foreign investment; reliance on, 107–108

Free market regime; Caribbean economic integration and the, 355–359; implication for the Caribbean, 350–351; protection strategies within, 21; strengthening the, 396–398

Free trade *see* Free market regime

Free Trade Area of the Americas (FTAA); xvi, 8, 15, 16, 50–51, 106, 335–337, 341, 354–355, 358, 360–363, 486–487

Gender; and capitalism, 387; issues in Jamaica, 212–213, 224–226; revolution, 197–199;

Girvan, Norman; defining the Caribbean, xix, 31–36

Global capitalism *see* Capitalism

Global economy; Caribbean dependence on, 108–109; strategic alliances within the, 23

Globalisation *see also* Free trade regime; and Caribbean political economy, 354–355, 592; benefits for the Caribbean, 112; and the cold war project, 388–389; defining, 295–298; development of, 353–355; and issues of governance, 302–303; implications for the Caribbean, xv–xvi, xxiv, 15–18, 51, 103, 142–144, 432–433; and national sovereignty, 302–303, 401–402, 431–432; process, 331; social effects of, 185–196; and technology, 304; widening development gap, 304–305

Globalisation with a human face, 193–194

Golding, Bruce; on Jamaican constitution reform, 261–262

Governance structures *see also* Westminster model, xiv; accountability in the, 256; challenge of multi-ethnic societies, 264–267; need for new, 24–25, 169–175, 243–246, 588–589; PPP as, 289–292

Government *see* governance structures

Government-private sector collaboration; need for, 94–95

Grant, Cedric; on the RNM, xxvi, 447–495

Group of 77; xvi, xxiv–xxv, 595

Guyana; art in socialist, 577–580

Higher education *see* University education

History education; in the Caribbean, 66–75

Hemispheric trading patterns, 335–337, 341–343, 355–359

Human Resource Development; as development strategy, 93–94, 375–376, 589, 593

Identity; concept of a Caribbean, 33–34, 164–167, 171–172; cultural, 39, 515–517; and intra-Caribbean migration, 89; and language, 180–181; preservation of the Caribbean, 346

Identity crisis; 54–75; role of the media in Caribbean, 5; slavery and the Caribbean; 55–58, 63–64

Information technology; changing, 138–139; defining, 126–127; opportunities in the Caribbean, 130–136; economic viability of, 127–130; and sustainable development, 127

Integration theory; on regionalism among less developed countries, 448; on the role of supra-national institutions, 447–457

Intellectual property; 115

International economic environment *see* globalisation

International economic relations *see* international relations;

International financial system; financial liberalisation within the, 409–410 impact on regional economies, 104–106, 298

International Monetary Fund (IMF); impact of structural adjustment programmes in the Caribbean, xii; role in restructuring global market economy, 396–398

International relations; changing nature of, xiv–xvi, 3, 8, 299–300, 306–307, 309–318; North Atlantic focus of Caribbean, 16–17; response of Caribbean community to new, 327–330

Internet; commercial activity facilitated by the, 129–130, 139, 297–298; and distance education, 137–146

International trade *see* International relations, Hemispheric trade

Jamaica Labour Party; on Jamaican constitution reform, 259–260

Jamaica; global repositioning strategy, 418–425; political tribalism in, 208; problems of social integration in Jamaica, 179–184, 207–232; race and class in, 207–208

Jamaica Welfare Ltd; 205–207, 229–230

Johnson, Anthony; on science & technology and sustainable development, xxi, 154–157

Knowledge–based community; developing a; 114–117, 593

Knowledge workers; phenomenon of, 298

Labour; and capitalism, 431–432; and technological displacement, 411–418

Language; expressing identity through, 180–181

Leadership; in twenty-first century Caribbean, 287–289; concept of, 246; by PPP, 289–292

Lewis, Vaughan; on Caribbean European relations, xxv

Liberal democracy; concept of, 388

Liberalism, theory of, 390

Liberalisation *see* Free trade regime

Literature; lost Caribbean, 519–523, 526–529; role of the intellectual in literature, 523–526; revitalisation of, xxviii

Lomé Convention; 8, 15, 16, 106, 358, 481–486; establishment and development of the, 363–365

Market; concept of, 386

McDonald, Ian; on the Caribbean creative achievement, 530–533

McIntyre, Sir Alister; and establishment of the RNM, 457–459; role in regional integration, 460–470

Media; and the identity crisis, 64–66

Migration; and global trends, 300–302, 343, 500–501; and identity, 88–89; as an integrative force, 80–90; intra-Caribbean, 81–90; and security issues, 370–371; and unemployment, 405; to the USA, 501–504

Mills, Professor Gladstone; on Jamaican constitution reform, 259; review of CARICOM by, 460

Mohammed, Patricia; on gender in the Caribbean, xxii, 196–202

Monetary/fiscal policy; need for independent, 97–98, 102–103

Multilateral Agreement on Investment (MAI); promoting globalisation, 402

Multinational corporations (MNCs); economic influence of, 305

Munroe, Trevor; on Caribbean political thought, xxiii, 237–247

Nanotechnology; and displacement of labour, 411–412

Narcisse, Carol; on social disintegration, xxii, 204–232

Nation states; in the context of capitalism, 389–393; and new constitutionalism, 397–398; fragmentation of; 300; and globalisation, 431–432

National Democratic Party; on Jamaican constitution reform, 261–262

Neo-liberalism; ideology of, 385–388, 396–404, 432; strategy, 402–404

New constitutionalism; concept of, 397–398

Nettleford, Rex; and the Caribbean creative imagination, 4–5; on constitution reform, 258–259

Non government organisations (NGOs); in community development, 267–270; emergence of, 303

Noguera, Felipe; on economic policy options, xx, 114–122
North America Free Trade (NAFTA), 50, 106, 335–337, 341–343, 361–362, 403–404, 461–463
Organisation of American States (OAS); Resolution 1080 and neo-liberal project, 398–401, 437n
Organisation of Eastern Caribbean States (OECS), economic performance of, 14
Organised crime; liberalisation and, 368–370
Panday, Basdeo; on Caribbean development, 1–6; on the creative imagination in the Caribbean, xvii–xviii; on TT constitution reform, 263
Panton, David; on politics of principled proactive pragmatism, xxiv, 286–292
Parliament; disadvantages of the size of Caribbean, 257
Participatory government; as development strategy, 170–172
Patterson, Orlando; on opportunities within the Caribbean diaspora, xxvii, 500–510
Patterson, Percival J; on Jamaican constitution reform, 259–260; and development of human resources, 7–11; on need for technological change, xviii
Peoples National Party; on Jamaican constitution reform, 260
Persaud, Bernadette; on evolution of Caribbean art, xxviii–xxix, 575–584
Pluralism *see also* Ethnic polarisation; in the Caribbean, 179–180
Political economy; trends in Caribbean, 350–351
Political integration *see* Regional governance
Political power, need for the decentralisation of; 169–171; as development strategy, 171–175
Political process; accountability in the, 256; challenges to the Caribbean, 237–243; need for minority rights in the, 251–252
Political systems *see* governance structures
Political thought; Caribbean contribution to twentieth century, 246–247, 248–272
Poverty; in the Caribbean, 190–191; in Jamaica, 215–216, 226–228
Power; theory of; 385
Premdas, Ralph; on the Caribbean diaspora, xxi
Prime Ministerial Sub-Committee on External Negotiations (PMSC), 452–453, 459, 464
Principled Proactive Pragmatism (PPP); defining, 289–292; and economic integration, 291–292
Racial stereotypes; and Caribbean identity crisis, 55–63
Ramchand, Kenneth; on the Caribbean creative imagination, xxvii, 513–529
Ramphal, Sir Shridath; leadership of the RNM by, 469–470; on negotiating strategy, 471–473
Regional economies; dependence on global economies; 108–109
Regional governance *see also* Political integration; issues relating to, 342–343, 345
Regional integration *see also*, cultural integration, economic integration, political integration; xvi, xviii, xxv; arguments for, 315–318, 344; biotechnology and, 152–153; challenges to, 48–50; defining, 37–38; failed attempts at, 38; history of, 356–359; historical linkages and, 49–50; opportunities for, 42–44, 50–52
Regional Negotiating Machinery (RNM); xvii, xxvi, 362; and CARICOM, 450–451; and the CCS, 475–477; establishment of the, 461–463, 466–468, 494–495; and the FTAA,

487–488; funding of the, 474, 489–490; leadership of the, 469–470, 490–491; and the Lomé IV negotiations, 481–486; mandate of the, 470–473; and national negotiators, 477–481, 492; negotiating strategy of the, 491–492; performance, 488–494; operationalisation of the, 474–488; and sectoral negotiators, 492–494; structure, 456, 463–468; and the WTO, 487–488

Regional security *see* Security issues

Regional trade agreements *see also* Hemispheric trade; 354–359

Reichhgelt, Han; on information technology in the Caribbean, xxi, 125–136

Religious practices; in Jamaica, 183–184

Rohlehr, Gordon; on Calypso and social change, xxviii, 542–574

Ross-Brewster, Havelock; on Union of West Indian States, xix, 37–44

Ryan, Selwyn; on Caribbean political thought, xxiii, 248–272

Science & Technology; as development tool, 9–10, 138–142; education, 114–117, 121–122, 135–136; policy, 407

Seaga, Edward; on Jamaican constitution reform, 259–260

Security issues; 309–310, 333–334; and capitalism, 401–402; impact of liberalization on, 368–373; influence of regional geopolitics on, 339; and vulnerability of Caribbean democracy, 351–352

Sexism, in slavery, 59–61

Shepherd, Verene; on the Caribbean identity crisis, xix, 53–75

Skin bleaching; and the Caribbean identity crisis, 54–56

Slave society, 71–75

Slavery; and the Caribbean identity crisis, 55–58; legacy of, 204–205

Social and economic conditions; instability of Caribbean, 352–353, 406–407; in Jamaica, 209–219

Social integration; and globalisation, 185–196; Jamaica's problems with, 179–184, 208–219

Social programmes; in Jamaica, 220–222

Socialism; role of art under, 576–580

Software engineering *see* computer programming

Sovereign autonomy; concept of, 390

State *see* Nation state

Stone committee; on Jamaican constitution reform, 262

Strategic global repositioning; defining, 311; of the Caribbean community, 311–313

Structural adjustment programmes; effect on Jamaica small farmers, 223–224; impact on the Caribbean, xii, xxii, 189–196, 407–408; implementation of, 350

Sustainable development; defining, 126; and economic development, 151–152, 153–156, 371–372

Squatting; in Jamaica; 219

Thomas, Clive; on impact of Caribbean economic policy, xx, 96–112

Technological advances; and globalisation, 298–298, 304; impact on labour of modern, 411–418

Treaty of Chaguaramas; and the CSME, 24–25

Trade preferences; erosion of, 16, 106, 307–308, 327, 354–355, 4005; Caribbean response to the erosion of, 332–333

Trade Related Intellectual Property Rights (TRIPS); 115

University education, 137–138; and technological development, 140–141, 144

University/industry cooperation; in biotechnology, 148–153

University of the West Indies (UWI); Biotechnology Centre, 149–150; and Caribbean governments, 4, 42; and cultural stimulation, xxviii, 5–6; and human resource development, xviii, xx, 10, 52, 589–590; and IT training, 135–136; and science education, 116; 121–122; implications of distance education for, 142–144

Urbanisation; the Caribbean experience, 200–202; and gender, 201–202

Uruguay Round of Multilateral Trade Negotiations; xv

USA; Caribbean migrants in the, 501–504; Caribbean relations, 333, 462–463; Cuba relations, 429; influence of ethnic groups on foreign policy in the, 506–507; national security strategy, 398–402

Washington Consensus; xviii–xix, 15, 94–95, 193

Watson, Hilbourne, on global neo-colonialism, xxvi, 382–440

West Indian Commission (WIC); establishment and role of the, 454–456

West Indian Federation; 356

West Indian Union; proposal for a, 40

Westminster Model *see also* Governance structures; xiv, xxiii, 24–25, 253; debate on replacement of, 258–267; threats to, 352

Williams, Denis; on role of art in socialist Guyana, 577–580

Williams, Eric; on minority rights in politics, 251–252, 253

Women; and capitalism, 387, 406–407; in Cuban labour force, 427–428; and gender revolution, 197–199; in Jamaica, 212–213; and labour, 201–202; racial stereotyping of slave, 59–62; in slave society

Working Group of Experts (WGE); 452–453

World Trade Organisation (WTO); xv, 3, 8, 103–106, 397, 405, 461–463; bias towards developed countries, 117–118; and MAI, 403–404

World Bank; impact of structural adjustment programmes in the Caribbean, xii; role in restructuring global market economy, 396–398